EVERYDAY
FRENCH COOKING
for the American Home

Also by Henri-Paul Pellaprat
(adapted by Avanelle Day)

MODERN FRENCH CULINARY ART

EVERYDAY FRENCH COOKING

for the
American Home

BY

HENRI-PAUL PELLAPRAT

EDITED BY RENÉ KRAMER AND DAVID WHITE

Recipes Adapted for the American Kitchen, and
with an Introduction, by Avanelle Day

An Alexis Gregory Book for

THE WORLD PUBLISHING COMPANY

New York and Cleveland

Published by The World Publishing Company
2231 West 110th Street
Cleveland, Ohio 44102

In cooperation with
Editions René Kramer and David White
A Helvetica Press Production

First World Printing 1968

Library of Congress Catalog Card Number: 68–28744

Text printed in the United States of America

The color illustrations were printed at
Heliogravure Centrale, S.A., Lausanne, Switzerland.

TYPOGRAPHIC DESIGN BY JEANETTE YOUNG

Editorial Supervision by Alice Roberts

CONTENTS

LIST OF ILLUSTRATIONS

vi

List of Illustrations

List of Illustrations

INTRODUCTION

Henri-Paul Pellaprat had three equal claims to greatness—as a chef, a teacher of cooking, and a writer of cookbooks. He began his apprenticeship as a pastry cook in 1881, at the age of twelve, worked under some of the finest chefs in Paris, and became chef in the restaurants Lucas Carton and Terminus Demain. For many years he was a teacher at the Cordon Bleu cooking school in Paris, and after his retirement in 1932, he devoted himself to recording his knowledge and skill in a series of famous cookbooks.

At the Cordon Bleu many of Pellaprat's students were housewives. While his *Art culinaire moderne* (published in the United States in 1966 as *Modern French Culinary Art*) is a monument to *la haute cuisine*, the elaborate and sophisticated cookery of the great houses and great restaurants of France, the present book embodies his appreciation of those housewives' needs. It is primarily concerned with the everyday cooking of the little bistros and the bourgeois homes where food is prepared with care and eaten with pleasure.

In the original French version, *Le nouveau guide culinaire*, of which the latest revision was edited by René Kramer and published in Lausanne in 1966, Pellaprat's intention is clearly indicated by the number of recipes titled "*à la ménagère*" or "*à la bonne femme*." He provides a recipe for a basic brown sauce (*Sauce Demi-Glace Ménagère*) worthy of the tradition of the classic brown sauces but much simpler and quicker in preparation. His suggestions for using leftovers are as practical as they are imaginative and French. All the recipes are simple enough to be followed by the average homemaker, French or American. In this American adaptation, they call for ingredients obtainable in supermarkets and equipment commonly available in the home. In addition, quantities and techniques have been converted into modern American terms, and the detailed instructions that the American cook expects but does not find in French cookbooks have been supplied.

Yet the great gastronomic tradition of France is reflected in this book as it is reflected in ordinary French cooking. The chapters on sauces and on culinary know-how (*Le savoir culinaire* in Pellaprat's original) provide an indispensable basis for home cooking French style. Once the housewife has become at ease with this, she may well wish to progress to the more elaborate recipes in *Modern French Culinary Art*.

AVANELLE DAY

EVERYDAY FRENCH COOKING
for the American Home

Menus and Wines

PLANNING THE MEAL

As every housewife knows, the preparation of any meal, from the simplest to the most elaborate, is preceded by a plan—in other words, by a menu. Today the number of dishes served has decreased considerably from former practice, but the general pattern and the gastronomical principles involved remain the same. The modern trend is toward simple, easily digested dishes—sautéed meats, poultry, grills, less elaborate desserts. Light, appetizing meals which do not overload the stomach are the housewife's aim.

The following rules are important in planning meals according to the principles of gastronomy:

1. Do not serve the same kind of meat or poultry twice at the same meal, or a dessert made with eggs after an egg entrée.
2. Vary the colors of the food—serve only one dish with a white sauce or only one with a brown sauce at any meal.
3. Vary the garnishes.
4. Vary the methods of preparation—do not serve poached chicken after poached fish.

5. Suit the menu to the season—serve thick soups, rich stews, lentil dishes, etc., in winter, lighter meals in warm weather.

6. Vary the vegetables. Do not served canned or frozen summer vegetables immediately after the fresh ones go out of season.

Family meals usually consist of three or four courses, depending on family habits, the time of year, and other factors. Some suggested menus for everyday meals are:

Cream of Celery Soup
Braised Veal with vegetables
Lattice-Top Apple Tart

Cheese Soufflé
Cold Beef Niçoise
Strawberries

Cannelloni
Grilled Veal Cutlets
Spinach
Fruit

Leeks Vinaigrette
Veal Scallops
Apricot Croûte

Stuffed Tomatoes Piedmontese Style

Niçoise Platter
Grilled Lamb Chops
Green beans
Straw Potatoes
Oranges Stella

Cod English Style
Boiled potatoes
Green salad
Fruit compote

Meals for guests or for family celebrations are naturally on a grander scale and should include the following courses:

Luncheon:
1. A cold hors d'oeuvre, or an egg or fish entrée.
2. A hot roast—meat, poultry, or game—with one or more vegetables, or a garnished grill. (In summer, cold meat or poultry with a salad.)
3. A light cooked dessert, a frozen dessert, a fruit compote, or assorted pastries.
4. Cheese.

Dinner:
1. Clear soup, cream soup, or an hors d'oeuvre such as melon, shellfish, or smoked salmon.
2. Fish, a hot entrée, or a vegetable platter.
3. A roast with vegetables, or, if a substantial entrée was served, cold meat or poultry with a salad.
4. A hot, cold, or frozen dessert, or fresh fruit (with cheese if desired).

Sample menus are:

LUNCHEON
Shrimp Cocktail
Roast Fillet of Beef
with vegetables
Château Potatoes
Chicory salad
Pears with Chocolate Sauce

DINNER
Consommé with port
Fillets of Sole with Mushrooms
Duck with Orange Sauce
Chestnut Purée
Pineapple Ninon

WINE WITH THE MEAL

To the French it is difficult, not to say impossible, to conceive of good food being served without appropriate wines. Even at an everyday meal, a glass of pleasant unpretentious wine imparts its glow to the family table; the choicer "Sunday bottle" or the fine vintage wine served in honor of friends or special occasions provides an indispensable complement to the dishes carefully and lovingly prepared by the mistress of the house.

In the United States the custom of serving wine with meals, once uncommon, is now spreading rapidly. Imported wines are more generally available, and American wine growers are producing excellent wines in increasing quantity and variety. As a guide to serving wines, the following suggestions will be helpful; for the choice of wines to accompany various dishes, see the table on pages 4–8.

Since wine is a living thing, moving tires it. After buying a bottle of wine, let it rest for several days—if it is an old wine, several weeks—before serving it. In countries where wine drinking has a long tradition, there are also traditional glasses for different kinds of wine—Bordeaux, Burgundy, Chablis, Rhine wines, Champagne, and so on. However, in the United States an all-purpose wine glass, resembling the Bordeaux glass in shape, is becoming popular. A wine glass should never be filled full.

For greatest enjoyment, wines should be served at the proper temperature for each type. Dry white wines should be pleasantly cool, not cold; they should generally be served at cellar temperature—50° to 55° F. Champagne can be colder—about 45° F., and the great rich white wines 40° to 45° F. Light red wines of the type drunk when young, such as Beaujolais, are also served at cellar temperature. Rich full-bodied red wines are served at room temperature, but this does not mean the temperature of the dining room. These wines should be given time to take on the temperature of the coolest room in the house. Red Burgundies should be brought to the table at a temperature of about 60° F.; they reach their full bouquet at about 65°. Red Bordeaux is served at 65° F.

Wines to Accompany Various Kinds of Foods

NOTE: Most American wines have the generic names of similar European wines (Burgundy, Claret, Sauterne, etc.) and can be substituted for these. For the use of American wines with varietal names, consult your wine merchant.

TYPE OF FOOD	WHITE WINES	RED WINES	ROSÉ WINES
Hors d'oeuvre, ham, sausage	LIGHT AND DRY WINES Bordeaux supérieur Entre-deux-Mers Aligoté Burgundy Petit Chablis White Mâcon Pouilly-Fumé, Sancerre Montlouis Edelzwicker Sylvaner	LIGHT WINES Bordeaux supérieur Burgundy Passe-tous-grains Givry-Mâcon Beaujolais Chinon, Bourgueil	Bordeaux clairet Burgundy rosé Anjou, Touraine Provence and Côtes-du-Rhône
Pâtés	DRY VINTAGE WINES Graves Montrachet Meursault Champagne Riesling SWEET VINTAGE WINES Sauternes Barsac Coteaux-du-Layon	GREAT GROWTHS OF: Médoc, Graves St. Emilion Pomerol Musigny Romanée-Conti Beaune, Volnay Hermitage Banyuls Grand Cru	
Entrées	DRY OR MELLOW WINES Graves, Cérons Puligny-Montrachet Meursault Champagne Vouvray, Saumur Anjou Riesling	SUPPLE WINES Margaux, Moulis Beaune, Savigny Mercurey Beaujolais Chinon, Bourgueil	FRUITY WINES Sancerre rosé Anjou or Touraine rosé Alsatian pinot rosé

TYPE OF FOOD	WHITE WINES	RED WINES	ROSÉ WINES
Oysters and other mollusks	DRY WINES Graves, Entre-deux-Mers Chablis, Pouilly-Fuissé Chassagne-Montrachet Puligny-Montrachet Champagne Nature Riesling Pouilly-Fumé Sancerre, Quincy Savennières Muscadet Cassis, Bandol Arbois		
Grilled or poached fish or crustaceans	DRY WINES Same as for mollusks		DRY ROSÉ WINES OF SOUTHERN FRANCE Cassis, Bandol Côtes-de-Provence Tavel, Lirac Côtes-du-Rhône
Fish or shellfish served in a sauce Highly seasoned sauces	FULL-BODIED DRY WHITE WINES Graves Chablis Meursault Chassagne-Montrachet Corton-Charlemagny Pouilly-Fuissé White Hermitage Condrieu Riesling Arbois yellow wine	FISH STEWS MADE WITH RED WINES Same wine as that used for cooking	

TYPE OF FOOD	WHITE WINES	RED WINES	ROSÉ WINES
Mild sauces	MELLOW OR SEMI-DRY WINES Monbazillac Vouvray Anjou Coteaux-du-Layon Gewurztraminer		
Grilled meat White meats: poultry, veal	Graves, Cérons Vouvray Anjou Champagne	FAIRLY LIGHT WINES Médoc and Graves Beaune, Savigny Beaujolais Chinon, Bourgueil Saumur-Champigny	
Red meats: beef, mutton		FULLY MATURE WINES Pauillac, St. Estèphe Graves St. Emilion, Pomerol Côtes-de-Beaune Côte-de-Nuits Morgon, Fleurie Moulin à Vent Hermitage Châteauneuf-du-Pape	
Meat served in a sauce Wine sauces	Same wine as that used for cooking		
Highly seasoned sauces, stews		FULL-BODIED, BUT NOT FROM GREAT GROWTHS Bordeaux supérieur Canon-Fronsac Santenay Mercurey Juliénas Côtes-du-Rhône Côtes-de-Provence Touraine-Amboise	
Mild sauces	Graves, Sauternes		

TYPE OF FOOD	WHITE WINES	RED WINES	ROSÉ WINES
	Montrachet Meursault Riesling Vouvray Anjou Champagne		
Game			
Game birds		Médoc, Graves, St. Emilion, Pomerol Chambolle-Musigny Vosne-Romanée Wines of the Côte-de-Beaune Beaujolais Arbois Hermitage, Cornas	
Furred game		Médoc and Graves, good years St. Emilion, Pomerol Wines of the Côte-de-Nuits Corton, Pommard Côtes-Rôties, Cornas Châteauneuf-du-Pape	
Cheese			
Hard or semihard cheeses		Médoc, Graves, St. Emilion, Pomerol Wines of the Côte-de-Beaune Beaujolais Chinon, Bourgueil	
Soft fermented cheeses		St. Emilion and Pomerol, good years Wines of the Côte-de-Nuits Côtes-de-Beaune, good years	

7

TYPE OF FOOD	WHITE WINES	RED WINES	ROSE WINES
		Named Beaujolais	
		Hermitage, Cornas, Côtes-Rôties	
		Châteauneuf-du-Pape	
		Bandol, Cassis	
		Banyuls, Grand Cru	
Blue-veined cheeses	Sauternes	Rich wines of the Côte-de-Nuits	
	Barsac	Côtes-du-Rhône	
	Meursault	Châteauneuf-du-Pape	
	Chassagne-Montrachet	Banyuls Grand Cru	
	White Hermitage		
	Condrieu		
	Jura yellow wine		
	Gewurztraminer		
Goat cheeses	Sancerre, Pouilly-Fumé, Quincy	Mercurey	Bordeaux clairet
	White Arbois	Mâcon	
		Beaujolais	
		Chinon, Bourgueil	
Desserts	Champagne	Maury	
	Sparkling wines made by the Champagne method	Rivesaltes	
		Grand-Roussillon	
	Sauternes, Barsac and all sweet white vintage Bordeaux	Banyuls	
	Monbazillac		
	Vouvray, Saumur		
	Coteaux-du-Layon		
	Gewurztraminer		
	Alsatian Muscatel		
	Muscatel wines of Southern France: Rivesaltes, Lunel, Frontignan, Beaumes-de Venise		

Culinary
Know-How

As a preparation for the recipes which follow, and as a convenience to the cook, certain basic information has been assembled in this chapter. This includes various methods of cooking applicable to many different foods, a list of herbs and spices with their culinary uses, and instructions for making doughs and batters, stocks, forcemeats, and marinades which are essential to the preparation of a wide variety of dishes.

Cooking Methods

Generally speaking, cooking is the application of heat, in various forms, to foods of animal and vegetable origin, to make them more wholesome, digestible, and flavorful. The various methods of cooking can be classified according to the cooking medium. These mediums are: water, steam, dry heat, fat, and combinations of two or more of these.

COOKING IN WATER

Boiling. Cooking in boiling water (bubbles of steam rise to the surface and break). Under standard atmospheric pressure pure water boils at 212° F. However, it boils at lower temperatures at high altitudes, and mixtures such as sugar syrups boil at higher temperatures. Boiling is used for the following purposes:

1. To make stock from bones where no meat is present, boiling being necessary to extract the flavor from the bones.
2. To reduce or concentrate meat stock or fish stock by evaporating part of the water. These robust-flavored reduced stocks are used in soups and sauces having meat or fish flavor, in braising, and in glazing.
3. To make vegetables more digestible by softening their cellulose and swelling (gelatinizing) their starch.
4. To cook cereals, pastas, and boiled dumplings.
5. To make sugar syrup, cooked candies and frostings, and meatless sauces and dessert sauces containing starch.

Parboiling. Partial cooking by boiling in water, used when another method is employed to complete the process or when strong flavors or water-soluble elements are to be removed and fresh water added to finish cooking.

Simmering. Cooking in very hot water below boiling point (180° to 210° F.). At simmering point tiny bubbles form slowly and break before they reach the surface. This slow method is used for making stocks from meats, chicken, or fish; for cooking tough cuts of meat, tongue, country-cured ham, dried beans and peas, and certain milk and egg dishes.

Poaching. Cooking in water or other liquid just below boiling point, either basting the food with the hot liquid or covering with a lid so the steam will perform a self-basting action. Foods cooked by this method include eggs, fish, vegetables, and some raw fruits.

Stewing. Cooking below boiling point in just enough liquid to produce steam. This method requires long, slow cooking in a saucepan or kettle covered with a tight-fitting lid; it is used for tough cuts of meat (cut into small pieces), poultry, certain vegetables, and fresh and dried fruits.

COOKING WITH STEAM

Steaming is cooking in moist heat without having the food in direct contact with water. Its advantage is that minerals, vitamins, and flavor are not destroyed to the extent that they are by boiling in water. There are three methods of steaming:

Steamer. Place the food in the perforated inset pan. Place the inset pan in the pan containing water, cover and bring to boiling point. The steam from the boiling water will pass through the perforations and cook the food. This is a long process, recommended for cooking vegetables, but not meats. Steamer pans designed for this method are available in houseware stores in various sizes, containing from one to three inset pans.

Waterless cooking. Steam is generated by the water that is in the food. The cooking is done over very low heat in a heavy-bottomed saucepan having a close-fitting lid. This method is excellent for mild-flavored vegetables and soft fruits such as plums, berries, and cherries.

Pressure saucepan. This method cooks food in a shorter time than does any other method, because the cooking is done in an atmosphere of steam at a temperature higher than the normal boiling point of 212° F. Foods suitable for cooking at such high pressure are tough meats and poultry, tongue, potatoes, and mature vegetables that require long cooking. Generally, pressure cooking is not recommended for quick-cooking vegetables.

COOKING WITH DRY HEAT

Dry-heat cooking is cooking with air as the medium of transferring heat, as in broiling, roasting, and baking.

Broiling. Cooking on a grill over an open fire, under the broiler unit of an electric or gas range, or in a skillet on top of the range (pan-broiling). Broiling is suited to small tender cuts of meat, such as steaks, chops, cutlets, and ham slices, as well as sausage and meat patties. When broiling pieces of meat, slash the fat around the edges to prevent curling.

When the broiler is used, food is placed on the rack in the broiler pan, with no water. Place the broiler 2 to 5 inches from the source of heat, the distance depending on the thickness of the cut. Cook the meat on one side, turn, and cook on the other side to the desired degree of doneness. Serve at once.

In pan-broiling, meat is put in a skillet and cooked on top of the stove, uncovered, without fat or liquid. Cook slowly, turning occasionally and pouring off fat as it accumulates, until the meat reaches the desired degree of doneness.

Roasting. Originally, roasting meant cooking meat on a spit over a hot fire, with someone in constant attendance to turn the meat frequently. This method went out of style with the development of ovens, but with the increased interest in outdoor cooking, and the availability of motor-driven spits, it has been revived. The size of the spit determines the size and weight of the meat it will accommodate. Consult the directions with the equipment to avoid overloading and to obtain best results. Spit-roasting has one disadvantage: the weight loss of the meat due to shrinkage.

Oven roasting is still the most generally used method of roasting. It is done in two ways: at constant low temperature (300° to 350° F.); and by searing at high heat and then reducing the cooking temperature. Research has proved that constant low heat gives more juicy and tender meat with less shrinkage, but the cooking time is longer and browning is insufficient. The latter objection may be overcome by increasing the temperature for a short time at the end of the roasting period. The searing method of roasting is still favored by French chefs and others for the flavor, aroma, and color of roasts so cooked. The meat is first seared in a pan on top of the stove over high heat, or placed in a very hot oven (450° to 500° F.) for the first 15 minutes of the cooking period, and the roasting finished at 350° F.

Baking. This method is essentially the same as roasting, but the term roasting is generally used to refer to meats (or chestnuts), and baking to breads, cakes, cookies, pies, rolls, and to some extent to vegetables and fruits. When food is baked a crust forms on the parts that are directly exposed to the hot air and on the bottoms and sides where the heat is so intense that it penetrates the pans.

Baking temperatures vary with the food being cooked. Therefore it is important to have well-insulated, thermostatically controlled ovens, particularly for batters and doughs, and for pastries, soufflés, and other dishes containing eggs or cheese, with which the cooking temperature means the difference between success and failure.

Fresh vegetables and fruits containing enough moisture to prevent drying, such as potatoes, onions, carrots, beets, apples, bananas, and pears, may be baked whole in their skins by direct oven heat, or they may be pared, sliced, and baked in a covered casserole. The casserole serves much the same purpose as the skins in holding in the steam. To prevent baked starchy vegetables from becoming soggy, open the skins when baking is finished to allow the steam to escape.

COOKING IN FAT

Deep-fat frying. Cooking foods in hot fat deep enough to allow the food to be completely submerged. Foods suitable for deep-fat frying are small units, such as doughnuts, croquettes, fritters, oysters, fish, soft-shell crabs, and some sliced vegetables, such as potatoes, onions, eggplant, and parsnips. The chief advantage of this method over pan-frying is that because of the high temperature the foods will absorb a minimum of fat during cooking.

Fats used in deep-fat frying should be flavorless and odorless, such as cottonseed, corn, peanut, and soybean oils, modern vegetable shortenings, or high-grade lard.

In the average home the best utensil for deep-fat frying is a deep kettle made of heavy aluminum or iron, equipped with a frying basket. The surest method of determining the temperature of the fat is to have a deep-fat thermometer clipped to the side of the pan or kettle. If observed closely, it protects against underheating or overheating the fat. If a thermometer is not available, rough tests may be made with a 1-inch cube of bread dropped into the fat. If the cube browns in 40 seconds, the temperature is suitable for cooked foods; if it browns in 60 seconds, for uncooked foods. Foods should be at room temperature, and all excess moisture should be removed to prevent cooling and spattering the fat. Raw vegetables, such as potatoes for chips or French fries, should be thoroughly dried between clean towels. The food may be first rolled in fine dry cracker crumbs or breadcrumbs, then dipped in egg beaten with milk, using 1 to 2 tablespoons of milk for each egg, and then rolled in crumbs again. Another method is to dip each piece of food in thin batter, using as little as possible in order to give a crisp, delicate crust.

To absorb the excess fat, drain the food on paper towels as soon as it is removed from the hot fat, placing it on the towels in a single layer—never piling pieces of food one on top of another.

Pan-frying. Cooking in a small amount of fat in an uncovered skillet over heat. This differs from pan-broiling in that the fat is permitted to accumulate in the pan and that meat and vegetables may first be floured and crumbed to give a brown, crisp crust.

Sautéing. The French word *sauté* literally means "jumped." This is cooking in a skillet lightly greased to make it possible to "flip" or turn the food without its sticking to the pan. The food is fried lightly and quickly and is turned several times in the process.

COMBINATION METHODS OF COOKING

Methods of cooking which consist of combinations of two of the methods already described include braising, pot-roasting, *étouffée*, *à la poele*, *au gratin*, and glazing.

Braising (*fricasseeing*). Food is first sautéed and then cooked in a small amount of liquid in a covered saucepan or Dutch oven (steaming).

Pot-roasting. A form of braising; this term is applied to cooking large pieces of meat. The meat is first browned and then cooked slowly in a covered pan either on top of the range or in the oven. Vegetables are sometimes added near the end of the cooking period.

Étouffée. This term, or sometimes *à l'étuvée,* is used in France for a method of cooking in a tightly closed vessel with a small amount of water, stock, or wine. Fat must be added if it is not already present in the food. During the cooking most of the water evaporates, leaving a rich reduced liquid. This method is suitable for meats, poultry, and vegetables.

À la poele. A French term applied to a method of pot-roasting meat or poultry which is a combination of pan-frying and steaming. The meat is browned in a heatproof casserole over high heat, then removed from the casserole and set aside. Sliced carrots, onions, and celery are cooked in the same fat in the casserole for 5 minutes over low heat, then the meat is returned to the casserole, and seasoned with salt and pepper and melted butter. The casserole is then covered and put into a slow oven (325° F.) to finish cooking.

Au gratin. This French term designates a dish in which the food is mixed with a sauce, covered with buttered breadcrumbs, and cooked in the oven until the food is done and a brown crust has formed over the top. This type of dish may be made with either raw or cooked foods. With the latter, the dish may also be browned under the broiler. This is the authentic method of preparing *au gratin* dishes. Another method, erroneously labeled *au gratin,* specifies the use of cheese. It is used mainly for potatoes and other vegetables and various kinds of seafood and meats. The method of preparation and cooking is the same, except that the top is sprinkled with grated cheese and breadcrumbs may be omitted if desired.

Glazing. Widely used in French cooking and to some extent in America, this is the application of a coating which gives food a smooth, glossy surface, improving its appearance and usually its flavor. Materials used for glazing include butter, thick sauces such as Béchamel or Mornay, grated cheese, reduced meat juices acquired in cooking, reduced meat stock, gelatin, jelly, honey, corn syrup, simple sugar syrups, sugar (granulated, brown, and confectioners'), and chocolate. Some of the methods of glazing hot and cold dishes follow.

Glazing with sauces:
1. Butter sauce. Cover food (fillet of sole, for example) heavily with melted butter. Put the dish in a large pan of cold water to prevent the butter from curdling and brown quickly in a preheated very hot broiler.
2. Thick sauces. Coat the food with a thick sauce, usually Béchamel or

Mornay, and sprinkle with grated cheese. Brown quickly in a preheated very hot broiler.

3. Meat juices. Baste meat or poultry (braised or roasted) with reduced juices acquired in cooking and then subject it to intense oven heat.

Glazing with jelly, honey, or syrup:

1. Ham. Mix equal parts of jelly, honey, or syrup and prepared mustard. Spread over the ham and bake it in a preheated moderate oven (325° to 350° F.) until glazed and browned. If mustard is not desired, replace it with water, using 1 tablespoon to each ½ cup jelly.
2. Cold desserts. Make the glaze with water, heat, and use to glaze cold pies and other cold desserts.

Glazing with sugar (one of the simplest methods):

1. Vegetables. Sprinkle granulated white or brown sugar over vegetables and place in a hot oven to glaze and brown.
2. Cake. Sprinkle white granulated sugar over cake. Bake in a preheated hot broiler (450° F.), leaving door open and watching closely, until sugar melts and forms a brown glaze.
3. Crème Brulée. Sift brown sugar over Crème Brulée (baked custard made with light cream and brown sugar). Then bake in a preheated very slow broiler (250° F.), leaving door open, until sugar melts and forms a smooth caramel topping.

For other glazes see various recipes.

Herbs and Spices

The skillful use of herbs and spices in seasoning food is one of the marks of a fine cook in any country. Culinary herbs are usually defined as the leaves of plants grown in temperate climates, used fresh or dried; spices as various parts of plants grown in tropical countries—seeds, roots, flowers, fruit, bark, etc.—dried and used either in whole or powdered form. However, the distinction is somewhat hard to make; hence the following list includes both, in alphabetical order, with their uses in cooking.

NAME AND DESCRIPTION	CULINARY USES
Allspice (*Toute-épice*). Berry with combined flavors of cinnamon,	Whole or ground: meats, gravies, pickles, curry powder, sausages.

clove, and nutmeg (not a blend of spices).

Ground: cakes, meatloaf, soups, salads.

Anise (*Anis*). Delicate, sweet fragrance, medicinal.

Seeds, whole or ground: soups, meats, pastries, breads, cheese, fruits. Leaves: salads, sauces, shellfish.

Basil (*Basilic*). Leaves. Sweet, fragrant.

Soups, sauces, sausages, pâtés, salads; popular in Italian cooking.

Bay leaves (*Laurier*). Strong, pungent; use with discretion.

Meat, poultry, fish, stews.

Caraway (*Carvi*, *Cumin des prés*). Seeds. Aromatic, distinctive flavor.

Austrian specialties, breads, cakes, cheese.

Cardamom (*Cardamome*). Seeds, whole or ground. Pleasantly aromatic, medicinal. Fruits containing 8 to 16 seeds are harvested before they have ripened, then dried in the sun and sometimes bleached.

Curries, syrups, sausages, pastries.

Cayenne pepper (*Poivre rouge*). Made from the dried ground pods (with seeds) of small very hot capsicums; not related to black or white pepper. To be used with discretion.

Barbecued or curried meats and poultry, cheese dishes, sauces.

Cinnamon (*Cannells*). Made from the bark of a tree of the laurel family, peeled, dried, and trimmed into quills. Both quills (sticks) and ground cinnamon are used. Delicate, sweet, aromatic.

Beverages, pastries, breads, fruits, preserves.

Chervil (*Cerfeuil*). Leaves and stalks. Mild, aromatic, pleasing shape.

Soups, sauces, salads, decoration of cold dishes.

Chives (*Ciboulettes*). Very mild onion flavor; slender tubular leaves.

Soup, hot or cold, cold sauces, salads, meat, fish, mixed with butter or cream cheese.

Cloves (*Clous de girofle*). Flower buds, picked just before opening and dried in the sun. Used whole or ground. Strong, aromatic, high oil content, medicinal.

Meats, vegetables, fruit, sauces, marinades and brines, pickles, preserves.

Coriander (*Coriandre*). Seeds. Very delicate aroma, sweetish taste.

Meats, cheeses, polenta, soups, salads, pickles, pastries.

Cumin (*Cumin*). Seeds. Sharp and spicy.

Appetizers, breads, fish, poultry, game, meats, vegetables.

Curry (*Cari*). Powder. A mixture of various spices. Hot, pungent; the strength of the flavor depends on the combination and the amount used.

Oriental dishes, curry sauces, meats, poultry, rice, eggs.

Dill (*Aneth*). Leaves and seeds. Fragrant, permeating flavor.

Soups, sauces, crayfish, salads, pickles (seed).

Fennel (*Fenouil*). Mild, fragrant, penetrating, resembles anise.

Leaves: sauces, decoration of cold dishes; seeds: liqueurs, cakes, candies. Stalks and root: as vegetable, in salads.

Garlic (*Ail*). Sections of bulb, whole, chopped or crushed. Strong, pungent, penetrating; to be used with discretion.

Meats, fish, poultry, vegetables, salad dressing.

Ginger (*Gingembre*). Root (rhizome) is used; the young shoots crystallized, preserved; the older roots dried or ground into powder. Very fragrant, pungent, medicinal.

Gingerbread, cakes, pastries, sausages, pickles, curries.

Horseradish (*Raifort*). Grated root. Strong, hot, pungent.

Sauces, meat dishes, marinades, pickles.

Mace (*Macis*). The dried outer shell of the kernel of the fruit of the nutmeg tree, flattened and dried or ground into powder. Fragrant; flavor between nutmeg and cinnamon but stronger. (See Nutmeg.)

Sweet baked goods, preserves, cheese, fruit, soups, sauces, meats, fish, shellfish, potatoes, other vegetables.

Marjoram (*Marjolaine*). Leaves. Odoriferous, fragrant. Related to oregano.

Soups, sauces, fish, meat preparations.

Mint (*Menthe*). Leaves. Mild, fragrant.

Soups, sauces, potatoes, other vegetables, lamb, jelly, vinegars.

Mustard (*Moutarde*). Two varieties, black (dark-brown seeds) and

Young leaves: salad, or cooked greens. Powder: vinegar, sauces, salad white (yellow seeds), are both used in preparing dry mustard (powder or mustard flour). The powder must be mixed with water to bring out its pungent flavor. Prepared mustards in paste form are widely available commercially; the formula varies with the manufacturer.

dressings, meats, eggs, pickles. Prepared mustard is used with meats or in sauces.

Nutmeg (*Muscade*). Seed or nut found inside the kernel of the fruit of the nutmeg tree (see Mace), dried. Formerly sold whole and grated at home; now available in powdered form. Delicate, pungent.

Cakes, fruit pies, fruits, vegetables, meats, sauces, soups, milk drinks.

Oregano (*Origan*). Leaves. Related to marjoram, but stronger and more pungent; use with discretion.

Indispensable in Italian cooking, especially pizza; bouquet garni, soups, sauces, fish, meat, potatoes, other vegetables.

Paprika. Red powder made from the ripe dried pods of the larger and sweeter varieties of capsicum; the color, flavor, and pungency vary with the exact variety used. Hungarian paprika has a distinctive sweet aroma. Spanish paprika is usually more pungent than American or Hungarian. Rich in vitamin C.

Hungarian dishes; as seasoning and decoration for hors d'oeuvre, fish, shellfish, meat, poultry, salads, vegetables.

Parsley (*Persil*). Several varieties. Sprigs and leaves usually used fresh, but dried leaves are available. Aromatic; contains minerals and vitamin C.

Bouquet garni, Maître d'Hôtel Butter, soups, salads, garnishes.

Pepper (*Poivre*). Dried berry of a tropical vine, available whole (peppercorns) or ground. Black peppercorns are the whole berries; white peppercorns are berries from which the outer husks have been removed. White pepper is milder and less

All foods except sweet pastries or desserts. To secure best flavor, either black or white peppercorns should be freshly ground in a pepper mill just before using. Commercially ground pepper loses flavor and is often adulterated. Whole pepper-pungent, and in Europe is much more popular than black; in America black pepper is much more used than white.

corns are used in soups, stews, sausages.

Poppy seeds (Pavot). Dried seed of the poppy plant, white to deep blue. Aromatic, flavor resembles walnut.

Breads, cakes, pastries, canapés, vegetables, sauces.

Rosemary (Romarin). Leaves. Strong and pungent.

Pork, lamb, mutton, duck, goose, infusions, vinegars, fish soups, sauces, risottos, sausages.

Saffron (Safran). The dried stamens of a variety of crocus, whole or powdered. Difficulty of harvesting makes saffron the most expensive of spices. Gives attractive yellow color to food. Aromatic, pungent, to be used sparingly.

Soups, sauces, risottos, bouillabaise, curries, pastries, preserves.

Sage (Sauge). Leaves. Medicinal, aromatic, astringent; bitter if used to excess.

Sausages, fish, pork, goose, duck, brines and marinades.

Savory (Sarriette). Leaves. Rather peppery and piquant. Summer savory is known in some countries as the bean herb. Winter savory is similar but has a stronger aroma.

Green beans, peas, mushrooms, soups, sauces, meats.

Shallots (Échalotes). Member of the onion family, but with very delicate flavor. Bulbs.

Many culinary uses, especially fish, meat dishes, poultry, sauces.

Spring onions (Ciboules). Also called green onions or scallions. Odoriferous, mildly pungent. Bulbs and leaves.

Peas, salads, egg dishes.

Tarragon (Estragon). Leaves. Fragrant, taste and smell resembling anise.

Soups, sauces, eggs, fish, meat and poultry dishes, mustard, preserves, vinegar, mixed with butter, decoration of cold dishes.

Thyme (Thym). Leaves. Fragrant, pungent.

Most culinary preparations; salads, marinades, vinegar.

Turmeric (Curcuma). Powder made from the dried root of a plant of the ginger family. Color varies from light yellow to orange. Sweet, tangy flavor.

A main ingredient of curry powder; Oriental dishes, fish, shellfish, meats, pickles, sauces.

Vanilla (Vanille). Pod (bean) of a climbing orchid. Used whole, powdered, or as an extract. The most fragrant of culinary spices.

Pastries, confectionery, ice cream.

Basic Recipes

DOUGHS AND BATTERS

An important factor in French cuisine is the number of different dough and batter preparations, which are used in a great many ways. The two basic ingredients of all these preparations are flour and liquid, combined in varying amounts to obtain the characteristics desired for each type. Also, each type is mixed by a different method and to a different degree in order to obtain the texture and tenderness required for the particular product. For yeast doughs considerable kneading is necessary to develop the gluten (the protein in flour that gives it the elastic property). For quick doughs and batters, only a very little mixing is required. Rich, quick pastry should never be kneaded; it must be handled as little as possible in order to obtain a tender, flaky product.

⚜ BRIOCHE DOUGH (*Pâte à Brioche*)
(French Method)

Since brioche dough is soft, it should be refrigerated several hours or overnight to make it firm enough to handle.

1 package active dry yeast
lukewarm water
2 tablespoons sugar
3¼ cups sifted all-purpose flour
¾ teaspoon salt

2 large eggs, beaten
¾ cup (1½ sticks) butter, softened
1 egg yolk
1 tablespoon water

Place the yeast, ¼ cup lukewarm water, and 1 teaspoon of the sugar in a small mixing bowl. Let stand 5 minutes to soften. Stir in ¾ cup of the flour to make a soft dough. Shape into a ball. With scissors, cut a cross in the center top of the dough. Place the dough in a bowl and pour in enough lukewarm water to cover it. Cover the bowl and let the dough rise until it is bubbly, spongy, and has doubled in size, about 35 minutes. This is known as ferment or sponge.

Meanwhile mix together in a mixing bowl the remaining sugar, 1¾ cups of the flour, and the salt. Add the beaten eggs and mix until all the flour has been absorbed by the eggs. This dough is very stiff, but do not add liquid of any kind. Knead the dough, with both hands, on a flat surface until the dough is smooth, satiny, bouncy, and leaves the hands clean, about 10 minutes. Add the butter and stir as much of it in as possible. Then, with the hands, work the dough until it is as smooth as possible and has the consistency of pound-cake batter. Stir in ½ cup of the remaining flour. Stir and knead the dough about 5 minutes.

Drain all the water possible from the ferment, being careful not to drain off any particles of the ferment that might be floating in the water. Add the ferment to the dough and mix well without beating. Stir in the remaining ¼ cup flour. The dough will be a little sticky. Shape it into a ball and put it in a clean buttered bowl. Cover it with a tight-fitting lid or tie a piece of foil over the top of the bowl. Refrigerate overnight to make the dough easier to handle. Shape three-fourths of the dough into 18 balls, golf-ball size, and put them in well-greased 2½-inch cupcake pans. Dampen a finger and make a depression in the center of each ball. Shape the remaining dough into ½- to ¾-inch pear shapes and insert the pointed ends well into the depression of the larger balls, forming a topknot. With scissors make 4 or 5 slits in the dough of the larger balls around the topknots, an equal distance apart. Beat the egg yolk with the 1 tablespoon water and brush over the rolls. Cover the rolls and let them rise in a warm place 1 hour or until they have doubled in size. Bake in a preheated hot oven (400° F.) 10 to 12 minutes. Makes 18 rolls.

⚜ BRIOCHE DOUGH
(Quick Method)

2 envelopes active dry yeast
½ cup lukewarm water
2 tablespoons sugar
3½ cups sifted all-purpose flour
¾ teaspoon salt

2 large eggs
¾ cup (1½ sticks) butter, softened
1 egg yolk
1 tablespoon water

Combine the yeast, the ½ cup water, and 1 teaspoon of the sugar in a small mixing bowl and let stand 5 minutes to soften. Stir in ½ cup of the flour. Cover and let the mixture rise in a warm place (80° to 85° F.) until it is bubbly and has doubled in size. This is known as ferment or sponge. Reserve

2 tablespoons of the remaining flour for later use and put the rest of the flour in a mixing bowl. Add the remaining sugar (5 teaspoons), and the salt. Stir in the fermented yeast mixture. Beat the batter 2 minutes. Beat in the eggs, one at a time. Add the butter and stir and beat until it is thoroughly blended with the dough, using the hands if necessary. Sprinkle the reserved 2 tablespoons flour on a flat surface and turn out the dough onto it. Knead 5 minutes. Put the dough in a buttered bowl, turning it over so that the greased side is up. Cover the dough and let it rise in a warm place until it has doubled in size, about 1 hour. Knead the dough 2 minutes, then cover and let it rest 10 minutes. Shape three-fourths of the dough into 18 2-inch balls and put them in buttered 2½-inch cupcake pans. Dampen a finger and make a depression in the center of each ball. Roll the remaining dough into 18 pear shapes and push the small ends well into the centers of the larger balls to form topknots. With scissors cut 4 slits in the dough of each of the larger balls around the topknots. Beat the egg yolk with the 1 tablespoon water and brush it over the rolls. Cover the rolls and let them rise in a warm place until doubled in size, about 30 minutes. If topknots have shifted during the rising period, replace them in the centers of the large balls. Bake in a preheated hot oven (400° F.) 10 to 12 minutes. Makes 18 rolls.

❧ Filled Brioche Fritters

Make Brioche Dough, using either method. Chill the dough for several hours or overnight. Roll half the dough to ⅛-inch thickness into a rectangle or square. Mark it in 2-inch squares and drop ¾-inch balls of filling (made of meat, fish, shellfish, egg, cheese, fruit, jam, etc.) on the squares. Dip a finger or a pastry brush in water and moisten the dough around the filling. Roll the remaining dough the same thickness and size as the first half and place it on top. With a finger, press down the dough around each ball of filling. Cut out the fritters with a 1½- or 2-inch biscuit cutter. Place them on a tray covered with waxed paper, cover them with a towel, and let them rise 30 minutes in a warm place (80° to 85° F.). Fry the fritters until golden in deep fat preheated to 375° F. Drain on paper towels. Fritters with a sweet filling should be sprinkled with confectioners' sugar. Makes approximately 2 dozen fritters.

❧ CHOU PASTE (*Pâte à Choux*)
(Cream-Puff Paste)

Pâte à choux (Chou Paste) has many practical applications in French cooking. It may be baked just as it is and filled with pastry cream or whipped cream to serve as dessert. Or the paste may be mixed with cheese to make a tasty hors d'oeuvre; mixed with forcemeat to make quenelles and mousses; or beaten with mashed potatoes and used to make Gnocchi (Italian dumplings), or to make Dauphine potatoes by shaping the mixture into balls, dipping them in beaten egg, then in fine breadcrumbs, and frying them in deep fat.

1 cup water
½ cup (1 stick) butter
¼ teaspoon salt

1 cup sifted all-purpose flour
4 large eggs

Place the first 3 ingredients in a 1-quart saucepan. Bring to boiling point. Remove from heat and stir in all the flour at one time, using a wooden spoon. Beat vigorously. Return to heat and stir and cook over low heat until the mixture forms a very stiff ball and leaves the sides of the pan. Remove from heat. Beat in the eggs, one at a time, beating in each until it is completely absorbed before adding another. Continue beating until the dough is shiny and satiny and breaks into strands. Do not overbeat, as this reduces the volume and affects the consistency needed for piping the mixture.

⚜ Cream Puffs

Squeeze the Chou Paste from a pastry bag, or drop by rounded tablespoonfuls, 2 inches apart onto ungreased baking sheets. Bake in a preheated hot oven (400° F.) 30 to 35 minutes, or until golden. Do not underbake. Turn off heat. Prick the puffs with a knife to allow steam to escape, and leave them in the oven 20 minutes to dry out the centers and to cool. Split and fill with creamed mixtures for entrées or with cream fillings, etc., for desserts. Makes 12 large puffs.

⚜ Small Hors d'Oeuvre Puffs

Drop the Chou Paste from a teaspoon and bake only 20 to 25 minutes. This recipe will make 24 small puffs.

⚜ Eclairs

Shape the Chou Paste into finger lengths on an ungreased baking sheet. Bake and cool as for Cream Puffs. Fill with French Pastry Cream and frost the tops with melted semisweet chocolate or with other chocolate or caramel icing. Makes 12 eclairs.

⚜ CHOU PASTE FOR FRITTERS (*Pâte à Choux pour Beignets Soufflés*)

Add 2 teaspoons sugar and 1 teaspoon vanilla extract to the recipe for Chou Paste. Drop the paste from a tablespoon into deep fat preheated to 370° F. Fry until brown on all sides. Drain on paper towels. Serve hot, sprinkled with confectioners' sugar, or serve with Vanilla Sauce. Or fill the fritters with well-drained cooked fresh fruit or canned fruit.

23

⚜ French Crullers

Fill a pastry bag with the Chou Paste mixture in the preceding recipe. Pipe the dough into ring shapes and fry in preheated deep hot fat (370° F.). Drain on paper towels and sprinkle with confectioners' sugar.

⚜ FRITTER BATTER (*Pâte à Frire*)

1 cup sifted all-purpose flour
½ teaspoon salt
1 large egg, slightly beaten

¾ cup milk
1 tablespoon butter, melted

Sift the flour and salt together. Combine the egg, milk, and butter, and stir into the dry ingredients. Use to cover vegetables such as sliced onions, sliced zucchini or summer squash, cauliflower, spinach leaves, or okra; shrimp or other shellfish; and Cheddar cheese cubes, for frying. Fry in deep hot fat preheated to 370° F. 3 to 4 minutes. Drain on paper towels. Makes approximately 6 portions.

⚜ Sweet Fritter Batter

To the flour in Fritter Batter, add 2 tablespoons sugar and 1 teaspoon double-acting baking powder. Use to make fruit fritters.

⚜ PLAIN PASTRY DOUGH (*Pâte Brisée*)

For a 9-inch pastry shell:

1 cup sifted all-purpose flour
¼ teaspoon salt
¼ cup (½ stick) butter

1½ tablespoons vegetable shortening
about 3 tablespoons cold water

Sift the flour and salt into a mixing bowl. Add the butter and shortening and with a pastry blender or two knives cut it in until the mixture resembles coarse meal. Add water and blend it in quickly, using a tossing motion. Press the dampened particles together into a ball. Roll into a circle ⅛ inch thick and 2 inches larger in diameter than the pie plate. Carefully fold the dough into quarters and place it into a 9-inch pie plate. Unfold and fit it loosely in the plate without stretching or pulling the pastry. Trim the edges of the pastry ½ inch larger than the outside rim of the plate. Flute or crimp the edge with the fingers or a fork. If a filling is to be baked in the shell, bake as directed in each recipe. If the crust is to be filled after it has been baked, prick the bottom and sides of the pastry with a fork, then fit a smaller pan or bean bag into the pie crust. Bake in a preheated hot oven (425° F.) 12 to 15 minutes, removing the smaller pan or bean bag after the pastry has baked 10 minutes. Bake until golden brown. Makes one 9-inch crust. For a 2-crust 9-inch pie, double the ingredients, except use only about 5 tablespoons cold water. Mix and roll as above.

⚜ SWEET PIE PASTRY (*Pâte Sucrée*)

1½ cups sifted all-purpose flour
⅓ cup sifted confectioners' sugar
⅛ teaspoon salt

½ cup (1 stick) butter
3 tablespoons milk or water

Sift the flour, sugar, and salt together into a mixing bowl. Add the butter and cut it in with a pastry blender or two knives until the mixture resembles coarse meal. Add the milk or water. Mix lightly to form a dough.

For individual tart shells, divide the dough into 8 equal parts. Roll each ¹⁄₁₆ to ⅛ inch thick. Fit into tart pans measuring 3½ inches across the top and 2 inches across the bottom. Prick the bottom and sides of the pastry with a fork at intervals to prevent blistering. Bake in a preheated moderate oven (350° F.) 15 to 20 minutes. Cool completely, then remove the tart shells from the pans. Fill with pastry cream or fruit fillings. Makes 8 tart shells.

For a 9- or 10-inch pie, roll the pastry to ⅛-inch thickness and fit it into a 9- or 10-inch pie plate. Trim the dough, as for Plain Pastry, turn under, and flute the edge. Prick bottom and sides with a fork. Bake as for tart shells.

⚜ PUFF PASTRY (*Pâte Feuilletée*)
(Puff Paste)

This is a basic recipe. Puff Pastry should not be made on a hot day because the butter will melt and soak into the flour, making the pastry heavy. The butter, water, and lemon juice should be thoroughly chilled and the dough thoroughly kneaded to make it more stretchable. Be sure to seal the edges firmly. The dough should be refrigerated 30 minutes after each rolling to make it more flexible for additional rolling and folding, and to help prevent the butter from breaking through the thin layer of dough. Since folding and rolling the dough results in pastry that rises high, it should be rolled and chilled no more than 7 times, or the dough will become tough.

2 sticks (1 cup) butter
1¾ cups sifted all-purpose flour
½ teaspoon salt

½ cup plus 2 teaspoons ice water
¾ teaspoon lemon juice

Cut each stick of butter into 3 lengthwise strips. Place the 6 strips close together on a piece of waxed paper to form a rectangle. Refrigerate until ready to use. Sift the flour with the salt into a mixing bowl. Combine the ice water and lemon juice and add to the flour, stirring and tossing it in with a fork, to form a dry dough. Knead the dough on a *very* lightly floured board 10 minutes, then cover and let rest 15 minutes. Roll out the dough into a 16- by 6-inch rectangle on a *very* lightly floured board with a *very* lightly floured rolling pin. Place the chilled butter strips on half of the dough, leaving a ½-inch margin of dough at the edges. Fold the other half of the dough over the butter. Press the edges together firmly with the fingers to seal. Tap the dough lightly with the rolling pin to flatten the butter. Roll out lengthwise into a rectangle 18 by 6 inches, having the folded side nearest you. Fold the dough, from the short side, into thirds, making the dough into a 3-layer 6-inch square. Be sure that the edges and corners are even and square. Press the edges firmly with the fingers to seal in the butter and the air. Wrap in waxed paper and refrigerate 30 minutes. Roll out the dough again into an 18- by 6-inch rectangle, having the pastry board and rolling pin floured *very* lightly. Fold, seal edges, and wrap as before and again refrigerate for 30 minutes. Repeat this procedure 5 more times. This pastry may be wrapped in foil and kept refrigerated until ready to use. Puff Pastry may also be frozen and stored in the freezer. Use Puff Pastry for making Patty Shells, Vol-au-Vents, Pastry Horns for cream filling, pie crust, Palm Leaves, Croissants, etc., according to directions in the individual recipes.

⚜ PATTY SHELLS (*Bouchées*)

Make the recipe for Puff Pastry and divide it into thirds. Roll one portion at a time, keeping the others refrigerated until ready to use. Roll pastry to ⅛-inch thickness on a lightly floured board. For each patty shell, cut three 3-inch pastry circles, using a sharp 3-inch fluted cooky cutter. (For 8 patty shells, 24 circles.) Place 8 of the pastry circles on an ungreased baking sheet. Brush the surface of each with 1 egg yolk beaten with 1½ teaspoons cold water. Do not let egg drip on the sides. Using a 2-inch cutter, cut out centers of 8 pastry circles, making a ring as for doughnuts. Place one ring on each of the pastry circles on the baking sheet. Brush with egg yolk. Press a 1½-inch cooky cutter into the centers of remaining 8 pastry circles, but do not cut through. Place these on top of the first ring. Brush with egg yolk. Bake in a preheated very hot oven (450° F.) for 10 minutes. Reduce heat to moderate (350° F.) and bake 20 minutes or until shells are golden. Remove the indented centers of the top layer with a pointed knife. Return the shells to the 350° F. oven and bake 10 minutes longer to dry out centers. Fill the shells with creamed mixtures such as chicken, shrimp, etc. Garnish tops with removed centers. Makes 8 patty shells.

Crêpes, Pancakes, and Waffles

French crêpes are very thin pancakes made from batter containing less flour and more eggs and milk than the batter for American pancakes. They are always very thin with a delicate fine-grained texture which is as smooth to the palate as a creamy custard. (The American pancake is thicker and has a coarser texture.)

The French use crêpes for making hors d'oeuvre, entrées, and desserts and, cut into strips or fancy shapes, such as hearts or diamonds, as a garnish in soup. The batter for dessert crêpes contains sugar while that for entrée and soup crêpes does not. Crêpes may be made ahead of time and reheated before serving.

Pancakes and waffles are made from batter thin enough to pour. The perfect pancake is golden and tender. The perfect waffle is light, porous, and crisp.

Heavy, tough pancakes result from too much stirring of the batter. The thicker the batter the less it can be stirred and the more likely it is to produce heavy, tough pancakes. If the griddle is too hot the pancakes will be spotted and unevenly browned.

Waffles are baked in electrically heated waffle irons, which are usually thermostatically controlled. However, if yours is not, care must be taken that the iron is heated to the correct temperature. This is reached when a drop of water sputters when dropped on the surface. If the iron is too hot the waffle will stick and become too brown; if too cold, the waffle will be tough and underbaked. The waffle batter should only partly fill each compartment of the iron. Keep the cover closed and bake the waffle until the steam is no longer visible.

Leftover pancake and waffle batter made with double-acting baking powder can be kept covered in the refrigerator for several days.

⚜ CRÊPES FOR CONSOMMÉ

1 large egg
dash salt
2 tablespoons flour

½ cup milk, or ¼ cup milk and ¼ cup chicken stock
½ teaspoon chopped parsley

Beat the egg and add the salt, flour, and ¼ cup milk. Beat the mixture only until it is smooth, since overbeating the egg produces tough crêpes. Stir in the remaining ¼ cup milk or the ¼ cup chicken stock and the parsley. Let the batter stand 2 hours. Heat a 6-inch skillet or a special French crêpe frying pan and butter it lightly. For each crêpe pour in 2 tablespoons batter. Quickly rotate the skillet to spread the batter uniformly. Cook over direct moderate heat 1 to 2 minutes or until the crêpe has browned underneath and bubbles have formed over its top surface. Turn and cook ½ to 1 minute to brown the other side. Transfer the crêpes as they are cooked to a larger pan lined with a clean towel. Cut into julienne strips or into fancy shapes with tiny assorted cooky cutters. Serve in consommé. Makes about 5 crêpes.

⚜ PLAIN PANCAKE BATTER (*Pâte à Crêpes Ordinaires*)

1½ cups sifted all-purpose flour
2 tablespoons sugar
½ teaspoon salt
2½ teaspoons double-acting baking
   powder

2 eggs, beaten
1¼ cups milk
3 tablespoons butter, melted

Sift the first 4 ingredients together into a mixing bowl. Combine the beaten eggs and the milk and add to the dry mixture. Add the melted butter. Mix only until ingredients are blended. (The batter will be a little lumpy.) Let the batter stand 2 hours. Use ¼ cup batter for each pancake. Bake on a hot, lightly greased griddle. (The griddle is hot enough when cold water dropped on the surface spurts or boils rapidly.) Turn the pancakes when bubbles form over the surface. Turn only once during baking. Serve dredged with confectioners' sugar or spread with jam. Makes twelve 5-inch pancakes.

⚜ FRENCH DESSERT PANCAKES (*Crêpes*)

1 cup sifted all-purpose flour
½ teaspoon salt
1 tablespoon sugar
¼ teaspoon double-acting baking
   powder

3 eggs, beaten
2 cups milk
1 teaspoon vanilla extract
2 tablespoons butter, melted

Sift the first 4 ingredients together into a mixing bowl. Set aside. Combine the beaten eggs with the milk and vanilla extract and add to the flour mixture. Add the melted butter and mix only until ingredients are blended. Let the batter stand 2 hours. For each pancake pour 2 tablespoons batter into a hot, lightly greased 6-inch skillet or Crêpes Suzette pan. Quickly rotate the pan to spread the batter over the bottom uniformly. Cook over moderately low heat until the underside is brown and bubbles form over the top. Turn to brown the other side. As the pancakes are cooked, stack them on a clean towel in a baking pan, sprinkling confectioners' sugar over each. Cover. Shortly before serving, heat in a preheated moderate oven (350° F.) 10 minutes or until hot. Before serving spread each pancake with jam or stewed fruit or with honey, syrup, or a dessert sauce, and roll it up. Makes approximately 20 pancakes.

⚜ WAFFLES (*Gauffres*)

2 cups sifted all-purpose flour
3 teaspoons double-acting baking
   powder
1 teaspoon salt

3 eggs, separated
1¾ cups milk
6 tablespoons butter, melted

Sift the first 3 ingredients together into a mixing bowl. Beat the egg yolks until they are light and lemon-colored. Mix them with the milk and add to the dry ingredients. Add the melted butter and stir only until the ingredients are blended. Beat the egg whites until they stand in soft stiff peaks and fold them into the batter. Bake in hot waffle irons until medium brown in color. Makes approximately 6 waffles.

❧ RICH DESSERT WAFFLES

1 cup sifted cake flour	1 teaspoon salt
1 tablespoon sugar	2 large eggs, separated
1 teaspoon double-acting baking powder	1 cup heavy cream
	½ teaspoon vanilla extract

Sift the first 4 ingredients together into a mixing bowl. Beat the egg yolks until light and lemon-colored, then add the cream and vanilla extract and beat well. Add to the dry ingredients. Mix only until ingredients are blended. Beat the egg whites until they stand in soft stiff peaks and fold them into the batter. Spoon the batter into preheated waffle irons, being careful not to fill the compartments completely. Bake 3 to 4 minutes or until the steam subsides. Serve with Lemon Sauce, Chocolate Sauce, Orange Sauce, or any other sauce desired. Makes 3 to 4 waffles.

STOCKS

Stocks are used for braising meats and vegetables and as the liquid for making meat-, poultry-, and fish-flavored sauces, soups, and stews. They are made by simmering (not boiling) bones, meat, poultry, or fish, vegetables, herbs, and spices in water for several hours. Stocks of stronger flavor are obtained by removing the bones, meat, and vegetables after the stock is cooked, straining the stock, and then cooking it down to smaller volume. This essence is used for making aspics, glazing, and as a flavor-booster in sauces. The best stocks are made from cracked beef bones and veal bones; beef, veal, or poultry; soup vegetables (onions, leeks, carrots, celery, mushroom stems); herbs and spices. Starchy or strong-flavored vegetables should not be used. For fish stocks, see Chapter 8.

⚜ PLAIN WHITE STOCK (*Fond Blanc Ordinaire*)

3 pounds shoulder of veal
4 pounds knuckle of veal
4 pounds chicken giblets, or backs,
    necks, and wings
3 tablespoons salt
about 6 quarts of cold water

2 medium-sized carrots
2 medium-large onions
4 leeks
4 ribs celery
large bouquet garni

Bone the meat and tie it up with a string. Crack the bones, wash the chicken parts, and place all in a 12-quart saucepan. Add the salt. Add the water, having it cover the ingredients by 1 full inch. Bring to boiling point. Skim off and discard scum that has risen to the surface. Peel the carrots and onions and add along with the celery and bouquet garni. Wash the leeks thoroughly and add. Bring to boiling point, partially covered with the lid. Reduce heat and simmer 4 hours or more, never allowing the water to boil. Add boiling water if water evaporates to the level of the ingredients. Remove the meat and bones and cool stock enough that it can be strained. Then strain through two thicknesses of cheesecloth first wrung out in cold water. Refrigerate the stock uncovered until the fat has hardened on the surface and can be lifted off. If desired, the fat can be removed while the stock is hot. Use for making Velouté Sauce, gravies, aspics, and soups. Makes about 4 quarts.

⚜ CLEAR BROWN STOCK (*Fond Brun Clair*)

5 pounds lean beef soup meat
6 pounds knuckle of veal
1 pound rind of salt pork
2 pounds each beef and veal bones
3 tablespoons shortening or suet
2 large carrots

2 medium-large onions
about 7 quarts cold water
3 tablespoons salt
large bouquet garni
1 large clove garlic

Cut the meat and pork rind in large pieces. Crack the bones. Peel and slice vegetables. Brown all, including bones, in shortening or suet, in a large pan in the oven. Then transfer to a 12-quart kettle and add 2 quarts of the water and the salt. Simmer 1 hour, having the pot partially covered with a lid. Add the remaining water, or enough to cover the ingredients by 1 full inch. Add the bouquet garni and garlic. Simmer 5 or more hours, removing the scum from the surface from time to time. Remove the meat and bones from the stock, strain and skim off fat as described for Plain White Stock (see preceding recipe). Use in making brown sauces, braising, for stews, and in meat jellies. Makes about 4 quarts.

FORCEMEATS

Forcemeats (*farces*) are made of finely ground meat, poultry, liver, close-grained fish, shellfish, seasonings, and sometimes Panada, a mixture similar to Chou Paste. Panada acts as a binding agent and also gives body. Forcemeats are used for making quenelles, mousses, mousselines, pâtés, loaves, molds, vol-au-vents, borders, garnishes, canapés, spreads, and stuffings.

❧ COOKED FORCEMEAT (*Farce au Gratin*)

½ pound fat salt pork, diced fine
1 pound liver—poultry, veal, or game
—thinly sliced
2 tablespoons chopped shallots or
small white onions

1 small bay leaf
2 tablespoons chopped parsley
½ teaspoon dried thyme, or 1½ tablespoons chopped fresh thyme
¼ teaspoon ground black pepper

Cook the salt pork over medium-low heat until all the fat has been rendered. Remove the pork. Strain the fat and return it to the skillet. Add the liver, the chopped shallot or onion, and the bay leaf. Stir and cook over medium heat until the liver has browned lightly. Add the remaining ingredients. Stir and cook 1 to 2 minutes. Remove and discard the bay leaf. Lift out the liver and the chopped shallots or onion and put through a food chopper twice, using the finest blade, or grind in an electric blender. (If a blender is used, grind one-third of the liver at a time.) Add the fat from the skillet. Beat well with a wooden spoon. Use for stuffing game, as a spread for canapés, or as a filling for fritters or turnovers. Makes approximately 2 cups.

❧ QUENELLE FORCEMEAT WITH PANADA

1 pound (2 cups ground) boneless,
raw white meat of poultry, veal, or
dry, firm-textured fish, with gristle
and fat removed
½ teaspoon salt
¼ teaspoon ground black pepper

⅛ teaspoon ground nutmeg
1 cup cold Flour Panada (page 32)
½ cup (1 stick) soft butter
2 large whole eggs and 2 large egg
yolks

Put the poultry, veal, or fish through a food chopper twice, using the finest blade. Add the seasonings and beat well. Add the Flour Panada, and beat it into the meat with a wooden spoon. Beat in the butter. Beat in the whole eggs and egg yolks, one at a time. Put the forcemeat through a sieve. Test the consistency by shaping a spoonful of the mixture into a small ball or cylinder and poaching it in simmering water. If it disintegrates, beat in 1 or 2 more egg yolks; if the mixture is too dry, beat in a little cream, 1 tablespoon at a time. Test after each addition. Shape into Quenelles and poach.

✤ HOW TO SHAPE AND POACH QUENELLES

The size and shape of Quenelles depends upon the way they are to be used. There are four methods of shaping them: with spoons, by hand, in molds, or by forcing the mixture through a pastry bag.

Spoon Method. Wet a soup spoon or dessert spoon and measure out a rounded spoonful of cold forcemeat. Smooth the top with the inverted bowl of another spoon of the same size which has been dipped in very hot water. Loosen the dumpling from the first spoon and slide it into simmering water or broth. Simmer, uncovered, 15 to 20 minutes. If the water is allowed to boil, Quenelles are likely to split.

Shaping by Hand. Measure out a rounded soup spoon or dessert spoon of forcemeat and roll it with the palms of the hands on a floured board to form a 2½-inch cylinder. Simmer as for spoon-shaped Quenelles.

In Molds. Forcemeat for garnishes may be shaped like large olives, using the spoon method, or cooked in individual flared, round, or boat-shaped molds. First butter the molds generously and make a simple design on the bottom of each with bits of truffle or ripe olive. Fill the molds generously with forcemeat, making sure there are no air spaces along the sides. Poach in simmering water as for spoon-shaped Quenelles. The Quenelles will unmold themselves and float to the surface of the liquid.

With a Pastry Bag. Place a round ½-inch tube in a large pastry bag and put the forcemeat into the bag. Pipe small round, or 1½-inch elongated, Quenelles onto the bottom of a buttered saucepan or skillet. Cover with simmering water or broth and poach as for spoon-shaped Quenelles.

To make Quenelles for soup, put forcemeat through a pastry bag fitted with a small tube, moving the bag a short distance back and forth to give the Quenelles a slight curl. These are sometimes called Caterpillar Dumplings. Cover with simmering water or stock and cook, uncovered, 12 to 15 minutes. Serve in soup.

✤ FLOUR PANADA (*Panada pour Farce à la Farine*)

½ cup water
3 tablespoons butter

¼ teaspoon salt
1 cup sifted all-purpose flour

Mix the first 3 ingredients in a 1-quart saucepan. Bring to boiling point. Remove from heat and beat in all the flour at one time, using a wooden spoon. Continue beating about 1 minute. Return to heat. Stir and cook slowly for

5 minutes or until the mixture forms a ball and leaves the sides of the pan. Remove from heat and spread the mixture on a buttered plate. Cover with buttered paper to prevent crusting over the top. Refrigerate until thoroughly chilled. Mix with twice-ground meat, chicken, liver, game, or fish as specified in each recipe. Makes 1 cup.

⚜ Milk Panada

In the recipe for Flour Panada, replace the water with milk.

⚜ Egg Panada

Make Panada, using milk instead of water. Before adding the flour, add 1 large whole egg and beat it in well. Proceed as in the recipe for Flour Panada. Use with fish forcemeats and fish pastries.

MARINADES

A marinade is a highly seasoned liquid, cooked or uncooked, made with vinegar or wine and water or bouillon with seasonings. It is used to tenderize less tender cuts of meat, to add flavor, and to increase the keeping qualities of the food. The length of time for marinating depends upon the type of food and the size of the pieces into which the food is cut.

⚜ UNCOOKED MARINADE (*Marinade Crue*)

1 cup sliced carrots
½ cup sliced onion
2 shallots, chopped
6 whole black peppercorns, crushed
4 juniper berries (if available)
2 whole cloves
¼ cup chopped parsley
1 bay leaf

½ teaspoon dried thyme, or 2 teaspoons chopped fresh thyme
⅓ cup wine vinegar
2 cups dry white wine, or 1 cup wine and 1 cup beef bouillon
1 teaspoon salt
¼ cup salad oil or olive oil

Put half the carrots, half the onion, and half the shallots in the bottom of a roasting pan and place the meat to be marinated on top. Add all the remaining ingredients except the oil. Pour the oil over the part of the meat that is not covered by the marinade to prevent the meat from turning dark. Refrigerate. Allow small pieces (chops, cutlets, noisettes, Shish Kebabs, etc.) to marinate in the refrigerator 12 to 24 hours; larger pieces 2 to 3 days, turning the meat often. Makes about 2½ cups.

❧ COOKED MARINADE (*Marinade Cuite*)

Use all the same ingredients as in Uncooked Marinade, but increase the vinegar to ⅔ cup and the wine to 2¼ cups and add ½ cup water to allow for evaporation during cooking. Put all the ingredients except the oil into a large kettle. Bring the mixture to boiling point and simmer 10 minutes. Cool. Put the meat in a deep bowl, pour in the marinade, and sprinkle the oil over the part of the meat not covered with marinade. Refrigerate. Marinate larger pieces of meat 24 to 36 hours, smaller pieces 8 to 10 hours, turning the meat frequently in the marinade.

If you are in a hurry, pour the hot marinade over the meat, sprinkle with oil, and marinate larger pieces 12 to 24 hours, smaller pieces 4 to 5 hours.

Sauces

Sauces play an important role in French cooking. They serve to enhance and complement the flavor and texture of the food they accompany. They should never disguise or mask the natural flavor of the food.

In France, the term "sauce" covers dessert sauces, gravies, and salad dressings as well as the sauces used in cream soups, entrées, vegetables, meats and some hors d'oeuvre. In this book, dessert sauces are in Chapter 15; most others are in this chapter, but see Chapter 14 for additional salad dressings.

Although there are hundreds of different French sauces, they are all derived from a few basic sauces. Some of these are made with roux and stock; others are emulsion sauces and butters or butter sauces.

Sauces with a roux base are often enriched with egg yolk, cream, and additional butter.

To prevent the hot sauce from coagulating the egg yolk when it is added, mix the yolk with 1 to 2 tablespoons of cream and gradually beat in a little of the hot sauce. Then stir the mixture into the remaining hot sauce. Cook only to boiling point, stirring constantly.

If a sauce containing cream is to be reduced, use light cream. If a sauce is enriched with heavy cream, add it last.

Sauces are often finished with a little butter after they are cooked to improve the flavor and to give additional thickness. As stirring reduces the thick-ening quality of the butter, instead swirl the pan in a circular motion to blend in the butter. Remove the saucepan from the heat before the butter is com-pletely melted. This method gives the sauce a better flavor and a slightly thicker consistency.

Roux. There are two kinds of roux, white and brown.

To make a white roux, blend flour with butter and gently cook and stir until the mixture is foamy, taking care not to brown it. This cooking elimi-nates the disagreeable pasty taste of raw flour. White roux is the basis of all white sauces.

Brown roux may be made with lard, unsalted beef or pork drippings, cooking oil, or clarified butter (butter melted and the liquid poured off with-out disturbing the sediment). In sauces used on foods of delicate flavor, such as eggs, clarified butter is preferable. The fat is cooked slowly in a heavy saucepan with a little diced onion, carrot, etc., until the vegetables are soft, but not browned. Then it is blended with flour and stirred and cooked very slowly until the flour has browned, being careful not to burn it. Brown roux is the basis of *Sauce Espagnole,* the great brown sauce from which Demi-Glace Sauce (page 44) is made.

Roux may be prepared ahead of time and stored in a covered jar in the refrigerator or freezer to use as needed.

Stocks. These are also of two general types, white and brown.

White stock is made by simmering cubed meat and cracked bones from veal, chicken, or fish in water. Veal and chicken stocks are simmered for several hours; fish stocks cook in less time. Soup vegetables—carrots, onions, celery—and herbs are added. The stock should be skimmed occasionally while it is cooking and again after it has been strained through a fine sieve or through cheesecloth. White stock should be clear and as light as possible.

Brown stock is made with cubed beef and veal meat and cracked bones sprinkled with a little melted fat and browned in the oven, stirring occasion-ally to brown uniformly, then simmered in water, with soup vegetables and herbs. Skim and strain the stock as for white stock. Brown stock should be amber-colored and transparent. (For recipe see page 30.)

⚜ HOW TO REFRIGERATE SAUCES

Most sauces can be made ahead of time and reheated before using. Such sauces as Velouté, Demi-Glace, and Tomato, may be stored in the refrigerator for several weeks and used as needed. However, sauces containing milk, eggs, and cream should not be kept longer than 24 hours. To store sauces, put them in clean jars and pour a layer of melted shortening over them. Cover tightly and refrigerate.

CLASSIFICATION OF BASIC SAUCES

The two great basic white sauces are Béchamel, made with white roux and milk, and Velouté, made with white roux and white stock (chicken, veal, or fish).

The two leading French brown sauces are *Sauce Espagnole*, made from brown roux and brown stock or bouillon and simmered several hours, and Demi-Glace Sauce, which in France is made by combining equal quantities of *Sauce Espagnole* and brown stock and then simmering long enough to reduce the quantity to a little less than one-half the original amount. See Demi-Glace Sauce, Home Style (page 44) for a simplified version.

Basic Tomato Sauce is made with brown roux, tomatoes, brown stock, and coarsely diced carrots, celery, and onions, simmered about 2 hours and strained through a fine sieve, rubbing through as much of the vegetable pulp as possible.

Hollandaise, the basic cooked emulsion-type sauce, is made with egg yolks, butter, and lemon juice, cooked over hot (not boiling) water until the mixture thickens.

Mayonnaise, the basic cold emulsion-type sauce, is made by gradually beating oil into a mixture of egg, lemon juice or vinegar, and seasonings.

Butters and Butter Sauces are of two types, cold and hot. Cold butter sauces are made with softened butter into which various seasoning ingredients, such as anchovies, herbs, spices, purées, and/or lemon juice, are blended. Hot butter sauces consist of melted butter browned and seasoned as desired with herbs, spices, almonds or other nuts, lemon juice, etc.

Basic Sauces and Some Derivatives

The following chart shows how easily a basic sauce can be made into a different sauce by the addition of a few simple ingredients.

BASIC SAUCE	SAUCE VARIATION	INGREDIENTS ADDED
Béchamel	Aurora	tomato sauce, tomato purée, or tomato paste, and additional butter
	Caper	capers and parsley
	Egg	chopped hard-cooked eggs and parsley
	Mornay	grated cheese, cream, and egg yolk

37

Velouté	Poulette	heavy cream, egg yolk, chopped mushrooms, and lemon juice
	Suprême	cream, lemon juice, and additional butter
Demi-Glace	Bordelaise	red wine, herbs, beef marrow, butter, and additional stock
	Gratin	mushrooms, shallots, white wine, tomato paste, parsley, and additional butter
	Piquante	shallots, parsley, chives, gherkins, wine, vinegar, and additional butter
	Robert	tomato sauce, mustard, onion, white wine, wine vinegar, parsley, sour pickle, and butter
Hollandaise	Béarnaise	chervil, parsley, tarragon, and tarragon vinegar
	Mousseline	whipped cream
Mayonnaise	Cocktail Sauce	catsup, whipped cream, cognac, and sherry
	Rémoulade	mustard and capers; other herbs, as chervil, tarragon, spinach, or watercress, if desired
Vinaigrette	Ravigote	capers, chervil, chives, parsley, tarragon, onion
Cold Butter	Anchovy Butter	anchovy paste or mashed anchovies and lemon juice
	Maître d'Hôtel Butter	parsley, lemon juice, salt and pepper
Hot Butter	Brown Butter	melted butter cooked until nut-brown
	Black Butter	melted butter cooked until dark-brown, almost black

WHITE SAUCES

White sauces are used as the base for cream soups, for soufflés, with chicken, eggs, fish, shellfish, veal, vegetables and certain hors d'oeuvre.

⚜ BÉCHAMEL SAUCE (*Sauce Béchamel*)

2 tablespoons butter
2 tablespoons flour
1 cup hot milk

¼ teaspoon salt or salt to taste
ground white pepper to taste

Melt the butter in a 3-cup saucepan. Remove pan from the heat and blend in the flour. Return to heat and stir. Cook until the mixture is frothy. Add all the hot milk at one time. Beat the sauce vigorously with a wire whisk or a wire hand eggbeater. Stir and cook the sauce over moderate heat 1 to 2 minutes or until the sauce has thickened. Add salt and pepper. Makes approximately 1 scant cup.

⚜ AURORA SAUCE (*Sauce Aurore*)

1 cup Béchamel Sauce   2 tablespoons butter
1 to 2 tablespoons thick tomato sauce
   or tomato purée

Mix the Béchamel Sauce with enough tomato sauce or tomato purée to give the sauce a rosy color. Stir and cook until the sauce is hot, 3 to 4 minutes. Remove the sauce from the heat and blend in the butter. Serve with eggs and poultry. This sauce may also be made with Velouté Sauce or with Fish Velouté Sauce to serve with fish. Makes 1 cup.

⚜ CAPER SAUCE (*Sauce aux Câpres*)

2 cups Béchamel Sauce   1 tablespoon chopped parsley
2 tablespoons capers

Combine the Béchamel Sauce and capers in a small saucepan. Stir and cook 2 to 3 minutes—only until the sauce is hot. Add the parsley. Serve with fish or poultry. Makes 2 cups.

⚜ CREAM SAUCE (*Sauce Crème*)

2 cups Béchamel Sauce   ½ cup heavy cream

Cook the Béchamel Sauce over low heat, stirring frequently, until it has reduced to 1 ½ cups. Stir in the cream. Serve with eggs, chicken, fish, shellfish, and vegetables. Makes 2 cups.

⚜ EGG SAUCE (*Sauce aux Oeufs Durs*)

This sauce is especially good on poached codfish.

4 hard-cooked eggs, chopped   ½ teaspoon salt, or salt to taste
2 cups hot Béchamel Sauce   ⅛ teaspoon ground white pepper
1 tablespoon chopped parsley

Add the eggs to the Béchamel Sauce and cook only until the sauce is hot. Stir in the remaining ingredients. Makes 3 cups.

⚜ MORNAY SAUCE (*Sauce Mornay*)

1 large egg yolk	2 tablespoons grated Parmesan cheese
2 tablespoons light cream	or Swiss cheese
1 cup hot Béchamel Sauce	salt and ground white pepper to taste

Put the egg yolk and cream in a 3-cup saucepan. Mix well. Gradually stir in the Béchamel Sauce. Stir and cook the mixture 1 to 2 minutes. Do not boil. Remove the pan from the heat and fold in the cheese, using a spoon. Add salt and pepper to taste. Never beat this sauce after the cheese is added or it will become a thick paste. Makes approximately 1¼ cups.

⚜ SHRIMP SAUCE (*Sauce Crevette ou Joinville*)

¼ pound cooked shrimp or prawns	dash cayenne
2 cups hot Béchamel Sauce	salt and ground white pepper to taste
3 tablespoons heavy cream or butter	

Chop the shrimp or prawns fine, crush, and add to the hot Béchamel Sauce. Stir and cook 2 to 3 minutes over moderately low heat. Strain the sauce through a fine sieve. Add the remaining ingredients. Serve with eggs, fish, or shellfish. If a delicate pink sauce is desired, add 1 or 2 drops red food coloring. Makes 2¼ cups.

⚜ VELOUTÉ SAUCE (*Sauce Velouté*)

2 tablespoons butter	¼ teaspoon salt
2 tablespoons flour	ground white pepper to taste
1 cup hot light stock, or 1 chicken	1 egg yolk (optional)
bouillon cube dissolved in 1 cup	4 tablespoons heavy cream (optional)
hot water	

Melt the butter in a 3-cup saucepan. Remove pan from the heat and blend in the flour. Return to heat; stir and cook until the mixture is frothy. Add all the hot stock or hot water in which the bouillon cube is dissolved. Beat the sauce vigorously with a wire whisk or a wire hand eggbeater. Stir and cook the sauce over moderate heat 1 to 2 minutes or until it has thickened. Add salt and pepper. If a richer sauce is desired, blend the egg yolk with 2 tablespoons of the cream, stir in a little of the hot sauce, and then mix with the rest of the hot sauce. Bring the sauce to boiling point (do not boil) and add the remaining cream. Makes approximately 1¼ cups.

40

⚜ WHITE BERCY SAUCE (*Sauce Bercy*)

1 shallot or green onion (white part only), chopped fine
4 tablespoons (½ stick) butter
½ cup dry white wine
½ cup fish stock

1 cup Velouté Sauce, made with fish stock
1 tablespoon chopped parsley
salt and ground white pepper to taste

Cook the chopped shallot or onion in 1 tablespoon of the butter 2 minutes—only until soft, not browned. Add the wine and stock and boil the mixture until it has reduced to ½ cup. Add the Velouté Sauce and mix well. Stir and cook 3 to 4 minutes. Remove the pan from the heat and add the parsley and salt and pepper to taste. Swirl in the remaining 3 tablespoons butter. Serve with fish and shellfish. Makes approximately 1 ½ cups.

⚜ POULETTE (MUSHROOM) SAUCE (*Sauce Poulette*)

1½ cups Velouté Sauce
½ cup chopped mushrooms
1 large egg yolk

4 tablespoons heavy cream
1 teaspoon lemon juice
salt and ground black pepper to taste

Put the Velouté Sauce and the mushrooms in a 1-quart saucepan, mix well, and cook over low heat 10 minutes, stirring frequently. Combine the egg yolk and 2 tablespoons of the cream, stir in a little of the hot sauce, and then mix with the rest of the hot sauce. Bring the sauce to boiling point (do not boil). Blend in the remaining 2 tablespoons cream, the lemon juice, and salt and pepper to taste. Serve with sweetbreads, calves' brains, fish, and poultry. Makes approximately 1 ½ cups.

⚜ SAUCE SUPRÊME (*Sauce Suprême*)

1½ cups Velouté Sauce made with chicken stock
½ cup light cream

1 teaspoon lemon juice
salt and ground white pepper to taste
1 tablespoon butter

Pour the Velouté Sauce and the cream into a 3-cup saucepan and mix well. Stir and cook the sauce rapidly until it is reduced to 1 ½ cups, or until it coats a metal spoon, being careful that it does not burn or stick to the saucepan. Remove the sauce from the heat and stir in the lemon juice, salt and pepper, then swirl in the butter. Serve with eggs, poultry, and vegetable dishes. Makes approximately 1 ½ cups.

⚜ WHITE TARRAGON SAUCE (*Sauce Blanche à l'Estragon*)

1 cup Velouté Sauce
1 teaspoon chopped fresh tarragon, or
   ¼ teaspoon dried tarragon
1 large egg yolk

4 tablespoons heavy cream
salt and ground white pepper to taste

Put the Velouté Sauce and the tarragon in a 3-cup saucepan. Stir and cook over moderately low heat 2 to 3 minutes or until the sauce is hot. Blend the egg yolk with 2 tablespoons of the cream, stir in a little of the hot sauce, and then mix with the rest of the hot sauce. Bring the sauce to boiling point (do not boil). Add the remaining 2 tablespoons cream and salt and pepper to taste. Serve with boiled chicken or poached fish. Makes approximately 1 cup.

⚜ COLBERT SAUCE (*Sauce Colbert*)

3 to 4 tablespoons meat glaze, or 2 to
   3 tablespoons beef extract
1 tablespoon white stock or water
¼ pound (1 stick) butter
dash cayenne
dash ground nutmeg

salt and ground black pepper to taste
1 tablespoon lemon juice
1 tablespoon Madeira (optional)
1 tablespoon chopped parsley
1 teaspoon chopped fresh tarragon, or
   ¼ teaspoon dried tarragon

Put the first 3 ingredients in a 3-cup saucepan and cook over low heat or hot water until the butter is melted. Remove from heat and set aside until cold. Stir in the remaining ingredients. Serve with fish, roasted meat, and vegetables. Makes approximately ⅔ cup.

⚜ SOUBISE (ONION) SAUCE (*Sauce Soubise*)

½ cup coarsely chopped onion
2 tablespoons butter
1½ cups hot Béchamel Sauce or
   Velouté Sauce

salt and ground white pepper to taste
¼ cup heavy cream

Cook the onion over moderate heat in 1 tablespoon of the butter until soft, but not browned. Add the Béchamel or Velouté Sauce and simmer 10 to 15 minutes, stirring occasionally. Add salt and pepper to taste. Strain through a fine sieve. Add the cream and heat ½ minute or only until sauce is hot. Remove the saucepan from the heat and swirl in the remaining 1 tablespoon butter. Use with eggs, fish, lamb, and some beef dishes. Makes approximately 1½ cups.

⚜ PLAIN WHITE SAUCE (*Sauce Blanche Ménagère ou Bâtarde*)

This sauce can replace Hollandaise Sauce (page 52) in everyday cookery, since Hollandaise is too expensive for daily use by the economy-minded housewife. It can be made in 5 minutes. Serve with fish, eggs, and such vegetables as artichokes, asparagus, broccoli, cauliflower, etc.

6 tablespoons (¾ stick) butter
4 tablespoons flour
1⅓ cups hot water
1 egg yolk

¼ teaspoon salt or salt to taste
ground white pepper to taste
lemon juice or vinegar to taste

Melt 4 tablespoons (½ stick) of the butter in a 3-cup saucepan. Remove from heat and blend in the flour. Measure out 2 tablespoons of the hot water, set this aside, and add the remaining water to the roux. Mix well. Bring the mixture to boiling point, stirring constantly, and boil 1 minute. Remove the sauce from the heat. Blend the egg yolk with the reserved 2 tablespoons water and beat in a little of the hot sauce. Then gradually stir the egg mixture into the rest of the hot sauce. Stir and cook 1 minute. Season to taste with salt, pepper, and lemon juice, or vinegar. Finish the sauce by swirling the remaining 2 tablespoons butter into it. Makes approximately 1⅓ cups.

⚜ Mustard Sauce (*Sauce Moutarde*)

Mix 1 teaspoon powdered mustard with 1 tablespoon water and let stand 5 minutes to develop the flavor of the mustard. Add to 1 cup Plain White Sauce and mix well. Serve with eggs, ham, beef, and pork. Makes 1 cup.

⚜ WHITE WINE SAUCE (*Sauce au Vin Blanc*)

½ cup chopped mushroom stems
½ cup dry white wine
1½ cups reduced fish stock
3 tablespoons butter
1 tablespoon flour

2 egg yolks
⅓ cup heavy cream
1 teaspoon lemon juice
salt to taste
ground white pepper to taste

Combine the mushroom stems, wine, and ½ cup of the fish stock in a small saucepan. Cook over moderate heat until the mixture has reduced to ½ cup. Strain and set aside.

Melt 1 tablespoon of the butter in a 1-quart saucepan and remove from the heat. Blend in the flour and cook, stirring constantly, 1 to 2 minutes or until the mixture is frothy. Add the remaining 1 cup fish stock and the reduced wine and fish stock mixture. Stir and cook slowly 10 minutes or until the mixture coats a metal spoon rather thickly. Blend the egg yolks with 2 tablespoons of the cream, add to the sauce, and bring the mixture to boiling point. Stir in the lemon juice and the remaining cream and heat ½ minute. Season to taste with salt and white pepper. Swirl in the remaining 2 tablespoons butter. Serve with fish. Makes approximately 1½ cups.

BROWN SAUCES

The classic French versions of *Sauce Espagnole* and *Sauce Demi-Glace*, from which most other brown sauces are derived, require more preparation time than the average housewife is willing or able to spend. For home use, the following recipe, which is easily made and relatively economical, is a satisfactory replacement.

⚜ DEMI-GLACE SAUCE, HOME STYLE, OR BASIC BROWN SAUCE
(*Sauce Demi-Glace Ménagère, ou Sauce Brune de Base*)

¼ cup fat (lard, unsalted beef or pork
    drippings, or clarified butter)
2 tablespoons flour
5 cups brown stock or bouillon

4 tablespoons tomato paste
salt and ground black pepper to taste
2 tablespoons butter (optional)

Melt the fat in a 2-quart saucepan and remove from the heat. Add the flour and mix well. Stir and cook the mixture over *very* low heat until it is nutbrown, being careful not to burn it. Gradually stir in the stock or bouillon and the tomato paste, using a wire whisk. Bring the sauce to boiling point over moderately low heat, stirring frequently. Reduce heat to low, and simmer sauce 30 to 40 minutes or until the quantity is reduced to 2½ cups, skimming off and discarding the fat as it forms over the surface. Season to taste with salt and pepper. Remove the sauce from the heat, and if desired drop in 2 tablespoons butter and swirl the pan to blend the butter with the sauce. This sauce should be of medium thickness. Any that is not used at once may be refrigerated to use as needed. (*See* How to Refrigerate Sauces, page 36.) Makes approximately 2½ cups.

⚜ BORDELAISE SAUCE (*Sauce Bordelaise*)

1 shallot, or 1 green onion (white part
    only), chopped fine
½ small bay leaf
1 cup dry red wine
1⅓ cups Demi-Glace Sauce
1 sprig fresh thyme, or ¼ teaspoon
    dried thyme

2 tablespoons butter
2 ounces beef marrow
hot stock, bouillon, or water
1 tablespoon chopped parsley
salt and ground black pepper to taste

Combine the first 3 ingredients in a 1-quart saucepan and boil the mixture until the quantity is reduced to ½ cup. Add the Demi-Glace Sauce and thyme and mix well. Cook the mixture over moderately low heat, stirring frequently, until the quantity is reduced to 1 cup, about 10 minutes. Add the butter and strain the sauce. Dice the beef marrow, using a sharp knife dipped in hot water, put it in a small saucepan, and add enough hot stock, bouillon, or water to cover it. Cover the saucepan and let stand for 5 minutes or until the marrow has softened. Drain well and add to the sauce. Add the parsley and season to taste with salt and black pepper. Serve over grilled steak. Makes approximately 1¼ cups.

⚜ CHASSEUR SAUCE I (*Sauce Chasseur I*)

1 cup chopped mushroom caps or stems

1 shallot, or 1 green onion (white part only), chopped fine

1 tablespoon cooking oil or olive oil

2½ tablespoons butter

½ cup dry white wine

1½ cups Demi-Glace Sauce

1 tablespoon tomato paste

1 tablespoon chopped parsley

1 teaspoon each chopped fresh chervil and tarragon, or ¼ teaspoon each dried chervil and tarragon

salt and ground black pepper to taste

Heat the oil and ½ tablespoon of the butter and cook the mushrooms and shallot or onion in it 4 to 5 minutes or until the mushrooms are soft. Add the wine. Cook until the liquid is reduced to ¼ cup. Stir in the Demi-Glace Sauce and tomato paste. Cook over low heat for 5 minutes, stirring frequently. Add the herbs, salt, and pepper and mix well. Add the remaining butter and swirl the pan to blend the butter with the sauce. Serve with fowl and small cuts of meat. Makes 1¾ cups.

⚜ SAUCE DIABLE (*Sauce Diable*)

A hot brown sauce for grilled chicken, pigeon, pork chops or roast pork, and leftover meats.

2 shallots or green onions (white part only), chopped fine

2 tablespoons butter

1¼ cups dry white wine

½ cup Demi-Glace Sauce

¾ teaspoon chopped fresh chervil, or ¼ teaspoon dried chervil

ground black pepper to taste

dash cayenne

dash Worcestershire sauce

Melt the butter over moderate heat, add the shallots or onions, and cook until they are pale brown. Add the wine. Cook uncovered over low heat about 15 minutes or until the liquid is reduced to one-half the original amount. Add the Demi-Glace Sauce and mix well. Simmer about 4 to 5 minutes. Add the chervil, black pepper to taste, cayenne, and Worcestershire Sauce. Makes approximately 1 cup.

⚜ GRATIN SAUCE (*Sauce Gratin*)

½ cup chopped mushroom caps and
    stems
2 tablespoons butter
2 shallots or 2 green onions (white
    part only), chopped fine

¼ cup dry white wine
1¼ cups Demi-Glace Sauce
2 teaspoons tomato paste
1 tablespoon chopped parsley

Cook the mushrooms in the butter until they are tender. Add the shallots or onions and the wine. Simmer the mixture, uncovered, until it is reduced to one-half the original quantity. Add the Demi-Glace Sauce and tomato paste and cook, uncovered, 2 to 3 minutes. Strain through a fine sieve. Heat and add the parsley. Makes approximately 1⅓ cups.

⚜ ITALIAN SAUCE (BROWN MUSHROOM SAUCE) (*Sauce Italienne*)

½ cup finely chopped mushrooms
2 tablespoons salad oil or olive oil
¼ cup finely chopped ham
2 shallots, or 2 green onions (white
    part only), chopped fine
½ cup dry white wine or Marsala

1⅓ cups Demi-Glace Sauce
2 tablespoons tomato sauce
2 tablespoons chopped parsley
salt and freshly ground black pepper
    to taste

Brown the mushrooms lightly in the oil. Add the ham and shallots or onions and cook for 2 minutes over moderate heat. Add the wine and cook, uncovered, until the liquid is reduced to one-half the original quantity. Add the Demi-Glace Sauce, tomato sauce, and parsley. Season to taste with salt and black pepper. Simmer, uncovered, 5 minutes. Serve over pastas, eggs, sautéed liver, and leftover meats, poultry, or fish. Makes approximately 1 cup.

⚜ LYONNAISE SAUCE (*Sauce Lyonnaise*)

This sauce is suitable for small cuts of meat, especially for leftover meats, and for vegetables.

3 tablespoons chopped onion
2 tablespoons butter
¼ cup wine vinegar
¼ cup dry white wine

1 cup Demi-Glace Sauce
1 tablespoon tomato purée
salt and freshly ground black pepper
    to taste

Cook the onion in butter until soft; do not let brown. Add the vinegar and wine and cook, uncovered, over moderate heat until the liquid is reduced to one-half the original amount. Add the Demi-Glace Sauce and tomato purée, bring the sauce to boiling point, and cook 1 minute, stirring frequently. Season to taste with salt and black pepper. Strain or not as desired. Makes approximately 1¼ cups.

❧ PERIGUEUX SAUCE (*Sauce Perigueux*)

½ cup Madeira
1¼ cups Demi-Glace Sauce
2 tablespoons finely chopped truffles

salt and freshly ground black pepper
  to taste
2 tablespoons butter

Boil the Madeira until it has reduced to ¼ cup. Add the Demi-Glace Sauce, mix well, and cook the mixture, uncovered, over low heat for 10 minutes. Remove the saucepan from the heat and skim off and discard fat from the surface. Stir in the truffles. Season to taste with salt and black pepper. Swirl in the butter. Serve with eggs, fish, meat, and poultry. Makes approximately 1 cup.

❧ PIQUANT SAUCE (*Sauce Piquante*)

1 shallot, or 1 green onion (white part
  only), chopped fine
1 tablespoon butter
¼ cup dry white wine
2 tablespoons wine vinegar
1¼ cups Demi-Glace Sauce

1 tablespoon chopped chives
1 tablespoon chopped parsley
1¼ tablespoons chopped gherkin
  pickles
salt and freshly ground black pepper
  to taste

Cook the shallot or onion in butter 2 to 3 minutes or until soft but not brown. Add the wine and vinegar and cook the mixture until it has reduced to one-half the original volume. Stir in the Demi-Glace Sauce, bring the sauce to boiling point, and boil ½ minute. Remove the saucepan from the heat and stir in the remaining ingredients. Serve over pork and leftover meats. Makes approximately 1¼ cups.

❧ POIVRADE SAUCE FOR GAME
(*Sauce Poivrade pour Gibier à Poil*)

This is a peppery sauce for furred game. The marinade in which the meat has been tenderized is used in the sauce.

1 to 2 pounds game trimmings (bones,
  giblets, and meat)
6 tablespoons salad oil or olive oil
2 tablespoons butter
½ cup diced carrots
½ cup chopped onion
½ cup flour
3 cups brown stock or bouillon
1 cup tomato purée
1 bay leaf

2 stalks parsley
½ cup wine vinegar
½ cup of the marinade used for the
  game
8 whole black peppercorns, crushed
1 sprig fresh thyme, or ¼ teaspoon
  dried thyme
½ cup dry red wine
salt to taste

Put the game trimmings in a large shallow pan, sprinkle with 2 tablespoons of the oil, and put in a preheated very hot oven (450° F.) until browned. Remove from the oven and set aside. Put the remaining 4 tablespoons oil and the butter in a heavy 2-quart saucepan. Heat, add the carrots and onions, and cook until the vegetables have browned lightly. Remove the saucepan from the heat and blend in the flour. Return to heat; stir and cook until the flour is golden-brown. Remove from heat and gradually beat in the stock or bouillon and the tomato purée. Add the bay leaf, parsley, and browned game trimmings. Simmer, uncovered, 1½ hours, stirring and skimming occasionally. In another saucepan simmer the vinegar, marinade, crushed peppercorns, and thyme until the liquid is reduced to one-third the original amount, then add the mixture to the sauce. Remove and discard the game trimmings from the sauce. Cook the sauce, uncovered, 30 minutes over low heat. Strain the sauce and stir in the wine. Add salt to taste. Makes approximately 3 cups.

⚜ Venison Sauce (*Sauce Chevreuil*)

In the recipe for Poivrade Sauce, replace the ½ cup wine vinegar with ½ cup dry red wine. Continue as directed in the recipe. Season with a dash of cayenne, ¼ teaspoon sugar, and salt and freshly ground black pepper to taste. Makes approximately 3 cups.

⚜ SAUCE ROBERT (*Sauce Robert*)

⅓ cup finely chopped onion
1 tablespoon butter
4 tablespoons wine vinegar
½ cup dry white wine
1 cup Demi-Glace Sauce
2 tablespoons Tomato Sauce (page 50) or canned tomato sauce
1 tablespoon prepared mustard
1 tablespoon chopped parsley
1 tablespoon chopped sour cucumber pickle
salt and ground black pepper to taste

Cook the onion in the butter, without browning, until soft. Add the vinegar and wine and cook until reduced to three-fourths the original amount. Add the Demi-Glace Sauce and Tomato Sauce. Simmer, uncovered, 10 minutes, stirring frequently. Add the remaining ingredients. Use with meats. Makes approximately 1¼ cups.

⚜ BROWN TARRAGON SAUCE (*Sauce à l'Estragon*)

Suitable for poached or baked eggs, scallops, fried chicken, veal, rabbit, chops or cutlets, leftover meats, and braised vegetables.

1 shallot, or 1 green onion (white part only), chopped fine
1 tablespoon chopped fresh tarragon, or 1 teaspoon dried tarragon
1 cup dry white wine
2 cups Demi-Glace Sauce

1 teaspoon chopped parsley or chopped fresh tarragon
2 tablespoons butter

Put the first 3 ingredients in a 3-cup saucepan and cook, uncovered, 15 minutes or until the wine is reduced to 3 tablespoons. Strain the liquid into a 1-quart saucepan, pushing as much as possible of the shallot or onion and tarragon through the sieve. Stir in the Demi-Glace Sauce and cook 2 to 3 minutes or only until the sauce is hot. Remove from heat. Add the parsley or 1 teaspoon additional fresh tarragon. Add the butter and swirl it in. Makes 2 cups.

⚜ CURRY SAUCE

This sauce is used in making Anglo-Indian dishes.

1 cup finely chopped onion
3 tablespoons clarified butter or salad oil
2 tablespoons flour
2 to 3 teaspoons curry powder
½ cup finely chopped cooking apple
3 tablespoons tomato purée
2¼ cups Brown Stock (page 30)
1 teaspoon grated dried orange peel
1 small clove garlic, minced

1 teaspoon salt, or salt to taste
¼ cup coconut milk, or ¼ cup evaporated milk

Cook the onion in the butter or oil over moderate heat 6 to 8 minutes, until it is soft but not browned. Sprinkle with the flour and curry powder. Stir and cook the mixture 5 minutes over moderately low heat, without browning. Add the next 6 ingredients and cook, uncovered, over low heat 40 minutes. Add the coconut milk or evaporated milk and heat only to boiling point (do not boil). Serve with beef, chicken, lamb, mutton, firm-fleshed fish, boiled rice, and pilaf. Makes approximately 3 cups.

TOMATO SAUCES

⚜ TOMATO SAUCE (*Sauce Tomate*)

This is the basic French recipe.

½ cup diced carrot
½ cup diced celery
½ cup diced onion
1 leek or green onion (white part only), chopped
1 clove garlic, cut in half
3 tablespoons drippings from salt pork or pork rind
½ cup flour
3 cups tomato purée, or 1½ cans (6 ounces each) tomato paste

3½ cups brown stock or bouillon, or 3 bouillon cubes and 3½ cups water
1 bay leaf
6 whole black peppercorns
2 teaspoons salt or salt to taste
½ teaspoon sugar
1 teaspoon chopped fresh thyme, or ¼ teaspoon dried thyme
2 tablespoons butter

Cook the first 5 ingredients in the pork drippings until the vegetables take on a slight color. Remove and discard the garlic. Remove from heat and blend in the flour. Stir and cook over low heat 4 to 5 minutes or until flour is brown. Add the next 6 ingredients. Slowly bring mixture to boiling point, reduce heat, and simmer, covered, 1½ to 2 hours, stirring frequently to prevent scorching. Or cover the saucepan and cook the sauce in a preheated slow oven (325° F.) 1½ to 2 hours. Since tomato sauces scorch easily the oven method is preferable. Add the thyme 10 minutes before cooking time is up. Strain the sauce through a fine sieve, adjust the seasoning, and reheat. Finish off the sauce by swirling in the butter. Makes approximately 4½ cups.

VARIATIONS

⚜ Tomato-Sherry Sauce

Add ¼ cup dry sherry to 2 cups Tomato Sauce. Heat and serve with fish or shellfish.

⚜ Tomato-Mushroom Sauce

Cook 1 cup sliced mushrooms and 1 chopped shallot in 2 tablespoons butter, olive oil, or salad oil over moderate heat for 5 minutes or until the vegetables are tender. Add 2 cups Tomato Sauce. Cover and simmer 10 minutes, stirring frequently. Adjust seasonings. Serve with spaghetti, fish, shellfish, and leftover meats.

⚜ Spaghetti Sauce

Cook ½ pound (1 cup) ground chuck and ⅓ cup chopped green pepper in 1 tablespoon olive oil or salad oil over moderate heat until meat is brown and pepper is soft. Add 3 cups Tomato Sauce. Cover and simmer 10 minutes, stirring frequently. Adjust seasonings.

⚜ FRESH TOMATO SAUCE ITALIAN STYLE
(*Sauce aux Tomates Fraiches à l'Italienne*)

½ cup diced carrots
¾ cup chopped onion
1½ ounces streaky salt pork, diced
3 tablespoons butter
¼ cup flour
5 medium-sized fresh tomatoes, diced

2 stalks parsley
6 whole black peppercorns
1 to 2 teaspoons salt, or salt to taste
3½ cups brown stock or bouillon, or
    3 bouillon cubes and 3½ cups water
½ teaspoon sugar

Put the carrots, onion, salt pork, and 1½ tablespoons of the butter in a heavy 2-quart saucepan. Cook over moderate heat, stirring frequently, only until the mixture begins to brown (do not brown). Remove the saucepan from the heat and blend in the flour. Stir and cook over moderately low heat until flour is brown, 2 to 3 minutes. Add the tomatoes, parsley, peppercorns, 1 teaspoon salt, and the stock, bouillon, or bouillon cubes and water, and mix well. Cover, bring to boiling point, reduce heat to low, and simmer 1 hour. Or, if desired, cook 1 hour in a preheated slow oven (325° F.). Add the sugar and additional salt to taste. (If bouillon cubes are used, less salt is required). Strain the sauce through a fine sieve. Reheat and swirl in the remaining 1½ tablespoons butter. Makes approximately 2½ cups.

⚜ BOLOGNESE SAUCE (*Sauce Bolognaise*)

This is a meat sauce to serve with pastas.

2 tablespoons olive oil or salad oil
¼ cup diced carrot
¼ cup diced celery
¼ cup chopped onion
¼ cup finely chopped ham
½ pound (1 cup) ground chuck
1½ teaspoons salt, or salt to taste
⅓ cup dry red wine
1½ teaspoons flour

1 cup (8-ounce can) tomato purée, or
    2 tablespoons tomato paste
1 cup brown stock or canned bouillon,
    or 1 bouillon cube and 1 cup water
¼ teaspoon dried marjoram
¼ teaspoon dried thyme
⅛ teaspoon ground black pepper
dash of ground nutmeg

Heat the oil in a saucepan and cook the carrots, celery, onion, and ham in it until they are golden brown. Add the chuck and cook until it turns gray.

Stir in 1½ teaspoons salt and the wine and cook the mixture until most of the liquid has evaporated. Remove the saucepan from the heat and blend in the flour. Cook ½ minute. Add the tomato purée or tomato paste and the stock, bouillon, or bouillon cube and water. Mix well. Bring the sauce to boiling point, reduce heat, and cook very slowly until the mixture is reduced to a smooth purée (about 1½ hours), adding a little more stock if needed. Add the seasonings and adjust the salt. Serve with pastas. Makes approximately 2 cups.

⚜ PROVENÇAL TOMATO SAUCE (*Sauce Provençale*)

⅓ cup olive oil or cooking oil
¼ cup chopped onion, or 3 chopped
   shallots
1 small clove garlic
3 pounds (12 small or 9 medium-
   sized) tomatoes, diced, or 1 quart
   canned tomatoes

1 cup veal stock
½ cup chopped parsley
1 teaspoon sugar
salt and ground black pepper to taste

Heat the oil and cook the onion or shallots and the garlic in it until onion is soft, but not browned. Remove and discard the garlic. Add the tomatoes, stock, parsley, and sugar. Cook the mixture, stirring frequently, over low heat 40 to 50 minutes, or until the sauce has thickened. Add salt and pepper to taste. Strain through a sieve. Use with eggs, chicken, fish, meat, and vegetables. Makes approximately 3 cups.

COOKED EMULSION SAUCES

⚜ HOLLANDAISE SAUCE (*Sauce Hollandaise*)

¾ cup (1½ sticks) butter
3 large egg yolks, well beaten

4 teaspoons lemon juice
dash each salt and cayenne

Divide the butter into 3 equal parts (¼ cup each). Put 1 part into the top of a double boiler and add the egg yolks and lemon juice. Cook over hot water (not boiling), beating constantly with a wire whisk, until the butter is melted. Add the second ¼ cup butter and continue beating and cooking until the mixture thickens, never allowing the water to boil. Then add the last ¼ cup butter. Stir and cook until the sauce has thickened. Remove from heat and stir in the salt and cayenne. Should the Hollandaise mixture curdle, add 1½ tablespoons boiling water, beating constantly to rebuild the emulsion. Serve with fish, shellfish, and vegetables. Or, if desired, use as the base for one of the following sauces. Makes ¾ cup.

52

⚜ BÉARNAISE SAUCE (*Sauce Béarnaise*)

¾ cup Hollandaise Sauce
1 tablespoon tarragon vinegar
1 teaspoon chopped parsley

1 teaspoon each chopped fresh chervil and tarragon, or ¼ teaspoon each dried chervil and tarragon

Combine all ingredients. Serve with baked, broiled, or poached fish and meat. Makes ¾ cup.

⚜ CHORON SAUCE (*Sauce Choron*)

Make Béarnaise Sauce as directed but omit the herbs and stir in 1½ teaspoons tomato purée, or more if desired. Serve with chicken, fish, and vegetables. Makes ¾ cup.

⚜ MOUSSELINE SAUCE (*Sauce Mousseline*)

¾ cup Hollandaise Sauce

3 tablespoons stiffly whipped cream

Make the recipe for Hollandaise Sauce. At the last moment fold in the whipped cream. Serve on fish, soufflés, or boiled or steamed vegetables. Makes 1 cup.

⚜ ORANGE HOLLANDAISE (*Sauce Maltaise*)

This is an orange-flavored Hollandaise Sauce. In France, blood-red oranges are used for it, but since these oranges are not generally available in the United States, navel oranges or tangerines may be substituted. This sauce is especially good on asparagus, broccoli, and cauliflower.

¾ cup Hollandaise Sauce
2 tablespoons orange juice or tangerine juice

½ teaspoon grated orange rind or tangerine rind

Combine all ingredients. Makes a generous ¾ cup.

COLD SAUCES

⚜ MAYONNAISE

2 large egg yolks, or 1 large whole egg
½ teaspoon salt, or salt to taste
¼ teaspoon paprika
1/16 teaspoon ground white pepper

dash cayenne
2 tablespoons lemon juice or vinegar
1 cup salad oil or olive oil

Put the first 5 ingredients in a 1-quart mixing bowl and mix well. Using an electric beater or rotary beater, beat in 1 tablespoon of the lemon juice or vinegar. Gradually beat in oil, ½ teaspoon at a time, until ¼ cup has been added. Then beat in another ¼ cup of the oil, 1 to 2 tablespoons at a time, beating well after each addition. Add the remaining tablespoon lemon juice or vinegar. Beat in the rest of the oil (½ cup). Transfer the mayonnaise to a jar, cover, and refrigerate until ready to use. Makes 1½ cups.

⚜ BLENDER MAYONNAISE

½ teaspoon powdered mustard
1 teaspoon water
½ teaspoon salt, or salt to taste
⅟₁₆ teaspoon ground white pepper

dash cayenne
2 large egg yolks, or 1 large whole egg
2 tablespoons lemon juice or vinegar
1 cup salad oil or olive oil

Soak the mustard in the water 5 minutes to develop the flavor. Put it in the blender container and add the next 5 ingredients and ¼ cup of the oil. Cover and turn on the motor at high speed. Then quickly turn off the motor. Set the motor at high speed again and add the remaining ¾ cup oil in a steady, gradual stream. Turn off the motor. Transfer mayonnaise to a jar, cover, and refrigerate until ready to use. Makes 1¼ cups.

⚜ COATING MAYONNAISE

Put 1½ teaspoons unflavored gelatin and 2 tablespoons cold water in a custard cup. Mix well and let the mixture stand 5 minutes to soften the gelatin. Place the custard cup in a pan of hot water (not boiling) and let it stand until the gelatin has melted. Stir the melted gelatin into 1 cup mayonnaise. Use to coat cold dishes where regular mayonnaise may tend to slip off. Coating Mayonnaise may also be forced through a decorating tube to make designs on salads and cold mousses. Makes 1 cup.

⚜ COCKTAIL SAUCE I

1 cup thick mayonnaise
2 tablespoons catsup, or catsup to
   taste

1 tablespoon each cognac and sherry
3 tablespoons whipped cream

Combine the mayonnaise and catsup. Fold in the cognac, sherry, and whipped cream. Serve with hors d'oeuvre cocktails made of fish, shellfish, or shredded chicken. Makes approximately 1⅓ cups.

✤ GREEN MAYONNAISE (*Sauce Vert*)

2 stalks parsley
8 watercress leaves
5 small spinach leaves

¼ teaspoon salt
boiling water
1 cup mayonnaise

Strip the leaves from the parsley and discard the stems. Put the leaves in a small bowl with the watercress and spinach leaves, and the salt, and cover with boiling water. Cover the bowl and steep the herbs 5 minutes. Drain off the hot water and rinse in cold water. Squeeze out the excess water and rub the wilted leaves through a sieve. Blend with the mayonnaise. Serve with fish and shellfish. Other fresh herbs, such as chives, chervil, dill, or tarragon, may be used in this sauce. Makes 1 cup.

✤ RÉMOULADE SAUCE (*Sauce Rémoulade*)

1 tablespoon Dijon-type prepared
  mustard
1 cup mayonnaise
2 tablespoons capers

1 tablespoon fresh chervil, spinach, tarragon, and/or watercress (optional)

Blend the mustard with the mayonnaise. Squeeze out the capers in a clean cloth to extract the excess liquid. Fold the capers and the other herbs (if used) into the sauce. Serve with fish and shellfish. Makes a generous cup.

✤ TARTARE SAUCE (*Sauce Tartare*)

1 large cold hard-cooked egg
1 tablespoon Dijon-type prepared
  mustard
1 large raw egg yolk
2 tablespoons lemon juice or vinegar
1 cup olive oil or salad oil
2 tablespoons capers

2 tablespoons finely chopped sour pickle
2 tablespoons chopped fresh herbs (parsley, chives, tarragon, or chervil)
½ teaspoon salt, or salt to taste

Mash the yolk of the hard-cooked egg in a 1-quart bowl. Add the mustard and blend until the mixture is free of lumps. Stir in the raw egg yolk. Add the lemon juice or vinegar and beat ½ minute. Gradually beat in oil, ½ teaspoon at a time, until ¼ cup has been added. Then beat in another ¼ cup of oil, 1 to 2 tablespoons at a time, beating well after each addition. Beat in the remaining ½ cup oil. Put the capers and pickles in a clean towel or cloth and squeeze out the excess liquid. Add to the sauce. Put the hard-cooked egg white through a sieve and add, along with the chopped herbs. Season to taste with salt. Serve with cold fish, shellfish, meats, and vegetables. Makes 1¼ cups.

⚜ VINAIGRETTE SAUCE OR BASIC FRENCH DRESSING
(*Sauce Vinaigrette*)

2 tablespoons wine vinegar, or 1 tablespoon wine vinegar and 1 tablespoon lemon juice
6 tablespoons olive oil or salad oil
¼ teaspoon salt
⅛ teaspoon freshly ground black
pepper

¼ teaspoon powdered mustard soaked
in ½ teaspoon water (optional)
1 tablespoon chopped fresh parsley
and/or other fresh herbs, such as
chervil, chives, basil, tarragon,
thyme, marjoram, or 1 teaspoon
dried herbs (optional)

Place the first 4 ingredients in a mixing bowl. Add the mustard if used. Beat
with a rotary beater or a wire whisk. If fresh herbs are used, add them just
before tossing the dressing with the salad. Add dried herbs (if used) along
with the salt and pepper before mixing. Serve with asparagus, broccoli, cauliflower, string beans, boiled fish, calf's head, calf's brains, and salads. Makes
½ cup.

⚜ RAVIGOTE SAUCE (*Sauce Ravigote*)

½ cup Vinaigrette Sauce
½ teaspoon chopped capers
½ teaspoon chopped onion

½ teaspoon each chopped fresh chervil, chives, parsley, and tarragon,
or ¼ teaspoon dried herbs

Combine all ingredients. If desired, the sauce may be thickened with mayonnaise. Serve with calf's head, leftover meat, or leftover fish. Makes ½ cup.

BUTTERS AND BUTTER SAUCES

⚜ BROWN BUTTER (*Beurre Noisette*)

Melt butter over very low heat until it is hazelnut brown. Serve over fish
and vegetables. (It is important that this butter be browned over very low
heat for best flavor.) To serve over grilled fish, allow 2 teaspoons browned
butter per serving. For 6 servings of cooked vegetables, allow ¼ cup browned
butter.

⚜ BLACK BUTTER (*Beurre Noir*)

Melt ½ cup (1 stick) butter and cook over moderately low heat until dark
brown, being careful not to burn the butter. Remove from heat. Add 2

tablespoons chopped parsley and lemon juice to taste. Use for calves' brains and vegetables. Makes ½ cup.

⚜ CLARIFIED BUTTER

Melt butter in a saucepan over hot water or very low heat. Pour off or siphon off the clear liquid butter and discard the milky sediment left in the bottom of the saucepan. Use for some sauces, as Curry Sauce, and for some fine pastries.

⚜ THICKENED BUTTER (*Beurre Manié*)

Blend ¾ cup sifted flour with 1 cup (2 sticks) softened butter. Store in a covered jar in the refrigerator. Use for sauces and gravies. Makes approximately 1½ cups.

⚜ ANCHOVY BUTTER (*Beurre d'Anchois*)

1 tablespoon anchovy paste, or 2 canned anchovies, mashed

½ cup (1 stick) unsalted butter, softened
lemon juice to taste

Blend the anchovy paste or anchovies with the butter. Add lemon juice to taste. Use on broiled or poached fish. Makes ½ cup.

⚜ BERCY BUTTER (*Beurre Bercy*)

2 shallots, chopped fine
¾ cup dry white wine
¼ cup (½ stick) butter, softened

2 teaspoons finely chopped parsley
salt and ground black pepper to taste

Put the shallots and wine in a small saucepan and cook until the wine has reduced to 3 tablespoons. Cool the mixture. Mix the butter and parsley and gradually blend in the shallots and wine. Season to taste with salt and pepper. Serve on broiled steak and chops. Makes ⅓ cup.

⚜ GARLIC BUTTER (*Beurre d'Ail*)

2 large cloves garlic
½ cup (1 stick) butter, softened
salt and freshly ground black pepper
    to taste

2 tablespoons chopped parsley (optional)

Boil the unpeeled garlic in water to cover 5 or 6 seconds. Drain off the water, peel the garlic, and rinse in cold water. Cover garlic with water again, bring to boiling point, and boil ½ minute. Remove from water and rinse well. Put the garlic through a garlic press or pound it to a smooth paste in a mortar. Mix it with the butter, along with the parsley, if used. Season to taste with salt and pepper, and other herbs if desired. Use on steaks. Makes ½ cup.

✤ HERB BUTTER

Blend ¼ cup (½ stick) softened butter with any of the following herb combinations:

1 teaspoon chopped fresh rosemary, or ¼ teaspoon dried rosemary, and 1 tablespoon chopped parsley.

2 teaspoons chopped fresh thyme, or ½ teaspoon dried thyme, and 1 tablespoon chopped parsley.

2 teaspoons chopped fresh tarragon, or ¼ teaspoon dried tarragon, and 1 tablespoon chopped parsley.

2 tablespoons chopped watercress and 1 teaspoon chopped parsley.

1 tablespoon chopped parsley and 2 tablespoons chopped chives.

Makes approximately ¼ cup.

✤ HORSERADISH BUTTER (*Beurre de Raifort*)

Push 2 tablespoons prepared horseradish through a sieve and blend it with ½ cup (1 stick) softened butter. Season to taste with salt. Use for meats. Makes ½ cup.

✤ MAÎTRE D'HÔTEL BUTTER (*Beurre Maître d'Hôtel*)

Blend 2 tablespoons finely chopped parsley and 1 tablespoon lemon juice with ½ cup (1 stick) softened butter. Season to taste with salt and pepper. Serve on broiled steak, kidneys, brochettes, poultry, or fish. The butter should not melt until it comes in contact with the hot food. Makes ½ cup.

✤ MUSTARD BUTTER (*Beurre de Moutarde*)

2 teaspoons powdered English mustard	½ cup (1 stick) butter, softened
1 tablespoon water	salt to taste

Soak the mustard in the water for 5 minutes to develop the flavor. Gradually blend with the butter. Season to taste with salt. Serve on beef, fish, or ham, or use for canapés and sandwiches. Makes ½ cup.

⚜ **SARDINE BUTTER** (*Beurre de Sardine*)

Mash 2 sardines to a pulp and blend with ½ cup (1 stick) softened butter. Season to taste with lemon juice, salt, and freshly ground black pepper. Use on broiled or poached fish, or for canapés and sandwiches. Makes ½ cup.

⚜ **TARRAGON BUTTER** (*Beurre d'Estragon*)

Pour boiling water over ¼ cup fresh tarragon leaves and let stand 1 minute. Drain and rinse in cold water. Press the excess water out of the leaves and chop them fine. Blend with ½ cup (1 stick) softened butter and 1 tablespoon lemon juice. Put the butter through a sieve. Serve with broiled or poached chicken, fish, and shellfish. Makes approximately ⅔ cup.

⚜ **WATERCRESS BUTTER I** (*Beurre de Cresson I*)

Blanch a handful of watercress in boiling water, drain off the water, and blanch again. Rinse in cold water. Chop ½ cup of the leaves and stems and rub them through a fine sieve. Blend with ½ cup (1 stick) softened butter. Season to taste with salt and ground black pepper. Serve with fish. Makes approximately ⅔ cup.

⚜ **WATERCRESS BUTTER II** (*Beurre de Cresson II*)

Blend ½ cup finely chopped watercress leaves with ½ cup (1 stick) softened butter. Season with anchovy paste to taste. Serve with fish. Makes ⅔ cup.

⚜ **WINE BUTTER** (*Beurre Marchand de Vin*)

2 shallots, or 2 green onions (white
   part only), chopped fine
¼ cup dry red wine
1 tablespoon meat glaze, or ½ cup
   brown stock or bouillon

1/16 teaspoon ground black pepper
½ cup (1 stick) butter, softened
1 tablespoon chopped parsley
salt to taste

Place the first 4 ingredients in a small saucepan. Boil the mixture until the liquid has reduced to 2 tablespoons. Cool and strain. Gradually beat the cooled liquid into the butter. Beat in the parsley. Season to taste with salt. Serve on hamburgers, chops, steak, and liver. Makes approximately ½ cup.

✤ WHITE BUTTER SAUCE (*Sauce au Beurre Blanc*)

This sauce is good with fish, especially pike.

2 shallots, coarsely chopped
½ cup dry white wine or wine vinegar
6 tablespoons (¾ stick) butter

2 teaspoons chopped parsley
salt and freshly ground white pepper
  to taste

Cook the shallots and wine in a small saucepan until the liquid is reduced to 2 tablespoons. Cool. Strain out the shallots and discard them. Wash the butter in cold water, drain well, and stir until the butter is softened. Blend with the reduced wine and the remaining ingredients. Beat well. Makes approximately ½ cup.

Hors d'Oeuvre

An hors d'oeuvre (*or d'urv*, or *or doe'vr*, literally "outside the work") is an appetizer usually served before a meal. In French, the same spelling and pronunciation are used for both singular and plural. In English, the plural form is often spelled "hors d'oeuvres."

Hors d'oeuvre may be hot or cold. In choosing them, consider the menu of the meal that will follow. If the meal is to be hearty, the hors d'oeuvre should be light and delicate to avoid dulling the appetite. For a light luncheon or supper, the hors d'oeuvre may be more substantial or in a more generous assortment.

In France, hors d'oeuvre served as the first course for a luncheon or dinner are eaten at the table with a fork. (An exception is pâté, which the French like to spread on bread.) Hors d'oeuvre luncheons are not uncommon in France. The entrée for such a meal is a small hot hors d'oeuvre, sometimes preceded by a cold one, served with wine and followed by fresh fruit. Such a meal can be an attractive, economical way of making use of leftovers.

In the United States more elaborate meals are usually preceded by cocktails in the living room, accompanied by the kinds of hors d'oeuvre that are eaten without plates or forks. Hors d'oeuvre are also served at cocktail parties, fashionable in America though less popular in France.

Hors d'oeuvre, hot or cold, should be small in size, savory, not too rich, interestingly seasoned, and attractive in appearance.

CANAPÉS

Canapés are two-bite-sized open sandwiches that can be eaten with the fingers. They are served as appetizers or as cocktail accompaniments.

Canapé bases are made of firm-textured, day-old white or whole-grain bread, cut into small, attractive shapes, and either toasted, skillet-fried in butter, or deep-fat fried to prevent moist toppings from seeping through. Bases made of pumpernickel need not be toasted or fried, since the texture is firm and dry enough to withstand moist toppings. These bases may be spread with softened unsalted or salted butter or a seasoned butter compatible with the topping. If sliced meat, poultry, or fish is used as a topping, the slices should be very thin and cut to fit the base. Canapé spreads should be skillfully seasoned and spread to the edge of the bread.

Canapés should have attractive garnishes compatible with the flavors of the spreads—anchovies, black or green olives, hard-cooked eggs, mushrooms, pickled onion, pimiento, parsley, small shrimp, truffles, watercress, etc.

Canapés may be served either hot or cold.

⚜ ANCHOVY CANAPÉS (*Canapés aux Anchois*)

crustless white bread cut into 2½- by   softened butter
  1½-inch pieces   hard-cooked eggs
butter or oil   anchovy fillets
anchovy paste

Fry the bread in butter or oil. Cool. Spread with anchovy paste mixed with softened butter, using 1 tablespoon anchovy paste for each stick (¼ pound) butter. Chop the whites of the hard-cooked eggs fine and sieve the yolks. Garnish one end of each canapé with chopped egg white and the other with sieved yolk. Cross 2 flat anchovy fillets in the center of each. Chill. Allow 2 to 3 canapés per person.

⚜ ANCHOVY AND TOMATO CANAPÉS (*Canapés à la Niçoise*)

Cut unsliced bread into slices ½ inch thick, then cut out rounds 1½ inches in diameter. Fry the rounds lightly in hot olive oil or salad oil. (The centers should be soft.) Mix 1 tablespoon anchovy paste or 1 mashed anchovy fillet with ¼ cup (½ stick) softened butter and spread over the fried canapé bases. Cut cherry tomatoes, 1 inch in diameter, in slices ¼ inch thick, drain well, and place one slice on each canapé. Sprinkle with salt and ground pepper. Garnish each canapé with a small pitted black olive or green olive. Glaze with aspic. Chill. Allow 2 canapés per person. Makes 10 to 12 canapés.

⚜ COTTAGE CHEESE OR RICOTTA CHEESE CANAPÉS
(*Canapés au Fromage Blanc*)

sliced rye bread or other whole-grain
   bread, cut into assorted shapes
butter or oil
½ cup cottage cheese or ricotta cheese
1 teaspoon caraway seeds
1 teaspoon chopped chives

lemon juice to taste
salt to taste
paprika
chopped parsley or chives
clear aspic

Fry the bread in butter or oil. Put the cheese through a sieve and blend with the next 5 ingredients. Spread over the fried canapé bases. Garnish with chopped parsley or chopped chives. Glaze with clear aspic. Chill. Allow 2 canapés per person.

⚜ CREAM-CHEESE CANAPÉS (*Canapés au Petite-Suisse*)

Cut assorted shapes of bread and toast them or fry them in butter or olive oil or cooking oil. Combine 2 parts softened cream cheese with 1 part softened butter. Spread evenly over the prepared canapé bases. Cover one half of each canapé with waxed paper and sprinkle the other with paprika or chopped parsley. Remove and discard the paper, leaving one side of the canapé white and the other side red or green. Glaze with aspic. Allow 2 to 3 canapés per person.

⚜ HAM CANAPÉS (*Canapés au Jambon*)

Slice cold boiled or baked boneless ham ⅛ inch thick in 4- by 2½-inch pieces. Wrap each slice around a fresh cucumber or a cucumber pickle ¾ inch in diameter, or around a stick of firm-textured cheese, ½ by ½ inch by 4 inches. Wrap the rolls in foil or waxed paper and chill. To serve: Use canapé bases of buttered toast or fried bread. Place a slice of Ham Mousse (page 76) and a slice of hard-cooked egg on each. Cut the ham rolls crosswise into slices ⅛ inch thick and place a slice on each canapé. Glaze with aspic. Chill. Allow 2 canapés per person.

⚜ LETTUCE AND EGG CANAPÉS (*Canapés Printaniers*)

Spread slices of crustless bread with softened butter and cut each slice into 3 strips. Cut lettuce in julienne strips and mix with enough mayonnaise to make the mixture spread easily. Spread it over the buttered strips and arrange slices of hard-cooked egg on top. Sprinkle with chopped chives. Glaze with aspic. Chill. Allow 2 to 3 canapés per person.

⚜ LOBSTER AND LETTUCE CANAPÉS (*Canapés Bagration*)

These were named for a Russian general who fought against Napoleon. A salad and a soup are also named for him.

crustless white bread cut into strips about 1½ inches wide and 3 inches long	lettuce, cut into julienne strips
	thin slices of cooked lobster
	Coating Mayonnaise (page 54)
butter or oil	hard-cooked eggs, yolks and white sieved separately, or small pieces of lemon
softened butter	

Fry the bread in butter or oil. Spread thinly with softened butter. Place a layer of julienne strips of lettuce on each strip and cover with thin slices of cooked lobster, cut to fit the bread. Coat thinly with Coating Mayonnaise. Garnish each with sieved egg yolk and white, or with a small piece of lemon. Allow 2 canapés per person.

⚜ MEAT AND EGG CANAPÉS WITH HERBS
(*Canapés à la Ménagère*)

Fry squares of bread in butter. Combine ground leftover boiled or roast beef, chopped hard-cooked eggs, and chopped gherkin pickles with enough mayonnaise to make a mixture of spreading consistency. Season to taste with chopped parsley, chervil, thyme, and salt and ground black pepper. Spread the mixture over fried canapé bases. Decorate the top of each with a slice of cherry tomato. Glaze with aspic. Chill. Allow 2 canapés per person.

⚜ SARDINE CANAPÉS (*Canapés de Cannes*)

bread strips 1½ by 3 inches	chopped parsley
butter or oil	boned sardines
1 tablespoon lemon juice	paprika
6 tablespoons softened salted or un-salted butter	clear aspic

Fry the bread strips in butter or oil. Set aside. Blend the lemon juice with the butter and spread over the fried bread strips. Dip the edges of the strips in chopped parsley and place a boned sardine down the center of each strip. Sprinkle with paprika. Glaze with aspic. Chill. Allow 2 canapés per person.

❧ SHRIMP CANAPÉS (*Canapés Amiral*)

12 cooked peeled medium-sized
 shrimp
¼ cup (½ stick) butter, softened
1 teaspoon lemon juice

24 canapé bases, assorted sizes,
 toasted or fried
chopped parsley
24 small, cooked peeled shrimp
 clear aspic

Cut the medium-sized shrimp into small pieces and pound to a paste. Add the softened butter and lemon juice and mix well. Spread over one side of the canapé bases. Dip the edges of the bases in chopped parsley. Place a small cooked shrimp in the center of each. Coat the tops with clear aspic. Chill and serve cold. Makes approximately 2 dozen canapés of assorted sizes.

❧ SHRIMP AND EGG CANAPÉS (*Canapés Joinville*)

Fry rounds of bread in butter or oil and spread them with shrimp butter (see the preceding recipe). Dip the edges in chopped yolk of hard-cooked egg. Arrange very tiny peeled cooked shrimp in a circle on each round. Pipe a rosette of butter in the center of each. Glaze with aspic. Chill. Allow 2 to 3 canapés per person.

❧ SMOKED-SALMON CANAPÉS (*Canapés au Saumon Fumé*)

Fry rounds or squares of bread in butter, olive oil, or cooking oil. Spread thinly with butter seasoned with curry powder, prepared Dijon mustard, or powdered dry mustard and a few drops of lemon juice, or with plain butter. Cover with thin slices of smoked salmon cut to fit the bread. Garnish with slices of gherkin pickles or slices of hard-cooked egg. Glaze with aspic. Chill. Allow 2 to 3 canapés per person.

SANDWICHES

Party sandwiches should be small, dainty, colorful, and in assorted shapes. The bread for sandwiches should be firm-textured, thinly sliced, either white or dark, and not too fresh. The butter should be softened for easy spreading and for variety may be flavored with anchovies, curry powder, horseradish, mustard, chopped parsley, sardines, or chopped watercress. The fillings and the garnishes should be varied.

⚜ OPEN-FACED ANCHOVY SANDWICHES (*Sandwiches aux Anchois*)

6 tablespoons (¾ stick) butter, softened
2 tablespoons mashed anchovies or
  anchovy paste

4 thin slices white or dark bread,
  crusts removed
2 hard-cooked eggs
finely chopped parsley

Combine the butter and the anchovies or anchovy paste, mix well, and spread on the slices of bread. Chop the hard-cooked eggs fine and sprinkle over the top. Cut the sandwiches into triangles and garnish the edges with chopped parsley. Makes 16 sandwiches.

⚜ Open-Faced Anchovy and Egg Sandwiches
(*Sandwiches aux Anchois et Oeufs*)

Trim crusts from thin slices of white bread and spread with anchovy butter made as directed for Anchovy Sandwiches. Cut each slice into 4 equal squares, and place a slice of hard-cooked egg on each. Brush mayonnaise around the edges of the sandwiches and roll the edges in chopped parsley. Allow 3 sandwiches per person.

⚜ OPEN-FACED CHEESE SANDWICHES (*Sandwiches aux Fromage*)

2 teaspoons powdered mustard
1 tablespoon water
½ cup (1 stick) softened butter
thinly sliced white or dark bread,
  crusts removed

thinly sliced Gruyère, Cheshire, or
  Cheddar cheese
pimiento-stuffed green olives or pitted
  black olives

Soak the mustard in the water for 5 minutes and then blend it with the butter. Spread on one side of thinly sliced white or dark bread. Cover with thin slices of Gruyère, Cheshire, or Cheddar cheese, cut to fit the bread. Cut each slice into 4 triangles and garnish each with a slice of pimiento-stuffed green olive or pitted black olive. Allow 3 sandwiches per person.

⚜ OPEN-FACED CHICKEN SANDWICHES (*Sandwiches de Poulet*)

thinly sliced bread
softened butter
finely shredded lettuce
mayonnaise

thin slices of cold roast chicken
salt and ground black pepper
grapes, cut in half

Trim the crusts from the bread and spread one side of each slice with softened butter. Combine finely shredded lettuce with mayonnaise, using half as much lettuce as mayonnaise. Spread over the buttered side of the bread. Cover with thin slices of roast chicken cut to fit the bread. Sprinkle lightly with salt and ground black pepper. Cut each slice into 4 small square open-faced sandwiches. Garnish each with a seeded or seedless grape, cut in half. Allow 3 sandwiches per person.

❧ HAM SANDWICHES WITH MUSTARD BUTTER
(*Sandwiches au Jambon*)

2 teaspoons powdered mustard
1 tablespoon water
½ cup (1 stick) butter, softened

thinly sliced firm-textured white or
rye bread, crusts removed
thinly sliced cold lean ham

Soak the mustard in the water for 5 minutes and blend with the softened butter. Spread one side of each slice of bread with mustard butter. Cover half the slices with thinly sliced cold lean ham and top each with one of the remaining slices of buttered bread. Cut each sandwich into 3 lengthwise strips, making finger-length sandwiches. Allow 2 small sandwiches per person.

❧ LOBSTER SANDWICHES (*Sandwiches au Homard*)

¼ cup finely chopped watercress
½ cup (1 stick) butter, softened
thinly sliced firm-textured white
    bread, crusts removed

thinly sliced cooked lobster meat
salt and ground black pepper

Combine the watercress and the butter and spread on one side of each slice of bread. Cover half the slices with lobster and sprinkle them very lightly with salt and ground black pepper. Top each with one of the remaining slices of buttered bread and cut each sandwich into 4 triangles. Allow 3 small sandwiches per person.

❧ COLD-MEAT SANDWICHES (*Sandwiches de Charcuterie*)

2 tablespoons grated horseradish
½ cup (1 stick) softened butter
thinly sliced white or dark bread,
    crusts removed

sliced cold meat (ham, roast beef,
    veal, lamb, or pork, chicken, turkey,
    meat loaf, pâté, or sausage)
salt and ground black pepper
watercress

Combine the horseradish and the butter and spread over one side of each slice of bread. Cover half the slices with sliced cold meat. Sprinkle with salt and ground black pepper. Top each with one of the remaining buttered bread slices. Cut each sandwich into 3 lengthwise strips, making finger-length sandwiches. Garnish the top of each with 3 watercress leaves. Allow 2 sandwiches per person.

⚜ POULTRY-LIVER SANDWICHES (*Sandwiches de Foie de Volaille*)

⅓ cup toasted hazelnuts or almonds
½ cup (1 stick) butter, softened
thinly sliced firm-textured white or
   whole-wheat bread, crusts removed

½ pound chicken livers or turkey
   livers sautéed in butter
salt and ground black pepper
gherkin pickles, thinly sliced

Put half the nuts at a time into the glass container of an electric blender. Blend 4 to 6 seconds or until nuts are ground very fine. When all are ground, mix them with the butter. Spread one side of each slice of bread with the nut and butter mixture. Cover half the slices with thin slices of sautéed livers. Sprinkle lightly with salt and ground pepper. Top each with one of the remaining slices of buttered bread. Cut each sandwich into 4 triangles. Decorate the top of each triangle with a thin slice of gherkin pickle. Allow 3 small sandwiches per person.

⚜ Open-Faced Poultry-Liver Sandwiches

Grind the nuts and mix them with the butter as in the preceding recipe. Purée half the sautéed chicken or turkey livers at a time in the electric blender. Add the ground livers to the nut-and-butter mixture. Season to taste with salt and ground black pepper. Cut the bread into rounds with a 1½- or 2-inch cooky cutter. Spread with the liver-and-nut mixture. Garnish the tops with 2 to 3 slivers of toasted hazel nuts or almonds. Omit the pickles. Allow 2 to 3 sandwiches per person.

⚜ SARDINE SANDWICHES (*Sandwiches aux Sardines*)

¼ cup minced and sieved sardines
½ cup (1 stick) butter, softened
thinly sliced firm-textured bread,
   crusts removed

whole sardines packed in olive oil,
   drained
watercress

Blend the minced sardines with the butter and spread on one side of each slice of bread. Cover half the slices with drained whole sardines and watercress, and top each with one of the remaining slices of buttered bread. Cut each sandwich into 4 small square sandwiches. Decorate the tops of each small sandwich with 2 watercress leaves. Allow 2 to 3 small sandwiches per person.

⚜ TOMATO SANDWICHES (*Sandwiches à la Tomate*)

2 tablespoons grated horseradish
½ cup (1 stick) butter, softened
thinly sliced white or whole-wheat
   bread, crusts removed

firm ripe tomatoes
salt and ground black pepper
parsley

Combine the horseradish and butter, mix well, and spread on one side of each slice of bread. Slice the tomatoes ⅛ inch thick and place enough tomato slices on half of the bread slices to cover them. Sprinkle with salt and ground black pepper and cover with the remaining slices of buttered bread. Cut the sandwiches in half, diagonally. Decorate the top of each half with a bit of parsley. Allow 2 small sandwiches per person.

FISH AND SEAFOOD HORS D'OEUVRE

⚜ ANCHOVY MEDALLIONS (*Médaillons d'Anchois à la Niçoise*)

Anchovies are usually filleted and preserved in oil or brine. To remove the excess salt, soak the anchovies in olive oil or salad oil before serving.
  Thoroughly drain rolled anchovy fillets. Cut rounds of bread about 2 inches in diameter and ¼ inch thick and spread them with softened butter. Put a slice of hard-cooked egg on each and place a rolled anchovy in the center. Garnish with a slice of pitted black olive and a little chopped fresh tarragon or parsley. Allow 2 to 3 per person.

⚜ INDIVIDUAL HOT ANCHOVY PATTIES (*Petits Pâtés Chauds*)

Roll Puff Pastry (page 25) ⅛-inch thick on a lightly floured pastry board. Cut it into rounds, using a 2-inch fluted cooky cutter. On half the rounds place a rolled anchovy and dot it with ¼ teaspoon butter. If desired, season the butter to taste with finely chopped garlic or garlic powder. Moisten the edges of the rounds, cover each with one of the remaining rounds, and press the edges down firmly or crimp them with a fork. Arrange the patties on an ungreased cooky sheet. Beat an egg yolk with 1 tablespoon milk or water and brush the tops. Prick the tops in three places with a pointed knife. Bake in a preheated hot oven (425° F.) 12 to 15 minutes or until patties are golden brown. Serve hot. Makes approximately 3 dozen patties.

⚜ Pâté de Foie Gras Patties

In the recipe for Anchovy Patties, replace the anchovies and butter with a rounded ½ teaspoon pâté de foie gras and a slice of truffle. Cover and bake according to directions in the recipe.

⚜ ANCHOVY STICKS (*Allumettes aux Anchois*)

Puff Pastry (page 25)
flat anchovy fillets
chopped hard-cooked egg

chopped parsley
1 egg beaten with 1 tablespoon milk

Roll Puff Pastry ⅛ inch thick and cut it into strips 2½ by 3 inches. Drain the oil from flat anchovy fillets and roll them in chopped hard-cooked egg and chopped parsley. Place one on each strip of pastry and roll up the pastry strips, enclosing the fillets completely. Moisten the edges to seal them. Shape one end of each roll to simulate the head of a fish and the other end to simulate the fish's tail. Place the rolls on an ungreased baking sheet. Brush the tops with the egg beaten with milk and score with a sharp knife. Bake in a preheated hot oven (400° F.) 10 to 12 minutes. Allow 2 to 3 per person.

❧ ANCHOVY TOAST *(Toasts aux Anchois)*

Cut slices of firm-textured bread ¼ inch thick, and cut each slice into 3 lengthwise strips. Toast on both sides lightly and place a flat anchovy fillet on each. Fry dried breadcrumbs lightly in butter and sprinkle them over the anchovies. Place in a preheated very hot oven (450° F.) to brown lightly. Allow 2 to 3 per person.

❧ FISH IN COQUILLES *(Poisson en Coquille ou en Ravier)*

4 to 6 lettuce leaves
1 cup leftover cooked fish, or 1 can
   (7 ounces) tuna fish
1 tablespoon tomato purée
⅓ cup thick mayonnaise

salt and ground black pepper
2 hard-cooked eggs, sliced
2 tomatoes, sliced
toast

Shred the lettuce leaves and place them in the bottom of 4 scallop shells or oval hors d'oeuvre dishes. Flake and mash the fish. Combine the tomato purée and mayonnaise and add to the fish, mix, and season to taste with salt and pepper. Garnish with sliced hard-cooked eggs and tomatoes. Serve toast separately. Makes 4 servings.

❧ ASSORTED FISH HORS D'OEUVRE *(Hors d'Oeuvre de Poisson)*

Place poached or broiled fillet of sole in highly seasoned Tomato Sauce (page 50) with thinly sliced mushrooms. Serve hot.

Place coarsely chopped peeled, seeded tomatoes on 3- by 1½- by ½-inch slices of poached cod. Garnish with almond- or onion-stuffed green olives.

Cover poached fillets of fish (cod, haddock, halibut, or sole) with Tartare Sauce (page 55). Garnish with peeled, deveined, cooked shrimp or crayfish.

Arrange 2 cooked buttered asparagus tips each on 3- by 1½- by ½-inch slices of poached fish fillets (cod, haddock, halibut, or sole). *(See illustration, page 87.)*

⚜ MARINATED FRESH HERRING *(Harengs Frais Marinés)*

4 fresh herring, 5 to 6 ounces each, cleaned and dressed, heads removed
salt
ground black pepper
½ cup dry white wine
½ cup wine vinegar
¼ cup chopped celery tops
¼ cup sliced carrots

2 shallots or 2 small white onions, sliced
1 stalk parsley
6 whole black peppercorns
1 small bay leaf
¼ teaspoon dried thyme or 1 teaspoon chopped fresh thyme
2 tablespoons olive oil or salad oil

Sprinkle herring lightly with salt and pepper and let stand one hour. Place all the remaining ingredients, except the oil, in a saucepan. Cover and simmer 20 minutes. Arrange the herring in an oiled baking dish. Add the boiling marinade, sprinkle with oil, cover the baking dish with foil, and bake in a preheated moderate oven (350° F.) 12 minutes. Cool in the marinade. Serve cold. Makes 4 servings.

⚜ SMOKED HERRING FILLETS, RUSSIAN STYLE *(Filets de Harengs à la Russe)*

4 smoked herring fillets
2 ripe firm eating apples
1 small onion, chopped fine

¼ cup dry white wine
2 to 3 tablespoons olive oil or salad oil

Dip the herring fillets in boiling water and remove the skins. Cut the fillets into long strips and set them aside. Wash and core the apples but do not peel them. Dice the apples and mix with the chopped onion. Mound the mixture in the center of an oval-shaped hors d'oeuvre dish. Garnish with the herring strips in lattice fashion. Mix the wine and oil and sprinkle over all. Makes 6 servings.

⚜ SMOKED SALT HERRING FILLETS *(Filets de Harengs Saurs)*

6 smoked salt herring fillets
milk to cover
2 medium-sized onions, sliced thin
½ small bay leaf, crumbled
6 whole black peppercorns

1 teaspoon chopped fresh thyme or ¼ teaspoon dried thyme
⅓ cup dry white wine
2 tablespoons olive oil or salad oil

Cut the herring fillets into strips ½ inch wide. Soak them in enough milk to cover for 1 hour, or longer if herring is very salty. Remove the fillets from the milk and wipe them dry with a clean towel. Place in a pie plate a layer of herring, then a layer of onion slices, alternating until all are used. End with a layer of herring. Scatter the crumbled bay leaf, peppercorns, and thyme on top, sprinkle with the wine and oil, and marinate 24 hours. Makes 6 servings.

⚜ OYSTERS ON THE HALF SHELL (*Huîtres Hors d'Oeuvre Froids*)

Oysters should be fresh, cold, and opened just before serving for best flavor. Serve them on the deeper halves of the shells in a shallow bowl or soup plate on a bed of finely chopped ice. Sprinkle with fresh lemon juice and coarsely ground black pepper. Or, if desired, serve Shallot Vinegar or Tomato-Horseradish Sauce (see following recipes) in a very small bowl or glass placed in the center of each serving. Garnish with lemon wedges or parsley. The French serve buttered dark bread as an accompaniment to this dish. Allow 5 to 6 medium-sized oysters per serving.

⚜ Shallot Vinegar (*Essence d'Echalotes*)

Bring 1 cup wine vinegar to boiling point. Add 4 tablespoons chopped shallots and boil the mixture 5 minutes. Strain through a fine sieve. Makes approximately ⅔ cup.

⚜ Tomato-Horseradish Sauce

Combine ⅓ cup catsup, 3 tablespoons lemon juice, 1 tablespoon prepared horseradish, 1 teaspoon Worcestershire sauce, 3 to 4 drops Tabasco sauce, and salt to taste. This sauce is a favorite with shellfish for many Americans. Makes ⅔ cup.

⚜ SARDINES IN OIL (*Sardines à la Huile*)

Drain the oil from the sardines and arrange them in a fan shape on a long hors d'oeuvre dish. Sprinkle chopped parsley, chopped hard-cooked egg whites, and sieved hard-cooked egg yolks on the dish around the sardines to form a border, keeping the colors separate. Allow 3 medium-sized sardines or 5 small sardines per serving.

⚜ SARDINES WITH TOMATO SAUCE (*Sardines à la Tomate*)

shredded lettuce
1 cup Tomato Sauce (page 50) or
   canned tomato sauce
1 tablespoon chopped parsley
18 medium-sized sardines packed in oil

1 teaspoon each chopped fresh basil
   and tarragon, or ¼ teaspoon each
   dried basil and tarragon
6 strips green pepper
6 wedges hard-cooked egg

Place shredded lettuce on each of 6 salad plates. Set aside. Combine the tomato sauce and herbs and spoon the mixture over the lettuce. Drain the oil from the sardines and place 3 on each plate on top of the sauce. Garnish each plate with green pepper strips and a wedge of hard-cooked egg. Serve as an hors d'oeuvre. Makes 6 servings.

⚜ SMOKED-SALMON ROLLS (*Saumon Fumé en Roulades*)

1 can (7 ounces) tuna fish packed in oil
½ cup (1 stick) butter, softened
1 teaspoon lemon juice
salt and ground black pepper
12 thin slices, 3 by 3½ inches, smoked salmon

2 cups cold mixed diced cooked vegetables
6 tablespoons mayonnaise
12 thin disks of truffles, or 12 slices of black olives (optional)

Drain the oil from the tuna fish. Put the tuna fish in a bowl and flake and mash it with a fork. Add the butter and mix until a paste is formed. Blend in the lemon juice, and add salt and pepper to taste. Spread the mixture over the salmon slices and roll them up. Set aside. Combine the cooked vegetables and the mayonnaise and add salt and pepper to taste. Put the mixture in a rectangular serving dish and arrange the salmon rolls over the top. If desired, garnish each roll with a thin disk of truffle or a slice of black olive. Makes 6 servings.

⚜ SCALLOP COCKTAIL (American)

½ pound chilled cooked scallops
lettuce or Romaine

Cocktail Sauce II (see following recipe)

Cut large scallops in half; leave small scallops whole. Line sherbet glasses with lettuce or Romaine. Pile the scallops on top. Cover with Cocktail Sauce. Serve chilled as a cold hors d'oeuvre. Makes 6 servings.

⚜ Cocktail Sauce II

¼ cup catsup
2 tablespoons grated onion
2 tablespoons grated cucumber

lemon juice, salt, and black pepper to taste
1 tablespoon chopped parsley

Combine all ingredients. Chill. Serve over cooked scallops, shrimp, or lobster. Makes ½ cup.

73

⚜ SHRIMP OR LOBSTER COCKTAIL
(Cocktail de Crevettes ou de Homard)

½ cup mayonnaise
2 tablespoons whipped heavy cream
¼ cup tomato catsup
1 teaspoon cognac
1 teaspoon dry sherry

1 pound peeled cooked shrimp or
    diced cooked lobster
lettuce
4 or 5 pimiento-stuffed olives

Combine the first 5 ingredients. Mix half the sauce with the shrimp or lobster. Shred the lettuce fine and arrange it in the bottom of chilled glass compotes. Divide the shrimp or lobster mixture among the glasses. Spoon the remaining sauce over the top of each serving and garnish with a pimiento-stuffed olive. Serve as an appetizer. Makes 4 to 5 servings.

⚜ WHOLE SHRIMP OR PRAWNS *(Crevettes Roses)*

Place peeled cooked whole large shrimp or prawns in a bowl on cracked ice. Or, if desired, hang them around the rim of a dish containing sprigs of fresh parsley and Rémoulade Sauce (page 55) or Cocktail Sauce (pages 54, 73).

⚜ SHRIMP OR PRAWN COCKTAIL *(Cocktail de Crevettes)*

Place peeled cooked whole shrimp or prawns in cocktail glasses. Cover with Cocktail Sauce (pages 54, 73) or tomato-flavored mayonnaise. Serve as the appetizer course. Allow 6 per serving.

⚜ TUNA FISH BARQUETTES *(Barquettes de Thon)*

3 tablespoons butter
3 tablespoons flour
1½ cups hot milk or light stock
6½- or 7-ounce can tuna fish
2 tablespoons heavy cream

salt and ground white pepper to taste
24 small baked pastry boats made
    from Puff Pastry or plain rich
    pastry
12 flat anchovy fillets

Melt the butter in a 1-quart saucepan. Remove the pan from the heat and blend in the flour. Stir and cook until the mixture is frothy. Remove the saucepan from the heat and add all the milk or stock at one time. Beat the sauce vigorously with a wire whisk or wire hand eggbeater. Stir and cook over moderate heat 1 to 2 minutes or until the sauce has thickened. Drain the oil from the tuna fish, flake it, and add it to the sauce. Add the cream, salt, and pepper. Fill the pastry boats with this mixture. Cut the anchovy fillets in half and place a half on each boat. Serve hot. This amount will fill about 24 small barquettes.

❧ TUNA FISH SPREAD (*Crème de Thon*)

6½- to 7-ounce can white tuna fish
  packed in oil
2 tablespoons softened butter
½ teaspoon lemon juice

salt to taste
ground black pepper to taste
hard-cooked eggs
potato chips

Turn the tuna fish with the oil into a mixing bowl. Mash with a fork. Add the butter and mix to a purée. Add the lemon juice and salt and pepper to taste. Put the mixture in a small serving dish. Garnish with slices of hard-cooked egg or sieved hard-cooked eggs. Serve with potato chips. Makes 6 servings.

❧ Tuna Fish Spread Mirabeau (*Crème de Thon Mirabeau*)

Make Tuna Fish Spread according to the preceding recipe. Mound it in a serving dish and surround it with sliced tomatoes and pitted black olives or green olives. Allow one 6½- or 7-ounce can of tuna fish for 6 servings.

HAM HORS D'OEUVRE

❧ HAM ROLLS LUCULLUS (*Jambon en Roulades Lucullus*)

3½ ounces pâté de foie gras or
  chicken liver purèe
¼ cup (½ stick) butter, softened
2 to 3 tablespoons Madeira or dry
  sherry

8 thin slices (about 3 by 3½ inches)
  baked or boiled ham
half-set clear aspic

To make chicken liver purée, sauté the livers in butter, put them through a sieve or purée in a blender, and season to taste with salt and ground black pepper. Combine the pâté de foie gras or puréed chicken livers with the softened butter and add Madeira or sherry until the mixture is of spreading consistency. Spread it on the slices of ham and roll them up. Glaze with half-set aspic. Refrigerate until aspic is firm. Makes 4 servings.

❧ HAM ROLLS PRIMAVERA (*Jambon en Roulades Primavera*)

¼ pound mushrooms
about 2 teaspoons Dijon-type
  prepared mustard
½ cup thick mayonnaise

4 thin slices, 3 by 4 inches, baked or
  boiled ham
3 medium-sized tomatoes
2 large hard-cooked eggs
parsley

75

Wash the mushrooms, chop them fine, and mix them and the mustard with the mayonnaise, adjusting the mustard to taste. Spread the mixture on the slices of ham and roll them up. Arrange the rolls in the shape of a cross (+) in a round shallow dish. Cut the tomatoes and eggs in crosswise slices and arrange them alternately in the spaces between the ham rolls. Garnish with parsley. Makes 4 servings.

❧ HAM MOUSSELINES OR MOUSSE
(Mousselines ou Mousse de Jambon)

2 envelopes unflavored gelatin
1 cup cold port wine
2 cups hot beef or veal stock or bouillon
2½ cups finely ground cooked lean ham
½ cup (1 stick) butter, softened

2 tablespoons tomato purée
2 teaspoons paprika
1 cup cold Béchamel Sauce (page 38)
salt and ground black pepper to taste
½ cup heavy cream, whipped
½ tomato

In a 2-quart bowl soften the gelatin in the cold wine. Add the hot stock or bouillon and mix well. Place the bowl in ice water until the aspic begins to set. Reserve ½ cup liquid aspic and set aside at room temperature. Pour into 7 round or oval molds enough aspic to coat the bottom and sides. Chill the molds until the aspic is firm. Refrigerate the remaining aspic until it is firm and reserve it for later use.

The ham should be put through the food chopper 3 times, using the finest blade. Blend the ground ham with the softened butter, tomato purée, and paprika. Add the Béchamel Sauce and mix well. Chill the reserved ½ cup aspic until it begins to set, then fold it into the mixture. Season to taste with salt and pepper. Fold in the whipped cream. Spoon the mousse into the aspic-coated molds and chill until firm. Just before serving, break up the reserved aspic with a fork and scatter it over the bottom of a round serving plate. Unmold the individual molds of mousse and arrange them around the plate on top of the chopped aspic. Put a heaping teaspoon of the aspic on the cut side of the tomato half and place it in the center of the plate for a garnish. Makes 7 servings. (*See illustration, page* 87.) The ham mousse may be chilled in a 1½-quart mold instead of in small individual molds and sliced for serving.

MELONS

A good melon served as a first course can turn an otherwise humdrum meal into one that is very special. All melons appeal to the eye, the nose, and the palate. Some should be served chilled; others are best when merely cool.

Watermelons and honeydews are best when quite cold, while the bouquet of cantaloupe is more delightful if the fruit is served only moderately cool or at room temperature.

Melons may be sliced, diced, or cut into balls with a French melon-ball cutter. They may be flavored with lemon juice, lime juice, or orange juice, or port, sherry, Madeira, Cointreau, or Triple Sec. The same melon dishes may be served either as a first course or as a dessert. (*See illustration of melon balls on page 85.*)

MIXED HORS D'OEUVRE SALADS

⚜ COLD BEEF SALAD (*Salade de Boeuf*)

Beef from which stock was made is best to use in this salad. It should be cold and cut into julienne strips.

2 cups julienne strips cold cooked beef

2 tablespoons thinly sliced gherkins

1 tablespoon chopped onion

1 tablespoon chopped parsley

¼ cup julienne strips green pepper

¼ cup diced tomatoes

¼ cup Vinaigrette Sauce (page 56)

salt and ground black pepper to taste

Combine all ingredients and serve as a cold hors d'oeuvre. Makes 6 servings. (*See illustration, page 85.*)

⚜ DANISH-STYLE SALAD BOWL (*Ravier à la Danoise*)

This salad is served at room temperature.

3 medium-sized potatoes, peeled

salt

boiling water

¼ cup hot beef stock

3 tablespoons olive oil or salad oil

1 tablespoon wine vinegar

ground black pepper to taste

2 shallots or small white onions, chopped

3 tablespoons chopped parsley, or more

1 cup flaked cooked fresh salmon, or 1 can (6 to 7 ounces) salmon

mayonnaise

Place the potatoes in a saucepan with 1 teaspoon salt and boiling water to cover. Cover and cook 30 minutes or until potatoes are done. Drain off the water and save it for soup. Slice the potatoes ¼ inch thick. While they are still hot, add salt to taste, the beef stock, oil, wine vinegar, pepper, and chopped shallots or onions. Mix lightly and let the mixture stand at room temperature until the potatoes have absorbed all the liquid. Add 2 tablespoons of the parsley and mix lightly. Place the salad in the bottom of a large salad bowl. Season the salmon to taste with salt and pepper. (If canned salmon is used, drain and flake it.) Spread the salmon over the potato salad and coat lightly with mayonnaise. Sprinkle the remaining tablespoon chopped parsley, or more if desired, around the edges. Makes 6 servings.

⚜ SALAD ARGENTEUIL (*Salade Argenteuil*)

½ cup cooked sliced carrots
½ cup cooked sliced celery
½ cup cooked green beans or
   diced cooked turnip
½ cup cooked green peas
½ cup diced cooked ham
1 tablespoon chopped onion

½ cup mayonnaise
salt and ground white pepper to taste
tips from 1½ pounds asparagus,
   cooked
4 hard-cooked eggs, quartered
   lengthwise
pimiento

Have all the vegetables cold and well drained. Combine the first 8 ingredients in a salad bowl and mix lightly. Arrange the asparagus on top, with the tips pointed toward the sides of the bowl and the cut ends toward the center. Stand 4 egg quarters upright in the center of the bowl and arrange the remaining ones around the edge. Garnish with strips of pimiento. Makes 6 servings. (*See illustration, page 88.*)

⚜ NIÇOISE PLATTER (*Assiette Niçoise*)

shredded lettuce
6 medium-sized tomatoes, sliced
6 large sardines or 12 small
6-ounce can solid-pack tuna fish
4 hard-cooked eggs, sliced

18 to 24 anchovy fillets
green olives
black olives
Vinaigrette Sauce (page 56)

Arrange shredded lettuce on 6 salad plates. Arrange a sliced tomato in the center of each plate. Put a sardine on the lettuce on one side of the tomato and a portion of the tuna fish on the other. Arrange 3 to 4 anchovy fillets on each tomato. Garnish with hard-cooked egg slices and with green and black olives. Serve with Vinaigrette Sauce. Makes 6 servings. (*See illustration, page 86.*)

⚜ POULTRY SALAD (*Salade de Volaille*)

2½ cups julienne strips cold cooked
   chicken or turkey
½ cup julienne strips cold cooked ham
2 tablespoons chopped gherkins
1 tablespoon chopped parsley
1 teaspoon chopped fresh tarragon,
   or ¼ teaspoon dried tarragon

1 tablespoon wine vinegar
3 tablespoons olive oil or salad oil
salt and ground black pepper to taste
lettuce, shredded
1 or 2 hard-cooked eggs, sliced

78

Combine the first 8 ingredients and mix lightly. Arrange shredded lettuce in a shallow salad bowl. Put the salad on top, shape it into a mound, and garnish with slices of hard-cooked egg. Makes 6 servings.

STUFFED VEGETABLES

⚜ STUFFED ARTICHOKES (*Artichauts Farcis*)

Use 6 small artichokes. To prepare the artichokes, wash them, cut off the stems even with the base, and remove and discard the tough outer leaves. Cut off and discard the top third of each artichoke. If prickly ends of leaves are left, trim them off. Stand the artichokes upright in a saucepan just large enough for them to fit in snugly, or tie a string around each to hold it in shape. To prevent discoloration, rub lemon juice over the cut surfaces or fasten a thin slice of lemon onto the base of each artichoke with a toothpick. Sprinkle with 1 teaspoon salt and cover with boiling water. Cook, covered, 30 to 40 minutes or until artichokes are tender. They are done when a leaf pulls out easily. Remove the strings (if used) and place artichokes upside down to drain. Using a sharp knife, remove the prickly chokes in the centers and discard them. Put the artichokes into cold water to freshen them, then remove the leaves in the center so each artichoke forms a bowl. (Reserve the leaves for later use.) Fill the centers with Artichoke and Mushroom Salad à la Grecque or Rice Salad Manuela (see following recipes) or with other desired filling. Garnish with reserved artichoke leaves, if desired.

⚜ ARTICHOKE AND MUSHROOM SALAD À LA GRECQUE
(*Salade d'Artichauts et Girolles à la Grecque*)

6 small artichokes
6 small carrots
12 very small white onions
12 button mushroom caps
6 morels (if available), or 6 large mushroom caps
boiling water to cover
1 cup water
½ cup vinegar
½ cup olive oil or salad oil

1 rib celery, sliced
1 stalk parsley
½ teaspoon salt
1 bay leaf
2 teaspoons chopped fresh thyme, or ½ teaspoon dried thyme
6 whole black peppercorns
6 coriander seeds
12 green olives or black olives, pitted

Prepare the artichokes as directed in the preceding recipe. Scrape the carrots and cut into balls or into slices ½ inch thick and put them in a 2-quart sauce-

79

pan. Peel the onions, wash the button mushroom caps and the morels or large mushroom caps, and add to the carrots. Cover with boiling water and cook 1 minute. Drain and discard the water. Remove all the mushrooms and set them aside. Add the next 7 ingredients and the fresh thyme, if used, to the carrots and onions. Put the peppercorns and coriander seeds in clean cheese-cloth (with the dried thyme, if used), tie, and add. Cover the saucepan, bring the marinade to boiling point, reduce heat to moderate, and cook the vege-tables 5 minutes, then add all the mushrooms, and continue cooking only until vegetables are crisp-tender, 5 to 7 minutes. Remove the saucepan from the heat and cool the vegetables in the marinade. Remove the morels or large mushroom caps, slice, and return to the saucepan. Add the artichoke bowls, the artichoke leaves removed when shaping the bowls, and the olives. Cover and marinate 4 to 5 hours or overnight. Before serving, remove and discard the parsley stalk and the spice bag, and drain off the marinade. Fill the artichoke bowls with the vegetables. Arrange them on a platter and garnish with parsley. Serve chilled. Makes 6 servings. (*See illustration, page 86.*)

⚜ RICE SALAD MANUELA (*Salade de Riz Manuela*)

1 cup cooked rice	1 teaspoon water
½ cup diced cooked ham	1 teaspoon wine vinegar
¼ cup cold cooked peas	salt and ground black pepper to taste
¼ cup diced sweet red or green pepper	6 artichoke bowls prepared as in Stuffed Artichokes and marinated
1 tablespoon catsup	as in Artichoke Salad à la Grecque

Put the rice, ham, peas, and diced peppers in a mixing bowl. Combine the catsup, water, vinegar, salt, and pepper, and toss with the mixture. Spoon into the artichoke bowls. Makes 6 servings. (*See illustration, page 86.*)

This artichoke stuffing can also be served as a separate salad, mounded on a salad plate. Makes 4 servings.

⚜ STUFFED TOMATOES (*Tomates Garnies ou Farcies*)

Cold tomatoes stuffed with various salads are served as hors d'oeuvre, luncheon or supper entrées, or to garnish cold dishes. Choose firm ripe tomatoes, medium-sized and uniform in shape. Cut a slice from the stem end of each or cut them in crosswise halves. Carefully scoop out the pulp and seeds, leaving the cases intact. Sprinkle the inside of the cases lightly with salt and ground black pepper. Invert them on a wire rack to drain. Fill the cases with any desired salad mixture, such as chicken, egg, fish, shellfish, ham or other meat salad, rice, or potato or other vegetable salad. Decorate as de-sired with hard-cooked egg, black olives or green olives, gherkin pickle, truffles, small mushrooms, green pepper, parsley, or other fresh herbs. Allow 1 stuffed tomato per serving.

⚜ TOMATOES STUFFED WITH ASPARAGUS AND HAM
(*Tomates Argenteuil*)

6 uniform medium-sized tomatoes
salt and ground black pepper
1 cup cold diced cooked lean ham
1 cup cold diced cooked asparagus
  tips
1 teaspoon finely chopped onion

½ teaspoon Dijon-type prepared
  mustard
¼ cup mayonnaise
Coating Mayonnaise (page 54)
gherkin pickles
lettuce

Prepare tomatoes for stuffing according to the recipe for Stuffed Tomatoes. Combine the ham, asparagus tips, and onion. Blend the mustard with the mayonnaise, add it to the ham mixture, and mix lightly. Season to taste with salt and pepper. Spoon the mixture into the tomato cases. Coat thinly with Coating Mayonnaise. Garnish each with a slice of gherkin pickle. Serve on lettuce. Makes 6 servings.

⚜ TOMATOES STUFFED WITH CAULIFLOWER ⚜
(*Tomates Dubarry*)

6 uniform medium-sized tomatoes
salt and ground black pepper
1 head (1 pound) cauliflower
cold water to cover
2 teaspoons salt

boiling water to cover
mayonnaise
fresh chervil or parsley
lettuce

Prepare the tomatoes for stuffing according to the recipe for Stuffed Tomatoes. Remove the outside leaves from the cauliflower. Put the head with 1 teaspoon salt in cold water to cover and soak it 20 minutes. Drain the cauliflower, and break it into flowerets. Cover with boiling water and add the remaining 1 teaspoon salt. Cover, bring the water to boiling point, reduce heat, and simmer 5 minutes. Remove the cauliflower from the hot water and quickly rinse in cold water to stop the cooking process. Place a teaspoon of mayonnaise in the bottom of each tomato case. Sprinkle the caulifflowerets with a little black pepper and put them into the tomato cases. Spoon a little mayonnaise over the top of each case. Garnish with sprigs of chervil or parsley. Serve on lettuce. Makes 6 servings.

⚜ TOMATOES STUFFED WITH CHICKEN AND MUSHROOMS
(*Tomates Sevigné*)

6 uniform medium-sized tomatoes
salt and ground black pepper
1 cup diced cold cooked chicken
1 cup finely diced raw mushrooms
¼ teaspoon finely chopped onion

¼ teaspoon lemon juice
1 tablespoon chopped parsley
¼ cup mayonnaise
Coating Mayonnaise
green-pepper strips

81

Prepare tomatoes for stuffing according to the recipe for Stuffed Tomatoes. Combine the chicken, mushrooms, onion, lemon juice, parsley, mayonnaise, and salt and pepper to taste. Mix lightly but thoroughly. Spoon the mixture into the tomato cases. Cover the tops with Coating Mayonnaise. Decorate each with green-pepper strips in a lattice pattern. Serve on lettuce. Makes 6 servings.

⚜ TOMATOES STUFFED WITH MIXED VEGETABLE SALAD
(*Tomates à la Russe*)

6 uniform medium-sized tomatoes
salt and ground black pepper
1½ cups cold diced mixed cooked vegetables (carrots, celery, peas, potatoes, etc.)
1 teaspoon lemon juice

1 teaspoon finely chopped onion
¼ to ⅓ cup mayonnaise
6 slices hard-cooked egg
green-pepper strips
lettuce

Prepare the tomatoes for stuffing according to the recipe for Stuffed Tomatoes. Combine the vegetables, lemon juice, onion, and enough mayonnaise to bind the mixture and mix lightly. Season to taste with salt and pepper. Spoon the mixture into the tomato cases. Cover the tops with mayonnaise. Decorate each with a slice of hard-cooked egg and strips of green pepper. Serve on lettuce. Makes 6 servings.

⚜ TOMATOES STUFFED WITH RICE (*Tomates à l'Andalouse*)

6 uniform medium-sized tomatoes
salt and ground black pepper
2 tablespoons finely chopped Spanish onion
1 teaspoon olive oil or salad oil
1½ cups cold cooked rice
3 tablespoons finely chopped green pepper

1 teaspoon Dijon-type prepared mustard
⅓ cup mayonnaise
green-pepper strips
6 black olives, pitted
lettuce

Prepare tomatoes for stuffing according to the recipe for Stuffed Tomatoes. Cook the onions in the oil only until they are limp, *not browned*. Add to the rice. Add the chopped green pepper. Mix the mustard with the mayonnaise and blend with the rice mixture. Season with salt and pepper to taste. Spoon the mixture into the tomato cases. Decorate each with strips of green pepper and a black olive. Serve on lettuce. Makes 6 servings. (*See illustration, page 88.*)

⚜ TOMATOES STUFFED WITH TUNA FISH (*Tomates Beaulieu*)

6 uniform medium-sized tomatoes
salt and ground black pepper
wine vinegar
2 cans (6½ to 7 ounces each) tuna fish
   packed in oil

¼ cup (½ stick) softened butter
1 teaspoon lemon juice
4 tablespoons mayonnaise
1 hard-cooked egg
6 black olives or green olives, pitted

Prepare tomatoes for stuffing according to the recipe for Stuffed Tomatoes. Sprinkle the inside of the tomato cases lightly with salt, pepper, and a little wine vinegar and invert them on a wire rack to drain. Put the tuna fish with the oil in a mixing bowl. Mash with a fork. Add the butter and mix to a purée. Add the lemon juice and mayonnaise and salt and pepper to taste. Mix and spoon the mixture into the tomato cases. Chop the hard-cooked egg white fine and sprinkle an equal amount over the top of each tomato. Put the yolk through a sieve and sprinkle a little over the white right in the center. Decorate each with an olive. Makes 6 servings.

VEGETABLES À LA GRECQUE

The term "à la Grecque" is misleading, in that most dishes so designated are actually French rather than Greek in origin. The vegetables are simmered *only* until tender in a sauce made of bouillon or water, oil, vinegar, wine, lemon juice, herbs, and spices. Then the vegetables are cooled in the liquid and refrigerated several hours before serving. Vegetables à la Grecque are served as hors d'oeuvre or in salads.

⚜ ARTICHOKES À LA GRECQUE (*Artichauts à la Grecque*)

8 small artichokes
1 cup dry white wine
1 cup water
½ cup olive oil or salad oil
2 tablespoons lemon juice

1 small bay leaf
6 whole black peppercorns
¼ cup sliced fresh fennel or ⅛ teaspoon fennel seeds
salt to taste

Prepare the artichokes for cooking according to the recipe for Stuffed Artichokes (page 79). Put all the other ingredients in a 2-quart saucepan, bring to boiling point and boil 2 minutes. Add the artichokes and cook until the artichokes are tender, 30 to 40 minutes. Artichokes are done when a leaf pulls out easily. With a sharp knife remove the prickly chokes in the center and discard them. Return the artichokes to the cooking liquid and let them marinate until ready to serve. Serve cold with a little of the liquid. Makes 8 servings.

⚜ FENNEL À LA GRECQUE (*Fenouil à la Grecque*)

1¼ to 1½ pounds fennel	2 tablespoons lemon juice
salt	1 small bay leaf
boiling water to cover	6 whole black peppercorns
¾ cup bouillon or boiling water	6 coriander seeds
¾ cup dry white wine	¼ teaspoon dried chervil or thyme
¼ cup olive oil or salad oil	1 stalk parsley

Wash the fennel and cut the ribs into quarters lengthwise. Place in a saucepan with ½ teaspoon salt and enough boiling water to cover. Cover and boil 10 minutes. Drain off and discard water. Add remaining ingredients. Cover and cook *only* until fennel is tender, about 30 minutes. Add salt to taste. Remove the fennel. Strain the cooking liquid and simmer it until it has reduced to one-half the original quantity. Pour the liquid over the fennel, let cool, and then chill for several hours before serving. Serve with some of the liquid. Makes 6 to 8 servings.

VEGETABLES AS HORS D'OEUVRE

⚜ BEET SALAD (*Salade de Betterave*)

8 small beets, cooked	salt and ground black pepper to taste
1 tablespoon wine vinegar	6 medium-sized cooked potatoes,
Vinaigrette Sauce (page 56)	peeled
1 small white onion, sliced	

Peel the cooked beets and cut them into slices ¼ inch thick. Add the vinegar, Vinaigrette Sauce, onion, and salt and pepper to taste and marinate 2 to 3 hours. Turn the beets into a serving dish and just before serving arrange the cold cooked potatoes around the edge of the bowl. Makes 6 servings.

⚜ WHITE CABBAGE SALAD (*Salade de Chou Blanc*)

3 cups finely shredded cabbage	⅓ cup mayonnaise
2 tablespoons finely shredded onion	1½ teaspoons wine vinegar
2 tablespoons finely chopped parsley	salt and ground black pepper to taste

Use the firm white hearts of cabbage heads and shred them fine. Combine all ingredients and mix lightly. Makes 4 to 5 servings.

↑ Hard-Cooked Eggs with Tomatoes (page 139)

86 ↑ Salad Marguerite, Salad Orloff, Niçoise Platter   ↓ Stuffed Artichokes: with Artichoke and Mushroom
      (pages 399, 401, 78)   Salad à la Grecque, with Rice Salad Manuela (pages

88   ↑ Salad Argenteuil (page 78)   ↓ Tomatoes Stuffed with Rice (page 82)

⚜ RED CABBAGE SALAD *(Salade de Chou Rouge)*

4 cups finely shredded red cabbage
½ teaspoon salt
2 tablespoons wine vinegar

⅓ cup Vinaigrette Sauce (page 56)
ground black pepper to taste
shredded green peppers

Sprinkle the cabbage with salt and wine vinegar and toss lightly but thoroughly. Put the mixture in a 1½-quart heatproof bowl or saucepan, cover, and place on a hot-plate warmer or over a pan of hot water for about 10 minutes to soften the cabbage. Drain and cool. Add the Vinaigrette Sauce and pepper, toss, and turn into a serving dish. Sprinkle shredded green peppers around the edge of the salad. Makes 6 servings.

⚜ CELERIAC SALAD IN RÉMOULADE SAUCE
(Salade de Céleri-Rave en Rémoulade)

2½ cups julienne strips celeriac
boiling water
⅓ cup mayonnaise
½ to 1 teaspoon Dijon-type prepared
   mustard (to taste)

1 tablespoon chopped parsley
1 teaspoon each chopped fresh chervil
   and tarragon, or ¼ teaspoon each
   dried chervil and tarragon
salt and ground black pepper

Cover the celeriac strips with boiling water and let stand 5 minutes to remove the strong flavor of the celeriac and make it tender. Drain well. Cool. Combine the mayonnaise, mustard, and herbs, mix with the celeriac, and season the mixture to taste with salt and pepper. Makes 6 servings.

⚜ CELERY SALAD *(Salade de Céleri Blanc)*

Use only the tender inside ribs of the celery.

2 cups celery sticks
2 tablespoons chopped parsley
⅓ cup Rémoulade Sauce (page 55)

1 teaspoon each chopped fresh chervil
   and thyme, or ¼ teaspoon each
   dried chervil and thyme

Remove the tender inside ribs from the celery bunch, wash, and dry well. Cut the ribs into 2-inch lengths and cut these into strips of matchstick thickness. Combine the herbs with the Rémoulade Sauce, add the celery sticks, and mix lightly. Let the mixture stand 2 hours before serving. Makes 6 servings.

⚜ CUCUMBER SALAD *(Salade de Concombre)*

Peel 2 medium-sized cucumbers. Cut them in half lengthwise and carefully remove the seeds and water from the inside. Sprinkle with salt, preferably coarse salt if it is available. Pour enough water over the cucumbers to cover them and let them soak 1 hour. Drain well and press out excess water. Slice the cucumber halves very thin crosswise, and arrange them on an hors d'oeuvre dish. Mix 1 tablespoon wine vinegar, 3 tablespoons olive oil or salad oil, coarsely ground black pepper to taste, and a little chopped parsley, and sprinkle over the cucumbers. Makes 6 servings.

❧ POTATO SALAD (*Salade de Pommes de Terre*)

1 quart hot boiled potatoes sliced
  ¼ inch thick
salt to taste
ground black pepper to taste
¼ cup chopped onion
⅓ cup hot beef stock, bouillon, or dry
  white wine

¼ cup Vinaigrette Sauce (page 56)
1 teaspoon chopped fresh chervil or
  tarragon, or ¼ teaspoon dried
  chervil or tarragon
chopped parsley
lettuce

Combine the first 5 ingredients and mix lightly. Marinate several hours, until the potatoes have absorbed the liquid, adding the Vinaigrette Sauce gradually as the other liquid is absorbed. Before serving, add the herbs and mix carefully to avoid breaking the potato slices. Serve at room temperature on lettuce. Makes 6 servings.

❧ LEEKS VINAIGRETTE (*Poireaux à la Vinaigrette*)

8 leeks
hot water
1 teaspoon salt

boiling water
Vinaigrette Sauce (page 56)

Remove and discard the roots of the leeks. Cut off the green tops and reserve for stocks, soups, and salads. Wash the white part of the leeks thoroughly and split them lengthwise down the center to 3 inches from the root end. Tie the leeks in serving-size bundles as for asparagus (see page 350). Soak 30 minutes in enough hot water to cover them. Drain. Add the salt and enough boiling water to cover the leeks, cover, and cook for 30 minutes. Drain off the water and rinse with cold water. Drain again. Pour Vinaigrette Sauce over the leeks and serve. Makes 4 servings.

❧ MARINATED MUSHROOMS (*Champignons Marinés*)

¾ pound small firm mushrooms
boiling water to cover
½ teaspoon salt

¾ teaspoon powered mustard
2 teaspoons cold water
¾ cup Vinaigrette Sauce (page 56)

Wash the mushrooms, quarter them, and place in a saucepan. Cover with boiling water and add the salt. Cover and cook below boiling point for 5 minutes (do not boil). Drain off and discard the water. Rinse the mushrooms in cold water. Mix the mustard with the cold water and let the mixture stand 5 minutes for flavor to develop. Add to the Vinaigrette Sauce and pour the mixture over the mushrooms. Marinate 24 hours. Serve as an hors d'oeuvre. Makes 6 servings. (*See illustration, page 85.*)

❧ BLACK RADISHES VINAIGRETTE (*Radis Noirs en Vinaigrette*)

Wash and peel black radishes and cut them in crosswise slices. Cover with cold water, add ½ teaspoon salt, and let soak ½ hour. Drain the radishes, rinse in cold water, and dry between clean towels. Pour enough Vinaigrette Sauce (page 56) over the radishes *barely* to cover them and let them stand 2 hours. Black radishes may also be served peeled with salt and unsalted butter. Allow 1 cup sliced radishes for each 4 servings.

Entrées

Entrées may constitute the first course or the main course of a luncheon or supper or may be served after the soup at dinner in place of a fish course. Entrées contained in this chapter include croquettes, tarts, patties, etc., filled with various mixtures (these may also be used, in smaller sizes, as hot hors d'oeuvre); cheese dishes; dishes made with pastas, cereals, or rice; and, for special occasions, pâtés, terrines, and galantines. For most egg dishes served as entrées, see Chapter 6; see also Chapter 12, Leftovers.

Small Entrées or Hot Hors d'Oeuvre

These dishes may be served as entrées, or in smaller portions as hot hors d'oeuvre. They should always be served piping hot.

⚜ CHICKEN CROQUETTES (*Croquettes de Volaille*)

½ cup finely chopped celery
¼ cup finely chopped mushrooms
2 tablespoons finely chopped onions
 or shallots
4 tablespoons (½ stick) butter
4 tablespoons flour
1 cup hot milk
2 cups finely ground cooked chicken

1¼ teaspoons salt
¼ teaspoon ground black pepper
¼ teaspoon ground mace or nutmeg
1½ teaspoons lemon juice
3 large eggs
fine dry breadcrumbs
1 tablespoon milk or water
Tomato Sauce (optional; page 50)

Cook the celery, mushrooms, and onions or shallots in 2 tablespoons of the butter until soft, 4 to 5 minutes. Add the remaining 2 tablespoons butter and stir until it is melted. Blend in the flour. Stir and cook 1 to 2 minutes. Remove from heat and add all the milk. Beat well with a wire whisk. Return to heat. Stir and cook until the sauce is very thick, 2 to 3 minutes. Stir in the chicken, salt, pepper, mace or nutmeg, and the lemon juice. Beat 2 of the eggs, add, and mix well. Form the mixture, with the hands, into 12 cylinder- or pyramid-shaped croquettes. Roll them in breadcrumbs. Beat the remaining egg with the 1 tablespoon milk or water. Roll the croquettes in the mixture and then in breadcrumbs again and set them aside for 30 minutes for crumbs to dry. Fry about 3 croquettes at a time in deep fat preheated to 375° F. until they have browned. Drain on paper towels. Serve hot, with Tomato Sauce if desired.

To make chicken croquettes of hors d'oeuvre size, shape this mixture into ½-inch balls and crumb and fry them in the same way. Serve hot. Makes 12 croquettes or 8 dozen cocktail-size balls.

⚜ EGG PATTIES (*Chaussons aux Oeufs*)

4 hard-cooked eggs, diced
⅓ cup Béchamel (page 38) or Velouté
 Sauce (page 40)
1 tablespoon Tomato Sauce (page 50)
 or tomato purée
¼ cup sautéed diced mushrooms

1 tablespoon chopped parsley
salt to taste
ground white pepper to taste
Puff Pastry (page 25)
1 large egg yolk
1½ teaspoons water or milk

Combine the first 7 ingredients and heat in the top of a double boiler only until hot. Cool. Roll Puff Pastry ⅛ inch thick on a lightly floured pastry board. Cut it into circles, using a 2-inch fluted cooky cutter. Place a rounded teaspoon of the egg mixture in the centers of half of the pastry circles. Moisten the edges, cover each with one of the remaining pastry circles, and press the edges down firmly. Arrange on ungreased cooky sheets. Beat the egg yolk with the water or milk and brush over the tops of the patties. Prick the tops 3 times with the pointed tip of a knife. Bake in a preheated hot oven (425° F.) 12 to 15 minutes or until patties are golden. Serve hot. Makes approximately 3 dozen.

⚜ FISH BALLS (*Beignets de Poisson*)

2 cups leftover flaked cooked fish (salmon, halibut, turbot if available, hake, whiting, or cod)
2 cups dry mashed potatoes
1 teaspoon grated onion
1 teaspoon dried thyme or marjoram
2 tablespoons finely chopped parsley

1 teaspoon lemon juice
3 large eggs
salt and ground black pepper to taste
1 tablespoon milk
fine dry breadcrumbs, or flour
melted butter or Béchamel Sauce (page 38) (optional)

Combine the first 6 ingredients, 2 of the eggs, and salt and pepper. Mix well. Shape into 2-inch balls and flatten them to ½-inch thickness. Beat the remaining egg with the milk, dip the fish balls into the mixture, and then dip them in breadcrumbs or flour. Fry until brown in deep fat heated to 375° F. Drain on paper towels. Serve an an entrée with melted butter or Béchamel Sauce if desired. The mixture may also be made into 1-inch balls, fried the same way, and served as hot hors d'oeuvre. Makes 6 servings as an entrée, or about 3 dozen cocktail fish balls.

⚜ FISH SOUFFLÉ (*Soufflé de Poisson*)

This recipe may also be used to make a soufflé from leftover poultry, ham, sweetbreads, shellfish, or game.

3 tablespoons butter
3 tablespoons flour
1 cup milk
4 eggs, separated
¾ teaspoon salt
⅛ teaspoon ground white pepper

2 cups finely chopped cooked fish (cod, flounder, haddock, halibut, salmon, or tuna)
1 teaspoon lemon juice
½ teaspoon powdered mustard
1 teaspoon water
¼ teaspoon cream of tartar

Melt the butter in a saucepan. Remove from heat and blend in the flour. Add the milk gradually. Stir and cook until the sauce is of medium thickness. Beat the egg yolks until thick and lemon-colored. Add a little of the hot sauce to the egg yolks and then stir the yolks into the remaining sauce. Stir in salt and pepper. Purée the fish in an electric blender with a little of the hot sauce and the lemon juice, and add it to remaining sauce. Or put the fish through a food mill, and add the fish and lemon juice to the remaining sauce. Soak the mustard in the water 5 minutes, then stir it into the mixture. Beat the egg whites until they are foamy. Add the cream of tartar and continue beating until the whites stand in soft, stiff peaks. Carefully fold the whites into the mixture. Extend the top of a 1½-quart soufflé dish by tying a folded piece of foil 4 inches wide around the top to allow the soufflé room for expansion as it cooks. Butter *only* the bottom of the dish and turn the mixture into it. Place the dish in a pan of hot water and bake in a preheated slow oven (325° F.) 1½ hours, or until the soufflé is well puffed and browned. Serve immediately. Makes 6 servings.

❧ HOT HAM AND CHEESE SANDWICHES (*Croque-Monsieur*)

Cut firm-textured white bread in slices ¼ inch thick and remove the crusts. Dip the slices in melted butter and brown on both sides on a heavy griddle over moderate heat. Melt ½ pound diced Gruyère cheese with 2 tablespoons dry white wine over hot water (not boiling). Spread one side of each slice of sautéed bread with melted cheese. Make into sandwiches with a slice of grilled ham in the center of each. Serve very hot. To serve as a hot hors d'oeuvre, cut each sandwich into 4 squares or triangles. Allow 1 to 2 large sandwiches or 2 to 3 small sandwiches per person.

❧ MUSHROOM TARTLETS (*Croûtes aux Champignons*)

Plain Pastry Dough (page 24)
1¼ pounds mushrooms
3 tablespoons minced shallots or
   green onion
¼ cup (½ stick) butter
1 teaspoon lemon juice

3 tablespoons flour
1 cup hot chicken stock
¾ cup heavy cream
3 tablespoons dry sherry
salt and ground black pepper

Roll the pastry dough thin and line tartlet pans or molds. Set them aside. Wash, dry, and dice the mushrooms and sauté them gently with the shallots or green onion in the butter and lemon juice for 2 minutes. Remove pan from the heat and blend in the flour. Return to heat. Stir and cook 2 minutes. Remove from heat, add the stock, and mix well. Cook, stirring, until the sauce is smooth and thick. Stir in the cream and sherry. Season to taste with salt and pepper and bring the mixture to a boil, stirring constantly. Spoon the mixture into the tart shells and place the pans on a baking sheet. Bake in a preheated hot oven (400° F.) 12 minutes or until the pastry is brown. If desired, this mixture can be served in bread cases. Cut unsliced bread into slices 1 inch thick and cut out rounds from the slices with a 2- or 3-inch cooky cutter. Scoop out the centers of the rounds and save for breadcrumbs. Brush the rounds with melted butter and toast them in a preheated very hot oven (450° F.) or fry them in butter. Fill with the mushroom mixture. Serve the larger as a small entrée, the small ones as hot hors d'oeuvre. Makes 8 large or 18 small tartlets.

✿ ONION TART (*Tarte aux Oignons*)

3 large onions, sliced thin
3 tablespoons butter
Plain Pastry Dough (page 24) for a
   9-inch unbaked pie shell
3 large eggs, lightly beaten
¾ teaspoon salt

⅛ teaspoon ground white pepper
⅛ teaspoon ground mace
1½ cups light cream
chopped parsley
Poulette Sauce (optional; page 41)

Cook the onions in the butter in a skillet, stirring frequently, until they are soft and transparent but not browned. Line a 9-inch pie plate with the pastry and arrange the onions uniformly over the pastry. Mix the next 4 ingredients with ¼ cup of the cream. Heat the remaining cream and add to the egg mixture. Mix well and strain over the onions. Bake in a preheated hot oven (425° F.) 10 minutes. Reduce heat to 350° F. (moderate) and bake 30 to 40 minutes or until a knife inserted in the center comes out clean. Garnish with chopped parsley. Serve as a hot hors d'oeuvre or as a small hot entrée with Poulette Sauce. Makes 12 hors d'oeuvre servings or 6 small-entrée servings.

✿ PIZZA

Pizza is an Italian pie filled with vegetables cooked in oil, and garnished with cheese, Italian sausage, mushrooms, anchovies, olives, etc. The pastry is made of yeast dough. Pizza is served as a hot hors d'oeuvre or as an entrée for lunch or supper. (*See illustration, page 121.*)

✿ Pizza Dough (*Pâte à Pizza*)

1 envelope active dry yeast
1 cup lukewarm water
½ teaspoon sugar

½ teaspoon salt
about 3¼ cups sifted all-purpose flour

Combine the first 3 ingredients and let stand 5 minutes. Stir in the salt and 2 cups of the flour. Turn the dough onto a floured board and gradually knead in the remaining 1¼ cups flour. Knead until the dough is smooth and satiny. Cover and let the dough rise until it has doubled in size. Place the dough on a lightly floured board and pound it lightly with a rolling pin to deflate it. Cover and let the dough rise 30 minutes. Roll and stretch the dough to ⅛ inch thickness and line a 12-inch lightly oiled pizza pan. (There will be a small piece of dough left, which may be made into rolls or smaller pizzas.) Chill until ready to spread with filling.

⚜ Pizza Filling

¼ cup finely chopped onion
⅛ teaspoon finely chopped garlic
5 tablespoons olive oil or salad oil
2 cups drained canned Italian tomatoes
2 tablespoons tomato paste
1½ teaspoons dried oregano leaves
½ teaspoon each salt and sugar
⅛ teaspoon ground black pepper

½ pound Mozzarella cheese, sliced thin
1 2-ounce can anchovy fillets
¼ pound Italian sausage, sliced
1 4-ounce can sliced buttered mushrooms, or ½ cup sliced fresh mushrooms cooked in butter
½ cup grated Parmesan cheese

Cook onion and garlic in 2 tablespoons of the hot oil until onion is transparent, 2 to 3 minutes (do not brown). Break up the tomatoes with a fork and add to the onions along with the tomato paste and seasonings. Stir and cook 5 minutes. Cool. Spread over the unbaked pizza crust. Arrange Mozzarella cheese slices over the top. Place anchovies, sausage, and mushrooms over the cheese in any desired pattern. Sprinkle with ¼ cup of the Parmesan cheese. Drizzle with the remaining 3 tablespoons oil. Bake in a preheated hot oven (400° F.) 25 to 30 minutes, or until crust is brown and the edges crisp. Sprinkle with the remaining ¼ cup Parmesan cheese. Serve hot. Makes filling for a 12-inch pizza.

⚜ RICE TIMBALES MILANESE STYLE
(*Timbales de Risotto à la Milanaise*)

Season 2 cups cooked rice with ¼ teaspoon ground nutmeg. Pack it into 4 buttered 6-ounce timbale molds (custard cups). Melt 6 tablespoons butter and spoon 1½ tablespoons over each. Set the molds in a pan of hot water and cover with foil to prevent the top of the rice from drying. Bake in a preheated moderate oven (350° F.) 20 to 30 minutes. In the meantime, cut 4 rounds of cooked lean ham, ¼ inch thick and the same size as the top of the timbales, and arrange them on a platter. Unmold a timbale over each slice. Garnish the tops with diced tomatoes. Serve very hot. Makes 4 servings. (*See illustration, page 123.*)

⚜ SAVORY TURNOVERS (*Les Rissoles*)

These small turnovers may be made from leftover Puff Pastry or Plain Pastry Dough. They may be filled with mixtures made from leftover chicken, meat, fish, foie gras, mushrooms, shellfish, etc., and are equally good fried in deep fat or baked in the oven. Allow 2 to 3 turnovers per person. (*See illustration, page 121.*)

Roll Puff Pastry (page 25) ⅛ inch thick or Plain Pastry Dough (page 24) 1/16 inch thick on a lightly floured postry board. Cut the dough into circles, using a 2½- or 3-inch fluted cooky cutter. Place a rounded ½ teaspoon of filling (see following recipes) in the center of each circle. Moisten the edges and fold the pastry over the filling to make half-moon shapes. Press the edges together with the index finger or crimp them with a fork. Beat 1 egg with 1 tablespoon water or milk and brush over the tops of the turnovers. Prick the tops with the tines of a fork. Place the turnovers on ungreased cooky sheets. Bake in a preheated hot oven (425° F.) 8 to 10 minutes or until browned, or fry until browned in deep fat preheated to 375° F. Drain on paper towels.

FILLINGS FOR TURNOVERS

⚜ Curried Ham Filling

1 cup ground cooked lean ham
½ cup thick Velouté Sauce (page 40),
   or ½ cup sour cream and 1 tablespoon mayonnaise
1 teaspoon curry powder

¼ teaspoon each salt and powdered
   mustard
dash cayenne
1 teaspoon finely chopped onion
1/16 teaspoon minced garlic

Combine all ingredients and mix well. Use a rounded ½ teaspoon of this mixture for each turnover. Makes filling for 4 dozen turnovers.

⚜ Meat Filling

1 cup ground leftover beef, ham,
   lamb, or veal
2 tablespoons finely chopped onion
¼ teaspoon powdered mustard soaked
   5 minutes in 1 teaspoon water

¼ cup thick Velouté Sauce (page
   40), or ¼ cup sour cream
1 tablespoon chopped parsley
salt and ground black pepper to taste

Combine all ingredients and mix well. Use a rounded ½ teaspoon of this mixture for each turnover. Makes fiilling for approximately 3½ dozen turnovers.

⚜ Oyster Filling

Drain 25 small soup oysters well and cut each in half. Mix with ⅛ teaspoon ground black pepper, ¼ teaspoon each salt and celery seeds. Let stand 30 minutes. Use ½ oyster for the filling for each 2½-inch circle of pastry. Makes filling for 50 turnovers.

⚜ SHRIMP PATTIES (*Bouchées Joinville*)

Make 8 round or oval-shaped Patty Shells of Puff Pastry as directed in the recipe on page 26. Fill them with Shrimp Filling.

⚜ Shrimp Filling

2 cups peeled cooked small shrimp
½ cup sautéed diced mushrooms
1¼ cups Béchamel Sauce (page 38)
  or Velouté Sauce (page 40)

salt and ground white pepper to taste
1 tablespoon chopped parsley

Combine all ingredients and heat in the top of a double boiler. Fill the patty shells and serve hot. Makes 8 servings. (*See illustration, page 121.*)

⚜ TOMATO AND OLIVE TART (*Pissaladière ou Tarte Niçoise*)

Serve as a hot hors d'oeuvre or as a small entrée.

9-inch unbaked pie shell (see following recipe)
⅓ cup freshly grated Parmesan cheese
1½ cups chopped onion
2 tablespoons butter
2 cups diced tomatoes
¼ cup sliced black olives
1/16 teaspoon minced garlic

1 tablespoon olive oil or salad oil
½ teaspoon each dried oregano and
  dried rosemary, or 1½ teaspoons
  each fresh oregano and fresh rosemary
⅛ teaspoon ground black pepper
1 can (2 ounces) flat anchovy fillets
5 to 6 pimiento-stuffed green olives

Line a 9-inch pie plate with pastry, sprinkle with 3 tablespoons of the Parmesan cheese, and set aside. Cook the onions in the butter 4 to 5 minutes or until they are soft. Cool and spread over the cheese. Cook the tomatoes, olives, and garlic in the olive oil until all the excess moisture has evaporated, about 10 minutes. Spread over the onions. Bake in a preheated hot oven (425° F.) 30 minutes or until the pie is done. Sprinkle the top with the remaining cheese. Arrange the anchovies, in lattice fashion, over the cheese, having 4 strips in each direction. Cut each stuffed olive into 3 slices and place one in each lattice square. Serve warm. Makes 16 servings as an hors d'oeuvre or 6 servings as a small entrée.

⚜ Pastry for Tomato and Olive Tart

1½ cups sifted all-purpose flour
¾ teaspoon salt

½ cup shortening
about 4 tablespoons cold water

Sift the flour with the salt into a mixing bowl. Add the shortening and cut it in until the flour-coated particles are the size of beans. Sprinkle in the cold water—only enough to form a firm dough. Roll the pastry ¼ inch thick on a lightly floured pastry board. Place it in a 9-inch plate, turn under the pastry that hangs over the rim of the plate, and flute the edge or crimp it with a fork. Makes pastry for one 9-inch pie.

⚜ VOL-AU-VENT OF SWEETBREADS (*Vol-au-Vent Maison*)

A vol-au-vent is a puff-pastry case large enough to make several servings; it is usually filled with a mixture in a sauce.

3 pairs calf's sweetbreads
salt
lemon juice or vinegar
1 cup diced cooked chicken breasts
6 ounces mushrooms
1½ cups hot chicken stock
3 tablespoons butter

3 tablespoons flour
2 egg yolks
½ cup light cream
salt and ground white pepper to taste
1 large (8-inch) Vol-au-Vent case
  (page 25)

Soak the sweetbreads 15 to 20 minutes in cold salted water (1 teaspoon salt to 1 quart water). Rinse under cold running water and drain. Drop the sweetbreads in boiling acidulated water (1 teaspoon salt and 1 tablespoon lemon juice or vinegar to 1 quart water). The acid helps the sweetbreads retain their shape and whiteness. Cover, reduce heat, and simmer 20 minutes (do not boil). Remove the sweetbreads from the water, and while holding them under running cold water, slip off the membranes with the fingers. Cut out the dark veins and thick connective tissue, and cut the sweetbreads into cubes. Put them in a saucepan and add the chicken. Wash the mushrooms, put them in a saucepan in enough water to cover, and add ¼ teaspoon salt and 2 teaspoons lemon juice. Poach 5 to 6 minutes. Pick out 6 mushrooms of uniform size, flute them, and reserve to use as a garnish. Slice the remaining mushrooms and add them to the sweetbreads and chicken. Pour in ½ cup of the chicken stock, cover, and let steep while making the sauce.

Melt the butter in a saucepan. Remove from heat and blend in the flour. Stir and cook until the mixture foams. Remove from heat and add the remaining 1 cup hot chicken stock. Beat well with a wire whisk or a wire hand eggbeater. Stir and cook until the sauce is of medium thickness, 3 to 4 minutes. Beat the egg yolks with 2 tablespoons of the cream and stir into the hot sauce. Add the remaining cream and cook 1 minute (do not boil). Stir in the sweetbread mixture. Heat and season with salt and pepper. Heat the Vol-au-Vent case in the oven and fill it with the mixture. Garnish with the 6 poached fluted mushrooms. Makes 6 servings.

Cheese Dishes

When cooking with cheese there is one fundamental rule to follow. Use low to moderate heat and cook as short a time as possible. High heat and overcooking toughen cheese. Cheese used as an ingredient in a dish should be diced or grated first to speed the time of melting. Gruyère and Parmesan cheeses are favorites of continental cooks.

Many of the dishes in this section can also be served as hot hors d'oeuvre.

⚜ CHEESE BALLS OR CROQUETTES (*Croquettes au Fromage*)

6 large hot boiled potatoes, peeled
3 large eggs
1 teaspoon salt
¼ teaspoon ground white pepper
⅛ teaspoon ground nutmeg
5 tablespoons milk

½ cup grated Gruyère, Cheddar, or Parmesan cheese
8 cubes (¾ inch) Gruyère or Cheddar cheese
fine dry breadcrumbs

Mash the potatoes until they are smooth and fluffy. Beat in 2 of the eggs, the seasonings, and 4 tablespoons of the milk. Stir in the grated cheese. Shape the mixture around the cubes of cheese to form croquettes or balls. Beat the remaining egg with the remaining 1 tablespoon of milk. Roll the croquettes in breadcrumbs and then in the egg mixture, and then in breadcrumbs again. Fry in deep fat preheated to 375° F. until croquettes are golden. Drain on paper towels. If small balls are desired for cocktail accompaniments, shape the potato-cheese mixture around ½-inch cubes of cheese. Makes 8 large croquettes or 2 dozen 1¼-inch balls.

⚜ CHEESE CRUSTS (*Croûtes au Fromage*)

8 slices bread, ½ inch thick
6 tablespoons butter
4 tablespoons dry white wine
8 slices (about 8 ounces) Gruyère or Cheddar cheese

8 large slices tomato, ¼ inch thick (optional)
4 slices bacon, cut in half and partially cooked (optional)

Fry the bread in butter, turning to brown both sides. Arrange the slices on a baking sheet, sprinkle with wine, and cover each with a slice of cheese. If desired, garnish each with a slice of tomato and a half slice of bacon. Place in a preheated hot oven (425° F.) until cheese melts, about 5 minutes. Makes 4 servings.

⚜ CHEESE FONDUE (*Fondue au Fromage*)

The classic cheese fondue is cheese melted with wine. The best cheeses to use are imported Swiss Emmenthal or Gruyère; never use processed cheese. Use a dry white wine, such as Chablis, Fendant, Neuchâtel, Riesling, or Traminer. If the wine is reduced to about three-fourths the original quantity before adding the cheese, the fondue will have a more refined flavor. The addition of cream and butter gives a smoother consistency. Have all ingredients ready before starting the fondue and make it just before serving. Never allow the water under the casserole to boil.

3 cups (¾ pound) grated imported
  Gruyère or Emmenthal cheese
2 tablespoons flour
1 clove garlic
1¾ cups dry white wine
salt, ground white pepper, and ground
  nutmeg to taste

1½ tablespoons butter
¼ to ⅓ cup heavy cream
  cheese
3 tablespoons Kirsch
French bread

Mix the grated cheese and flour. Set aside. Boil the garlic and wine together until the wine is reduced to three-fourths the original quantity. Strain into a 1½-quart earthenware casserole. Discard the garlic. Place the casserole over hot (not boiling) water. Add ¼ cup of cheese at a time, stirring until each addition is completely mixed with the wine before adding another. When all the cheese has been blended in, add salt, pepper, and nutmeg to taste. Add the butter and 2 tablespoons of the cream. Mix well. Add the remaining cream gradually as the fondue thickens. Stir in the Kirsch.

To serve: Place the casserole on an electric warmer on the dining table. Cut French bread into cubes. Spear each cube with a fork and dunk in the fondue in a stirring motion. If the fondue becomes too thick, stir in a little more warm wine or cream. Makes approximately 6 servings. Fondue can also be made in a chafing dish at the table.

⚜ CHEESE FRITTERS I (*Beignets au Fromage I*)

1 cup sifted all-purpose flour
1 teaspoon double-acting baking
  powder
½ teaspoon salt
½ teaspoon powdered mustard
⅛ teaspoon ground white pepper

1 cup (¼ pound) grated Gruyère or
  Cheddar cheese
1 large egg, separated
2 tablespoons butter, melted
¼ cup beer
¼ cup water
Tomato Sauce (optional; page 50)

Sift the first 5 ingredients together into a mixing bowl. Add the cheese and mix well. Beat the egg yolk and mix with the remaining ingredients. Stir into the flour and cheese mixture. Beat the egg white until it stands in soft moist peaks and fold it into the mixture. Drop 1 tablespoon of the batter at a time into deep fat preheated to 375° F. Fry only until fritters are golden, 1 to 2 minutes. Drain on paper towels. Serve as a small hot entrée with Tomato Sauce. Or to serve as cocktail hors d'oeuvre, drop the batter from a teaspoon into the hot fat and fry until golden. Makes 8 large fritters or 2 dozen small fritters.

⚜ CHEESE FRITTERS II (*Beignets au Fromage II*)

¾ cup sifted all-purpose flour
¼ teaspoon salt
⅛ teaspoon ground nutmeg
dash cayenne
1 large egg, beaten

1 tablespoon butter, melted
½ cup beer at room temperature
1 egg white, stiffly beaten
about 1 cup cubed Gruyère or
   Cheddar cheese

Sift ½ cup of the flour with the salt, nutmeg, and cayenne. Add the egg and butter and mix lightly. Gradually stir in the beer, and mix until the batter is smooth. Let stand 1 hour. Fold in the egg white. Dredge the cheese cubes in the remaining flour and then coat them with the batter. Fry in deep fat pre-heated to 375° F. until golden. Drain on paper towels. Serve hot. Makes approximately 3 dozen.

⚜ SURPRISE FRITTERS (*Beignets Surprise*)

These delectable crisp puffed fritters are made of Chou Paste (page 22) with grated cheese, chopped ham, and almonds added.

¼ cup (½ stick) butter
½ cup water
¼ teaspoon salt
½ cup sifted all-purpose flour
2 large eggs

¼ cup grated Gruyère, Cheddar, or
   Parmesan cheese
¼ cup chopped cooked lean ham
2 tablespoons chopped blanched
   almonds
1 large egg white, stiffly beaten

Put the butter, water, and salt in a 1-quart saucepan. Bring to boiling point and remove from heat. Stir in all the flour at once. Put the saucepan over low heat and stir and beat with a spoon until the mixture leaves the sides of the pan in a smooth ball, and a metal spoon pressed into it leaves a clear impression (cooking time 2 to 3 minutes). Remove from heat and beat in the whole eggs, one at a time. Stir in the cheese, ham, and almonds. Fold in the egg white. Drop the batter from a teaspoon into deep fat preheated to 375° F. Fry until golden, 2 to 3 minutes. Serve piping hot. Makes approximately 3 dozen.

⚜ CHEESE RAMEKINS (*Ramequins de Fromage*)

A ramekin was originally a baked cheese preparation. Today the term means a tart or tartlet filled with cream cheese, or a small pastry made of cheese-flavored Chou Paste (page 22), similar in appearance to a cream puff. The term is also used for the individual earthenware dishes often used for baking and serving these foods.

1 cup water
½ cup (1 stick) butter
⅛ teaspoon salt
1 cup sifted all-purpose flour
4 large eggs
1 cup grated Gruyère or Cheddar
  cheese

1 egg, beaten
12 small cubes Gruyère or Cheddar
  cheese
Cream of Camembert (see following
  recipe)

Put the water, butter, and salt in a 1-quart saucepan and bring to boiling point. Remove from heat and stir in all the flour at one time, using a wooden spoon. Beat vigorously. Return the saucepan to the heat and stir and cook until the mixture leaves the sides of the pan and forms a stiff ball. Remove from the heat and beat in the eggs, one at a time, beating each until it is completely absorbed before adding another. Beat in the grated cheese. Put the mixture in a pastry bag and pipe it onto an ungreased baking sheet in puffs the size of apricots. Or, if desired, drop tablespoonfuls onto baking sheets. Brush with beaten egg. Insert a cube of Gruyère or Cheddar cheese in the top of each puff or tablespoonful. Bake in a preheated hot oven (425° F.) 20 to 25 minutes or until puffed and lightly browned. Reduce the heat to 375° F. (moderate) and bake 10 to 15 minutes or until the puffs are golden and firm and crusty to the touch. Make a 1-inch slit in the side of each puff to allow the steam to escape. Return the puffs to the oven, turn off heat and let them stand 10 minutes with the oven door slightly ajar. Fill with Cream of Camembert or other creamed cheeses. Serve hot. Makes 12 ramekins. (*See illustration, page 121.*)

⚜ Cream of Camembert (*Crème de Camembert*)

1 box (4 ounces) very ripe Camembert cheese
dry white wine

4 tablespoons (½ stick) unsalted
  butter, softened

Keep the cheese at room temperature until it is soft and runny. Place it in a bowl, peeled or unpeeled, and pour *only* enough wine over it barely to cover it. Cover and steep for at least 12 hours. Add the softened butter and work it in well to form a smooth paste. Use as a filling for Ramekins or shape the mixture into rounds and serve with crackers as an accompaniment to cocktails or as a dessert. Makes approximately 1 cup.

⚜ SOUFFLÉ CHEESE OMELETTE (*Omelette Soufflé au Fromage*)

4 large eggs, separated
½ teaspoon salt
1/16 teaspoon ground black pepper
¼ cup milk

½ cup grated Gruyère or Cheddar
  cheese
1 tablespoon butter
chopped parsley

Beat the egg yolks until they are thick and lemon-colored. Stir in the salt, pepper, milk, and cheese. Set aside. Beat the egg whites until they stand in soft stiff peaks (not dry) and fold them into the mixture. Melt the butter in an 8- or 9-inch skillet, and pour in the egg mixture. Cook over low heat 5 to 6 minutes or until the omelette is puffy and light brown on the bottom, lifting the omelette at the edges with a spatula to judge the color. Bake in a preheated slow oven (325° F.) only until a knife inserted in the center of the omelette comes out clean—12 to 15 minutes. Make a crease across the center with the back of a knife or with a spatula. Fold half the omelette over the other half. Sprinkle with chopped parsley. Serve immediately. Makes 4 servings.

⚜ CHEESE SOUFFLÉ (*Soufflé au Fromage*)

¼ cup (½ stick) butter
4 tablespoons flour
¼ teaspoon salt
1 cup hot milk

1 cup (¼ pound) grated Gruyère or
    Cheddar cheese
4 large eggs, separated
dash cayenne
¼ teaspoon cream of tartar

Melt the butter in a saucepan. Remove from heat and blend in the flour and salt. Return to heat and stir and cook 1 minute. Remove from heat and beat in milk. Cook, stirring constantly, until the sauce is of medium thickness. Blend in the cheese. Beat the egg yolks until they are thick and lemon-colored. Add a little of the hot sauce to the egg yolks and then stir the yolks into the remaining hot mixture. Add the cayenne. Beat the egg whites until they are foamy, add the cream of tartar, and beat until the whites stand in soft stiff peaks. Gently fold them into the mixture. Butter the bottom (not the sides) of a 1½-quart soufflé dish and pour in the mixture. Place the dish in a pan of hot water. Bake in a preheated slow oven (325° F.) 1¼ hours, or until the soufflé is well puffed and browned. Serve immediately. Makes 6 servings.

⚜ CHEESE TART (*Gâteau au Fromage*)

Plain Pastry Dough (page 24) or
    Puff Pastry (page 25) for a 9-inch
    pie crust
2 cups (½ pound) grated Gruyère
    cheese

1 tablespoon flour
3 eggs, beaten
1 cup milk or light cream
1/16 teaspoon each salt and ground
    white pepper

Line a 9-inch pie plate with pastry rolled ⅛ inch thick. Set aside. Mix the cheese with flour and sprinkle the mixture over the pastry. Combine the remaining ingredients and pour over the cheese. Bake in a preheated hot oven (425° F.) 15 minutes; reduce heat to 325° F. and bake 30 to 40 minutes or until a knife inserted in the center comes out clean. Serve hot or warm, never cold. Makes 4 to 6 servings.

ENTRÉES

⚜ QUICHE LORRAINE (*Quiche à la Lorraine*)

Plain Pastry Dough (page 24) for a
   9-inch pie crust
1 tablespoon bacon drippings
1 cup thinly sliced onions
1½ cups cubed Gruyère or Emmenthal cheese

4 slices crisp bacon, crumbled
4 large eggs, beaten lightly
1 cup each heavy cream and milk, or
   2 cups light cream
¼ teaspoon each ground nutmeg and
   ground white pepper

Line a pie plate with pastry and bake 5 minutes. Cook the onions in the bacon drippings until they are transparent. Cover the pastry with the cheese, onions, and crumbled bacon. Combine the remaining ingredients and pour over the top. Bake in a preheated very hot oven (450° F.) for 10 minutes, then reduce heat to 350° F. (moderate) and bake until a knife inserted in the center comes out clean—15 to 20 minutes. Serve as a hot hors d'oeuvre or as an entrée. Makes one 9-inch pie.

⚜ Quiche Lorraine Tartlets

Line six 3-inch tart pans with Plain Pastry Dough. Set aside. Prepare the Quiche Lorraine filling as in the previous recipe and ladle it into the pastry-lined tart pans. Bake as directed in the recipe. Serve hot. Makes 6 tartlets. (*See illustration, page 121.*)

⚜ SWISS CHEESE TARTLETS (*Tartelettes Suisses*)

Plain Pastry Dough (page 24)
¼ cup (½ stick) butter
4 tablespoons flour
2 cups light cream
½ teaspoon salt

¼ teaspoon powdered mustard
⅛ teaspoon ground white pepper
dash cayenne
2 large eggs, lightly beaten
1 cup grated Emmenthal cheese

Line small tartlet pans with thinly rolled pastry. Set aside. Melt the butter in a saucepan, remove from heat, and blend in the flour. Return to heat, stir and cook 1 minute. Remove from heat and add the cream. Stir and cook until the mixture is thick. Add seasonings. Blend a little of the hot mixture with the beaten eggs and add to the remaining hot mixture. Stir in the cheese. Spoon the mixture into the tartlet shells and place them on a baking sheet. Bake in a preheated hot oven (425° F.) 15 to 20 minutes, or until crust has browned. Cool 5 to 10 minutes before serving. Serve as hot hors d'oeuvre. Makes approximately 16 tartlets. This mixture can also be baked in a 9-inch pie shell and served as a hot entrée.

Pastas, Cereals, and Rice Dishes

This section includes recipes for entrées made with gnocchi, macaroni, noodles, polenta (cornmeal), and rice, as well as instructions for making homemade noodles.

GNOCCHI

Gnocchi are dumplings of Italian or Austro-Hungarian origin, made from Chou Paste, semolina, or sometimes potatoes. (Farina may be used instead of semolina, which is not available in the United States.) The paste is shaped into balls 1 to 1½ inches in diameter or into cylinders 3 by 1½ inches. These shapes are often made by piping the mixture through a pastry bag. Then the gnocchi are poached in lightly salted simmering water until they swell to almost twice their original size, rise to the top of the water, and turn over in the water easily. Gnocchi may be served as hot hors d'oeuvre or as a separate course with a sauce, such as Béchamel, to which cheese is added.

❧ CHEESE GNOCCHI (*Gnocchi au Fromage*)

¼ cup butter
½ cup hot water
¼ teaspoon salt
dash of ground nutmeg
½ cup flour
2 large eggs
1 cup grated Parmesan or Gruyère
  cheese

6 tablespoons butter
6 tablespoons flour
2 cups hot milk
½ cup hot heavy cream
salt and ground white pepper to taste
2 to 3 tablespoons butter, melted

Put the first 4 ingredients in a 1-quart saucepan and bring to boiling point. Remove the pan from the heat and add the ½ cup flour all at one time, stirring rapidly with a wooden spoon. Turn the heat to low and stir and beat until the mixture leaves the side of the pan in a smooth ball, and a metal spoon pressed into it leaves a clear impression (cooking time 2 to 3 minutes).

Remove from heat and beat in the eggs, 1 at a time, beating vigorously after each addition, until the paste is smooth. Beat in ¼ cup of the cheese. Shape into 1½-inch balls, or put the paste into a pastry bag and pipe 1½-inch lengths. Put the gnocchi into a 12-inch skillet of simmering salted water (½ teaspoon salt to 1 quart water). Simmer 10 to 15 minutes. Gnocchi are done when they have doubled in size and rise to the top of the water. Remove from water and drain on a rack or a clean towel.

Melt the 6 tablespoons butter in a 1½-quart saucepan. Remove from heat and blend in the 6 tablespoons flour. Stir and cook until the mixture is foamy. Remove from heat and add all the hot milk at one time. Beat vigorously with a wire whisk. Stir and cook 2 to 3 minutes or until the sauce is medium thick. Add the cream, salt, and pepper. Add the gnocchi and simmer about 5 minutes. Fold in ¼ cup of the remaining cheese. Turn into a buttered 10- by 6- by 2-inch baking dish. Sprinkle with the remaining ½ cup cheese and the melted butter. Bake in a preheated moderate oven (350° F.) 20 minutes. Serve as a hot entrée. Makes 4 servings.

⚜ BAKED CHEESE PUFFS (*Gougère au Fromage*)

Make a double recipe of Cheese Gnocchi (see preceding recipe), using 1 cup finely diced Gruyère cheese in the dough instead of grated cheese. With a tablespoon scoop out portions of dough the size of an egg and arrange them in a circle, close together, in a buttered 9-inch cake pan or pie plate. Smooth the top and around the inside of the circle with the back of a tablespoon. Brush with beaten egg. Sprinkle with ½ cup finely diced Gruyère cheese. Bake in a preheated hot oven (425° F.) 20 to 25 minutes or until the paste has puffed and browned lightly. Reduce the heat to 375° F. (moderate) and bake 10 to 15 minutes, or until the puffs are golden, crusty, and firm to the touch. Cut a 1-inch slit in the side of each to allow the steam to escape. Return the puffs to the oven, turn off heat, and let them stand 10 minutes with the door slightly ajar. Serve hot. Makes 6 to 8 servings.

⚜ GNOCCHI AU GRATIN (*Gnocchi au Gratin*)

2 cups milk
¼ teaspoon salt
1/16 teaspoon ground nutmeg
½ cup butter

2⅔ cups sifted all-purpose flour
6 large eggs
1¼ cups grated Parmesan cheese
Mornay Sauce (page 40)

Combine the first 4 ingredients in a 1½-quart saucepan. Bring the mixture to boiling point, then remove the saucepan from the heat, stir in the flour, and mix well. Return to the heat and stir and cook until the butter begins to ooze from the mixture, 5 to 8 minutes. Remove from the heat and beat in the eggs, one at a time, and 1 cup of the cheese. Let the mixture stand until it is cool enough to shape. Form the dough into 1¼-inch balls and drop them into boiling salted water (1 teaspoon salt to 1 quart water). Cook until they rise to the top of the water and are springy. Using a perforated spoon, remove the balls from the water, drain, and place them in a glass or earthenware baking dish. Cover them generously with Mornay Sauce and sprinkle with the remaining ¼ cup grated cheese. Bake in a preheated moderate oven (350° F.) 20 to 30 minutes. Makes 6 servings.

⚜ GNOCCHI ROMAN STYLE (*Gnocchi alla Romana*)

1½ cups water
1½ cups milk
1½ teaspoons salt
1 cup Cream of Wheat or farina
3 large eggs, beaten
7 tablespoons butter

2 cups (½ pound) grated Gruyère or Parmesan cheese
ground black pepper to taste
¼ cup bouillon or light stock
3 tablespoons fine dry breadcrumbs

Put the water, milk, and salt in a 2-quart saucepan. Bring to boiling point. Gradually stir in the Cream of Wheat or farina, being careful to avoid lumps. Stir and cook until the mixture has thickened. Beat a little of the hot cereal into the beaten eggs and then gradually beat them into the remaining hot cereal. Stir in 3 tablespoons of the butter, ½ cup of the cheese, and pepper to taste. Pour the mixture into a buttered and lightly floured large shallow pan, spreading it between ¼ and ½ inch thick. Cool. Cut into squares, or cut into rounds or shapes with cooky cutters. Arrange in layers in a buttered 10- by 6- by 2-inch baking dish, sprinkling part of the remaining cheese between the layers. Pour the bouillon or stock over the top. Mix the breadcrumbs with the remaining cheese and sprinkle over the top. Melt the remaining 4 tablespoons butter and pour over the crumbs and cheese. Bake in a preheated moderate oven (350° F.) 20 to 30 minutes or until golden brown. Serve as a hot entrée. Makes 6 servings.

⚜ GNOCCHI TART (*Croustade de Gnocchi*)

2 cups grated Gruyère cheese
½ recipe Chou Paste (page 22)
2½ cups hot Béchamel Sauce (page 38)

Plain Pastry Dough (page 24) for a 9-inch pie crust, using 1 cup flour
2 tablespoons butter, melted

Mix 1 cup of the cheese with warm Chou Paste. Shape into 1-inch balls and poach 10 to 15 minutes in a 12-inch skillet of simmering salted water (½ teaspoon salt to 1 quart water). Do not boil. Gnocchi are done when they are doubled in size and rise to the top of the water. Remove from the water, drain on a rack or clean towel, and add to 2 cups of the hot Béchamel Sauce. Add ¾ cup of the remaining cheese. Line a 9-inch pie plate with unbaked pastry and put in the gnocchi mixture. Spread with the remaining ½ cup Béchamel Sauce, and sprinkle with the melted butter and the remaining ¼ cup grated cheese. Bake in a preheated very hot oven (450° F.) 10 minutes, then reduce to 375° F. (moderate) and continue baking 30 to 40 minutes. Serve as an entrée. Makes 6 servings.

MACARONI

⚜ BAKED MACARONI AND CHEESE (*Macaroni au Gratin*)

½ pound macaroni
4 egg yolks, lightly beaten
2 cups light cream or milk
1½ cups coarsely shredded sharp
  Cheddar or Gruyère cheese
½ teaspoon salt

¼ teaspoon ground white pepper
½ teaspoon powdered mustard
¼ teaspoon paprika
4 tablespoons (½ stick) butter
1 cup soft breadcrumbs

Cook the macaroni according to package directions (macaroni should be slightly underdone). Drain well and turn into a buttered 1½-quart casserole. Combine the egg yolks with ¼ cup of the cream or milk and set aside. Heat the remaining cream or milk only until hot (do not boil), add the egg-yolk mixture, 1 cup of the cheese, the seasonings, and 1 tablespoon of the butter. Mix well and pour over the macaroni. Stir lightly with a fork to blend the sauce with the macaroni. Melt the remaining butter, mix it with the breadcrumbs and the remaining ½ cup cheese, and sprinkle over the macaroni. Bake in a preheated moderate oven (350° F.) 35 to 40 minutes or until crumbs have browned. Makes 6 servings.

⚜ MACARONI IN CHEESE SAUCE (*Macaroni au Fromage*)

½ pound macaroni
2 tablespoons butter
1½ tablespoons flour
1 cup milk, heated
½ teaspoon salt
¼ teaspoon powdered mustard

⅛ teaspoon ground white pepper
1/16 teaspoon ground nutmeg
¼ cup light cream
1 cup shredded Gruyère or Cheddar
  cheese

Cook the macaroni according to package directions (macaroni should be slightly underdone). Meanwhile melt the butter in a 1½-quart saucepan, remove from heat, and blend in the flour. Return to heat; stir and cook until the mixture is foamy. Remove from heat and beat in the hot milk, using a wire whisk. Return to heat; stir and cook 2 minutes or until the sauce is slightly thick. Combine the next 4 ingredients, mix well, and add to the sauce. Stir in the cream. Drain all the water from the macaroni, add the sauce, and simmer 3 to 4 minutes, tossing lightly with a fork to prevent scorching. Remove from heat and add the cheese. Mix lightly. Makes 6 servings.

NOODLES AND DISHES MADE WITH NOODLE DOUGH

❧ NOODLE DOUGH (*Pâte à Nouilles*)

Homemade noodles are far superior to packaged noodles.

3 cups (or more) sifted all-purpose flour

4 large eggs, unbeaten

Place 3 cups flour in a large mixing bowl. Add the eggs and mix with the hands until the dough is stiff enough to be gathered into a ball. Knead on a pastry board until all the crumbly particles have been incorporated. This dough should be very stiff; if necessary knead in a little more flour. Divide the dough into thirds. Roll one portion at a time into a very thin sheet with a lightly floured rolling pin. Cover with a clean towel and let stand 30 minutes. Then roll each sheet up as for a jelly roll and cut crosswise into wide or narrow strips as desired. Lay the strips out on ungreased baking sheets to dry well. Cover them with a clean towel. When noodles are thoroughly dry, store them in covered containers and use as needed. Makes about 1 pound.

❧ NOODLES BERNE STYLE (*Nouilles à la Bernoise*)

½ pound noodles (homemade or bought)
1½ quarts boiling water
1 teaspoon salt
4 tablespoons (½ stick) butter, melted

4 to 6 slices grilled ham
4 to 6 fried eggs
4 to 6 Mushroom-Stuffed Tomatoes (see following recipe)

Cook the noodles until tender in boiling water with the salt added. Drain well. Add the melted butter and toss lightly with a fork. Turn onto a warmed platter. Arrange 4 to 6 slices grilled ham over the top, and top each ham slice with a fried egg. Garnish the platter with Mushroom-Stuffed Tomatoes. Makes 4 to 6 servings. (*See illustration, page 122.*)

❧ Mushroom-Stuffed Tomatoes

2 to 3 firm ripe medium-sized tomatoes
salt and ground black pepper
soft breadcrumbs

1 teaspoon finely chopped onion
⅓ to ½ cup finely chopped mushrooms
1 tablespoon butter

Wash the tomatoes, remove stem ends, cut in half crosswise, and scoop out the center pulp, leaving a shell ¼ inch thick. Sprinkle inside the shells with

111

salt and black pepper, and invert them on a tray to drain. Chop the pulp and mix with an equal amount of soft breadcrumbs. Sauté the onion and mushrooms in butter, using ⅓ cup mushrooms for 4 servings or ½ cup mushrooms for 6 servings. Add to the tomato-breadcrumb mixture. Season to taste with salt and black pepper. Fill the tomato shells with the stuffing and bake in a preheated moderate oven (375° F.) 20 minutes. Makes 4 to 6 servings.

⚜ NOODLES BOLOGNESE STYLE (*Nouilles à la Bolognaise*)

½ cup finely chopped onion
½ cup shredded carrots
¼ cup finely chopped celery
1 small clove garlic, chopped fine
2 tablespoons olive oil or salad oil
½ pound (1 cup) ground lean beef
¼ cup finely chopped ham, or 1 strip bacon, diced
⅓ cup dry red wine
1 tablespoon flour
½ cup finely chopped mushrooms

1 cup tomato purée
½ cup bouillon
½ teaspoon sugar
2 tablespoons tomato paste
salt
ground black pepper to taste
¾ teaspoon dried thyme or marjoram
¹⁄₁₆ teaspoon ground nutmeg
½ pound noodles (homemade or bought)
2 tablespoons butter

Cook the first 4 ingredients in the oil until the vegetables are soft, 4 to 5 minutes. Add the beef and the ham or bacon. Stir and cook until the beef loses its pink color. Add the wine and cook until it has evaporated. Blend in the flour and mushrooms. Stir and cook 3 minutes. Add the next 4 ingredients, mix well, bring to boiling point, reduce heat, and simmer 30 to 40 minutes or until the sauce has thickened. Season to taste with salt and black pepper. Add the thyme or marjoram and the nutmeg. Cook 1 to 2 minutes.

Meanwhile, cook the noodles until tender in 1½ quarts boiling water with ½ teaspoon salt added. Drain well. Add the butter and toss lightly. Serve the sauce in a sauce boat. Makes 6 servings. (*See illustration, page 124.*)

⚜ RAVIOLI ITALIAN STYLE (*Ravioli à l'Italienne*)

Noodle Dough (page 111)
Ravioli Filling (see following recipe)
hot broth or hot water

melted butter, Brown Butter (page 56), or Tomato Sauce (page 50)
grated Parmesan cheese

Make the Noodle Dough, divide in half, and roll each half on a lightly floured surface into a square as thin as it can be made without breaking the dough. Drop Ravioli Filling from a teaspoon, in small mounds, 2 inches apart, on one sheet of dough. Cover with the second sheet, and with the index finger press the dough firmly around each mound. Cut the dough between the mounds with a pastry cutter or a sharp-pointed knife. Boil the squares in hot broth or water to cover about 12 minutes, or until the dough is thoroughly cooked but not mushy. Serve with melted butter, Brown Butter, or Tomato Sauce, and grated Parmesan cheese. Makes 12 servings.

⚜ Ravioli Filling (*Farce de Ravioli*)

1 tablespoon butter
1 cup sieved chopped cooked spinach,
   drained
1 cup ground leftover cooked beef,
   veal, or chicken

1 raw egg yolk
1 hard-cooked egg yolk, sieved
salt, ground black pepper, and ground
   nutmeg to taste
½ cup grated Parmesan cheese

Melt the butter in a 1½-quart saucepan. Add the spinach and cook until it is very dry. Add all the remaining ingredients and mix well. Use as a filling for Ravioli, Cannelloni, or turnovers. Makes about 2 cups.

⚜ STUFFED CANNELLONI (*Cannelloni Farcis*)

Cannelloni are made by poaching squares or rectangles of thinly rolled noodle dough, rolling the pieces around a filling, then dotting the rolls with butter, sprinkling with grated cheese, adding a sauce if desired, and browning in the oven. Fillings for Cannelloni are made of various cheeses, meats, poultry, fish, shellfish, or vegetables. They should be fresh, delicately seasoned and blended with a sauce compatible with the main ingredient. The same fillings may be used for Ravioli.

Noodle Dough (page 111)
Chicken or Veal Filling (see following
   recipe)

2 cups Béchamel Sauce (page 38)
½ cup grated Parmesan cheese
butter

Divide the Noodle Dough into 3 equal parts. Roll one part at a time into paper-thin strips 4 inches wide. Straighten the edges by trimming them with scissors or a sharp knife. Cut the strips into 6- or 4-inch rectangles. Drop 4 pieces at a time into rapidly boiling water, reduce heat, and simmer 8 to 10 minutes. Using a perforated spoon or skimmer, remove the pieces from the water. Drain well. Spread the hot cooked strips of dough between two moist towels and let them stand while preparing the filling.

    Spread the center of each cooked strip of noodle dough with Chicken or Veal Filling. Roll the long way, pinch the dough at the ends to hold in the filling, and place the rolls side by side, seam down, in a buttered baking dish. Cover with Béchamel Sauce, sprinkle with grated Parmesan cheese, and dot with butter. Bake in a preheated moderate oven (375° F.) 20 minutes. Serve hot as an entrée. Makes 6 servings. (*See illustration, page 123.*)

⚜ Chicken or Veal Filling

6 chicken livers
1 small white onion, chopped
½ small clove of garlic, chopped
3 tablespoons butter
1½ cups diced cooked chicken or veal

½ teaspoon dried thyme, or 2 teaspoons chopped fresh thyme
salt and ground black pepper to taste
2 eggs, beaten

113

Sauté the chicken livers, onion, and garlic in the butter 5 to 6 minutes, or until the livers lose their pink color. Put the mixture through a food chopper along with the chicken or veal, using the finest blade. Add the remaining ingredients and mix well. Use as a filling for Cannelloni, Ravioli, or turnovers. Makes about 2 cups.

POLENTA

Polenta, one of Italy's staple foods, is yellow cornmeal made into a porridge, which when cold may be sliced, fried, and served with Brown Butter and grated Parmesan cheese. Polenta is also made into entrée pies, using boiled polenta for the bottom and top crusts with a filling of meat, mushrooms, cheese, etc. Boiled polenta can also be baked in the oven with ham or other meats or with cheese or tomato sauce. In the Lombardy and Veneto sections of Italy, boiled polenta often replaces bread in the menu.

⚜ BOILED POLENTA

This dish is more commonly known in the southern part of the United States as cornmeal mush.

4 cups water   1 cup yellow or white cornmeal
1 teaspoon salt

Put 2 cups of water and the salt in the top part of a double boiler. Bring the water to boiling point over direct heat. Mix the cornmeal with the remaining 2 cups cold water and add to the boiling water. Reduce heat and stir and cook until the mixture boils. Place over boiling water, cover, and cook 45 to 50 minutes, stirring frequently to prevent lumping. Serve hot with butter or light cream or milk, or if desired serve hot with butter and grated Parmesan, Gruyère, or Cheddar cheese. Makes approximately 4 cups.

VARIATIONS

⚜ Baked Polenta with Cheese

Add 1 cup grated Cheddar, Gruyère, or Parmesan cheese to the hot Polenta, and turn the mixture into a well-buttered 1½-quart baking dish. Cover and bake in a preheated slow oven (325° F.) 1 hour. Unmold on a warmed platter.

⚜ Polenta Sautéed in Butter

Put Boiled Polenta in a well-buttered 9- by 5- by 3-inch loaf pan. Cover the pan with foil, tie it in place, and bake in a preheated moderate oven (350° F.) until the Polenta becomes quite dry, 30 to 40 minutes. Cool several hours or overnight. Unmold and cut into slices ¼ inch thick. Fry in butter until golden brown, turning to brown both sides. Serve hot, sprinkled with grated Cheddar or Gruyère cheese.

RICE

There are three basic methods of cooking rice: boiling in salted water, as is done primarily in Europe and the United States; boiling and then frying as is done in Far Eastern countries; frying and then boiling, a method used in the Near Eastern countries. This last method is by far the simplest one for obtaining fluffy rice with every grain standing apart. Rice used for making desserts should be cooked to a softer texture than rice for entrées.

⚜ RICE—NEAR EASTERN METHOD

1 cup raw long-grain rice	2¼ cups boiling water
water to cover	1 teaspoon salt
2 tablespoons butter	1 teaspoon lemon juice

Soak the rice 30 minutes in water to cover. Drain well. Melt the butter in a saucepan. Add the rice, and stir and cook until rice begins to turn color and to stick to the bottom of the saucepan. Add the boiling water, salt, and lemon juice. Cover and cook, without stirring, 12 to 15 minutes or until the rice has absorbed all the water. If the rice is to be served separately, toss it lightly with 2 tablespoons butter, using a fork. Makes 6 servings.

⚜ RISOTTO WITH CÈPES OR MUSHROOMS (*Risotto aux Cèpes*)

1 cup raw long-grain rice	1½ cups thinly sliced cèpes or mushrooms
water to cover	
1 small white onion, chopped fine	2¼ cups hot beef broth or chicken broth
1 tablespoon olive oil or salad oil	
3 tablespoons dry white wine	½ teaspoon salt
4 tablespoons butter	⅓ cup grated Parmesan cheese

Soak the rice 30 minutes in water to cover. Drain well. Cook the onion in the oil until soft, 2 to 3 minutes. Add the wine and cook until about half of it has evaporated. Set aside. Melt 2 tablespoons of the butter in a 1½-quart saucepan. Add the drained rice and stir and cook over moderately low heat until the rice begins to color and stick to the bottom of the pan, about 3 minutes. Add the cooked onion, cèpes or mushrooms, broth, and salt. Cover and cook, without stirring, over moderately low heat 12 to 15 minutes, or until rice has absorbed all the liquid. Add the remaining 2 tablespoons butter and the cheese. Toss lightly with a fork. Makes 6 to 8 servings. (*See illustration, page 122.*)

⚜ MILANESE RISOTTO (*Risotto Milanaise*)

1 cup raw long-grain rice
cold water to cover
¾ cup dried boletus or dried mushrooms
hot water to cover
2 small white onions, chopped fine
5 tablespoons butter
⅓ cup dry white wine

2¼ cups hot beef broth or chicken
   broth
1 teaspoon lemon juice
½ teaspoon salt
¼ teaspoon crumbled saffron strands
⅛ teaspoon ground white pepper
⅓ cup grated Gruyère or Parmesan
   cheese

Soak the rice 30 minutes in cold water to cover. Drain well. Set aside. Soak the dried boletus or dried mushrooms 30 to 40 minutes in hot water to cover. Rinse well and set aside. Cook the onions in 1 tablespoon of the butter over moderately low heat 2 to 3 minutes or until soft. Add 2 more tablespoons of the butter to the onion and add the drained rice. Stir and cook over moderate heat until the rice begins to color and stick to the bottom of the pan, about 3 minutes. Add the wine and mix well. Stir in the boletus or mushrooms and the broth, lemon juice, salt, and saffron. Mix well. Cover and cook over moderately low heat 12 to 15 minutes or until the rice has absorbed all the liquid. Add the remaining 2 tablespoons butter, the white pepper, and the cheese. Toss lightly with a fork. Makes 6 servings.

⚜ RISOTTO PIEDMONT STYLE (*Risotto Piémontais*)

1 cup raw long-grain rice
cold water to cover
⅓ cup finely chopped onion
4 tablespoons butter
2 cups hot beef broth or chicken broth

¼ cup tomato purée
½ teaspoon salt
⅛ teaspoon ground black pepper
½ cup grated Parmesan cheese

Soak the rice 30 minutes in cold water to cover. Drain well. Cook the onion in 1 tablespoon of the butter over moderately low heat 2 to 3 minutes or until golden. Add 2 more tablespoons of the butter to the onion. Then add the drained rice. Stir and cook until the rice begins to color and stick to the bottom of the pan, about 3 minutes. Add the broth, tomato purée, and salt and mix well. Cover and cook over moderately low heat 12 to 15 minutes or until the rice has absorbed all the liquid. Add the remaining 1 tablespoon butter, the black pepper, and the cheese. Toss lightly with a fork. Diced ham tossed in butter, mussels, peas, or truffles may be added to this dish along with the cheese. Makes 6 servings.

❧ PILAF (*Riz Pilaf*)

1 cup raw long-grain rice	1 teaspoon lemon juice
cold water to cover	1 stalk parsley
4 tablespoons butter	¼ teaspoon dried thyme or rosemary
2¼ cups chicken broth or veal stock	dash ground red pepper
½ teaspoon salt	¾ cup cooked green peas (optional)

Soak the rice 30 minutes in cold water to cover. Drain well. Melt 2 table-spoons of the butter in a 1½-quart saucepan and add the drained rice. Stir and cook over moderately low heat until the rice begins to color and stick to the bottom of the pan, about 3 minutes. Add the next 5 ingredients. Cover and cook over moderate heat 12 to 15 minutes or until the rice has absorbed all the liquid. Remove and discard the stalk of parsley. Add the remaining 2 tablespoons butter and a dash of red pepper. Toss lightly with a fork. If desired, add ¾ cup cooked green peas along with the red pepper and butter. Makes 6 servings.

Pâtés, Terrines, and Galantines

In French, the word *pâté* means "pie." Although it formerly included vegetable and fruit pies, the use of the term is now limited to fillings made of ground meat, fish, poultry, game, or liver, surrounded (top, bottom, and sides) with a pastry crust, and served either hot or cold.

A pâté becomes a terrine when the pastry is omitted and the filling is baked in a dish called a "terrine," which is lined with thin slices of salt pork or bacon. The top is also covered with salt pork or bacon. Terrines are always served cold.

Through usage, the term pâté has been broadened to include both true pâtés and terrines. Restaurants which serve the true pâtés usually list them on the menu as *pâté en croûte* (in crust).

Galantines are made of boned poultry or meat, stuffed with mixtures similar to those used in pâtés and terrines, rolled, and cooked in rich stock.

PÂTÉS IN CRUST

❧ PASTRY FOR PÂTÉ IN CRUST (*Pâte à Pâté*)

4 cups sifted all-purpose flour
1 teaspoon salt
1 cup (2 sticks) butter

1 cup lard
about ½ cup water

Sift the flour and salt together into a mixing bowl. Add the butter and lard, and cut it in until the mixture reaches coarse crumb consistency. Sprinkle in enough cold water to make a dough that is manageable. Chill at least 2 hours.

❧ HOW TO LINE A PÂTÉ MOLD

Use a loaf pan or mold 9½ by 5 by 3 inches. Roll out pâté pastry ¼ inch thick, flour lightly, and mark out the shape of the bottom of the loaf pan or mold on it four times. Cut off one of the four portions and set it aside to use for the lid. Butter the pan and flour it lightly. Fit the pastry into the pan, pressing it firmly into the corners with a piece of pastry dough or with the fingers. Trim the edges evenly, leaving a ½-inch border. Fill with forcemeat as specified in the recipe you are making, packing it in well. Press the edges of the pastry inward upon the filling. Roll the reserved piece of pastry ⅛ inch thick, cut it to fit the top of the pan, moisten the under edges, and lay it over the filling. Crimp the edges with a pastry crimper or with the tines of a fork dipped in flour. Decorate the top as desired with pastry leaves, flowers, stars, crescents, or circles made from the leftover dough. With a fork prick the crust in several places to allow for the escape of steam. Make a hole in the center of the pastry and insert a funnel of foil or waxed paper to provide space for fat to rise during baking. Beat 1 egg with 1 tablespoon milk and brush the top crust with the mixture.

❧ HOW TO BAKE AND COOL PÂTÉ

Bake pâté in a preheated moderate oven (350° F.) 30 to 35 minutes per pound. The pâté is done when the fat which rises in the funnel is perfectly clear. If the crust tends to brown too fast, cover with foil or buttered brown paper.

Remove the pâté from the oven and pour aspic through the funnel to fill the air spaces and the space between the filling and crust formed during baking. Cool slowly to room temperature, then refrigerate at least 24 hours. To serve, turn out on a tray and cut into slices.

❦ RABBIT PÂTÉ (*Pâté de Lapin*)

3 to 4 pounds ready-to-cook rabbit
boneless lean fresh pork
boneless lean veal
2 tablespoons olive oil or salad oil
¼ cup chopped parsley
¼ cup sliced onion
½ cup sliced carrots
1 clove garlic, quartered
¾ cup dry white wine
2 tablespoons cognac

¾ pound lean fresh pork
1 pound fresh pork fat
1 teaspoon salt
½ teaspoon dried thyme or marjoram
1 small white onion, sliced
4 stalks parsley
1 Pastry for Pâté in Crust (page 118)
2 truffles, chopped (optional)
1 egg, beaten with 1 tablespoon milk

Remove the sinews from the rabbit, if this has not already been done. Cut the meat from the loin and the tender parts of the legs into narrow strips. Weigh this meat and add an equal amount each of lean fresh pork and veal, also cut in narrow strips. Add the next 5 ingredients, ¼ cup of the wine, and 1 tablespoon of the cognac. Cover and refrigerate overnight, turning the meat in the marinade 3 to 4 times.

Cut the rest of the rabbit from the bones and put it, along with the rabbit liver and heart, the ¾ pound fresh lean pork, and the fresh pork fat, through a food chopper twice, using the finest blade. Add the remaining ½ cup wine and 1 tablespoon cognac, the salt, and the thyme or marjoram, and mix well. Cover with slices of onion and the 4 stalks parsley. Cover the bowl tightly and refrigerate overnight. When ready to bake the pâté, remove and discard the onion and parsley, drain the marinade from the sliced meat into the force-meat, and mix well.

Make Pastry for Pâté in Crust and line a 9½- by 5- by 3-inch loaf pan or mold according to previous directions. Spread a layer of forcemeat 1 inch thick over the bottom. Lay half the strips of rabbit, pork, and veal on the forcemeat. Sprinkle with half the chopped truffles, if used. Repeat with another layer of forcemeat and then with the remaining strips of meat and chopped truffles. Cover with the rest of the forcemeat and top with pastry as directed. Bake, add aspic, and cool. To serve, turn the pâté out onto a tray and slice. Makes 12 to 15 servings.

❦ VEAL LOAF IN CRUST (*Pâté de Veau en Croûte*)

½ pound lean ham, sliced ¼ inch thick
¼ pound lean veal, sliced ¼ inch thick
⅓ cup cognac
½ pound finely ground fat salt pork
2 pounds finely ground lean veal
2 tablespoons chopped parsley
1 small white onion, chopped fine
2 large eggs, lightly beaten
1½ teaspoons salt

¼ teaspoon ground black pepper
⅓ cup heavy cream
1 Pastry for Pâté in Crust (page 118)
2 truffles, sliced (optional)
1 egg beaten with 1 tablespoon milk
Sherry-flavored Aspic (page 400)
parsley
1 small tomato

Marinate the ham and veal slices in the cognac for 1 hour. Mix the next 8 ingredients together in a mixing bowl. With a wooden spoon, beat the mixture until it is light and fluffy. Line a 9½- by 5- by 3-inch loaf pan with Pastry for Pâté in Crust as directed in How to Line a Pâté Mold. Spread half the forcemeat over the bottom of the pastry-lined pan. Cover with marinated slices of ham, veal, and ham, in that order. Cover with the rest of the forcemeat. If truffles are used, push them into the forcemeat down the center of the pan. Top with pastry, brush with beaten egg, bake, add aspic, and cool according to previous directions. To serve, turn out onto a tray and slice. Garnish the tray with parsley and the tomato. Makes 12 to 15 servings. (*See illustration, page 303.*)

⚜ PANTIN PÂTÉ (*Pâté Pantin*)

This is a long narrow loaf which is baked on a cooky sheet instead of in a loaf pan. It requires a rather firm dough.

Marinated Meat Strips (see following recipe)
1 recipe Pastry for Pâté in Crust
1 medium-sized onion, minced
2 tablespoons butter
¾ pound (1½ cups) finely ground lean pork
¾ pound (1½ cups) finely ground lean veal
1 pound (1 cup) finely ground fresh pork fat

2 teaspoons salt
¼ teaspoon ground black pepper
½ teaspoon dried thyme, or 2 teaspoons chopped fresh thyme
⅛ teaspoon ground ginger
⅛ teaspoon crushed garlic
½ cup cognac or Madeira
3 large eggs
Sherry-flavored Aspic (page 400)

Marinate the strips of meat according to the following recipe. Make Pastry for Pâté in Crust and chill it for 2 hours. Cook the onion in the butter over low heat 10 minutes or until onion is soft but not browned. Put the onion into a mixing bowl and add the next 8 ingredients. Pour the cognac or Madeira into the skillet in which the onion was cooked and cook 3 to 4 minutes or until the volume is reduced to ¼ cup. Add to the bowl of ingredients. Beat 2 of the eggs lightly and add. Stir until all ingredients are blended. Then, with a wooden spoon, beat vigorously until the texture of the mixture is light and fluffy. (There is no danger of overbeating this mixture. To test for seasoning, cook a very small amount over surface heat and taste. Add more seasoning if needed.) Refrigerate in a covered bowl if not used immediately. Roll three-fourths of the pastry into a rectangle ⅛ inch thick on a floured 15½- by 12-inch cooky sheet. (Put a wet towel under the cooky sheet to prevent it from slipping.) Trim the edges of the rectangle to make them straight. (Reserve the pastry trimmings.) Spread a layer of forcemeat about ½ inch thick down the center of the pastry, leaving a border of pastry 2 to 2½ inches wide all around the filling. Over the forcemeat place the marinated

↑ Savory Turnovers, Quiche Lorraine Tartlets,
Shrimp Patties, Cheese Ramekins (pages 97, 106, 98, 103)

↓ Pizza (page 96)

↑ Noodles Berne Style (page 111) ↓ Risotto with Cèpes or Mushrooms (page 115)

Rice Timbales Milanese Style (page 97)

↓ Stuffed Cannelloni (page 113) *123*

124   ↑ Scrambled Eggs Catalan Style (page 144)   ↓ Noodles Bolognese Style (page 112)

strips of meat. Cover with another ½-inch layer of forcemeat. Fold the sides of pastry over the filling, having the edges slightly overlapping. Then turn up the two ends of the pastry. Moisten the edges of the pastry and press them down to form a tight seal. Roll the rest of the pastry into a rectangle ⅛ inch thick on a lightly floured pastry board. Cut this rectangle a little smaller than the top of the filled rectangle and place it on top to form a lid. Roll the pastry trimmings ⅛ inch thick, shape them into leaves, stars, crescents, circles, etc., and arrange them as desired over the top. Beat the remaining egg until foamy and brush it all over the pastry. Make 2 or 3 slits in the top of the crust to allow for the escape of steam. Make a hole in the center and insert a funnel of foil or waxed paper. Leave the pâté on the cooky sheet, and bake, pour in aspic, cool, and refrigerate, according to previous directions. If pastry tends to brown too fast, cover it with foil. Makes 10 to 12 servings.

⚜ Marinated Meat Strips

¼ pound lean veal, lean pork, poultry, or rabbit
¼ teaspoon salt
¹⁄₁₆ teaspoon ground black pepper

¼ cup cognac or Madeira
1 tablespoon finely chopped onion
⅛ teaspoon dried thyme
dash of ground ginger

Cut the meat into strips ½ inch wide and ¼ inch thick. Marinate in the remaining ingredients at least 2 hours.

⚜ Pantin Pâté Turnovers

Make Pastry for Pâté in Crust and roll it ⅛ inch thick. Using a 5-inch saucer as a guide, cut the pastry into rounds. Make the forcemeat for Pantin Pâté, but omit the strips of meat. Spread a ½-inch layer of forcemeat over half of each round and fold the other half over the forcemeat. Moisten the edges of the turnovers with water and press them down with the tines of a fork dipped in flour to form a tight seal. Prick the tops to allow for the escape of steam. Place the turnovers on a cooky sheet and bake in a preheated hot oven (400° F.) 10 minutes. Reduce heat to 350° F. (moderate) and bake 40 minutes. If the turnovers tend to brown too fast, cover them with foil. Makes approximately 12 turnovers.

TERRINES

⚜ HOW TO BAKE AND COOL A TERRINE

Terrines have the same filling as pâtés. Line a terrine mold or other earthenware casserole with very thin slices of fat salt pork before filling with alternate layers of forcemeat and sliced meat. Cover the top with more thin slices of fat salt pork and if desired place a bay leaf and a sprinkling of dried or fresh thyme on the top. Cover with the lid and tie 2 thicknesses of foil over it. Place the mold in a pan of hot water, having the water about halfway up the sides of the mold, and place it in a preheated oven (for temperatures and baking times, see individual recipes). Add more hot water to the pan as it evaporates.

Check the terrine after cooking 50 minutes. The terrine is done if the mixture shrinks from the sides of the mold and the fat that has come to the top is clear. Take the pan out of the oven, remove the mold from the water, and take off the lid. Remove and discard the bay leaf and fat salt pork from the top. Weight the top of the terrine with a heavy plate or a wooden block cut to fit the top of the mold. Cool slowly to room temperature—several hours or overnight. Refrigerate 12 to 24 hours, keeping the weight on top.

⚜ HOW TO UNMOLD AND SERVE A TERRINE

A terrine (pâté) may be served directly from the mold (terrine) without unmolding, or it may be unmolded by dipping the dish quickly into very hot water, loosening the edges of the pâté with a spatula, and inverting the dish on a platter. The slices of salt pork are then removed and the excess fat wiped off. The terrine may be sliced or returned to the mold for serving. Or it may be returned to the mold and aspic flavored with sherry, Madeira, or port poured over it, chilled again until the aspic is firm, and then turned out onto a chilled platter and sliced.

⚜ PORK-LIVER TERRINE (*Terrine de Foie de Porc*)

1¼ pounds pork liver
1 small white onion
2 slices white bread soaked in milk
1 pound pork sausage, uncooked
½ clove garlic, mashed
2 large eggs, well beaten
1 teaspoon salt
½ teaspoon ground black pepper

⅛ teaspoon ground ginger
½ cup brandy or dry sherry
1 bay leaf
½ teaspoon dried thyme, or 2 teaspoons fresh thyme
½ to ¾ pound fat salt pork, sliced thin

Cook the liver in hot water to cover 2 to 3 minutes to set the juices. Drain, wipe dry, and put the liver and the onion through a food chopper, using the finest blade. Squeeze all the milk out of the bread, fluff it with a fork, and add to the liver. Stir in the next 7 ingredients. With a wooden spoon, beat the mixture until it is fluffy. Line the bottom and sides of a 5-cup terrine mold, casserole, or loaf pan with slices of fat salt pork. Add the terrine mixture and place the bay leaf on top. Sprinkle with the thyme. Cover with salt pork slices. Cover the terrine with the lid, tie 2 layers of foil over it, and place in a pan of hot water. Bake in a preheated moderate oven (350° F.) 1½ to 2 hours, adding more hot water to the pan as it evaporates. Following previous directions, open, cool, refrigerate, unmold, slice, and serve. Makes 8 to 10 servings.

⚜ PORK LIVER PÂTÉ CHARCUTIER STYLE
(*Pâté de Foie Genre Charcutier*)

This pâté is almost as good as that made of goose liver.

2 pounds pork liver
¾ pound lean pork
¾ pound fat salt pork
1 small white onion
1 small clove garlic
1 tablespoon flour

1 teaspoon salt
½ teaspoon ground thyme
1 tablespoon finely chopped parsley
2 large eggs
¼ pound salt pork

Put the first 5 ingredients through a food chopper, using the finest blade. Blend in the flour and seasonings and mix well with a wooden spoon. Beat in the eggs, one at a time. Line the bottom and sides of a 9- by 3- by 3-inch loaf pan with thin slices of salt pork. Fill the pan with the mixture. Cover the top with thin slices of salt pork. Cover the loaf pan with foil and set it in a larger pan containing boiling water. Bake in a preheated moderate oven (350° F.) 1¾ to 2 hours. Cool. Unmold and cut the pâté into slices for serving. The pâté will keep in the refrigerator about 10 days. Makes 1 loaf 9 by 5 by 3 inches.

⚜ VEAL TERRINE (*Terrine de Veau*)

¾ pound lean veal, coarsely ground
¾ pound lean fresh pork, coarsely ground
½ pound fat fresh pork, coarsely ground
2 small white onions, chopped fine
1 shallot, chopped fine (if available)
½ clove garlic, mashed
1½ teaspoons salt

¼ teaspoon ground black pepper
½ teaspoon poultry seasoning
½ cup dry white wine
1 large egg, well beaten
½ to ¾ pound fat salt pork, sliced thin
½ teaspoon dried thyme, or 2 teaspoons fresh thyme
1 bay leaf

Combine the first 11 ingredients and mix well. With a wooden spoon, beat the mixture until it is light and fluffy. Line the bottom and sides of a 5-cup terrine, casserole, or baking dish with thin slices of fat salt pork. Fill with the mixture. Sprinkle with thyme and place a bay leaf on the top. Cover with the rest of the salt pork slices. Adjust the cover and tie 2 thicknesses of foil tightly over the top. Place in a pan of hot water. Bake in a preheated moderate oven (350° F.) 1½ to 2 hours, adding more hot water as it evaporates. Following the previous directions, open, cool, refrigerate, unmold, slice, and serve. Makes 8 to 10 servings.

GALANTINES

Serve Galantines at cold buffets or as a first course accompanied with buttered toast.

⚜ HOW TO ROLL AND COOK A GALANTINE

Generously butter a large clean cloth or several thicknesses of cheesecloth and spread on a flat surface. Lay the skin of the fowl on the cloth with the outside down and spread with other ingredients as directed in individual recipes. By lifting the edge of the cloth and pulling gently, carefully shape the arrangement into a firm roll, drawing the edges of the skin together to form a sausage-shaped roll. Sew the skin together along the length of the roll and at the ends. Wrap the roll tightly in the cloth, making sure it is smooth and even, and tie it in the middle and at the ends with string.

Place the roll and the other ingredients, as specified, in a large kettle and pour in stock to cover. Cover the kettle, bring to boiling point, reduce heat, and simmer according to individual recipes. Cool the galantine in the stock, then remove it, unroll, and roll again in a clean cloth. Weight it with a plate and let it stand for 2 hours or longer.

Make clear aspic from the stock in which the galantine was cooked. Remove the cloth and the threads with which the skin was sewed. Glaze the roll with aspic. Chill until firm and cut in thin slices for serving.

⚜ GALANTINE OF CHICKEN (*Galantine de Poularde*)

6-pound ready-to-cook roasting
    chicken
2 pounds veal shank
1 calf's foot (optional)
½ pound boneless lean pork
½ pound boneless lean veal
½ pound salt pork, cubed
3 tablespoons cognac, sherry, or
    Madeira
1½ teaspoon salt
¼ teaspoon ground mace

1 teaspoon ground thyme
½ cup heavy cream
¼ pound fatback
¼ pound cooked tongue or ham
1 truffle, chopped (optional)
⅓ cup pistachio nuts
1 stalk parsley
1 carrot
½ cup sliced onion
½ cup sliced celery

Ask the butcher to bone the chicken for you. Make a rich stock from the chicken bones, veal shank, and the calf's foot if available. Reserve. Split the boned chicken down the whole length of the back and open it out flat, skin side up. Starting at the back, with a sharp knife carefully cut the skin away from the meat, removing the skin in one piece. Be careful not to pierce the skin. Trim the skin at the legs and wings, leaving enough to cover the openings. Cut the meat of the breast and the tenderloin under the breast and that of the legs into thin slices and set aside. Put the remaining chicken meat and the lean pork and veal through a food chopper twice, using the finest blade. Add the next 6 ingredients and mix well.

Place the chicken skin, outside down, on a buttered clean cloth (see preceding directions) and spread it with the meat mixture. Cut the fatback and tongue or ham into strips and arrange them in alternate layers over the meat. Between the layers sprinkle chopped truffles, if used. Sprinkle with pistachio nuts. Cover with slices of chicken.

Following the previous directions, make the arrangement into a roll and place it in a large kettle, with the parsley, carrot, onion, celery, and hot stock to cover. Cover and simmer 1¼ hours; then cool, glaze, chill, and slice. Makes approximately 8 servings.

⚜ GALANTINE OF VEAL (*Galantine de Veau*)

3½ pounds breast of veal	¾ pound lean ham, sliced
salt and ground black pepper	3 tablespoons pistachio nuts
1 teaspoon poultry seasoning	1 carrot, sliced
½ teaspoon crumbled dried rosemary, or 1½ teaspoons chopped fresh rosemary	⅓ cup sliced onion
	1 rib celery, sliced
1¾ pounds sausage	2 pounds veal shank
	aspic

Ask the butcher to bone the veal and reserve the bones. Make a rich stock from the bones and reserve it.

Spread the meat out flat (as with skin of a fowl; see previous directions, How to Roll and Cook a Galantine) and sprinkle it with salt, pepper, and herbs. Spread the sausage over the veal, leaving a 1-inch border all around. Cut the ham into strips 4 inches long and 1 inch wide and arrange these in rows down the length of the veal. Sprinkle with pistachio nuts.

Following the previous directions, make the meat into a roll and place it, with the vegetables and veal shank, in a large kettle. Pour in hot stock to cover. Cover the kettle, bring to boiling point, reduce heat, and simmer 2 hours. Cool, glaze, chill, and slice, according to previous directions. Makes 12 to 15 servings.

Eggs
and Egg Dishes

Eggs, because of the large number of ways in which they can be prepared and served, have universal appeal for family meals. Eggs may be baked, fried, scrambled, soft-cooked, hard-cooked, made into omelettes, and used as an ingredient in many kinds of cooking—sauces, soufflés, desserts, cakes, etc.

There is one fundamental rule to follow in all forms of egg cookery: cook with low to moderate heat (never high) and for the exact time specified in the recipe. A properly cooked egg has a tender white and a smooth yolk. Overcooking produces a tough, watery product.

Eggs of various kinds are consumed in all parts of the world. Hens' eggs, however, are the most commonly used. In this book the term egg refers to hens' eggs, unless otherwise specified.

POACHED EGGS

❧ HOW TO POACH EGGS

Pour into a skillet enough water to cover the eggs and add ¼ teaspoon vinegar for each cup water. Heat the water just to boiling point. Break 1 egg at a time into a saucer and slip it into the water. When all are in, reheat water to simmering point. Cover the skillet, remove from heat, and let stand 3 to 5 minutes, until eggs are of desired firmness. For breakfast, sprinkle with salt and ground black pepper to taste and serve on buttered toast. Allow 1 to 2 eggs per person. Poached eggs served for breakfast may or may not have the whites trimmed, but if they are used as a hot or cold entrée, always trim the uneven edges of the whites off neatly with a sharp knife or kitchen shears.

⚜ POACHED EGGS AURORA (*Oeufs Pochés Aurore*)

8 poached eggs
8 slices buttered toast
salt and ground black pepper to taste
1½ cups hot Béchamel Sauce (page 38) or Velouté Sauce (page 40)

1½ to 2 tablespoons tomato purée or reduced tomato sauce
2 tablespoons butter
2 hard-cooked egg yolks, sieved

Place 1 poached egg on each piece of buttered toast and sprinkle with salt and pepper to taste. Combine the hot Béchamel or Velouté Sauce with the tomato purée or tomato sauce and the butter. Spoon the sauce over the eggs. Sprinkle with sieved hard-cooked egg yolk. Serve for special breakfasts, lunch, or supper. Makes 4 to 8 servings.

⚜ POACHED EGGS WITH CARDINAL SAUCE
(*Oeufs Pochés à la Cardinal*)

Follow the recipe for Poached Eggs Aurora. Use Velouté Sauce made with fish stock and replace the tomato purée or tomato sauce and the 2 tablespoons butter with 3 tablespoons cooked puréed lobster coral or lobster meat mixed with 3 tablespoons butter. Stir in ¼ cup heavy cream. Spoon the sauce over the eggs. Omit the hard-cooked egg yolks, and if desired sprinkle with 1 tablespoon chopped truffles. Makes 4 to 8 servings.

⚜ POACHED EGGS WITH HAM OR BACON
(*Oeufs Pochés au Jambon ou au Lard*)

4 to 8 hot poached eggs
4 to 8 slices fried ham, or 8 to 16 thin slices crisply fried bacon

salt and ground pepper to taste
4 to 8 teaspoons ham or bacon drippings or melted butter

Place 1 poached egg on each slice of ham or on each 2 slices of bacon. Sprinkle with salt and pepper to taste. Spoon 1 teaspoon ham or bacon drippings or 1 teaspoon melted butter over each egg. Serve for breakfast. Allow 1 or 2 eggs per serving.

⚜ POACHED EGGS AND HAM IN RAMEKINS
(*Oeufs Pochés en Cocotte au Jambon*)

4 thin slices baked or boiled ham
4 cold poached eggs

1 cup liquid clear aspic
parsley

Line the bottoms of 4 cocottes with thinly sliced baked or boiled ham. Place 1 cold poached egg in each and pour ¼ cup aspic over each egg. Refrigerate until aspic is firm. Serve in the cocottes or turn out onto a chilled platter. Garnish with parsley. Makes 4 servings.

⚜ POACHED EGGS PORTUGUESE STYLE
(*Oeufs Pochés à la Portugaise*)

¾ cup long-grain rice
1½ cups light stock or bouillon
3 tablespoons tomato purée
4 hot poached eggs

salt and ground black pepper to taste
½ cup Mornay Sauce (page 40)
½ cup grated Gruyère or Cheddar
  cheese

Cook the rice according to package directions, but use stock or bouillon instead of water and omit the salt. Add the tomato purée and toss the rice lightly with a fork. Turn the rice onto a heatproof platter, and arrange the poached eggs over it. Shake salt and pepper lightly over the eggs. Coat with the Mornay Sauce, sprinkle with grated cheese, and bake in a preheated hot oven (425° F.) 5 to 10 minutes or until the cheese has melted and is flecked with brown. Makes 4 servings.

⚜ EGGS POACHED IN RED WINE (*Oeufs Pochés en Matelote*)

8 eggs
dry red wine
1 tablespoon flour
1½ tablespoons softened butter
¾ cup sliced mushrooms

2 cups boiling water
salt
ground black pepper to taste
8 slices bread
butter

Poach the eggs in simmering dry red wine instead of in water and vinegar. Remove the eggs from the wine with a slotted spoon and keep them warm. Boil the wine until it is reduced to 1 cup. Strain it. Blend the flour with the softened butter and add to the wine. Stir and cook until the sauce is of medium thickness. Poach the mushrooms in 2 cups boiling water with ½ teaspoon salt added. Remove the mushrooms from the water with a slotted spoon, drain them well, and add them to the sauce. Season to taste with salt and pepper. Fry the bread slices in butter and arrange them on a warmed platter. Place a poached egg on each slice. Cover with the wine-mushroom sauce. Serve for lunch or supper. Allow 1 or 2 eggs per serving.

⚜ POACHED EGGS RUSSIAN STYLE
(*Oeufs Pochés en Cocotte à la Russe*)

3 cups liquid aspic about as thick as fresh egg whites

4 truffle slices, or 4 sautéed mushroom slices with stem attached

4 cold poached eggs

⅓ cup each hot cooked green peas and diced cooked carrots, potatoes, turnips, and green beans

3 tablespoons Vinaigrette Sauce (page 56)

salt and ground black pepper to taste

⅓ cup each diced cold cooked ham and tongue

⅓ cup mayonnaise

4 anchovy fillets

2 hard-cooked eggs

Coat 4 cocottes with aspic and chill until the aspic is almost firm. Put 1 thin slice of truffle or sautéed mushroom in the bottom of each cocotte. Chill 5 to 10 minutes. Coat the cocottes with another layer of aspic and chill until firm. Place 1 cold poached egg in each cocotte and pour in enough aspic to fill the cocotte. Refrigerate until aspic is firm. Chill all the remaining aspic until firm. Combine the hot cooked vegetables with the Vinaigrette Sauce and salt and pepper to taste, and marinate 2 hours. Add the ham, tongue, and mayonnaise to the vegetable mixture, mix lightly and place in a mound in the center of a round serving plate. Garnish with anchovy fillets and slices of hard-cooked egg. Unmold the cocottes and place them around the salad. Break up the remaining jellied aspic with a fork, and spoon it onto the plate around the eggs. Makes 4 servings.

⚜ POACHED EGGS WITH SHRIMP (*Oeufs Pochés Joinville*)

3 tablespoons butter

3 tablespoons flour

¾ cup hot fish stock

¾ cup hot milk or hot light cream

salt and ground black pepper to taste

½ teaspoon lemon juice

½ cup diced cooked shrimp

2 cups bread cubes fried in butter (croutons)

8 poached eggs

8 cooked, peeled, and deveined whole shrimp

paprika

Melt the butter in a 1-quart saucepan. Remove from heat and blend in the flour. Return to heat; stir and cook until the mixture is foamy, 1 to 2 minutes. Remove from heat, pour in all the stock and milk or cream, and beat vigorously with a wire whisk or a wire hand eggbeater. Return to heat and stir and cook until sauce is of medium thickness. Add salt and pepper to taste, and the lemon juice and diced shrimp. Heat. Spread the fried croutons on a warmed platter and arrange the poached eggs on top. Coat the eggs with the hot shrimp sauce and pour the remaining sauce around them. Garnish each egg with a whole cooked shrimp. Sprinkle with paprika. Serve for lunch or supper. Makes 4 to 8 servings.

⚜ POACHED EGGS WITH SPINACH (*Oeufs Pochés à la Florentine*)

1½ packages (15 ounces) frozen spinach, or 2 pounds fresh spinach,
cooked
6 tablespoons butter
salt and ground black pepper to taste

6 hot poached eggs
¾ cup Mornay Sauce (page 40)
¼ cup grated Gruyère or Cheddar
cheese
¼ cup fine dry breadcrumbs

Drain the cooked spinach well and sauté it in 2 tablespoons of the butter.
Season to taste with salt and black pepper. Place in a shallow 1-quart baking
dish. Arrange the poached eggs over the top. Coat with the Mornay Sauce.
Sprinkle with the cheese and breadcrumbs. Melt the remaining 4 tablespoons
butter and pour over the top. Place in a preheated very hot oven (450° F.)
for 5 minutes or until browned. Serve as a luncheon or supper dish. Makes
6 servings.

⚜ POACHED EGGS WITH TARRAGON (*Oeufs Pochés à l'Estragon*)

Poach the eggs and place them on croutons fried in butter or in buttered
cocottes (small oval or round individual baking dishes). Coat them with hot
Velouté Sauce mixed with chopped fresh tarragon or dried tarragon (1 teaspoon chopped fresh or ¼ teaspoon dried tarragon to 1 cup sauce). Garnish
with chopped parsley or with blanched tarragon leaves arranged to form a
star. Serve hot for lunch or supper. Allow 1 to 2 eggs per person.

⚜ TARRAGON POACHED EGGS IN RAMEKINS
(*Oeufs Pochés en Cocotte à l'Estragon*)

2 cups liquid Tarragon Aspic (see
following recipe)
6 cold poached eggs

salt and ground white pepper to taste
fresh tarragon leaves, or fresh parsley

Coat the bottoms and sides of 6 individual ramekins or cocottes with Tarragon
Aspic that is about the consistency of fresh egg whites. Chill until aspic is
firm. Coat again with aspic and chill again until aspic is set. Place 1 cold
poached egg in each ramekin and sprinkle it lightly with salt and pepper.
Finish filling the ramekins with the remaining aspic. Refrigerate until aspic
is firm. Just before serving, unmold onto a chilled serving dish. Garnish with
fresh tarragon leaves, if available, or with fresh parsley. Makes 6 servings.

⚜ Tarragon Aspic

See recipe for Aspic, page 400. Steep 2 teaspoons chopped fresh tarragon or

¾ teaspoon dried tarragon 5 to 8 minutes in the hot water or stock used for making the aspic. Strain and add to the softened gelatin.

⚜ POACHED-EGG TARTLETS (*Oeufs Pochés Sigurd*)

4 baked plain pastry tartlet cases, 3 inches in diameter
⅓ cup sliced mushrooms
1½ tablespoons butter
4 teaspoons diced onion
4 poached eggs
salt and ground black pepper
½ cup hot Béchamel Sauce (page 38)

2 tablespoons heavy cream
1 teaspoon paprika
4 sautéed mushroom caps
1 teaspoon prepared horseradish

Bake the tartlet cases and set them aside. Cook the sliced mushrooms in 1 tablespoon of the butter; cook the onion separately in the remaining ½ tablespoon butter. Just before serving, poach the eggs, drain them well, and place 1 in each case. Sprinkle lightly with salt and pepper. Spoon over each 1 teaspoon cooked onion and 1 tablespoon cooked sliced mushrooms. Combine the Béchamel Sauce, cream, and paprika and heat about ½ minute, then spoon the sauce over the eggs. Garnish each egg with a sautéed mushroom cap, topped with about ¼ teaspoon horseradish. Serve for luncheon or supper. Makes 4 servings.

⚜ POACHED-EGG AND CHICKEN TARTLETS (*Croustades d'Oeufs Pochés à la Reine*)

6 baked plain pastry tartlet cases, 3 inches in diameter
6 medium-sized mushrooms with stems
4 tablespoons butter
1 shallot, chopped fine
⅓ cup Madeira wine or dry sherry
1 cup Demi-Glace Sauce (page 44)

½ teaspoon salt
ground black pepper to taste
6 eggs
1 cup finely ground cooked chicken

Bake the tartlet shells and set them aside. Put the chicken through the food chopper 3 times, using the finest blade. Set aside. Remove the stems from the mushroom caps (reserving the caps), chop the stems fine and sauté them in 2 tablespoons of the butter, 4 to 5 minutes, stirring frequently. Add the shallot, wine, and Demi-Glace Sauce. Stir and cook 6 to 7 minutes. Add salt and pepper. Just before serving, poach the eggs, drain them well, and place 1 in each case. Add the ground chicken to the sauce, heat, and spoon into the baked pastry cases. Sauté the mushroom caps in the remaining 2 tablespoons butter until they have browned lightly. Place one on each tartlet. Serve at once. Makes 6 servings.

SOFT-COOKED EGGS (*Oeufs Mollets*)

⚜ HOW TO SOFT-COOK EGGS IN THE SHELL

Place eggs in a saucepan with enough water to cover them to a depth of about 1 inch. Cover, bring to boiling point, remove from heat, and let stand in the water 3 to 5 minutes, allowing the longer time for a larger number of eggs or for firmer consistency.

Serve soft-cooked eggs for breakfast or make them into hot or cold dishes for lunch, supper, or a buffet. If soft-cooked eggs are to be peeled, let them stand 5 to 6 minutes and then plunge them into cold water. Allow 1 to 2 eggs per person.

⚜ EGGS MORNAY (*Oeufs Mornay*)

12 eggs, soft-cooked, poached, or
  hard-cooked
4 tablespoons butter
4 tablespoons flour
2 cups hot milk
1 raw egg yolk, beaten lightly

1 cup grated Gruyère or Cheddar
  cheese
salt and ground white pepper to taste
Buttered Soft Breadcrumbs (see following recipe)

Cook the eggs by whichever method you prefer. If they are cooked in the shells, peel them; if hard-cooked, cut them in halves. Set them aside. Melt the butter in a 1-quart saucepan. Remove from heat and blend in the flour. Return to heat. Stir and cook until the mixture is foamy. Remove from heat and add all the hot milk at one time. Beat vigorously with a wire whisk or wire hand beater. Return to heat. Stir and cook until the sauce is medium-thick. Remove from heat. Gradually beat a little of the hot sauce into the beaten egg yolk and then add it to the remaining hot sauce. Stir in ½ cup of the grated cheese and salt and pepper to taste. Place 2 eggs in each of 6 buttered individual baking dishes. Divide the sauce evenly over the servings. Sprinkle with the remaining grated cheese and Buttered Soft Breadcrumbs. Brown *quickly*, 5 to 10 minutes, in a preheated very hot oven (450° F.). As soon as the crumbs have browned remove the dishes from the oven to avoid toughening the eggs. Serve at once. Makes 6 servings.

⚜ Buttered Soft Breadcrumbs

Melt 1 tablespoon butter or margarine and mix with ½ cup soft fresh breadcrumbs.

⚜ VIRGINIA CLUB SOFT-COOKED EGGS
(Oeufs Mollets Virginia Club)

6 cold medium-soft-cooked eggs
2 cups well-drained canned whole-kernel corn or whole corn kernels cut from ears of cooked corn
⅔ cup mayonnaise

salt and ground black pepper to taste
watercress
3 medium-sized tomatoes
olive oil or salad oil
black olives

Peel the eggs and set them aside. Mix the corn with ¼ cup of the mayonnaise, season to taste with salt and pepper, put on a plate, and chill. Just before serving, divide the corn equally on 6 serving plates. Coat the eggs with the remaining mayonnaise and place 1 on each serving of corn. Arrange a small bunch of watercress on each plate. Peel the tomatoes, cut them in half, and place 1 half tomato on each bunch of watercress. Sprinkle the tomatoes with salt, pepper, and oil. Garnish with black olives. Serve cold for a buffet, lunch, or supper. Makes 6 servings.

HARD-COOKED EGGS *(Oeufs Durs)*

Hard-cooked eggs, correctly prepared, are firm, tender, and appetizing in appearance. High temperature and/or long cooking make egg whites tough and rubbery, produce hard spots in the yolks, and cause the formation of green discoloration on the outside of the yolks. Immediately after the eggs are done, cool them by placing them in cold water, to prevent discoloration. Use hard-cooked eggs in hot and cold entrées, salads, sandwiches, canapés and garnishes.

⚜ HOW TO HARD-COOK EGGS IN THE SHELL

Place eggs in a saucepan with sufficient water to cover them to a depth of 1 inch. Cover, bring to boiling point, remove from heat, and let stand, covered, for 20 minutes. Then cool in cold water immediately.

⚜ HARD-COOKED EGGS AURORA *(Oeufs Durs Aurore)*

6 hard-cooked eggs
1¼ cups hot Béchamel Sauce (page 38)
salt and ground black pepper

½ cup grated Gruyère or Cheddar cheese
hot Tomato Sauce (page 50)

Slice 4 of the eggs and the 2 remaining egg whites and add to the Béchamel Sauce. Set the 2 remaining yolks aside for later use. Season the sauce to taste with salt and black pepper. Put the mixture in a buttered 1-quart casserole and sprinkle with the grated cheese. Cook in a preheated slow oven (325° F.) until the cheese is melted and flecked with brown. Sieve the 2 remaining egg yolks over the cheese. Surround the center of the top with a ribbon of Tomato Sauce. Serve as an entrée for lunch or supper. Makes 4 servings.

⚜ HARD-COOKED EGGS WITH BÉCHAMEL SAUCE
(Oeufs Durs à la Béchamel)

1¼ Cups Béchamel Sauce (page 38)	salt and ground black pepper to taste
1½ tablespoons butter	4 slices toast or 4 baked patty shells
6 hard-cooked eggs	parsley

Combine the Béchamel Sauce with the butter and heat until butter is melted. Slice the eggs and add. Season to taste with salt and black pepper. Heat, without boiling, only until hot. Serve on toast or in patty shells. Garnish with parsley. Makes 4 servings.

Cold Hard-Cooked Egg Dishes

Cold hard-cooked eggs may be coated with aspic flavored with a little tarragon infusion, Madeira, or any good dry white wine. Cold hard-cooked eggs so coated retain their fresh, appetizing appearance. Eggs in aspic are served as an hors d'oeuvre or the entrée for a luncheon or supper, or used to garnish cold meat, poultry, or fish platters.

⚜ HARD-COOKED EGGS WITH FOIE GRAS
(Oeufs Durs au Foie Gras)

4 hard-cooked eggs	aspic, flavored with white wine or
4 slices of truffle	tarragon and about the thickness
foie gras purée	of fresh egg whites

Put a peeled hard-cooked egg in each of 4 custard cups. Surround each with a ring of foie gras purée put through a pastry bag. Garnish each egg with a slice of truffle. Finish filling the cups with aspic. Chill until aspic is firm. Unmold onto a serving plate and serve for a buffet, lunch, or supper. Makes 4 servings.

❧ HARD-COOKED EGGS WITH MAYONNAISE
(*Oeufs Durs à la Mayonnaise*)

Cut hard-cooked eggs in lengthwise halves and arrange them attractively in a dish, cut side down. Cover them with mayonnaise and garnish with sliced gherkins, blanched chervil, tarragon, or chopped parsley. Allow 1 egg per serving. (*See illustration, page 85.*)

❧ HARD-COOKED EGGS MENTON STYLE
(*Oeufs Durs à la Mentonaise*)

6 hard-cooked eggs
¾ cup cold cooked fish or drained
   canned tuna fish
2 to 3 tablespoons mayonnaise

salt
ground black pepper
6 anchovy fillets
12 black olives, pitted

Cut the eggs into lengthwise halves. Remove the yolks and put them through a fine sieve. Flake the fish, add it to the yolks, and work the mixture into a paste. Put this through a sieve, then mix it with the mayonnaise and salt and black pepper to taste. Spoon the mixture into a pastry bag and pipe it into the egg whites. Cut the anchovy fillets in half and roll each half around a pitted black olive. Place an anchovy-wrapped olive on each stuffed half egg. Makes 3 to 6 servings.

❧ HARD-COOKED EGGS SWEDISH STYLE
(*Oeufs Durs à la Suédoise*)

sliced hard-cooked eggs
small tomatoes, 1½ inches in diameter,
   sliced thin
powdered mustard

cold water
Vinaigrette Sauce (page 56)
thin onion rings

Arrange hard-cooked egg slices and tomato slices alternately on a platter. Combine powdered mustard with twice as much cold water, let stand 5 minutes to develop the flavor, and add to Vinaigrette Sauce to taste. Sprinkle the sauce over the tomatoes and eggs. Garnish with onion rings. Allow 1 egg and 1 tomato per serving.

❧ HARD-COOKED EGGS WITH TOMATOES (*Oeufs Durs Mistral*)

Cut cold hard-cooked eggs into lengthwise halves, and sprinkle the cut sides with salt and ground black pepper. Coat the uncut sides with mayonnaise and place the eggs, cut side down, on tomato slices ¼ to ½ inch thick. Arrange on a tray and garnish each egg with half of a pimiento-stuffed olive, cut lengthwise. Cover the center of the tray with additional tomato slices, sprinkle with chopped parsley, and pile black olives in the center. Allow 2 slices of tomato and 2 egg halves per person. (*See illustration, page 85.*)

⚜ HARD-COOKED EGGS VINAIGRETTE
(*Oeufs Durs à la Vinaigrette*)

Slice 8 hard-cooked eggs and arrange them on a platter. Sprinkle with Vinaigrette Sauce (page 56) to taste. Garnish with chopped parsley. Makes 4 servings.

FRIED EGGS (*Oeufs sur le Plat*)

See also Baked Eggs, page 141.

⚜ HOW TO FRY EGGS

Eggs fried by any of the following methods will be tender and not greasy. Allow 1 or 2 eggs per serving.

⚜ Fried Eggs I

Heat butter, bacon drippings, or other fat in a skillet, using only enough to grease the bottom of the pan. Break the eggs into a saucer, one at a time, and slip them into the pan. Sprinkle with salt and ground black pepper. Cover pan tightly and cook over very low heat 2 to 3 minutes or until the egg whites are firm and the yolks are covered with a film of coagulated white.

⚜ Fried Eggs II

Prepare pan and eggs as for Fried Eggs I. Add 1 to 2 tablespoons hot water, cover pan tightly, and steam over very low heat until eggs are cooked as desired.

⚜ Fried Eggs III

Prepare pan and eggs as for Fried Eggs I. Cook over very low heat until eggs have cooked underneath, 1 to 2 minutes. Turn eggs over and cook on the other side about 1 minute.

⚜ FRIED EGGS WITH BLACK BUTTER
(*Oeufs sur le Plat au Beurre Noir*)

6 tablespoons butter
8 eggs

salt and ground black pepper to taste
1 tablespoon wine vinegar

Brown 4 tablespoons of the butter in a 10-inch skillet. Break the eggs into the butter. Cover and cook over low heat 2 to 3 minutes or until egg whites are firm and the yolks are coated with a film of coagulated white. Sprinkle the eggs with salt and pepper and arrange them on a serving dish. Meanwhile brown the remaining 2 tablespoons butter in a small saucepan until it begins to turn black. Add the vinegar, heat, and pour over the eggs. Makes 4 to 8 servings.

BAKED EGGS

Eggs may be baked in a large casserole or in individual casseroles, with sauces or other ingredients. They are cooked in a slow oven (325° F.). See recipes for baking times.

⚜ EGGS BERCY (*Oeufs sur le Plat Bercy*)

4 to 8 eggs
salt and ground black pepper to taste
4 to 8 chipolata sausages, grilled

½ to ¾ cup Tomato Sauce (page 50)
chopped parsley

Break the eggs into a saucer, one at a time, and slide them into a buttered casserole. Sprinkle with salt and pepper. Place grilled sausages between the eggs. Cook, uncovered, in a preheated slow oven (325° F.) 12 to 18 minutes or until the whites are firm and the yolks are cooked as desired. Surround the eggs with hot Tomato Sauce. Sprinkle with chopped parsley. Serve for lunch or supper. Makes 4 to 8 servings.

⚜ EGGS WITH MUSHROOMS (*Oeufs sur le Plat aux Champignons*)

¾ pound small mushrooms
2 tablespoons butter
salt and ground black pepper
½ cup Béchamel Sauce (page 38)

⅓ cup light cream
½ teaspoon lemon juice
4 large eggs

Wash the mushrooms. Remove the stems and save them for soups or sauces. Cook the mushroom caps in the butter with ½ teaspoon salt and a dash of black pepper for 5 minutes or until they are soft, stirring frequently. Add the Béchamel Sauce and cream. Simmer 10 minutes. Remove from heat and add the lemon juice. Pour the mixture into 4 individual baking dishes. Make a hollow in the center of each and break an egg into it. Sprinkle the eggs with salt and black pepper. Bake, uncovered, in a preheated slow oven (325° F.) 12 to 18 minutes or until eggs are cooked to desired consistency. Serve for lunch or supper. Makes 4 servings.

❧ EGGS WITH PARMESAN CHEESE (Oeufs sur le Plat au Parmesan)

¾ cup grated Parmesan cheese
8 eggs

ground black pepper to taste
4 tablespoons (½ stick) butter

Sprinkle the bottom of a buttered baking dish with half the cheese. Break the eggs over the cheese, sprinkle them with ground black pepper and the remaining cheese, and dot with butter. Cover and bake in a preheated slow oven (325° F.) 8 to 10 minutes or until eggs are cooked as desired. The whites should be firm and the yolks soft. Serve for breakfast, lunch, or dinner. Makes 4 to 8 servings.

❧ SHIRRED EGGS

8 slices bacon
8 eggs

salt and ground black pepper to taste
2 tablespoons butter

Fry the bacon until it is about three-fourths done. Arrange the slices in a shallow 9-inch baking dish, cake pan, or pie plate. Break the eggs over the bacon. Sprinkle with salt and black pepper. Dot with butter. Bake in a preheated slow oven (325° F.) 8 to 10 minutes or until eggs are cooked as desired. The whites should be firm and the yolks soft. Makes 4 to 8 servings.

EGGS EN COCOTTE (Oeufs en Cocotte)

A cocotte is a small oval or round individual casserole in which food is baked and served. It may be made of earthenware, glass, or metal. Food cooked in such a vessel is usually called "en cocotte."

❧ HOW TO COOK EGGS EN COCOTTE

Warm the cocotte dishes and butter them. Break 1 egg into each dish and place the dishes in a shallow pan of hot water. Cook over surface heat for 2 to 3 minutes, never allowing the water to boil. Cover the dishes with foil or a cooky sheet and finish cooking in a preheated slow oven (325° F.), about 3 to

4 minutes. The egg whites should be firm and the yolks soft. Sprinkle with salt and ground black pepper to taste. Allow 1 to 2 eggs per person.

⚜ EGGS EN COCOTTE WITH CREAM (*Oeufs en Cocotte à la Crème*)

Warm the cocottes and pour in hot light cream to a depth of ⅛ inch. Break the eggs into the cocottes and sprinkle with salt and ground black pepper to taste. Cook as in basic recipe 3 minutes over low surface heat and 5 minutes in a preheated slow oven (325° F.). Allow 1 to 2 eggs per person.

⚜ EGGS EN COCOTTE WITH SPINACH
(*Oeufs en Cocotte à la Florentine*)

1 10-ounce package frozen spinach
2 tablespoons butter
6 eggs
salt and ground black pepper to taste

6 tablespoons warmed heavy cream
6 tablespoons grated Gruyère or Cheddar cheese

Cook and season the spinach according to package directions. Drain well and sauté in butter 2 to 3 minutes. Spread the spinach over the bottoms and sides of 6 cocotte dishes. Break 1 egg into each cocotte. Sprinkle with salt and pepper. Cook as in the basic recipe 3 minutes over surface heat. Then pour 1 tablespoon warmed heavy cream over each egg and sprinkle with 1 table-spoon grated cheese. Cover and cook 5 minutes in a preheated slow oven (325° F.). Makes 6 servings.

SCRAMBLED EGGS (*Oeufs Brouillés*)

⚜ HOW TO SCRAMBLE EGGS

Break the desired number of eggs into a bowl. Add milk or light cream in the following proportions: for Creamy Scrambled Eggs, 1 tablespoon milk or light cream for each egg; for Dry Scrambled Eggs, ½ tablespoon milk or light cream for each egg. Beat the mixture *only* until whites and yolks are blended. If flecks of egg whites are preferred in scrambled eggs, omit the milk or cream and beat the eggs *very slightly*. Season to taste with salt and ground black pepper. Heat a small amount of butter or other fat in a skillet until melted. Pour in the egg mixture. Stir and cook slowly until the eggs are set, but still moist (soft-firm). Scrambled eggs may also be cooked in a little butter in the top of a double boiler over simmering water (not boiling). Allow 1 to 2 eggs per person.

143

⚜ SCRAMBLED EGGS WITH CROUTONS
(Oeufs Brouillés aux Croutons)

8 large eggs	1 tablespoon butter
⅓ cup light cream	30 white-bread croutons fried in butter
salt and ground black pepper to taste	

Beat the eggs lightly; add the cream, salt, and black pepper. Melt the butter in an 8-inch skillet and pour in the egg mixture. Stir and cook over low heat until eggs begin to set. Add the croutons. Continue cooking until eggs are soft-firm. Serve on a warmed platter for breakfast, luncheon, or supper. Makes 6 servings.

⚜ SCRAMBLED EGGS WITH CHEESE *(Oeufs Brouillés au Fromage)*

In the preceding recipe replace the croutons with ½ cup grated Gruyère or Cheddar cheese. Serve over slices of cheese. Serve for breakfast, luncheon, or supper. Makes 4 to 6 servings.

⚜ SCRAMBLED EGGS CATALAN STYLE
(Oeufs Brouillés à la Catalane)

1 green sweet pepper, 3 to 3½ inches long	8 large eggs
2 tablespoons butter	4 tablespoons light cream
1 medium-sized tomato, peeled and diced	salt and ground black pepper to taste

Wash the pepper and remove seeds and pith. Cut the pepper into julienne strips 1½ inches long and cook in butter over medium heat, stirring frequently, until wilted, 5 to 8 minutes. Add the tomato and cook 2 to 3 minutes or until most of the moisture has evaporated. Beat the eggs and cream together *only very slightly*. Add to the pepper and tomatoes and mix. Cook, stirring, until the eggs are soft-firm. Add salt and black pepper to taste. Serve hot for lunch or supper. Makes 4 to 6 servings. *(See illustration, page 124.)*

⚜ SCRAMBLED EGGS WITH MUSHROOMS
(Oeufs Brouillés aux Champignons)

1 cup thinly sliced mushrooms	¼ cup light cream or milk
2 tablespoons butter	salt and ground black pepper to taste
8 large eggs	

Sauté the mushroms in the butter until they have browned. Beat the eggs lightly, add the cream or milk, and mix *only* until blended. Pour the mixture into the skillet over the mushrooms. Add salt and pepper. Stir and cook over low heat until eggs are soft-firm. Serve for breakfast, lunch, or supper. Makes 6 servings.

⚜ SCRAMBLED EGGS WITH SHRIMP (*Oeufs Brouillés aux Crevettes*)

8 large eggs
⅓ cup light cream
½ pound peeled, deveined cooked
   shrimp

salt and ground black pepper to taste
2 tablespoons butter

Beat the eggs lightly. Add the cream, shrimp, salt, and black pepper. Melt the butter in an 8-inch skillet. Add the mixture and cook until eggs are soft-firm, stirring constantly. Serve for special breakfasts, luncheon, or supper. Makes 6 servings.

OMELETTES

There are recipes for two basic types of omelettes in this book: French (plain), and American (puffy). The French Omelette is made with whole eggs beaten only enough to blend the whites with the egg yolks, with no additional liquid. The American Puffy Omelette is made by beating the whites and yolks separately with 1 tablespoon liquid to each egg. Both types of omelettes are folded.

A variety of other foods, sauces, etc., may be added to omelettes, either cooked with the eggs or used as a filling which is added after the omelette is cooked and just before it is folded (see Omelette Additions, pages 147–148).

⚜ FRENCH OMELETTE

4 large eggs
½ teaspoon salt

dash ground black pepper
about 1½ tablespoons butter

Beat the eggs only until the whites and yolks are mixed. Add the salt and pepper and stir only until ingredients are blended. Melt the butter in an 8- or 9-inch skillet. Pour in the egg mixture. Cook over moderately low heat. As the omelette cooks, lift the edges and turn them toward the center so the uncooked mixture flows under the cooked portion. Cook only until the bottom is light brown and the top is set. Make a crease across the center with a spatula or the back of a knife. Fold half the omelette over the other half. Serve immediately on a warmed platter. Serves 2. If desired, a filling may be spread on one side of the omelette just before it is folded or a sauce served over it.

❧ AMERICAN PUFFY OMELETTE (*Omelette Mousseline*)

A puffy omelette (American) should have fine uniform air cells throughout, a soft, puffy, moist texture, and a tender light golden-brown crust. Cooking too long or at too high temperature causes the bottom of the omelette to become tough and heavy, and the omelette may fall and be tough and dry.

6 large eggs	ground black pepper to taste
½ teaspoon salt	2 tablespoons butter
6 tablespoons light cream	

Separate the eggs and put whites and yolks in separate bowls. Add the salt to the egg whites and beat until soft, stiff, moist (not dry) peaks form. Add the cream and pepper to the egg yolks and beat until they are thick and lemon-colored. Fold the yolks into the beaten whites. Melt the butter in an 8- or 9-inch skillet and pour in the omelette mixture. Cook over low surface heat 5 to 6 minutes or until omelette is puffy and light brown on the bottom; lift the edges with a spatula to judge the color. Put in a preheated slow oven (350° F.) and bake *only* until a knife inserted in the center comes out clean, 12 to 15 minutes. Make a crease across the center with the back of a knife or with a spatula. Fold half of the omelette over the other half. Serve promptly on a warmed platter. Makes 4 generous servings.

❧ KIDNEY OMELETTE (*Omelette aux Rognons*)

3 lamb's kidneys	2 tablespoons butter
cold water	½ cup Madeira Sauce (page 294)
salt	ground black pepper
2 tablespoons chopped shallots or onions	French Omelette or Puffy Omelette
	chopped parsley

Put the kidneys into enough cold water to cover them, and ¾ teaspoon salt, and soak 2 hours. Remove from water, rinse in cold water, and wipe dry. Cut the kidneys into crosswise slices, removing all the fat and membrane. Sauté the chopped shallots or onions in the butter for 2 minutes or until soft. Add the kidneys and cook 10 minutes, or until kidneys are tender, adding additional butter if necessary. Add the Madeira Sauce and season to taste with salt and ground black pepper. Prepare and cook a French Omelette or an American Puffy Omelette. Spread half the kidney mixture over one side and fold the other half over it. Transfer the omelette to a warm platter. Make an incision in the top of the omelette and spoon in the remaining kidney mixture. Sprinkle with chopped parsley. Serve at once. Makes filling for 2 to 3 servings.

OMELETTE ADDITIONS

Any of the following combinations may be used with French Omelettes. Each recipe makes enough for 2 servings.

⚜ Bacon (*Au Lard*)

Dice 4 slices of bacon and cook in an omelette pan until crisp. Drain off excess fat. (Do not add butter.) Beat the eggs with salt and black pepper and pour over the bacon. Cook as instructed in the recipe for French Omelette.

⚜ Cheese (*Au Fromage*)

Add ½ cup grated Gruyère, Parmesan, or Cheddar cheese to the eggs before they are beaten. Cook quickly according to the directions for French Omelette.

⚜ Ham (*Au Jambon*)

Heat ½ cup cooked diced ham in a buttered omelette pan. Pour the beaten eggs over it and cook as directed for French Omelette.

⚜ Herb (*Aux Fines Herbes*)

Add 1 tablespoon finely chopped fresh parsley and ¼ teaspoon each dried or 1 teaspoon each fresh finely chopped chervil, chives, and tarragon, before beating the eggs. Cook quickly according to directions for French Omelette.

⚜ Mushroom (*Aux Champignons*)

Sauté ¾ cup sliced mushrooms in 1 tablespoon butter 3 to 5 minutes in the omelette pan. Beat the eggs with 1 tablespoon chopped parsley and pour them over the mushrooms in the hot pan. Cook quickly according to directions for French Omelette.

⚜ Onion (*Lyonnaise*)

Sauté 1 cup sliced onions in 2 tablespoons butter in the omelette pan. Beat 1 tablespoon chopped parsley with the eggs and pour the mixture over the onions in the hot omelette pan. Cook according to directions for French Omelette.

⚜ Potato (*Parmentier*)

Sauté ¾ cup diced cooked potatoes in 2 tablespoons butter in an omelette pan. Pour the beaten eggs into the hot pan over the potatoes. Cook according to the directions for French Omelette.

⚜ Potato and Bacon (*À la Paysanne*)

Sauté potatoes as in the preceding recipe. Crumble 4 slices crisp bacon and add. Pour the beaten eggs into the hot pan over the potatoes and bacon. Cook according to the directions for French Omelette.

⚜ Shrimp (*Aux Crevettes*)

Sprinkle 1 cup deveined peeled shrimp with salt and ground black pepper. Cook in 2 tablespoons butter over medium-low heat until they turn pink. Spoon half the shrimp over one side of a French Omelette (or an American Puffy Omelette). Fold the other half of the omelette over the shrimp and transfer it to a warmed platter. Make an incision in the top of the omelette and fill it with the remaining cooked shrimp. Serve at once.

7

Soups

Because of their endless variety and nutritive value, soups may be served for lunch, supper, or dinner. A hearty soup, served in sufficient quantity, needs only a salad and a light dessert, such as cheese and fruit with wine, to make a complete luncheon or supper. Light soups, such as bouillon, consommé, and broth, are appropriate to serve as an appetizer course for dinner or a formal luncheon or supper.

Soups may be classified as clear soups (bouillon, consommé, and broth), cream soups (with or without vegetables), thick soups with a vegetable-purée base, and unstrained vegetable soups.

CLEAR SOUPS

❧ BASIC BROTH (*Grand Marmite*)

2 pounds lean soup meat
1 shinbone of beef
2½ quarts cold water
2 teaspoons salt
2 leeks
1 rib of celery
1 cup diced turnip
1 cup sliced carrots

1 large onion studded with 2 whole cloves
1 clove of garlic
½ bay leaf
6 peppercorns
1 tablespoon chopped fresh or 1 teaspoon dried thyme

149

Place the meat and shinbone in a 6-quart saucepan. Add the water and salt. Cover and bring to boiling point. Skim. Add all the remaining ingredients except the thyme. Simmer 3½ hours. Add thyme 10 minutes before cooking time is up. Cool. Remove the meat and bones. Strain the broth through 2 thicknesses of cheesecloth or through a very fine sieve. Makes approximately 2 quarts broth.

⚜ CONSOMMÉ (*Consommé*)

1 pound ground lean beef
2 egg whites
1 leek, shredded
1 carrot, grated

2 quarts stock from Basic Broth (page 149)
1 tablespoon chopped fresh or 1 teaspoon dried thyme or chervil

Mix the beef with the egg whites, leek, and carrot. Skim off all fat from the broth and mix with the beef and vegetables. Cover. Slowly bring to boiling point, stirring frequently. Simmer gently for 50 minutes. Add the herbs 10 minutes before cooking time is up. Cool. Remove the meat. Strain through 2 thicknesses of cheesecloth or through a very fine sieve. Serve hot. Makes 3½ pints.

⚜ NOODLE SOUP (*Potage aux Vermicelles ou aux Pâtes d'Italie*)

2 ounces vermicelli or fine noodles
5 cups boiling bouillon or Brown
   Stock (page 30)

salt and ground black pepper to taste

Carefully add the vermicelli or fine noodles to the boiling bouillon or stock. Boil gently, uncovered, 10 to 15 minutes, or until pasta is tender. Add salt and pepper to taste. Serve hot. Makes 4 servings.

⚜ TAPIOCA SOUP (*Potage au Tapioca*)

3 tablespoons quick-cooking tapioca
4 cups boiling bouillon or Brown
   Stock (page 30)

salt and ground black pepper to taste

Carefully sprinkle the tapioca into the boiling bouillon or soup stock, stirring to prevent the tapioca from lumping. Cover and boil gently for 6 to 8 minutes. Add salt and black pepper. If the soup is not to be used at once, keep it covered to prevent an unattractive skin from forming over the surface. Makes 4 to 5 servings.

CREAM SOUPS

Cream of rice and cream of barley form the basis of most French cream soups. Vegetables for vegetable cream soups should first be cooked a few minutes in water and then finish cooking in the soup.

⚜ CREAM OF OATMEAL SOUP
(*Crème d'Avoine ou de Flocons d'Avoine*)

3¼ cups milk
2 cups (1 pint) bouillon or Brown Stock (page 30)
¾ cup uncooked oatmeal

¼ cup heavy cream
salt and ground black pepper to taste
small fried croutons

Combine 1¼ cups of the milk and the bouillon or stock in a 3-quart saucepan and heat to boiling point. Mix the remaining 2 cups cold milk with the oatmeal and carefully stir the mixture into the boiling liquid. Stir and cook slowly 15 to 20 minutes. Skim. Add the cream, salt, and black pepper. Serve in bowls with fried croutons. Makes 4 servings.

⚜ CREAM OF RICE SOUP (*Crème de Riz*)

¼ cup (½ stick) butter
3 tablespoons cream of rice or rice flour
4¼ cups veal or beef bouillon or stock
½ cup milk

1 egg yolk
¼ cup heavy cream
salt and ground white pepper to taste
fried small croutons

Soften the butter in a small saucepan. Gradually blend in the cream of rice or rice flour to form a roux. Stir and cook the mixture over low heat 2 minutes. Pour the bouillon or stock into a 2-quart saucepan, add the roux, and beat with a wire whisk or wire hand eggbeater until the mixture is smooth. Bring to boiling point, then reduce heat and simmer 25 minutes, stirring frequently. Skim. Add the milk and heat. Mix the egg yolk with the cream and pour it into a soup tureen. Add the hot soup. Season to taste with salt and white pepper. Serve in bowls with fried croutons. Makes 4 to 5 servings.

⚜ CREAM OF BARLEY SOUP (*Crème d'Orge*)

In the preceding recipe replace cream of rice or rice flour with ¼ cup pearl barley. Continue as directed in the recipe. Cook 3 tablespoons pearl barley in bouillon or stock 45 minutes or until done. Use to garnish the soup. Serve with fried croutons. Makes 4 to 5 servings.

❧ CREAM OF ASPARAGUS SOUP (*Crème d'Asperges*)

1½ pounds asparagus
boiling water or stock
salt
¼ cup (½ stick) butter
3 tablespoons cream of rice

6¼ cups bouillon or light stock
½ cup hot milk
2 large egg yolks
⅓ cup heavy cream
ground white pepper

Wash the asparagus, break off and discard the tough ends, and remove the scales. Cut 1¼ pounds of the asparagus into small pieces. Put the cut asparagus and the remaining whole asparagus tips in a saucepan with ½ inch boiling water or stock and ½ teaspoon salt. Cook, covered, 5 to 6 minutes. Set aside.

Soften the butter in a small saucepan and blend in the cream of rice to form a roux. Stir and cook the mixture over low heat for 2 minutes. Put the bouillon in a 2-quart saucepan, add the roux, and bring the mixture to boiling point, stirring constantly. Add the diced cooked asparagus (save the whole cooked asparagus tips for later use). Cook the soup, uncovered, over *very low* heat 20 to 30 minutes or until the asparagus is very soft. Put the soup through a fine sieve or blend in an electric blender. Add the hot milk and heat the soup 1 minute. Mix the egg yolks with the cream and stir into the hot soup. Season to taste with salt and white pepper. Garnish the soup with the reserved asparagus tips. Makes 6 to 8 servings.

❧ CREAM OF CELERY SOUP (*Crème de Céleri*)

2 cups diced celery or celeriac
1 cup boiling water
2 tablespoons (¼ stick) butter
5 cups Cream of Rice Soup (page 151)

2 large egg yolks
1 scant cup heavy cream
salt to taste
ground white pepper to taste
fried croutons

Cook the celery or celeriac in boiling water in a covered saucepan for 5 minutes. Drain off the water. Add the butter and cook, covered, for 5 minutes or until the celery or celeriac is very soft. Put it through a sieve or blend it in an electric blender, a little at a time, to form a purée. Add the purée to the Cream of Rice Soup. Stir and cook 5 minutes over medium-low heat. Mix the egg yolk with the cream, add to the soup, and heat 2 minutes. Season to taste with salt and white pepper. Serve in bowls with fried croutons. Makes 6 to 8 servings.

⚜ CREAM OF PEA SOUP (*Crème Clamart*)

2¼ pounds green peas
1 cup boiling water or stock
salt
2¼ cups milk
4¼ cups bouillon or Brown Stock
  (page 30)

3 tablespoons cream of rice
½ teaspoon sugar
2 large egg yolks
⅓ cup heavy cream
ground black pepper to taste
shredded lettuce

Shell the peas and put them in a saucepan with the boiling water or stock and ½ teaspoon salt. Cover and cook 6 to 8 minutes, or until peas are tender, lifting the cover 2 to 3 times to help the peas retain their green color. Drain the peas, saving some of the water or stock. Put the peas through a sieve, or purée them in an electric blender, ½ cup at a time, with 2 tablespoons of the reserved cooking water. Put the pea purée, 2 cups of the milk, and 4 cups of the bouillon or stock in a saucepan and heat to boiling point. Mix the remaining ¼ cup milk with the cream of rice and add it to the soup. Add the sugar. Stir and cook 10 minutes, or until the soup has thickened slightly. Blend the egg yolks with the cream and mix with the soup. Season to taste with salt and black pepper. Garnish with shredded lettuce cooked 1 minute in the remaining ¼ cup bouillon or soup stock. Makes 8 servings.

⚜ CREAM OF CAULIFLOWER SOUP (*Crème Dubarry*)

1 small head (1¼ pounds) cauliflower
boiling water or Plain White Stock
  (page 30)
salt
6 tablespoons butter
6 tablespoons flour

1¼ cups milk
5 cups bouillon or Plain White Stock
2 large egg yolks
¼ cup heavy cream
ground white pepper
fried croutons or cooked cauliflower

Remove and discard the large coarse leaves from the cauliflower. Break the head into flowerets and put them in a saucepan with 1 inch boiling water or light stock and ½ teaspoon salt. Cover, bring to boiling point, and continue cooking gently 8 to 10 minutes. Drain off and discard the water and set the cauliflower aside.

Melt the butter in a 2-quart saucepan, remove from heat, and blend in the flour. Add the milk and the bouillon or stock, mix well and cook, uncovered, 5 minutes or until the mixture has thickened slightly. Put the cooked cauliflower through a sieve or purée it in an electric blender, a little at a time. Add to the soup. Heat 1 to 2 minutes. Blend the egg yolks with the cream and mix with the hot soup. Season to taste with salt and white pepper. Serve hot in bowls, garnished with fried croutons or cooked cauliflowerets. Makes 6 to 8 servings.

153

⚜ CREAM OF LETTUCE SOUP (*Crème de Laitue*)

1 medium-sized head Romaine or
  green iceberg lettuce
boiling water
4½ to 5 cups Cream of Rice Soup
  (page 151)
½ cup milk

salt
ground white pepper
1 large egg yolk
¼ cup heavy cream
fried croutons or boiled rice

Wash and shred the lettuce, and put it in a 2-quart saucepan with ½ inch boiling water. Cover and cook 5 minutes. Drain and rinse in cold water. Then squeeze the lettuce to remove all the water and add it to the Cream of Rice Soup. Put the mixture through a sieve, or purée it in an electric blender, a little at a time. Stir in the milk and heat only until the mixture is hot. Season to taste with salt and white pepper. Blend the egg yolk with the cream and mix with the soup. Serve with croutons or boiled rice. Makes 6 servings.

VEGETABLE-PURÉE SOUPS

⚜ DRIED-BEAN SOUP (*Potage Soissonnais*)

1½ cups dried white beans or kidney
  beans
4 cups boiling water
½ cup sliced onion
½ cup sliced carrots
salt

4 cups bouillon or Brown Stock (page
  30)
1 cup milk
ground black pepper
3 tablespoons butter
¼ cup heavy cream
fried croutons

Wash the beans and place them in a 2-quart saucepan. Add the boiling water, cover, and boil 2 minutes. Turn off heat and let the beans stand in the hot water 1 hour. Add the onion, the carrots, and 1 teaspoon salt. Cook, covered, 1 hour or until beans are tender, adding additional hot water if necessary. Push the mixture through a fine sieve, or purée it in an electric blender, a little at a time. Add the bouillon or stock and the milk and bring to boiling point. Season to taste with salt and black pepper. Stir in the butter and cream. Garnish with fried croutons. Makes 6 servings. If desired, replace the dried beans in this recipe with 3 cups shelled fresh beans cooked in water until they are soft enough to purée.

⚜ CARROT SOUP WITH RICE (*Potage Crécy au Riz*)

4 slices lean bacon
⅓ cup chopped onion
5½ cups sliced carrots
3 tablespoons butter
8½ cups bouillon or Brown Stock
   (page 30)

⅓ cup raw long-grain rice
¼ cup heavy cream
salt and ground black pepper to taste
8 tablespoons boiled rice

Dice the bacon and cook it with the onions until onions are limp, 2 to 3 minutes. Add the carrots and butter. Cover the saucepan and let stand over very low heat 5 to 10 minutes. Add the bouillon or stock and the raw rice. Cover and simmer 1 hour. Strain the soup through a fine sieve, pushing as much of the vegetables and rice through as possible. If the soup is too thick, thin it to desired consistency with a little additional bouillon or soup stock. Add the cream and season to taste with salt and black pepper. Garnish each serving with 1 tablespoon boiled rice. Makes 8 servings.

⚜ THICK POTATO SOUP (*Potage Parmentier*)

3 leeks, white part only
2 tablespoons butter
7 medium-sized (2¼ pounds)
   potatoes
bouquet garni
salt

hot water
bouillon, Brown Stock (page 30), or
   water
ground black pepper
¼ cup heavy cream
croutons fried in butter

Dice the leeks and sauté them in butter until they have turned a light golden color. Peel and quarter the potatoes and add them to the leeks along with the bouquet garni, 1 teaspoon salt, and just enough hot water to cover the vegetables. Cover and cook slowly for 1 hour. Remove the bouquet garni. Strain the mixture through a fine sieve, pushing as much of the potatoes and leeks through as possible. Thin the mixture to desired consistency with a little bouillon, brown stock, or water. Add salt and black pepper to taste and the cream. Serve with croutons. To vary this soup, replace the croutons with grated Parmesan cheese, crumbled crisp bacon, fried onion rings, chopped parsley, diced cooked carrots, or grated raw carrots. Makes 8 servings.

⚜ SPLIT-PEA SOUP (*Potage Saint-Germain*)

2 cups (1 pound) split peas
cold water
6½ cups bouillon or brown stock
1 leek or scallion, green part only
1 cup diced onion
1 carrot, sliced

4 slices (10 inches long) bacon or
   lean salt pork, diced
3 tablespoons butter
bouquet garni
salt and ground black pepper to taste
¼ cup heavy cream

155

Wash the peas and soak them for 1 hour in only enough water to cover them well. Add the bouillon or stock, cover, and bring the mixture to boiling point. Skim off and discard the scum. Slice the leek or scallion and cook it with the onion, carrot, and bacon or salt pork in 1 tablespoon of the butter until the vegetables are soft. Mix with the peas. Add the bouquet garni. Cook, covered, over low heat or in a preheated slow oven (325° F.) 1 to 2 hours or until the vegetables are soft and mushy. Remove the bouquet garni. Push the mixture through a fine sieve or purée it in an electric blender, a little at a time. Season to taste with salt and black pepper. Stir in the cream and the remaining 2 tablespoons butter. Serve hot. Makes 8 servings.

⚜ PUMPKIN SOUP (*Soupe au Potiron*)

While this soup can be made with canned pumpkin, fresh pumpkin gives it a more delicate flavor and is preferred by the best French home cooks.

2 teaspoons finely chopped onion
2 teaspoons butter
1 cup cooked mashed fresh pumpkin,
    or 1 cup canned pumpkin
2⅔ cups hot chicken stock
1 tablespoon flour

1 teaspoon salt, or salt to taste
⅛ teaspoon each ground ginger and
    ground mace
1 cup top milk or light cream
1 large egg, beaten
chopped chives or parsley

Cook the onion in the butter until soft, about 2 minutes. Mix with the pumpkin and the stock in the top of a double boiler or in a saucepan. Blend the flour with the salt and spices and stir into the pumpkin mixture. Combine the milk or cream with the beaten egg and add. Cook, stirring frequently, over hot water or over low heat 5 to 10 minutes, or until hot. Serve hot, garnished with chopped chives or parsley. Makes 4 servings.

UNSTRAINED VEGETABLE SOUPS

⚜ CABBAGE SOUP (*Soupe aux Choux*)

2¼ pounds fresh or smoked pork
    hocks
½ pound pickled pigs' feet
6 cups cold water
2 cups sliced carrots
1 cup diced turnips
1½ cups sliced leeks (white part only),
    or 1½ cups diced onion

4 medium-sized potatoes, diced
½ pound sausage
salt
1 head (1½ pounds) cabbage,
    quartered
ground black pepper to taste

Rinse the meat and place it in a 4-quart saucepan or soup kettle. Add the water, cover, and cook over moderately low heat for 1½ hours. Remove and discard the scum. Add the carrots, turnips, leeks or onion, potatoes, and sausage, with 1 teaspoon salt. Cook, covered, 30 minutes. Add the cabbage and cook, covered, 20 minutes. Season to taste with salt and black pepper. Serve hot, in soup plates, with some meat and some vegetables in each. Makes 8 to 10 servings.

⚜ **JULIENNE SOUP** (*Potage Julienne*)

2 medium-sized carrots
1 turnip, 2½ inches in diameter
¼ small head of cabbage
⅓ cup thinly sliced onion
2 small leeks, white part only
¼ cup (½ stick) butter, or the fat removed from the soup stock

7 cups (3½ pints) Brown Stock (page 30)
½ teaspoon sugar
¼ teaspoon ground black pepper
salt to taste
chopped chervil or parsley

Pare the carrots and turnips and cut them into julienne strips. Cut the cabbage into julienne strips. Place all the vegetables and the butter or the fat removed from the Brown Stock in a 4-quart saucepan. Add the stock. Cover. Cook over low heat 25 to 30 minutes or until vegetables are tender. Add the sugar, pepper, and salt. Cover and simmer 10 minutes. Serve hot in bowls, sprinkled with chopped chervil or parsley. Makes 8 servings.

⚜ **MINESTRONE MILANESE STYLE**
(*Soupe aux Légumes à la Milanaise*)

¼ pound lean salt pork, diced
½ cup sliced onion
2 tablespoons olive oil or salad oil
2 tablespoons butter
2 medium-sized potatoes, diced
1 cup diced celery
1 cup sliced carrots
½ cup raw rice
2 quarts bouillon or Brown Stock (page 30)

2 cups shredded cabbage
1 cup cooked kidney beans
½ cup chopped parsley
2 tablespoons chopped fresh basil, or 2 teaspoons dried basil
1 small clove garlic, chopped fine
salt and ground black pepper to taste
grated Parmesan cheese

Cook the salt pork in enough water to cover it in a covered saucepan for 30 minutes. Put the onion and the oil and butter in a 4-quart saucepan or soup kettle and cook 2 to 3 minutes, or until the onions are golden brown. Add the cooked salt pork, the potatoes, celery, carrots, rice, and bouillon or stock. Cook, covered, over gentle heat for 45 minutes. Add all the remaining ingredients except the Parmesan cheese and cook, covered, 10 minutes. Serve hot or cold. Sprinkle each serving with 1 tablespoon grated Parmesan cheese. Makes 10 to 12 servings.

⚜ ONION SOUP WITH CHEESE (*Soupe à l'Oignon au Fromage*)

Serve in individual soup bowls with covers.

2 large onions
4 tablespoons butter or more
1 tablespoon flour
3½ cups water, bouillon, or Brown
  Stock (page 30)

salt and ground black pepper to taste
4 thin slices French bread
4 thin slices Gruyère cheese

Peel the onions and slice thin. Put them in a 2-quart saucepan with 3 table-spoons of the butter. Cook slowly until onions are golden but not browned. Dust the onions with flour; stir and cook until flour has browned. Add the water, bouillon, or stock, and salt and ground black pepper to taste. Cook, covered, 10 to 15 minutes. Meanwhile, put in each soup bowl 1 slice French bread, 1 slice cheese, and 1 pat butter. Pour in the hot soup, cover the bowls, and let stand 5 minutes before serving. If pieces of onion are not desired, strain the soup into the bowls. Makes 4 servings.

⚜ Onion Soup "Gratinee" (*Soupe à l'Oignon "Gratinée"*)

Make the preceding recipe using 1 additional tablespoon flour. Pour the soup into a casserole or ovenproof tureen, sprinkle generously with grated Gruyère or Parmesan cheese, and place it in a preheated very hot oven (450° F.) until the cheese melts, if Gruyère is used, or browns, if Parmesan is used. Makes 4 servings.

⚜ SIMPLE POT-AU-FEU (*Pot au Feu Simple*)

10 pounds beef shinbones
1½ pounds lean soup meat
4½ quarts cold water
2½ teaspoons salt
2½ cups diced carrots
1 large onion studded with 4 whole
  cloves

3 leeks
1 cup diced turnip
1 cup diced celery
1 bouquet garni
1 pound chicken giblets

Crack the bones and put them in an 8-quart saucepan. Cut the meat into 2-inch pieces and add to the bones. Add the water and salt. Cover and bring to boiling point. Skim. Add the remaining ingredients. Bring to boiling point and skim again. Simmer 3 hours. Cool. Remove the meat and bones. Skim off all fat. Serve hot. Strained, this is an excellent broth for preparing Consommé. Makes 3 quarts of broth.

⚜ SOUP SAVOYARD (*Soupe Savoyarde*)

¼ pound diced fat salt pork
½ celery root
2 leeks (white part only), sliced
1½ cups diced onion
1½ cups diced raw turnip
6½ cups water or brown stock
3 medium-sized potatoes, sliced thin

salt
2½ cups hot milk
ground black pepper
6 to 8 slices French bread
butter, softened
grated Gruyère or Parmesan cheese

Fry the salt pork lightly in a 3-quart saucepan. Add all the vegetables except the potatoes. Cover and cook over *very low* heat 10 minutes, stirring frequently. Add the water or stock. Cover and cook 20 to 25 minutes. Add the potatoes and 1 teaspoon salt, cover, and continue cooking 10 to 15 minutes, or until the potatoes are tender. Stir in the hot milk. Season to taste with salt and black pepper. Spread the bread slices with softened butter and sprinkle them with grated cheese. Put one in each soup plate and pour the hot soup over it. Makes 8 to 10 servings.

Fish

Both fish and shellfish are excellent sources of good-quality protein, many valuable minerals, and essential B complex vitamins. Their fat content is generally lower than that of meat and other quality protein foods. Because of their high protein and low calorie content, fish and shellfish are of value in many special diets. In addition, the protein of fish and shellfish is easily digested and readily available to the body. Fish is marketed in the following forms:

Whole fish are sold just as they come from the water. They must be scaled and eviscerated, and, if desired, the head, tail, and fins removed. They may be baked whole, split, or cut into serving-size portions. Small fish, such as smelts, are usually cooked with the head and tail intact.

Drawn fish have been eviscerated before they are marketed. The fish butcher generally removes the scales, head, and fins at the customer's request. The fish is split and cut into serving-size portions in preperation for cooking. Drawn fish intended for baking need the scales removed.

Dressed or pan-dressed fish are scaled and eviscerated, and the head, tail, and fins removed. Small fish are cooked as purchased. Larger dressed fish may be baked as purchased, or cut into steaks or serving-size pieces.

Fish steaks are cross-sectional slices of large dressed fish. They are ready to cook as purchased, or large ones may be divided into serving-size pieces. They are boneless except for the cross-section of backbone.

Single fillets are the sides of a fish cut separately lengthwise away from the backbone. Fillets are almost boneless. They may be skinned or cooked with the skin on, but the scales must be removed. No other preparation is necessary before cooking.

Butterfly fillets are the two fillets held together by uncut flesh and skin.

Fish sticks are pieces of fish cut from fillets or steaks into lengthwise or crosswise portions of uniform length and width.

BASIC METHODS OF COOKING FISH

The basic methods of cooking fish are poaching, broiling, pan-frying, oven-frying, deep-fat frying, baking, braising, steaming, stewing, and in chowders.

⚜ COURT BOUILLON

Court bouillons are liquids cooked only a short time with seasonings. Their composition varies with their use, from simple acidulated water (water with vinegar, lemon juice, or wine, and salt) to more highly seasoned preparations of stocks, herbs, spices, and vegetables. Fish court bouillon is used as the liquid for poaching, braising, and marinating fish.

Court bouillon for fish may be used hot or cold, depending upon the kind and size of the fish. Cold court bouillon is used for cooking large fish (salmon, trout, pike, etc.), since the cooking time is long enough to allow the vegetables in the stock to be cooked at the same time. Court bouillons for small fish, fillets, and steaks must be cooked first to allow the vegetables and condiments to impart their flavor to the fish. The court bouillon should be very hot when the fish is put into it.

One rule must be observed in cooking fish in liquid: the liquid must be kept at the simmering point and never allowed to boil while the fish is cooking; otherwise the fish will disintegrate.

½ cup diced celery
⅓ cup each diced carrots and onion
1½ tablespoons cooking oil or butter
⅔ cup dry white wine, or 3 tablespoons vinegar or lemon juice
2 stalks parsley
1 small bay leaf
1 whole clove
2 teaspoons chopped fresh thyme, or ½ teaspoon dried thyme

1½ tablespoons salt
2 pounds fish trimmings (head, tails, and fins), tied in cheesecloth bag
2 quarts cold water
6 whole black peppercorns

Cook the celery, carrots, and onion in the oil or butter in a 3-quart saucepan until the vegetables are limp but not browned. Add all the remaining ingredients except the peppercorns. Cover and slowly bring to boiling point. Reduce the heat and simmer (do not boil) 30 minutes. Add the peppercorns 10 minutes before cooking time is up. Cool. Remove the fish trimmings and strain the Court Bouillon through a double thickness of cheesecloth. Makes approximately 2 quarts.

⚜ ACIDULATED WATER

To each quart of water add 1½ tablespoons of salt and 3 tablespoons vinegar, lemon juice, or dry wine.

⚜ SIMPLE FISH STOCK

To each quart of cold water add 1 pound fish trimmings (heads, tails, fins, bones), tied in a cheesecloth bag, and 1 tablespoon salt. Bring to boiling point, reduce heat, and simmer 30 minutes. Strain.

⚜ FISH STOCK WITH VEGETABLES AND CONDIMENTS

1½ tablespoons butter	1 rib of celery, quartered
3 pounds fish trimmings (heads, bones, tails, and fins), tied in a cheesecloth bag	1 small bay leaf
	½ teaspoon dried thyme
	3 stalks parsley
2 quarts cold water	2 teaspoons salt
¼ cup each diced carrots and onion	4 whole black peppercorns

Melt the butter in a soup kettle. Add all the remaining ingredients except the peppercorns. Slowly bring to boiling point, reduce heat, and simmer, with cover ajar, for 30 minutes. Add the peppercorns 10 minutes before cooking time is up. Strain. This stock will keep in the refrigerator for 1 week. If desired, it may be frozen in containers and defrosted as needed. Makes approximately 2 quarts.

⚜ BROILED OR GRILLED FISH

This method is chiefly used for fresh fish fillets or defrosted frozen fillets, small and medium-sized whole fish, fish steaks, and slices of large fish.

Cut the fish into serving-size pieces. Small fish, such as whiting and butterfish, should be split and left whole. Sprinkle both sides with salt and ground black pepper. Place the fish on a preheated greased broiler rack. Brush with melted butter, using 4 tablespoons (½ stick) for each 2 pounds fish. Sprinkle with lemon juice. Place in the broiler 4 inches from the source of heat. Broil 5 to 8 minutes. Turn carefully, brush the other side with butter, sprinkle with lemon juice, and broil 5 to 8 minutes, or until fish is flaky. Transfer the fish carefully to a warmed platter and serve immediately, with Herb Butter or Béarnaise Sauce if desired. Allow 1½ pounds fish for 4 servings.

⚜ BRAISED FISH

This is an excellent method of cooking large whole fish such as carp, halibut, pike, salmon, sturgeon, and trout.

1 cup sliced carrots
½ cup sliced onion
1 shallot, or the white part of 1 green onion, sliced
4 tablespoons (½ stick) butter, melted
¼ cup coarsely chopped parsley
4- to 5-pound whole fish, dressed (carp, halibut, pike, salmon, sturgeon, or trout)

salt and ground black pepper
3 strips bacon or salt pork, 4 inches long
dry red or white wine, and/or Court Bouillon or Fish Stock
2 teaspoons cornstarch
4 tablespoons (¼ cup) heavy cream

Toss the first 3 ingredients with the melted butter and the parsley. Butter a baking dish that can be used for cooking over surface heat and is large enough to accommodate the fish. Spread the butter and vegetable mixture over the bottom of the dish. Sprinkle the skin and the inside of the fish lightly with salt and black pepper. Place the fish on the vegetables. Make 3 slashes ¼ inch deep across the top of the fish, brush it with melted butter, and lay the strips of bacon or salt pork on top. Pour in wine, Court Bouillon, or Fish Stock (or equal parts of wine and Court Bouillon or Fish Stock) to fill the pan to half the thickness of the fish. Place the baking dish over surface heat and bring the liquid to boiling point. Then place the dish in a preheated slow oven (325° F.) and cook only until the fish flakes when tested with a fork (30 to 40 minutes), basting the fish 3 times with the cooking liquid. Transfer the fish to a warmed platter. Boil the pan liquid, uncovered, until it has reduced to one-half the original amount. Blend the cornstarch with 2 tablespoons of the cream and mix with the reduced liquid. Stir and cook 2 minutes. Add the remaining cream and serve over the fish. Makes 4 to 5 servings.

⚜ DEEP-FAT-FRIED FISH

This method is especially suitable for cooking dressed whole small fish, fish fillets, fish sticks, and fish steaks. (*See* Deep-Fat Frying, page 12.)

1½ pounds fillets, steaks, or pan-dressed fish
¾ teaspoon salt
⅛ teaspoon ground black pepper

1 medium-sized egg, beaten lightly with 2 teaspoons water or milk
¾ cup fine dry breadcrumbs, cracker crumbs, or Batter (see following recipe)

Cut the fish into serving-size pieces. Sprinkle both sides with salt and black pepper. Dip the fish into the beaten egg and then roll it in crumbs or batter. Place one layer of fish at a time in a frying basket, lower it into deep fat preheated to 375° F., and fry 3 to 6 minutes or until fish is golden brown. Remove from fat and drain on paper towels. Serve promptly. Makes 4 servings.

⚜ Batter for Frying Fish

1 large egg	½ cup milk
½ teaspoon salt	½ cup sifted all-purpose flour

Beat the egg, salt, and milk together. Add all the flour at one time, mix, and beat until smooth. Use as a coating for fish, shellfish, chicken, vegetables, etc., for pan-frying or deep-fat-frying. Makes enough batter for 4 to 6 servings.

⚜ OVEN-FRIED FISH

1½ pounds fish fillets or steaks	flour or fine dry breadcrumbs
1 teaspoon salt	3 tablespoons butter, melted
⅛ teaspoon ground black pepper	
milk	

Cut the fish into serving-size piece. Add the salt and black pepper to the milk and mix well. Dip the fish into the milk and then roll it in flour or breadcrumbs. Place the fish in a well-buttered baking pan and spoon the melted butter over it. Place the pan on the top rack of a preheated very hot oven (500° F.). Bake 10 to 12 minutes or until the fish flakes when tested with a fork. Serve at once on a warm platter, plain, or with a sauce. Makes 4 servings.

⚜ PAN-FRIED FISH (*Les Poissons à la Meunière*)

1½ pounds dressed fish	about ⅓ cup flour, fine dry bread-
1 teaspoon salt	crumbs, cracker crumbs, or corn-
¼ teaspoon ground black pepper	meal
1 large egg, lightly beaten	1 tablespoon butter
3 tablespoons milk	2 tablespoons shortening
	lemon wedges

Cut the fish into serving-size pieces. Rub both sides with the salt and black pepper. Beat the egg with the milk, and dip the fish into the mixture, then roll it in flour, breadcrumbs, cracker crumbs, or cornmeal. Heat the butter and shortening in a 9- or 10-inch skillet and fry the fish over moderate heat, turning carefully to brown both sides, until the fish has browned and is flaky. Cooking time is about 10 minutes, depending upon the thickness of the fish. Drain on paper towels. Serve promptly, garnished with lemon wedges. Makes 4 servings.

⚜ POACHED FISH

Fish may be poached in Court Bouillon or fish stock, or wine, or a combination of broth and wine, either in the oven or by simmering over surface heat. Either method is especially adapted to small fish, fish fillets, and fish steaks.

⚜ Oven Method of Poaching Fish

¼ cup diced onion
1 shallot, diced
1½ pounds fish fillets or fish steaks
salt and ground white pepper

Court Bouillon or Simple Fish Stock
  (pages 161–162), or dry white wine
2 teaspoons cornstarch
4 tablespoons (¼ cup) heavy cream

Scatter the onion and shallot over the bottom of a buttered shallow 9-inch baking dish and spread the fish over them. Sprinkle the fish lightly with salt and white pepper. Pour in sufficient Court Bouillon, fish stock, or wine nearly to cover the fish. Cover the baking dish with buttered paper or foil. Bake in a preheated slow oven (325° F.) *only* until fish flakes when tested with a fork, about 15 minutes. Drain the liquid from the baking dish into a small saucepan. Boil it to reduce it slightly. Blend the cornstarch with 2 tablespoons of the cream, add to the reduced liquid, and mix well. Stir and cook 2 minutes. Add the remaining cream and salt and pepper to taste. Serve over the fish. Makes 4 servings.

⚜ Simmering Method of Poaching Fish

1½ pounds fish fillets

1½ quarts boiling Court Bouillon, Simple Fish Stock, or Acidulated Water (see pages 161–162)

Cut the fish into serving-size pieces and place them on a plate. Tie the plate in cheesecloth. Lower the plate of fish into the boiling liquid, reduce heat, and simmer (never boil) 10 minutes or until fish is flaky when tested with a fork. Carefully remove the fish to a warm platter. Serve with Herb Butter; Curry or Tarragon Sauce; Hollandaise, Béarnaise, Rémoulade, or Tartare Sauce (see Index). Makes 4 servings.

⚜ STEAMED FISH

3 pounds dressed whole fish or 1½
  pounds fish steak or fillets
salt

ground black pepper
hot water

Sprinkle the fish with salt and black pepper. Wrap it in a piece of cheesecloth and tie the ends. Place a rack or trivet in a Dutch oven or saucepan, pour in hot water to the level of the rack, and place the fish on the rack. Cover tightly. Steam whole fish 30 minutes, steaks or fillets 12 minutes, or until fish flakes when tested with a fork. Open the cheesecloth and carefully transfer the fish to a warm platter. Remove skin and bones, if desired. Serve with Egg Sauce (page 39) or Herb Butter (page 58). Makes 4 servings.

BASS (*Bar*)

There are many varieties of bass, both marine and freshwater. It is a delicately flavored fish which lends itself to numerous methods of preparation. Small bass may be grilled, pan-fried, deep-fat-fried, or poached; larger ones may be poached, braised, or baked, with or without stuffing. Bass may also be served cold with Vinaigrette Sauce (page 56) or Rémoulade Sauce (page 55).

✣ BAKED BASS (*Bar Rôti*)

4-pound dressed bass or gray mullet
salt and ground black pepper to taste
olive oil or salad oil
flour

melted butter
Herb Butter (page 58)
boiled potatoes

Rub the fish with salt and black pepper, brush it with oil, and roll it in flour. Place in a well-buttered baking dish large enough to accommodate the fish. Bake in a preheated moderate oven (350° F.) 25 to 30 minutes or until the fish flakes when tested with a fork, basting with melted butter 3 times. Serve with Herb Butter and boiled potatoes. Makes 4 servings.

✣ SEA BASS À LA GRECQUE (*Bar à la Grecque*)

1 quart mussels
Court Bouillon (page 161)
⅓ cup Vinaigrette Sauce (page 56)
½ pound small whole mushrooms

2 tablespoons chopped parsley
2-pound sea bass, dressed
2 medium-sized tomatoes
6 pitted black olives

Scrub the mussels thoroughly and steam them in Court Bouillon in a covered kettle until the shells open, 8 to 10 minutes. Cool them in the broth. Drain off the liquid. Remove the mussels from the shells and remove and discard the beards. Add the mussels to the Vinaigrette Sauce. Cook the mushrooms in boiling water 1 to 2 minutes, drain, rinse in cold water, and add to the Vinaigrette Sauce with the parsley. Chill 30 minutes. Poach the sea bass in Court Bouillon as directed for Poaching Fish. Cool in the Court Bouillon. Cut the fish into serving portions. Arrange the mussel and mushroom salad on a serving platter and place the fish on top. Garnish with tomato wedges and ripe olives. Makes 4 servings. (*See illustration, page 191.*)

BRILL (*Barbue*)

Brill is a flat marine fish related to turbot. It is more abundant in European waters than in the Atlantic Ocean, though brill caught in the Atlantic is more highly esteemed. The flesh is delicate and light, similar to sole. Brill is a luxury fish and may be prepared in the same way as sole, flounder, and turbot.

⚜ BROILED BRILL (*Barbue Grillé*)

Cut the fish into serving portions. Sprinkle both sides lightly with salt and ground white pepper. Place on a greased broiler rack. Brush with melted butter, using 4 tablespoons for each 2 pounds of fish. Sprinkle with lemon juice. Place the broiler 4 inches from the source of heat. Broil 5 to 8 minutes. Turn carefully, brush the other side with butter, sprinkle with lemon juice, and broil 5 to 8 minutes or until fish is flaky. Transfer the fish carefully to a warmed platter and garnish with parsley. Serve with Béarnaise Sauce (page 53) or Hollandaise Sauce (page 52) or melted seasoned butter. Makes 6 servings.

BURBOT (*Lotte de Rivière*)

Burbot, a member of the cod family, is a freshwater fish of the Northern Hemisphere. In the United States it is sometimes called freshwater cusk. It can be prepared in the same ways as cod, haddock, or hake, except that it should never be fried, because it gives off too much moisture. Burbot liver, highly prized by connoisseurs, is prepared in the same way as roe but must be poached longer. In Europe the liver is sometimes poached in white wine and made into pâté.

⚜ FILLETS OF BURBOT (*Filets de Lotte Dugléré*)

1 medium-sized onion, diced	⅓ cup dry white wine
4 medium-sized tomatoes, chopped	4 tablespoons butter
2 tablespoons chopped parsley	1 tablespoon tomato paste
1½ pounds dressed burbot	1 tablespoon flour
salt and ground black pepper	3 tablespoons fine dry breadcrumbs

Place the onion, tomatoes, and parsley in an 8- by 8- by 2-inch baking dish. Cut the fish into 4 serving portions and rub both sides with salt and black pepper. Arrange over the vegetables. Add the wine and place ½ tablespoon of the butter on each portion of fish. Bake, uncovered, in a preheated moderate oven (350° F.) 20 minutes or until the fish flakes when tested with a fork. Transfer the fish to a heatproof platter and keep it warm. Cook the pan liquid over surface heat to reduce it to one-half the original amount. Add the tomato paste. Blend the flour with 2 tablespoons of the butter and add to the reduced liquid. Stir and cook 1 minute or until the mixture has thickened. Pour over the fish. Sprinkle with breadcrumbs and dot with the rest of the butter. Brown under broiler heat or in a preheated hot oven (425° F.) Makes 4 servings.

CARP (*Carpe*)

Carp, a freshwater fish, was originally introduced from China. Today it is so common in the United States that it is sometimes considered a nuisance because it crowds out other fish.

Carp weighing between 2 and 8 pounds are available in many of the Middle Atlantic and Midwestern states from November through March. The meat is lean and has a muddy taste. Seasoned fishermen sometimes keep carp in clean, fresh water a month or so before eating them. Carp may be bought whole or in fillets or steaks, fresh, frozen, and smoked. It may be fried, poached, or stuffed and baked.

⚜ CARP À LA MARINIÈRE (*Carpe à la Marinière*)

4 pounds carp
salt and ground black pepper
¾ pound mushrooms, sliced
2 shallots or small white onions, sliced
1 cup dry white wine
¼ cup hot water

2 tablespoons chopped parsley
2 tablespoons fine dry breadcrumbs
¼ cup (½ stick) butter, softened
8 fried smelts or other very small fried fish
lemon wedges

Ask the butcher to scale and clean the carp. Sprinkle each side lightly with salt and black pepper. Place the fish in a baking dish and surround it with the sliced mushrooms and shallots or onions. Sprinkle with salt and black pepper. Pour in the wine and hot water. (Do not cover the fish with the liquid.) Sprinkle the fish with chopped parsley. Blend the breadcrumbs with the butter and spread over the fish. Bake in a preheated moderate oven (350° F.) 30 to 35 minutes or until the fish flakes when tested with a fork. Just before serving, arrange the smelts or other small fish around the carp, being careful not to immerse them in the sauce. Garnish with lemon wedges. Makes 4 servings.

COD, HADDOCK, HAKE (*Cabillaud, Aiglefin, Colin*)

These three fishes belong to the same family. All have white, lean, fragile flesh, and they may be used interchangeably in most recipes. All are good fried, baked, in stews, in croquettes, cakes, or patties, and poached in Court Bouillon or Fish Stock and served with Rémoulade or Tartare Sauce. Dried salt codfish is called *morue* in France, and dried hake is called *merluche*. In Scotland smoked haddock is called finnan haddie.

⚜ FRIED COD WITH TARTARE SAUCE
(*Cabillaud Frit, Sauce Tartare*)

1½ pounds cod
salt and ground black pepper to taste
1 large egg, beaten with 1 tablespoon milk or water

fine dry breadcrumbs
fried or fresh parsley
Tartare Sauce (page 55)

Cut the fish into serving-size portions ½ inch thick. Sprinkle both sides lightly with salt and black pepper. Beat the egg with the milk or water and dip the pieces of fish into the egg and then roll them in bread crumbs. Let the fish stand 20 minutes. Fry in deep fat preheated to 375° F. or pan-fry in shallow fat (shortening or salad oil), turning to brown both sides. Drain on paper towels. The fish may be rolled in flour instead of in egg and breadcrumbs and pan-fried in shallow fat. Serve on a warmed platter garnished with fried or fresh parsley. Serve Tartare Sauce separately. Makes 4 servings.

⚜ COD LYONNAISE STYLE (*Cabillaud à la Lyonnaise*)

1½ pounds cod
salt and ground black pepper to taste
milk
flour

4 tablespoons (½ stick) butter
4 small white onions, sliced
fried parsley or fresh parsley
lemon wedges

Cut the fish into serving-size pieces ½ inch thick. Sprinkle both sides with salt and black pepper. Dip the slices in milk and then roll them in flour. Pan-fry the fish in 3 tablespoons of the butter, adding it as needed, browning both sides. Sprinkle lightly with salt and arrange on a warmed platter. Meanwhile fry the onions in the remaining 1 tablespoon butter in a separate pan and spread them over the fish. Garnish with fried parsley or fresh parsley and lemon wedges. Makes 4 servings.

⚜ COD MISTRAL (*Cabillaud Mistral*)

1½ pounds cod steaks, cut ½ inch thick
salt and ground black pepper to taste
flour
3 tablespoons oil or shortening
2 medium-large tomatoes

¾ cup sliced mushrooms
⅓ cup dry white wine
½ small clove garlic, crushed
½ cup fresh breadcrumbs
3 tablespoons butter, melted
chopped parsley

Cut the fish into 4 servings. Rub both sides with salt and black pepper. Roll the pieces in flour and fry over moderate heat in the oil or shortening until browned on both sides. Transfer the fish to a baking dish. Peel and seed the tomatoes and dice coarsely. Mix with the mushrooms, wine, garlic, and salt and black pepper to taste. Bring to boiling point and pour over fish. Mix the breadcrumbs with the melted butter and sprinkle over the top. Cook in a preheated moderate oven (350° F.) 30 minutes or until crumbs are brown. Serve hot as an entrée, sprinkled with chopped parsley. Makes 4 servings.

⚜ HAKE OR COD WITH EGG SAUCE (*Colin à la Sauce aux Oeufs*)

1½ pounds fresh hake or cod fillets or steaks
Court Bouillon (page 161) or Simple Fish Stock (page 162)
½ teaspoon powdered mustard

1 teaspoon water
1 cup Béchamel Sauce (page 38)
3 hard-cooked eggs
1 tablespoon chopped parsley
salt and ground white pepper to taste

Cut the fish into 4 servings. Poach in Court Bouillon or Fish Stock (see Poached Fish, page 165). Drain well and place on a warmed platter. Soak the mustard in the water for 5 minutes and add to the Béchamel Sauce. Chop 2 of the eggs and blend with the sauce along with the parsley and salt and white pepper to taste. Serve over the fish. Slice the remaining hard-cooked egg and arrange the slices over the fish. Makes 4 servings.

⚜ POACHED HAKE OR COD ENGLISH STYLE (*Colin à l'Anglaise*)

2 pounds fresh hake or cod
boiling Simple Fish Stock (page 162), or boiling water with 1 tablespoon vinegar
6 servings boiled potatoes

2 lemons
parsley
2 strips tomato or pimiento
6 tablespoons butter, melted

Poach the fish in boiling Fish Stock, or in salted water with 1 tablespoon vinegar (see Poached Fish, page 165). Drain the fish well. Carefully transfer it to a warmed platter, and arrange boiled potatoes on each side. Cut 1 of the lemons into thin slices and arrange on top of the fish. Cut the remaining lemon in half, notch the edges, and put one half at each end of the platter with parsley. Decorate the lemon halves with a strip of tomato or pimiento. Serve the melted butter in a separate bowl. Makes 6 servings. (*See illustration, page 191.*)

⚜ HAKE OR COD WITH MORNAY SAUCE
(*Colin ou Cabillaud Mornay*)

½ cup dry white wine
1½ pounds fresh hake or cod fillets
   or steaks
3 tablespoons flour
3 tablespoons butter, melted

¾ cup hot milk
½ cup grated Gruyère or Cheddar
   cheese
salt and ground white pepper to taste
buttered soft breadcrumbs

Pour the wine into a 9-inch skillet and bring to boiling point. Arrange the fish in a single layer in the wine, cover, and cook over moderately low heat until the fish flakes when tested with a fork, 5 to 6 minutes. Keep the fish warm while making the sauce. Blend the flour with the butter and stir and cook until the mixture is foamy, 1 to 2 minutes. Remove from heat and beat in the milk. Return to heat and cook until the sauce is very thick, stirring constantly. Thin the sauce with ⅓ cup of the wine in which the fish was cooked. Add the cheese and salt and white pepper to taste. Place the cooked fish in a buttered 9- by 9- by 2-inch baking dish, and pour the sauce over it. Sprinkle with buttered breadcrumbs. Brown quickly, about 10 minutes, in a preheated hot oven (425° F.). Makes 4 servings.

⚜ HAKE OR COD FILLETS BERCY (*Filets de Colin Bercy*)

2-pound whole cod or hake
salt and ground white pepper to taste
1 shallot or small white onion,
   chopped
4 tablespoons (½ stick) butter
⅓ cup dry white wine

1 cup Simple Fish Stock (page 162)
2 teaspoons lemon juice
2 tablespoons chopped parsley
1½ tablespoons flour
½ cup buttered soft breadcrumbs

Ask the fish butcher to remove the head, tail, fins and bones from the fish. Use these to make fish stock. (See Simple Fish Stock.) Cut the fish into 4 portions. Sprinkle both sides lightly with salt and white pepper and arrange in a buttered 8- by 8- by 2-inch baking dish. Cook the shallot or onion ½ minute in 1 tablespoon of the butter. Add the wine and cook the mixture until it has reduced to 3 tablespoons. Add the fish stock, lemon juice, and 1 tablespoon of the parsley. Soften the remaining 2 tablespoons butter, blend in the flour, and add to the wine and stock mixture. Mix well. Stir and cook until the sauce boils up twice. Add salt and white pepper to taste and the remaining 1 tablespoon butter, and pour the sauce over the fish. Sprinkle with buttered breadcrumbs. Bake in a preheated moderate oven (350° F.) 25 minutes or until the crumbs are brown and the fish flakes when tested with a fork. Sprinkle with the remaining 1 tablespoon chopped parsley. Serve promptly. Makes 4 servings.

⚜ BREADED HAKE OR COD FILLETS, ENGLISH STYLE
(*Colin ou Cabillaud à l'Anglaise*)

⅓ cup milk	fine dry breadcrumbs
½ teaspoon salt	2 tablespoons butter
⅛ teaspoon ground black pepper	Herb Butter (page 58), or melted
1½ pounds fresh hake or cod fillets	butter and lemon juice
flour	4 servings boiled potatoes
1 large egg white, beaten until frothy	

Combine the milk, salt, and pepper. Dip the fillets in the milk, then roll them in flour, dip them in the beaten egg white, and roll them in fine, dry breadcrumbs. Let stand 10 minutes. Pan-fry slowly in the butter, browning both sides. Or if desired, place the fish on well-buttered baking sheets and dot with butter. Bake in a preheated moderate oven (350° F.) 25 minutes or until the crumbs are brown. Serve with Herb Butter, or with melted butter and lemon juice, and accompany with boiled potatoes. Makes 4 servings.

⚜ HAKE OR COD FILLETS FLORENTINE STYLE
(*Filets de Colin à la Florentine*)

1 pound hake or cod fillets	dash ground nutmeg
fish stock	salt and ground black pepper to taste
1½ pounds fresh spinach, or 1 10-	1 cup Mornay Sauce (page 40)
ounce package frozen spinach	2 tablespoons dry white wine
5 tablespoons butter	3 tablespoons grated Gruyère or
¼ teaspoon sugar	Cheddar cheese

Poach fish fillets in stock (see Poached Fish). Cook the spinach, drain well, and heat with 3 tablespoons of the butter. Add the seasonings. Spread the spinach over the bottom of a well-buttered baking dish and arrange the fish over it. Combine the Mornay Sauce and the wine, stir and cook 2 minutes, and pour over the fish. Meanwhile melt the remaining 2 tablespoons butter. Sprinkle the fish with the melted butter and the grated cheese. Bake in a preheated hot oven (425° F.) 10 to 15 minutes, or brown under broiler heat. Makes 4 servings.

⚜ HAKE OR COD FILLETS PROVENÇAL
(Filets de Colin à la Provençale)

1½ pounds fresh cod or hake
dry white wine
½ teaspoon dried thyme
1 small bay leaf
1 shallot, chopped
salt and ground black pepper to taste
2 tablespoons chopped onion

1 tablespoon olive oil or salad oil
2 medium-sized tomatoes
¹⁄₁₆ teaspoon crushed garlic
1 tablespoon chopped parsley
2 tablespoons fine dry breadcrumbs
2 tablespoons butter, melted

Cut the fish into serving portions ½ inch thick, and put them in an ovenproof dish with the wine, ¼ teaspoon of the thyme, the shallot, ½ bay leaf, salt and black pepper. Poach as in Oven Method of Poaching Fish (page 165). Arrange the fish on a warmed platter and keep warm. Reserve the wine. Brown the onion in the oil in a 1-quart saucepan. Peel, seed, and dice the tomatoes, and add to the onion. Stir in the garlic, parsley, the remaining ¼ teaspoon thyme, the remaining ½ bay leaf, and ⅓ cup of the wine from the poached fish. Bring to boiling point and boil briskly for 5 minutes or until the sauce has thickened. Add salt and black pepper to taste. Pour the sauce over the fish. Mix the breadcrumbs with melted butter and sprinkle them on top. Brown in a preheated moderate oven (350° F.) 15 minutes. Makes 4 servings. *(See illustration, page 190.)*

⚜ COD OR HAKE FILLETS PORTUGUESE STYLE
(Cabillaud ou Colin à la Portugaise)

1½ pounds cod or hake fillets
salt
ground black pepper
4 tablespoons (¼ cup) olive oil or
salad oil
¼ cup chopped onion

3 medium-sized tomatoes, peeled and
seeded
½ small clove garlic, crushed
⅓ cup dry white wine
½ teaspoon sugar
chopped parsley

Sprinkle the fish fillets with ¾ teaspoon salt, ⅛ teaspoon black pepper, and 2 tablespoons of the oil. Place in a baking dish. Put the remaining 2 tablespoons oil in a saucepan with the onion, tomatoes, and garlic. Stir and cook 5 to 6 minutes or until tomatoes are soft and the mixture has thickened. Add the wine, the sugar, and salt and pepper to taste. Pour over the fish. Bake in a preheated moderate oven (350° F.) 25 minutes. Serve hot as an entrée, sprinkled with chopped parsley. Any fish fillets may be prepared the same way. Makes 4 servings.

⚜ **POACHED HAKE OR COD STEAKS** (*Darnes de Colin Pochées*)

Allow ⅓ to ½ pound fish per serving. Poach the fish in boiling Court Bouillon (page 161) or Acidulated Water (page 162) as directed in the Simmering Method for Poaching Fish (page 165). Sprinkle with lemon juice to taste. Garnish each serving with a whole mushroom cap, cooked in butter. Serve with melted butter. (*See illustration, page 192.*)

⚜ **COLD HAKE OR COD RUSSIAN STYLE** (*Colin Froid à la Russe*)

Any cooked fish may be used for this dish.

1 pound hake or cod all in 1 piece with the skin on	½ teaspoon salt
	4 servings Russian Salad (page 402)
boiling water	mayonnaise
2 teaspoons vinegar	4 anchovy fillets

Place the fish in boiling water, reduce the heat, add the vinegar and salt, cover, and simmer 15 minutes or until the fish flakes when tested with a fork. Drain the water from the fish and remove the skin and bones. Chill. Place fish on a chilled platter. Arrange Russian Salad at each end of the platter. Decorate with mayonnaise piped through a pastry bag. Garnish as desired with the anchovy fillets. Makes 4 servings.

⚜ **CODFISH WITH CREAM** (*Morue à la Crème*)

1 pound dried salt codfish	½ cup light cream
milk	¼ teaspoon vinegar
flour	ground black pepper to taste
3 tablespoons butter	chopped parsley

Soak the codfish in cold water 12 hours or overnight. Remove from the water, rinse in fresh cold water, and wipe dry. Cut into serving portions. Dip the pieces in milk, then in flour, and fry slowly in the butter until pale brown on both sides. Transfer to a warmed platter. Pour the cream into the skillet, add the vinegar, and boil briskly 2 minutes. Season with black pepper to taste. Pour over the fish. Sprinkle with chopped parsley. Serve hot. Makes 4 servings.

⚜ **CODFISH À LA MÉNAGÈRE** (*Morue à la Ménagère*)

1 pound dried salt codfish	¾ cup hot milk
hot water to cover	¼ cup hot fish liquor
¼ cup finely chopped onion	salt and ground white pepper to taste
3 tablespoons butter	4 medium-large hot boiled potatoes
2 tablespoons flour	

Soak the codfish 24 hours in cold water, changing the water 5 times. Cut the fish into 3 or 4 pieces and put them in a saucepan with sufficient hot water to cover. Cook, uncovered, below boiling point 10 to 15 minutes or until the fish flakes. Remove from the water and drain well. Reserve ¼ cup of the liquid. Keep the fish warm. Cook the onion in the butter until soft, without letting it brown. Remove from heat and blend in the flour. Cook over medium-low heat, stirring constantly, until the mixture is foamy. Beat in the milk and the fish liquor. Cook, stirring constantly, until the sauce is of medium thickness. Season to taste with salt and white pepper. Slice the potatoes and arrange them on a platter. Sprinkle them with salt and white pepper. Flake the hot fish, arrange it over the potatoes, and cover with the hot sauce. Makes 4 servings.

⚜ SAUTÉED CODFISH AND TOMATOES (*Morue Sautée aux Tomates*)

1 pound dried salt codfish	½ small clove garlic, crushed
flour	¼ teaspoon sugar
4 tablespoons butter	3 tablespoons chopped parsley
4 medium-sized tomatoes	salt and ground black pepper to taste

Soak the codfish in cold water 24 hours, changing the water 5 times. Drain off the water and wipe the fish dry. Cut it into 4 serving portions. Roll the pieces in flour and brown them slowly in the butter, turning to brown both sides. Transfer to a warmed platter and keep warm. Peel, seed, and chop the tomatoes. In the same skillet, cook the tomatoes, garlic, sugar, and 1 tablespoon of the parsley until the tomatoes are soft. Season to taste with salt and black pepper. Pour the mixture over the codfish and sprinkle with the remaining 2 tablespoons chopped parsley. Serve hot. Makes 4 servings.

⚜ BAKED SMOKED HADDOCK (*Finnan Haddie*)

Soak 1½ pounds finnan haddie 2 hours in enough cold water to cover it. Drain. Cut the fish into 6 portions and place in a buttered baking dish. Brush with melted butter and pour in sufficient hot milk to cover the fish. Bake in a preheated moderate oven (350° F.) for 20 minutes. Transfer the drained fish to a warmed platter and serve with Parsley Butter, made by mixing 1 tablespoon chopped parsley with ¼ cup (½ stick) softened butter. Accompany with potatoes. Makes 6 servings.

EEL (*Anguille*)

Eel is an elongated fish with a smooth skin, often without scales or fins. The flesh is delicately flavored, especially when the eel is caught in fast-running

175

water. Eel may be fried, broiled, poached in Court Bouillon, or used as an ingredient in Bouillabaisse. The average market sizes of American eels are: small, under 1 pound; medium, 1 to 2 pounds; large, 3 to 5 pounds.

⚜ FRIED EEL (*Anguille Frite*)

Cut a dressed 2-pound eel into 3-inch lengths. Dry the pieces. Beat 1 egg with 1 tablespoon milk and dip the pieces in it, then roll them in fine dry bread-crumbs or cornmeal. Fry in deep fat preheated to 375° F. 2 to 5 minutes or until browned. Drain on paper towels. Or, if desired, pan-fry in a small amount of shortening or salad oil 5 to 8 minutes, turning to brown both sides. Serve plain or with Vinaigrette Sauce, Tomato Sauce, Sauce Diable, or Herb Butter (see Index). Makes 4 servings.

⚜ GRILLED EEL WITH TARTARE SAUCE (*Anguille Grillée Tartare*)

1 medium-sized onion, sliced	1¼ cups dry red wine
1 shallot, chopped	1 large egg white, beaten until foamy
1 small clove garlic, chopped	fine dry breadcrumbs
2 stalks parsley	olive oil or salad oil
1½ pounds dressed freshwater eel	fried parsley or fresh parsley
1 teaspoon salt	Tartare Sauce (page 55)

Place the first 4 ingredients in a deep 9-inch skillet. Cut the eel into serving portions, rub both sides with salt, and put the pieces in the skillet over the vegetables. Add the wine, cover, and cook below boiling point 20 minutes or until the eel flakes when tested with a fork. Remove the eel from the skillet and wipe the pieces dry. Dip them in the egg white and then roll them in breadcrumbs. Fry in deep fat preheated to 375° F., or pan-fry in shallow hot fat, browning both sides. Serve garnished with fried parsley or fresh parsley. Pass Tartare Sauce in a separate bowl. Makes 4 servings.

⚜ EEL IN GREEN SAUCE (*Anguille au Vert*)

This is a Belgian dish.

1½ pounds dressed freshwater eel	⅓ cup dry white wine
6 tablespoons butter	hot water to cover
½ cup chopped parsley	3 egg yolks, beaten lightly
1 tablespoon chopped sorrel (sour-	1 teaspoon cornstarch or potato starch
grass)	2 tablespoons lemon juice
1 tablespoon chopped fresh chervil	ground black pepper to taste
1 teaspoon chopped fresh sage	2 carrots cut in julienne strips, cooked
1 teaspoon chopped fresh savory	chopped parsley
salt	

Cut the eel into serving-size pieces. Melt the butter in a 9-inch skillet and add the eel. Sprinkle with the herbs and ½ teaspoon salt. Pour in the wine and add enough hot water to cover. Cover and simmer 20 to 25 minutes. Blend the egg yolks with the cornstarch or potato starch and the lemon juice and gradually mix with a little of the eel liquor. Add to the eel and simmer 1 minute (do not boil). Season to taste with black pepper and salt if needed. Rearrange the eel attractively in the skillet and spoon some of the sauce over it. Garnish with the cooked carrot julienne strips and chopped parsley. Serve hot or cold. Makes 6 servings. (*See illustration, page 226.*)

⚜ POACHED EEL (*Anguille Pochée*)

1½ pounds dressed eel	1 teaspoon salt
¼ cup sliced onion	boiling water
1 stalk parsley	lemon slices
2 teaspoons vinegar or lemon juice	4 tablespoons (½ stick) butter, melted
3 whole black peppercorns	

Cut the eel into serving-size pieces and place in a saucepan with the next 5 ingredients and boiling water to cover. Simmer 10 to 15 minutes or until the eel flakes when tested with a fork. Transfer to a serving dish and garnish with lemon slices. Serve with melted butter. Makes 4 servings.

⚜ EEL STEW BURGUNDY STYLE
(*Anguille en Matelote à la Bourguignonne*)

In French cookery a *matelote* is a fish stew cooked in red or white wine.

1 medium-sized onion, sliced	¼ pound mushrooms, sliced
1 shallot, chopped	10 small white onions, cut in half
1 small clove garlic, chopped fine	4 tablespoons butter
2 stalks parsley	2 tablespoons flour
1½ pounds dressed freshwater eel	½ teaspoon caramel or Kitchen
1 teaspoon salt	Bouquet
¼ cup liqueur brandy (optional)	ground black pepper to taste
1¼ cups dry red wine	croutons fried in butter

Put the first 4 ingredients in a deep 9-inch skillet. Cut the eel into finger-sized strips, rub with the salt, and put in the skillet over the vegetables. Place the pan over the heat. If brandy is used, add it and ignite it. Pour in the wine. Cover and cook 20 minutes over moderately low heat. Transfer the strips of eel to a warmed serving dish and keep warm. Reserve the liquid in the skillet. Cook the mushrooms and white onions in 2 tablespoons of the butter 10 minutes, then add them to the liquid in the skillet. Cook, uncovered, until the liquid has reduced slightly. Soften the remaining 2 tablespoons butter, blend with the flour, then blend the mixture with the liquid in the skillet. Stir and cook 2 to 3 minutes or until the liquid has thickened slightly. Color the sauce with a little caramel or Kitchen Bouquet. Season to taste with additional salt and black pepper. Pour over the eel. Garnish with butter-fried croutons. Makes 4 servings.

FLOUNDER

The name flounder is applied to a number of American and European flatfish. Flounder is often sold as sole, but the true European sole belongs to a different family. The American summer flounder is also called plaice but is not the same species as the European plaice (*carrelet*). Generally speaking, any of the flatfish designated as flounder, plaice, or sole can be used interchangeably in recipes. See Sole.

⚜ .FLOUNDER AU GRATIN

2 whole dressed summer flounder (plaice), 1 pound each
salt and ground black pepper to taste
¼ pound mushrooms, sliced
5 tablespoons butter
1 tablespoon flour

⅓ cup dry white wine
⅓ cup water
2 tablespoons tomato purée
½ cup soft breadcrumbs
chopped parsley

Sprinkle the whole dressed fish lightly with salt and black pepper and lay them in an oblong baking dish. Cook the mushrooms in 3 tablespoons of the butter until soft, 4 to 5 minutes. Sprinkle with flour and mix well. Stir in the wine, water, and tomato purée, and season to taste with salt and black pepper. Pour over the fish. Sprinkle with breadcrumbs and dot with the remaining 2 tablespoons butter. Bake in a preheated moderate oven (350° F.) 30 minutes or until crumbs are brown. Sprinkle with parsley. Serve at once. Makes 4 servings.

HERRING (*Hareng*)

Herring is a deep-sea fish, 10 to 12 inches long. It is abundant in the North Atlantic and North Pacific and is considered one of the world's most important seafoods. Since the flesh is fat and has a strong flavor it tastes best when highly seasoned. Fresh herring may be baked, broiled, fried, and used in salads, but herring is really at its best pickled, salted, and smoked. Kippered herring is lightly smoked herring, which must be kept refrigerated until ready to use. In America young fresh herring are canned extensively as sardines.

⚜ **GRILLED FRESH HERRING WITH MUSTARD SAUCE**
(*Harengs Grillés à la Sauce Moutarde*)

1½ pounds dressed herring
¾ teaspoon salt
¼ teaspoon ground black pepper

flour, or cornmeal and flour
Mustard Sauce (page 43)

Cut the herring into serving portions. Rub both sides with salt and black pepper. Roll the pieces in flour, or in a mixture of half flour and half corn-meal. Brown on both sides in oil or shortening. Serve with Mustard Sauce. Makes 4 servings.

MACKEREL (*Maquereau*)

There are several species of mackerel. All have firm-textured flesh, are extremely oily, and deteriorate rapidly when removed from the water. The common mackerel caught in the North Atlantic usually runs about 12 inches long. The Spanish mackerel, abundant in the Western Hemisphere, usually weighs from 3 to 10 pounds. The flesh of the male mackerel is said to have better flavor than that of the female. The general rule for cooking mackerel is to cook it as simply as possible, since it is rich in its own fat and flavor. Mackerel is harder to digest than fish with low-fat content. It is available fresh, smoked, salted, and pickled.

⚜ **FRIED MACKEREL** (*Maquereaux Frite*)

Allow 1 pound pan-dressed mackerel per serving. Prepare as in recipe for Pan-Fried or Oven-Fried Fish (page 164). Sprinkle with melted butter and chopped parsley.

⚜ **POACHED LARGE MACKEREL WITH PARSLEY SAUCE**
(*Gros Maquereaux Bouillis, Sauce Persil*)

Allow ⅓ to ½ pound sliced large mackerel per serving. Prepare according to either Oven Method or Simmering Method for Poached Fish (page 165). Make Béchamel Sauce (page 38) with half fish stock and half milk and add 1 tablespoon chopped parsley. Serve separately.

⚜ **MACKEREL VINAIGRETTE** (*Maquereaux à la Vinaigrette*)

Poach whole or sliced mackerel in Acidulated Water (with vinegar, page 162) as in Poached Fish (page 165). Drain. Remove skin and place the fish on a platter. Mix 1 tablespoon chopped parsley with 3 tablespoons Vinaigrette Sauce (page 56) and pour over the fish. Serve hot or cold. Allow ⅓ to ½ pound per serving. The fish may be cut in smaller pieces and served cold as an hors d'oeuvre. (*See illustration, page 85.*)

⚜ **FILLETS OF MACKEREL MIREILLE**
(*Filets de Maquereaux Mireille*)

1¾ pounds dressed mackerel	1 shallot, chopped
salt	1 small whole clove garlic
ground black pepper	¼ pound mushrooms, sliced
flour	1 tablespoon wine vinegar
4 tablespoons oil or shortening	3 medium-sized tomatoes, sliced
1 medium-sized onion, sliced	chopped parsley

Cut the mackerel into serving portions. Rub both sides with salt and black pepper. Roll the pieces in flour. Heat 2 tablespoons of the oil or shortening, and brown the pieces on both sides. Transfer the fish to a warmed platter and keep it warm. Pour 1 tablespoon of the remaining oil or shortening into the skillet, heat, and add the onion, shallot, garlic, mushrooms, and ¼ teaspoon salt. Stir and cook 5 minutes or until the mushrooms are tender and onion is limp. Remove and discard the garlic. Sprinkle the mixture with the vinegar and heat ½ minute. Pour over the fish. Sauté the tomatoes in the same skillet in the remaining 1 tablespoon oil or shortening. Arrange the sautéed tomatoes around the fish, sprinkle them with salt and black pepper, and scatter chopped parsley on top. Makes 4 servings.

MULLET

The name mullet is applied to the gray mullet (French *mulet, muges*) and the striped mullet, an important food fish in the southern part of the United States, and also to the red mullet (French *rouget*, from its color), which is a different species, not found in America. Recipes for bass may be used for gray mullet or striped mullet (see Bass). The red mullet of the Mediterranean is considered a great delicacy by connoisseurs and is sometimes eaten without being cleaned or scaled.

⚜ RED MULLET MONTE CARLO (*Rougets Monte Carlo*)

4 red mullet, ½ to ¾ pound each
2 teaspoons anchovy paste
½ cup (1 stick) butter, softened
4 slices toast

1½ tablespoons chopped parsley
2 teaspoons lemon juice
Straw Potatoes (page 387)

Broil the mullet as in the recipe for Broiled Fish (page 162). Mix the anchovy paste with ¼ cup (½ stick) of the butter and spread on 4 slices of hot toast. Place the fish on the toast. Melt the remaining ¼ cup (½ stick) butter, combine with the parsley and lemon juice, and spoon over the fish. Serve with Straw Potatoes. Makes 4 servings.

⚜ HOT RED MULLET NIÇOISE (*Rougets Chauds à la Niçoise*)

4 red mullet, ¾ pound each
salt and ground black pepper
flour
2 to 3 tablespoons oil or shortening

3 medium-sized tomatoes
½ small clove garlic, crushed
4 anchovy fillets
12 green olives, stoned

Rub each side of the fish with salt and black pepper, roll the fish in flour, and fry in hot oil or shortening, adding it as needed. Arrange the fish on a warmed platter and keep warm. Peel, seed, and chop the tomatoes. Using the same skillet in which the fish was fried, cook the tomatoes and garlic about 5 minutes. Season to taste with salt and black pepper. Pour over the fish. Garnish with anchovies and olives. Makes 4 servings.

⚜ RED MULLET PROVENÇAL STYLE (*Rougets à la Provençale*)

3 medium-sized tomatoes
5 tablespoons olive oil or salad oil
½ small clove garlic
1 tablespoon chopped parsley
½ teaspoon sugar

salt and ground black pepper
4 red mullet, ¾ pound each
flour
3 tablespoons fine dry breadcrumbs
2 tablespoons butter

Peel, seed, and chop the tomatoes. Heat 2 tablespoons of the oil in a 1-quart saucepan and cook the tomatoes 5 minutes with the garlic. Remove and discard the garlic. Add the parsley, sugar, and salt and ground black pepper to taste. Keep warm. Rub salt and black pepper on each side of the fish, roll them in flour, and fry in a skillet in the remaining 3 tablespoons hot oil, adding oil as needed. Spread half of the cooked tomatoes over the bottom of a heat-proof platter, add the fish, and cover with the remaining tomatoes. Sprinkle with breadcrumbs, dot with butter, and brown in a preheated hot oven (425° F.) or under broiler heat. Makes 4 servings.

⚜ COLD RED MULLET NIÇOISE (*Rougets Froids à la Niçoise*)

4 dressed red mullet, ½ pound each
4 small white onions, sliced
1 cup dry white wine
salt

3 medium-sized tomatoes, peeled and
    sliced
ground black pepper to taste
lemon slices

Place the mullet and 2 of the onions in a 9-inch skillet. Pour in the wine and sprinkle with ¼ teaspoon salt. Bring the wine to boiling point, reduce heat, and simmer only until the fish flakes when tested with a fork, about 10 minutes. Carefully remove the fish from the liquid and place it on a cold platter. Cook the poaching liquid until it is reduced to one-half the original amount. Cool. Pour over the cold fish. Arrange the sliced tomatoes and the remaining 2 sliced onions over the fish. Sprinkle lightly with salt and black pepper. Garnish with lemon slices. Makes 4 servings.

PERCH (*Perche*)

Perch, a popular freshwater fish, resembles trout and can be cooked in many of the same ways, although the flesh is less delicate. Small perch are usually fried in deep fat; medium-sized ones are filleted and pan-fried in butter; large ones may be stuffed and cooked like shad.

⚜ BOUQUET OF FRIED FISH (*Buisson ou Friture de Poissons Frits*)

This method of cooking and serving fish is especially suitable for small fish, such as perch, smelts, butterfish, sand eel, sunfish, etc.

Clean, wash, and dry small whole fish. Dip them in milk, roll them in flour, and fry them in deep fat preheated to 375° F. Or, if desired, pan-fry in shallow fat (shortening, olive oil, or salad oil), turning to brown both sides. Drain on paper towels. Sprinkle lightly with salt and ground black pepper to taste. Arrange fish on a warmed platter in the form of a bouquet, and garnish with fried or fresh parsley and lemon wedges. Serve promptly. Allow 1½ pounds fish for 4 servings.

⚜ DEEP-FAT-FRIED SMALL FRESHWATER FISH
(*Petite Friture de Rivière ou de Lac*)

Use perch or any small whole fish. Allow ¾ pound per serving. Dip the fish in salted milk (1 teaspoon salt to 1 cup milk) and roll them in flour. Fry not more than 3 or 4 at a time in deep fat preheated to 375° F. until the fish are golden. Drain on paper towels. Sprinkle with black pepper. Arrange the fish on a serving dish and garnish with fried or fresh parsley and notched lemon halves. Serve promptly. (*See illustration, page 225.*)

PIKE (*Brochet*)

Pike is a freshwater fish, of which there are several species, all good eating. The largest of the pike family, the muskellunge, called "muskies" for short, weigh up to 80 pounds and live in the Great Lakes. The great northern pike, next in size, is found in the lakes of Wisconsin and Minnesota. Since both of these are too big to cook whole, they are cut into steaks. The smallest of the pike family is the pickerel; the average market weight is 1 to 2 pounds. Since the flesh of all pike is lean and dry, it should be served with a good sauce or cooked in plenty of butter.

The popular fish called yellow pickerel or walleyed pike is not a pike at all, but a large perch. Its flesh is not so dry as that of true pike.

⚜ BLANQUETTE OF PIKE (*Brochet en Blanquette*)

2½ pounds dressed boned pike
salt
4 tablespoons (½ stick) butter
2 tablespoons flour
½ cup dry white wine
½ cup hot water

12 small white onions, parboiled
½ pound small mushroom caps
2 tablespoons chopped parsley
2 egg yolks
⅓ cup heavy cream
ground white pepper to taste

Cut the pike into slices ¾ inch thick and sprinkle salt over each side. Cook the slices in the butter without browning, about 5 minutes. Sprinkle with flour and cook 1 to 2 minutes. Add the wine, hot water, onions, mushroom caps, and parsley. Cover and simmer 10 to 15 minutes or until the onions are tender. Transfer the fish and vegetables to a serving dish and keep warm. Blend the egg yolks with the cream, add to the sauce, mix well, and cook slowly 1 to 2 minutes. Adjust salt and add white pepper to taste. Pour the sauce over the fish and vegetables. Serve hot. Makes 6 servings.

⚜ PIKE WITH WHITE BUTTER (*Brochet au Beurre Blanc*)

2 pounds dressed pike
hot Simple Fish Stock (page 162) to
cover

Maître d'Hôtel Butter (page 58) or
Tarragon Butter (page 59)
parsley

Put the pike in a 10- or 12-inch skillet with barely enough Simple Fish Stock to cover it. Slowly bring to boiling point, reduce heat, and simmer until the fish flakes when tested with a fork. Transfer the fish to a warmed platter and quickly remove the skin. Serve with Maître d'Hôtel Butter or Tarragon Butter. Garnish with parsley. Makes 4 servings.

SALMON AND SALMON TROUT
(*Saumon, Truite Saumonée*)

Salmon, one of the most delicious of all fish, is characterized by its orange-pink color. This large fish may be served whole, or sections or steaks may be cut from the center. Salmon trout, also called European sea trout, a related species not found in America, is interchangeable with salmon in many recipes. See also Trout.

⚜ SALMON OR SALMON TROUT IN COURT BOUILLON
(*Truite Saumonée au Court Bouillon*)

3½ to 4 pounds salmon, or 1 dressed
    salmon trout, 3½ to 4 pounds
1¾ cups Court Bouillon (page 161)
1¾ cups Velouté Sauce (page 40)

2 large egg yolks
1 tablespoon butter
chopped parsley

Place the fish in a saucepan large enough to accommodate it. Pour in the Court Bouillon. Bring to boiling point, reduce heat, and simmer until the fish flakes when tested with a fork. Transfer fish to a warmed platter and keep warm. Reduce the Court Bouillon to one-half the original amount and mix 1½ cups of the Velouté Sauce with it. Blend the egg yolks with the remaining ¼ cup Velouté Sauce and add to the bouillon. Stir and cook ½ minute. Swirl in the butter. Pour over the fish. Sprinkle with chopped parsley. If desired, serve with Hollandaise Sauce, Mousseline Sauce, or Shrimp Sauce (see Index). Makes 6 servings.

⚜ SALMON OR SALMON TROUT CUTLETS BELLEVUE
(*Tranches de Truite Saumonée en Bellevue*)

6 salmon or salmon trout cutlets, ½
    pound each
Court Bouillon (page 161)
6 thin tomato slices
6 thin cucumber slices
6 thin truffle or black olive slices

6 hard-cooked eggs
salt and ground black pepper to taste
prepared Dijon mustard to taste
⅔ cup mayonnaise
12 small peeled cooked shrimp or
    shrimp tails

Poach the salmon or salmon trout in Court Bouillon as in directions for Poached Fish, Simmering Method (page 165). With a perforated spoon, remove the fish from the liquor, drain well, remove the skin and arrange the fish on a cold platter. Place 1 slice each tomato, cucumber, and truffle or black olive on each of the cutlets. Cut the hard-cooked eggs in half, remove the yolks, put them through a sieve, season to taste with salt, black pepper, and mustard and mix with 2 tablespoons of the mayonnaise. Put the mixture into a pastry bag with a fluted tip and pipe it into the egg whites. Garnish the eggs with small shrimp or shrimp tails and place them on the platter around the fish. Serve the remaining mayonnaise in a separate bowl. Makes 6 servings.

SHAD (*Alose*)

⚜ BAKED SHAD (*Alose Rôtie*)

3- to 3½-pound dressed shad
1 teaspoon salt
⅛ teaspoon ground black pepper
¼ small clove garlic, minced

4 tablespoons (½ stick) butter, melted
2 tablespoons lemon juice or lime juice
chopped parsley

Split the shad along the back and remove the large bone. Combine the salt, pepper, and minced garlic and rub the mixture into both sides of the fish. Combine the melted butter and the lemon juice or lime juice and brush the mixture over both sides of the fish. Reserve the remainder of the mixture. Place the shad in a buttered baking dish. Bake in a preheated moderate oven (350° F.) 30 to 35 minutes or until the fish has browned and flakes when tested with a fork, basting at 10-minute intervals. Transfer the fish to a warmed platter and pour the remaining butter and lemon sauce over it. Sprinkle with chopped parsley. Makes 4 servings.

⚜ BROILED SHAD (*Alose Grillée*)

2- to 2½-pound dressed shad
salad oil
½ teaspoon salt

¼ teaspoon ground black pepper
3 tablespoons butter, melted
Herb Butter (page 58)

Split the fish, oil it lightly, and rub both sides with the salt and black pepper. Put the fish in a preheated oiled broiler pan, skin side up. Place the pan in the broiler 3 inches from the source of heat. Broil 5 to 8 minutes, baste with melted butter, and turn carefully. Brush the other side with melted butter and cook about 5 minutes or until the fish has browned and flakes when tested with a fork. Serve immediately with Herb Butter. Makes 4 servings.

SKATE *(Raie)*

Skate, belonging to the ray family, is a flat and scaleless fish caught off the New England and Middle Atlantic coasts. It has well-developed pectoral winglike fins and a long, rather thick tail.

Skate must be absolutely fresh. Otherwise, it gives off an odor of ammonia which makes it unfit for human consumption. Its methods of preparation are limited. Since the flesh is lean, skate should be prepared with cream or a butter sauce. It is served with ordinary butter in England and with black butter in France. Cold poached skate is good in salads, especially when garnished with capers.

⚜ SKATE WITH BLACK BUTTER *(Raie au Beurre Noir)*

Cut 1½ to 1¾ pounds skate wings into convenient eating-size pieces. Poach them in Simple Fish Stock (page 162) as directed for Poached Fish, Simmering Method (page 165). Remove the pieces from the stock, using a slotted spoon. Scrape both sides of the pieces with a knife to remove the skin, and arrange them on a warmed platter. Sprinkle with salt and ground black pepper. Serve with Black Butter (page 55). Makes 4 servings.

⚜ DEEP-FAT-FRIED SKATE *(Raie Frite)*

For frying in deep fat, very tiny whole skate are best. Larger skate may be used if cut in small pieces but are not as good.

Skin 1½ to 1¾ pounds skate. If small, leave them whole; if large cut into chunks. Soak the skate 1 hour in cold boiled milk. Remove from milk, drain, and roll lightly in flour. Fry in deep fat preheated to 375° F. until browned. Drain on paper towels. Sprinkle with salt and ground black pepper. Serve with melted butter and Tomato Sauce (page 50), or with fried parsley and lemon. Makes 4 servings.

SOLE

True sole, a flatfish native to European waters, is considered the finest of flatfish. Its flesh is white, firm, and delicate. It may be fried, poached, braised, broiled, or otherwise cooked in ways similar to those used for preparing brill, flounder, whiting, and freshwater trout. European sole is exported to the United States but is not generally available. Most fish sold in America as "sole" is actually flounder or other flatfish. The two most common varieties of flounder in American waters are sold under the commercial names of "gray sole" and "lemon sole," the latter being more delicate and more flavorsome. See also Flounder.

⚜ BROILED SOLE (*Soles Grillées*)

4 fillets of sole, ½ pound each	olive or salad oil
salt and ground black pepper	parsley and lemon wedges
flour	

Score the fillets lightly in crisscross fashion on both sides. Sprinkle them with salt and black pepper, dredge in flour, and sprinkle with oil. Put them on an oiled broiler pan and place in the broiler 4 inches from the source of heat. Broil 5 to 8 minutes or until browned, sprinkling with oil once. Turn carefully, sprinkle with oil, and broil 5 to 8 minutes or until browned. Transfer to a warmed platter. Garnish with parsley and lemon wedges. Makes 4 servings. (*See illustration, page 189.*)

⚜ DEEP-FAT-FRIED SOLE WITH LEMON

Allow 1 sole weighing ½ pound per serving. Dip the fish in lightly salted milk, roll them in flour, and shake off surplus flour. Fry until golden brown in deep fat preheated to 375° F. Drain on paper towels. Sprinkle salt and black pepper lightly on both sides of the fish. Put a handful of thoroughly dried washed parsley in the fat and remove it immediately with a perforated spoon or skimmer. Arrange the fried parsley and slices of lemon around the fish as a garnish.

⚜ PAN-FRIED SOLE (*Soles à la Meunière*)

4 fillets of sole, ½ pound each	flour
1 teaspoon salt	6 tablespoons (¾ stick) butter
¼ teaspoon ground black pepper	2 lemons
milk	chopped parsley

Rub both sides of the fillets with the salt and black pepper. Dip them in milk and then roll in flour. Brown on both sides in 4 tablespoons of the butter, adding it as needed. Transfer the fish to a warmed platter. Squeeze the juice from 1 lemon over the fish. Brown the remaining 2 tablespoons butter in the frying pan and pour it over the fish. Sprinkle with chopped parsley. Cut the remaining lemon into wedges to garnish the fish. Makes 4 servings.

⚜ SOLE IN WHITE WINE (*Filets de Sole au Vin Blanc*)

2 whole sole, 14 ounces each, or 8
    fillets, 4 ounces each
salt
ground white pepper
1 shallot or small white onion,
    chopped

¾ cup dry white wine
Simple Fish Stock (page 162)
3 tablespoons butter
3 tablespoons flour
1 cup hot milk
2 tablespoons cream

Sprinkle the fish with salt and white pepper. If fillets are used, fold them in half and beat them lightly with the palm of the hand to flatten them. Put the sole in a buttered baking dish. Add the chopped shallot or onion, the wine, and only enough fish stock barely to cover the sole. Cover the baking dish with foil or buttered paper. Cook in a preheated slow oven (325° F.) 15 to 20 minutes or only until the fish flakes when tested with a fork. Drain the liquor off the fish into a saucepan and boil until it is reduced to ⅓ cup. Melt the butter in a separate saucepan, remove from heat, and blend in the flour. Return to heat; stir and cook until the mixture foams, 1 to 2 minutes. Remove from heat and beat in the milk. Cook until sauce is medium-thick. Stir in the ⅓ cup reduced fish stock. Add salt and pepper to taste and the cream. Spoon over the poached sole. Makes 4 servings.

⚜ FILLETS OF SOLE BURGUNDY STYLE
(*Filets de Sole à la Bourguignonne*)

2 fillets of sole, ½ pound each
salt and ground black pepper
¾ cup dry red wine
2 teaspoons flour
2 tablespoons butter, softened

1 teaspoon caramel, or ½ teaspoon
    Kitchen Bouquet
16 small white onions, boiled
¼ pound whole button mushrooms,
    sautéed

Rub both sides of the fillets with salt and black pepper. Place in a buttered deep 8-inch baking dish. Add the wine. Cover and simmer 8 to 10 minutes or until the fish flakes when tested with a fork. Drain off the cooking liquid, strain it into a saucepan, and cook until the quantity has reduced to one-half the original amount. Blend the flour with the butter and add to the reduced cooking liquid. Mix well. Stir and cook 2 minutes or until thickened. Color with caramel or Kitchen Bouquet. Season to taste with salt and black pepper. Transfer the fish to a warmed platter and surround it with the boiled onions and sautéed mushrooms. Coat the fish and vegetables with the sauce. Makes 4 servings.

Fish Cakes (page 339)

↓ Broiled Sole (page 187)

↑ Hake or Cod Fillets Provençal (page 173)

↓ Paupiettes of Fillets of Sole au Gratin (page 19

↑ Sea Bass à la Grecque (page 166)

↓ Poached Hake or Cod English Style (page 170)

↑ Poached Hake or Cod Steaks (page 174)

↓ Vol-au-Vent of Fillets of Sole (page 193)

⚜ VOL-AU-VENT OF FILLETS OF SOLE (*Croustade de Filets de Sole*)

Puff Pastry (page 25)	Sole and Shrimp Ragout (see follow-
2 eggs, beaten	ing recipe)

Make a double recipe of Puff Pastry. Roll one-fourth of the dough into a 10-inch circle ⅛ inch thick. Cut out a 9-inch circle, using a round 9-inch cake pan as a guide. (Save all the trimmings of the dough to use later.) Place the dough on a baking sheet and prick it all over with a fork to permit it to rise uniformly. Make a ball of paper 6 inches in diameter, wrap it in tissue paper or foil, and tie it with string. Place the ball in the center of the circle of dough. Brush the edges of the dough with water. Roll one-half of the remaining dough into a 13-inch circle ⅛ inch thick and cut it into a 12-inch circle, using a 12-inch plate as a guide. Fit the dough over the paper ball and press the edges down well all around. Brush the entire surface with beaten egg. Roll one-third of the remaining dough ⅛ inch thick. Cut a 4-inch circle using a 4-inch lid or bowl as a guide and place it in the center of the top of the dome. Roll the rest of the dough into a 10-inch circle and cut out a 9-inch circle, leaving a ring 1 inch wide. Place this ring around the dome. Roll all the reserved trimmings of the dough ⅛ inch thick and cut it into circles, crescents, and narrow strips, using scalloped cooky cutters and a pastry cutter. Place these cutouts as desired on the puff-pastry dome and around the edge. Prick the pastry with a fine needle in several places. Brush the entire surface with beaten egg.

Bake the pastry in a preheated hot oven (400° F.) 20 to 25 minutes. If the pastry tends to brown too much, cover it with foil or brown paper. Remove the pastry from the oven and let it cool. Using a sharp-pointed knife, cut around the edge of the dome, being careful not to cut into the base crust. Carefully lift off the dome and set it aside. Remove and discard the paper ball. Fill the center of the pastry with Sole and Shrimp Ragout. Cover with the dome. Makes 8 servings. (*See illustration, page 192.*)

⚜ Sole and Shrimp Ragout

8 fillets of sole, 4 ounces each	3 tablespoons flour
salt and ground white pepper	1 cup hot milk
½ cup dry white wine	½ pound diced cooked shrimp
Simple Fish Stock (page 162)	½ pound mushrooms, quartered and
4 tablespoons butter	blanched

Sprinkle the sole fillets with salt and white pepper, roll them up, and pin the ends with toothpicks. Place in a buttered 10-inch skillet. Pour in the wine and only enough Simple Fish Stock barely to cover the sole. Bring the liquor to boiling point, reduce heat, and simmer 10 minutes or only until the sole flakes when tested with a fork. Let the rolls cool in the liquor until they are cold, then remove them from the liquor, and cut them into slices ¼ inch thick. Set aside. Boil the liquor until it is reduced to ½ cup and set aside. Melt 3 tablespoons of the butter. Remove from heat and blend in the flour. Return to heat; stir and cook 1 to 2 minutes or until the mixture foams. Remove from heat and beat in the hot milk and the reserved ½ cup hot sole liquor. Cook until the sauce is medium thick. Add the remaining 1 tablespoon butter, the sliced sole, diced shrimp, and blanched mushrooms. Season to taste with salt and white pepper. Heat. Use to fill a large Puff-Pastry case (page 25), or, if desired, serve on rice or in Patty Shells (page 26). Makes 8 servings.

⚜ FILLETS OF SOLE FLORENTINE STYLE
(Filets de Sole Gratinés à la Florentine)

1¼ pounds fresh spinach, or 1 10-ounce package frozen spinach, cooked	4 fillets of sole, ⅓ pound each
	1 shallot, chopped
2 tablespoons butter	¾ cup dry white wine
½ teaspoon sugar	1 cup Mornay Sauce (page 40)
salt and ground black pepper	⅓ cup grated Cheddar or Gruyère cheese

Season the cooked spinach with the butter, sugar, and salt and black pepper to taste. Spread it over the bottom of a buttered 8- by 8- by 2-inch baking dish. Sprinkle the sole lightly with salt and black pepper. Place it in a buttered baking pan with the shallot. Pour in the wine. Cover the pan with foil or buttered paper. Poach in a preheated slow oven (325° F.) 15 minutes or until the fish flakes when tested with a fork. Remove the fillets from the liquor and drain them on a clean towel to absorb the moisture. Arrange them over the spinach. Cover completely with Mornay Sauce. Sprinkle with the cheese. Brown in a preheated hot oven (400° F.). Makes 4 servings.

⚜ FILLETS OF SOLE MORNAY *(Filets de Sole Mornay)*

4 fillets of sole, ½ pound each	¾ cup Mornay Sauce (page 40)
salt and ground black pepper	¼ cup grated Cheddar or Gruyère cheese
1 cup dry white wine	

Sprinkle the fillets lightly with salt and black pepper. Heat the wine in a 9-inch skillet, add the fish, and simmer 10 minutes or until the fish flakes when tested with a fork. Transfer the fish to a buttered heatproof platter. Boil the pan liquor until it is reduced to one-half the original amount. Add to the Mornay Sauce and spread over the fish. Sprinkle with the grated cheese and brown under broiler heat. Makes 4 servings.

⚜ FILLETS OF SOLE MURAT *(Filets de Sole Murat)*

4 fillets of sole, ⅓ pound each	4 medium-sized potatoes, peeled and diced
salt and ground black pepper	
⅓ cup milk	4 tablespoons butter
flour	4 raw artichoke bottoms
about 5 tablespoons oil or shortening	2 firm ripe tomatoes, thickly sliced
	chopped parsley

Cut the fillets into lengthwise halves. Add ¼ teaspoon salt and ⅛ teaspoon black pepper to the milk. Dip the fish in the seasoned milk, and roll it in flour. Fry in 3 tablespoons of the oil or shortening until crisp and brown. Set them aside in a warm place. Parboil the potatoes 2 to 3 minutes, drain, and wipe dry with a paper towel. Toss with 2 tablespoons of the butter, and cool. Fry the potatoes in the remaining oil or shortening until browned, using as little as possible. Keep warm. Dice the artichoke bottoms and cook in 1 tablespoon of the remaining butter. Mix lightly with the potatoes and fish, and put all into a serving dish. Fry the tomatoes in the remaining 1 tablespoon butter and arrange them on top of the dish. Sprinkle lightly with salt, black pepper, and chopped parsley. Makes 4 servings.

⚜ FILLETS OF SOLE WITH MUSHROOMS
(Filets de Sole aux Champignons)

1½ pounds fillets of sole	½ pound mushrooms, sliced
salt and ground black pepper	1 tablespoon lemon juice
½ cup dry white wine	1 tablespoon flour
5 tablespoons butter	chopped parsley

Sprinkle the fillets on both sides with salt and black pepper and place them in a buttered baking dish. Pour in the wine. Bake in a preheated moderate oven (350° F.) 25 minutes or until the fish flakes when tested with a fork, basting once with the wine. Dot the fish with 2 tablespoons of the butter. Brown in the broiler 4 inches from the source of heat. Arrange the fish in a ring on a warmed serving plate. Reserve the liquid. Meanwhile, sauté the mushrooms in 1 tablespoon of the remaining butter. Sprinkle them with the lemon juice and salt and black pepper to taste. With a perforated spoon, transfer the mushrooms to the center of the serving plate. Blend the flour with the remaining 2 tablespoon butter and add to the fish pan liquid. Mix well and boil 2 minutes or until thickened. Season with salt and black pepper. Spoon the sauce over the fish only, sprinkle the mushrooms with chopped parsley. Makes 4 servings.

⚜ FILLETS OF SOLE WITH MUSSELS *(Filets de Sole à la Dieppoise)*

2 quarts unshucked mussels	3 tablespoons flour
1 shallot, chopped	½ cup hot mussel liquor
¾ cup dry white wine	½ cup hot milk
4 fillets of sole, ⅓ pound each	¼ cup heavy cream
salt and ground white pepper	chopped parsley
3 tablespoons butter	

Wash the mussels and steam them with the shallot in the wine (see directions for Washing and Steaming Mussels, page 213). Remove the mussels from their shells, strain the liquor, sprinkle a little over the mussels, and keep them warm. Reserve the remaining liquor. If the fillets are thin, fold them and flatten them slightly with the palm of the hand. Arrange them in a buttered baking dish. Melt the butter in a 1-quart saucepan. Remove from heat and blend in the flour. Return to heat; stir and cook until the mixture foams. Beat in the ½ cup hot mussel liquor and ½ cup hot milk. Cook 1 to 2 minutes or until the sauce is medium thick, stirring constantly. Season to taste with salt and ground white pepper. Add the cream. Pour the sauce over the fish. Cover with foil or buttered paper and bake in a preheated slow oven (325° F.) 15 to 20 minutes or until the fish flakes when tested with a fork. Sprinkle with chopped parsley. Surround the fillets with the mussels. Makes 4 to 8 servings.

⚜ FILLETS OF SOLE ORLY (*Filets de Sole Orly*)

The term Orly, in French cooking terminology, is applied to skinned fillets of fish dipped in batter and fried in deep fat, usually served with tomato sauce.

8 fillets of sole, ¼ pound each
1 teaspoon salt
¼ teaspoon ground black pepper
1½ tablespoons lemon juice

2 tablespoons chopped parsley
Batter for Frying Fish (page 164)
Tomato Sauce (page 50)

Marinate the fillets 1 hour in the salt, black pepper, lemon juice, and parsley. Dip the fish in Batter for Frying Fish and fry until browned in deep fat preheated to 375° F. Drain on paper towels. Serve hot, with Tomato Sauce in a separate bowl. Makes 4 servings.

⚜ PAUPIETTES OF FILLETS OF SOLE AU GRATIN
(*Paupiettes de Filets de Sole au Gratin*)

12 fillets of sole, ¼ pound each
salt and ground black pepper
¾ pound fish (haddock, salmon, whiting, etc.)
1 tablespoon minced onion
½ cup chopped parsley
2 large eggs

1½ cups dry white wine or Simple Fish Stock (page 162)
2 tablespoons butter
2 tablespoons flour
½ cup hot milk
½ cup grated Cheddar or Gruyère cheese

Wipe the fillets of sole dry and beat them lightly with a heavy, wide knife blade or a mallet. Sprinkle with salt and black pepper and set aside. Put the ¾ pound of fish through a food chopper, using the finest blade. Add the onion and parsley and put the mixture through a food chopper twice more. Beat in the eggs, beating and pounding the mixture to a smooth paste. Add salt and black pepper to taste. Spread the mixture uniformly over the sole fillets and roll them up. Pin the ends with toothpicks. Place the rolls in a buttered heatproof dish. Pour in the wine or fish stock. Cover the dish, bring the liquid to boiling point over medium heat, reduce heat, and simmer 10 minutes or until the fish flakes when tested with a fork, basting frequently with the wine or stock. Transfer the fillets to a warmed platter. Keep warm. Reserve the liquor. Melt the butter in a 1-quart saucepan, remove from heat, and blend in the flour. Return to heat; stir and cook until the mixture foams. Remove from heat and beat in the hot milk and ¾ cup of the poaching liquor. Cook until the sauce is medium thick, stirring constantly. Blend in the cheese. Add salt and pepper to taste. Pour over the fish rolls. Brown under a preheated broiler. Makes 6 servings. (*See illustration, page 190.*)

⚜ FILLETS OF SOLE WITH SHRIMP
(*Filets de Sole aux Crevettes dits Joinville*)

4 fillets of sole, ⅓ pound each
salt and ground white pepper
1 shallot, chopped
¾ cup dry white wine
1 cup Hollandaise Sauce (page 52),
  or 1 cup Béchamel Sauce (page
  38) and 2 tablespoons butter

⅓ cup finely chopped shrimp
1 teaspoon tomato paste (optional)
chopped parsley
½ pound deveined, peeled, cooked
  shrimp

Fold the fillets of sole if they are thin and flatten them slightly with the palm of the hand. Arrange them in a buttered baking dish and sprinkle with salt, white pepper, and the chopped shallot. Pour in the wine. Cover with buttered paper or foil and bake in a preheated slow oven (325° F.) only until the fish flakes when tested with a fork, about 15 to 20 minutes. Remove the fish, drain it on a clean towel to absorb the moisture, and arrange it on a warmed platter. Keep warm. Boil the fish liquor until it is reduced to one-half the original amount. Measure out ⅓ cup and add to the Hollandaise Sauce, or the Béchamel Sauce and butter, and the chopped shrimp. Season to taste with salt and white pepper. Add the tomato paste if a pink-colored sauce is desired. Spoon the sauce over the fish. Sprinkle with chopped parsley. Surround the fish with the peeled and deveined cooked shrimp. Makes 4 servings.

TROUT (*Truite*)

Freshwater trout, a fish related to salmon, is found in brooks, rivers, and lakes in North America. There are many varieties, all delicious, though trout caught in mountain streams is particularly prized. Freshwater trout can be used in recipes for salmon or salmon trout.

⚜ TROUT IN CREAM (*Truite à la Crème*)

6 dressed whole trout, ½ pound each
salt
ground black pepper
chopped parsley
2 tablespoons lemon juice

hot water
1 cup heavy cream
¾ cup soft breadcrumbs
2 tablespoons butter

Sprinkle the trout with salt and black pepper and place them in a buttered baking dish large enough to accommodate them. Sprinkle them with parsley and lemon juice. Pour in just enough hot water to cover the bottom of the dish. Bake in a preheated slow oven (325° F.) 25 to 30 minutes or only until the fish flakes when tested with a fork. Drain the liquor from the fish into a saucepan and blend in the cream. Cook over surface heat until the liquid is reduced to one-half the original amount. Season to taste with salt and black pepper. Pour into the baking dish over the fish. Sprinkle with the bread-crumbs. Dot with the butter. Brown in a preheated broiler. Serve hot. Makes 6 servings.

⚜ FRIED TROUT (*Truite à la Meunière*)

½ teaspoon salt
½ cup milk
4 dressed whole trout, ½ pound each
flour

2 to 3 tablespoons butter
lemon slices
parsley

Add the salt to the milk and dip the trout into it, then roll them in flour. Brown on both sides in butter over moderate heat, adding butter as needed. Transfer to a warmed platter. Garnish with lemon slices and sprinkle with chopped parsley. Decorate the platter with a bunch of fresh parsley. Makes 4 servings. (*See illustration, page 226.*)

⚜ POACHED BLUE RIVER TROUT (*Truite de Rivière au Bleu*)

Blue river trout must not be killed until just before they are to be cooked. If the blue color is desired, do not scale the fish, since the scales give the fish its color.

4 dressed whole blue river trout, ½ pound each
Court Bouillon (page 161) or Simple Fish Stock (page 162)

¼ cup (½ stick) butter and 2 table-spoons lemon juice (optional)
Hollandaise Sauce (optional; page 52)

Poach the fish in boiling Court Bouillon or Simple Fish Stock according to the directions for the Simmering Method of Poaching Fish (page 165). Transfer the fish to a warmed platter and pour in a little of the poaching liquor. If desired, serve with melted butter and lemon juice, or with Hollandaise Sauce. Makes 4 servings.

⚜ TROUT IN ASPIC (*Truite en Gelée*)

8 dressed whole river trout, ½ pound
  each, heads attached
Court Bouillon (page 161) or Simple
  Fish Stock (page 162)
6 shrimp or crayfish, poached and
  peeled

4 hard-cooked eggs, cut in half
8 tomato slices
truffles or black olives
½ cup aspic
parsley
mayonnaise

Wash the trout. Tie the heads to the tails with string to form rings. Poach slowly in Court Bouillon or Simple Fish Stock as directed for Poached Fish, Simmering Method (page 165). Cool the trout in the bouillon or stock. Remove from the stock, drain well, and wipe dry with a clean towel. Simmer the shrimp or crayfish, in the same bouillon or stock, only until they turn a deep pink, about 5 minutes. Place the trout on a cold platter and arrange the shrimp or crayfish at one end. Place a hard-cooked egg half on each of 8 tomato slices and arrange them around the trout and shrimp or crayfish. Decorate the eggs with a piece of truffle or a slice of black olive. Coat the whole with aspic. Garnish the dish with fresh parsley. If desired, serve additional sliced tomatoes in a separate dish. Serve with mayonnaise. Makes 8 servings.

TUNA (*Thon*)

Tuna (called tunny in England) is a mackerel-like fish widely distributed in warm and temperate seas. It is caught in the Atlantic and Pacific oceans and the Mediterranean. There are many species, ranging in size from 4 pounds to 1000 pounds. The flesh of tuna is firm and oily and resembles veal in flavor. It is available fresh, canned, smoked, and salted. Fresh tuna steaks are as highly esteemed as fresh swordfish steaks.

⚜ TUNA BORDEAUX STYLE (*Thon à la Bordelaise*)

1½ pounds fresh tuna
salt and ground black pepper
2 tablespoons oil
4 tablespoons butter
½ cup thinly sliced onion
2 shallots, chopped

5 medium-sized tomatoes, peeled,
  seeded, and quartered
⅓ cup Demi-Glace Sauce (page 44)
⅓ cup dry white wine
2 cups quartered mushrooms
chopped parsley

Rub the tuna lightly with salt and black pepper. Brown on both sides in the oil and 2 tablespoons of the butter. Add onion, shallots, tomatoes, Demi-Glace Sauce, and wine. Cover and cook over moderate heat until the fish flakes when tested with a fork. Transfer the fish to a warmed platter and keep it warm. Cook the sauce until the quantity has reduced to three-fourths the original amount. Meanwhile sauté the mushrooms in the remaining 2 tablespoons butter and add them to the sauce. Add salt and black pepper to taste. Heat ½ minute. Pour over the fish. Sprinkle with chopped parsley. Makes 6 servings.

⚜ GRILLED TUNA (*Thon Grillé*)

Sprinkle thick slices of tuna lightly with salt and black pepper. Brush olive oil or salad oil over both sides and arrange the fish in an oiled broiler pan. Place in the broiler oven 4 inches from the source of heat. Broil 5 to 8 minutes. Brush with melted butter and turn carefully. Brush the other side with melted butter, sprinkle with lemon juice, and broil 5 to 8 minutes or only until the fish is flaky. Carefully transfer the fish to a warmed platter and serve immediately with melted butter or Tartare Sauce (page 55), accompanied with boiled potatoes. Allow ⅓ pound per serving.

⚜ TUNA MÉNAGÈRE (*Thon à la Ménagère*)

Ménagère in French means housewife, or, as an adjective, thrifty or frugal. As a culinary term, *à la ménagère* is applied to economical dishes.

2 pounds fresh tuna, cut in slices ½ inch thick
salt
ground black pepper
4 tablespoons (½ stick) butter
⅓ cup chopped onion
about 1 tablespoon flour

⅓ cup each dry white wine and water
3 tablespoons tomato paste
2 tablespoons lemon juice
1½ cups sliced mushrooms, or 1½ cups peeled and seeded diced tomatoes, cooked in butter

Place the fish in a saucepan, cover with cold water, bring to boiling point, reduce heat, and simmer 4 to 5 minutes. Remove the fish from the water, drain, season lightly with salt and black pepper, and brown on both sides in 2 tablespoons of the butter. Melt the remaining 2 tablespoons butter in a casserole. Add the onion, mix well, sprinkle with the flour, and stir and cook 1 minute. Add the wine and water. Cook until the sauce has reduced to three-fourths the original quantity. Stir in the tomato paste and lemon juice. Add the tuna, cover, and cook in a preheated moderate oven (350° F.) 15 minutes or until the fish flakes when tested with a fork. Transfer the fish to a warmed platter and keep it warm. Add the mushrooms or tomatoes to the sauce and bring to boiling point. Adjust seasonings and pour the sauce around the fish. Makes 6 servings.

TURBOT (*Turbot*)

Turbot is a large European flatfish, with white, firm, flaky flesh and a delicate flavor. Halibut may be substituted in recipes calling for large turbot or turbot steaks, flounder in recipes for small turbot.

⚜ POACHED TURBOT (*Turbotin Poché*)

Wash the fish and soak it in cold water 1 hour or longer. Place it in a large saucepan or a fish kettle. Cover well with cold water. Add 1 teaspoon salt for each quart water used. (Do not add any other seasoning or any vegetables, which might detract from the delicate flavor of the fish.) Add 1 cup milk to retain the white color of the flesh. Simmer very gently, uncovered, *only* until the fish flakes when tested with a fork. Turn off the heat. Cool a 5-pound turbot in the liquid 20 minutes; a smaller turbot or a piece of turbot 12 to 15 minutes. Remove from the liquor. Drain on a clean towel to absorb the moisture. Put the turbot on a platter and serve with Hollandaise Sauce (page 52) or melted butter. Allow ½ pound boneless turbot, or 1 pound turbot with bone in, per serving.

⚜ GRILLED CHICKEN TURBOT (*Turbotin Grillé*)

Chicken turbot are small turbot, weighing 3 pounds or less. They may be prepared according to any turbot recipe.

Score both sides of a dressed chicken turbot. Sprinkle lightly with salt and ground white pepper. Brush with melted butter and cook according to directions for Broiled Fish (page 162). Serve with melted butter or Béarnaise Sauce (page 53) and boiled potatoes. Allow ½ pound boneless fish, or 1 pound fish with bone in, per serving.

⚜ FILLETS OF TURBOT MORNAY (*Filets de Turbot Mornay*)

In the recipe for Fillets of Sole Mornay (page 194), replace the sole with fillets of turbot. Makes 4 servings.

WHITING (*Merlan*)

The European whiting is caught in the English Channel and in the Baltic Sea. The American whiting, also known as the silver hake, is caught off the New England coast. Its flesh is lean, fine-textured, and flavorful and is best pan-fried or broiled in plenty of butter. Whiting is also available smoked.

⚜ BAKED WHITING (*Merlan Rôti*)

4 dressed whiting, ½ pound each
1 shallot, chopped
salt and ground black pepper to taste
⅓ cup dry white wine

chopped parsley
2 tablespoons fine dry breadcrumbs
2 tablespoons butter

Split the fish down the back, remove the spines, and set the fish aside. Sprinkle the chopped shallot over the bottom of a buttered baking dish. Season the fish lightly with salt and black pepper, fold them into their original shape, place them over the shallot, and pour the wine over them. Sprinkle with parsley and the breadcrumbs. Dot with the butter. Bake in a preheated moderate oven (350° F.) 25 minutes or until the fish flakes when tested with a fork. Makes 4 servings.

⚜ BREADED WHITING MAÎTRE D'HÔTEL
(*Merlans Panés à la Maître d'Hôtel*)

Allow 1 dressed fish (½ pound) per serving. Split the whiting down the back and remove the spines. Rub both sides of the fish with salt and ground black pepper. Dip in milk and roll in flour, then dip in egg beaten with water (1 tablespoon to 1 egg) and roll in fine dry breadcrumbs. Fry until browned in deep fat preheated to 375° F. Drain on paper towels. Serve with Maître d'Hôtel Butter (page 58).

⚜ DEEP-FAT-FRIED WHITING (*Merlans Frites*)

Allow 1 dressed fish (½ pound) per serving. Dip the whole fish in milk, then roll in flour, and fry in deep fat preheated to 375° F. Drain on paper towels. Sprinkle lightly with salt and serve with Rémoulade Sauce (page 55), or sprinkle with lemon juice and chopped parsley.

FISH STEWS

⚜ MOSELLE FISH STEW (*Matelote de Moselle*)

¾ pound each carp, pike, and eel
6 tablespoons butter
½ pound button mushrooms
1 tablespoon lemon juice
hot water
6 shallots, chopped
2 tablespoons cognac
1 cup dry white wine
1 small clove garlic, chopped

¼ cup chopped parsley
salt
12 small white onions
2 tablespoons flour
2 egg yolks
⅓ cup light cream
ground black pepper to taste
crescent-shaped croutons fried in
   butter

Cut all the fish into 1½-inch chunks. Fry the carp and pike lightly in 2 tablespoons of the butter, adding the butter as needed. Reserve the eel for later use. Put the mushrooms, 1 tablespoon of the butter, and the lemon juice in a 3-quart saucepan. Pour in *only* enough hot water barely to cover them. Simmer, uncovered, 5 minutes. Add the browned carp and pike and the shallots. Set aside. Brown the eel lightly in 1 tablespoon of the butter in a skillet. Add the cognac, warm over *very low* heat, ignite, and pour in the wine. Stir and scrape all particles from the bottom of the pan. Add the eel to the fish and mushrooms. Stir in the garlic, parsley, and 1 teaspoon salt. Cover and cook slowly 15 to 18 minutes. Transfer the fish, eel, and mushrooms to a warmed platter, cover loosely with foil, and keep warm. Add the onions to the stock, cover, and cook 20 minutes, or until onions are soft. Transfer the onions to the platter. Blend the flour with the remaining 2 tablespoons butter, blend with the stock, and boil 1 to 2 minutes. Beat the egg yolks with the cream, add to the stock, and heat ½ minute. Adjust the salt and add black pepper to taste. Spoon the sauce over the fish and vegetables. Garnish the dish with butter-fried croutons. Makes 4 servings. (*See illustration, page 225.*)

⚜ RIVER FISH STEW, BURGUNDY STYLE (*Pauchose*)

This dish is a Burgundian specialty made with white wine.

¾ pound each carp, eel, perch, and
   trout
salt
3 ounces salt pork, sliced
1 clove garlic
24 small white onions
¾ pound button mushrooms
⅓ cup chopped parsley

1 cup dry white wine
2 tablespoons cognac
2 tablespoons flour
3 tablespoons butter, softened
ground black pepper
Croutons Fried in Garlic Butter (see
   following recipe)

Wash the dressed fish quickly in cold water, cut it into chunks, rub with 1 tablespoon of salt, and set aside. Fry the salt pork in a 3-quart saucepan until crisp. Remove and save for later use. Add the fish to the hot pork drippings, along with the garlic, onions, mushrooms, parsley, and wine. Bring to boiling point, uncovered. Meanwhile, heat the cognac in a small pan and *just* as the wine comes to boiling point, add the hot cognac and ignite. Cover and cook the mixture slowly for 25 minutes (do not boil). Blend the flour with the butter and add to the mixture. Remove and discard the garlic. Simmer until the sauce has thickened, 1 to 2 minutes. Serve with Croutons Fried in Garlic Butter. Makes 8 servings.

⚜ Croutons Fried in Garlic Butter

Fry 1 clove garlic in 4 tablespoons (½ stick) butter. Remove and discard the garlic. Add 1 cup bread cubes and stir and fry over medium heat until the cubes have browned. Sufficient for 8 servings.

Shellfish
and Frogs' Legs

Shellfish

Shellfish are divided into two classes: crustaceans, which include crabs, crayfish, lobster and rock lobster, shrimp, scampi, and prawns; and mollusks, which include clams, mussels, oysters, scallops, and squid. In this chapter shellfish are arranged in alphabetical order by name.

CLAMS (*Palourdes, Praires*)

The clam is a bivalve mollusk, found only in salt water. There are two well-known species: the round, hard-shell clam and the long, soft-shell clam. The hard-shell clam is often called by its Indian name quahaug, or quahog. Small hard-shell clams, known as cherrystones, are eaten raw in the same way as oysters, and may also be cooked in the same ways as oysters. The little-neck clam is the smallest of the hard-shell variety, and the chowder clam the largest. The long soft-shell clams, also known as steamers, are more easily digested than the hard-shell varieties, and are therefore more desirable for steaming, baking at clambakes, and deep-fat frying.

Clams are available shucked and in the shell. If the recipe calls for shucked clams, buy them by the pint or quart. If they are to be served in the shell, buy them by the dozen, quart, peck, or gallon. Always make sure the shells are tightly closed except for the protruding neck, which should withdraw into the shell when touched. Reject any that are broken or partially opened.

❧ CLAMS ON THE HALF SHELL

Allow 6 little-neck or cherrystone clams per serving. Ask the fish butcher to open the clams for you. Leave them in the deeper half of the shells and arrange each serving on a bed of cracked ice in a soup plate. In the center of each plate, put a small glass or lettuce cup filled with a cocktail sauce. Garnish with lemon wedges and parsley.

❧ STEAMED CLAMS

Allow 1 quart soft-shell clams in the shell per person. Scrub the clams under running cold water until they are free of sand. Place the clams in a large kettle with ½ cup boiling water for each 4 quarts of clams. Cover and steam *only* until the shells open. Serve the clams in soup plates. Serve with melted butter to which a little lemon juice has been added. Strain the broth through fine cheesecloth and serve it in cups with a thin slice of lemon floating on top. Each person shells his own clams and dips them into the broth and then into the lemon butter. Provide finger bowls, or paper napkins, or finger towels wrung out in hot water.

❧ CLAM BISQUE (American)

1 pint (2 cups) shucked hard-shell clams	1¾ cups milk, heated
4 tablespoons (½ stick) butter, melted	⅔ cup light cream, heated
½ teaspoon minced onion	1 teaspoon salt, or salt to taste
1/16 teaspoon minced garlic	¼ teaspoon ground nutmeg
3 tablespoons flour	⅛ teaspoon ground white pepper

Remove the necks from the clams and put the necks through the food chopper, using the coarsest blade. Add the chopped necks to the rest of the clams in their juice, cover, and cook *just* below boiling point 5 minutes or until clams are tender. *Do not boil.* Remove from heat and set aside. Mix the melted butter with the onion, garlic, and flour in a 1½-quart saucepan. Stir and cook until the mixture foams. Remove from heat and beat in the hot milk. Cook over low heat until the sauce begins to thicken, stirring constantly. Add the hot cream and heat. Stir in the clams and seasonings and heat gently—if the bisque is allowed to boil, it will curdle. Serve promptly, garnished with chopped parsley. Makes 6 servings.

CRABS *(Crabes, Tourteaux)*

There are four principal species of crabs caught in the salt waters of North America: blue crab, Dungeness crab, king crab, and rock crab. Crabs are available live, cooked in the shell, cooked and frozen; as fresh cooked crab meat and canned crab meat. Canned crab meat is usually sold in 5-, 6½-, and 13-ounce cans. Fresh crab meat may be purchased by the pound or half pound in several grades.

Hard-shell crabs are available all year round but are more plentiful during the summer months. Since hard-shell crabs do not ship well, they are generally sold in the area in which they are caught.

The term soft-shell crab is applied to any crab that is molting—that is, shedding its hard shell, leaving a soft one underneath. Most of the soft-shell crabs coming to the market are blue crabs, which constitute about three-fourths of all crabs marketed in the United States.

Fresh hard-shell and soft-shell crabs should be alive at the time of cooking. Cooked crab meat must be refrigerated, iced, or frozen from the time it is cooked to the time it is used.

⚜ BOILED HARD-SHELL CRABS

Wash the crabs in plenty of cold water and scrub them with a brush. Rinse well in cold water. Plunge the live crabs, head first, into enough rapidly boiling water to cover them completely. Add 1 tablespoon salt for each 1 quart water. Simmer 15 to 20 minutes or only until the shells turn red. Drain and hold under running cold water. Drain again and let the crabs cool, resting on their claws. Break off the claws close to the body, crack them with nut crackers, and remove all the meat. Break off the tail or the pointed apron. With both hands, pull the upper and lower shells apart, beginning at the tail. Wash away loose matter under running cold water. Remove the membranous covering along the edges. Using a pointed knife, remove the meat between the sections and the cartilage. Keep the pieces whole if possible. Save the roe and liver to garnish crab-meat salad. Six crabs make about 1 cup meat.

⚜ BOILED SOFT-SHELL CRABS

Wash the crabs in cold water several times. Place the live crabs on a board, face down. With scissors, make an incision straight across each crab just back of the eyes and cut out the face. Lift the pointed ends of the shells and scrape out the spongy portion. Turn the crabs on their backs and cut off the tails. Wash thoroughly under running cold water. Plunge the cleaned crabs in enough boiling water to cover them. Add 1 teaspoon salt for each quart water. Cover and simmer 15 minutes. Drain. Serve hot with melted butter and lemon juice, or Herb Butter (page 58). Or chill and serve with lemon juice and mayonnaise. Allow 2 crabs per person.

⚜ CRABS MORNAY (Crabes ou Tourteaux Mornay)

meat of 6 medium-sized cooked crabs, or 1 cup cooked crab meat	salt and ground black pepper to taste
	⅓ cup grated Cheddar cheese
1½ cups Mornay Sauce (page 40)	3 tablespoons butter, melted
¾ teaspoon lemon juice	¾ cup soft breadcrumbs

Combine the crab meat, Mornay Sauce, and lemon juice. Add salt and pepper to taste. Spoon the mixture onto 4 well-buttered crab shells or coquilles. Sprinkle with the grated cheese. Mix the melted butter with the breadcrumbs and sprinkle over the cheese. Bake in a preheated moderate oven (350° F.) 30 minutes or until crumbs are brown. Makes 4 servings.

⚜ KING CRAB, RUSSIAN STYLE (Tourteau à la Russe)

1½ cups cold cooked crab meat	lemon juice to taste
1½ cups cold cooked mixed vegetables (diced carrots, peas, potatoes, celery, and string beans)	mayonnaise
	fresh chervil, parsley, or tarragon leaves
salt and ground black pepper to taste	2 hard-cooked eggs, sliced

Combine the crab meat, vegetables, and salt, black pepper, and lemon juice to taste with about ⅓ cup mayonnaise. Spoon into crab shells or coquilles. Coat with mayonnaise. Garnish with chervil, parsley, or tarragon leaves and slices of hard-cooked eggs. Makes 6 servings.

CRAYFISH (Écrevisses)

The crayfish, also called crawfish, is a small freshwater crustacean similar in structure to its large cousin, the lobster. Its average length is about 6 inches.

Crayfish

Crayfish are rare in the northeastern part of the United States but are readily obtainable in the South and West. The flesh is somewhat firm and delicately flavored and may be used interchangeably with shrimp in many recipes.

⚜ HOW TO CLEAN AND COOK CRAYFISH

Use only live crayfish, allowing 6 to 8 per person. Wash the crayfish in cold water 5 to 6 times or until the water is clear. Remove the intestinal tract by inserting a knife tip under the intestine in the middle of the tail and pulling the intestine out gently, holding it between the knife and the index finger. Rinse the crayfish in cold water and immediately drop into boiling Court Bouillon (page 161) or boiling Acidulated Water (page 162) to prevent the body liquids from escaping through the body opening. Cover and simmer 5 to 10 minutes—*only* until the crayfish turn red. Cool in the cooking liquid. Serve cold on a bed of cracked ice, garnished with parsley. Eat with the fingers. Or, if desired, serve them steaming in their shells, swimming in their own juices.

Cooked crayfish may be shelled and made into numerous dishes by combining with various sauces, etc.

⚜ CRAYFISH IN COURT BOUILLON
(*Écrevisses au Court-Bouillon ou à la Nage*)

24 to 32 live crayfish	2 stalks parsley
1½ quarts water	½ bay leaf
1 small onion, sliced	½ teaspoon dried thyme
1 small carrot, diced	1½ teaspoons salt
1 shallot or green onion, chopped	¾ cup dry white wine

Wash and eviscerate the crayfish and reserve. Place all ingredients except the crayfish and the wine in a 6-quart saucepan. Cover and cook until vegetables are tender. Add the wine and bring the mixture to boiling point. Add the crayfish immediately while the liquid is boiling. Cover and simmer 5 to 10 minutes or *only* until the crayfish turn red. Remove from the court bouillon and serve in the shells; eat with the fingers. If desired, accompany with melted butter seasoned to taste with dill. Makes 4 to 5 servings.

⚜ CRAYFISH, BORDEAUX STYLE (*Écrevisses à la Bordelaise*)

24 live crayfish	3 tablespoons brandy
2 small white onions, minced	⅓ cup dry white wine
1 small carrot, finely diced	⅓ cup Velouté Sauce (page 40)
2 shallots, or white parts of 2 green onions, minced	salt and ground black pepper to taste
4 tablespoons butter	¼ teaspoon meat glaze
	parsley

Wash and eviscerate the crayfish and reserve. Brown the vegetables in 3 table-spoons of the butter. Add the crayfish and cook *only* until the crayfish turn red. Add the brandy, heat, and ignite. Stir in the wine, Velouté Sauce, and salt and black pepper to taste. Simmer 10 minutes. Transfer the crayfish to a dish. Add the meat glaze to the pan liquid and cook until the liquid is reduced to three-fourths the original amount. Add the remaining 1 tablespoon of the butter to the sauce and pour the sauce over the crayfish. Sprinkle with chopped parsley. Makes 4 servings.

LOBSTER AND ROCK LOBSTER
(*Homard et Langouste*)

The true northern lobster, the king of shellfish, is a crustacean native to the North Atlantic. One species is found in the cold waters off the North American coast from Labrador to North Carolina; another is found off the coast of northern Europe. The most important sources of lobster in the United States are Nova Scotia and Maine.

The shell of the true lobster is smooth and the claws large with pincers of unequal size. Lobsters are available throughout the year but are most plentiful in summer when they come closer inshore. Lobster must be alive and active at the time of cooking, with the tail curling under the body rather than hanging down when picked up. Live lobsters that are bought from the fish markets usually weigh from 1 to 3 pounds and are graded in four sizes: chicken, ¾ to 1 pound; quarters, 1¼ pounds; large, 1½ to 2¼ pounds; and jumbos, 2½ pounds and over.

Lobsters are also available cooked whole in the shells. They should have a fresh "seashore odor" and be bright red in color. The tail should spring back quickly after it has been pulled straight. Cooked lobster picked from the shells is marketed fresh, frozen, and canned. Frozen lobster meat is also available in 6-, 14- and 16-ounce cans.

The flesh of the northern lobster is highly esteemed for its delicate and savory flavor. That of the female is considered finer than that of the male. In the opening of the female there is likely to be roe, or coral, which turns red when cooked and is used to garnish the lobster dish and to color the sauce. In both male and female, the liver, called tomally, is delicious.

Rock lobster, also known as spiny lobster, is almost worldwide in its distribution, being found in tropical, subtropical, and temperate waters of the Atlantic, Pacific, and Indian oceans and in the Mediterranean Sea. It is readily distinguished from the true northern lobster by the absence of heavy claws, by prominent spines on its body and legs, and by its long antennae. The flesh is less flavorsome than that of true lobster but can be prepared in the same ways. Frozen rock lobster tails are popular in the United States.

⚜ BOILED LOBSTER WITH BUTTER OR MAYONNAISE

Allow 1 small live lobster or half of a large one per person. Grasp the lobster by the body with the claws away from you so it cannot nip you. Plunge it, head first, into enough rapidly boiling salted water to cover it (1 tablespoon salt to 1 quart water). Cover the kettle. Return to boiling point and simmer 20 minutes. Remove the lobster from the water and drain well. Place the lobster on its back. With a sharp knife or kitchen shears, cut it in half lengthwise and spread it open. Remove the stomach, which is just below the head, and the intestinal vein, which runs from the stomach to the tip of the tail. Do not discard the coral röe or the green liver; both are delicious. Crack the claws. Arrange the lobster on a platter. Garnish with lemon wedges and parsley. Serve hot with melted butter, or cold with mayonnaise. Lobster can be cooked in Court Bouillon instead of unsalted water.

For recipes specifying cooked lobster meat, cool the cooked lobster and remove the meat. Two lobsters, 1 pound each, yield approximately ½ pound cooked lobster meat.

⚜ BROILED LIVE LOBSTER

Allow 1 small live lobster or half of a large one per person. Place the lobster on its back. Insert a sharp knife between the body shell and tail segment, cutting down to sever the spinal cord. Cut the lobster in half lengthwise. Remove the stomach, which is just below the head, and the intestinal vein, which runs from the stomach to the tip of the tail. Do not discard the liver or the coral roe. Crack the claws. Spread the lobster open as flat as possible on a broiler pan. Brush the meat with melted butter. Sprinkle with salt and ground black pepper. Broil about 4 inches from the source of heat for 12 to 15 minutes or until lobster has browned lightly. Sprinkle with a little paprika. Arrange the lobster on a platter and garnish with lemon wedges and parsley. Serve with lemon butter made by mixing ¼ cup (½ stick) melted butter with 1 tablespoon lemon juice.

⚜ LOBSTER FRA DIAVOLO (*Homard Fra Diavolo*)

1 cooked lobster, 1½ pounds	¼ cup chopped parsley
2 tablespoons butter, melted	¼ teaspoon dried marjoram
3 medium-sized tomatoes, peeled, seeded, and chopped	salt and ground black pepper to taste
	lemon wedges
1 small clove garlic, split in half	parsley
2 tablespoons olive oil	cooked rice

211

Cut the lobster in half lengthwise and arrange it in a shallow heatproof dish. Brush with the melted butter and bake in a preheated slow oven (325° F.) 10 to 15 minutes or until the lobster is warm. Sauté the tomatoes and garlic in hot olive oil and add the herbs, salt, and pepper. Remove the garlic and pour the sauce over the lobster. Garnish with lemon wedges and parsley. Serve with cooked rice. Makes 3 servings.

⚜ LOBSTER RUSSIAN STYLE (*Homard ou Langouste à la Russe*)

2 boiled lobsters, weighing 1¼ pounds each
2 cups mixed cold, cooked, diced vegetables
about ⅓ cup mayonnaise
salt and ground black pepper to taste
½ teaspoon lemon juice

4 hard-cooked eggs, sliced
truffles or black olives
lemon wedges, slices, or curls

Split each lobster in half lengthwise and arrange them on a bed of lettuce. Combine the vegetables, mayonnaise, salt, pepper, and lemon juice and spoon an equal amount of the mixture onto each of the lobster halves. Arrange the slices of hard-cooked eggs on top. Garnish the egg slices with bits of truffle or black olives. Decorate the platter with lemon wedges, slices, or curls. Makes 4 servings. (*See illustration, page 227.*)

⚜ GARNISHED ROCK LOBSTER (*Langouste en Bellevue*)

1 rock lobster, 2½ pounds
lettuce
truffles or ripe olives
salad oil
2 cups mixed cold, cooked, diced vegetables

mayonnaise
½ teaspoon lemon juice
salt and ground black pepper
2 hard-cooked eggs, sliced
2 medium-sized tomatoes, sliced

Boil and drain the rock lobster according to the recipe for Boiled Lobster. Cut the membrane under the tail with scissors in such a way that the tail meat can be taken out in one piece, without breaking or damaging the shell. Place a bed of lettuce on a large fish platter and put the shell on it, with the tail spread out. Cut the tail flesh into nice slices and arrange them down the middle of the shell so they overlap, from the feelers to the tail. Place a thin slice of truffle or black olive on each and brush with oil so the dish will retain its fresh look. Mix the vegetables with ⅓ cup of mayonnaise, the lemon juice, and salt and black pepper to taste. Place a mound of vegetables on each side of the shell and decorate with hard-cooked egg slices and tomato slices. Serve more mayonnaise in a separate dish. Makes 4 servings.

MUSSELS (*Moules*)

Although mussels are consumed in great quantities in France and Italy, they have not yet become widely popular in America. They are found mostly in the markets that cater to the foreign population of the larger cities.

Mussels are one of the world's most plentiful and delicious shellfish. The meat is a creamy golden-yellow, tender and sweet as a small clam. Mussels may be prepared in ways similar to those used for clams and oysters.

⚜ HOW TO WASH MUSSELS

Put the mussels in a colander and hold them under running cold water to rinse off all the loose dirt and mud. Then scrub the shells with a stiff brush and scrape them with a knife to remove all seaweed, slime, and dirt that has adhered to the shells. Rinse well under running cold water. With scissors trim off the beard that protrudes from the closed shell. Soak mussels 2 hours in cold water to rid the interior of possible sand and to get rid of some of the salty flavor. Then put them in a colander and rinse again in cold running water.

⚜ STEAMED MUSSELS (*Moules à la Marinière*)

Mussels should be cooked only until the shells open, about 8 to 10 minutes. Put the mussels in a large kettle with only enough water or wine to create steam. Add a little parsley and freshly ground black pepper. Cover the kettle tightly and steam until the shells open, shaking the kettle occasionally up and down and sideways to cook all the mussels uniformly. Transfer the mussels to another pan and cover tightly to keep hot. Strain the broth through a fine sieve or thick cheesecloth.

To serve, put the mussels in soup plates, heat the broth, and pour it over them. With fingers or an oyster fork, pick the mussels out of the shells. The shells are discarded in a dish provided for the purpose. Provide each person with a spoon for drinking the broth, a large napkin, and a finger bowl, or a finger towel wrung out in hot water for cleaning the fingers. Allow 1 quart of mussels per person.

213

⚜ MUSSELS CREOLE STYLE (*Moules à la Créole*)

2 cups shucked raw mussels
½ cup dry white wine
2 tablespoons finely chopped onion
2 tablespoons butter
½ teaspoon curry powder

2 cups cold cooked rice
olive oil or salad oil to taste
wine vinegar to taste
salt and ground black pepper to taste

Scrub and clean the raw mussels thoroughly. Open the shells with a knife. Discard the shells and set the mussels and the liquor aside. Put the wine, onion, butter, and curry powder in a saucepan, bring to boiling point, and boil 1 minute. Add the shucked mussels. Strain the mussel liquor through fine cheesecloth to be sure that all sand is removed. Add the liquor to the mixture. Cover and cook 2 to 3 minutes over low heat. Put the rice in a serving dish. With a slotted spoon lift out the mussels and arrange them over the rice. Cook the liquor 1 to 2 minutes to reduce the quantity slightly and pour it over the mussels and rice. Sprinkle with oil, vinegar, salt, and black pepper to taste. Serve chilled. Makes 4 servings.

⚜ MUSSELS ITALIAN STYLE (*Moules à l'Italienne*)

3 quarts thoroughly scrubbed and
  cleaned mussels in the shells
½ teaspoon dried thyme
¼ teaspoon ground black pepper
2 tablespoons chopped parsley

6 to 8 fresh tomatoes, or 1 cup tomato
  purée
2 tablespoons butter
salt and ground black pepper to taste
pinch of saffron
¼ teaspoon sugar

Place the first 4 ingredients in an 8-quart heavy saucepan. Cover and cook, without liquid, until the mussel shells are wide open, about 10 minutes. Drain the juice from the mussels and strain it into a saucepan. Keep the mussels warm. If fresh tomatoes are used, chop them fine, press through a sieve, and add to the mussel juice. Or add the tomato purée if that is used. Add the butter. Cook over high heat until the sauce has reduced to two-thirds the original amount. Season with salt and pepper, saffron, and sugar. Serve the sauce in small individual dishes. Serve the mussels in the shells in soup plates; they are dipped into the sauce as they are eaten. Makes 4 servings.

⚜ MUSSELS WITH MAYONNAISE (*Moules à la Mayonnaise*)

3 quarts thoroughly scrubbed and
  cleaned mussels in the shells
¾ cup dry white wine or water
2 tablespoons reduced mussel liquor
¾ cup mayonnaise

¼ teaspoon powdered mustard
½ teaspoon water
8 small boiled potatoes
Vinaigrette Sauce (page 56)
chopped parsley

Place the mussels and the wine or water in a 6-quart saucepan. Cover and simmer over low heat 8 to 10 minutes or *only* until the shells open. Remove the mussels from the shells and chill them. Strain the liquor through fine cheesecloth and cook until it has reduced to 2 tablespoons. Add the reduced mussel liquor to the mayonnaise. Soak the mustard for 5 minutes in the ½ teaspoon water, blend it with the mayonnaise, and add to the mussels. Place the mussels in a serving dish. Dip the potatoes in Vinaigrette Sauce and place them on the dish around the mussels. Sprinkle with chopped parsley. Serve chilled. Makes 4 servings.

❦ PILAF OF MUSSELS ORIENTAL STYLE
(*Pilaf de Moules à l'Orientale*)

3 quarts thoroughly scrubbed and
  cleaned mussels in the shells
5 tablespoons butter
1 shallot, sliced
1 stalk parsley
3 whole black peppercorns
¾ cup dry white wine
3 tablespoons flour
1¼ cups mussel liquor

½ cup light cream
⅛ to ¼ teaspoon crumbled saffron
  strands
1 tablespoon hot water
¾ teaspoon salt, or salt to taste
⅛ teaspoon ground black pepper
3 cups hot cooked rice
chopped parsley

Place the mussels, 2 tablespoons of the butter, and the shallot, parsley, peppercorns, and wine in a 6-quart saucepan. Cover and steam over low heat 8 to 10 minutes or *only* until the shells open. Remove the mussels from the shells, discard the shells, and set the mussels aside. Strain the liquor and set aside. Melt the remaining 3 tablespoons butter in a saucepan. Remove from heat and blend in the flour. Return to heat; stir and cook 1 minute or until the mixture foams. Remove from heat and add 1¼ cups of the mussel liquor. Stir and cook 1 minute or until the sauce begins to thicken. Add the cream. Stir and cook until the sauce is medium thick. Dissolve the saffron in the hot water and blend it with the sauce. Add the mussels and heat. Season with salt and black pepper. Shape the hot cooked rice in a ring on a serving plate. Fill the center with the creamed mussels. Sprinkle with chopped parsley. Makes 6 servings.

❦ MUSSELS POULETTE (*Moules à la Poulette*)

3 quarts mussels, prepared according
  to recipe for Steamed Mussels
  (page 213)
2 tablespoons butter
3 tablespoons flour
mussel liquor

¾ cup light cream
1 egg yolk
salt and ground black pepper to taste
2 tablespoons chopped parsley
4 servings Pilaf (page 117)

Prepare Steamed Mussels and strain the liquor. Melt the butter in a 1-quart saucepan. Remove from heat and blend in the flour. Return to heat; stir and cook 1 minute or until the mixture foams. Remove from heat and add the strained mussel liquor and ½ cup of the light cream. Return to heat; stir and cook 1 to 2 minutes or until the mixture is of medium thickness. Beat the egg yolk with the remaining ¼ cup light cream and gradually stir into the hot sauce. Cook only until hot. Season to taste with salt and ground black pepper. Add 2 tablespoons chopped parsley and the shelled mussels. Serve with Pilaf. Makes 4 servings.

⚜ MUSSEL SALAD À LA GRECQUE (*Salade de Moules à la Grecque*)

1 cup shucked steamed mussels, chilled	3 tablespoons olive oil or salad oil
	salt and ground black pepper to taste
1 cup sliced blanched mushrooms	4 large slices tomato
1 small white onion, sliced	4 blanched artichoke hearts
1 tablespoon lemon juice	parsley

Combine the mussels, mushrooms, onion, lemon juice, oil, salt, and pepper. Set aside. Arrange the tomato slices on a platter and place an artichoke heart on each. Sprinkle lightly with salt and black pepper and top with the mussel and mushroom salad. Garnish with parsley. Makes 4 servings.

OYSTERS (*Huîtres*)

Oysters may be eaten at any season of the year but are not considered best in flavor during the spawning season, which is from May through August. Oysters are eaten raw, roasted, steamed, baked, escalloped, creamed, fried, in stews, in stuffings, etc. They should be cooked at low temperature only until they are plump and the edges begin to curl. Overcooking results in tough, rubbery oysters.

Oysters are marketed live in the shells, shucked (fresh or frozen), and in cans (whole oysters, smoked, or in stew). They are graded according to size: extra large, large, medium, small, and extra small. The form and size in which oysters should be purchased are determined by the method of preparation; for example, for serving on the half shell, buy large oysters in the shell; for stew, the small or extra small oysters are appropriate.

Oysters purchased in the shell should be alive with the shells closed. If the shells gape and do not close quickly in handling, discard them. If the recipe specifies shucked oysters, buy them by the pint or quart. The contents should include not more than 10 per cent clear liquid by weight. Oysters should be gray in color.

For Oysters on the Half-Shell, see page 72.

⚜ **OYSTERS MORNAY** (*Huîtres Mornay*)

20 to 24 small shucked oysters in their
 liquor
¾ cup Béchamel Sauce (page 38)
1 large egg yolk

½ cup grated Gruyère or Cheddar
 cheese
salt and ground black pepper to taste
lemon juice

Cook the oysters in the liquor over very low heat or hot water *only* until the
edges curl. Drain off and discard the liquor. Add ¼ cup of the Béchamel
Sauce to the oysters. Beat the egg yolk and ¼ cup of the cheese into the remaining ½ cup Béchamel Sauce. Season to taste with salt, black pepper, and
lemon juice. Put 1 teaspoon of the sauce into each of 4 heatproof individual
serving dishes and then put 5 to 6 oysters in each dish. Cover with the sauce.
Sprinkle with the remaining ¼ cup cheese. Brown quickly under broiler
heat. Serve at once. Makes 4 servings.

SCALLOPS (*Pétoncles*)

Scallops are available in two varieties: large or "sea" scallops and small or
"bay" scallops. The sea scallop's shell is saucer-shaped and ranges in size from
that of a saucer to that of a dinner plate. In Europe and the West Indies the
whole scallop is eaten, but in the United States, only the juicy adductor
muscle, or "eye," is used. Sea scallops are taken from the waters of the
northern and Middle Atlantic states, with the vast majority coming from
the waters at New Bedford, Massachusetts.

Bay scallops are sweeter than sea scallops and much smaller, attaining a
maximum width of 4 inches, with the adductor muscle, which is the only part
eaten, about ½ inch wide. Bay scallops are found in inshore bays and estuaries
from New England to the Gulf of Mexico.

Scallops are available throughout the year. They are marketed fresh or
frozen but only in the form of ready-to-cook meat, as they are opened,
packed, and iced at sea. Both fresh scallops and thawed frozen scallops should
have a "sweetish" odor. When bought in packages, they should be practically
free of liquor.

Scallops contain good-quality protein, minerals, and vitamins and very
little fat. They may be deep-fat-fried, pan-fried, made into soup, main dishes,
salads, or served as the appetizer course.

In France, scallops are called *Coquilles Saint-Jacques* because the pilgrims
who visited the shrine of Saint James of Compostella ate the scallops as a
penance instead of eating meat. The shells were fastened to the pilgrims' hats
and brought home with them. Scallop shells (*coquilles*) are used as dishes for

cooking and serving not only scallops and other seafoods but various other creamed mixtures, and the term coquilles is applied to any food so served.

❧ BAKED SCALLOPS (*Coquilles Saint-Jacques*)

This is a delicious dish appropriate for the first course of a meal.

42 uncooked bay scallops	1/16 teaspoon minced fresh garlic
6 tablespoons butter	1/16 teaspoon ground black pepper
1 teaspoon minced onion	3/4 teaspoon lemon juice
1 teaspoon chopped chives	1/4 teaspoon salt
2 teaspoons finely chopped parsley	1/2 cup soft breadcrumbs
1/8 teaspoon dried tarragon	

Arrange 7 scallops in each of 6 buttered scallop shells (coquilles) or individual casseroles. Set aside. Soften 3 tablespoons of the butter and blend with all the other ingredients except the breadcrumbs. Put 1 teaspoon of the butter mixture on each shell or casserole. Melt the remaining 3 tablespoons butter, mix with the breadcrumbs, and sprinkle over the scallops. Bake in a preheated very hot oven (500° F.) 5 minutes. Makes 6 servings.

❧ BOILED SCALLOPS

1 pound fresh or frozen scallops	2 tablespoons salt (omit if Court
1 quart boiling water or Court	Bouillon is used)
Bouillon (page 161)	

If frozen scallops are used, thaw them first. Remove and discard all particles of shell and wash the scallops in cold water. Place them in a saucepan with the boiling water and salt, or with 1 quart Court Bouillon. Simmer 3 to 4 minutes, depending upon the size. Drain and use in recipes calling for cooked scallops. Makes approximately 1/2 pound cooked scallops.

❧ SCALLOPS COOKED IN WINE

1 quart fresh or frozen scallops	dry white wine

If frozen scallops are used, thaw them first. Remove any particles of shell and wash the scallops in cold water. Drain well. Place the scallops in a saucepan with barely enough wine to cover. Bring the wine slowly to boiling point, reduce heat, and simmer 8 to 10 minutes. Remove the scallops. If they are large, slice them. Use in any recipe specifying scallops cooked in wine.

✤ DEVILED SCALLOPS (*Coquilles Saint-Jacques à la Diable*)

2 pounds fresh or frozen scallops
¼ cup chopped onion
6 tablespoons butter
4 tablespoons flour
1 teaspoon prepared Dijon-type
  mustard

½ teaspoon Worcestershire sauce
1 teaspoon salt
dash cayenne
1 tablespoon chopped parsley
¾ cup soft breadcrumbs

If frozen scallops are used, thaw them first. Remove and discard any particles of shell and wash the scallops in cold water. Drain well. Chop the scallops and cook with the onion in 4 tablespoons (½ stick) of the butter 3 to 4 minutes, stirring frequently. Blend in all the remaining ingredients except the breadcrumbs. Stir and cook until thick, 2 to 3 minutes. Divide the mixture among 6 buttered scallop shells (coquilles) or individual casseroles. Melt the remaining 2 tablespoons butter, mix with the breadcrumbs, and sprinkle over the scallops. Bake in a preheated moderate oven (350° F.) 20 to 25 minutes or until crumbs are brown. Makes 6 servings.

✤ SCALLOPS AND MUSHROOMS IN WINE SAUCE
(*Coquilles Saint-Jacques à la Parisienne*)

1 quart fresh or frozen bay scallops
1 small white onion, chopped
2 tablespoons chopped parsley
dry white wine to cover
¼ pound mushroom caps, sliced
1 shallot, chopped (optional)
7 tablespoons butter
2 tablespoons hot water

2 tablespoons flour
1 cup scallop-wine stock
2 tablespoons heavy cream
salt and ground black pepper to taste
1 tablespoon chopped truffle
  (optional)
½ cup grated Gruyère cheese
½ cup soft breadcrumbs

Cook the scallops with the onion and parsley in *only* enough wine barely to cover them, as directed for Scallops Cooked in Wine. Reserve the stock. Simmer the mushrooms, and the shallot if used, in 1 tablespoon of the butter and 2 tablespoons hot water 8 to 10 minutes. Drain off the liquid, add to the scallop-wine stock, and boil until the quantity is reduced to one-half the original amount. Set aside. Melt 3 tablespoons of the butter in a 1-quart saucepan. Remove from heat and blend in the flour. Strain the scallop-wine stock, heat, and add 1 cup of it to the butter and flour mixture. Beat with a wire whisk until smooth. Cook over moderate to low heat until the sauce is medium thick, stirring frequently. Remove from heat, add the cream, 1 table-spoon of the butter, salt and pepper to taste, and truffles, if used. Add the scallops and mushrooms to the sauce and heat about 2 minutes. Stir in ¼ cup of the cheese and adjust seasonings. Spoon the mixture into 6 buttered scallop shells or ramekins. Sprinkle the tops with the rest of the grated cheese. Melt the remaining 2 tablespoons butter, mix with the breadcrumbs, and sprinkle on top of the cheese. Place under broiler heat until the tops have glazed and browned. Makes 4 servings.

⚜ SCALLOPS À LA DUCHESSE (*Coquilles Saint-Jacques à la Duchesse*)

Prepare the recipe for Scallops and Mushrooms in Wine Sauce. Fill 6 buttered scallop shells with the mixture. Put 2 cups Duchess Potatoes (page 383) in a pastry bag and pipe a border around each shell. Brush the potatoes lightly with milk. Sprinkle the scallop mixture with grated Gruyère or Cheddar cheese and buttered soft breadcrumbs. Cook under broiler heat until browned. Makes 6 servings.

⚜ SCALLOPS WITH TARTARE SAUCE
(*Coquilles Saint-Jacques à la Tartare*)

2 pounds fresh or frozen scallops
1 egg, beaten
1 tablespoon milk
1 teaspoon salt
1/16 teaspoon ground black pepper
1/2 cup flour
1/2 cup fine dry breadcrumbs
Tartare Sauce (page 55)

If frozen scallops are used, thaw them first. Remove and discard any particles of shell and wash the scallops in cold water. Drain well. Cut large scallops in half. Combine the beaten egg, milk, salt, and pepper. Combine the flour and breadcrumbs. Dip the scallops in the egg mixture and then roll them in the flour and breadcrumbs. Let them stand 15 to 20 minutes so crumbs will dry. Pan-fry or deep-fat-fry. Serve with Tartare Sauce. Makes 6 to 8 servings.

⚜ Pan-Fried Scallops

Place the crumbed scallops in a heavy skillet which contains 2 tablespoons hot oil or vegetable shortening. Fry over moderate heat until brown on one side, turn and brown on the other side. Add more oil or shortening if needed. Drain on paper towels.

⚜ Deep-Fat-Fried Scallops

Fry the crumbed scallops in deep fat preheated to 350° F. 2 to 3 minutes or until browned. Drain on paper towels.

SHRIMP, PRAWNS (*Crevettes, Langoustines*)

Shrimp, one of the most esteemed of the shellfish family, are tender and white-meated with a distinctive flavor. Thanks to modern fishing and marketing methods, they are marketed in all parts of the United States every season of the year.

There are various species of shrimp, which, when caught, range in color from greenish gray to brownish red. However, when cooked, they differ little in flavor and appearance and may be used interchangeably in recipes.

Shrimp are graded according to size: jumbo, large, medium, and small. Jumbo shrimp run 15 or fewer per pound while the smallest run 60 or more per pound. A very large shrimp, available in some markets in the larger cities, is known as the colossal or giant and runs 10 or fewer per pound. This variety comes from European and Indian waters and is sold mostly to fancy restaurants and hotels. The larger shrimp are more expensive than the smaller ones but require less time to prepare. Shrimp may be purchased fresh, raw or cooked, either in the shells or peeled and deveined. Shrimp are also available in frozen form: raw or cooked in the shells; raw or cooked, peeled and deveined; breaded, peeled, deveined, and ready for cooking, according to package directions. Shrimp are also available in 4½-, 5- and 6½-ounce cans, either packed in brine or dry. Pickled, smoked, and dried shrimp are available in specialty food stores and in markets catering to the foreign population.

Prawns (French, *langoustines;* Italian, *scampi*) are similar to shrimp but belong to a different genus. They are prepared in the same ways.

⚜ HOW TO COOK SHRIMP

Shrimp may either be cooked in the shells and peeled later, or peeled before cooking. If they are cooked in the shells more salt is used; otherwise the method is the same and the decision entirely a matter of preference. To obtain ½ pound cooked, peeled, and deveined shrimp, purchase 1 pound raw shrimp in the shells.

⚜ How to Cook Shrimp in the Shells

1 pound raw unpeeled shrimp	8 teaspoons or 2⅔ tablespoons salt
3 cups boiling water	

Wash the shrimp and add them to the boiling water. Stir in the salt. Cover, bring to boiling point, reduce heat, and simmer until the shrimp turn red, about 5 minutes. Drain and let cool enough to handle. Peel the shrimp and remove the vein. Rinse in cold water and chill.

⚜ How to Cook Peeled Shrimp

4 teaspoons salt
3 cups boiling water

1 pound shrimp, peeled and deveined

Add the salt to the boiling water. Then add the shrimp. Cover, bring the water to boiling point, reduce heat, and simmer 5 minutes. Remove from the water, drain, and chill.

⚜ FRIED SHRIMP (*Crevettes Frits*)

1 pound raw shrimp, peeled and
  deveined
4 tablespoons butter, melted

1 tablespoon lemon juice
¼ teaspoon salt
dash ground black pepper or cayenne

Wash the shrimp and dry thoroughly on paper towels. Fry in hot melted butter until browned on both sides, turning frequently. Transfer the shrimp to a warmed platter. Add the remaining ingredients to the butter in which the shrimp were cooked, and pour over the shrimp. Makes 4 servings.

⚜ PRAWNS OR SHRIMP CHÂTEAU BOUSCAT
(*Langoustines Château Bouscat*)

1 envelope unflavored gelatin
¼ teaspoon powdered mustard
¼ cup cold water
1¼ cups boiling water
2 tablespoons sugar
2 tablespoons lemon juice
½ teaspoon salt
⅛ teaspoon ground white pepper

2 cups cold, cooked, diced, mixed
  vegetables
15 prawns or jumbo shrimp, cooked,
  peeled, and deveined
20 medium shrimp, cooked, peeled,
  and deveined
11 black olives, pitted and cut in half
Coating Mayonnaise (page 54)
parsley

Mix the gelatin, mustard, and ¼ cup cold water together, and let stand 5 minutes. Add the boiling water, sugar, lemon juice, salt, and white pepper. Chill until the mixture is about as thick as fresh egg whites. Fold in the vegetables. Turn the mixture into a lightly oiled 1-quart mold. Refrigerate until the salad is firm. Unmold the salad onto a serving plate. Arrange the prawns or jumbo shrimp around the salad and the medium shrimp over the top as shown in the illustration (page 228). Decorate with black olives and pipe rosettes of Coating Mayonnaise between the prawns or jumbo shrimp. Garnish the base of the salad with parsley. Decorate each end of the tray with an arrangement of 5 medium shrimp and ½ black olive. Makes 4 to 6 servings.

⚜ SHRIMP PILAF (*Pilaf de Crevettes*)

1 cup long-grain rice
2 cups cold water
5 tablespoons butter
2 cups boiling chicken stock or
    bouillon
¾ teaspoon salt
¼ teaspoon ground white pepper
1 teaspoon lemon juice
1 teaspoon curry powder

2 tablespoons finely chopped onion
2 tablespoons flour
¾ cup hot shrimp stock, fish stock, or
    chicken stock
⅓ cup heavy cream
½ pound cooked, peeled, and
    deveined shrimp
salt and ground black pepper to taste

Soak the rice in the cold water at least 30 minutes. Drain well. Melt 2 table-spoons of the butter in a 1½-quart saucepan. Add the rice. Stir and cook over moderately low heat 4 to 5 minutes or until rice is dry and begins to stick to the pan. Pour in the boiling stock or bouillon. Add the salt, pepper, and lemon juice, cover, and cook, without stirring, 12 to 15 minutes or until rice is almost tender and has absorbed all the liquid. Turn off heat and let the rice stand, covered, while preparing the shrimp.

    Melt the remaining 3 tablespoons butter in a 1-quart saucepan. Add the curry powder and onion. Stir and cook 2 to 3 minutes or until onion is limp and transparent. Remove from the heat and blend in the flour. Return to heat; stir and cook 1 to 2 minutes. Remove from heat and beat in the hot stock. Cook over moderately low heat until the sauce is medium thick. Add the cream and heat 1 minute. Stir in the shrimp and salt and pepper to taste. Turn the hot cooked rice onto a serving plate and shape it into a ring. Fill the center with the creamed shrimp. Garnish the dish with shrimp tails or heads, if available. Serve hot. Makes 4 to 6 servings. Other shellfish can also be used for this dish. (*See illustration, page 228.*)

⚜ CURRIED SCAMPI OR SHRIMP BROCHETTES
(*Scampi en Brochettes au Curry*)

8 jumbo scampi or shrimp, peeled and
    deveined
4 slices bacon, cut in half
4 tablespoons butter
1 teaspoon curry powder
¼ teaspoon salt

1 cup hot cooked rice
1 tablespoon narrow strips pickled red
    sweet pepper or pimiento
1 tablespoon julienne strips cooked
    ham

Wrap each scampi or shrimp in ½ slice bacon and thread them on skewers. Melt 2 tablespoons of the butter in a small saucepan, add the curry powder and salt, and stir and cook ½ minute. Brush the curry butter over both sides of the scampi or shrimp, and arrange them on an oiled broiler pan. Broil 3 inches from the source of heat 4 to 5 minutes. Brush both sides again with curry butter, turn, and broil the other side 3 to 4 minutes. Toss the rice with the strips of pickled pepper or pimiento and ham and the remaining 2 tablespoons butter. Spoon the rice into a serving dish. Arrange the skewers of scampi or shrimp on the rice. Makes 2 servings. (*See illustration, page 227.*)

Squid (*Supions*)

The squid, or calamar or calamary, is a cephalopod mollusk, one of a group which includes the octopus, cuttlefish, and nautilus. The squid has a soft, elongated body built around a thin, transparent, flexible, pen-shaped shell. Its head has ten arms or tentacles with suction cups at their tips. It feeds on fish and can hide from its enemies by changing color quickly and by ejecting a black sepia (ink) to cloud the water. This sepia is used as an artists' color and sometimes in cooking the squid meat.

Squid inhabit most of the warm and temperate seas, and the several species vary in size from less than 1 inch to the giant squid which may have tentacles 30 feet long. The common squid is about 2 feet long and is bluish or purple in color. A variety which is found in the Mediterranean is about 10 inches long when full grown. The flesh of the squid is sweet, rather rich, and is considered by some as a great delicacy. Squid is available fresh, frozen, canned, and dried, but only in markets catering to the foreign trade.

⚜ HOW TO PREPARE SQUID FOR COOKING

Wash the squid thoroughly. Cut off and discard the head. Cut off the tentacles, put them in hot water, and pull off the veiling and the suction cups. The tentacles may be chopped and used in stuffing for squid and in stews. Slit the pouch down the middle and carefully pull out the intestines and the pen, a thin spiny translucent rod, being careful not to puncture the ink sac at the base of the head. Place the squid in warm water to remove the purplish outside skin. Remove or retain the ink sac (most squid fanciers feel that the ink adds flavor to the dish). Wash the squid in cold running water to remove all particles of grit and sand. Squid may be broiled, fried, stuffed, or made into stews. Allow ½ pound of squid per serving.

⚜ DEEP-FAT-FRIED SQUID (*Supions Frites*)

Allow ½ pound squid per serving. Cut squid into serving-size pieces, sprinkle with salt and ground black pepper, and roll in flour. Fry in deep fat preheated to 375° F., having the frying kettle semi covered to prevent the fat from splashing. Drain on paper towels. Serve at once while squid is very crisp.

↑ Deep-Fat-Fried Small Freshwater Fish (page 182)

↓ Moselle Fish Stew (page 203)   225

226 ↑ Eel in Green Sauce (page 176) ↓ Fried Trout (page 198)

↑ Curried Scampi or Shrimp Brochettes (page 223)

↓ Lobster Russian Style (page 212)

↑ Shrimp Pilaf (page 223) ↓ Prawns or Shrimp Château Bouscat (page 222)

Frogs' Legs

The bullfrog or bellowing frog native to the United States is about twice the size of the European frog (French *grenouille*). Only the legs of frogs are eaten and even the large ones contain no more than a tidbit of meat. The meat resembles chicken in texture and is regarded as a delicacy. Allow about 6 American frogs' legs or 12 European frogs' legs per serving.

Frogs' legs may be obtained ready to cook, fresh or frozen. If you prepare them yourself, cut off the hind legs close to the frog's body. Wash the legs in cold water and strip off the skin as you would pull off a glove. Cut off and discard the feet and soak the legs 2 hours in very cold water, changing the water often, then drain and dry thoroughly.

⚜ FRIED FROGS' LEGS (*Grenouilles Frites*)

Dip the legs in milk and dredge in flour seasoned with salt and ground black pepper. Pan-fry in hot shortening or oil 8 to 10 minutes or until browned on all sides. Serve in the same way as Southern fried chicken.

⚜ FROGS' LEGS FRITTERS (*Grenouilles en Beignets*)

24 prepared frogs' legs	¾ teaspoon salt
1½ tablespoons lemon juice or vinegar	¼ teaspoon ground black pepper
¼ cup olive oil or salad oil	1 recipe Fritter Batter (page 24)
2 teaspoons chopped parsley	fried parsley

Marinate the frogs' legs 1 hour in the next 5 ingredients. Wipe the legs dry, dip in Fritter Batter, and fry until brown in deep fat preheated to 375° F. Drain on paper towels. Serve as an entrée or as a hot hors d'oeuvre. Garnish with fried parsley. Makes 4 servings.

⚜ SAUTÉED FROGS' LEGS WITH HERBS
(*Grenouilles Sautées Fines Herbes*)

¼ small clove garlic	¼ cup dry white wine
1 tablespoon olive oil or salad oil	salt and ground black pepper
1 shallot, chopped	chopped parsley
2 tablespoons butter	lemon wedges
24 dressed frogs' legs	

229

Fry the garlic in the oil until it begins to turn color, then remove and discard it. Add the shallot and butter and cook about ½ minute. Add the frogs' legs and fry until golden on all sides. Transfer the legs to a warmed platter. Mix the wine with the butter in the skillet and bring the mixture to boiling point. Boil ½ minute. Sprinkle the legs with salt and black pepper and chopped parsley. Pour the wine-butter sauce over them. Serve with lemon wedges. Makes 4 servings.

Meats

The meats principally considered in this chapter are beef, veal, lamb and mutton, and pork. These meats are esteemed for their flavor as well as for their food value and should be purchased with thrift and cooked with care. Cuts from different animals and from different parts of the same animal differ in flavor, tenderness, and proportions of bone and gristle. Therefore, it is important that the consumer know both how to buy meat and how to cook it. While methods of cutting meat and the names of the cuts vary from country to country and even in different parts of the same country, the general principles are the same. This book uses American terms for cuts of meat.

This chapter also includes a section on variety meats and one on furred game.

Beef (*Boeuf*)

Beef is the flesh of mature cattle (steers, heifers, and cows). The highest grades of beef are from steer and heifers (baby beef) bred and fed for meat production. However, the tenderloin of cows is usually preferable to that of steers, because the fat layer is thinner. (The fat layer serves as an insulator against oven heat. A thicker layer prolongs the cooking time.) Cow's tenderloin is also less expensive, since the short loin of steer is the source of porterhouse and T-bone steaks, and the remainder of the short loin has to be sold as strip steaks at a lower price. The remaining meat of the cow is made into various kinds of processed meats.

Tender cuts of beef, as a rule, come from the ribs and loins which make up about one fourth of the carcass. These cuts are: steaks—porterhouse, T-bone, club, pinbone, sirloin, and rib; and roasts—standing rib, rolled rib, bottom sirloin, fillet. The less tender cuts come from the rest of the animal. These are: steaks—chuck, blade, flank, arm, full round, bottom round, and top round; pot roast—blade roast, arm pot roast, standing and boneless rump roast, and tip roast; stew meat—neck, plate, brisket, flank, heel of round.

Beef of good quality is well marbled with fat and has a moderately thick covering of fat over the exterior and a much thinner covering over the interior surface of the ribs. The lean meat is firm, fine-grained, and velvety in appearance. The bones of older animals are porous and red.

The three methods of cooking meat are dry heat, moist heat, and frying. Cuts from the loin are tender, because they contain little connective tissue. These cuts should be cooked by dry heat (open-pan roasting, broiling, and frying). Cuts from the remainder of the carcass are less tender, because they contain much connective tissue, and should be cooked by moist-heat methods (braising and cooking in liquid, as pot roast, stews, etc.).

❧ BEEFSTEAK (*Beefsteak*)

The amount of steak to allow per person depends upon the amount of bone and fat the meat contains. Purchase ⅓ to ½ pound boneless steak per person; ½ to ¾ pound bone-in steak per person. Slash the fat edge in several places to prevent the meat from curling. Broil the meat, using one of the following methods:

❧ Oven-Broiling Method

Set the oven control to "Broil" 5 to 10 minutes before the meat is placed under the heat. (Preheating time varies with the stove.) Place the steaks on the broiler rack and slip the rack in the broiler about 3 inches from the source of heat. Turn the steak when the upper side is nicely browned, using tongs or inserting a fork in the fat. Sprinkle the cooked side with salt and ground black pepper. Turn the meat and cook until it has reached the desired degree of doneness: rare, approximately 5 minutes on each side; medium-rare, 7 to 8 minutes on each side; well done, about 10 minutes on each side. Sprinkle with salt and pepper. Serve on a heated platter with Maître d'Hôtel Butter (page 58). Garnish as desired.

⚜ Pan-Broiling or Pan-Frying

This is a convenient method, popular in France, for broiling a small steak or a thin steak. Rub the bottom of a heated heavy skillet with a piece of suet or a little butter. Place the steak in the skillet. Cook slowly on one side and then the other, turning as often as necessary to insure uniform cooking. Pour off the fat as it accumulates in the pan. (Do not cover the pan or add water.) Definite times for pan-broiling are difficult to give. To test for doneness, cut a small gash near the bone and note the color of the interior. Rare meat will be uniformly red throughout; medium-rare will be uniformly light pink in the interior; well-done will be brownish-gray throughout and will have very little juice. Sprinkle with salt and ground black pepper. Serve on a hot platter with Maître d'Hôtel Butter (page 58). Garnish as desired.

⚜ GRILLED BEEF WITH TARTARE SAUCE
(Boeuf Grillé au Sauce Tartare)

4 steaks, 6 ounces each, ½-inch thick, cut from the top round	1½ tablespoons butter
salt and ground black pepper	1½ tablespoons olive oil or salad oil
about 6 tablespoons flour	Tartare Sauce (page 55)

Sprinkle both sides of the steaks with salt, black pepper, and enough flour to cover them lightly on both sides. Heat the butter and oil in a heavy 10-inch skillet. Add the steaks and cook uncovered over moderate heat until browned; turn and brown the other side. Reduce heat and continue cooking, uncovered, until steaks are tender, turning occasionally to cook them uniformly. Serve with Tartare Sauce. Makes 4 servings.

⚜ GRILLED CHATEAUBRIAND *(Chateaubriand Grillé)*

Chateaubriand, which is cut from the middle of the fillet, is the tenderest and most flavorful of all beefsteaks.

1 Chateaubriand steak, 2½ to 3 inches thick	Béarnaise Sauce (page 53)
butter, olive oil, or salad oil	Soufflé Potatoes (page 386) or Potatoes Pont-Neuf (page 386)
salt and ground black pepper	parsley

Spread the steak generously with butter or brush with oil on all sides. Place it on the broiler rack in a preheated broiling oven and broil 6 minutes. Transfer steak to a pan, sprinkle lightly with salt, and again spread it with butter or brush with oil. Reduce the heat to 350° F., and continue cooking in the broiling oven about 15 minutes if rare steak is desired; 20 minutes for medium-rare. Again sprinkle lightly with salt and with black pepper. Serve with Béarnaise Sauce and Soufflé Potatoes or Potatoes Pont-Neuf. Garnish with parsley. Makes 2 servings.

❧ ENTRECÔTE WITH BÉARNAISE SAUCE
(Entrecôte à la Béarnaise)

Entrecôte is a French cut which is not usually available in the United States; it is the boneless meat between the ribs, and is about 1 inch thick. The American cuts that come closest to it in tenderness and flavor are sirloin without the tenderloin, or rib steak with or without the bone.

2 entrecôte steaks (or sirloin or rib steaks), 1 pound each, cut 1 inch thick	2 tablespoons salad oil
	3 tablespoons hot water
	salt and ground black pepper to taste
5 tablespoons butter	Béarnaise Sauce (page 53)

Trim any excess fat from the steaks and make a small incision around them, in the layer of gristle between the fat and the meat. This prevents them from curling. Dry the meat thoroughly. Heat 3 tablespoons of the butter and the 2 tablespoons oil in a skillet. When the butter foam begins to subside, add the steaks and sauté each side 3 to 4 minutes, regulating the heat so the fat will not burn. The steak is medium-rare when bubbles of red juice begin to appear on the surface. Transfer steaks to a hot platter and keep hot. Skim off and discard the fat from the pan juices and add 3 tablespoons hot water. Mix well and cook ½ minute. Stir in the remaining 2 tablespoons butter. Bring to boiling point. Add salt and black pepper to taste. Sprinkle the steaks with salt and black pepper and pour the pan juices over them. Serve with Béarnaise Sauce. Makes 4 to 6 servings.

❧ Entrecôte with Bordelaise Sauce (Entrecôte à la Bordelaise)

Grill entrecôte steaks as directed in the preceding recipe. Poach slices of beef marrow in boiling salted water (½ teaspoon salt and 2 cups water) and place one on each serving of grilled entrecôte steak. Serve Bordelaise Sauce (page 44) in a separate bowl, or pour the sauce over the steak.

❧ Entrecôte with Maître d'Hôtel Butter (Entrecôte à la Maître d'Hôtel)

Grill entrecôte steaks as directed in the recipe for Entrecôte with Béarnaise Sauce. Arrange them on a warmed platter. Serve with Maître d'Hôtel Butter (page 58). Garnish with watercress.

⚜ Entrecôte with Wine Sauce (*Entrecôte à la Marchand de Vin*)

Broil entrecôte steaks according to directions in the recipe for Entrecôte with Béarnaise Sauce. Transfer the steaks to a warmed platter and keep them warm. Add ⅔ cup dry red wine to the skillet. Then add 1 sliced shallot and salt and ground black pepper to taste. Bring the mixture to boiling point and boil 1 minute. Stir in 1 tablespoon each butter and chopped parsley, and lemon juice to taste. Pour over the steaks.

⚜ ENTRECÔTE MIRABEAU (*Entrecôte Mirabeau*)

2 entrecôte steaks (or boneless sirloin or rib steaks), 1 pound each,
cut 1 inch thick
15 flat anchovy fillets

3 tablespoons butter, softened
24 pimiento-stuffed olives, sliced
watercress

Trim and flatten the steaks and place them on an oiled broiler rack. Blend 1 anchovy fillet with the butter and spread over the steaks. Place the rack in a preheated broiler oven 3 inches from the source of heat. Broil 5 minutes on each side for rare meat; 7 to 8 minutes for medium-rare; 10 minutes for well-done. Transfer the steaks to a warmed platter and arrange the remaining anchovies over the steaks in lattice pattern. Place slices of pimiento-stuffed olive in the squares. Garnish the platter with watercress and olives. Makes 6 servings.

⚜ SAUTÉED BEEF LYONNAISE (*Boeuf Sauté à la Lyonnaise*)

2 cups thinly sliced onion
3 tablespoons butter
salt and ground black pepper to taste

1½ pounds boneless sirloin or rib
steak, cut 1 inch thick
3 tablespoons dry white wine
parsley

Sauté the onion in 1½ tablespoons of the butter and sprinkle them with salt and black pepper. Cut the meat into 4 steaks. Using a separate heavy skillet, brown the steaks in the remaining 1½ tablespoons butter. Sprinkle them with salt and black pepper. Transfer them to a warmed platter. Pour the wine into the skillet, bring to boiling point, promptly spoon it over the steaks, and top them with the sautéed onion. Garnish with parsley. Makes 4 servings.

⚜ SIRLOIN STEAK NIÇOISE (*Tranche d'Aloyau à la Niçoise*)

Broil or pan-broil sirloin steak to the desired doneness (see Beefsteak, page 232). Sprinkle the steak with salt and ground black pepper and transfer to a hot platter. Surround it with Grilled Tomatoes (page 392) and Straw Potatoes (page 387). Garnish with parsley. Allow 1½ pounds steak for 4 servings.

❧ SLICED FILLET OF BEEF WITH CREAM
(*Emincé de Filet de Boeuf à la Crème*)

1½ pounds fillet of beef cut from the narrow part of the fillet	salt and ground black pepper
3 tablespoons butter	⅓ cup light cream
	2 tablespoons chopped parsley

Cut the beef into thin slices. Melt the butter in a heavy skillet and brown the slices quickly on both sides. Arrange the slices on a warmed platter, sprinkle them with salt and ground black pepper, and keep them warm. Pour the cream into the skillet and add salt and black pepper to taste, and the parsley. Bring to boiling point and serve immediately over the hot meat. Makes 4 servings.

❧ TOURNEDOS WITH BÉARNAISE SAUCE
(*Tournedos à la Béarnaise*)

Tournedos are small steaks cut from the fillet. They should be cooked rare or medium-rare, never well-done.

4 tournedos, 4 to 5 ounces each	4 tablespoons Béarnaise Sauce (page 53)
salt	
6 tablespoons butter, softened	watercress
4 slices firm-textured white bread	Château Potatoes (page 382)
ground black pepper	

Tie a string around each steak to hold it in shape. Sprinkle both sides of the steaks with salt and spread one side with softened butter. Broil in a preheated oven broiler 3 minutes for rare; 4 to 5 minutes for medium-rare. Turn, spread the uncooked side with butter and broil the same length of time as before. Or, if desired, pan-broil over surface heat, using the same cooking time as for oven broiling. Cut pieces of white bread the same shape and size as the steaks and fry them in the remaining butter (about 3 tablespoons), browning both sides. Remove the strings from the steaks and place one steak on each piece of bread. Sprinkle with black pepper. Top each with 1 tablespoon Béarnaise Sauce. Garnish with watercress. Serve with Château Potatoes. Makes 4 servings.

❧ TOURNEDOS À LA CHASSEUR

4 tournedos, 4 to 5 ounces each	4 slices firm-textured bread
5 tablespoons butter, softened	Chasseur Sauce II (see following recipe)
1½ tablespoons olive oil or salad oil	chopped parsley
salt	

Tie a string around each steak to hold it in shape. Melt 1½ tablespoons of the butter, mix it with the oil, and brush over both sides of the steaks. Sprinkle them with salt and arrange them on the broiler pan. Broil in a preheated broiler 3 minutes for rare; 4 to 5 minutes for medium-rare. Turn the steaks, brushing both sides with the oil and butter mixture. Broil the same length of time as before. Or, if desired, pan-broil over surface heat, using the same cooking time as for oven broiling. Cut pieces of bread the same size and shape as the steaks and fry them in the remaining butter, browning them on both sides. Cut the strings around the steaks and remove them. Place the steaks on the pieces of bread and coat with Chasseur Sauce II. Serve sprinkled with parsley. Makes 4 servings.

⚜ Chasseur Sauce II (*Sauce Chasseur II*)

2 tablespoons thinly sliced mushrooms
1 teaspoon finely chopped shallot or
  white onion
2 teaspoons salted butter
⅓ cup dry white wine
1 tablespoon tomato purée

¾ cup Demi-Glace Sauce (page 44)
1 teaspoon unsalted butter
½ teaspoon finely chopped parsley
⅛ teaspoon dried tarragon
salt to taste

Cook the mushrooms and shallot or white onion in the salted butter until they are limp and transparent. Add the wine and cook the mixture until it has reduced to one-half its original volume. Add the tomato purée and Demi-Glace Sauce. Mix well and bring the mixture to boiling point twice. Remove from the heat and beat in the unsalted butter, the parsley and tarragon, and salt to taste. Makes about ⅔ cup.

⚜ TOURNEDOS CHÂTEAU FIGEAC (*Tournedos Château Figeac*)

4 tournedos, 4 to 5 ounces each
4 tablespoons butter, softened
salt and ground black pepper
Bordelaise Sauce (page 44)
12 mushrooms caps sautéed in butter

24 tiny boiled carrots or 2-inch
  lengths of carrot, buttered
4 buttered cooked artichoke bottoms,
  each filled with buttered asparagus
  tips

Prepare and broil the steaks according to the recipe for Tournedos with Béarnaise Sauce. Sprinkle the steaks with black pepper, arrange them on a warmed platter, and spoon Bordelaise Sauce over them. Place 3 mushroom caps on each. Garnish the platter with the cooked carrots, arranged in groups of 4 around the steaks, alternating with the artichoke bottoms filled with asparagus tips. Makes 4 servings. (*See illustration, page 262.*)

⚜ TOURNEDOS CLAMART (*Tournedos Clamart*)

4 tournedos, 4 to 5 ounces each
6 tablespoons butter, softened
salt and ground black pepper
4 pieces firm-textured bread cut to
   fit the steaks

4 baked 2-inch tart shells
1 cup buttered cooked peas
Noisette Potatoes (page 385)

Prepare and broil the steaks according to the recipe for Tournedos with Béarnaise Sauce, using 3 tablespoons of the butter. Sprinkle with salt and black pepper. Fry the bread in the remaining 3 tablespoons butter, browning both sides. Place a steak on each piece and arrange on a warmed platter. Fill the tart shells with the cooked peas and sprinkle the peas with some of the pan drippings from the steak. Arrange the tart shells around the steaks. Serve with Noisette Potatoes. Makes 4 servings.

⚜ TOURNEDOS MARIE-LOUISE (*Tournedos Marie-Louise*)

4 tournedos, 4 to 5 ounces each
7 tablespoons butter, softened
salt and ground black pepper
4 pieces firm-textured white bread cut
   to fit the steaks

Demi-Glace Sauce (page 44)
4 tablespoons grated onion
4 cooked artichoke bottoms
4 small buttered mushroom caps
Duchess Potatoes (page 383)

Prepare and broil the steaks according to the recipe for Tournedos with Béarnaise Sauce, using 3 tablespoons of the butter. Sprinkle the steaks with salt and black pepper. Fry the bread in 3 tablespoons of the remaining butter, browning both sides. Place a steak on each piece and arrange them on a warmed platter. Coat the steaks with hot Demi-Glace Sauce. Cook the onion 2 to 3 minutes over low heat in the remaining 1 tablespoon butter and divide it equally among the 4 artichoke bottoms. Garnish each with a mushroom cap. Place them on the platter around the steaks. Surround with Duchess Potatoes. Makes 4 servings.

⚜ TOURNEDOS PORTUGUESE STYLE (*Tournedos à la Portugaise*)

4 tournedos, 4 to 5 ounces each
2 tablespoons olive oil or salad oil
salt and ground black pepper
4 pieces firm-textured bread cut to fit
   the steaks
6 tablespoons butter

⅓ cup dry white wine
2 tablespoons tomato purée
4 tomato halves, stuffed with sautéed
   mushrooms
Château Potatoes (page 382)

Prepare and broil the steaks according to the recipe for Tournedos with Béarnaise Sauce, using 3 tablespoons of the butter. Sprinkle with salt and black

238

pepper. Fry the bread in the remaining 3 tablespoons butter, browning both sides, place a steak on each slice, and put them in a circle on a warmed platter. Add the wine to the drippings in the broiler pan or skillet and boil the mixture over surface heat until it has reduced to one-half the original volume. Add the tomato purée, bring to boiling point, and spoon the sauce over the steaks. Place a mushroom-stuffed tomato half on each steak. Fill the center of the platter with Château Potatoes. Makes 4 servings.

⚜ TOURNEDOS WITH TARRAGON (*Tournedos à l'Estragon*)

4 tournedos, 4 to 5 ounces each
6 tablespoons butter, softened
salt and ground black pepper
4 pieces firm-textured bread, cut to fit
   the steaks

8 tarragon leaves (or 4 parsley
   leaves)
Tomato Gravy (see following recipe)
baked potatoes

Prepare and broil the steaks as in the recipe for Tournedos with Béarnaise Sauce, using 3 tablespoons of the butter. Sprinkle with salt and black pepper. Fry the bread in the remaining 3 tablespoons butter, browning both sides, place a steak on each piece, and arrange them on a warmed platter. Decorate each steak with 2 tarragon leaves in the form of a cross or with a piece of parsley. Serve with Tomato Gravy and baked potatoes. Makes 4 servings.

⚜ Tomato Gravy

¼ cup finely chopped onion
¼ cup finely chopped green pepper
3 tablespoons butter
3 tablespoons flour
⅛ teaspoon powdered mustard

½ cup water
1¼ cups tomato purée
1 teaspoon each sugar and salt
dash cayenne
1/16 teaspoon ground black pepper

Sauté the onion and green pepper in the butter. Remove from heat and blend in the flour. Return to heat; stir and cook until the mixture foams. Meanwhile soak the mustard in the water for 5 minutes. Add to the mixture along with the remaining ingredients. Mix well. Stir and cook until the sauce is medium thick. Makes about 1½ cups.

⚜ FONDUE BOURGUIGNONNE (*Fondue Bourguignonne*)

This dish, like Cheese Fondue (page 101), is of Swiss origin.

2 pounds sirloin steak
1½ cups salad oil
salt and ground black pepper

assorted cold sauces—Mayonnaise,
   Aurora, Mustard, Rémoulade, Vin-
   aigrette Sauce, catsup, etc. (see
   Index)

Cut the raw meat into ½-inch cubes and string the cubes on wooden skewers (do not use metal skewers). Put the skewered meat on a platter. Heat the oil in a heatproof dish and place it in the center of the table on a hot plate or over an alcohol lamp. The guests dip their own pieces of skewered meat into the hot oil and cook them as desired (rare, medium, or well done). Provide salt, black pepper, and a selection of sauces, each in a separate bowl. The pieces of meat are removed from the skewer and speared with forks for dipping into the desired sauce. Makes 6 servings.

⚜ BRAISED STUFFED BEEF ROLLS ORIENTAL STYLE
(*Paupiettes de Boeuf à la Orientale*)

Paupiettes, sometimes called birds or olives, are thin serving-size slices of meat, poultry, or fish wrapped around a stuffing and braised in wine and bouillon or stock.

8 slices round steak cut 5 by 3 inches
   and ¼ inch thick
salt
ground black pepper
½ cup finely chopped onion
½ cup finely chopped mushroom
   stems
3 tablespoons butter
1 cup (½ pound) ground ham
½ cup (¼ pound) ground raw veal
½ small clove garlic, crushed
½ teaspoon dried thyme leaves

1 egg, beaten lightly
2 tablespoons oil
½ cup each sliced onions and diced
   carrots
2 tablespoons flour
2 tablespoons tomato purée
¾ cup each dry white wine and
   bouillon
2 stalks parsley
2 cups hot cooked rice
8 sautéed small mushroom caps
8 sautéed slices of tomato

Flatten the slices of meat with a wooden mallet, sprinkle with salt and black pepper, and set them aside. Cook the chopped onion and mushroom stems in 1 tablespoon of the butter 4 to 5 minutes. Add the next 5 ingredients, and ½ teaspoon salt and ⅛ teaspoon black pepper. Mix well. Divide the mixture into 8 rolls of equal size and place one on the lower third of each slice of meat. Roll the meat around the stuffing. Tie the rolls at both ends and in the middle with clean white string. Brown the rolls in the oil and the remaining 2 tablespoons butter in a heavy skillet, transfer them to a casserole, and brown the sliced onion and carrots in the skillet. Then blend in the flour and stir and cook slowly until browned, 2 to 3 minutes. Add to the casserole, scraping in all the browned particles from the bottom of the skillet. Add the tomato purée, wine, bouillon, and parsley. Cover and simmer 1 hour or until meat is tender. Arrange the rolls on a bed of hot rice. Top each with a sautéed mushroom cap. Garnish the platter with the sautéed sliced tomatoes. Strain the gravy, pushing as much of the vegetables through as possible, adjust seasonings, and heat. Serve in a separate bowl. Makes 4 servings.

⚜ FLANK STEAK COOKED WITH BEER
(Carbonade de Boeuf à la Bière)

4 boneless flank, round, or chuck steaks, cut to ½ or ¾ inch thick, 6 ounces each
salt and ground black pepper
3 tablespoons shortening
1½ cups chopped onion
¾ cup beer

1 stalk parsley
¾ cup Demi-Glace Sauce (page 44), or ¾ cup bouillon
1 tablespoon cornstarch and 2 tablespoons water (optional)
boiled potatoes

Sprinkle the steaks with salt and ground black pepper. Sauté in 2 tablespoons of the shortening. Sauté the onion in the remaining 1 tablespoon shortening. Place half the onions on the bottom of a casserole and arrange the steaks over them. Cover with the remaining onions. Sprinkle lightly with salt and black pepper. Add the beer, parsley, and the Demi-Glace Sauce or bouillon. Cover and cook in a preheated slow oven (300° F.) 2 hours. Skim off and discard the fat from the pan liquid. If bouillon was used, blend the cornstarch with the water and add to the liquid to thicken it. Bring the gravy to boiling point. Serve with boiled potatoes. Makes 4 servings.

⚜ HAMBURGER STEAK *(Beefsteak Haché)*

Allow 1 pound ground lean beef for 3 large hamburgers or 4 medium-sized ones.

1 pound ground chuck or other lean beef
1 tablespoon finely chopped onion
1 large egg

¾ teaspoon salt
⅛ teaspoon ground black pepper
butter
¼ cup sour cream (optional)

Combine the first 5 ingredients. Shape into 3 steaks ½-inch thick, or 4 smaller steaks. Brown on both sides in butter in a heavy skillet, keeping the inside slightly underdone, if desired. Pour the browned frying butter over the steaks. Or, if desired, add the sour cream to the butter left in the skillet, season with salt and black pepper to taste, and pour it over the meat. Makes 3 or 4 servings.

⚜ ROAST FILLET OF BEEF *(Filet de Boeuf Rôti)*

Fillet of beef is also called the tenderloin.

Trim the fat and connective tissue from a beef fillet roast and lard it with larding pork, or tie thin strips of fat salt pork or beef suet around it. If a meat thermometer is used, insert it in the thickest part of the roast. Place the roast in a preheated very hot oven (450° F.). Cook a 4- to 6-pound roast 45 to 60 minutes, a half tenderloin (2 to 3 pounds) 45 to 50 minutes, or to 140° F.

on a meat thermometer. Serve with the pan juices or spread with meat glaze or beef extract. Allow ½ pound per serving.

⚜ FILLET OF BEEF WITH MADEIRA (*Filet de Boeuf au Madère*)

3-pound fillet of beef, 3 inches in
   diameter
1 medium-small onion, sliced
1 medium-small carrot, sliced
3 tablespoons butter
salt and ground black pepper

1½ cups Demi-Glace Sauce (page
   44), or 1½ cups bouillon
½ cup Madeira
2 tablespoons tomato purée
½ cup sliced mushrooms
1 tablespoon cornstarch

Ask the butcher to trim and lard the fillet. Brown the fillet, onion, and carrot in 2 tablespoons of the butter. Drain off and discard all fat from the pan. Sprinkle the meat and vegetables with salt and black pepper. Add the Demi-Glace Sauce or bouillon, ⅓ cup of the wine, and the tomato purée. Cook over surface heat until simmering point is reached. Cover and continue cooking in a preheated moderate oven (350° F.) 50 to 60 minutes, never allowing the liquid around the roast to boil. Baste the meat with the cooking liquid 3 to 4 times. Transfer the roast to a warm platter and keep warm. Skim the fat from the braising liquid and discard it. Boil the liquid until it has reduced to about three-fourths its original volume. Meanwhile, sauté the mushrooms in the remaining 1 tablespoon butter. Blend the cornstarch with the remaining Madeira and add to the sauce along with the mushrooms. Simmer 2 to 3 minutes. Adjust seasonings. Spoon 2 to 3 tablespoons of the sauce over the fillet and serve the rest in a sauceboat. Makes 6 to 8 servings.

⚜ BRAISED BEEF BOURGEOISE
(*Pointe de Boeuf Braisée à la Bourgeoise*)

2 pounds rolled boneless shoulder of
   beef
salt and ground black pepper
beef suet, or 1 tablespoon shortening
   or lard
1 cup beef stock or water
2 carrots, sliced
½ cup chopped onion
1 tablespoon each cornstarch and
   water

½ clove garlic
1 tablespoon butter
2 cups diced peeled tomatoes
¼ teaspoon sugar
¼ cup soft breadcrumbs
chopped parsley
4 buttered boiled potatoes
2 cups braised celery

Rub the meat with salt and black pepper. Brown it on all sides in beef suet, shortening, or lard in a Dutch oven. Add the beef stock or water, carrots, and onion. Cover and simmer 1½ to 2 hours or until the meat is tender. Transfer the meat to a warmed platter and keep it warm. Skim off and discard the fat from the pan liquid. Strain the liquid, pushing as much of the vegetables through as possible. Blend the cornstarch with the water and add to the pan liquid. Stir and cook until boiling point is reached. Adjust seasonings. Remove from heat. Slice the meat and arrange the slices in a ring on a platter. Keep warm. Cook the garlic in the butter 1 minute. Remove and discard garlic. Add the tomatoes and sugar and cook 6 to 7 minutes. Stir in the bread crumbs and add salt and black pepper to taste. Put the mixture in the center of the platter and sprinkle with chopped parsley. Spoon the gravy over the meat. Garnish the platter with boiled potatoes and braised celery. Makes 4 servings.

⚜ BRAISED BONELESS ROUND ROAST
(*Aiguillette de Boeuf Braisée*)

3 pounds boneless top round or bottom round roast	1 cup Demi-Glace Sauce (page 44), or 1 cup bouillon
salt and ground black pepper	2 stalks parsley
2 tablespoons lard or shortening	1 rib celery, quartered
½ cup sliced onion	6 to 8 medium-sized potatoes, braised
½ cup sliced carrots	12 medium-sized carrots, braised
2 cups dry white wine or water	12 small white onions, braised

Ask the butcher to lard the roast with strips of fat salt pork. Rub the outside of the meat with salt and black pepper and brown it on all sides in lard or shortening, along with the sliced onion and carrots. Pour off the excess fat, add the wine or water, and cook the meat, uncovered, until the liquid has reduced to one-half the original amount. Pour the Demi-Glace Sauce or bouillon over the meat. Add the parsley and celery. Cover and cook slowly 2½ to 3 hours, turning the meat 3 to 4 times. Transfer the meat to a warm platter and keep it warm until ready to serve. Skim excess fat off and discard from the cooking liquid. Strain the liquid and if it is not thick enough, boil a few minutes to reduce it to the desired consistency. Serve it in a gravy boat. Garnish the platter with the braised vegetables. Makes 6 to 8 servings.

⚜ ROAST EYE OF ROUND (*Rôti Rond de Gîte à la Noix*)

3- to 4-pound eye of round beef roast	½ cup bouillon or water
salt and ground black pepper	2 small white onions, sliced
2 tablespoons shortening, oil, or beef suet	2 small carrots, sliced
	⅓ cup dry white wine

Sprinkle the roast with salt and ground black pepper. Brown it in the shortening, oil, or suet. Add the bouillon or water, onions, and carrots. Cover and cook 30 minutes in a preheated slow oven (325° F.). Remove the cover and continue to cook 1¼ to 1¾ hours or until roast is tender. Transfer the roast to a warmed platter. Skim off and discard the excess fat from the pan juices. Add the wine to the pan juices and cook over surface heat until the quantity is reduced to half the original volume. Strain the gravy and season to taste with salt and black pepper. Cut the roast in thin slices and serve the gravy over the meat. Makes 6 to 8 servings.

⚜ FRENCH POT ROAST (*Boeuf à la Mode*)

4 pounds top round or bottom round
  roast
salt and ground black pepper
beef suet, or 2 tablespoons shortening
¼ cup brandy, warmed
1 cup dry red wine
1 cup beef stock or water

1 calf's foot (if available)
12 small white onions
8 carrots, peeled and cut in half
2 tablespoons butter
1 tablespoon potato starch or cornstarch
2 tablespoons water

Ask the butcher to lard the roast. Rub salt and black pepper over all sides. Brown in beef suet or shortening in a Dutch oven. Drain off all surplus fat. Pour the warmed brandy over the roast and ignite. Add the wine and stock or water. Split the calf's foot, cover with boiling water, cook slowly 5 minutes, remove from water, and add to the roast. Cover and cook slowly 1½ hours. Brown the onions and carrots in the butter and add them to the roast. Cover and cook slowly 1 hour or until meat and vegetables are tender. Transfer the meat to a warm platter and surround it with the vegetables. Blend the starch with the water, add to the pan liquid, and bring to boiling point. Boil until the gravy has thickened slightly. Adjust the salt. Spoon some of the gravy over the roast and serve the remainder in a sauceboat. Makes 6 to 8 servings.

⚜ FRENCH-STYLE BOILED DINNER (*Pot-au-Feu*)

Pot-au-Feu is a family-style boiled dinner consisting of meat and vegetables cooked slowly in the same pot. This dish provides soup (which may be served as the first course with toast, boiled rice, or pasta) and meat and vegetables for the entrée. The meat may consist of beef and chicken or chicken giblets. In certain regions of France other meats, such as fresh pork, veal, and dry country sausage are added to the pot. The meat is served with a sauce, such as Mustard, Tomato, Caper, Rémoulade, or Béarnaise Sauce (see Index). Any leftover stock may be used in the soup or sauce.

244

3 pounds pot roast (brisket, chuck, or bottom round)

3 pounds beef shin bones or veal knuckle

3 quarts cold bouillon, or 3 quarts cold water and 6 bouillon cubes

4 stalks parsley

4 ribs celery, quartered

3 medium-sized onions, each studded with a whole clove

3 leeks (optional)

1 bay leaf

6 whole black peppercorns

2 cloves garlic

3- to 4-pound fricassee chicken or 1 pound chicken giblets

8 carrots, peeled and cut in half

6 medium-small turnips, peeled and quartered

8 medium-sized onions, peeled

6 parsnips, peeled and cut in half

6 medium-sized potatoes peeled and cut in half

1 pound dry link sausage

salt to taste

6 to 8 cabbage wedges

Trim off the excess fat from the meat. Place the meat in a 10-quart kettle with a cover. Add the shin bones or veal knuckle and the bouillon or the water and bouillon cubes. Tie the next 7 ingredients in a piece of cheesecloth that has been rinsed in water and add the bag to the kettle. Cover, bring to boiling point, reduce heat and simmer 1 hour, leaving the cover ajar, and skimming 2 to 3 times. Add the chicken or chicken giblets. Simmer, partly covered, 1 hour. Put the carrots, turnips, onions, parsnips, and potatoes in a washed cheesecloth bag, tie, and add, along with the sausage. Add salt to taste. Simmer, partially covered, 1 hour or until meat and vegetables are tender, skimming occasionally. Add the cabbage and simmer 20 minutes. To serve, remove the meat, chicken or chicken giblets, and sausage and arrange them on a large warmed platter. Lift out the cabbage and the bag of vegetables and arrange them attractively around the meat. Spoon some of the stock over all. Keep warm. Serve the broth for the soup course in individual bowls with toasted French bread, cooked rice, or noodles. Sprinkle the broth with chopped parsley. Serve one or more of the sauces listed above with the meat course. Makes 6 to 8 servings.

⚜ BEEF BOURGUIGNONNE (*Boeuf à la Bourguignonne*)

2 pounds boneless beef (rump or chuck)

flour

2 tablespoons olive oil, salad oil, or shortening

1 small clove garlic

1¼ cups Burgundy

hot water

½ small bay leaf

1¼ teaspoons salt, or salt to taste

2 stalks parsley

1½ strips bacon, diced

18 small white onions

1 tablespoon tomato paste

½ teaspoon dried thyme

¼ teaspoon ground black pepper

18 mushroom caps

2 tablespoons butter

245

Cut the beef into 1-inch cubes and roll them in flour. Brown on all sides in the hot oil or shortening. Add the garlic and cook with the meat 1 minute. Remove the garlic. Put the meat into a 2-quart casserole. Add the wine and enough hot water barely to cover the meat. Add the bay leaf, salt, and parsley. Cover and cook in a preheated slow oven (325° F.) 2 hours. Fry the bacon briefly, then add the onions and cook until they have browned lightly on all sides. Add to the casserole and cook, covered, ½ hour, or until onions and meat are tender. Stir in the tomato paste, thyme, and black pepper. Cook another 10 minutes. Adjust the salt. Cook the mushroom caps in the butter and arrange them over the top of the casserole. Serve from the casserole. Makes 4 to 5 servings.

❧ MARINATED BEEF CASSEROLE (*Boeuf en Daube*)

2 pounds boneless shoulder or other lean beef	1½ teaspoons salt
	6 whole black peppercorns
narrow strips of fat salt pork (optional)	dry red wine
	¼ cup tomato purée
1 cup sliced onion	1 tablespoon potato starch or corn-
1 cup sliced carrots	starch
2 stalks parsley	2 tablespoons water

The meat may be left in one piece or cut into large cubes. If the meat lacks fat, lard the whole piece or thread a piece of fat salt pork through each cube. Place the meat in a heavy saucepan that has a close-fitting cover. Add the next 5 ingredients and pour in just enough wine barely to cover. Marinate 2 hours. Cover the saucepan tightly and simmer for ½ hour, then add the tomato purée and simmer 1 hour more. When the meat is tender, skim off and discard the excess fat. Blend the starch with 2 tablespoons water and add to the sauce. Mix well, and cook 5 minutes. Adjust salt and serve hot. Makes 6 servings.

❧ HUNGARIAN GOULASH (*Goulasch à la Hongroise*),

3 pounds lean chuck or stew meat	2 teaspoons salt
2 tablespoons shortening or lard	2 stalks parsley
2 cups chopped onion	½ teaspoon cumin seed
3 tablespoons tomato purée	2 tablespoons Hungarian paprika
⅓ cup hot water or bouillon	¼ teaspoon dried marjoram leaves
1-pound can tomatoes	buttered boiled potatoes

Cut the meat into 1½-inch cubes. Melt the shortening or lard in a heavy Dutch oven, add the onion, and cook slowly until they are soft, 5 to 6 minutes. Add the beef. Stir and cook only until meat is lightly browned. Stir in the tomato purée, the water or bouillon, and the canned tomatoes. Add the salt, parsley, and cumin seed. Cover and cook over low heat 2 hours or until meat is tender. Stir in the paprika and marjoram, cover, and cook 15 minutes. Adjust the salt. Serve with buttered boiled potatoes. Makes 6 servings.

⚜ COLD BEEF NIÇOISE (*Boeuf Froid à la Niçoise*)

1 pound boneless sliced roasted or braised beef	4 medium-sized tomatoes
2 cups cold cooked green beans	2 hard-cooked eggs, sliced
¼ cup Vinaigrette Sauce (page 56)	7 strips red sweet pepper
	salt and ground black pepper

Arrange the slices of beef in the center of a platter. Toss the beans lightly with the Vinaigrette Sauce and place half of them at each end of the platter. Slice the tomatoes and arrange them around the sides of the beef. Place slices of hard-cooked egg alternately with red sweet pepper strips down the center of the beef. Makes 4 servings. (*See illustration, page 261.*)

⚜ FRENCH POT ROAST IN ASPIC (*Boeuf à la Mode en Gelée*)

2 calf's feet, split in half	1 recipe French Pot Roast (page 244)
4 ounces pork rinds (if available)	parsley

Make the recipe for French Pot Roast. Simmer 2 additional calf's feet and the pork rinds (if available) with the calf's foot called for in the original recipe and add the roast. When the meat and vegetables are done, remove them from the stock. Cut the carrots in slices or strips and arrange them and the onions in an attractive pattern in the bottom of a large bowl or mold. Skim off the fat from the stock, strain the stock, and pour enough over the vegetables to cover them generously. Chill until the stock is firm. Cool and slice the meat. Finish filling the bowl or mold with sliced cold beef and the meat cut from the calf's feet. Pour in enough strained stock to come about ½ inch to 1 inch above the meat. Chill until the stock is firm, about 12 to 24 hours. Unmold onto a large serving plate. Garnish with parsley. Makes 6 to 8 servings.

⚜ MOLDED BEEF IN ASPIC (*Turban de Boeuf à la Gelée*)

1 envelope unflavored gelatin	2 gherkin pickles, sliced
¼ cup cold water or bouillon	salt and ground black pepper to taste
1½ cups hot bouillon, or 1½ cups hot water and 1½ beef bouillon cubes	2 cups Potato Salad (page 90)
1 pound cold boneless braised lean beef	1 cup cold cooked green beans
¼ pound cold cooked lean ham	2 tablespoons Vinaigrette Sauce (page 56)
2 hard-cooked eggs, coarsely chopped	parsley
2 tablespoons chopped parsley	1 tomato wedge

Soften the gelatin in the cold water or bouillon. Add the hot bouillon or the hot water and bouillon cubes. Mix well. Chill until the mixture is about as thick as fresh egg whites. Cut the beef and ham into matchlike strips and fold the strips into the gelatin mixture along with the chopped eggs, parsley, and pickles. Add salt and pepper to taste. Turn the mixture into a lightly oiled 5-cup ring mold. Refrigerate 5 to 6 hours or until the gelatin is firm. Unmold the ring onto a serving plate. Fill the center of the mold with Potato Salad. Toss the cooked beans with Vinaigrette Sauce and arrange them around the Potato Salad. Garnish the center with parsley and the tomato wedge. Makes 6 servings. (*See illustration, page 261.*)

Veal (*Veau*)

The term *veal* refers to the flesh of calves up to 1 year of age. The lean meat of veal is grayish-pink in color, fine in grain, and fairly firm with a velvety texture. It is not marbled with fat as in beef.

Veal is the most delicately flavored of all meats and harmonizes with the flavors of many foods. It may be oven-roasted, pot-roasted, braised, made into stews, or ground and used for meat loaf or meat balls. Since veal contains very little fat, it should never be broiled. Both the French and the Italians are famous for delicious veal dishes.

⚜ VEAL CUTLETS WITH CREAM
(*Côtelettes de Veau en Cocotte à la Crème*)

4 veal cutlets
salt and ground black pepper to taste
2 tablespoons butter

¼ cup light cream
Château Potatoes (page 382)
chopped parsley

Sprinkle the cutlets with salt and black pepper. Brown them on both sides in butter in a heatproof casserole or a skillet over moderate heat. Add the cream and simmer, uncovered, 10 minutes or until the veal is tender. Adjust seasonings. Sprinkle with chopped parsley and serve in the casserole or on a warmed platter. Accompany with Château Potatoes. Makes 4 servings.

⚜ GRILLED VEAL CUTLETS (*Côtelettes de Veau Grillées*)

4 veal cutlets, cut ½ inch thick
salt and ground black pepper
flour

3 to 4 tablespoons butter
Maître d'Hôtel Butter (page 58)

Sprinkle the cutlets with salt and black pepper and dredge them in flour. Fry them in butter, adding it as needed, in a heavy skillet over moderate heat until they have browned on both sides. Serve with Maître d'Hôtel Butter. Makes 4 servings.

✤ VEAL CUTLETS MÉNAGÈRE
(Côtelettes de Veau en Cocotte à la Ménagère)

4 veal cutlets, cut ½ inch thick
salt and ground black pepper
6 tablespoons butter
12 very small white onions

8 carrots, peeled and quartered
8 medium potatoes, peeled
½ cup dry white wine or bouillon

Sprinkle the cutlets with salt and black pepper. Brown them on both sides in 2 tablespoons of the butter in a heavy skillet or heatproof casserole. In another skillet, brown the vegetables in the remaining 4 tablespoons butter. Arrange them around the cutlets. Add the wine or bouillon, cover, and simmer 30 minutes. Adjust seasonings. Makes 4 servings.

✤ VEAL CUTLETS SAUTÉED WITH HERBS
(Côtelettes de Veau Sautée aux Fines Herbes)

4 veal cutlets, ½ inch thick
salt and ground black pepper
flour
4 tablespoons butter

1½ tablespoons chopped parsley
¼ teaspoon dried thyme leaves, or 1
  teaspoon chopped fresh thyme

Sprinkle the cutlets with salt and ground black pepper, dredge them in flour, and brown them on both sides in a heavy skillet in 2 tablespoons of the butter. Transfer the cutlets to a warmed platter. Add the remaining 2 tablespoons butter and the herbs to the skillet. Heat until the butter foams, then pour over the cutlets. Makes 4 servings.

✤ VEAL CUTLETS WITH VEGETABLES
(Côtelettes de Veau Bonne Femme)

12 very small white onions
¼ pound button mushrooms,
  quartered
5 tablespoons butter
8 cups medium-small potatoes, peeled
  and quartered

salt
ground black pepper
flour
4 veal cutlets, cut ½ inch thick
1 slice bacon, diced
½ cup stock, bouillon, or water

Sauté the onions and mushrooms together in 2 tablespoons of the butter and transfer them to a casserole with a cover. To the same skillet, add 2 more tablespoons of the butter and brown the potatoes. Add them to the casserole.

Sprinkle with ½ teaspoon salt and ⅛ teaspoon black pepper. Sprinkle the cutlets with salt and black pepper and roll them in flour. Put the remaining 1 tablespoon butter and the diced bacon in the skillet, add the cutlets, and brown them over moderate heat. Arrange the cutlets over the vegetables in the casserole. Pour the stock, bouillon or water into the skillet, bring to boiling point, and pour it over the casserole. Cover and cook in a preheated slow oven (325° F.) 30 minutes. Makes 4 servings.

⚜ VEAL MEDALLIONS VERONESE STYLE
(Médaillons de Veau Véronèse)

Medallions of veal are round slices cut from the choicest part of the fillet.

8 medallions of veal, cut thin
salt and ground black pepper
flour
3 tablespoons olive oil or salad oil
7 tablespoons butter

8 thin slices raw ham, cut 1 inch larger in diameter than the medallions
6 ounces hot cooked green noodles
1 medium-sized tomato, peeled and coarsely chopped
4 black olives, pitted

Place the veal medallions between pieces of waxed paper and flatten them with a mallet. Sprinkle them with salt and black pepper and dredge them in flour. Heat the oil and 2 tablespoons of the butter in a heavy 10-inch skillet. Add as many pieces of veal at a time as the skillet will accommodate. Brown on both sides, remove from the skillet, and keep warm. When all the veal is browned, fry the ham in the same skillet, browning lightly on both sides. Place a medallion on each piece of ham. Toss the hot noodles with 2 tablespoons of the remaining butter and turn them out onto a warmed platter. Arrange the ham and veal medallions on top. Garnish each medallion with coarsely chopped tomato and half of a pitted black olive. Melt the remaining 3 tablespoons butter, heat until it has browned, and pour it over all. Makes 4 servings. (*See illustration, page 264.*)

⚜ VEAL SCALLOPS CORDON BLEU
(Escalopes de Veau Cordon Bleu)

Veal scallops (French, *escalopes*; Italian, *scaloppini*; British, collops) are slices of veal cut from the leg and pounded very thin between pieces of waxed paper with a wooden mallet or the flat side of a cleaver.

12 veal scallops, 2 ounces each
salt and ground black pepper
6 thin slices ham
6 thin slices Gruyère or Cheddar cheese

flour
2 eggs, beaten
fine dry breadcrumbs
about 4 tablespoons (½ stick) butter

Pound the scallops very thin and sprinkle them with salt and black pepper. Sandwich 1 slice ham and 1 slice cheese between each 2 scallops. Fasten by pinning with toothpicks or small skewers. Dredge the scallops in flour and dip them in the beaten eggs and then in breadcrumbs, patting them a little to make the crumbs adhere. Let stand 15 to 20 minutes to dry. Brown first on one side and then on the other in the butter, adding it as needed. Makes 6 servings.

⚜ VEAL SCALLOPS CHASSEUR (*Escalopes de Veau à la Chasseur*)

4 veal scallops cut ½ inch thick, 4½ ounces each
salt and ground black pepper
flour
3 tablespoons butter
1 tablespoon olive oil or salad oil
8 medium-sized mushroom caps, sliced

2 shallots, or ½ small white onion, chopped
½ cup dry white wine
¾ cup veal stock or bouillon
4 button mushroom caps, sautéed in butter
2 teaspoons cornstarch
2 tablespoons water

Pound the scallops very thin, as directed for Veal Scallops Cordon Bleu. Sprinkle with salt and black pepper and dredge with flour. Sauté in 2 tablespoons of the butter and the 1 tablespoon oil 5 to 6 minutes on each side or until the scallops are golden brown. Remove the scallops to a warmed platter and keep them warm. In the same skillet cook the sliced mushrooms slowly until they are tender. Add the shallots or onion and cook until wilted. Return the scallops to the skillet, pour in the wine and stock or bouillon, and cook over moderate heat until the liquid has reduced to half the original quantity. Arrange the scallops in a ring on a warmed platter with the mushrooms in the center. Top each scallop with a sautéed button mushroom cap. Mix the cornstarch with the water, add to the sauce in the skillet, and cook 1 minute. Swirl in the remaining 1 tablespoon butter and adjust the seasonings. Pour over the scallops. Makes 4 servings.

⚜ VEAL SCALLOPS ENGLISH STYLE
(*Escalopes de Veau à l'Anglaise*)

4 scallops of veal, 5 ounces each
salt and ground black pepper
flour
1 large egg white

2 tablespoons salad oil or olive oil
fine dry breadcrumbs
2 tablespoons butter
1 tablespoon lemon juice

Pound the scallops very thin, as directed for Veal Scallops Cordon Bleu. Sprinkle them with salt and black pepper and dredge them in flour. Beat the egg white with 1 tablespoon of the oil and dip the scallops in the mixture, then roll them in breadcrumbs and let them stand 15 minutes to dry. Heat the remaining 1 tablespoon oil and the butter in a heavy skillet. Add the scallops and brown them on both sides over moderate heat. Sprinkle with the lemon juice and the pan drippings. Serve with potatoes and green beans or other vegetables. Makes 4 servings.

⚜ VIENNESE VEAL CUTLETS (*Wiener Schnitzel*)

4 veal scallops, 5 ounces each
salt and ground black pepper
1 egg, beaten
1½ tablespoons flour

¼ cup fine dry breadcrumbs
3 tablespoons butter
4 thin slices lemon

Pound the scallops thin as directed for Veal Scallops Cordon Bleu. Sprinkle with salt and ground black pepper. Mix the flour with the breadcrumbs. Dip the scallops in the beaten egg and then in the flour mixture. Brown on both sides in the butter in a heavy skillet over moderate heat. Transfer to a hot platter and top each scallop with a lemon slice. Makes 4 servings.

⚜ BRAISED VEAL BIRDS (*Paupiettes de Veau Braisées*)

4 veal scallops
salt and ground black pepper to taste
½ pound ground lean raw pork
1 tablespoon finely chopped onion
1 tablespoon finely chopped parsley
½ teaspoon dried thyme leaves
1 egg
2 tablespoons heavy cream

1 small white onion, sliced
1 small carrot, sliced
2 tablespoons butter
1 cup bouillon or water
1½ teaspoons cornstarch
1 tablespoon water
mashed potatoes or boiled rice

Sprinkle the scallops with salt and black pepper. Mix together the next 4 ingredients. Beat in the egg and then gradually beat in the cream. Add salt and ground black pepper to taste. (To test the seasonings, fry a bit of the mixture until done and taste it.) Spread an equal amount of the meat mixture over each scallop, using all of it. Roll up in jelly-roll fashion. Tie each end and the middle of the rolls with clean white string. Brown the rolls along with the sliced onion and carrot in the butter in a skillet. Add the bouillon or water. Cover and cook in a preheated slow oven (325° F.) 1 hour, basting 2 to 3 times with pan liquid. Skim off the fat from the liquid. Blend the cornstarch with the 1 tablespoon water, add to the pan liquid, and stir and cook 1 to 2 minutes or until the liquid has thickened slightly. Adjust seasonings. Serve the rolls and sauce over mashed potatoes or boiled rice. Makes 4 servings.

✤ BRAISED VEAL BIRDS À LA GRECQUE
(Paupiettes de Veau Braisées à la Grecque)

4 thin veal scallops
salt
ground black pepper
⅔ cup chopped onion
4 tablespoons butter
1¾ cups soft breadcrumbs
1½ tablespoons chopped parsley

¼ teaspoon dried thyme
4 thin slices raw ham
¾ cup veal stock or bouillon
¼ cup tomato purée
cooked rice
1½ teaspoons cornstarch
1 tablespoon water

Sprinkle scallops with salt and black pepper. Cook the onion in 2 tablespoons of the butter until they are limp, 4 to 5 minutes. Add the breadcrumbs, parsley, and thyme, and salt and black pepper to taste. Spread an equal amount of the mixture over each scallop, using all of it. Cover with one of the slices of ham. Roll up in jelly-roll fashion and tie each end and the middle of the rolls with clean white string. Brown the rolls in the remaining 2 tablespoons butter, adding it as needed. Add the veal stock or bouillon and the tomato purée. Cover and cook in a preheated slow oven (325° F.) 1 hour, basting occasionally with the cooking liquid. Arrange the rolls on a mound of cooked rice. Skim off the fat from the pan liquid. Blend the cornstarch with the water, add to the liquid, and stir and cook until it has thickened slightly. Add salt and black pepper to taste. Serve the gravy over the rolls and rice. Makes 4 servings.

✤ VEAL ROLLS IN POTATO NESTS *(Nids d'Hirondelles)*

Literally translated, the French name of this dish means "Swallows' Nests." It consists of thin veal scallops, each spread with cooked chopped onion and parsley and topped with a thin slice of ham and a hard-cooked egg, then rolled, tied, and braised in wine and bouillon. For serving, the rolls are cut in half and each half put in a nest of mashed potatoes.

4 thin scallops of veal, 4 to 5 ounces
  each
salt and ground black pepper
2 tablespoons finely chopped onion
2 tablespoons finely chopped parsley
3 tablespoons butter
4 thin slices raw lean ham
4 medium-sized hard-cooked eggs
flour

2 medium-sized carrots, sliced
8 small white onions, whole
¼ cup dry white wine
½ cup bouillon
fluffy mashed potatoes
2 teaspoons potato starch or cornstarch
2 tablespoons water

Pound the scallops very thin, as directed for Veal Scallops Cordon Bleu. Sprinkle with salt and ground black pepper. Cook the chopped onion and

253

parsley in 1 tablespoon of the butter about 2 minutes. Spread an equal amount of the mixture on each scallop, using it all. Cover each with a thin slice of ham, and top with a hard-cooked egg. Roll up in jelly-roll fashion and tie clean white string around each end and the middle of the rolls. Brown the rolls, along with the carrots and whole onions, in the remaining 2 tablespoons butter in a Dutch oven over moderate heat. Add the wine and ½ cup of the bouillon. Cover and cook in a preheated slow oven (325° F.) 30 minutes. Add the remaining bouillon and cook, covered, 30 minutes longer. Allow the veal rolls to cool 15 minutes. Then remove the strings, cut the rolls in half, and place each half in a nest of fluffy mashed potatoes. Adjust seasonings in the liquid. Blend the potato starch or cornstarch with the water, and add to the pan liquid. Stir and cook 1 to 2 minutes. Serve the gravy in a separate bowl. Makes 4 servings.

⚜ ROAST FILLET OF VEAL WITH STRAW POTATOES
(*Noix de Veau Rôtie, Pommes Paille*)

1 whole fillet of veal, 4 to 5 pounds, larded
1½ teaspoons salt
¼ teaspoon ground black pepper
6 tablespoons (¾ stick) butter, melted
1 medium-sized onion, sliced
1 medium-sized carrot, sliced

½ cup bouillon
6 medium-sized tomatoes
1 tablespoon potato starch or cornstarch
2 tablespoons water
Straw Potatoes (page 387)
chopped parsley

Ask the butcher to lard the veal for you. Rub 1 teaspoon of the salt and the black pepper over the veal and place it in a Dutch oven or roasting pan. Pour the melted butter over the veal and brown it over moderate heat. Add the onion and carrot, and brown them in the same butter. Pour in the bouillon. Cover, bring the bouillon to boiling point, reduce heat, and simmer 1½ hours, basting frequently. Score the stem ends of the tomatoes in the shape of a cross (+) to a depth of ¼ inch and sprinkle them with the remaining salt. Place them around the meat. Cover and cook until a skewer inserted in the center of the veal shows beads of clear liquid when it is withdrawn, about 20 minutes. Transfer veal and tomatoes to a warmed platter. Skim off and discard the fat from the liquid; if the liquid is too thick, thin it with a little bouillon. Strain and heat. Blend the potato starch or cornstarch with the water, add to the liquid, and stir and cook 1 to 2 minutes. Adjust seasonings. Surround the veal and tomatoes with Straw Potatoes. Sprinkle with chopped parsley. To serve, slice the veal thin and pass the gravy in a separate bowl. Makes 6 to 8 servings.

⚜ ROAST LOIN OF VEAL (*Longe de Veau Rôti*)

Ask the butcher to give you the bones from the roast and use them to make stock for the gravy.

5-pound boned veal loin roast
salt and ground black pepper
thin strips of salt pork

3 tablespoons flour
2 cups veal stock or bouillon
⅓ cup sautéed mushrooms (optional)

Sprinkle the veal with salt and black pepper and cover it with thin strips of salt pork. Put it fat side up on a rack, in a roasting pan. Cook, uncovered, in a preheated moderate oven (375° F.) 18 to 20 minutes per pound, or to 180° F. on a meat thermometer, if one is used. Add a little water to the roasting pan if the fat tends to scorch. Transfer meat to a hot platter and keep it warm. Blend the flour with ⅓ cup of the stock or bouillon, add to the pan drippings, and mix well, scraping up all the browned bits from the bottom of the pan. Add the remaining veal stock or bouillon. Bring the mixture to boiling point and boil 1 to 2 minutes, stirring constantly. Add sautéed mushrooms if desired. Makes 10 to 12 servings.

⚜ Roast Loin of Veal with Kidneys (*Rognonade de Veau Rôti*)

Have the butcher cut a 5-pound boned loin of veal with kidneys attached. Roast it as directed for Roast Loin of Veal. Make gravy from the pan drippings as directed. Makes 10 to 12 servings.

⚜ RUMP OF VEAL WITH MUSHROOMS (*Fricandeau à l'Oseille*)

The French version of this dish is made with sorrel (*oseille*); since sorrel is not readily available in the United States, mushrooms have been substituted in this recipe.

2 pounds rump of veal, larded
1 ounce salt pork, thinly sliced
1 medium-sized onion, sliced
2 medium-sized carrots, sliced
2 stalks parsley
2 ribs celery, quartered

½ bay leaf
1 teaspoon salt
1 cup bouillon
¼ teaspoon ground black pepper
2 cups sliced mushrooms sautéed in butter

Ask the butcher to lard the veal. Line the bottom of a roasting pan with the salt pork, put in the next 5 ingredients, and lay the veal on top. Sprinkle with the salt. Cook over moderately low heat until the vegetables begin to brown. Add the bouillon, cover, and cook in a preheated moderate oven (350° F.) 1 hour, basting frequently with the pan liquid. Transfer the veal to a warmed platter, slice it, and keep it warm. Skim off the fat from the pan liquid and discard it. Add the black pepper and bring the liquid to boiling point over surface heat. Boil, uncovered, 1 to 2 minutes. Serve the sliced veal on the sautéed mushrooms. Pass the gravy separately in a gravy boat. Makes 4 servings.

⚜ RUMP OR LOIN OF VEAL COOKED IN A CASSEROLE
(Quasi ou Longe de Veau en Casserole)

4 pounds rump or loin of veal
2 teaspoons salt
18 small white onions
10 medium-sized carrots
3 tablespoons butter or oil
⅓ cup water

¼ teaspoon ground black pepper
2 cups quartered sautéed mushrooms
8 artichoke bottoms cooked in butter,
   or 8 small boiled potatoes
8 tomato halves, grilled

Rub the meat with the salt and place it in a Dutch oven. Slice 2 each of the onions and carrots and add them to the veal along with the butter or oil. Cook over moderate heat until veal and vegetables have browned. Add the water. Cover tightly and simmer slowly about 2 hours. Cut the remaining onions and carrots in quarters and add them with the black pepper. Cook about 30 minutes longer, or until the veal is fork-tender. Transfer the meat and vegetables to a warmed platter. Garnish with the sautéed mushrooms, the artichoke bottoms or potatoes, and the grilled tomatoes. Makes 8 servings. (*See illustration, page 263.*)

⚜ RUMP OF VEAL WITH ONIONS AND CHESTNUTS
(Noix de Veau en Casserole à la Grand-mère)

2 pounds rump of veal, larded
1 teaspoon salt
⅛ teaspoon ground black pepper
5 tablespoons butter
18 small white onions
24 chestnuts

salad oil
½ bay leaf
1 rib celery with leaves
2 stalks parsley
1 cup veal stock or water
2 tablespoons tomato purée

Ask the butcher to lard the veal. Rub ½ teaspoon of the salt and the black pepper over the veal. Brown in 2 tablespoons of the butter in a Dutch oven. Brown the onions separately in the remaining 3 tablespoons butter and add them to the veal. Slit the chestnuts with a sharp paring knife and coat them with salad oil. Put them in a shallow baking pan and bake in a preheated very hot oven (450° F.) 20 minutes. Cool. Remove shells and skins with a sharp paring knife, and add the chestnuts to the veal. Add the remaining ½ teaspoon salt and all the remaining ingredients. Cover, bring the stock or water to boiling point, reduce heat, and simmer 1½ hours, or until veal is tender. Makes 6 servings.

⚜ ROLLED STUFFED VEAL *(Roulade de Veau)*

3-pound slice of shoulder of veal, cut ½ inch thick
salt
ground black pepper
½ pound sausage meat
½ cup finely chopped onion
¼ clove garlic, crushed
1 shallot, chopped (optional)
5 slices white bread
bouillon or milk

½ teaspoon dried marjoram, or 1½ teaspoons chopped fresh marjoram
2 tablespoons chopped parsley
2 tablespoons (¼ stick) butter
2 medium-sized onions, sliced
2 medium-sized carrots, sliced
1 cup bouillon
¼ cup tomato sauce
1 tablespoon cornstarch
2 tablespoons water

Flatten the veal with a mallet or the flat side of a cleaver. Sprinkle both sides with salt and black pepper. Brown the sausage in a heavy skillet and drain off and discard excess fat. Add the onion, garlic, and shallot (if used) and cook them with the sausage 4 to 5 minutes. Put the bread in enough bouillon or milk to cover it, soak 5 minutes, squeeze dry, and crumble it into the sausage mixture. Add the marjoram and parsley and season the mixture to taste with salt and black pepper. Spread the mixture over the veal. Roll up in jelly-roll fashion and tie loosely at each end and in the middle. Brown the roll in the butter in a Dutch oven. Add the sliced onions and carrots, the 1 cup bouillon, and the tomato sauce. Cover, bring the mixture to boiling point, reduce heat, and simmer 1½ to 2 hours or until the veal is tender when tested with a fork. Transfer the veal and vegetables to a warmed platter. Skim off the fat from the pan liquid and discard it. Blend the cornstarch with the water and mix with the pan liquid. Stir and cook 2 to 3 minutes. Serve the gravy in a separate bowl. Makes 6 to 8 servings.

⚜ VEAL MARENGO *(Sauté de Veau Marengo)*

2 pounds shoulder of veal
1 teaspoon salt
1 tablespoon each butter and salad oil or olive oil
2 medium-sized white onions, chopped
1 small clove garlic, crushed
1 tablespoon flour

⅓ cup dry white wine
2 tablespoons tomato purée
¼ cup bouillon or water
4 tablespoons chopped parsley
¼ pound small mushrooms
¼ teaspoon ground black pepper
heart-shaped croutons fried in butter

Cut the meat into 2-inch pieces, sprinkle with the salt, and brown in the butter and oil in a Dutch oven. Add the onions and stir and cook till they begin to color, about 5 minutes. Add the garlic and the flour, mix well, and stir and cook until flour begins to brown. Add the wine, tomato purée, bouillon or water, and 2 tablespoons of the parsley. Cover, and simmer 1 hour. Wash the mushrooms and add them along with the black pepper. Cover and cook 30 minutes, or until veal is tender. Skim off and discard the fat from the sauce. Adjust the salt. Serve with heart-shaped croutons fried in butter. Garnish with the remaining 2 tablespoons chopped parsley. Makes 4 servings.

⚜ BLANQUETTE OF VEAL (*Blanquette de Veau*)

2 pounds breast of veal
cold water
salt
2 stalks parsley
2 ribs celery, cut in quarters
16 small white onions
2 tablespoons flour

2 tablespoons (¼ stick) butter, softened
1 large egg yolk
¼ cup heavy cream
½ pound button mushrooms sautéed in butter
¼ teaspoon ground white pepper
chopped parsley

Cut the veal into 1½-inch pieces and put it in a 4-quart saucepan or Dutch oven with 1 quart cold water. Bring the water to boiling point and simmer 5 to 6 minutes. Drain off the water and rinse the veal in running cold water. Add 1 teaspoon salt, 1 quart cold water, and the parsley stalk and celery. Cover and cook over low heat 1 hour. Add the onions and cook 30 minutes. Blend the flour with the butter and add to the veal. Mix well and cook until the sauce has thickened slightly. Blend the egg yolk with the cream and stir into the stew. Add the mushrooms and white pepper and cook below boiling point 1 to 2 minutes. Adjust the salt. Sprinkle with chopped parsley. Makes 4 servings.

⚜ VEAL RAGOUT WITH VEGETABLES (*Ragoût de Veau aux Légumes*)

2 pounds shoulder or breast of veal
2 tablespoons (¼ stick) butter
flour
1 teaspoon salt
2 cups bouillon
8 small white onions
8 medium-sized carrots, sliced

2 ribs celery, sliced
2 medium-sized tomatoes, diced
½ teaspoon ground black pepper
2 teaspoons potato starch or cornstarch
2 tablespoons light cream

Cut the veal into 1½-inch pieces. Melt the butter in a Dutch oven or heavy 4-quart saucepan, add the veal, toss lightly, and cook until the meat begins to color. Add the flour and salt and mix well to coat the meat. Pour in the bouillon, cover, bring to boiling point, reduce heat, and simmer 50 minutes. Add the vegetables and the black pepper, cover, and cook 30 minutes, or until meat and vegetables are tender. Combine the potato starch or cornstarch with the cream, add to the ragout, mix well, and cook 2 to 3 minutes. Makes 4 to 6 servings.

⚜ STUFFED BREAST OF VEAL *(Poitrine de Veau Farcie)*

3 pounds breast of veal
salt
ground black pepper
4 slices white bread
bouillon or milk
½ pound pork sausage
⅓ cup finely chopped onion

2 tablespoons finely chopped parsley
¼ cup finely chopped celery tops
1 egg, beaten lightly
¼ teaspoon ground sage
½ cup bouillon, stock, or water
3 carrots, peeled and quartered
4 onions, cut in half

Bone the veal breast and make a slit in the underside to form a pocket. (Or ask the butcher to do this for you.) Sprinkle the inside of the pocket and the outside of the meat with salt and black pepper. Dip the bread in bouillon or milk, squeeze it dry, and crumble it over the sausage. Add the next 5 ingredients and salt and black pepper to taste and mix well. (To test stuffing for seasonings, cook a small amount in a little butter over low surface heat, then taste.) Fill the pocket with the stuffing mixture. Fasten the opening together with skewers or sew it up with a needle and thread. Place the meat in a casserole. Add the bouillon, stock, or water and the onions and carrots. Cover and cook in a preheated slow oven (325° F.) 1½ to 2 hours or until meat is done. Serve with the braised vegetables. This dish may also be served cold. Makes 8 servings.

⚜ VEAL TENDRONS BRAISED WITH VEGETABLES
(Tendrons de Veau à la Paysanne)

Tendrons are strips of breast of veal cut the breadth of the breast and 1½ to 2 inches wide. They are delicious braised in the oven.

1½ pounds breast of veal
salt
ground black pepper
2 tablespoons lard or oil
1 cup sliced carrots

1 cup sliced onion
1 cup diced turnip
½ cup dry white wine
1 cup bouillon
¼ cup tomato purée

Cut the veal into strips the breadth of the breast and 1½ to 2 inches wide. Sprinkle with salt and black pepper. Brown on both sides in the lard or oil in a Dutch oven over moderate heat. Cover with the vegetables and sprinkle with ¾ teaspoon salt and ¼ teaspoon ground black pepper. Pour in the wine and cook uncovered over surface heat until the wine evaporates. Add the bouillon and tomato purée. Cover and cook in a preheated slow oven (325° F.) 1½ hours or until meat is very tender. Remove the tendrons and vegetables to a serving dish. Skim the fat off the liquid and boil the liquid until it is reduced to half the original quantity. Pour it over the tendrons. Serve accompanied by potatoes, beans, or peas cooked separately. Makes 4 servings.

⚜ KNUCKLE OF VEAL (*Osso Buco*)

2½ pounds knuckle of veal
1¼ teaspoons salt
⅓ cup flour
3 tablespoons each butter and salad
   oil
1 small clove garlic, crushed
1 medium-sized carrot, finely diced
⅓ cup chopped celery

1 cup dry white wine
2 tablespoons tomato paste
bouillon, rich stock, or water
4 tablespoons chopped parsley
1 teaspoon grated lemon rind
1 tablespoon each cornstarch and
   water
3 lemon slices

Have the butcher saw the veal knuckle into 8 slices of equal thickness. Combine the salt and flour and roll the slices in the mixture. Heat the butter and oil in a Dutch oven or heavy skillet. Put in as many of the slices at a time as the pan will accommodate. Brown on both sides. When all the slices are browned, add the next 5 ingredients and enough bouillon, stock, or water to half cover the meat. Bring the mixture to boiling point, reduce heat, and simmer, covered, about 1 hour or until the meat is tender but not falling off the bones. Add 2 tablespoons of the parsley and the grated lemon rind. Blend the cornstarch and water, add to the veal, and cook 2 to 3 minutes. Transfer the veal to a warm platter and spoon some of the gravy over it. Sprinkle with the remaining 2 tablespoons chopped parsley. Garnish with the lemon slices. Makes 4 servings. (*See illustration, page 264.*)

⚜ GROUND-VEAL CUTLETS POJARSKI
(*Côtelettes de Veau Pojarski*)

3 slices day-old bread
¼ cup milk, bouillon, or stock
1¼ pounds ground veal
2 small white onions, chopped very
   fine
4 tablespoons (½ stick) butter

1 teaspoon salt
⅛ teaspoon ground black pepper
1 egg
1 tablespoon milk
fine dry breadcrumbs
4 sticks macaroni 2 inches long

Soak the bread in the milk, bouillon, or stock 5 minutes. Squeeze out the liquid and crumble the bread into the ground veal. Sauté the onions in 1 tablespoon of the butter, 3 to 4 minutes, or until they are limp, and add them to the veal. Add the salt and black pepper and mix well. Shape the mixture into 4 pear-shaped cutlets. Beat the egg with the 1 tablespoon milk, and dip the cutlets into the mixture, then roll them in the dry breadcrumbs, and let them stand 15 minutes for the crumbs to dry. Brown the cutlets on both sides over moderate heat in the remaining 3 tablespoons butter, adding it as needed. Arrange the cutlets on a warmed round serving plate. Insert a stick of macaroni into the small end of each to simulate the bone, and put a frill on each, if desired. Serve at once, with boiled potatoes and one or more cooked vegetables. Makes 4 servings.

↑ Molded Beef in Aspic (page 247)

↓ Cold Beef Niçoise (page 247)

262   ↑ Braised Sweetbreads Jardinière (page 292)

↓ Tournedos Château Figeac (page 237)

↑ Rump or Loin of Veal Cooked in a Casserole (page 256)

↑ Veal Medallions Veronese Style (page 250)   ↓ Knuckle of Veal (page 260)

↑ Pork Chops with Apples (page 278) ↓ Leg of Lamb Boulangère (page 271)

↑ Pork Medallions Hungarian Style (page 279)

↓ Braised Ham (page 284) **267**

↑ Glazed Pork Chops (page 278)   ↓ Garnished Sauerkraut (page 357)

⚜ VEAL CUTLETS WITH VEGETABLES IN ASPIC
(*Côtes de Veau à la Printanière en Gelée*)

4 veal cutlets, 4 to 5 ounces each
salt and ground black pepper
flour
4 tablespoons (½ stick) butter
1 veal knuckle, cut into pieces
6 carrots, cut into 2-inch pieces
12 small white onions
1 bay leaf

½ teaspoon dried thyme, or 2 teaspoons chopped fresh thyme
1 envelope unflavored gelatin
¼ cup cold veal stock
1¾ cup hot veal stock
½ cup cold cooked green peas
parsley

Sprinkle the cutlets with salt and black pepper and dredge them with flour. Melt the butter in a Dutch oven or a heavy 4-quart saucepan, add the cutlets, and brown them on both sides. Add the next 5 ingredients. Add ½ teaspoon salt and enough veal stock to cover the veal and vegetables. Cover and simmer, stirring occasionally, 1 hour or until the veal is tender. Drain off the stock, skim off and discard the fat, and strain the stock. Soften the gelatin in the cold veal stock and dissolve it in the hot veal stock. Season to taste with salt and black pepper. Cool slightly and pour a layer ¼ inch thick in a 5-cup ring mold. Chill until the aspic is set. Place the 4 cutlets on the aspic. Arrange half the carrots and onions and half the separately cooked peas between the cutlets in an attractive design. Cover with a layer of aspic. Chill until aspic is set. Arrange the remaining cooked vegetables in an attractive design over the firm aspic. Chill until thoroughly set. Unmold onto a serving plate, and gar-nish the plate with parsley. Makes 4 to 6 servings.

⚜ COLD VEAL SWEDISH STYLE (*Veau à la Suédoise*)

2 celery roots
½ teaspoon salt
boiling water
1 large eating apple, thinly sliced
4 tablespoons mayonnaise

8 slices cold roast veal
Tartare Sauce (page 55)
2 tomatoes, sliced
2 hard-cooked eggs, sliced

Cook the celery roots with the salt in boiling water to cover until they are tender. Remove them from the water, rinse in cold water, and cool. Cut them into julienne strips, add the apple slices and the mayonnaise, mix lightly, and mound in the center of a serving plate. Arrange the veal slices around the salad. Spread the veal with thick Tartare Sauce. Garnish the platter with sliced tomatoes and sliced hard-cooked eggs. Makes 4 servings.

Lamb, Mutton (*Agneau, Mouton*)

Lamb is the flesh of young sheep; mutton that of mature sheep. The flesh of lamb varies in color from light pink to dark pink. It is fine-grained, and the fat is clear, creamy, white, and soft-brittle. Mutton may be distinguished from lamb by its light-red to dark-red color and by its whiter and more brittle fat. As the animal ages, the color of the flesh deepens, the meat is not as juicy as that from young animals, and it has a stronger flavor.

Most of the sheep's flesh sold for meat in the United States is lamb, mutton being available only on special order. However, in Europe, mutton is popular and many delectable dishes have been created with mutton as well as with lamb. In America the favorite ways of cooking the tender cuts of lamb are roasting and broiling; the less tender cuts are braised or made into stews.

⚜ ROAST LEG OF LAMB OR MUTTON (*Gigot de Mouton Rôti*)

Trim off all but a thin layer of fat from a 6- to 7-pound leg of lamb or mutton. Rub it with salt and ground black pepper. Make 4 slits in various places in the roast and insert ½ clove of garlic in each. Place the roast in a roasting pan, along with the bones included in the package. Roast, uncovered, using either of the following methods:

French Two-Temperature Method. Cook meat in a preheated very hot oven (450° F.) 15 minutes, then reduce heat to 350° F. (moderate). For medium-rare, cook 10 to 12 minutes per pound, for well-done, cook 13 to 15 minutes per pound.

American Low-Temperature or One-Temperature Method. Cook meat in a preheated slow oven (325° F.). For medium-rare cook 30 minutes per pound, or to 175° F. on a meat thermometer; for well-done, 35 minutes per pound, or to 180° F. on the thermometer.

Remove the bones from around the roast and discard them. Transfer the roast to a warmed platter and keep it warm. Makes about 8 to 10 servings.

Make Gravy according to following recipe and serve separately.

⚜ Gravy

Skim the fat off the pan drippings and discard it. Blend 1 tablespoon cornstarch with 2 tablespoons water, add to the roasting pan, and mix well. Stir in 1½ cups water or stock. Stir and cook until the gravy has thickened. Season to taste with salt and ground black pepper.

⚜ LEG OF LAMB BOULANGÈRE (*Gigot d'Agneau à la Boulangère*)

6- to 7-pound leg of lamb, with extra bones and trimmings
salt
ground black pepper
2 cloves garlic

6 each medium-sized potatoes and onions, parboiled
lamb stock made from the extra bones and trimmings
watercress or parsley

Prepare the leg of lamb with salt and pepper and garlic as for Roast Leg of Lamb or Mutton and cook by either roasting method until it is about three-fourths done. Meanwhile make stock with the bones and trimmings. Slice the parboiled potatoes and onions and put them around the roast. Sprinkle the vegetables with salt and ground black pepper. Continue cooking until the lamb and vegetables are done. Transfer the lamb to a warmed platter and surround it with the vegetables. Make the gravy in the roasting pan, scraping up all the browned bits. Blend 1½ tablespoons cornstarch with ¼ cup cold lamb stock or water and pour the mixture into the pan. Mix well. Add 2 cups hot lamb stock. Stir and cook until the gravy is of desired consistency. Season to taste with salt and black pepper. Serve the gravy in a separate bowl. Garnish the meat with watercress or parsley. Makes 8 to 10 servings. (*See illustration, page 266.*)

⚜ ROAST LEG OF LAMB OR MUTTON BRETON STYLE (*Gigot de Mouton à la Bretonne*)

6- to 7-pound leg of lamb or mutton
salt
ground black pepper
2 cloves garlic
3 small white onions, chopped fine
3 tablespoons pan drippings from the roast

3 tablespoons tomato purée
½ cup bouillon
8 to 10 servings cooked whole tender green beans
chopped parsley

Prepare the leg of lamb or mutton for roasting with salt, black pepper and garlic as directed for Roast Leg of Lamb or Mutton, and roast the meat, using either of the methods described. Transfer the roast to a warmed platter and keep it warm. Brown the onions in a saucepan in the pan drippings. Add the tomato purée and bouillon. Stir and cook until the sauce has reduced to medium thickness. Season it to taste with salt and ground black pepper, and pour it over the cooked green beans. Sprinkle with chopped parsley. Serve with the roast. Makes 8 to 10 servings.

⚜ LEG OF LAMB ENGLISH STYLE (*Gigot de Pré-Salé à l'Anglaise*)

Pré-salé is the name given in France to young sheep pastured in salt meadows near the sea; the flesh has unusual delicacy and flavor.

6-pound leg of lamb, boned	4 stalks parsley
butter	2 ribs celery, quartered
flour	8 carrots, quartered
boiling water	16 small white onions
salt	8 medium-sized turnips, quartered
1 bay leaf	1 pound green beans
8 whole black peppercorns	Caper Sauce (see following recipe)
3 whole cloves	

Ask the butcher to bone the lamb. (Save the bones and trimmings for use in cooking the lamb.) Rub butter over a piece of clean cheesecloth large enough to wrap the lamb and sprinkle it with flour. Place the meat in the center of the cloth, bring the sides and corners up over the top of the meat, and tie with a string. Place the bundle in a large kettle and pour in enough boiling water to cover. Add 1 teaspoon salt for each quart of water used. Tie the lamb bones and trimmings, the bay leaf, black peppercorns, cloves, parsley, and celery in a piece of clean cheesecloth and add to the kettle. Simmer, partly covered, 20 minutes per pound, or until lamb is tender. Tie the carrots, onions, turnips, and green beans in a cheesecloth bag and add to the kettle 30 minutes before cooking time is up. Arrange the lamb and vegetables on a warmed platter. Make Caper Sauce with the stock from the kettle and serve over the meat. Makes 8 servings.

⚜ Caper Sauce for Leg of Lamb English Style

3 tablespoons butter	1 teaspoon cold water
2 tablespoons flour	1 teaspoon lemon juice
2 cups stock in which the leg of lamb was cooked	2 teaspoons wine vinegar
	1 tablespoon heavy cream
¼ teaspoon powdered mustard	¼ cup chopped capers

Melt 2 tablespoons of the butter in a 1-quart saucepan. Blend in the flour. Stir and cook until the mixture has lightly browned. Remove from heat and beat in the 2 cups lamb stock from the kettle. Stir and cook the mixture 1 to 2 minutes. Soak the powdered mustard in the water for 5 minutes, then add to the sauce. Stir in the lemon juice, wine vinegar, and cream. Cook 1 minute. Just before serving, add the remaining 1 tablespoon butter and the capers. Serve over the lamb roast. Makes about 2 cups sauce.

⚜ LAMB CHOPS OR MUTTON CHOPS
(*Côtelettes d'Agneau ou de Mouton*)

4 loin lamb or mutton chops, 6 ounces
   each
salt and ground black pepper

1 tablespoon butter
Maître d'Hôtel Butter (page 58)
Worcestershire sauce

Ask the butcher to remove the bone from the boned end of the chops. Roll the boned ends inward and hold them in place with skewers or toothpicks. Rub both sides of the chops with salt and black pepper. Pan-fry in butter, turning to brown both sides. Transfer the chops to a warmed platter. Garnish with Maître d'Hôtel Butter and with a few drops of Worcestershire sauce. Serve promptly with some of the pan drippings. Makes 4 servings. (*See illustration, page 265.*)

⚜ BRAISED LAMB CHOPS CHAMPVALLON
(*Côtelettes d'Agneau Braisées Champvallon*)

8 shoulder lamb chops
salt and ground black pepper
2 tablespoons butter

1 cup sliced onion
3 medium-sized potatoes, sliced
bouillon or broth

Rub the chops with salt and black pepper. Pan-fry them in the butter in a heavy skillet, turning to brown both sides. Transfer the chops to a baking dish and cover them with the sliced onion and potatoes. Sprinkle with salt and black pepper and pour in enough bouillon or broth to cover. Bring the liquid to boiling point over surface heat. Cover and place in a preheated slow oven (325° F.). Cook 1 hour. Serve from the baking dish. Makes 4 servings.

⚜ GRILLED RIB LAMB CHOPS (*Côtelettes d'Agneau Grillées*)

8 rib lamb chops, cut 1 inch thick
salt and ground black pepper
1 tablespoon butter

1 tablespoon olive oil or salad oil
buttered cooked green beans
Straw Potatoes (page 387)

Rub both sides of the chops with salt and black pepper. Heat the butter and oil in a heavy skillet and sauté the chops, turning to brown both sides. Or, if desired, melt the butter, mix with the oil, brush the chops with the mixture, and place them in a preheated oven broiler 3 inches from the source of heat and broil 6 to 7 minutes on each side. Serve with green beans and Straw Potatoes. Makes 4 servings.

⚜ LAMB CHOPS WITH RICE AND PEPERONATA SAUCE
(*Côtelettes d'Agneau au Riz, Sauce Peperonata*)

4 loin lamb chops, or 8 rib lamb chops
salt and ground black pepper
1 tablespoon butter
1 tablespoon olive oil or salad oil
4 tablespoons grated Parmesan cheese

2 cups hot cooked rice
Grilled Tomatoes (page 392)
Peperonata Sauce (see following recipe)

Rub both sides of the chops with salt and black pepper. Heat the butter and oil in a heavy skillet, and sauté the chops, turning to brown both sides. Sprinkle the chops with grated Parmesan cheese and arrange them over a bed of hot rice. Garnish with Grilled Tomatoes. Serve Peperonata Sauce in a separate bowl. Makes 4 servings. (*See illustration, page 265.*)

⚜ Peperonata Sauce

¼ cup chopped onion
2 tablespoons olive oil or salad oil
1 clove garlic, crushed
¾ cup finely diced sweet green peppers

3 medium-sized tomatoes, peeled, seeded, and diced
¼ cup bouillon
¼ teaspoon sugar
salt and ground black pepper

Cook the onions until soft in the olive oil or salad oil, without letting them brown. Add the garlic. Stir in the green peppers. Add the tomatoes, bouillon, and sugar. Cover and simmer 30 minutes. Season to taste with salt and ground black pepper. Serve separately with lamb chops or over the chops. Makes about 1½ cups.

⚜ BREAST OF LAMB OR MUTTON WITH TARTARE SAUCE
(*Poitrine de Mouton Tartare*)

2 medium-sized onions
4 whole cloves
½ cup sliced celery
¼ cup chopped parsley
4 cups beef broth or stock
salt and ground black pepper to taste

2 cups shredded cabbage
3 pounds breast of lamb or mutton
powdered mustard
fine dry breadcrumbs
3 tablespoons salad oil or shortening
Tartare Sauce (page 55)

Stud the onions with 2 whole cloves each and place in an 8-quart soup kettle with the celery, parsley, broth or stock, and salt and black pepper. Cover and simmer 30 minutes. Add the cabbage and simmer 20 minutes. Add the breast of lamb or mutton. Cover and simmer 1½ hours, or until the meat is tender. Transfer the meat to a large platter, reserving the stock and vegetables.

Remove the bones from the meat and cool the meat under the pressure of a heavy plate or dish. Sprinkle the meat lightly with mustard and breadcrumbs. Brown it in the hot oil or shortening, adding it as needed. Cut the meat into 2-inch squares and serve it with Tartare Sauce. Skim off the fat from the broth and serve it and the vegetables in bowls, sprinkled with chopped parsley, as the soup course. Makes 6 servings.

⚜ CASSOULET OF LAMB OR MUTTON (*Cassoulet à la Ménagère*)

1 cup (½ pound) dried navy beans
4 cups cold water
1 medium-large whole onion
3 whole cloves
1 clove garlic
2 fresh pork hocks
2 pounds boneless shoulder of lamb or mutton
2 tablespoons cooking oil, lard, or shortening

½ cup chopped onion
1 teaspoon powdered mustard
2 teaspoons cold water
4 teaspoons salt
½ teaspoon ground black pepper
½ cup tomato purée or tomato sauce
1 cup bouillon
8 carrots, quartered

Wash the beans, changing the water 3 to 4 times. Place them in a 4-quart saucepan with the cold water. Bring the water to a full rolling boil and boil 2 minutes. Remove beans from the heat and let them soak 1 hour. Do not drain. Stud the whole onion with the cloves and add to the beans, along with the garlic and pork hocks. Cover and cook over moderately low heat 2 hours or until beans are tender but do not break. Cut the lamb or mutton into 2-inch pieces and brown in the oil, lard, or shortening. Add the chopped onions, cook until the onions are soft, and then add the meat and onions to the beans. Soak the mustard in the 2 teaspoons cold water for 5 minutes, and add to the beans and lamb. Add the next 4 ingredients. Mix well, being careful not to break the beans. Cover and cook 1½ hours in a preheated slow oven (325° F.). Add the carrots and cook 30 minutes longer. Serve from the casserole. Makes 6 to 8 servings.

⚜ MARINATED LAMB OR MUTTON PROVENÇAL STYLE
(*Daube de Mouton à la Provençale*)

3 pounds boneless shoulder of lamb or mutton
2 cups dry red wine
3 tablespoons olive oil or salad oil
1 carrot, diced
4 small white onions, chopped
¼ cup chopped parsley
1 clove garlic, quartered

3 ready-to-cook lamb's feet, split
hot water
3 teaspoons salt, or salt to taste
½ teaspoon ground black pepper
1 bay leaf
4 fresh tomatoes, diced, or 2 cups canned tomatoes

Cut the lamb or mutton into 1½-inch pieces and place in a casserole with the next 6 ingredients. Marinate 24 hours. Pour hot water to cover over the lamb's feet and simmer 5 minutes, then transfer the feet to the lamb casserole. Add the remaining ingredients and cover the casserole tightly. Cook in a preheated slow oven (300° F.) 4 hours. Skim off the fat and serve the meat from the casserole with the liquid. Makes 8 servings.

⚜ LAMB OR MUTTON RAGOUT WITH DRIED BEANS
(*Haricot de Mouton*)

The term *haricot* for a ragout is believed to be a corruption of *halicot*, from *halicotor*, to chop fine; it does not refer to the French *haricot* meaning "bean." The beans in this recipe are substituted for the turnips more commonly used in a haricot.

2 pounds boneless shoulder of lamb or mutton

4 tablespoons salad oil, lard, or shortening

2 tablespoons flour

1 clove garlic, crushed

1½ cups hot water

½ cup tomato purée

2 teaspoons salt

¼ teaspoon ground black pepper

3 stalks parsley

1 tablespoon dark caramel, or 1 teaspoon Kitchen Bouquet

12 small white onions

6 medium-sized potatoes, cut in half

¼ teaspoon sugar

1½ cups cooked dried navy beans or pea beans

chopped parsley

Cut the meat into 1½-inch pieces and brown in 2 tablespoons of the oil, lard, or shortening in a Dutch oven. Stir in the flour and cook until the flour is brown. Add the next 7 ingredients, cover, and cook slowly for 1¼ hours. Brown the onions and potatoes in the remaining 2 tablespoons oil, lard, or shortening with the sugar and add to the meat. Cover and continue cooking 30 minutes or until vegetables and meat are tender. Add the cooked dried beans and cook 5 minutes. Sprinkle with chopped parsley. Makes 6 servings.

⚜ Lamb or Mutton Ragout (*Navarin d'Agneau ou Ragôut de Mouton*)

The term *navarin* is properly used only for mutton or lamb ragouts like the one in this recipe.

Use the same ingredients and method of cooking as in the recipe for Lamb or Mutton Ragout with Dried Beans, but omit the beans and, along with the onions and potatoes, brown 6 carrots and 6 small white turnips, all cut in half. Proceed according to the recipe. Makes 6 servings.

Pork (*Porc*)

Most pork available in the markets of the United States comes from hogs 6 to 12 months old and is tender. Of all the pork produced in this country, only about 30 per cent is sold as fresh pork. The rest is either cured as ham or bacon, rendered into lard, or made into sausage. Since the flesh is quite uniform in quality, there are fewer grades than in other meats. Pork is fine-grained, free from excessive moisture, relatively firm, and ranges in color from grayish pink in the younger animals to a delicate rose in the older ones.

Pork should be thoroughly cooked, both to develop its rich flavor and to destroy a microscopic parasite, *Trichinella spiralis*, often embedded in the muscle tissue of hogs, which may cause a condition known as trichinosis if eaten by humans. Fresh pork is well-done when it is gray with no tinge of pink.

⚜ ROAST LOIN OF PORK (*Carré de Porc Rôti*)

5 pounds center-cut loin of pork
1½ teaspoons salt
¼ teaspoon ground black pepper
¼ teaspoon ground ginger
1 tablespoon cornstarch

2 cups water
Parsley Potatoes (page 385)
Green Peas English Style (page 379)

Ask the butcher to saw through the bone of the loin in several places to make carving easier. Combine the salt, pepper, and ginger and rub over the outside of the roast. Place the meat on a rack in a roasting pan, fat side up. Cook, uncovered, in a preheated moderate oven (350° F.) 30 minutes per pound, or until the meat thermometer registers 185° F. Transfer the roast to a hot platter, and let it rest 15 minutes in a warm place. This will make the meat easier to carve. Pour off and discard the excess fat from the pan drippings. Blend the cornstarch with the 2 cups water and stir into the drippings, and cook 1 to 2 minutes. Adjust the seasoning. Garnish the roast with Parsley Potatoes and Green Peas English Style. Serve the gravy in a separate bowl. Makes approximately 10 servings.

❧ PORK CHOPS WITH APPLES *(Côtelettes de Porc aux Pommes)*

4 center-cut loin pork chops, 6 ounces
   each
salt and ground black pepper
⅛ teaspoon ground ginger
½ cup hot water, stock, or bouillon

2 medium-sized baking apples
sugar
2 teaspoons cornstarch
¼ cup cold water

Trim excess fat from pork chops and rub them on both sides with salt, black pepper, and ginger. In a heavy skillet, heat a piece of the pork fat long enough to grease the bottom and then remove it. Place the chops in the skillet and cook 15 to 20 minutes over moderate heat, turning them to brown both sides. Pour in the water, stock, or bouillon. Cover and bake in a pre-heated moderate oven (350° F.) 30 minutes. Peel and core the apples, cut them in half crosswise, and slice the halves ½ inch thick. Place ½ apple on each pork chop and spoon pan drippings over them. Cover and continue to cook 30 minutes, or until apples are tender but still hold their shape. Sprinkle the apples with a little sugar, but avoid sprinkling it on the meat. Put the skillet under the broiler and cook only long enough to brown and glaze the apples. Blend the cornstarch with the cold water, add to the pan drippings, and cook 1 to 2 minutes. Serve a spoonful of the sauce over each chop. Makes 4 servings. (*See illustration, page 266.*)

❧ GLAZED PORK CHOPS *(Côtelettes de Porc Glacées)*

2 thick center-cut loin pork chops, ¾
   pound each
salt and ground black pepper
⅛ teaspoon ground ginger
flour
2 tablespoons lard or shortening

½ cup hot water
⅓ cup dry white wine
Parsley Potatoes (page 385)
Grilled Tomatoes (page 392)
Green Peas English Style (page 379)

Trim off and discard the excess fat from the pork chops. Rub salt, black pepper, and ginger over both sides of the chops, dredge them with flour, and brown in the lard or shortening in a heavy skillet over moderately low heat. Add the hot water, cover, and cook 1 hour or until chops are tender. Trans-fer the chops to a warmed platter. Skim off and discard the excess fat from the pan drippings. Pour in the wine, bring to boiling point, and boil 1 to 2 min-utes. Pour the sauce over the chops. Serve with Parsley Potatoes, Grilled Tomatoes, and Green Peas English Style. Makes 4 servings. (*See illustration, page 268.*)

⚜ PORK MEDALLIONS HUNGARIAN STYLE
(*Médaillons de Porc à la Hongroise*)

8 round slices of pork cut from the tenderloin, 2 ounces each

garlic salt, or 1 small clove garlic, cut in half

3 tablespoons butter

1 medium-small sweet green pepper

1 medium-small sweet red pepper

1 medium-sized onion, sliced thin

1 red tomato, cut in coarse strips

1 yellow tomato, cut in coarse strips

1 to 2 tablespoons dry white wine

paprika

Sprinkle the pork slices lightly with garlic salt, or rub them on both sides with the cut garlic clove and discard it. Brown the slices on both sides in the butter, adding it as needed. Transfer the slices to a warmed dish and keep warm. Cut the peppers into julienne strips, add them, along with the onion, to the skillet in which the pork was browned, and sauté, adding more butter if needed. When the peppers and onion are half cooked, add the tomatoes, arrange the pork medallions on top of the vegetables, cover, and cook 30 minutes. Transfer the meat to a warmed platter. Pour the wine over the vegetables and cook slowly 5 minutes. Spoon the vegetables over the pork, and sprinkle lightly with paprika. Makes 4 servings. (*See illustration, page 267.*)

⚜ GARNISHED ROAST TENDERLOIN OF PORK
(*Filet de Porc Rôti, Garni*)

Pork tenderloin is the most tender and the most expensive of all pork cuts. The tenderloin is 9 to 12 inches long and weighs ¾ to 1½ pounds. It is usually cut in slices which are flattened to make larger, thinner pieces. It may also be braised whole over surface heat or in the oven, and cut in thin slices after it is cooked.

2 pork tenderloins, 1 pound each

1 clove garlic, cut in half

salt and ground black pepper

2 teaspoons lard or shortening

1 small white onion, sliced

1 medium-sized carrot, sliced

½ cup bouillon or water

4 to 6 medium-sized tomatoes, left whole

⅓ cup dry red or white wine

4 baked tart shells filled with buttered cooked carrots and peas

chopped parsley

Rub the tenderloins with the cut garlic clove and then with salt and black pepper. Discard the garlic. Brown them on all sides in the lard or shortening in a heavy skillet over moderate heat, then transfer to a casserole. In the same skillet, brown the sliced onion and carrot, and add them to the casserole, scraping up all the browned particles from the bottom of the pan and adding them. Pour in the bouillon or water. Cover and bake in a preheated moderate oven (350° F.) 40 minutes. Add the tomatoes and cook covered 20 to 30 minutes or until the pork is tender. Remove the meat and tomatoes to a warmed platter. Skim off the fat from the pan drippings and discard it. Add the wine, bring the mixture to boiling point, and boil 3 to 4 minutes. Strain, adjust seasoning, and serve in a sauceboat. Slice the pork thin and garnish the platter with the filled tart shells. Sprinkle the meat with chopped parsley. Makes 4 servings.

❧ PORK ROLLS PARMENTIER (*Roulades de Porc Parmentier*)

8 large thin slices pork tenderloin, 3 ounces each
salt and ground black pepper
½ pound pork sausage
1 small white onion, chopped fine
2 tablespoons chopped parsley

2 tablespoons lard or shortening
⅓ cup dry white wine
2 cups hot diced potatoes cooked in butter
1 tablespoon tomato purée

Flatten the pork tenderloin slices with a mallet or with the flat side of a cleaver. Sprinkle with salt and black pepper. Combine the sausage, onion, and parsley and spread an equal amount over each tenderloin, using it all. Roll up the tenderloins jelly-roll fashion and tie each end with white string. Brown the rolls on all sides in hot lard or shortening. Add the wine, cover, and cook slowly 1 hour. Remove the strings and place the rolls on a warmed platter. Garnish with the cooked diced potatoes. Add the tomato purée to the pan drippings, bring to boiling point, adjust seasonings, and pour the sauce over the meat. Makes 4 servings.

❧ PORK COUNTRY STYLE (*Potée Paysanne*)

This dish is made on the same principle as French-Style Boiled Dinner (*Pot au Feu*). The meat and vegetables are served as an entrée; the stock makes an excellent soup.

½ pound lean salt pork
2½ pounds boneless shoulder of pork
cold water
salt
1 or 2 links pork sausage

6 medium-sized potatoes
12 small white onions
6 medium-sized carrots, cut in half
6 wedges cabbage
¼ teaspoon ground black pepper

Soak the salt pork 1 hour in enough cold water to cover it. Place the salt pork and the shoulder of pork in a 4-quart saucepan or soup kettle. Add 1 quart cold water and 2 teaspoons salt. Partly cover the kettle and bring the water to boiling point. Reduce heat and simmer 1½ hours. Skim off scum and excess fat and discard. Add the sausage and potatoes. Cook 30 minutes. Add the carrots and onions and cook 30 minutes more. Add the cabbage and black pepper and cook 15 minutes more, or until the meat and vegetables are done. Remove the meat from the stock, slice it, and put the slices on a warmed platter. Arrange the vegetables around the meat. Skim off the excess fat from the stock, adjust the seasoning, and serve as soup. Makes 6 servings.

✤ PORK RAGOUT (*Ragoût de Porc*)

In the recipe for Lamb or Mutton Ragout (page 276) replace the lamb or mutton with lean shoulder or neck of pork. Continue according to the recipe.

H A M (*Jambon*)

A ham is the hind leg of a hog. There are several kinds available in the markets in the United States. They are:

Fresh Ham, sometimes called pork leg roast. It is neither cured nor smoked and should be thoroughly cooked.

Country Ham, usually heavily cured and/or smoked. It requires soaking or parboiling before being baked, or it may be fully cooked in water or other liquid, and eaten as boiled ham, or, if desired, baked a short time with a glaze.

Cook-Before-Eating Ham or Uncooked Smoked Regular Ham. Ham that has been cured, smoked, and heated to an internal temperature of at least 137° F. It must be thoroughly cooked (see timetable on page 283).

Fully Cooked Ham. Ham that has been heated to an internal temperature of 148° F. It may be served without further cooking; however, the flavor is improved if the ham is cooked before serving (see timetable on page 283).

Canned Hams. Fully cooked, boneless whole hams, weighing from 6½ to 12 pounds. Smaller cans containing 1½ pounds fully cooked, boneless pieces of ham are also available. The ham may be eaten without further cooking or may be glazed and baked about 10 minutes per pound. Ham in cans is either domestic or imported from France, Holland, Poland, and other countries.

Picnic Ham, which is actually not ham but is cut from the shoulder of a hog. It is available fresh or smoked and should be thoroughly cooked.

Canned Picnic Hams. These are smoked and cooked; they range in weight from 4½ to 8 pounds.

Be sure to read the label on the ham or the attached tag, so that you will know whether you are buying a ham that must be thoroughly cooked or one that may be eaten without further cooking. If there are no cooking directions, ask the butcher to tell you what kind of ham you are buying.

✤ HOW TO BAKE A COOK-BEFORE-EATING MILD CURED HAM

Place the ham, skin side up, on a rack and set it in a shallow baking pan. Insert a meat thermometer into the center of the thickest part of the ham, being careful that it does not touch the bone. Roast, without water or other liquid, uncovered, in a preheated slow oven until the meat thermometer registers 160° F., or gauge the time by the timetable on page 283. Pour off all the drippings in the pan. Remove all the rind and some of the fat, if it is too thick. Score the fat side (cut the fat into diamond shapes with a sharp knife) and stud each diamond with a whole clove. Spread with one of the ham glazes (page 283) or pour Madeira wine over the ham and sprinkle it lightly with white or brown sugar. Bake the ham in a preheated hot oven (400° F.) 15 to 20 minutes or until a brown glaze has formed. Allow about ½ pound uncooked ham per serving.

⚜ HOW TO COOK AN OLD-FASHIONED COUNTRY-CURED HAM

Soak an old-fashioned country-cured ham for 24 hours in enough cold water to cover it. Remove the ham from the water and saw off the knuckle bone. Put the ham in a large kettle and cover it with cold water, partly cover the kettle, and bring the water to boiling point. Reduce heat and simmer until the ham is done, allowing 20 minutes per pound. If the ham is to be served hot, remove it from the water and drain it well. Remove the skin and trim off the excess fat. Place the ham on a rack, fat side up, in a shallow baking pan, and pour 1 cup Madeira or white wine over it. Sprinkle lightly with brown sugar. Bake in a preheated slow oven (325° F.) 45 minutes, basting frequently with the wine and pan drippings. The ham should be glazed to a golden brown. If desired, the ham may be served cold without a glaze; in this case it should be cooled in the liquor. Allow ½ pound uncooked ham per serving.

To Test Ham for Doneness. Pull the small bone next to the large one at the shank end. When it is loose and slips out easily the ham is done. Since piercing releases the juices, a fork or other pointed object should never be used to test a ham for doneness.

⚜ HOW TO GLAZE A FULLY COOKED READY-TO-EAT HAM

If there are directions on the wrapper of a fully cooked ready-to-eat ham, follow them to the letter. If there are no directions, place the ham, fat side up, on a rack in a shallow roasting pan. Insert a meat thermometer through the fat side of the thickest part of the ham, being careful that it does not touch the bone. Bake the ham, uncovered, with water or other liquid. Gauge the cooking time by the timetable on page 283, or cook until the meat thermometer registers 130° F. Take the ham from the oven, remove the thermometer, pour off pan drippings and pull or cut off the rind. If there is a very thick layer of fat, cut off some of it. Score the fat side of the ham (cut the fat into diamond shapes with a sharp knife, only about ¼ inch deep). Stud each diamond with a whole clove, if desired. Cover with one of the following glazes, and bake the ham in a preheated hot oven (400° F.) 15 to 20 minutes or until it has browned and glazed. Allow ½ pound ham per serving.

Timetable for Baking Commercially Cured Hams

	Approximate Weight (Pounds)	Oven Temperature (°F.)	Approximate Total Cooking Time (Hours)	Meat Thermometer Reading (°F.)
HAM				
Uncooked				
(*Cook-Before-Eating*)				
Whole	12	325	3½	160
Half	6	325	2½	160
End	4	325	¾ (45 minutes)	160
Picnic	4 to 6	325	2½ to 3	170
Fully Cooked				
Whole	10 to 12	325	2½ to 2¾	130
Half	5 to 8	325	1¾ to 2	130
Picnic	4 to 6	325	1¾ to 2¼	130

GLAZES FOR HAMS

⚜ Madeira and Sugar

Pour ½ to 1 cup Madeira wine (amount depends upon the size of the ham) over the ham and sprinkle with a little white or brown sugar. The French prefer this glaze to the sweeter coatings popular in America.

⚜ Mustard and Jelly or Molasses

Combine equal amounts of prepared mustard and currant jelly or molasses and spread over the ham.

⚜ Honey or Corn Syrup and Orange Juice

Combine ½ cup honey or light corn syrup, ½ cup orange juice, and 1 cup light brown sugar and spoon over the ham.

⚜ Apple Cider and Marmalade

Combine ½ cup orange, apricot, peach, or pineapple marmalade with ½ cup apple cider or apple juice and spread over the ham.

⚜ Cranberry Jelly and Corn Syrup

Combine 1 cup cranberry jelly and ½ cup light corn syrup and spread over the ham.

⚜ BRAISED HAM (*Jambon Braisé*)

8- to 10-pound boiled ham	maraschino cherries
1½ cups Madeira or champagne	Poached Apples (page 307)
confectioners' sugar	chutney
1 cup Demi-Glace Sauce (page 44)	boiled white onions
pineapple rings	whole cloves

Remove the rind from the ham and take off some of the fat if the fat layer is thick. Score the fat. Place the ham in a roasting pan just big enough to fit it and to allow room for basting. Pour the Madeira or champagne over the ham. Cook, uncovered, in a preheated moderate oven (350° F.) 30 minutes, basting frequently with the wine from the pan. Sprinkle the ham with confectioners' sugar and cook 30 minutes longer, or until the ham has browned and glazed. Remove from the oven and let the ham rest 25 to 30 minutes before carving. Skim off and discard the fat from the pan liquor. Add the Demi-Glace Sauce to the pan, mix well, and cook over surface heat, stirring often, until the sauce has reduced to the desired consistency. Adjust the seasonings and serve in a separate bowl. Put ham on a warm platter. Garnish with pineapple rings with centers filled with maraschino cherries, Poached Apples with centers filled with chutney, and boiled white onions each stuck with a whole clove. Makes 16 to 20 servings. (*See illustration, page 267.*)

SAUSAGE

⚜ BLOOD SAUSAGE WITH APPLES (*Boudin aux Pommes de Reinette*)

Peel baking apples and slice ½ inch thick, allowing 2 medium-sized apples for 4 servings. Sauté the apples in butter in a skillet. Place them on a warm platter and keep them warm. Cut blood sausage in uniform pieces, allowing 8 pieces for 4 servings. In the same skillet, cook the sausage slices in only enough butter to prevent them from sticking. When they have browned lightly, place the slices on top of the apples. Serve promptly for supper or lunch.

⚜ GRILLED SAUSAGE WITH CABBAGE
(Saucisses Grillées aux Choux)

12 links pork sausage
boiling water
1 head (2 pounds) cabbage

½ teaspoon sugar
½ teaspoon salt
ground black pepper

Prick the sausage links with a fork and arrange them in a 10- by 6- by 2-inch baking pan. Pour in 2 tablespoons boiling water. Cook in a preheated hot oven (400° F.) 30 minutes or until sausages are brown. (Reserve the fat.) Meanwhile, chop the cabbage coarsely and cook it with the sugar and salt in ½ inch boiling water in a covered saucepan 8 to 10 minutes, or only until the cabbage is crisp-tender. Toss the cabbage lightly with black pepper to taste and 2 tablespoons of the sausage fat. Put the cabbage in a shallow dish and arrange the sausage links around it. Makes 6 servings.

⚜ POTTED PORK *(Rillettes)*

Rillettes are a French specialty made of lean and fat pork cooked with salt, black pepper, thyme, bay leaf, and water, then ground fine or pounded in a mortar, put into jars and sealed with a thin layer of fat. Rillettes should be stored in the refrigerator until ready to use.

1½ pounds fresh lean pork
2 pounds fat pork (fatback)
½ teaspoon ground black pepper
1½ teaspoons salt

¾ teaspoon ground thyme
1 bay leaf
¼ cup finely chopped parsley
1 cup boiling water

Dice the lean pork and the fat pork fine and place in a heavy-bottomed saucepan. Add the remaining ingredients. Cook over low heat until all the water has evaporated, and the meat and fat are browned, stirring occasionally. Place a colander over a bowl, turn the cooked mixture into the colander, and let drain until all the fat has drained out. Reserve the fat, discard the bay leaf, and put the meat through a food chopper, using the finest blade. Measure 1 cup of the fat that was drained from the meat and reserve. Stir the remaining fat back into the mixture, mix well, and pack into small jars. Pour the reserved fat over the top and cover the jars with lids that fit them. Refrigerate until ready to use. Serve as a pâté. Fills approximately 4 jars holding ½ pint each.

Variety Meats

Organs and other parts of an animal that cannot be classed as regular cuts are known in the United States as variety meats, in England as offal, and in France as *abats de boucherie*. Variety meats contribute important nutrients, since they contain the same food elements as those found in lean meat, and some, such as liver, are superior sources of important minerals and vitamins. Most are also economical.

The method of preparing variety meats is determined by the physical structure of each type. Precooking is sometimes necessary. Since the same organs of different animals are cooked in the same ways, variety meats are grouped according to type instead of being included under the names of the animals.

BRAINS

❧ CALF'S BRAINS IN BLACK BUTTER
(Cervelles de Veau au Beurre Noir)

1 pound calf's brains	1 teaspoon salt
cold water	⅛ teaspoon ground black pepper
Acidulated Water (page 162)	11 tablespoons butter
ice water	1 tablespoon wine vinegar
½ cup flour	1 teaspoon capers (optional)

Soak the calf's brains in cold water 1 hour. Drain, rinse, and drop into boiling salted Acidulated Water to cover (1 tablespoon lemon juice or vinegar and ½ teaspoon salt to each 2 cups water). Simmer gently 15 to 20 minutes. Drain the brains, cover them with ice water, and let them stand until they have cooled completely. Dry them with a clean towel. Mix the flour, salt, and pepper and dredge the brains with the mixture. Sauté the brains in 3 tablespoons of the butter and remove them to a heated platter. Put the 8 tablespoons (1 stick) remaining butter in the skillet in which the brains were sautéed and heat it until the butter begins to brown. Remove from heat, add 1 tablespoon wine vinegar, and heat until the mixture begins to foam. Pour it over the brains immediately. Serve at once. If desired, sprinkle 1 teaspoon capers over the brains before pouring the butter over them. Makes 4 servings.

FEET

❖ CALVES' FEET VINAIGRETTE (*Pieds de Veau Vinaigrette*)

2½ pounds ready to cook calves' feet
cold water to cover
½ lemon
3 tablespoons flour
2 medium-sized onions, sliced

1 medium-sized carrot, sliced
1 teaspoon salt
Vinaigrette Sauce (page 56)

Put the calves' feet in a 4-quart saucepan with enough cold water to cover them. Bring the water to boiling point and boil for 5 minutes. Remove the saucepan from the heat, drain off the water, and rinse the feet under running cold water. Drain them and rub with the half lemon. Return them to the saucepan. Add the flour, onions, carrot, salt, and enough cold water to cover them. Bring the water to boiling point, reduce heat, and simmer, covered, 3 hours. Remove the feet from the cooking liquid and cut them into 1½-inch slices. So that they will remain soft, add the slices to the Vinaigrette Sauce while they are still hot. Sprinkle with finely chopped parsley and with 1 to 2 tablespoons of the cooking liquid. Serve hot or cold. Makes 4 servings.

❖ PIGS' FEET SAINTE-MENEHOULD
(*Pieds de Porc Sainte-Menehould*)

6 pigs' feet
water
1 cup dry white wine
1 carrot, sliced
1 medium-sized onion, sliced
2 stalks parsley
coarsely ground black pepper

¾ cup (1½ sticks) butter, melted
fine dry breadcrumbs
6 portions mashed potatoes
6 portions cooked green peas

Split the pigs' feet, tie them back together, and place them in a large saucepan. Add water to cover. Add the next 5 ingredients. Cover, bring to boiling point, and simmer until the feet are tender. Remove the feet from the stock and pull out the bones. Spread the feet on a board, place another board on top of them, put a weight on it, and let stand in a cool place overnight. Sprinkle the feet with pepper, dip them in melted butter, and roll them in breadcrumbs, pressing down the crumbs. Fry in a heavy skillet in the remaining butter until browned on both sides, adding the butter as needed. Serve with mashed potatoes and green peas. Makes 6 servings.

287

⚜ PIGS' FEET IN MADEIRA SAUCE (*Pieds de Porc au Madère*)

4 pigs' feet (cleaned, split, and ready
  to cook)
salt
water
1 tablespoon lard or shortening
1 bay leaf
½ teaspoon dried thyme
4 whole black peppercorns

3 whole cloves
½ cup dry white wine
1 tablespoon tomato purée
Madeira Sauce (page 294)
sautéed or boiled potatoes

Sprinkle the pigs' feet with salt and let them stand 2 to 3 days in a cold place
or in the refrigerator. Wash the salt off the pigs' feet and place them in a
saucepan with enough cold water to cover them. Cover, bring to boiling point,
reduce heat and simmer 1 hour. Pour off the water and rinse the feet in cold
water. Melt the lard or shortening in a casserole or Dutch oven, add the pigs'
feet, the next 6 ingredients, and enough water to cover them. Cover the
casserole tightly and simmer 2 hours, adding more water if needed. Drain off
the water, add the Madeira Sauce, and simmer 30 minutes. Serve hot with
sautéed or boiled potatoes. Makes 6 servings.

HEAD

⚜ CALF'S HEAD VINAIGRETTE (*Tête de Veau Vinaigrette*)

1 calf's head
cold water
2 onions
6 whole cloves
2 ribs celery with tops
2 carrots, quartered
1 leek (if available)
3 stalks parsley

10 whole black peppercorns
2 tablespoons salt
1 tablespoon lemon juice or vinegar
½ cup Vinaigrette Sauce (page 56)

Ask the butcher to cut, clean, and bone a calf's head. Soak the meat, the skin
of the head, the tongue, and the brains 2 hours in enough cold water to cover.
Stud the onions with 3 cloves each and put them in a large saucepan. Add the
next 7 ingredients and 2 quarts cold water. Cover, bring to boiling point, and
boil 5 minutes. Add the meat and the skin of the head, partly cover, and
simmer 40 minutes. Add the tongue and simmer 1 hour. Add the brains and
simmer 20 minutes. Transfer the brains to a bowl and let them cool. Cool the
meat and the tongue in the cooking broth, then remove them from the broth.
Arrange the meat on a platter. Skin the tongue and discard the skin. Slice the

tongue and place it on the platter with the meat. Dice the brains, add to the Vinaigrette Sauce, and spoon over the platter of sliced tongue and meat. Makes 6 servings.

HEART

⚜ PAN-FRIED CALF'S HEART (*Coeur de Veau*)

2 calf's hearts
5 tablespoons olive oil or salad oil
salt
ground black pepper
⅛ teaspoon dried thyme leaves

½ small clove garlic
2 anchovy fillets, chopped
1½ teaspoons lemon juice
chopped parsley

Slice the calf's hearts thin into a mixing bowl. Add 2 tablespoons of the oil, ½ teaspoon salt, ⅛ teaspoon black pepper, and the thyme. Mix well. Marinate 1 hour, turning the slices frequently. Sauté the garlic in the remaining 3 tablespoons oil, then remove and discard. Add the heart slices to the hot oil and brown them well on both sides, turning them frequently, and cooking them approximately 8 minutes in all. Add the chopped anchovy fillets and cook 1 minute longer. Transfer the heart slices and anchovies to a warmed platter. Sprinkle lightly with salt, black pepper, the lemon juice, and parsley. Serve promptly. Makes 4 servings.

KIDNEYS

⚜ BEEF KIDNEYS AND MUSHROOMS WITH MADEIRA
(*Rognons de Boeuf au Madère et aux Champignons*)

1½ pounds beef kidneys
3 tablespoons vinegar
cold water
salt and ground black pepper
flour
5 tablespoons butter or salad oil

1½ cups sliced mushrooms
¼ cup Madeira
⅓ cup bouillon or beef broth
1 tablespoon tomato purée (optional)
½ teaspoon dried thyme leaves
chopped parsley

Remove all membrane and fat from the kidneys. Place them in a small mixing bowl with the vinegar and enough cold water to cover. Let them stand 2 hours. Drain off the water. Rinse the kidneys in cold water and wipe dry. Slice thin, sprinkle with salt and black pepper, and dredge the slices in flour. Heat 4 tablespoons of the butter or oil in a skillet and brown the slices quickly on both sides. In a separate skillet, sauté the mushrooms in the remaining 1 tablespoon butter or oil. Add them to the kidneys. Add the Madeira, the bouillon or beef broth, the tomato purée (if used), and the thyme. Cover and simmer 15 minutes. Remove cover and simmer until sauce is reduced to the desired thickness. Adjust seasonings. Sprinkle with chopped parsley. Serve promptly. Makes 4 to 5 servings.

⚜ VEAL KIDNEYS ENGLISH STYLE (*Rognons de Veau à l'Anglaise*)

4 veal kidneys
salt and ground black pepper
flour
1 large egg, beaten with 1 tablespoon
  olive oil or salad oil

fine dry breadcrumbs
juice of ½ lemon
chopped parsley

Remove most of the fat from the kidneys and discard it. Cut the kidneys in half. Sprinkle with salt and black pepper. Roll in flour, in egg beaten with oil, and then in breadcrumbs. Press the crumbs down with the hands to make them stick to the kidneys and let stand 15 minutes to dry. Place the kidneys in a hot well-buttered baking dish and bake in a preheated hot oven (400° F.) 20 minutes. Or, if desired, broil them 3 inches from the source of heat for 6 minutes on each side, or until browned. Serve sprinkled with a little lemon juice and chopped parsley. Makes 4 servings.

⚜ SAUTÉED VEAL KIDNEYS (*Rognons de Veau Sautés*)

4 veal kidneys
salt and ground black pepper
4 tablespoons (½ stick) butter
2 cups thinly sliced mushrooms

⅓ cup dry white wine or Madeira
chopped parsley
Pilaf (page 117)

Trim the surplus fat from the kidneys and discard it. Split the kidneys in half lengthwise but do not cut them all the way through. Open them so they will lie flat. Sprinkle them with salt and black pepper and rub flour over the surface. In a heavy skillet melt the butter, add the kidneys, and cook, partly covered, 10 to 12 minutes on each side, or until they are golden brown. Transfer the kidneys to a warmed serving platter and keep them warm. Sauté the mushrooms in the pan residue. Add the wine and cook, uncovered, until the liquid has reduced to half the original amount. Pour over kidneys. Sprinkle with chopped parsley. Serve with Pilaf. Makes 4 servings.

❧ SAUTÉED LAMB KIDNEYS TURBIGO (*Rognons Sautés Turbigo*)

8 lamb kidneys
milk
salt and ground black pepper
flour
5 tablespoons butter
1 tablespoon olive oil or salad oil
4 slices buttered toast

4 links chipolata sausages, grilled
¾ cup bouillon or beef stock
¼ cup light cream
¼ cup tomato purée
2 tablespoons finely chopped onion
¼ cup finely chopped mushrooms
chopped parsley

Cut the kidneys in half lengthwise, cover them with milk, and let soak 2 hours. Remove the kidneys from the milk and wipe them dry. Sprinkle them with salt and black pepper and roll them in flour. Brown them on both sides in 2 tablespoons of the butter and the 1 tablespoon of oil. Arrange the toast on a warmed platter and place 2 kidneys and a grilled sausage on each. Using the same skillet, melt 2 tablespoons of the butter, blend in 2 tablespoons flour, and cook until the flour browns. Add the bouillon or stock. Stir and cook until the sauce has thickened. Pour in the cream and cook 1 minute, stirring constantly. Blend in the tomato purée. Melt the remaining 1 tablespoon butter in a small saucepan, add the onion, and cook 1 minute. Stir in the mushrooms and cook until they are tender. Add the onion and mushrooms to the sauce, and cook 1 minute. Add salt and black pepper to taste. Spoon the sauce over the kidneys. Sprinkle with chopped parsley. Makes 4 servings.

LIVER

❧ CALF'S LIVER ENGLISH STYLE (*Foie de Veau à l'Anglaise*)

8 slices bacon
2 tablespoons (¼ stick) butter
4 slices calf's liver
flour

salt and ground black pepper to taste
parsley
½ lemon, notched
buttered boiled potatoes

Fry the bacon in a skillet until it is crisp. Transfer it to a warmed platter and keep it warm. Drain off half of the bacon drippings; discard or save, as preferred. Add the butter to the remaining drippings in the skillet and heat until the butter melts. Dredge the liver with flour and brown it on both sides in the hot bacon fat and butter. Remove the liver to the warmed platter, sprinkle with salt and black pepper, and garnish each slice with 2 strips of the bacon. Decorate the platter with parsley and the notched lemon half. Serve with buttered boiled potatoes. Makes 4 servings. (*See illustration, page 263.*)

OXTAIL

⚜ OXTAIL STEW (*Queue de Boeuf en Hochepot*)

2 pounds oxtail
2 tablespoons lard or shortening
2 pig's feet (if available), cut into pieces
1 pig's ear (if available), cut into pieces
3 medium-sized onions, sliced
2 medium-sized carrots, sliced
2 cups hot water or hot bouillon
½ teaspoon salt, or salt to taste

¼ teaspoon ground black pepper
3 carrots, quartered
1 cup sliced celery
2 tablespoons tomato paste
8 chipolata sausages (optional)
1 tablespoon cornstarch, blended with 2 tablespoons cold water
boiled potatoes
chopped parsley

Cut the oxtail into 1½-inch pieces and place in a Dutch oven with the lard or shortening, pig's feet and ear (if available), sliced onions, and sliced carrots. Cook until all have browned lightly, stirring frequently. Add the hot water or bouillon and salt. Cover and simmer over low heat 2½ hours, or until meat is almost tender. Add the pepper, quartered carrots, celery, tomato paste, and the sausage, if used. Cover and cook 20 to 30 minutes. Thicken the stew with the blended cornstarch. Cook until the sauce is translucent and slightly thick. Adjust the salt. Serve in a large deep dish surrounded with boiled potatoes. Sprinkle with chopped parsley. Makes 6 servings.

SWEETBREADS

⚜ BRAISED SWEETBREADS JARDINIÈRE
(*Ris de Veau Braisé à la Jardinière*)

1 pound calf's or lamb's sweetbreads
cold water
salt
1 medium-sized onion, sliced
2 medium-sized carrots, sliced
2 ribs celery, sliced

¾ cup bouillon or chicken broth
4 servings each buttered cooked green beans, green peas, and carrots
Braised Lettuce (page 375)

Soak the sweetbreads 15 to 20 minutes in cold salted water (1 teaspoon salt to 1 quart water). Rinse under running cold water and drain. Cover with fresh cold salted water, bring it slowly to boiling point, and then simmer 5 minutes.

Remove from heat and drain off the water. Cover the sweetbreads with cold water to cool them. When they are cold, remove them from the water and cut away and discard the dark veins and thick connective tissue, but do not remove the membranes around the sweetbreads. Press the sweetbreads under a weight for 1 hour to break the fibers and to prevent shrinkage during cooking. This process also makes the sweetbreads easier to handle when cooking and more attractive when they are served. Place the sliced onion, carrots, and celery in the bottom of a Dutch oven or casserole and arrange the sweetbreads on top of the vegetables. Pour in the bouillon or broth, cover, and cook 30 to 40 minutes in a preheated moderate oven (350° F.). Place the sweetbreads in the center of a warmed platter. Arrange Braised Lettuce, beans, peas, and carrots in mounds around them. Serve immediately. Makes 4 servings. (See illustration, page 262.)

⚜ SCALLOPED SWEETBREADS IN CREAM
(Escalopes de Ris de Veau à la Crème)

1½ pounds calf's or lamb's sweetbreads
salt
ground black pepper
flour

4 tablespoons (½ stick) butter
½ cup heavy cream
brandy
lemon juice
1 cup sliced poached mushrooms

Blanch the sweetbreads according to the directions in the preceding recipe and remove and discard the dark veins and thick connective tissue. Do not remove the membranes. Cut the sweetbreads into slices ½ inch thick, sprinkle with salt and black pepper, and dredge with flour. Cook the slices in a heavy skillet in the butter until they are tender, turning to brown both sides. Transfer to a warmed platter and keep them hot. Pour the cream into the skillet and mix well with the pan residue. Simmer until the sauce is slightly thick. Season to taste with salt and black pepper, brandy, and lemon juice. Add the mushrooms, heat, and pour the sauce over the sweetbreads. Makes 6 servings.

TONGUE

⚜ BEEF TONGUE WITH MADEIRA SAUCE
(Langue de Boeuf, Sauce Madère)

4-pound smoked beef tongue
water to cover
1 onion studded with 2 whole cloves
1 clove garlic
2 ribs celery with leaves

½ cup sliced carrots
6 whole black peppers
1 small bay leaf
Madeira Sauce (see following recipe)

Place all ingredients except the Madeira Sauce in a 6-quart saucepan. Cover and simmer 3 to 4 hours or until tongue is tender. Cool the tongue in the stock. When cool, remove the tongue to a tray. Cut off the bones and gristle at the thick end. Slit the skin from the tip end of the tongue to the thick end and pull it off with the aid of a paring knife. Return the tongue to the stock and reheat. Slice and serve with Madeira Sauce. Makes approximately 8 servings.

⚜ Madeira Sauce

2 tablespoons finely chopped onion
2 tablespoons beef, veal, or pork drippings
2 tablespoons flour

2 cups Brown Stock (page 30)
2 tablespoons tomato purée
salt and ground black pepper
⅓ cup Madeira

Brown the onion in the drippings. Add the flour and cook, stirring, until the roux is brown. Stir in the stock and tomato purée and simmer, uncovered, until sauce has reduced to about 1 cup, stirring occasionally. Add salt and black pepper to taste and stir in the Madeira. Makes about 1⅓ cups.

⚜ CALF'S TONGUE DUCHESS STYLE
(*Langue de Veau à la Duchesse*)

Calf's tongues weigh ½ pound to 2 pounds and are available fresh in the markets of larger cities. Allow 1 pound calf's tongue for each 4 servings.

1 pound calf's tongue
cold water
1 tablespoon lemon juice or vinegar
salt
2 medium-sized onions, diced
3 medium-sized carrots, diced
2 shallots, diced (optional)
2 tablespoons olive oil or salad oil

1½ cups bouillon or beef stock
¼ cup tomato sauce
4 whole black peppercorns
2 tablespoons flour
⅓ cup dry white wine
1 to 2 gherkins, chopped
chopped parsley
Duchess Potatoes (page 383)

Soak the tongue for 1 hour in 1 quart cold water and the lemon juice or vinegar. Drain, cover with 1 quart fresh cold water, and add 1 teaspoon salt. Cover and parboil 15 to 20 minutes or until the skin can be removed easily from the tongue. Drain. Cut off the tongue root, and remove the skin (see directions under Beef Tongue). Brown the tongue and the vegetables in the oil, add the bouillon or stock, tomato sauce, and peppercorns. Cover and cook in a preheated moderate oven (350° F.) 1 to 1½ hours or until the tongue is tender. Remove the tongue from the pan liquid and keep it warm. Skim off and discard the fat from the pan liquid. Blend the flour with the wine until smooth and add to the pan liquid. Stir and cook 2 to 3 minutes. Add salt to taste, and the gherkins and parsley. Slice the tongue and arrange the slices down the center of a warmed heatproof platter. Edge the dish with

Duchess Potatoes put through a pastry bag. Put the platter in a very hot oven just to brown the potatoes. Spoon the sauce over the tongue. Serve at once. Makes 4 servings.

⚜ LAMB'S TONGUES (*Langues d' Agneau*)

There are three methods of preparing lamb's tongues. For each, allow ½ pound lamb's tongue per serving.

First Method: Boil the tongues in Court Bouillon (page 161) and serve hot on a puréed vegetable (peas, green beans purée, mashed carrot, turnip, or potatoes). Season to taste with salt and black pepper.

Second Method: Put the tongues in a saucepan and pour in enough cold water to cover. Bring the water to boiling point and boil 5 to 10 minutes. Cool the tongues in the broth, then transfer to a plate, and remove the skins. Brown the tongues in shortening, allowing 1 tablespoon shortening per serving. For 4 servings, mix 2 tablespoons flour, ½ teaspoon salt, and ⅛ teaspoon ground black pepper and sprinkle the mixture over the tongues. Add 2 stalks parsley, ½ cup water, and ¼ cup tomato purée, cover, and simmer 1 hour or until tongues are tender. Serve with the pan liquid, cooked vegetables, and rice or potatoes.

Third Method: Boil the tongues in Court Bouillon, cool in the broth, and remove the skins. Cut the tongues into lengthwise slices ½ inch thick. Dip the slices into beaten egg, roll them in breadcrumbs, and pan-fry in melted butter, browning both sides.

TRIPE

Tripe is the wall of the stomach of cud-chewing animals. There are three kinds: plain tripe from the smooth first stomach; honeycomb tripe from the second stomach (this is considered the best variety and is called honeycomb because it is full of pockets on one side and smooth on the other); and the type called the "need," which comes from the fourth stomach (sometimes called the rennet stomach).

Beef tripe is the most popular. However, pork and sheep tripe are also used in some places. Sheep tripe, called Haggis, is used in Scotland, and pork tripe is used in the southern part of the United States. Both France and Italy are famous for their tripe dishes.

To cook tripe from scratch is a long and laborious task. Precooked fresh tripe is available in markets today, but it needs further cooking. Pickled tripe is also available, but must be soaked several hours before using. Canned tripe, ready to heat, is also available. A real connoisseur of tripe would use only the fresh precooked tripe.

❧ TRIPE CAEN STYLE (*Tripes à la Mode de Caen*)

This is the favorite tripe dish of France. Tripe is best prepared in a large quantity. Since it keeps well, it may be reheated without loss of flavor.

4 pounds precooked fresh tripe
2 calf's feet, washed and split
3 medium-sized onions, sliced
3 large carrots, sliced
3 stalks parsley
4 leeks (white part only), sliced
7 ounces beef kidney fat

5 whole black peppercorns
4 whole cloves
1½ teaspoons salt
1 clove garlic
¾ cup brandy
beef stock or water
baked potatoes or boiled potatoes

Wash the tripe and cut it into 2-inch squares. Put half the tripe in the bottom of a 3-quart casserole. Add the next 10 ingredients. Cover with the remaining tripe. Add the brandy and enough beef stock or water to cover the tripe completely. Cover and seal the casserole hermetically with dough. (This is done by mixing 2 cups flour with enough cold water to make a very stiff paste, shaping the paste into a roll, and pressing it in place around the casserole where the cover meets the dish.) Place the casserole over surface heat and bring the liquid *only* to boiling point. Put the casserole in a preheated slow oven (300° F.), and continue cooking about 12 hours or overnight. Never open the casserole or disturb the tripe while it is cooking. Transfer the tripe to another casserole. Remove the calf's feet, pick off the meat, and add it to the tripe, discarding the bones. Skim off and discard the fat from the liquid. Strain the stock over the tripe. Heat. Serve very hot from the casserole, accompanied by baked or boiled potatoes. Makes 8 to 10 servings.

❧ TRIPE LYONNAISE STYLE (*Tripes à la Lyonnaise*)

This dish is renowned all over the world. It originated in Lyon, a city famous for its very fine cuisine and the superior food products of its area.

1¼ pounds precooked fresh tripe
water or stock to cover
5 tablespoons butter
2 medium-sized onions, thinly sliced
½ pound mushrooms, sliced

2 tablespoons wine vinegar
3 tablespoons tomato purée
   (optional)
salt and ground black pepper to taste
1 tablespoon chopped parsley

Cook the tripe slowly in water or stock to cover for 3 to 4 hours, or until it is tender. Cool. Cut the tripe in 3- by 1-inch pieces and drain them well. Cook the pieces in 2 tablespoons of the butter until golden brown, turning the pieces frequently. In another skillet, cook the onions in 2 tablespoons of the butter until they are golden, and add them to the tripe. Put the mushrooms and the remaining 1 tablespoon butter in the onion skillet, cook 5 minutes or until the mushrooms are tender, and add them to the tripe and onions. Stir in the remaining ingredients. Heat the mixture and serve with baked, boiled, or sautéed potatoes. Makes 4 servings.

Furred Game

Game (French *gibier*) is the term applied to wild birds and animals which are hunted, and to their flesh when used as food. The flesh has a stronger flavor than that of domesticated birds and animals. Of the smaller game animals, hare and rabbit are most common. Squirrel, which is hunted in many parts of the United States, is cooked in the same ways as young rabbit. Deer hunting is becoming increasingly popular in America, and venison is thus more readily available than it was at one time.

Game can usually be frozen satisfactorily. Small animals should be skinned and eviscerated, washed and dried thoroughly, cooled overnight, wrapped in freezer paper, and stored at a temperature of 0° F. or lower. Venison should be cut into steaks, roasts, etc., wrapped, and stored.

For Game Birds, see Chapter 11, Poultry, pages 309–337.

HARE AND RABBIT (*Lièvre et Lapin*)

Although the terms hare and rabbit are often used interchangeably in the United States, the two are different animals, although belonging to the same family. There are several breeds of each. Hares are usually larger than rabbits, with darker flesh and a gamier flavor. Both may be eaten soon after they are killed and may be prepared in the same ways.

A tender rabbit can be identified by its short neck, plump knees, and very flexible front legs. A tender hare may be recognized by its smooth coat and slender paws with claws hidden under the fur. As hares grow older, the claws grow and project slightly beyond the fur.

Domesticated rabbit may replace hare or wild rabbit in recipes. Rabbit is available in United States markets both fresh and frozen. Frozen rabbit is packaged in serving-size pieces, in packages weighing 2 to 3 pounds.

⚜ JUGGED HARE (*Civet de Lièvre*)

4½-pound hare
2½ cups dry red wine
⅓ cup fat rendered from salt pork
2 tablespoons flour
¼ cup brandy
water
1 tablespoon tomato purée

1 stalk parsley
1 clove garlic, crushed
1 teaspoon salt
¼ teaspoon ground black pepper
20 small white onions, peeled
½ pound mushrooms, caps and stems
⅓ cup heavy cream

Clean the hare, reserving the liver and blood. Cut the hare into serving-size pieces and marinate 24 hours in the wine. Remove the hare, reserving the marinade, wipe the pieces dry, and brown them in 3 tablespoons of the salt pork fat over high heat. Sprinkle with flour and let it brown. Add the brandy, heat, and ignite. Add the marinade and an equal amount of water, then add the next 5 ingredients. Cover, bring to boiling point, reduce heat and simmer 20 minutes. Brown the onions in the remaining salt pork fat and add them to the hare. Simmer 45 minutes. Wash the mushrooms and add. Cover and cook about 10 minutes, or until hare is becoming tender. Meanwhile dice the hare liver, add it, and cook about 5 minutes longer. Mix the hare's blood with a few spoonfuls of the sauce from the casserole, add, and stir. Remove and discard the parsley. Add the cream and heat (do not boil). Adjust the salt. Serve in a warmed deep dish, heaping the mushrooms in the center. Makes 6 to 8 servings.

⚜ RABBIT STEW (*Gibelotte de Lapin*)

1 dressed rabbit, 2¾ to 3 pounds
2 teaspoons salt
½ teaspoon ground black pepper
flour
3 to 4 tablespoons bacon drippings or
    salt pork drippings
¼ teaspoon finely chopped garlic

1 cup bouillon or chicken broth
1 cup dry red or white wine
12 small white onions
3 tablespoons butter
8 small new potatoes
1 tablespoon flour
chopped parsley

Cut the rabbit into serving-size pieces, rub with 1 teaspoon of the salt and ¼ teaspoon of the black pepper, and dredge with flour. Brown on all sides in 3 tablespoons of the bacon drippings or salt pork drippings. Add the garlic, bouillon or broth, and the wine. Cover, and simmer 1 hour. Brown the onions in 2 tablespoons of the butter and add to the rabbit, along with the potatoes and the remaining 1 teaspoon salt and ¼ teaspoon black pepper. Cover and cook 30 minutes or until rabbit and vegetables are tender. Transfer the rabbit and vegetables to a warmed serving dish. Blend the 1 tablespoon flour with the remaining 1 tablespoon butter to form a roux. Add to the liquid, mix well, and cook until the sauce bubbles. Pour over the rabbit. Sprinkle with chopped parsley. Makes 4 servings.

⚜ SMOTHERED RABBIT

This recipe originated in the southern part of the United States.

2 ready-to-cook rabbits, 1½ to 2 pounds each	4 tablespoons bacon drippings or shortening
salt and ground black pepper	hot water
flour	2 tablespoons flour
	½ cup milk

Wash the rabbits and cut them into serving-size pieces. Sprinkle with 1½ teaspoons salt and ½ teaspoon ground black pepper and rub it into the pieces. Dredge with flour. Brown in a heavy 10-inch skillet on all sides in bacon drippings or shortening, adding it as needed. Pour in 1½ cups hot water and add ¼ teaspoon salt. Cover and simmer 40 minutes or until the rabbit is tender. Transfer the rabbit to a warmed platter. Blend flour with the pan drippings and stir and cook until the mixture has browned. Stir in 1 cup water and the milk. Cook until the gravy begins to thicken. Season to taste with salt and black pepper. Serve the gravy in a sauceboat. Makes 6 to 8 servings.

⚜ SADDLE OF HARE OR RABBIT WITH MUSHROOMS
(*Râble de Lièvre aux Champignons*)

The saddle is the back of the hare or rabbit from the first ribs to the legs.

1 ready-to-cook saddle of hare or rabbit, weighing 1¾ to 2 pounds	4 whole black peppercorns, cracked
lardoons (thin, narrow strips of fat salt pork)	salt
¼ cup cognac	½ cup sliced mushroom caps and stems
½ cup dry white wine	3 tablespoons butter
1 shallot, finely diced	⅓ cup light cream
¼ teaspoon dried thyme, or 1 teaspoon chopped fresh thyme	ground black pepper
1 small bay leaf, crumbled	9 small mushroom caps, blanched
	chopped parsley

Lard the meat with lardoons and place it in a pan long enough to accommodate it. Add the next 6 ingredients and ½ teaspoon salt. Marinate 24 hours, turning the meat several times. Remove the saddle, place it on a rack in a roasting pan, pour in the marinade, cover, and cook in a preheated hot oven (425° F.) 20 minutes. Reduce heat to 325° F. (slow) and cook 1 hour or until the saddle is tender. Transfer saddle to a warmed platter and keep it warm. Strain the pan liquid and cook it over surface heat until it has reduced to ½ cup. Sauté the sliced mushrooms in 1 tablespoon of the butter and add them to the sauce. Stir in the cream and cook 1 to 2 minutes. Stir in 1 tablespoon of the remaining butter, adjust salt and black pepper, and pour the sauce onto the platter around the saddle. Sauté the blanched whole mushroom caps in the remaining 1 tablespoon butter and arrange them on top of the saddle along the center. Sprinkle chopped parsley over the sauce. Makes 4 servings. (*See illustration, page 302.*)

✤ Sweet-and-Sour Saddle of Hare or Rabbit
  (*Râble de Lièvre à l'Aigre-Doux*)

Follow the recipe for Saddle of Hare or Rabbit with Mushrooms, but omit the sautéed sliced mushrooms from the sauce and blend in 1 tablespoon red currant jelly (or more if desired). Serve over saddle of hare or rabbit with unsweetened applesauce to which lemon juice to taste has been added. Makes 4 servings.

✤ STUFFED RABBIT OR HARE MÉNAGÈRE
  (*Lapereau Farci à la Ménagère*)

1 dressed rabbit or small hare, 1¾ to 2 pounds
salt and ground black pepper
¼ pound pork sausage
¼ cup finely chopped onion
2 tablespoons finely chopped celery
2 cups toasted small bread cubes (croutons)
¹⁄₁₆ teaspoon minced garlic
½ teaspoon ground thyme
1 cup bouillon or chicken stock
2 slices salt pork or bacon
½ cup dry white or red wine
1 medium-sized onion, cut in half
1 medium-sized carrot, quartered

Wash and dry the rabbit or hare. Sprinkle the inside of the body cavity with salt and black pepper. Set aside. Brown the sausage with the onion and celery. Without draining off the fat, add the croutons, garlic, and thyme, and mix well. Blend in ¼ cup of the bouillon or chicken stock, ¼ teaspoon salt, and ⅛ teaspoon ground black pepper. Spoon the stuffing loosely into the body cavity. Close the body opening with skewers and lace tightly with string. Tie the legs in place. Rub the outside skin with salt and black pepper. Render the fat from the salt pork or bacon and use it to brown the rabbit on the two sides and back. Place the browned rabbit on a rack in a roasting pan and pour the pan drippings over it. Rinse the pan with the remaining bouillon or stock, and pour it over the rabbit. Add the wine, onion, and carrot. Cover and braise in a preheated slow oven (325° F.) for 2 hours or until the rabbit is tender, basting every 30 minutes with the pan liquid. Transfer the rabbit to a warmed platter. Make gravy from the pan liquid, using the following recipe, and serve it separately. Makes 3 servings.

✤ Gravy

Blend 1½ tablespoons cornstarch with 1 cup cold bouillon or chicken stock. Add to the pan drippings in the roasting pan. Stir and cook 1 to 2 minutes or until the gravy has thickened slightly. Season to taste with salt and ground black pepper. Makes about 1½ cups.

↑ Chicken Casserole Bonne Femme (page 311)

↓ Duck with Orange Sauce (page 322)

↑ Boiled Chicken with Rice (page 311)   ↓ Saddle of Hare with Mushrooms (page 299)

↑ Partridge Vigneronne (page 333)

↓ Veal Loaf in Crust (page 119)   303

↑ Braised Partridge with Cabbage (page 332) ↓ Roast Saddle of Venison (page 307)

❧ SAUTÉED RABBIT OR HARE CHASSEUR
(*Lapin Sauté à la Chasseur*)

2¾- to 3-pound rabbit or hare
1½ teaspoons salt
¼ teaspoon ground black pepper
flour
4 tablespoons shortening
2 shallots, or 1 small white onion, chopped

⅔ cup chicken broth, veal broth, or water
⅓ cup dry white wine
parsley
2 tablespoons tomato purée
½ pound mushrooms, sliced
2 tablespoons butter

Wash a dressed rabbit and cut into serving-size pieces. Sprinkle the pieces with salt and black pepper and dredge in flour. Heat the shortening in a heavy 10-inch skillet, add the rabbit, reduce heat to moderate, and brown the pieces on both sides. Add the shallots or onion and cook 3 to 4 minutes or until soft. Add the broth or water and the wine. Add 2 stalks of parsley and the tomato purée. Cover and cook over low heat 1 hour or until rabbit is tender. Brown the mushrooms in the butter and add to the rabbit. Skim off and discard the fat. Sprinkle the rabbit with 2 tablespoons chopped parsley. Makes 4 servings.

❧ WILD RABBIT JEANNETON (*Lapin de Garenne à la Jeanneton*)

2 wild rabbits, 2 pounds each
salt and ground black pepper
3 tablespoons salad oil or olive oil
3 tablespoons butter
3 shallots, or 2 small white onions, chopped
1 small clove garlic
2 medium-sized tomatoes, peeled and seeded, or 1 cup canned tomatoes

½ cup dry white or red wine
½ cup hot water
½ teaspoon dried thyme, or 2 teaspoons chopped fresh thyme
parsley
French-fried onion slices
croutons fried in butter

Skin and dress the rabbits, cut them into serving-size pieces, and sprinkle with 1½ teaspoons salt and ½ teaspoon ground black pepper. Brown on all sides in the oil and 2 tablespoons of the butter in a heavy 10- or 12-inch skillet. Add the shallots or onions, garlic, and tomatoes, and simmer 5 minutes. Remove and discard the garlic. Add the wine, water, thyme, and ¼ cup chopped parsley. Cover and cook slowly 1 hour or until rabbit is tender. Transfer the rabbit to a warmed platter. Strain the sauce. Adjust the salt and black pepper and swirl in the remaining 1 tablespoon butter. Pour over the rabbit and sprinkle with chopped parsley. Surround the rabbit with mounds of French-fried onions and croutons. Makes 6 to 8 servings.

VENISON (*Chevreuil*)

The term venison is broadly applied to the flesh of any antlered animal. It is the most highly prized of all furred game. Like beef, venison should be aged for a period of 2 to 4 weeks before cooking. Since its flesh, like other wild meat, lacks fat, most cuts should be larded with narrow strips of fat salt pork or covered with slices of fat salt pork. Chops and steaks from young, tender animals do not need larding; they need only to be cooked in plenty of butter. Less tender cuts and the flesh of older animals should also be marinated for several hours before cooking. The saddle of a young tender animal should not be marinated and should be cooked in a very hot oven only to the rare or medium-rare stage. A saddle weighing 5 to 6 pounds will cook very rare in 45 minutes to 1 hour in a preheated very hot oven (450° F.).

⚜ LEG OF VENISON MARY QUEEN OF SCOTS
(*Gigue de Chevreuil Marie-Stuart*)

6- to 7-pound leg of venison
2 cups dry red wine
1 cup beef bouillon
1 medium-sized onion, sliced
1 clove garlic, crushed
1 bay leaf

3 juniper berries (if available)
8 whole black peppercorns
1 teaspoon salt
lardoons, or 1 pound fat salt pork sliced
Poivrade Sauce (optional; page 47)

If the lower part of the leg is used, remove the shank bone. Place the meat in a large bowl or pan with the next 8 ingredients and marinate it 24 hours. Remove the meat, reserving the marinade. Skewer and tie the meat in a compact shape. Lard it or cover it with slices of salt pork. If a meat thermometer is used, insert it in the thickest part of the muscle, not touching a bone. Place the meat on a rack in a shallow roasting pan. Roast, uncovered, in a preheated very hot oven (450° F.) 20 minutes. Reduce heat to 325° F. (slow) and cook 15 to 18 minutes per pound, or to an internal temperature of 140° F. for very rare, 150° F. for medium well done. Strain the marinade and baste the meat with it several times during the roasting process. Transfer the meat to a heated platter. Remove and discard the fat from the pan drippings, heat the drippings and serve in a sauceboat. Or serve Poivrade Sauce separately. Makes 10 to 12 servings.

⚜ ROAST SADDLE OF VENISON *(Selle de Chevreuil Rôti)*

5- to 6-pound saddle of venison
salt and ground black pepper
slices of fat salt pork

Cream Pan Gravy (see following recipe)
Poached Apples (see recipe below)

Wipe the meat with a damp cloth and rub it with salt and black pepper. If a meat thermometer is used, insert it in the thickest part of the meat, not touching a bone. Place the meat on a rack in a shallow roasting pan and cover it with slices of salt pork. Roast, uncovered, in a preheated very hot oven (450° F.) 45 minutes (for very rare) to 1 hour (for medium). Or roast until the internal temperature is 140° F. on the meat thermometer for very rare; 150° F. for medium well done. Remove meat to a preheated platter. Make Cream Pan Gravy in the roasting pan. Garnish with Poached Apples and serve the gravy in a sauceboat. Makes 6 to 8 servings. (*See illustration, page 304.*)

⚜ Cream Pan Gravy for Venison

1 tablespoon finely chopped white onion
2 tablespoons butter
2 tablespoons flour

1 cup bouillon or beef stock
¾ cup heavy cream
salt and ground black pepper

Remove and discard all but 2 tablespoons fat from the roasting pan. Add the onion and butter. Stir and cook until onion is limp. Blend in the flour and stir and cook 1 to 2 minutes. Add the bouillon or beef stock. Stir and cook until the gravy begins to thicken. Add the cream and salt and black pepper to taste and mix well. Cook 1 to 2 minutes. Serve with roast venison. Makes enough for 6 to 8 servings.

⚜ Poached Apples

10 small Rome Beauty apples or other good baking apples
lemon juice
1 cup sugar

1½ cups water
1/16 teaspoon salt
red-currant jelly

Peel and core the apples. Brush them with lemon juice. In a 1½-quart saucepan, put 1 tablespoon lemon juice and the sugar, water, and salt and mix well. Stir and cook until boiling point is reached. Boil 1 minute. Add 5 apples at a time, partly cover the pan, and cook over moderate heat 10 to 15 minutes or until apples are tender. Transfer the apples to a plate so they can drain. Cook the rest of the apples in the same manner, drain, and cool. Fill the apples with red-currant jelly.

✤ VENISON CUTLETS (*Côtelettes de Chevreuil*)

8 cutlets from the tenderloin, ½ to ¾
   inch thick
⅓ cup olive oil or salad oil
salt and ground black pepper
flour
1 large egg, beaten lightly

fine dry breadcrumbs
4 tablespoons (½ stick) butter
8 mushroom caps, blanched
parsley
¼ cup red-currant jelly

Marinate the cutlets 1 hour in olive oil or salad oil. Remove them from the oil, drain well, sprinkle with salt and black pepper, dredge with flour, dip in the beaten egg, and then roll in breadcrumbs. Sauté in 3 tablespoons of the butter, adding it as needed, 10 to 12 minutes, turning the cutlets frequently. Transfer the cutlets to a warmed platter. Sauté the blanched mushroom caps in the remaining 1 tablespoon butter and place one on each cutlet. Garnish the platter with parsley. Mix the jelly with the pan drippings, bring to boiling point, and serve with the cutlets. Makes 4 servings.

Poultry

There are two simple, easy-to-follow rules for cooking poultry so that the meat will be tender, juicy, and thoroughly cooked. These rules apply to poultry of all ages.

Rule 1. Cook at moderate heat, since intense heat hardens and toughens the muscles and also drives out the juices and causes excessive shrinkage.

Rule 2. Cook the bird by the method best suited to its age and fatness. Well-fatted, tender, young birds are best suited for broiling, frying, and open-pan roasting. Older birds and lean young birds are best when braised in the oven or over surface heat in a covered roaster or Dutch oven. Very old birds should be cooked slowly for a long time in water or steam: they are best used in stews, fricassees, creamed dishes, and as a base for many casseroles and in other hot or cold dishes.

Poultry is perishable; raw poultry should be refrigerated, and cooked poultry cooled quickly, without cover or with cover ajar, if it is not eaten promptly.

CHICKEN

Probably the most popular kind of poultry the world over is chicken. The kinds available, with the dressed, cleaned, ready-to-cook weights, are:

Broiler-fryer (*poulet de grain* and *poulet de reine*)	1½ to 3 pounds
Roasting chicken (*poulet gras* or *poularde*)	3½ to 6 pounds
Capon (*chapon*), castrated male	4 to 8 pounds
Fricassee chicken or fowl (*poule de l'année*)	4½ to 5 pounds mature bird

⚜ HOW TO TRUSS CHICKEN OR TURKEY

Just before roasting a chicken or turkey, rub the crop and body cavities with salt and ground black pepper. The bird may be stuffed or not. If stuffing is used, spoon it into the body cavities loosely to allow room for expansion during cooking. Stuff the neck first, then pull the neck skin to the back, fold the ends of the skin under neatly, and pin it to the back skin with skewers. Turn the bird breast side up. Lift each wing and fold the tip under and press it against the back, akimbo style. This method eliminates the need of skewers for holding the wings in place and gives the bird a base on which to rest in the roasting pan and serving platter. Now put the stuffing into the body cavity loosely. Close the opening of the body cavity by inserting 3 or 4 skewers through the skin at the edge of one side of the opening, having them pass over the opening through the skin on the opposite side. Then draw the edges together by crisscrossing a string around the skewers as in lacing shoes. Tie the ends of the string together at the bottom of the opening and fasten them to the tailpiece. If the bird is not stuffed and there is a band of skin across the opening to the body cavity, push the ends of the legs under it. This holds the legs in place. Remove all skewers and strings before serving.

⚜ ROAST CHICKEN (*Poulet Rôti*)

This is a basic recipe for roast chicken without stuffing. If stuffing is desired, see Stuffings for Poultry (page 319). Select a young, well-fatted bird for roasting. The body should be well rounded, with a well-fleshed breast and a good coating of fat under the skin, with few blemishes or pin feathers.

Truss a 4- to 5-pound roasting chicken as in the preceding directions for How to Truss Chicken or Turkey. Sprinkle salt and ground black pepper over the skin of the chicken and then rub with softened butter. Place the chicken on a rack in a shallow baking pan. Bake, uncovered, in a preheated slow oven (325° F.) 3 hours, or until it does not show pink juice when pierced with a fork. Make stock with the giblets to use in the gravy. Baste the bird occasionally with melted butter and pan drippings. If the breast, legs, and wings tend to brown too fast, cover the chicken with foil. When the chicken is done, remove it from the oven, put it on a warmed platter, and let it stand in a warm place 20 minutes before carving. (Chicken is done when the thickest part of the drumstick is soft when pressed with the index finger and the leg moves up and down and twists easily out of the thigh joint.) Garnish the platter with parsley. Make gravy from the pan drippings and giblet stock and serve it in a sauceboat. Makes 6 servings.

⚜ BOILED CHICKEN WITH RICE (*Poule au Riz*)

3-pound ready-to-cook whole chicken
2 small white onions, sliced
2 medium-sized carrots, quartered
2 leeks or 2 green onions, white part only, sliced
4 whole black peppercorns
salt

3 to 4 cups chicken broth
1 cup white rice
3 tablespoons butter, melted
1 tablespoon cornstarch
1 egg yolk
¼ cup heavy cream

Place the first 5 ingredients in a large saucepan. Add ½ teaspoon salt and 2 cups of the chicken broth. Cover, bring the broth to boiling point, reduce heat, and simmer 1½ hours or until chicken is tender. Meanwhile, soak the rice 30 minutes in cold water to cover. Transfer the chicken to a warmed bowl and keep it warm. Strain the broth into a 1½-quart saucepan and add more broth if necessary to make 2½ cups. Drain off the water from the rice and toss the rice in the melted butter, coating every grain with butter. Add to the broth. Add ½ teaspoon salt. Cover, bring to boiling point, reduce heat, and simmer until rice is tender, about 12 minutes. Put the rice on a warmed platter and place the chicken on top. Garnish with the carrots which were cooked with the chicken. Blend the cornstarch with 1 cup of the remaining broth, bring to boiling point, and stir and cook 1 to 2 minutes. Blend the egg yolk with the cream and add to the sauce. Stir and cook 1 minute. Serve in a separate bowl. Makes 6 servings. (*See illustration, page 302.*)

⚜ CHICKEN CASSEROLE BONNE FEMME
(*Poulet de Grain en Cocotte à la Bonne-Femme*)

2½-pound ready-to-cook whole chicken
4 tablespoons (½ stick) butter
12 small white onions
2 carrots cut into 1-inch pieces
1 cup chicken stock or broth
4 thin strips salt pork

½ teaspoon salt
¼ teaspoon ground black pepper
½ pound whole medium-sized mushrooms
1 tablespoon cornstarch
2 tablespoons water

Truss the chicken as directed in How to Truss Chicken or Turkey. Do not stuff it. Brown the chicken all over in a Dutch oven or heavy skillet in 2 tablespoons of the butter. In another skillet brown the onions and carrots in the remaining 2 tablespoons butter. Put them in the Dutch oven around the chicken. Pour in the stock or broth. Place 2 strips of the salt pork across the breast of the chicken and 1 strip, lengthwise, on each leg. Sprinkle salt and black pepper over all. Cover and cook in a preheated hot oven (400° F.) 15 minutes. Add the mushrooms. Reduce heat to 325° F. (slow) and continue cooking 1½ hours or until the leg moves up and down and twists easily out of the thigh joint and the thickest part of the drumstick feels very soft when pressed with the index finger (cover finger with a paper towel or napkin to prevent burning). Transfer the chicken to a warmed plate and keep it warm. Blend the cornstarch with the water and mix with the pan liquid. Stir and cook 2 to 3 minutes, or until the sauce has thickened. Adjust seasonings. Remove the pork slices, skewers, and string, and place the chicken in a warmed casserole. Surround it with the vegetables and pour the gravy over all. Serve hot. Makes 4 to 5 servings. (*See illustration, page 301.*)

⚜ CHICKEN CASSEROLE COUNTRY STYLE
(*Poulet en Cocotte à la Paysanne*)

3-pound ready-to-cook whole chicken, trussed	3 medium-sized carrots, quartered
salt	3 medium-small white turnips, quartered
ground black pepper	1 cup chicken stock or broth
4 tablespoons (½ stick) butter	⅓ cup dry white wine
4 thin strips salt pork	1 tablespoon cornstarch
12 small white onions	2 tablespoons water

Do not stuff the chicken. Rub the outside skin with ½ teaspoon salt and ⅛ teaspoon pepper. Brown the whole chicken on all sides in 2 tablespoons of the butter in a Dutch oven. Place two strips of the salt pork over the breast, and one strip lengthwise over each leg. Melt the remaining 2 tablespoons butter, toss the vegetables in it, and put them in the Dutch oven around the chicken. Pour in the stock or broth. Sprinkle ½ teaspoon salt and ⅛ teaspoon black pepper over all. Cover and cook in a preheated hot oven (400° F.) 20 minutes. Reduce heat to 325° F. (slow) and continue to cook 1¾ hours, or until the leg moves up and down and twists easily out of the thigh joint and the thickest part of the drumstick feels soft when pressed with the index finger. Transfer the chicken to a warmed plate and keep it warm. Add the wine, bring the mixture to boiling point, and cook 2 to 3 minutes. Blend the cornstarch with the water and mix with the pan liquid. Stir and cook 2 to 3 minutes. Remove the pork slices, skewers, and string from the chicken and return it to the casserole. Season to taste with salt and ground pepper. Serve promptly. Makes 6 servings.

⚜ BLANQUETTE OF CHICKEN (*Poulet au Blanc*)

3- to 4-pound ready-to-cook fricassee chicken
1 medium-sized onion
3 whole cloves
4 whole black peppercorns
2 teaspoons salt
1 carrot, cut into 1-inch pieces
2 leeks or green onions (white parts only), sliced
2 stalks parsley

2½ cups chicken stock, or 2½ cups water and 2½ chicken bouillon cubes
¼ cup chicken fat skimmed from the broth
¼ cup flour
2 egg yolks
½ cup light cream
½ pound mushrooms, sliced
2 tablespoons butter

Cut the chicken into serving-size pieces and put them in a 4-quart saucepan or Dutch oven. Stud the onion with the cloves and add it to the chicken along with the next 6 ingredients. Cover, bring the stock to boiling point, reduce heat, and simmer 1 to 1½ hours or until chicken is tender. Skim off the fat from the broth and place ¼ cup of the fat in a 1-quart saucepan. Blend in the flour. Stir and cook until the mixture foams. Beat in 2 cups of the broth in which the chicken was cooked. Stir and cook until the sauce has thickened. Blend the egg yolks with the cream and add to the sauce. Stir and cook 1 minute (do not boil). Sauté the mushrooms in the butter and add them to the sauce. Adjust the seasonings. Remove and discard the studded onion and the parsley stalks from the chicken. Pour the sauce over the chicken and simmer 5 minutes, stirring frequently. Makes 6 servings.

⚜ CHICKEN FRICASSEE (*Poulet au Fricassée*)

3-pound ready-to-cook chicken
1 teaspoon salt
¼ teaspoon ground black pepper
flour
3 to 4 tablespoons butter
⅓ cup dry white wine
2 cups chicken broth, or 2 cups water and 2 chicken bouillon cubes

18 small white onions
2 sprigs parsley
1 bay leaf
½ pound mushrooms, sliced
½ teaspoon dried thyme leaves
1 egg yolk
⅓ cup heavy cream or milk
chopped parsley

Cut the chicken into serving-size pieces, rub with salt and black pepper, and dredge with flour. Cook in 3 tablespoons of the butter in a Dutch oven until chicken is *very lightly* browned, turning frequently, and adding butter if needed. Sprinkle with 1 tablespoon flour and mix it with the pan drippings. Add the wine, the broth or water and bouillon cubes, the onions, sprigs parsley, and bay leaf. Cover and cook 30 minutes over moderately low heat. Stir in the mushrooms and thyme. Cook 10 minutes. Blend the egg yolk with the cream or milk and mix with the sauce in the pan. Cook below the boiling point 3 to 4 minutes. Sprinkle with chopped parsley. Serve over rice or croutons. Makes 6 servings.

⚜ CHICKEN MARENGO (*Poulet Marengo*)

3-pound ready-to-cook chicken
2 teaspoons salt
ground black pepper
flour
4 tablespoons shortening, salad oil, or
    olive oil
¾ cup chopped onion

½ cup dry white wine
3 tablespoons tomato purée
1/16 teaspoon finely chopped garlic
2 tablespoons chopped parsley
½ teaspoon dried thyme leaves
½ pound mushrooms, diced
croutons fried in butter

Cut the chicken into serving-size pieces, rub with 1½ teaspoons of the salt and ¼ teaspoon black pepper, and dredge with flour. Brown in the shortening or oil. After the chicken has browned on one side, add the onion and turn the pieces to brown on the other side. When they are well browned, pour in the wine and boil until the wine has reduced to about 4 tablespoons. Stir in the tomato purée, garlic, and parsley. Cover and cook slowly for 20 minutes. Add the thyme and mushrooms and cook 10 minutes longer. Adjust seasonings. Skim off and discard the fat from the gravy. Transfer the chicken to a warmed platter, and pour the gravy over it. Surround with croutons. Makes 6 servings.

⚜ CHICKEN IN WINE DIJON STYLE (*Coq au Vin à la Dijonnaise*)

2½-pound ready-to-cook chicken
1½ teaspoons salt
¼ teaspoon ground black pepper
flour
2 tablespoons butter
1 tablespoon salad oil or olive oil
2 slices (1 ounce) salt pork, diced
16 small white onions

1 cup red Burgundy
2 stalks parsley
½ teaspoon mixed pickling spice, tied
    in a cheesecloth bag
1 tablespoon cornstarch
2 tablespoons water
chopped parsley

Cut the chicken into serving-size pieces, rub with the salt and black pepper, and dredge with flour. Brown on all sides in the butter and oil in a heavy skillet or Dutch oven. Add the diced salt pork and the onions and cook over moderate heat until the pork and onions have browned. Add the next 3 ingredients. Cover and simmer 20 minutes. Skim off and discard the fat from the cooking liquid. Blend the cornstarch with the water, add, and mix well. Cook 2 to 3 minutes. Remove and discard the parsley stalks and spice bag. Adjust seasonings. Sprinkle with chopped parsley. Makes 4 servings.

⚜ SAUTÉED CHICKEN BERCY (*Poulet Sauté Bercy*)

3-pound ready-to-cook young chicken
1½ teaspoons salt
¼ teaspoon ground black pepper
2 tablespoons olive oil or salad oil
2 tablespoons butter
4 shallots, or 2 small white onions, chopped

¾ cup dry white wine
¾ cup chicken broth, or ¾ cup water and 1 chicken bouillon cube
½ teaspoon lemon juice
½ pound mushrooms, coarsely chopped
chopped parsley

Cut the chicken into serving-size pieces. Rub with the salt and black pepper. Sauté in the oil and butter in a heavy skillet over moderate heat, turning to brown both sides. Reduce heat and cook 10 to 15 minutes or until chicken is tender. Transfer chicken to a warmed platter. In the pan drippings in the skillet sauté the shallots or onions until they begin to turn color. Add the wine and cook until the quantity is reduced to half the original volume. Add the next 3 ingredients and cook 5 minutes. Pour this sauce over the chicken. Sprinkle with chopped parsley. Makes 5 to 6 servings.

⚜ SAUTÉED CHICKEN PARMENTIER (*Poulet Sauté Parmentier*)

3-pound ready-to-cook young chicken
2 teaspoons salt
ground black pepper
flour
2 tablespoons shortening, salad oil, or olive oil

5 tablespoons butter
4 medium-sized potatoes, cubed and parboiled
1 small white onion, chopped fine
⅓ cup dry white wine
2 tablespoons chopped parsley

Cut the chicken into serving-size pieces, rub with 1½ teaspoons of the salt and ¼ teaspoon black pepper, and dredge with flour. Brown on all sides in the shortening or oil and 2 tablespoons of the butter, adding more as needed. Reduce heat and cook 15 minutes longer, or until chicken is tender, turning the pieces occasionally. Meanwhile sprinkle the remaining ½ teaspoon salt and black pepper to taste over the potatoes and sauté them in 2 tablespoons of the butter, adding the onion when the potatoes are about half done. Pile the chicken in the center of a warmed platter. Pour the wine into the skillet, stir in 1 tablespoon of the parsley, and cook 1 minute. Swirl in the remaining 1 tablespoon butter. Adjust seasonings and pour the sauce over the chicken. Surround the chicken with the sautéed potatoes and sprinkle them with the remaining parsley. Serve hot. Makes 6 servings.

⚜ SAUTÉED CHICKEN CHASSEUR (*Poulet Sauté à la Chasseur*)

3-pound ready-to-cook young chicken
1½ teaspoons salt
¼ teaspoon ground black pepper
flour
2 tablespoons olive oil or salad oil
2 tablespoons butter

½ cup dry white wine or chicken broth
Chasseur Sauce I (page 45)
chopped parsley
croutons fried in butter

Cut the chicken into serving-size pieces, rub with the salt and black pepper, and dredge with flour. Brown the pieces on both sides in the oil and butter in a heavy skillet or Dutch oven. Cover and cook in a preheated moderate oven (350° F.) 30 minutes. Transfer the chicken to a warmed deep platter and keep it warm. Skim off and discard the fat from the pan dippings. Add the wine or chicken broth and cook until the liquid has reduced to half the original volume. Add the Chasseur Sauce and heat 1 to 2 minutes. Pour the sauce over the chicken. Sprinkle with chopped parsley. Garnish with croutons. Makes 6 servings.

⚜ SAUTÉED CHICKEN PORTUGUESE STYLE
(*Poulet Sauté à la Portugaise*)

3- to 3½-pound ready-to-cook young chicken
salt
ground black pepper
6 tablespoons butter
½ cup dry white wine
1½ cups small mushrooms

1 tablespoon chopped onion
½ teaspoon sugar
1 cup drained canned tomatoes
3 Mushroom-Stuffed Tomatoes (page 111)
chopped parsley

Cut the chicken into serving-size pieces and rub with 1 teaspoon salt and ¼ teaspoon black pepper. Melt 4 tablespoons (½ stick) of the butter and dip the pieces in it. Place them in a buttered 13½- by 9- by 2-inch pan or baking dish and pour the wine over them. Cook in a preheated moderate oven (350° F.) 1 hour or until chicken is tender, basting frequently. Remove from the oven and let the chicken cool in the cooking liquid. Sauté the mushrooms and onion in the remaining 2 tablespoons butter. Add the sugar and canned tomatoes and season to taste with salt and black pepper. Cook 5 minutes, stirring occasionally. Heat the chicken in the cooking liquid and transfer it to a warmed platter. Cover with the mushroom and tomato mixture. Arrange the Mushroom-Stuffed Tomatoes on the platter around the chicken, and sprinkle the chicken with chopped parsley. Makes 6 servings.

⚜ CURRIED CHICKEN

1⅓ cups chopped onion
1 clove garlic, crushed
¼ cup peanut oil or clarified butter (ghee)
1 teaspoon turmeric
1 teaspoon ground cumin seeds
½ teaspoon ground ginger
½ teaspoon ground black pepper
½ teaspoon ground mustard
3 teaspoons ground coriander seeds

⅛ to ¼ teaspoons ground red pepper
1 stick cinnamon, 2 inches long
3 pounds chicken legs and breasts
3 teaspoons salt
1 cup hot water
¼ cup undiluted evaporated milk, or ¼ cup Coconut Milk (see following recipe)
1 teaspoon lemon juice
3 to 4 cups fluffy hot rice

Cook the onion and garlic in the oil or clarified butter, stirring constantly, 2 to 3 minutes. Add the turmeric and cook over moderately low heat about 10 minutes, or until onions are very soft, stirring constantly to prevent the turmeric from scorching. Add the remaining spices, and stir and cook 2 to 3 minutes. Rub the chicken with 2 teaspoons of the salt, add it to the onion mixture, and cook over moderate heat 10 to 15 minutes, or until the chicken has browned lightly. Add the remaining salt and the hot water. Cover and cook 45 minutes, or until the chicken is tender and the gravy has thickened. Remove the cover and cook 5 minutes longer. Remove and discard the cinnamon. Stir in the evaporated milk or Coconut Milk and the lemon juice just before serving. Serve with hot fluffy rice. Makes 6 servings.

⚜ Coconut Milk

To 1 cup freshly grated coconut add 1 cup boiling water and let stand 1 hour. Strain through clean cheesecloth, squeezing out every bit of the milk. Use in curries, puddings, custards, and cream desserts. Makes 1 cup.

⚜ CHICKEN PILAF ORIENTAL STYLE (*Pilaf de Poulet à l'Orientale*)

6 chicken drumsticks and 6 second joints
2 teaspoons salt
½ teaspoon ground black pepper
1 tablespoon olive oil or salad oil
4 tablespoons butter
½ cup finely chopped onion
1 cup raw long-grain rice

2½ cups chicken stock, or 2½ cups water and 2½ bouillon cubes
1/16 teaspoon crushed garlic
¼ teaspoon crushed saffron
¼ chopped parsley
¾ cup diced sweet green pepper
1 cup canned tomatoes, or 3 medium-sized tomatoes, peeled, seeded, and chopped

Rub the pieces of chicken with half the salt and half the black pepper. Brown them lightly on both sides in the oil and 2 tablespoons of the butter in a Dutch oven. Add the onions and cook them until they are soft. Soak the rice 30 minutes in enough cold water to cover it. Drain off the water and cook the rice in the remaining 2 tablespoons butter until it is dry and begins to stick to the bottom of the pan. Combine the chicken stock (or the water and bouillon cubes), the remaining 1 teaspoon salt and ¼ teaspoon black pepper, the garlic, saffron, and parsley, mix well, and pour over the rice. Blend the green pepper and tomatoes with the rice. Add the mixture to the chicken, cover, and cook in a preheated moderate oven (350° F.) 25 to 30 minutes, or until chicken and rice are tender. Serve hot. Makes 6 servings.

TURKEY

Turkey, traditional in the United States for Thanksgiving Day dinner, and also for Christmas and New Year's Day, is available fresh and frozen the year around. Turkey is trussed, stuffed, and roasted in the same way as chicken. Young turkeys may also be broiled or fried. When buying turkey, if the ready-to-cook weight is less than 12 pounds, allow ¾ to 1 pound per serving; if it is over 12 pounds, allow ½ to ¾ pound. Cold turkey yields more servings per pound than hot turkey. In France turkeys are known as *dindon* (turkey cock), *dinde* (hen turkey), and *dindonneau* (young turkey); recipes usually call for *dindonneau*, and if *dinde* is specified a young and small hen is usually meant. In America larger turkeys are more commonly served, but small turkeys are gaining in popularity. French and American methods of roasting turkey differ (see the following recipe for Roast Turkey). Either method may be used for turkey, capon, or large chickens. To make carving easier, allow the turkey to stand 20 to 30 minutes after it comes out of the oven.

⚜ ROAST TURKEY (*Dinde Rôti*)

To prepare turkey, see How to Truss Chicken or Turkey (page 310). If turkey is to be stuffed, see the following recipes, or use any other preferred stuffing. Roast according to either of the following methods:
French Two-Temperature Method. Lay the bird on its side on a rack in a roasting pan. Spread it generously with melted butter and lay thin slices of salt pork over the breast. Roast, uncovered, in a preheated hot oven (425° F.) for 15 minutes; turn on the other side and roast 15 minutes longer. Reduce heat to moderate (350° F.) and cook until turkey is done, turning from side to side and basting with pan drippings every 20 minutes, and allowing 20 min-

utes per pound total cooking time. Place the bird on its back for the last 15 minutes of cooking. If the pan drippings tend to burn, add a little water to the pan but be careful not to add enough to create steam. To test for doneness, pierce the thigh with a fork: if the juice runs out clear without a trace of pink the bird is done.

American One-Temperature Method. Place the turkey breast side up on a rack in a roasting pan. Spread with softened butter or shortening. Cut 3 or 4 thicknesses of cheesecloth large enough to cover the bird. Melt butter or shortening in hot water (¼ pound butter or shortening to each cup water), wring out the cheesecloth in this and spread it over the turkey. Put the turkey in a preheated slow oven (325° F.) and roast according to the following time-table:

6 to 8 pounds	3 to 4 hours
8 to 12 pounds	4 to 5 hours
12 to 16 pounds	5 to 6 hours
16 to 20 pounds	6 to 7½ hours
20 to 25 pounds	7½ to 8½ hours

If a meat thermometer is used, when it registers 190° to 195° F., the turkey should be done. If the breast and legs tend to brown too fast, cover these parts with foil. To test for doneness, move a leg joint up and down; if it moves easily or breaks, the turkey is done. Another test is to wrap a piece of paper towel or napkin around one's index finger and press the fleshy part of the drumstick; if it feels soft, the turkey is done.

STUFFINGS FOR POULTRY

⚜ Basic Bread Stuffing (American)

1 cup chopped onion
1 cup (2 sticks) butter
2½ quarts (10 cups) toasted soft breadcrumbs or toasted bread cubes (croutons)
3 teaspoons ground sage

1½ teaspoons salt
½ cup chopped parsley
¾ teaspoon ground black pepper
¾ cup turkey stock, or 1 chicken bouillon cube and ¾ cup hot water
½ cup finely chopped celery

Cook the onion in 2 tablespoons of the butter until it is limp. Add the remaining butter and heat until it is melted. Add the remaining ingredients and mix lightly but well. Stuff and truss the turkey and roast according to the American One-Temperature Method for Roast Turkey. Makes enough stuffing for a 12- to 15-pound bird.

⚜ Mushroom Stuffing

To the preceding recipe, add ½ pound chopped mushroom caps and stems and cook them with the onion.

⚜ Oyster Stuffing

Mix 1 cup finely chopped oysters, well drained, with the other ingredients for Basic Bread Stuffing.

⚜ Sausage Stuffing

Crumble ½ pound sausage meat and brown it in a skillet. Drain off the fat. Mix the sausage with the ingredients for Basic Bread Stuffing.

⚜ Chestnut Stuffing (*Aux Marrons*)

2 pounds chestnuts	3 cups soft breadcrumbs
water	1 teaspoon salt
chicken stock	½ teaspoon ground nutmeg
2 pounds sausage meat	¼ cup cognac

Cut a gash in the convex side of each chestnut with a sharp knife. Place the chestnuts in a saucepan with water to cover and bring to boiling point. Remove from heat (do not drain off water). Remove the chestnuts, one at a time, from the water and peel off the shells and inner skins while the nuts are hot. Cook the chestnuts in chicken stock to cover ½ hour or until the chestnuts are barely soft. Drain and chop fine. Crumble the sausage meat in a skillet, cook until browned, drain off the fat, and add the sausage to the chestnuts along with the rest of the ingredients. Mix lightly but well. Stuff and truss the turkey as directed in How to Truss Chicken or Turkey (page 310), and roast it according to either method for Roast Turkey. Makes enough stuffing for an 8- to 10-pound bird.

⚜ Liver and Mushroom Stuffing

1 turkey liver	4 cups soft breadcrumbs
6 chicken livers	1 teaspoon salt
2 stalks parsley	½ teaspoon ground black pepper
3 shallots	3 tablespoons turkey fat or butter,
¼ pound mushrooms	melted
1 medium-sized onion	¼ cup cognac
2 ribs celery with leaves	

Put the first 7 ingredients through a food chopper, using the medium blade. Add the remaining ingredients and mix well. Stuff and truss the turkey as directed in How to Truss Chicken or Turkey (page 310), and roast according to either method for Roast Turkey. Makes enough stuffing for a 10-pound bird.

DUCK (*Canard*)

The average ready-to-cook weight of ducks on the American market is 4 to 5 pounds; in Europe the weight ranges from 3½ to 6 pounds, depending upon the breed. Ducks may be roasted (stuffed or unstuffed), braised, or fricasseed. Stuffings suitable for duck are fruit, bread with fruit, sauerkraut, potatoes, or rice. Since duck has a large amount of fat, it is an efficient self-baster and no basting is required during cooking. The excess fat that accumulates in the roasting pan should be spooned or siphoned off and may be saved for cooking purposes.

Only young ducks should be cooked. French recipes usually specify *caneton* (duckling) rather than *canard* (duck). Allow 1 pound of duck per serving.

❧ ROAST DUCKLING (*Caneton Rôti*)

4-pound ready-to-cook duckling	1½ cups chicken stock or veal stock
salt and ground black pepper	orange slices
2 teaspoons cornstarch	parsley

Wash the duck, dry, and rub outside and inside with salt and black pepper. Truss the duck as directed in How to Truss Chicken or Turkey (page 310) and place it on a rack in a baking pan. Roast in a preheated slow oven (325° F.) 1½ hours. Using a baster, keep siphoning off the fat which accumulates in the pan. Save the fat for cooking purposes. When the duck is done, transfer it to a warmed platter and keep it warm. Skim off the remaining fat from the pan drippings. Blend the cornstarch with the stock and add to the pan. Stir and cook 2 minutes, or until the sauce has thickened. Adjust the seasonings and serve the sauce in a sauceboat. Garnish the duck platter with orange slices and parsley. Makes 4 servings.

❧ BRAISED DUCK WITH PEAS (*Canard aux Petits Pois*)

4-pound ready-to-cook duck	2 tablespoons flour
salt and ground black pepper	2 cups chicken broth or veal stock
2 tablespoons softened butter	¼ cup chopped parsley
4 slices salt pork	2 cups shelled fresh green peas or
24 small white onions	thawed frozen peas

321

Wash the duck and wipe it dry. Rub salt and black pepper over the outside skin and inside the cavities. Truss, rub the butter over the skin, and place the duck on a rack in a Dutch oven. Cook in a preheated very hot oven (450° F.) 25 to 30 minutes or until duck has browned. Transfer the duck to another pan and remove the rack. Arrange the sliced salt pork over the bottom of the Dutch oven and fry over moderate heat until it is crisp. Remove the crisp pork, add the onions, and cook them in the fat until they begin to color. Transfer the onions to the pan with the duck. Drain off all but 2 tablespoons of the fat and blend the flour with the remaining fat. Stir and cook until the flour is golden. Pour in the broth or stock, mix well, and cook until the sauce has thickened slightly, 4 to 5 minutes. Add the parsley. Return the duck and onions to the Dutch oven, cover, and cook over very low heat 1 hour or until duck is tender. Add the peas and cook 10 minutes. Adjust seasonings. Transfer the duck and vegetables to a warmed platter. Serve the sauce in a sauceboat. Makes 4 servings.

⚜ DUCK WITH OLIVES (*Canard aux Olives*)

4-pound ready-to-cook duck	½ cup dry white wine
salt	2 tablespoons chopped parsley
ground black pepper	2 dozen black olives or green olives,
1 tablespoon flour	pitted
¾ cup chicken stock or water	parsley sprigs

Wash the duck, dry it, and rub it outside and inside with salt. Truss it as directed in How to Truss Chicken or Turkey (page 310) and place it on a rack in a Dutch oven or casserole. Cook, uncovered, in a preheated very hot oven (450° F.) 20 to 25 minutes or until duck has browned. Remove the duck from the pan and pour off all but 2 tablespoons of the fat. Blend in the flour; stir and cook until flour is golden brown. Add the stock or water and the wine. Cook until the sauce has thickened, stirring frequently. Add the chopped parsley and salt and black pepper to taste. Return the duck to the Dutch oven. Cover and cook 1 hour or until duck is tender. Simmer the olives 5 minutes in water to cover to remove excess salt. Drain off the water and add the olives to the sauce. Transfer the duck to a warmed platter and pour the sauce over it. Garnish the platter with sprigs of parsley. Makes 4 servings.

⚜ DUCK WITH ORANGE SAUCE (*Canard à l'Orange*)

4-pound ready-to-cook duck	½ cup dry white wine
1½ teaspoons salt	2 medium-sized oranges
¼ teaspoon ground black pepper	water
1 tablespoon butter	2 tablespoons sugar
1 tablespoon flour	1¼ cups orange juice
1 cup chicken or veal stock	2 tablespoons lemon juice

Wash the duck, dry it, and rub it outside and inside with 1 teaspoon of the salt and the black pepper. Place the duck on a rack in a casserole or Dutch oven. Cook, uncovered, in a preheated very hot oven (450° F.) 20 to 25 minutes or until duck has browned. Remove the duck and the rack from the pan and pour off all but 1 tablespoon of the fat. Add the butter to the pan and heat until it is melted. Blend in the flour. Stir and cook over medium-low heat until the roux is light brown. Add the stock and wine and the remaining ½ teaspoon salt. Stir and cook until the sauce has thickened slightly. Return the duck to the pan, cover, and cook in a preheated moderate oven (350° F.) 45 minutes to 1 hour or until duck is tender. Meanwhile, cut the peel (zest) from the oranges, being careful not to include the white bitter portion. Cut the peel into narrow strips, place them in water to cover, and boil 3 minutes. Drain and set them aside. Peel off and discard the white bitter rind of the oranges. Divide the peeled oranges into sections and set them aside. When the duck is done, transfer it to a warmed platter and keep it warm. Skim off and discard all excess fat from the sauce. Cook the sauce over surface heat until the volume has reduced to 1 cup. Cook the sugar with ¼ cup water in a small saucepan until the syrup is straw-colored, then add it to the sauce. Stir in the orange juice and lemon juice. Bring the sauce to boiling point and boil 1 minute. Add the strips of orange peel. Spoon some of the sauce over the duck and garnish it with the orange sections. Serve the remaining sauce in a sauceboat. Makes 4 servings. (*See illustration, page 301.*)

⚜ SALMIS OF DUCK (*Salmis de Canard*)

Salmis is a French dish often made with game birds, but also with duck, guinea hen, and other flavorsome poultry.

1 4-pound duck, roasted
2 tablespoons butter
2 shallots, or 1 small white onion, chopped fine
1/16 teaspoon crushed garlic
1 cup duck gravy made from roasting pan drippings
1 tablespoon lemon juice
¼ teaspoon dried thyme leaves
⅛ teaspoon crumbled dried rosemary leaves

1 tablespoon chopped parsley
½ cup sliced mushrooms sautéed in butter
⅓ cup dry sherry
⅓ cup Madeira
4 slices crisp buttered toast, or 4 slices bread fried in butter
12 black olives
chopped parsley

Roast the duck and make gravy according to directions for Roast Duckling. Set aside. Melt the butter in a 1½-quart saucepan, add the shallots or onion, and cook until they are transparent. Add the garlic and cook ½ minute. Stir in the next 8 ingredients and cook 5 minutes, stirring frequently. Remove the wings and legs from the roast duck and reserve for other use. Slice the breast and add the slices to the sauce. Heat 1 to 2 minutes (do not boil). Serve on buttered toast or bread fried in butter. Garnish with black olives and chopped parsley. Makes 4 servings.

GOOSE

Goose (*oie*) may be roasted, braised, and otherwise cooked in the same manner as duck.

Since goose older than 10 months is likely to be tough, select a younger bird, weighing from 6 to 10 pounds, for roasting. It may be roasted stuffed or unstuffed. If stuffing is used, allow ½ cup per pound of goose. Braising is the recommended method of cooking goose weighing over 10 pounds.

Goose has a very large amount of fat and therefore is an efficient self-baster; no basting is required during cooking. The excess fat that accumulates in the roasting pan should be spooned or siphoned off and may be saved for cooking purposes.

Allow 1 to 1½ pounds ready-to-cook goose per serving.

⚜ ROAST GOOSE (American)

Wash and dry an 8- to 10-pound ready-to-cook goose. Remove all layers of the fat that clings to the inside of the body cavities and save it for other cooking purposes. Rub the outside skin and inside the body cavities of the goose with 1 tablespoon lemon juice and salt and ground black pepper. If desired, put 2 teaspoons caraway seeds in the cavity, or put in an onion, a quartered apple, and a sliced rib of celery, to be discarded after the goose is cooked. Truss the goose as directed in How to Truss Chicken or Turkey (p. 310) and place it on its back on a rack in a roasting pan. Roast, uncovered, in a preheated slow oven (325° F.) 3½ to 3¾ hours, keeping the fat that accumulates in the roasting pan siphoned off with a baster; reserve the fat for other cooking purposes. (If goose tends to brown too quickly, cover it loosely with foil.) Make stock from the goose neck and giblets and reserve. When the goose is done, transfer it to a warmed platter and keep it warm. Skim off all the fat from the pan drippings. Blend 2 tablespoons flour with 2 cups of the stock and blend with the pan drippings. Stir and cook until the gravy has thickened slightly. Chop the giblets and add ½ cup to the gravy, adjust seasonings, and serve the gravy in a sauceboat. Garnish the goose and the platter with parsley and spiced apples or pears. Makes 8 to 10 servings.

⚜ ROAST GOOSE (French) (*Oie Rôti*)

Prepare and truss an 8- to 10-pound ready-to-cook goose for roasting as in the preceding recipe for Roast Goose (American). Lay the goose on its side on a rack in a roasting pan and pour ½ cup hot water into the pan. Roast the bird uncovered in a preheated hot oven (425° F.) for 1 hour. Prick the skin of the goose to allow the fat to seep out more freely. Turn the bird on its other side. Continue to cook, turning and basting every 30 minutes, allowing 15 minutes per pound total cooking time. Make stock with the goose neck and giblets and reserve. To test the goose for doneness, pierce the second joint. It is done if the juice which runs out is as clear as water. Then turn the bird on its back and cook 15 minutes longer, or until it has browned. If goose tends to brown too fast during cooking, cover it loosely with foil. Remove the goose to a warmed platter. Skim the fat from the pan drippings. Blend 4 teaspoons cornstarch with 2 cups of the goose stock and mix with the pan drippings. Stir and cook 4 to 5 minutes, adjust seasonings, and serve the gravy in a sauceboat. Garnish the goose with parsley. Makes 8 to 10 servings.

⚜ ROAST GOOSE WITH CHESTNUT STUFFING
(*Oie Farcie aux Marrons*)

2 pounds chestnuts
water to cover
chicken stock or goose stock
1 pound bulk sausage meat
1 teaspoon poultry seasoning
¼ cup cognac

salt and ground black pepper
8- to 10-pound ready-to-cook goose
1 cup hot water
1 tablespoon cornstarch
watercress or parsley

Using a pointed knife, slit the shells of the chestnuts on the convex side. Place them in a saucepan, cover with water, and bring to boiling point. Remove from the heat (do not drain off water). Remove chestnuts one at a time from the water and peel off shells and inner skins while nuts are hot. Cook the chestnuts in chicken or goose stock to cover ½ hour, or only until they are barely soft. Drain and chop fine. Brown the sausage meat, drain off the fat, and add the sausage to the chestnuts, along with the poultry seasoning, cognac, and salt and black pepper to taste. Mix well and stuff into the crop and body cavities of the goose. Close openings with skewers and twine. Truss as directed in How to Truss Chicken or Turkey (page 310). Rub the outside skin of the goose with salt and ground black pepper. Place the goose, breast side up, on a rack in a roasting pan. Pour the hot water into the pan. Roast in a preheated slow oven (325° F.) 3½ to 4 hours or until goose is tender and browned, adding more water to the pan as it evaporates. Siphon off the fat as it accumulates in the pan. Make stock with the goose neck and giblets and reserve. When the goose is done, transfer it to a warmed platter and keep it warm. Blend the cornstarch with 1½ cups of stock and add to the pan drippings. Cook 2 to 3 minutes, stirring in all the browned bits from the bottom of the pan. Season to taste with salt and black pepper. Garnish the goose with watercress or parsley. Serve the gravy in a sauceboat. Makes 8 to 10 servings.

⚜ GOOSE WITH SAUERKRAUT (*Oie à la Choucroute*)

½ cup diced salt pork	2 teaspoons caraway seeds
2 medium-sized onions, chopped fine	6 cups well-drained sauerkraut
2 medium-sized apples, chopped fine	8- to 10-pound ready-to-cook goose
salt and ground black pepper	1 to 2 tablespoons lemon juice
½ teaspoon dried thyme leaves	dry red wine

Fry the salt pork in a large heavy skillet. Add the onions and apples and cook over moderate heat until the mixture begins to color. Add salt and black pepper to taste. Add the next 3 ingredients and mix well. Rub the inside of the goose with lemon juice and salt and black pepper. Stuff the cavities loosely with the sauerkraut mixture. Close the openings with skewers and twine. Truss as directed in How to Truss Chicken or Turkey (page 310). Rub the outside skin of the goose with lemon juice, salt, and black pepper. Place the goose on a rack, breast side up, in a roasting pan. Roast in a preheated slow oven (325° F.) 3½ to 3¾ hours, basting with wine at 30-minute intervals, using ¾ to 1 cup. Transfer the goose to a heated platter. Skim off all excess fat from the pan drippings and reduce the sauce, over brisk heat, to ¾ cup. Pour the sauce around the goose and serve promptly. Makes 8 to 10 servings.

GUINEA FOWL

Guinea fowl (*pintade*) is native to Africa, and was known to the Romans as Numidian or Carthage hen. It is now raised in many parts of the world. The flesh is delicate, resembling that of pheasant, to which the guinea fowl is related. Fully grown guinea fowl can be prepared in any way suitable for chicken. If guinea fowl is roasted, it should be basted frequently with pan drippings, wine, or stock, or the back, breast, and legs should be covered with thin slices of fat salt pork, since the flesh is rather dry. Allow 1 pound of guinea fowl per serving.

❧ ROAST GUINEA HEN (*Pintade Rôti*)

2 ready-to-cook guinea hens, 2 pounds
   each
2 teaspoons salt
1 teaspoon ground black pepper
2 medium-sized onions

2 ribs celery, sliced
2 carrots, peeled and quartered
2 stalks parsley
softened butter
8 thin strips of fat salt pork

Wash the guinea hens and wipe them dry. Rub the inside of the body cavities with some of the salt and black pepper. Put 1 each of the vegetables into the body cavity of each guinea hen. Close the openings with skewers and lace tightly with twine. Truss as directed in How to Truss Chicken or Turkey (page 310). Rub the skin with the rest of the salt and black pepper. Place the birds, breast side down, on a rack in a shallow baking pan. Place a strip of salt pork across the back of each bird. Bake, uncovered, in a preheated moderate oven (350° F.) 45 minutes. Turn the birds over and place strips of salt pork across the breasts and lengthwise on the legs. Bake 45 to 50 minutes or until the birds are tender. Serve with gravy made from pan drippings. Makes 4 to 6 servings.

❧ GUINEA-HEN CASSEROLE

1 clove garlic
¼ cup olive oil or salad oil
2 tablespoons finely chopped green
   sweet pepper
2 tablespoons finely chopped onion
2 guinea hens, 2 pounds each
salt and ground black pepper
¼ cup cognac
dry white wine

18 black olives, pitted
½ cup sliced mushrooms
1 small bay leaf
¾ teaspoon dried tarragon, or 1 tablespoon chopped fresh tarragon
1/16 teaspoon ground nutmeg
2 tablespoons heavy cream
watercress

In a casserole which has a cover and which can be used over surface heat, cook the garlic in the oil 1 minute. Add the green pepper and onion and cook until they are soft and translucent. Remove and discard the garlic. Cut the guinea hens into serving-size pieces, rub them with 1 teaspoon salt and ¼ teaspoon black pepper, and in the same casserole brown the pieces on all sides over low heat. Heat the cognac in a small saucepan, pour it over the guinea hens and ignite it. Pour in enough white wine almost to cover. Add the olives, mushrooms, and bay leaf. Cover the casserole and cook over low heat 25 to 30 minutes, or until the pieces of guinea hen are tender. Add the tarragon and nutmeg and cook 10 minutes longer. Transfer the guinea-hen pieces to a warmed platter. Cook the pan liquid over brisk heat until it has reduced by

327

one-half. Stir in the cream. Adjust seasonings. Return the guinea-hen pieces to the sauce, garnish with watercress, and serve at the table from the casserole. Makes 4 servings.

⚜ SAUTÉED BREAST OF GUINEA HEN
(*Suprêmes de Pintade Sautés*)

2 guinea hens, 2 pounds each
salt and ground black pepper
⅛ teaspoon ground ginger
about 2 cups heavy cream
flour
4 tablespoons (½ stick) butter

2 tablespoons salad oil
4 slices fried ham
2 tablespoons flour
¼ cup dry sherry
chopped parsley

Remove the breasts from the guinea hens, leaving the wings attached. Reserve the rest of the birds for another meal. Split the breasts. With kitchen shears cut off the first 2 wing joints, leaving the big wing bone attached to the breast. Remove the skin and small bones from the breasts, leaving intact the main bone that runs lengthwise of the breasts. This helps the breast to hold its shape. Sprinkle the breasts with salt and black pepper and the ginger, dip them in heavy cream, and then in flour, and brown in a skillet in the butter and oil, adding it as needed. Transfer the breasts to a baking dish and pour the pan juices over them. Bake, uncovered, in a preheated hot oven (400° F.) 30 to 40 minutes or until the breasts are tender, basting frequently with the pan drippings. Place each breast on a slice of fried ham. Remove all but 2 tablespoons of the fat from the baking dish. Blend the flour with the remaining fat and stir and cook until the roux begins to color. Gradually stir in the remaining heavy cream (about 1½ cups) and the sherry. Adjust seasonings. Strain the sauce and spoon it over each serving. Garnish with chopped parsley. Serve promptly. Makes 4 servings.

PIGEONS AND SQUAB

Very young pigeons are called squabs. The average weight of squabs is about 1 pound and they are tender and delicious. French recipes usually specify *pigeonneau* (squab). Allow 1 squab or pigeon per serving.

⚜ SAUTÉED SQUAB (*Pigeonneaux Sautés*)

Clean and split 4 squabs and sprinkle them with salt. Melt ½ stick butter or enough to cover the bottom of a 9-inch skillet generously. Arrange the squabs skin side down in the pan. Sauté them until they are golden brown on both sides. Reduce heat, partly cover the skillet, and cook 20 to 30 minutes or until squabs are tender. Transfer the squabs to a serving platter and pour the melted butter from the pan over them. Pour ⅓ cup stock or water into the skillet, bring to boiling point, and boil until the volume is reduced to one-half, stirring in all the brown bits in the skillet. Adjust salt and add ground black pepper to taste. Pour over the squabs. Makes 4 servings.

⚜ STUFFED PIGEON (*Pigeon Farci*)

4 ready-to-cook young pigeons
2 tablespoons lemon juice
salt and ground black pepper
12 chicken livers, cut in half
4 tablespoons (½ stick) butter
⅔ cup finely chopped mushrooms

½ cup ground lean ham
⅓ cup chopped blanched almonds
½ teaspoon dried thyme leaves
8 thin slices fat salt pork
watercress

Rub the inside of the body cavities of the dressed pigeons with 1 tablespoon of the lemon juice and salt and black pepper. Cook the chicken livers in a skillet in 2 tablespoons of the butter until barely done. Transfer them to a wooden bowl and chop them fine. In the same skillet, sauté the mushrooms in the remaining 2 tablespoons butter. Add to the livers along with the ham, almonds, and thyme. Season to taste with salt and black pepper. Stuff the mixture lightly into the body cavities of the pigeons. Close the openings with skewers and lace them tightly with twine. Tie the legs together. Rub the skin with the remaining 1 tablespoon lemon juice and salt and black pepper. Place the pigeons on a rack, breast side up, in a shallow baking pan. Cover the breasts with thin slices of fat salt pork. Roast in a preheated slow oven (325° F.) 1 hour, or until pigeons are done, basting occasionally with pan drippings. Serve hot or cold, garnished with watercress. Makes 4 servings.

Game Birds

The same methods of cooking can be used interchangeably for most game birds. Game birds are usually lean and should be larded with salt pork or bacon before they are roasted.

WILD DUCK (*Canard Sauvage*)

Wild duck is one of the most popular of game birds. Mallard, the commonest species, is an ancestor of the domesticated duck. There are many other species of wild duck and related waterfowl; all are cooked in the same ways.

⚜ BROILED WILD DUCK (*Canard Sauvage Grillée*)

1½-pound ready-to-cook wild duck, halved
1 tablespoon baking soda
¼ cup (½ stick) butter

½ teaspoon salt
⅛ teaspoon ground black pepper
2 tablespoons currant jelly, melted (optional)

Rub the entire duck with the baking soda and rinse well. Combine the butter, salt, and black pepper and brush the mixture over the entire surface of the duck halves. Place the halves on a broiler rack, skin side down, and set the broiler 6 inches from the source of the broiler heat, or if a gas broiler is used, set the thermostat to 400° F. Broil 10 to 15 minutes, depending on the desired doneness, brushing occasionally with the butter mixture. Turn the halves and broil 10 to 15 minutes longer, brushing with the butter mixture. Transfer to a heated platter and brush with melted currant jelly, if desired. Makes 2 servings.

⚜ ROAST WILD DUCK (*Canard Sauvage Rôti*)

1½-pound ready-to-cook wild duck
½ teaspoon salt
¹⁄₁₆ teaspoon ground black pepper
1 medium-sized apple, sliced
1 rib celery, sliced
1 small white onion, sliced

3 juniper berries (optional, available at drugstores and health food stores)
2 slices fat salt pork
½ cup dry white wine
cooked wild rice

Sprinkle the outside skin and the inside of the body cavities with the salt and ground black pepper. Mix the next 4 ingredients and stuff the cavities with the mixture. Close the opening with skewers and lace tightly with twine. Truss as directed in How to Truss Chicken or Turkey (page 310). Place the duck on a rack in a shallow baking pan. Cover the breast with the salt pork slices. Roast in a preheated very hot oven (450° F.) for 40 minutes, basting frequently with the wine. If well-done duck is desired, roast 10 to 20 minutes longer. When the duck is done, remove the skewers and twine. Cut the duck into 2 servings and place them on a heated platter. If gravy is desired, make it from the pan drippings and chicken or veal stock. Serve with wild rice. Makes 2 servings.

Duck and other game birds may also be stuffed with Wild Rice Stuffing (see following recipe).

⚜ Wild Rice Stuffing

1 cup wild rice	1 cup chopped onion
6 cups boiling water	½ cup finely chopped green pepper
1 teaspoon salt	¼ teaspoon ground black pepper
½ cup cooked chopped mushrooms	½ teaspoon dried thyme leaves
¼ cup (½ stick) butter	¼ cup chopped parsley

Soak the wild rice 30 minutes in 2 cups of the boiling water in a covered bowl. Drain off the water and repeat the process two more times. Drain the wild rice well after the last soaking period. Add the remaining ingredients and mix well. Use as a stuffing for wild duck, wild goose, and other wild birds. Makes 4 cups stuffing.

PARTRIDGE

In French, young partridges are *perdreaux*, older ones *perdrix*. The bird called partridge in the United States is not a true partridge but belongs to the ruffed grouse family. It is found in woodland areas from the Mississippi Valley to the mountains of Georgia and northeastward into Canada.

The principal species of true partridges found in France is the common gray partridge. Another and larger variety is the red-legged partridge of southern France. European partridges especially suitable for breeding commercially in the United States are Bohemian, English, and Hungarian.

A young partridge has plump legs and a breastbone that bends and breaks easily. It is more desirable for roasting than the older birds. Tie the legs and wings close to the body, and roast, stuffed or not as desired, in an uncovered roasting pan. The older birds may be made into delectable braised dishes. The average partridge weighs from 12 to 14 ounces. Allow 1 partridge per person.

Partridge, pheasant, grouse, and quail may be cooked in the same ways. Partridge should age at least 4 days to develop its delicate flavor, while grouse may be eaten within 24 hours of killing.

⚜ ROAST PARTRIDGE (*Perdreaux Rôtis*)

Age cleaned partridges in the refrigerator or other cold place for 4 days. Rub them inside and out with lemon juice, salt, and ground thyme. Then rub the outside with softened butter and tie a thin slice of fat salt pork around each bird. Place the partridges on their sides in a heated roasting pan. Roast, uncovered, in a preheated very hot oven (450° F.) 15 minutes. Turn and roast on the other side 15 minutes. Then turn the partridges on their backs and roast 10 to 15 minutes. To test partridge for doneness, lift the bird and hold it tail down. Juice will run out and when it is clear as water without a pink tinge the bird is done. Remove the strings and salt pork and place the partridges on a warmed platter. Garnish with watercress and croutons fried in butter. Serve with wild rice, mushrooms, pan drippings, and red-currant jelly. Allow 1 partridge per serving.

⚜ BRAISED PARTRIDGE WITH CABBAGE
(*Perdreaux aux Choux*)

1 head (1½ pounds) green cabbage	2 ribs celery with leaves, quartered
4 partridges, dressed and then aged for 4 days	1 medium-sized onion
3 to 4 tablespoons hot bacon fat	salt and ground black pepper
6 ounces salt pork, sliced	½ pound stuffed sausage, in small links or in 1 piece
2 carrots	4 juniper berries (if available)
2 stalks parsley	boiling bouillon or water

Separate the cabbage into leaves and parboil them in boiling water to cover 6 minutes. Drain off the water and cut out the stalks from the cabbage leaves. Put half the cabbage in the bottom of a roasting pan or Dutch oven. Tie the wings of the partridges close to the bodies and brown the birds in a heavy skillet in the hot bacon fat, adding it as needed. Put the partridges on the cabbage in the roasting pan. Add the next 5 ingredients and sprinkle with salt and black pepper. Add the sausages and the juniper berries, if used. Cover with the remaining cabbage. Pour in enough boiling bouillon or water to come halfway up the cabbage. Cover and bake in a preheated very slow oven (250° F.) for about 3 hours. To serve, mound the cabbage in the center of a serving plate. Surround it with slices of the salt pork and ¼-inch-thick slices of sausage or sausage links, alternating the pork and the sausage. Slice the carrots and arrange them around the cabbage at the top of the pork and sausage slices. Place the partridges on top of the cabbage. Makes 4 servings. (*See illustration, page 304.*)

✤ **PARTRIDGE VIGNERONNE** (*Perdreaux à la Vigneronne*)

3 partridges, dressed and then aged for 4 days
3 slices fat salt pork or bacon
salt and ground black pepper to taste
6 tablespoons butter, softened

3 slices bread fried in butter
½ cup dry white Burgundy
⅓ cup game stock made from partridge giblets
green seedless grapes

Tie the partridge legs close to the bodies. Cover the breast of each bird with a slice of salt pork or bacon and tie the slices in place. Sprinkle the birds with salt and black pepper, spread with 3 tablespoons of the softened butter, place on their sides on a rack, and put the rack in a roasting pan. Roast the birds, uncovered, in a preheated hot oven (400° F.) 30 to 40 minutes, basting with butter 2 or 3 times. Roast on the other side, 10 to 15 minutes. Remove the salt pork or bacon slices and reserve them. Discard the strings. Turn the birds on their backs and cook 5 to 10 minutes or until they have browned. (If the breasts tend to brown too much, cover them with foil.) Continue to roast until the birds are tender. Place a bird on each piece of fried bread, arrange on a warmed platter, and keep warm. Pour off the fat from the roasting pan. Add the wine, game stock, and ⅓ cup grapes. Cook 4 to 5 minutes, stirring in all the crusty brown bits in the bottom of the roasting pan. Add the remaining 1 tablespoon butter and heat 1 minute. Trim the slices of salt pork or bacon used on the breasts of the birds and place one on each partridge. Adjust seasonings in the sauce and serve in a sauceboat. Garnish the platter with a cluster of green seedless grapes. Serve with mashed potatoes. Makes 3 servings. (*See illustration, page 303.*)

PHEASANT (*Faisan*)

The pheasant is a beautiful grouselike bird native to Southern Asia. The male is almost as gaily colored as a peacock, with a tail constituting two-thirds of its 3-foot total length. Its average weight is from 2¾ to 5 pounds. The female is smaller, weighing 2 to 3 pounds, with a shorter tail and modest brown plumage. By true connoisseurs the flesh of the female pheasant is more highly esteemed than that of the male.

Pheasants are shot by sportsmen as game and are also available dressed and smoked, and in frozen form, either plucked or in full plumage. Pheasants brought in by huntsmen should be aged to bring out the flavor of the bird. Young pheasants should age 4 days, while older birds do not reach their peak delicacy until they have aged 1 week or until the tail feathers can be plucked easily. While some gourmets insist that pheasants be aged longer, the aging periods mentioned are sufficient for most of us.

Young pheasants can be readily distinguished from the older birds by feeling the beak and examining the feathers on the wingtip. The upper part of the younger bird's beak is pliable, while in the older bird it is rigid. The feathers on the wingtip of the younger bird are pointed; in the older bird they are rounded. Young birds may be roasted; older birds should be marinated and cooked in moist heat.

Pheasants are lean and should be larded for cooking. Recipes for pheasant, partridge, and grouse may be used interchangeably.

⚜ ROAST PHEASANT (*Faisan Rôti*)

Select a young pheasant, clean it, and age it 4 days in the refrigerator or other cool place. Tie the wings and legs close to the body. Sprinkle the whole bird with salt and ground black pepper. Cover the breast completely with slices of fat salt pork or bacon and tie them in place with a string. Rub the outside skin with salad oil or softened butter, and place the bird on its side on a rack in a heated shallow baking pan. Roast, uncovered, in a preheated very hot oven (450° F.) for 15 minutes, basting once with salad oil or melted butter. Turn the bird onto the other side, baste with salad oil or melted butter, and roast 15 minutes longer. Then turn the bird onto its back, baste again with salad oil and melted butter, and roast 15 more minutes or until the bird is done. To test for doneness lift the bird and hold its tail down to let the juice run out. It is done when the juice is clear without a pink tinge. Transfer the bird to a warmed platter. Pour off the fat from the pan. Add to the pan drippings ¾ cup water or ¾ cup stock made from the giblets. Simmer, stirring in the brown bits that cling to the bottom of the roasting pan, until the volume is reduced to ½ cup. Season to taste with salt and ground black pepper. Quickly stir in 1 tablespoon butter. Serve in a sauceboat. Garnish the platter with watercress.

Note: If more than one bird is roasted in the same pan, increase the liquid in the gravy by ¼ cup for each bird and cook until the volume is reduced to three-fourths the original quantity. Allow one 2-pound bird for 2 servings.

⚜ SALMIS OF PHEASANT (*Salmis de Faisan*)

2 young pheasants
2 tablespoons salad oil or bacon drippings
salt
1 cup cold water
¼ cup finely chopped onion
1 shallot, chopped (optional)
1 small clove garlic, mashed

1½ tablespoons flour
⅓ cup each dry red wine and dry white wine
2 tablespoons tomato purée
½ cup sliced mushrooms
1 tablespoon butter
2 tablespoons chopped parsley
Rouennaise (see following recipe)

Roast the pheasants according to the directions for Roast Pheasant. Cut the breasts and legs from the roast pheasants and set aside. Cut the remaining carcasses into very small pieces and set aside. Cut the heads, necks, and giblets into very fine pieces and brown in 1 tablespoon of the oil or bacon drippings. Add ½ teaspoon salt, the cut-up carcasses, and the cold water. Bring to boiling point and simmer, covered, 1½ hours. Cool the stock without removing the bones. Set aside.

To make the sauce, cook the onion until it is golden in the remaining 1 tablespoon oil or bacon fat. Add the shallot, if used, the garlic, and the flour. Stir and cook 2 minutes. Pour in the wine and stir and cook until the mixture has thickened. Strain the stock and add ¾ cup to the sauce. Stir in the tomato purée. Cover and simmer 30 minutes. Meanwhile sauté the mushrooms in the butter for 5 minutes. Add them to the sauce, and simmer 5 minutes more. Slice the breast and leg meat and add the slices to the sauce along with the parsley. Cook 1 minute. Serve on toast spread with Rouennaise. Makes 4 servings.

⚜ Rouennaise

2 tablespoons diced salt pork	1 teaspoon salt
1 cup chicken livers	⅛ teaspoon ground black pepper
¼ teaspoon poultry dressing	2 tablespoons dry sherry

Fry the salt pork in a heavy skillet until it is very crisp. Add the next 4 ingredients. Cook over very high heat 4 minutes, stirring frequently. Pour in the sherry and mix well. Turn out the mixture into a wooden bowl and pound it with a mallet until it is soft. Then rub it through a sieve to make a paste. Spread on toast and serve with game. Makes approximately ½ cup.

QUAIL (*Cailles*)

The American quail belongs to the American partridge family. It is a little larger than the common European quail. Since this white-fleshed, delicate-flavored bird tastes best when fresh, it should be dry-plucked, cleaned, and refrigerated promptly after killing. Like other game birds, quail is lean and should be larded with fat salt pork or bacon for cooking. Allow 1 bird per serving.

⚜ ROAST QUAIL (*Cailles Rôties*)

Dry-pluck and dress quail as soon after killing as possible. Sprinkle the inside of the body cavity and the outside skin with salt and black pepper. Wrap the quail in grape leaves, if available, then in slices of fat salt pork, and tie the slices in place with string. Place the quail, breast side up, on a rack in a heated, shallow, open pan and spread quail with softened butter. Roast, uncovered, in a preheated very hot oven (450° F.) 20 to 25 minutes or until the quail is tender. Remove the salt pork and the grape leaves, if used. Cook the quail 5 to 10 minutes more or until it is brown, basting once with the pan drippings. Serve on buttered toast with gravy, or on toast spread with Rouennaise (page 335). Allow 1 quail per serving.

⚜ Quail Gravy

Pour ½ cup water or chicken stock or game stock into the baking pan. Simmer, stirring in all the brown bits that have stuck to the baking pan. Add 1 tablespoon dry sherry or dry white wine. Season to taste with salt and black pepper.

⚜ QUAIL TURKISH STYLE (*Cailles à la Turque*)

Other small birds may also be cooked in this way.

4 quail	2 cups hot chicken broth or bouillon
salt and ground black pepper	3 tablespoons tomato purée
4 tablespoons (½ stick) butter	parsley
1 cup raw long-grain rice	

Dry-pluck and dress the birds as soon as possible after killing. Tie the legs and wings close to the bodies. Sprinkle with salt and ground black pepper, and brown on all sides in 2 tablespoons of the butter. Meanwhile, soak the rice 30 minutes in enough cold water to cover it. Drain well. Melt the remaining 2 tablespoons butter in a 2-quart baking dish which has a cover. Add the rice. Stir and cook until rice is dry and begins to stick to the bottom and sides of the pan. Arrange the browned quail on top of the rice. Rinse the skillet in which the quail were browned with the chicken stock or bouillon and add the tomato purée, and salt and black pepper to taste. Pour the sauce over the rice and quail. Cover and cook in a preheated moderate oven (350° F.) 25 minutes or until rice and quail are tender. Remove the cover and cook 10 minutes longer. Garnish with parsley. Serve promptly from the baking dish. Makes 4 servings.

WOODCOCK (*Bécasse*)

Woodcock is regarded in France as the choicest of game birds. The American woodcock belongs to a different species. Woodcock should be aged 3 or 4 days before cooking.

⚜ ROAST WOODCOCK *(Bécasse Rôti)*

Sprinkle the inside of the body cavity and the outside skin of dressed wood-cock with salt and ground black pepper. Tie the legs and the wings close to the bodies. Wrap the birds in slices of fat salt pork and tie them in place with string. Spread each bird with about 1½ teaspoons softened butter. Place the birds on a rack in a shallow open baking pan. Roast, uncovered, 10 to 15 minutes, depending on the degree of rareness desired. Remove the birds from the pan and keep them warm.

Pour ½ cup chicken broth or water into the baking pan and simmer until the volume has reduced to ¼ cup. Add 1 tablespoon butter and heat only until it is melted. Adjust seasonings. If desired, add 3 to 4 juniper berries to the gravy at the time the chicken broth or water is added. (The berries may be purchased at health food stores and drug stores.) Remove the salt pork from the birds and discard the strings. Place each bird on a slice of buttered toast and spoon gravy over the top. Allow 1 woodcock per serving.

Note: Snipe may be roasted and served in the same way.

Leftovers

No good thrifty French cook would ever be guilty of wasting leftovers (*les restes*). On the contrary, the French housewife is known for her imagination and ingenuity in converting them into flavorful and attractive dishes. In most cases, her leftovers appear in a form as acceptable as that in which the ingredients were first served. She uses them to dress up omelettes, to give variety and flavor to soufflés, to make croquettes and casseroles, to vary her sauces, and in other interesting ways.

FISH

✤ COLD FISH WITH MAYONNAISE (*Poisson Froid à la Mayonnaise*)

cold cooked fish
1 tablespoon chopped gherkins
1 tablespoon wine vinegar
¼ cup mayonnaise
salt and ground black pepper to taste

Coating Mayonnaise (page 54)
4 radish roses
2 medium-small tomatoes, sliced
2 teaspoons capers

Remove the skin and bones from cold cooked fish and flake the fish. Add the next 3 ingredients, mix, and season to taste with salt and black pepper. Put the mixture on a serving plate and shape it to look like a fish. Mask with Coating Mayonnaise. Garnish the dish with radish roses and tomato slices. Sprinkle with capers. Makes 4 servings.

❋ FISH CAKES *(Bitok de Poisson)*

This is an excellent method of using leftover cooked fish, such as cod, haddock, halibut, salmon, tuna, etc. Canned fish can also be used.

2 cups flaked fish, cooked or canned	flour
3 tablespoons flour	1 large egg, beaten with 1 tablespoon milk or water
3 tablespoons butter, melted	fine dry breadcrumbs
1 cup milk	shortening or salad oil
2 large egg yolks	strips of tomato or red or green pepper
1 teaspoon salt	lemon wedges
⅛ teaspoon ground black pepper	
1½ teaspoons lemon juice	

Flake the fish, removing all bones, and set aside. Blend the 3 tablespoons flour with the 3 tablespoons melted butter in a saucepan. Stir and cook over moderately low heat until the mixture is foamy, 1 to 2 minutes. Remove from heat, add the milk, and beat with a wire whisk or a wire hand eggbeater. Return to heat; stir and cook until the sauce is very thick. Mix the flaked fish with the egg yolks and the salt and add to the sauce. Mix well. Stir and cook until the mixture is pastelike. Remove from heat and stir in the black pepper and lemon juice. Transfer the mixture to a shallow pan or platter and refrigerate until the mixture can be shaped into cakes. Using a tablespoon, make egg-shaped cakes, or if desired make round cakes and flatten them to ½ inch thickness. Roll the cakes in flour, then in the beaten egg, and then in breadcrumbs. Let the cakes stand 30 minutes. Fry in deep fat preheated to 375° F. Or if desired, pan-fry in shallow fat (shortening or salad oil), turning to brown all sides. Transfer the cakes to a warmed platter. Decorate with strips of tomato or strips of red or green sweet pepper and lemon wedges. Serve for lunch or supper. Makes 6 servings. (*See illustration, page 189.*)

BEEF

⚜ SMALL MEAT BALLS *(Fricadelles ou Boulettes)*

2½ cups ground leftover cooked beef	salt and ground black pepper
1 medium-sized white onion	Duchess Potatoes (page 383)
2 to 3 tablespoons bacon drippings, lard, or shortening	2 tablespoons chopped parsley
1 egg	flour
	Tomato Sauce (page 50)

Put the beef through a food chopper, using the finest blade. Set aside. Put the onion through the food chopper, then cook it in 1 tablespoon of the bacon drippings, lard, or shortening until it is soft. Add to the beef, along with the egg, salt and black pepper to taste, the Duchess Potatoes, and the parsley. Mix well. On a floured board shape the mixture into 3-inch patties. Fry in the fat, adding more as needed, until the patties are brown, turning them to brown both sides. Serve hot with Tomato Sauce. Makes 4 servings.

⚜ SMALL MEAT BALLS WITH PIQUANT SAUCE
(*Boulettes de Boeuf en Sauce Piquante*)

1 cup ground leftover cooked beef
½ pound sausage meat
3 tablespoons finely chopped onion
1 shallot (if available), chopped
1/16 teaspoon minced garlic
2 tablespoons chopped parsley
1 egg

3 slices white bread
stock or bouillon
salt to taste
flour
shortening, lard, or cooking oil
Piquant Sauce (page 47)

Put the beef, sausage meat, onion, shallot (if available), garlic, parsley, and egg in a mixing bowl. Soak the bread 10 minutes in enough stock or bouillon to cover it, squeeze dry, and crumble over the ingredients in the bowl. Add salt to taste. Mix well. (To test for salt, fry a small bit of the mixture in a skillet and taste. Add more salt if needed.) Shape the mixture into 1-inch balls, roll them in flour, and brown on all sides in hot shortening, lard, or oil. Serve Piquant Sauce in a separate bowl. Makes 6 servings.

⚜ BEEF HASH PARMENTIER (*Hachis Parmentier*)

2 medium-sized onions, chopped fine
2 tablespoons bacon drippings or lard
1 teaspoon flour
⅓ cup dry white wine
1¾ cups bouillon
3 cups ground leftover cooked beef

2 tablespoons tomato purée
3 medium-sized potatoes
salt and ground black pepper to taste
2 tablespoons butter, melted
1 egg yolk beaten with 1 tablespoon water

Cook the onions in the bacon drippings or lard until they are soft, then sprinkle them with the flour. Mix well. Add the wine, 1½ cups of the bouillon, the beef, and the tomato purée. Cook uncovered, 40 minutes, stirring occasionally. Meanwhile peel, boil, and mash the potatoes. Add 1 tablespoon of the butter, the remaining ¼ cup bouillon, and salt and black pepper to taste. Beat until fluffy. Season the meat mixture to taste with salt and black pepper. Turn it into a 10- by 6- by 2-inch baking dish. Spread the mashed potatoes over the meat, covering it completely. Bake in a preheated moderate oven (350° F.) 10 minutes. Then brush the potatoes with the remaining 1 tablespoon melted butter and then with the beaten egg yolk and water to help the potatoes brown with more color. Continue baking 30 minutes or until potatoes are brown. Makes 4 to 5 servings.

⚜ BEEF AND ONION STEW (*Miroton de Boeuf*)

Miroton is a stew made from cooked meat and onions; the name is at least 200 years old.

2 cups sliced onion
2 tablespoons butter, lard, or
   shortening
2 tablespoons flour

2 cups hot bouillon, or 2 cups water
   and 2 beef bouillon cubes
1 pound sliced cold braised beef
salt and ground black pepper to taste
about ¼ cup dry white wine

Gently brown the onion in the butter, lard, or shortening. Dust with the flour and stir and cook until the flour begins to turn golden. Add the bouillon or water and bouillon cubes. Cook until the sauce begins to thicken, stirring frequently. Add the beef and simmer, covered, 20 to 30 minutes. Season to taste with salt and black pepper. Just before serving, sprinkle with a little dry white wine. Serve hot. Makes 4 servings.

VEAL

⚜ CASSEROLES SUZANNE (*Cassolettes Suzanne*)

This dish may also be made with beef, poultry, fish, or shellfish.

10-ounce package frozen spinach,
   cooked, or 1½ cups cooked fresh
   spinach
4 tablespoons butter
salt and ground black pepper
½ cup chopped mushrooms
2 tablespoons flour

½ cup veal stock or chicken broth
½ cup milk or light cream
2 cups diced leftover cooked veal
4 tablespoons grated Gruyère or
   Cheddar cheese
4 mushroom caps, sautéed

Drain the cooked spinach and sauté it in 2 tablespoons of the butter. Season to taste with salt and black pepper. Spoon the spinach into 4 buttered individual casseroles or scallop shells. Cook the chopped mushrooms in 1 tablespoon of the butter 4 to 5 minutes. Add the remaining 1 tablespoon butter and heat until it is melted. Remove from heat and blend in the flour. Stir and cook 1 to 2 minutes. Remove from heat and stir in the veal stock or chicken broth and the milk or cream. Cook, stirring constantly, 2 to 3 minutes or until medium thick. Add the veal and season to taste with salt and black pepper. Spoon the mixture over the spinach and sprinkle the top of each serving with 1 tablespoon grated cheese. Place under broiler heat to melt and brown the cheese. Garnish each with a sautéed mushroom cap. Makes 4 servings.

⚜ VEAL COQUILLES MORNAY (*Coquilles de Veau Mornay*)

3 tablespoons butter	½ cup sliced mushrooms
3 tablespoons flour	½ cup grated Gruyère or Cheddar
¾ cup milk or light cream	cheese
¾ cup veal stock or chicken broth	¾ pound sliced leftover cooked veal
salt and ground black pepper to taste	½ cup grated soft breadcrumbs

Melt the butter in a 1-quart saucepan. Remove from heat and blend in the flour. Stir and cook 1 to 2 minutes or until the mixture begins to foam. Add the milk or light cream and the stock or broth. Stir and cook until the sauce is medium thick. Season to taste with salt and black pepper. Add the mushrooms and ¼ cup of the cheese. Divide half of the mixture among 4 buttered individual casseroles or scallop shells. Arrange veal slices over each serving and cover with the remaining sauce. Combine the remaining ¼ cup cheese with the breadcrumbs and sprinkle an equal amount over each dish. Bake in a preheated moderate oven (350° F.) 30 minutes or until browned. Makes 4 servings.

⚜ CREAMED VEAL PIEDMONTESE STYLE
(*Émincé de Veau à la Piémontaise*)

2½ cups hot cooked rice	2 cups diced cooked veal
2 tablespoons tomato purée	1 cup Béchamel Sauce (page 38) or
1 cup thinly sliced mushrooms	Madeira Sauce (page 294)
1 tablespoon chopped onion	salt and ground black pepper to taste
2 tablespoons (¼ stick) butter	

Combine the hot rice and the tomato purée, mixing lightly. Spoon the mixture into a buttered 5-inch ring mold and place the mold in a pan of hot water to keep warm. Sauté the mushrooms and onion in the butter and add them and the veal to the Béchamel Sauce or Madeira Sauce. Heat. Add salt and black pepper to taste. To serve, unmold the rice onto a warm serving plate and fill the center with the creamed mixture. Makes 6 servings.

⚜ VEAL CROQUETTES (*Croquettes de Veau*)

2 cups coarsely ground cold leftover cooked veal	salt and ground black pepper to taste flour
1 cup finely chopped mushrooms	1 whole egg beaten with 1 tablespoon
1 tablespoon butter	water
1 tablespoon flour	fine dry breadcrumbs
¼ cup veal stock or chicken broth	Tomato Sauce (page 50)
1 egg yolk	

Place the first 6 ingredients in a 1½-quart saucepan. Stir and cook over medium-low heat until the mixture leaves the sides of the pan. Remove from heat and season to taste with salt and pepper. Cool. Shape the mixture into croquettes. Roll them in flour, dip in the egg beaten with water, and then roll in breadcrumbs. Let the croquettes stand about 10 minutes. Fry in deep fat preheated to 375° F., 3 to 4 minutes. Drain on paper towels. Serve with Tomato Sauce. Makes 4 servings.

⚜ SLICED VEAL IN CREAM SAUCE (*Émincé de Veau à la Crème*)

2 pounds cooked roast veal, sliced thin
salt and ground black pepper
4 tablespoons (½ stick) butter
1 small white onion, chopped
3 tablespoons dry white wine

½ cup light cream
1 teaspoon beef extract (meat glaze)
¼ teaspoon lemon juice
½ pound thinly sliced mushrooms, sautéed (optional)

Sprinkle the veal slices with salt and black pepper. Sauté them quickly in 3 tablespoons of the butter, adding it as needed. Transfer the slices to a warm platter and keep them warm. In the same skillet sauté the onion in the remaining 1 tablespoon butter until it begins to color lightly. Add the wine and bring it to boiling point. Add the cream and beef extract, mix well, bring to boiling point, and boil 1 to 2 minutes. Adjust the seasonings and add the lemon juice, and, if desired, the sautéed mushrooms. Pour over the veal slices. Makes 6 servings.

⚜ VEAL-STUFFED TOMATOES (*Tomates à la Bonne-Femme*)

1½ slices bread
milk or bouillon
1 cup ground leftover roast veal
2 shallots, or 1 small white onion, chopped
1 tablespoon chopped parsley

1 egg
salt and ground black pepper to taste
4 medium-sized tomatoes
2 tablespoons butter, melted
½ cup soft breadcrumbs
Tomato Sauce (optional; page 50)

Soak the bread in milk or bouillon for 5 minutes. Squeeze it dry and add to the meat. Add the next 3 ingredients and mix well. Season to taste with salt and black pepper. Wash the tomatoes, cut them in half, and scoop out the centers. Sprinkle the shells with salt and pepper. Drain. Fill with the meat mixture. Combine the butter and breadcrumbs and sprinkle over the tomatoes. Place in a buttered baking dish. Bake in a preheated moderate oven (350° F.) 30 minutes or until crumbs have browned. Serve with Tomato Sauce, if desired. Makes 4 servings.

343

LAMB OR MUTTON

⚜ MINCED LAMB OR MUTTON (*Hachis du Mouton*)

1 small white onion, chopped fine
1 tablespoon butter
2½ cups finely diced leftover cooked
   lamb or mutton
2 shallots or the white parts of 2
   green onions, chopped fine

2 tablespoons chopped parsley
about 2 tablespoons bouillon or water
salt and ground black pepper to taste
croutons fried in butter
Tomato Sauce (page 50)

Cook the chopped onion in the butter without letting it turn color. Add the next 5 ingredients. Cook over medium-low heat 5 minutes or until hot, adding more bouillon or water if the mixture is too dry. Serve hot with croutons and Tomato Sauce. Makes 4 servings.

⚜ SLICED MUTTON OR LAMB WITH MUSHROOMS
(*Émincé du Mouton aux Cèpes*)

1 small white onion, chopped fine
2 shallots, or the white part of 2
   green onions, chopped fine
1 cup sliced mushrooms
2 tablespoons butter
1 tablespoon flour
1 cup dry white wine or veal stock

1 cup bouillon
2 tablespoons tomato purée
salt and ground black pepper to taste
8 slices leftover cooked leg or
   shoulder of lamb or mutton
chopped parsley

Sauté the first 3 ingredients in the butter. Sprinkle with the flour. Stir and cook until flour has browned. Add the wine or veal stock and cook until the liquid has reduced to one-half the original amount. Add the bouillon and tomato purée. Stir and cook 5 minutes. Add salt and pepper to taste. Add the meat and cook over low heat 5 minutes. Turn into a warmed serving dish and sprinkle with chopped parsley. Makes 4 servings.

TONGUE

⚜ SLICED TONGUE WITH TARTARE SAUCE
(*Langue en Tranches Tartare*)

Cut leftover cooked beef tongue into slices ¼ inch thick. Roll the slices in flour, then dip in beaten egg (1 egg beaten with 1 tablespoon water) and fine dry breadcrumbs. Fry in a little melted butter or salad oil or olive oil, browning both sides. Serve hot with cold Tartare Sauce (page 55). Allow 2 slices per serving.

GAME

⚜ CANAPÉS SAINT HUBERT (*Canapés Saint-Hubert*)

Use any leftover cooked game (birds, venison, wild rabbit or hare). Chop fine. Mix with Madeira, and stir in enough Demi-Glace Sauce (page 44) to make the mixture the consistency of thick vegetable soup. Stir and cook over low heat until the mixture is the thickness of a purée. Remove the crusts from slices of bread and fry the slices in butter. Spread them with the game purée. Decorate each slice with a sautéed button mushroom cap or with a bit of truffle. Serve hot as an entrée, or cut the bread in fancy shapes and serve as hot hors d'oeuvre. Allow 1 whole slice of bread per serving or 2 to 3 small hors d'oeuvre per person.

⚜ COLD SADDLE OF VENISON (*Selle de Chevreuil*)

Slice cold leftover cooked fillet of venison and coat the slices with currant jelly or apple jelly. Serve with a mushroom salad. Allow 2 slices venison per serving.

CHICKEN

⚜ CHICKEN IN ASPIC (*Aspic de Poulet*)

1 envelope unflavored gelatin
¼ cup cold chicken broth or water
1½ cups hot chicken broth
1 teaspoon lemon juice
½ teaspoon onion juice (optional)
salt and ground black pepper to taste

1½ cups julienne strips leftover cooked chicken
½ cup julienne strips leftover cooked ham
2 hard-cooked eggs, diced
parsley

Soak the gelatin in the cold chicken broth or water 5 minutes. Stir in the hot chicken broth (heated to just below boiling point), the lemon juice, onion juice (if used), and salt and black pepper to taste. Chill until the mixture is the thickness of fresh egg whites. Fold in the next 3 ingredients. Rinse a 1-quart mold in cold water and fill it with the aspic mixture. (If desired, replace the gelatin aspic with 1¾ cups reduced rich chicken or veal stock.) Chill until the aspic is firm. Unmold onto a tray. Arrange parsley around the edge of the mold. Makes 6 servings.

❧ CHICKEN SALAD MONA LISA (*Cassolettes de Poulet Joconde*)

12 cold cooked asparagus tips, or 1
    cup blanched and chopped mush-
    rooms
3 tablespoons Vinaigrette Sauce
    (page 56)

1 cup finely chopped cold leftover
    cooked chicken
mayonnaise
1 medium-sized tomato
1 hard-cooked egg, cut into 4 slices
salt and ground black pepper

Marinate the asparagus or mushrooms in the Vinaigrette Sauce at least 30 minutes. Drain and arrange in the bottom of a shallow round bowl. Cover with the chicken. Coat with mayonnaise. Cut the tomato into 4 uniform slices and arrange them over the top of the salad. Top each slice with a slice of hard-cooked egg. Sprinkle tomato and egg lightly with salt and black pepper. Makes 4 servings.

Vegetables

While vegetables (*les legumes*) are becoming increasingly important in the diets of people all over the world, there are probably more different varieties produced and served in the United States and France than in any other country. The American home cook is likely to cook vegetables with little water and only for a short time, in order to preserve the vitamins and minerals. The French homemaker, on the other hand, does not hesitate to soak, blanch, mash, squeeze, trim, or carve vegetables when these processes will result in a more flavorful and attractive dish. For an example of an attractive French vegetable platter, *see illustration, page 370.*

ARTICHOKES (*Artichauts*)

❧ HOW TO COOK ARTICHOKES

Allow 1 large artichoke or 2 small ones to a serving. Wash the artichokes, cut off the stems even with the base, and remove and discard the tough outer leaves. Cut off and discard the top third of each artichoke; if any prickly ends of the leaves are left, trim them off. Stand the artichokes upright in a sauce-pan just large enough for them to fit snugly, or tie a string around each one to hold it in shape. To prevent discoloration, rub lemon juice over the cut surfaces or fasten a thin slice of lemon onto the base of each artichoke with a toothpick or small skewer. Pour in boiling water to cover and add 1 tea-spoon salt. Cover and cook 40 minutes to 1 hour or until artichokes are tender. They are done when a leaf will pull out easily. Remove the strings, if used, and place the artichokes upside down to drain. Using a sharp knife, remove the prickly choke in the center that covers the heart; this is discarded. Serve with melted butter, Hollandaise Sauce, Mousseline Sauce, Vinaigrette Sauce, Plain White Sauce (see Index), or with one of the following:

❧ Lemon Butter

Melt ½ cup (1 stick) butter and add 1½ tablespoons lemon juice and a dash of ground black pepper.

❧ Parsley Butter

Melt ½ cup (1 stick) butter and add 2 tablespoons chopped parsley, 1 tea-spoon lemon juice, and a dash of ground black pepper.

❧ ARTICHOKES MIREILLE (*Artichauts Mireille*)

8 small artichokes	¼ teaspoon salt
⅓ cup olive oil or salad oil	1/16 teaspoon ground black pepper
⅔ cup hot bouillon or chicken broth	⅛ teaspoon sugar
8 small white onions	chopped parsley
3 medium-sized tomatoes	

Cut off the stems and tops of the artichokes and trim off the tips of the leaves. Wash well. Put them in a casserole with the oil and hot bouillon or broth and the onions. Peel the tomatoes, seed, quarter, and add. Sprinkle with the salt, black pepper, and sugar. Cover the casserole and bake in a preheated hot oven (425° F.) 40 minutes or until vegetables are tender. Sprinkle with chopped parsley and serve from the casserole. Makes 4 servings.

❧ ARTICHOKE BOTTOMS (*Fonds d'Artichauts*)

Wash 4 large or 8 medium-small artichokes. Cut off the stem even with the base. Trim the bottoms and rub them with lemon juice to prevent discolora-tion. Using a sharp knife, cut off the leaves about ½ inch from the base. Blend 1 tablespoon flour with ¼ cup water in a saucepan. Add 4 cups more water, bring to boiling point, and add artichoke bottoms along with 1 teaspoon salt and 1 teaspoon lemon juice. Cover and cook over moderate heat 30 minutes or until the bottoms are tender. Remove them from the water and drain well. Brown 2 tablespoons butter in a skillet, add the artichoke bottoms, and sauté a few minutes on each side. Or if desired, do not sauté but serve the artichoke bottoms with melted butter, Parsley Butter, Lemon Butter, Hollandaise Sauce, or Vinaigrette Sauce (see Index). Makes 4 servings.

⚜ Artichoke Bottoms Clamart *(Fonds d'Artichauts Clamart)*

Prepare and cook artichoke bottoms as directed in the recipe for Artichoke Bottoms. Fill them with hot green peas. Serve with Brown Butter (page 56). Allow 1 to 2 large artichoke bottoms per serving.

⚜ ARTICHOKE BOTTOMS AU GRATIN
(Fonds d'Artichauts au Gratin)

1 cup 1-inch pieces of cooked asparagus, or 6 large or 12 small cooked cauliflowerets
salt and ground black pepper to taste

6 large or 12 small cooked Artichoke Bottoms
½ cup Mornay Sauce (page 40)
3 tablespoons butter, melted
3 tablespoons grated Parmesan cheese

Season the asparagus or cauliflower to taste with salt and black pepper. Divide the asparagus among the cooked artichoke bottoms, or put 1 caulifloweret on each. Cover with the Mornay Sauce and sprinkle with the melted butter and grated Parmesan cheese. Bake in a preheated very hot oven (450° F.) 10 minutes or until the tops are flecked with brown. Serve promptly. Makes 6 servings. *(See illustration, page 371.)*

⚜ ARTICHOKES STUFFED WITH MUSHROOMS
(Artichauts Farcis à la Barigoule)

4 large artichokes
7 tablespoons butter
1½ cups chopped mushrooms
⅓ cup shredded cooked ham
2 tablespoons finely chopped onion or shallots
2 tablespoons tomato purée
2 tablespoons chopped parsley

4 tablespoons fine dry breadcrumbs
salt and ground black pepper to taste
4 strips bacon
⅓ cup dry white wine
½ cup bouillon or chicken broth
1½ tablespoons olive oil or salad oil
1½ tablespoons flour

Prepare and cook artichokes as in How to Cook Artichokes (page 347). Remove them from the water and place them upside down on a rack to drain thoroughly. Pull out the center leaves and remove the chokes.

Melt 2 tablespoons of the butter in a saucepan. Add the next 3 ingredients, cook 2 minutes, and then add 1 tablespoon each of the tomato purée, parsley, and breadcrumbs. Stir and cook 2 to 3 minutes. Season to taste with salt and black pepper. Stuff the artichokes with this mixture. Tie a strip of bacon around each artichoke and arrange the artichokes in a buttered casserole. Add the wine, the bouillon or broth, the oil, and the remaining 1 tablespoon each of tomato purée and parsley. Mix the remaining 3 tablespoons breadcrumbs with 3 tablespoons melted butter and sprinkle over the artichokes. Cover with foil or buttered brown paper. Bake in a preheated very hot oven (500° F.) for 5 minutes. Reduce heat to 350° F. (moderate) and bake 30 to 40 minutes longer. Transfer the artichokes to a warmed serving dish. Remove and discard the bacon. Blend the flour with the remaining 2 tablespoons butter and add to the liquor in the casserole. Stir and cook the mixture 2 or 3 minutes or until thickened. Add salt and black pepper to taste, and pour the sauce into the bottom of the serving dish. Makes 4 servings.

ASPARAGUS (*Asperges*)

⚜ HOW TO COOK ASPARAGUS

Allow 2 pounds asparagus for 4 generous servings.
French Method. Wash the asparagus, peel the spears, tie in serving-size bundles, and cook 10 to 18 minutes or only until barely tender, in a large amount of boiling salted water, using 1½ teaspoons salt to 1 quart water. Remove asparagus from the water immediately and drain well. Place it on a dish covered with a clean towel or put it in a special dish equipped with a rack to permit thorough drainage. Asparagus may be served hot or cold with various sauces. Peeled asparagus cooks more quickly than the unpeeled. The spears can be eaten down to the butt end and they retain their natural green color and texture.
American Methods. The American cook uses one of two methods of cooking asparagus, neither of which specifies peeling. Select firm, crisp stalks, with moist cut ends and compact closed tips. If possible, select spears of uniform thickness so that they will all finish cooking at the same time. Break the asparagus at the point where the stalk becomes tender, remove the scales, and wash thoroughly.

First method—tie the spears in serving-size bundles and stand them in the bottom part of a double boiler, tip ends up. Add ½ teaspoon salt and boiling water to a depth of 2 inches. Cover with the inverted top part of the double boiler. Boil 15 to 20 minutes. By this method the tips are not overcooked before the ends are done.

Second method—lay cleaned asparagus in a skillet, add ½ teaspoon salt, and pour in boiling water to a depth of 1 inch. Bring to boiling point, un-covered, and cook 5 minutes. Cover and cook 5 to 10 minutes; the time depends upon the size and natural tenderness of the asparagus. Remove from the water with a slotted pancake turner.

Asparagus cooked by any of these methods may be served with melted butter, Hollandaise Sauce, Béarnaise Sauce, Mousseline Sauce, Caper Sauce, Lemon Butter (page 348), Parsley Butter, Brown Butter, or Mustard Butter (see Index).

⚜ ASPARAGUS FLEMISH STYLE (*Asperges à la Flamande*)

Cook 2 pounds asparagus by any of the methods under How to Cook Aspar-agus. Melt 6 tablespoons (¾ stick) butter and mix with 2 finely chopped hard-cooked eggs. Serve over the cooked asparagus. Makes 4 servings.

⚜ ASPARAGUS MILANESE STYLE (*Asperges à la Milanaise*)

Place 2 pounds cooked asparagus on a heatproof oval platter, with the ends in the center and the tips at each end. Sprinkle with ⅓ cup grated Gruyère or Parmesan cheese, and pour 2 tablespoons Brown Butter (page 56) over all. Cook in a preheated very hot oven (450° F.) 5 minutes or until the cheese melts and begins to brown. Makes 4 servings.

⚜ ASPARAGUS VINAIGRETTE (*Asperges Vinaigrette*)

Serve Vinaigrette Sauce (page 56) from a sauceboat over lukewarm cooked asparagus. Allow ½ cup Vinaigrette Sauce for 4 servings of asparagus.

⚜ CREAMED ASPARAGUS TIPS (*Pointes d'Asperges à la Crème*)

1¾ pounds asparagus
1 cup Béchamel Sauce (page 38)
3 tablespoons light cream
¼ teaspoon sugar
1 egg yolk
salt and ground black pepper

Wash the asparagus and cut the tip ends into pieces ¾ inches long. Using one of the methods given under How to Cook Asparagus, cook the asparagus until it is tender. Drain well and add to the Béchamel Sauce, along with 2 table-spoons of the light cream and the sugar. Simmer, uncovered, 10 minutes. Blend the egg yolk with the remaining 1 tablespoon light cream and add to the sauce. Stir and cook 1 to 2 minutes (do not boil). Season to taste with salt and black pepper. Makes 4 servings.

❧ SAUTÉED ASPARAGUS TIPS

Sauté 2 pounds cooked asparagus tips in 3 tablespoons butter. Season to taste with salt and ground black pepper. Garnish with chopped parsley. Makes 4 servings.

BEANS (*Haricots*)

❧ BROAD BEANS (*Fèves*)

Broad beans are the common bean of Europe. They can be prepared in the same ways as lima beans.

2 cups shelled young broad beans or
   lima beans
boiling water
salt

1 tablespoon butter
2 tablespoons heavy cream (optional)
1/16 teaspoon ground black pepper

Wash the beans and place them in a saucepan with 1 inch boiling water and ½ teaspoon salt. Cover, bring to boiling point, and cook 20 minutes or until beans are tender. Drain well. Add the butter, heavy cream (if used), and black pepper. Mix lightly. Heat ½ minute. Adjust salt. Serve promptly. Makes 4 servings.

❧ CREAMED GREEN BEANS, FRENCH STYLE
(*Haricots Verts à la Crème*)

The French cooks boil green beans in plenty of water to retain their green color.

1 pound green beans
1 teaspoon salt
boiling water
2 tablespoons butter

1/16 teaspoon ground black pepper
⅓ cup heavy cream, or ½ cup
   Béchamel Sauce (page 38)

Wash the green beans, cut off the tips, and place the beans in a saucepan with the salt and boiling water to cover generously. Boil, uncovered, until beans are tender, about 20 minutes. Drain off water. Shake the pan gently over low heat 1 to 2 minutes to dry the beans. Add the butter, black pepper, and cream or Béchamel Sauce. Heat 1 to 2 minutes, or, if cream is used, until it thickens. Makes 5 to 6 servings.

⚜ GREEN BEANS PORTUGUESE STYLE
(Haricots Verts à la Portugaise)

¼ pound salt pork	½ teaspoon salt
1 pound green beans	½ teaspoon sugar
2 medium-sized tomatoes	⅛ teaspoon ground black pepper
¾ cup bouillon	chopped parsley

Dice the salt pork and scatter it over the bottom of a flameproof 1½-quart casserole. Wash the green beans, cut off the tips, cut the beans into 1-inch pieces, and place them in the casserole over the pork. Peel, seed, and cube the tomatoes and strew over the beans. Add the bouillon, salt, sugar, and black pepper. Bring to boiling point over surface heat. Cover and cook in a preheated moderate oven (350° F.) 30 to 40 minutes or until beans are tender. Sprinkle with chopped parsley. Makes 6 servings.

⚜ WAX BEANS OR GREEN BEANS BRETON STYLE
(Haricots Blancs à la Bretonne)

1 pound wax beans or green beans	1 small white onion, chopped
1 teaspoon salt	3 tablespoons tomato purée or tomato
boiling water	sauce
2 tablespoons butter or bacon	⅛ teaspoon ground black pepper
drippings	chopped parsley

Wash the beans and cut off the tips. If the beans are young and tender, leave them whole; if they are older, cut them into 1-inch pieces. Place the beans in a 1½-quart saucepan with 1 teaspoon salt and 1 inch boiling water. Bring to boiling point and cook, uncovered, 5 minutes. Cover and cook 10 minutes or until beans are almost tender. Drain off the water and dry the beans with a clean towel. Cook the onion in the butter or bacon drippings until soft. Add the beans, tomato purée or tomato sauce, and black pepper, cover, and simmer 5 minutes or until beans are tender. Turn into a serving dish. Sprinkle with chopped parsley. Makes 5 to 6 servings.

⚜ RED KIDNEY BEANS WITH WINE *(Haricots Rouges au Vin)*

The red kidney beans available in the United States are the same as the French *haricots rouges*. Cook fresh red beans in the same way as fresh green beans, dried red beans like dried white beans.

1 pound fresh red kidney beans
salt
boiling water
1 small white onion, chopped
2 tablespoons bacon fat or ham fat

1 tablespoon flour
½ cup dry red wine
2 strips crisp bacon, crumbled, or ½
   cup diced cooked ham

Prepare the beans and cook with 1 teaspoon salt in 1 inch boiling water according to the directions in the preceding recipe. Set aside. Cook the onion in the bacon or ham fat until golden. Sprinkle with the flour, mix well, add the wine, and cook 5 minutes over low heat. Add the beans and simmer 5 minutes. Adjust salt. Sprinkle with crumbled crisp bacon or diced cooked ham. Makes 6 servings.

THE CABBAGE FAMILY (*Choux*)

The cabbage family is very large; it includes Brussels sprouts, green (white) and red cabbage, cauliflower, kohlrabi, and others. All are delicious and all lend themselves to a number of different recipes.

⚜ SAUTÉED BRUSSELS SPROUTS (*Choux de Bruxelles Sautés*)

1 pound Brussels sprouts
cold water
salt
boiling water

3 tablespoons butter
ground black pepper to taste
chopped parsley

Wash the Brussels sprouts, remove and discard damaged leaves, and soak the sprouts 20 minutes in 1 quart cold water and 1 teaspoon salt. Rinse in cold water. Place in a 1½-quart saucepan with 1 inch boiling water and ½ teaspoon salt. Cook, uncovered, 5 minutes. Cover and cook 10 to 15 minutes or until barely tender. Drain well. Sauté in the butter, adding it as needed. Transfer the Brussels sprouts to a serving dish and sprinkle with black pepper and chopped parsley. Makes 4 to 5 servings.

⚜ CABBAGE ENGLISH STYLE (*Choux Verts à l'Anglaise*)

Cabbage cooked in this way is as easy to digest as spinach.

1 medium-sized head cabbage
boiling water
½ teaspoon salt

1/16 teaspoon ground black pepper
2 tablespoons butter

354

Remove any damaged cabbage leaves, wash the head, and cut it into wedges. Place the wedges in a large saucepan and add ½ inch boiling water and the salt. Cover, and cook 10 to 12 minutes or until cabbage is tender. Drain off the water and add the black pepper and butter. Makes 4 servings.

❧ BRAISED CABBAGE (*Choux Verts Braisés*)

1 medium-sized head cabbage	2 tablespoons chopped parsley
2 tablespoons ham fat	4 slices lean salt pork or ham
1 medium-sized white onion	½ teaspoon salt
1 whole clove	⅛ teaspoon ground black pepper
1 medium-sized carrot, sliced	hot bouillon
1 rib celery, sliced	

Remove and discard any damaged leaves from the cabbage and cut the head into wedges. Remove the stalks. Set aside. Spread the bottom of a 1½-quart casserole with the ham fat. Stud the onion with the clove and place in the casserole over the fat. Add the carrot, celery, and parsley and arrange the cabbage wedges on top. Place a slice of salt pork or ham over each wedge. Sprinkle with the salt and black pepper. Pour in enough hot bouillon to half cover the cabbage. Cover with foil and braise in a preheated moderate oven (350° F.) until the cabbage has absorbed the bouillon, about 1 hour. Makes 4 servings.

❧ CABBAGE AU GRATIN (*Choux au Gratin*)

1 medium-sized head cabbage	½ cup milk or light cream
boiling water	½ cup beef stock or veal stock
salt	1/16 teaspoon ground black pepper
4 tablespoons butter	½ cup grated Cheddar cheese
2 tablespoons flour	½ cup soft breadcrumbs

Remove and discard any damaged leaves from the cabbage and cut the head into wedges. Cut out the stalks and shred the cabbage coarsely. Place it in a 2-quart saucepan with ½ inch boiling water and ½ teaspoon salt. Cook 5 minutes uncovered, then cover and cook 5 to 8 minutes or until cabbage is tender. Rinse the cabbage in cold water, drain well, and squeeze out excess water. Set aside. Melt 2 tablespoons of the butter in a 1-quart saucepan. Remove pan from heat and blend in the flour. Return to heat; stir and cook until the mixture is foamy. Remove from heat and add the milk or cream and the stock. Return to heat; stir and cook until the mixture is of medium thickness, 3 to 4 minutes. Add ½ teaspoon salt, the black pepper, and ⅓ cup of the cheese. Add the cabbage and turn into a buttered 1½-quart casserole. Sprinkle with the rest of the cheese and the breadcrumbs. Dot with the remaining 2 tablespoons butter. Bake in a preheated moderate oven (350° F.) 30 minutes or until browned. Makes 4 servings.

⚜ STUFFED CABBAGE (*Chou Farci*)

1 large head green cabbage
boiling water
salt
3 slices white bread soaked in water
1 pound ground lean pork
¼ pound ground chuck or veal
2 small onions, chopped fine
¼ teaspoon ground black pepper
¾ teaspoon dried marjoram
1 large egg
2 tablespoons chopped parsley
2 to 3 slices bacon or thinly sliced salt
   pork

1 cup veal or beef stock, or more
1½ tablespoons flour
1½ tablespoons butter
2 tablespoons tomato paste

Wash the cabbage head and remove enough of the center to make a cavity large enough to hold the stuffing. (Save the center to use for other purposes.) Place the cabbage head in a deep saucepan. Pour in enough boiling water to cover and add 1 teaspoon salt for each quart of water used. Bring the water to boiling point, reduce heat, and simmer, covered, 10 minutes. Remove the cabbage from the water and invert it to drain well. Squeeze the bread dry. Mix it with the next 7 ingredients and 1½ teaspoons salt. Spoon the mixture into the cavity of the well-drained cabbage head. Tie the strips of bacon or salt pork around the head, or fasten them in place with toothpicks. Put the cabbage in a Dutch oven or large heavy saucepan. Pour in 1 cup stock. Cover, bring the stock to boiling point, reduce heat, and simmer the cabbage 45 to 50 minutes, adding additional stock if needed. Blend the flour with the butter to form a roux and add it to the cooking stock. Add the tomato paste. Add additional stock if a thinner sauce is desired. Adjust seasonings and cook 1 to 2 minutes. Spoon some of the sauce over each serving. Makes 6 servings.

⚜ Stuffed Cabbage Rolls (*Roulades de Choux Farcis*)

Remove 6 large green outer leaves from the cabbage head. Cut out the thick part of each leaf. Simmer 5 minutes in enough boiling water to cover them. Remove from water, drain well, and dry. Make the stuffing as in the preceding recipe. Spoon an equal amount onto each leaf, using it all. Fold the sides of the leaf over the stuffing and roll up from the end. Arrange the rolls, seam side down, in a buttered 10- by 6- by 2-inch baking dish. Pour in the stock and bake in a preheated moderate oven (350° F.) 30 minutes. Make the sauce as in the preceding recipe, and serve over the rolls. Makes 6 servings. (*See illustration, page 369.*)

❧ DOLMAS (*Petits Choux Farcis Dits Dolmas*)

½ cup raw rice
8 large green outside cabbage leaves
boiling water
¼ teaspoon salt
cold water
⅓ cup finely chopped onion
3 tablespoons butter, olive oil, or salad oil
2 cups (1 pound) ground lean raw lamb
1½ teaspoons salt
1 teaspoon paprika

¼ teaspoon ground black pepper
⅛ teaspoon crushed garlic
2 tablespoons tomato juice or bouillon
¼ cup chopped parsley
3 thin slices salt pork
2 medium-sized tomatoes, sliced
1 cup veal stock or beef stock
8 thin slices lemon
1 teaspoon lemon juice

Soak the rice 30 minutes in cold water to cover. Meanwhile, simmer the cabbage leaves 5 minutes in boiling water to cover, with the ¼ teaspoon salt. Remove the leaves from the water, drain well, and dry. With scissors, cut out the thick part of the leaves. Set the leaves aside. Cook the onion in the butter or oil until golden. Drain the rice, add to the onion, and stir and cook the rice until it is dry and begins to stick to the bottom of the pan. Add the next 7 ingredients, mix well, and put an equal amount of the stuffing on each of the cabbage leaves, using all the stuffing. Fold the sides of the leaves over the stuffing, and roll them up loosely from the ends. Place the rolls, side by side, in a buttered 10- by 6- by 2-inch baking dish, seam sides down. Arrange the salt pork and tomatoes over the rolls. Pour the stock over all. Cover lightly with foil. Bake in a preheated slow oven (300° F.) 1½ hours. Transfer the rolls to a serving dish and garnish each with a lemon slice. Boil the cooking liquor until it has reduced to one-half the original amount. Add the lemon juice and pour over the cabbage rolls. Serve promptly. Makes 4 servings.

❧ GARNISHED SAUERKRAUT (*Choucroute Garnie*)

4 cups sauerkraut
3 ounces fat bacon rind
3 ounces lean salt pork
6 frankfurters
1 ham knuckle
2 carrots, peeled and cut in half

2 medium-sized onions
2 whole cloves
6 whole black peppercorns
¼ teaspoon salt or salt to taste
½ cup dry white wine
6 boiled potatoes

Wash the sauerkraut in cold water and with the hands squeeze out excess water. Using a 1½-quart casserole with a lid, place the bacon rind in the bottom and put half the sauerkraut on top. In the center of the casserole place the salt pork, frankfurters, ham knuckle, and carrots. Add the remaining sauerkraut. Stud the onions with the cloves and add. Add the peppercorns and sprinkle with salt. Pour the wine over all. Cover with the casserole lid and then tie a piece of foil over the top. Braise in a very slow oven (275° F.) 3 hours. Serve with boiled potatoes. Makes 6 servings. (*See illustration, page 268.*)

⚜ RED CABBAGE FLEMISH STYLE (*Chou Rouge à la Flamande*)

1 large head red cabbage
1 tablespoon wine vinegar
⅛ teaspoon ground black pepper
½ teaspoon salt

1/16 teaspoon ground cinnamon
4 tablespoons (½ stick) butter
2 medium-small apples
sugar

Remove all damaged leaves from the cabbage, cut it into quarters, and cut out and discard stalks and large ribs. Wash the cabbage, cut it into julienne pieces, and put them in a well-buttered casserole. Sprinkle with the vinegar, black pepper, salt, and cinnamon. Dot with the butter. Stir the mixture 2 or 3 times with a spoon. Place cover on the casserole, and tie foil over the top. Bake in a preheated moderate oven (350° F.) 2 hours. Peel, core, and quarter the apples. Roll the quarters in sugar and bury them evenly in the cabbage. Cook, covered, 30 minutes longer. Makes 6 servings.

⚜ RED CABBAGE WITH RED WINE (*Chou Rouge au Vin Rouge*)

1 large head red cabbage
4 slices salt pork, diced
¼ cup chopped onion
2 tablespoons flour

½ teaspoon salt
⅛ teaspoon ground black pepper
½ cup dry red wine

Remove all damaged leaves from the cabbage head. Cut the head into quarters, remove the stalks and thick ribs, wash the sections and cut into coarse julienne strips. Set aside. Cook the salt pork until it is crisp and golden. Add the onion and cook until limp. Blend in the flour. Add the cabbage, salt, and black pepper. Cover and cook over surface heat until cabbage is tender. Add the wine, cover, and cook in a preheated moderate oven (350° F.) 40 minutes. Adjust seasonings. Serve promptly. Makes 4 servings.

⚜ CAULIFLOWER (*Chou-Fleur*)

1 medium-small head cauliflower
boiling water
salt

Hollandaise Sauce (page 52) or
Mousseline Sauce (page 53)
chopped parsley

Remove and discard the coarse leaves from the cauliflower. Soak it in cold salted water (1 teaspoon salt for each quart water) for 20 minutes. Drain and rinse in cold water. Place the whole cauliflower head in a deep saucepan. Add 1 teaspoon salt and boiling water to cover. Cook, uncovered, 5 minutes. Cover and cook 15 to 20 minutes or until cauliflower is tender. Transfer the cauliflower to a serving dish and mask with Hollandaise Sauce or Mousseline Sauce. Sprinkle with chopped parsley. Makes 4 to 5 servings.

⚜ CAULIFLOWER AU GRATIN (*Chou-Fleur au Gratin*)

4 tablespoons butter
2 tablespoons flour
½ cup milk
½ cup beef stock or veal stock
¼ teaspoon salt
1/16 teaspoon ground black pepper

½ cup grated Gruyère or Cheddar cheese
1 medium-sized head cauliflower, cooked
½ cup soft breadcrumbs

Melt 2 tablespoons of the butter in a 1-quart saucepan. Remove from the heat and blend in the flour. Return to heat; stir and cook until the mixture foams, 1 to 2 minutes. Add the milk and stock. Stir and cook 3 to 4 minutes or until the sauce is of medium thickness. Add the salt and black pepper and ⅓ cup of the cheese. Place the whole cooked cauliflower in a 1-quart casserole, pour the sauce over it, and sprinkle it with the rest of the cheese and the breadcrumbs. Dot with the remaining 2 tablespoons butter. Cook in a preheated moderate oven (350° F.) 30 minutes or until browned. Makes 4 to 5 servings.

⚜ CAULIFLOWER POLONAISE (*Chou-Fleur à la Polonaise*)

The term *à la Polonaise* is applied to dishes garnished with breadcrumbs fried in butter.

1 medium-sized head cauliflower, cooked
½ cup soft breadcrumbs

5 tablespoons butter
1 hard-cooked egg, chopped
1 tablespoon chopped parsley

Place the hot cooked whole head of cauliflower in a warm round serving dish. Brown the breadcrumbs in the butter and just before serving pour them over the cauliflower. Sprinkle with chopped hard-cooked egg and chopped parsley. Serve promptly. Makes 4 to 5 servings.

⚜ KOHLRABI (*Choux-Raves*)

Kohlrabi is a variety of cabbage with a stem that is swollen in the shape of a small turnip and a cabbagelike leaf. It may be prepared in the same ways as celeriac or turnips. In eastern France kohlrabi is used for making excellent sauerkraut.

Allow 1 medium-sized kohlrabi per serving.

CARROTS (*Carottes*)

⚜ CARROTS CHANTILLY (*Carottes Chantilly*)

1 pound young tender carrots	⅓ cup heavy cream
salt	ground black pepper
½ teaspoon sugar	2 cups hot cooked peas
boiling water	2 tablespoons butter
⅓ cup Béchamel Sauce (page 38)	

Wash and scrape the carrots and cut them into 2-inch pieces. Place in a saucepan with ½ teaspoon salt and the sugar. Pour in boiling water to a depth of 1 inch. Cover, bring to boiling point, and cook 10 minutes or only until carrots are crisp-tender. Drain. Add the Béchamel Sauce and cream and cook, uncovered, stirring frequently, until the sauce is very creamy, 2 to 3 minutes. Add black pepper to taste and adjust the salt. Turn the carrots into the center of a warmed serving dish. Toss the peas with the butter, season to taste with salt and black pepper, and arrange them in the dish around the carrots. Makes 6 servings.

⚜ CREAMED CARROTS (*Carottes à la Crème*)

1 pound young tender carrots	salt and ground black pepper
boiling water to cover	½ teaspoon sugar
3 tablespoons butter	⅓ cup heavy cream

Wash the carrots and trim both ends, but leave them whole with skins on. (If large old carrots are used, they must be peeled and sliced.) Blanch in boiling water for 5 minutes, rinse under running cold water, and if carrots were not peeled slip off the skins. Sauté the carrots in the butter in a heavy skillet. Sprinkle with salt, pepper, and the sugar. Cover and cook slowly 5 minutes. Add the cream, cover, and simmer until carrots are tender. Makes 4 servings.

⚜ GLAZED CARROTS (*Carottes Glacées*)

1 pound young tender carrots	3 tablespoons butter
1 tablespoon sugar	boiling bouillon, broth, or water
¼ teaspoon salt	chopped parsley

Wash and scrape the carrots. Leave whole if small, cut in lengthwise halves if medium-sized or large. Place the carrots in a saucepan with the sugar, salt, and butter and barely enough boiling bouillon, broth, or water to cover. Cook, uncovered, until carrots are crisp-tender and the liquid is reduced to a syrupy consistency, giving the carrots an attractive glaze. Turn the carrots into a warmed serving dish and sprinkle with parsley. Makes 4 servings.

❧ CARROTS COOKED WITH POTATOES (*Carottes Panachées*)

4 medium-sized carrots
4 potatoes, 1½ inches in diameter
¾ teaspoon salt

boiling water
2 tablespoons butter
1½ tablespoons chopped parsley

Wash and peel the carrots and the potatoes and cut them into slices ⅛ inch thick. Place them in a 1½-quart saucepan with salt and ½ inch boiling water. Cover, bring to boiling point, and cook 8 minutes or only until carrots and potatoes are tender. Drain off water. Add the butter and parsley. Toss lightly. Makes 4 servings.

❧ CARROTS VICHY (*Carottes Vichy*)

16 young tender carrots
3 tablespoons butter
½ teaspoon salt
1 teaspoon sugar

boiling water
⅟₁₆ teaspoon ground black pepper
chopped parsley

Wash and scrape the carrots, slice thin, and place in a saucepan with the butter, salt, and sugar. Add enough boiling water barely to cover them. Cover the pan, bring to boiling point, and boil rapidly until carrots are about half done. Remove the cover and cook until all the liquid has evaporated and you can hear the carrots sizzling in the butter. Add the black pepper and parsley, toss lightly, and transfer the carrots to a serving dish. Makes 4 servings.

CELERY AND CELERIAC
(*Céleri en Branches et Céleri-Rave*)

Celeriac or celery root (*céleri-rave*) is the subtly flavored, tough, knobby root of one variety of celery. To make celeriac easier to peel, to soften it, and to make the flavor more delicate, slice it first and then peel the slices. Blanch them 1 to 2 minutes in boiling water, and then rinse in cold water if the celeriac is to be used raw, or marinate in salt and lemon juice, using 1½ teaspoons salt and 1½ teaspoons lemon juice to 1 pound celeriac. All recipes for raw and cooked celery may also be applied to celeriac.

❧ CELERIAC FRITTERS (*Céleri-Rave en Beignets*)

2 celeriac, cut in ½-inch crosswise slices and peeled	flour
boiling water to cover	1 large egg, beaten
½ teaspoon salt	fine dry breadcrumbs
	lightly seasoned tomato sauce

Slice and peel the celeriac. Place the slices, the salt, and boiling water to cover in a 1-quart saucepan. Cover and cook 20 minutes or until celeriac is almost tender. Drain well. Roll the celeriac slices in flour; then, taking a tablespoonful at a time, dip in the beaten egg and roll in fine dry breadcrumbs. Fry in deep fat preheated to 375° F. Drain on paper towels. Serve with a lightly seasoned tomato sauce. Makes 4 servings.

❧ CELERIAC MÉNAGÈRE (*Céleri-Rave à la Ménagère*)

2 celeriac, cut in 2-inch pieces and peeled	2 medium-sized carrots, sliced
boiling water to cover	2 tablespoons butter
½ teaspoon salt	2 medium-sized tomatoes
2 small white onions, sliced	salt and ground black pepper to taste
	¼ cup bouillon

Place the first 3 ingredients in a 1-quart saucepan. Cover and let stand 15 minutes over very low heat. Drain well. Set aside. Cook the sliced onions and carrots in the butter in a baking pan until lightly browned. Add the celeriac. Peel and seed the tomatoes, cut them into quarters, and arrange them on top. Sprinkle with salt and ground black pepper. Pour the bouillon over all. Bake in a preheated moderate oven (350° F.) 20 to 30 minutes or until vegetables are tender. Makes 4 servings.

❧ Celery Ménagère

In the preceding recipe replace the celeriac with 1½ cups 1-inch pieces of celery ribs. Makes 4 servings.

❧ CELERIAC WITH PARMESAN CHEESE
(*Céleri-Rave au Parmesan*)

3 celeriac, cut into 2-inch pieces and peeled	2 tablespoons flour
boiling water to cover	½ cup milk or light cream
salt	½ cup chicken broth or veal stock
2 tablespoons butter	6 tablespoons grated Parmesan cheese
	1/16 teaspoon ground black pepper

Cook the celeriac in boiling water with ½ teaspoon salt until tender. Melt the butter in a 1-quart saucepan. Remove the pan from the heat and blend in the flour. Stir and cook 1 to 2 minutes or until the mixture foams. Add the milk or light cream and the broth or stock. Stir and cook until the mixture is of medium thickness, about 4 minutes. Add 3 tablespoons of the cheese, the black pepper, and salt to taste. Drain the celeriac and add to the sauce. Turn into a buttered 1-quart casserole. Sprinkle with the remaining grated cheese. Brown under broiler heat. If desired, replace the Parmesan cheese with the same amount of grated Gruyère cheese. Makes 4 servings.

⚜ CELERY WITH GRAVY *(Céleri en Branches au Jus)*

8 ribs of celery
boiling water
2 small white onions, sliced
1 medium-sized carrot, sliced

ground black pepper
½ cup rich bouillon
veal gravy

Wash the celery, remove the leaves, and cut each rib into 4 piéces. Put the celery in a saucepan, pour in boiling water to cover, and let stand 15 minutes over the lowest heat possible. Drain. Transfer the celery to a 1-quart casserole. Cover with the sliced onions and carrots. Sprinkle with black pepper. Pour in the bouillon. Cover and cook over very low heat until vegetables are tender, about 30 minutes. Drain off the bouillon. Serve with good veal gravy. Makes 4 servings.

⚜ CELERY MILANESE STYLE *(Céleri en Branches à la Milanaise)*

10 ribs of celery, cut in 1-inch pieces
½ inch boiling water, veal stock, or
   chicken stock
½ teaspoon salt

2 tablespoons butter
¼ cup grated Parmesan cheese
chopped parsley

Place the celery, the boiling water or stock, and the salt in a 1½-quart saucepan. Cover and cook 15 to 20 minutes or until celery is tender. Drain well. Add the butter, cover, and let stand until butter is melted. Turn into a warmed serving dish. Sprinkle with grated Parmesan cheese and chopped parsley. Makes 4 servings.

CHESTNUTS *(Marrons)*

⚜ HOW TO PEEL CHESTNUTS

Four methods of peeling chestnuts follow.
Skillet. Slit each chestnut with a sharp knife. Put them in a skillet with enough

oil to coat them. Stir and cook over moderate heat about 10 minutes. Let cool. When chestnuts are cool enough to handle, remove the shells and skins with a sharp knife.

Oven. Slit the chestnuts and coat them with oil as in the skillet method. Bake in a preheated very hot oven (450° F.) 20 minutes. Cool. Remove shells and skins with a sharp knife.

Deep Fat. Cut all around the chestnuts with a sharp knife. Place a few of them at a time in a wire basket or sieve, and immerse them in deep fat preheated to 375° F. until the shells open of their own accord. Drain the chestnuts well on paper towels. When cool enough to handle, remove shells and skins.

Boiling. Slit each shell and place chestnuts in boiling water to cover. Boil 20 minutes. Drain and cool. Peel off shells and skins.

⚜ BRAISED CHESTNUTS (*Marrons Braisés*)

Peel 1½ pounds chestnuts, using one of the preceding methods. Place them in a buttered casserole with 1 rib of celery cut into quarters. Sprinkle with ¼ teaspoon salt. Add enough strong veal stock to cover the chestnuts. Cover and bake in a preheated moderate oven (350° F.) 45 to 50 minutes or until chestnuts are tender. Adjust the salt. Serve with game, poultry, or meat. Makes 6 servings.

⚜ CHESTNUT PURÉE (*Purée de Marrons*)

2 pounds chestnuts, peeled	2 tablespoons butter
1 slice celeriac, or ¼ cup sliced celery	stock, milk, or heavy cream
boiling bouillon, or boiling water and	
½ teaspoon salt	

Place the chestnuts, celeriac or celery, and 1 inch boiling bouillon or water in a saucepan. Add salt if water is used. Cover. Bring to boiling point and cook 15 to 20 minutes or until the chestnuts are soft enough to put through a sieve or food mill. Purée the chestnuts. Add the butter. Thin with stock, milk, or cream to the consistency desired. Serve hot. Makes 6 servings.

CHICORY AND ENDIVE (*Chicorée et Endive*)

The three commonly used plants of the chicory family are often confused because the common names differ in different countries and are sometimes interchanged.

Belgian or French endive, or *witloof chicory,* has fleshy (blanched) leaves in

tight, slender, pointed heads, 4 to 6 inches long and 1 to 2 inches wide.
Chicory, or curly endive, has narrow, finely cut, curly leaves in a loose head, dark green shading to butternut yellow or white at the center.
Escarole, or *broad-leaf endive,* resembles chicory in shape and color, but the leaves are broad and curled at the edges.

All types of chicory have a slightly bitter flavor. The plants are most often used in salads, but they also may be cooked. Recipes for cooking all three varieties are grouped here.

⚜ BOILED CHICORY (*Chicorée Cuite*)

2½ pounds chicory (curly endive)
boiling water to cover
salt

1 cup Béchamel Sauce (page 38)
¹/₁₆ teaspoon ground nutmeg
¹/₁₆ teaspoon ground black pepper

Wash the chicory. Cut off the white parts of the leaves and reserve for salads. Place the green portions in a large saucepan, cover with boiling water, and add 1 teaspoon salt to each 1 quart water. Cover and cook until the chicory is very tender. (To test for tenderness, eat a leaf.) Drain, rinse in cold water, and squeeze out excess water with the hands. Chop fine, add the Béchamel Sauce, and simmer 3 to 4 minutes. Add salt to taste, and the nutmeg and black pepper. Serve as a vegetable. Makes 4 servings.

⚜ CREAMED CHICORY (*Chicorée à la Crème*)

2¼ pounds chicory (curly endive)
1 pound escarole (broad-leaf endive)
boiling water to cover
salt
1½ tablespoons flour
1½ tablespoons softened butter

½ cup bouillon
¹/₁₆ teaspoon ground black pepper
½ cup Béchamel Sauce (page 38)
2 tablespoons light cream
croutons fried in butter

Wash the chicory and escarole. Cut off the white parts of the leaves and re-serve for salads. Place the green portions in a 2½-quart saucepan with boiling water to cover, 1 teaspoon salt to each quart water. Cover and cook about 1 hour. Drain off the water, and rinse well in cold water. With the hands, squeeze out all the liquid. Chop the greens medium-fine. Blend the flour with the butter and add to the greens. Add the bouillon, the black pepper, and salt to taste. Turn into a buttered 1½-quart casserole. Cover and braise in a pre-heated moderate oven (350° F.) 45 minutes. Then transfer to another pan and add the Béchamel Sauce and cream. Cook over low heat 3 to 4 minutes. Serve surrounded with fried croutons. Makes 5 to 6 servings.

❧ BRAISED ENDIVE (*Endives Braisées*)

4 large or 8 small heads Belgian
  endive
3 tablespoons butter
¼ teaspoon salt

1 tablespoon lemon juice
3 tablespoons boiling water
chopped parsley
about ½ cup leftover gravy (optional)

Trim the base of the endive heads and discard any damaged or wilted leaves. Hold the heads, one at a time, under cold running water, and drain them well. Spread 1 tablespoon of the butter over the bottom of a 10- by 6- by 2-inch baking dish. Split large endives in half lengthwise and leave small ones whole. Put a layer of endive on the bottom of the dish. Sprinkle with salt and lemon juice, and dot with 1 tablespoon butter. Repeat with a second layer of endive, using the remaining butter. Add the boiling water. Cover the baking pan with foil and simmer over moderately low heat 10 minutes. Remove the foil, bring to boiling point, and cook until the liquid is reduced to 2 tablespoons. Place a piece of foil directly over the endive. Then cover the baking dish with another piece of foil. Bake in a preheated moderate oven (350° F.) for 1 hour. Remove the foil which covers the casserole but leave the foil over the endive, and bake 30 minutes. Remove the foil, sprinkle with chopped parsley, and serve promptly. Or if desired, heat leftover gravy, pour it over the endive, and place it under the broiler briefly to brown. Sprinkle with chopped parsley and serve. Makes 4 servings.

❧ HAM AND ENDIVE AU GRATIN (*Endives au Jambon Gratinées*)

4 large heads Belgian endive
4 tablespoons butter
1 cup Béchamel Sauce (page 38)
4 slices lean ham

⅓ cup grated Gruyère or Cheddar
  cheese
2 tablespoons chopped parsley

Trim the base of the endive heads and discard any damaged leaves. Wash and cook in 2 tablespoons softened butter according to directions for Braised Endive. Spread ⅓ cup of the Béchamel Sauce over the bottom of a 10- by 6- by 2-inch baking dish. Roll each braised endive in a slice of cooked ham, and place the rolls in the dish over the sauce. Stir 3 tablespoons of the cheese into the remaining ⅔ cup Béchamel Sauce and pour over the endives. Sprinkle the top with the remaining cheese. Dot with the remaining 2 tablespoons butter. Brown under moderate broiler heat. Sprinkle with chopped parsley. Makes 4 servings.

366

EGGPLANT (*Aubergines*)

⚜ FRIED EGGPLANT (*Aubergines à la Meunière*)

1 medium-large eggplant
1½ teaspoons salt
flour
⅔ cup fine dry breadcrumbs
⅓ cup grated Parmesan cheese

¼ teaspoon ground black pepper
1 large egg yolk
1 tablespoon milk
oil, lard, or vegetable shortening

Wash the eggplant, cut into crosswise slices ½ inch thick, and remove the peel. Sprinkle the slices with ¾ teaspoon of the salt and let them drain 30 minutes. Wipe dry and dredge with flour. Mix the remaining ¾ teaspoon of the salt with the breadcrumbs, cheese, and black pepper and set aside. Beat the egg yolk with the milk. Set aside. Roll the floured eggplant slices in the breadcrumb mixture, then dip in the beaten egg and milk, and again roll in the crumb mixture. Fry until golden in ¼ inch hot oil, lard, or vegetable shortening, about 4 to 5 minutes on each side. Makes 4 to 5 servings.

⚜ EGGPLANT FRIED IN DEEP FAT (*Aubergines Frites*)

1 large eggplant
1 large egg
1 tablespoon milk
1 teaspoon salt

⅛ teaspoon ground black pepper
fine dry breadcrumbs or fine cracker
   crumbs

Wash the eggplant and cut into crosswise slices ½ inch thick. Peel the slices and cut crosswise into finger-length strips ½ inch wide. Set aside. Beat the egg with the milk, salt, and black pepper, and dip the eggplant strips into the mixture. Then roll the strips in breadcrumbs or cracker crumbs. Set aside 10 minutes to dry. Then fry until golden in deep fat preheated to 350° F. Drain on paper towels. Makes 4 to 5 servings.

⚜ EGGPLANT PROVENÇAL STYLE (*Aubergines à la Provençale*)

1 large eggplant
salt
flour
olive oil or salad oil

3 medium-sized tomatoes
ground black pepper
½ small clove garlic, crushed
chopped parsley

367

Wash the eggplant, cut it into crosswise slices ½ inch thick, remove the peel and cut the slices into ½-inch cubes. Sprinkle the cubes with ¼ teaspoon salt and let stand 20 minutes. Dredge the cubes in flour and sauté in about ¼ cup hot oil, adding it as needed. In the meantime, peel, seed, and quarter the tomatoes, and, in a separate pan, sauté them quickly in 2 tablespoons hot oil. Add the tomatoes to the eggplant and mix quickly. Season to taste with salt, black pepper, and garlic. Cook the vegetables together 5 minutes. Turn into a serving dish and sprinkle with chopped parsley. Makes 4 servings.

⚜ STUFFED EGGPLANT BOSTON STYLE
(*Aubergines Farcies à la Boston*)

3 medium-small eggplants
½ cup olive oil or salad oil
⅓ cup Béchamel Sauce (page 38)
1 egg, beaten lightly

salt and ground black pepper
1 cup grated Gruyère or Cheddar cheese
⅓ cup heavy cream

Wash the eggplants and cut them in lengthwise halves. Make several crosswise cuts in the meat with a knife, without piercing the skin. Pour the oil into a baking pan large enough to accommodate the eggplants and heat it. Place the eggplants, cut side down, in the hot oil and bake them until the meat can be easily scooped out, leaving the shell intact. Chop the eggplant meat and mix well with the Béchamel Sauce, beaten egg, salt and black pepper to taste, and ½ cup of the cheese. Stuff the shells with this mixture, sprinkle with the remaining grated cheese, and place them in a baking pan. Brown in a preheated hot oven (400° F.). Salt the cream lightly and just before serving pour a little over the top of each eggplant half. Makes 6 servings.

FENNEL (*Fenouil*)

Fennel, which somewhat resembles celery, is a plant of Italian origin not very common in the United States. It has an anise flavor. The fleshy bulbous stem at the base of the leaf stalk may be prepared like celery. The feathery leaves are used as a condiment in dishes where an anise flavor is desired. These leaves may be dried for use as a seasoning when fresh fennel is out of season.

⚜ FENNEL PROVENÇAL STYLE (*Fenouil à la Provençale*)

3 stalks (1 pound) fennel
boiling water to cover
5 tablespoons butter
¼ cup bouillon
1 small onion, chopped fine

½ clove garlic, crushed
2 cups diced fresh tomatoes or canned tomatoes
salt and ground black pepper to taste
½ teaspoon sugar (optional)

↑ Assortment of Potatoes: Soufflé, Pont Neuf, Chips, Straw, Wafers, Potato and Raisin Croquettes (pages 386, 386, 387, 387, 387, 388)   ↓ Vegetable Platter (page 347)

Stuffed Zucchini Oriental Style (page 396)

↓ Artichoke Bottoms au Gratin (page 349) 37**1**

↑ Salad with Hard-Cooked Eggs (page 402)   ↓ Stuffed Tomatoes Piedmont Style (page 393)

Separate the fennel stalks into ribs, wash thoroughly, and discard any that are tough. Cut the ribs into 1-inch lengths, cover with boiling water, and let stand for 5 minutes. Drain well. Melt 4 tablespoons (½ stick) of the butter in a heavy saucepan, add the fennel and then the bouillon, cover, and cook very slowly 30 to 40 minutes or until fennel is tender. Sauté the onion and garlic in the remaining 1 tablespoon butter until the onion begins to color. Add to the fennel, along with the remaining ingredients. Cover and cook 10 minutes. Makes 4 to 5 servings.

JERUSALEM ARTICHOKES (*Topinambours*)

Jerusalem artichokes are tubers of firm consistency which resemble globe artichokes in flavor, although they are an entirely different vegetable.

⚜ HOW TO COOK JERUSALEM ARTICHOKES

To prepare Jerusalem artichokes, peel the tubers carefully and drop them in cold water immediately to prevent discoloration. Then blanch briefly in boiling water, drain, and simmer in butter until tender. Season to taste with salt and ground black pepper. Or, if desired, serve with Béchamel Sauce (page 38).

Large Jerusalem artichokes may be sliced, blanched, dipped in Fritter Batter (page 24) and fried in hot deep fat. They may also be cooked in boiling water until tender, drained, and puréed. The sliced cooked tubers may be chilled and put into vegetable salads.

LEEKS (*Poireaux*)

⚜ BOILED LEEKS (*Poireaux en Branches*)

4 bunches leeks	3 tablespoons butter
½ teaspoon salt	ground black pepper to taste
boiling water	chopped parsley

Cut off and discard the green tops of the leeks and the whiskers from the root ends. Remove one or two layers of the white skin. Wash the leeks in luke-warm water and rinse under cold running water to make sure all sand is removed. Drain. Place the leeks in a saucepan with the salt. Pour in boiling water to a depth of 1 inch. Cover and cook 15 to 20 minutes or until leeks are barely tender. Drain well. Add the butter and black pepper. Cover and let stand 2 to 3 minutes or until the butter melts. Transfer to a warm serving dish and sprinkle with chopped parsley. Serve as a vegetable. Makes 6 servings.

❧ BRAISED LEEKS (*Poireaux Braisés*)

12 large leeks, white parts only
boiling water
salt
1 tablespoon butter

1 tablespoon flour
½ cup bouillon
⅛ teaspoon ground black pepper
1 teaspoon lemon juice

Place the leeks in a casserole and cover with boiling water. Add ½ teaspoon salt and let stand 2 to 3 minutes. Pour off the water. Melt the butter, blend in the flour, and cook until the mixture is golden. Add the bouillon and cook 1 minute. Add the black pepper and season to taste with salt. Pour over the leeks. Cover with foil. Cook in a preheated slow oven (300° F.) 1½ to 2 hours or until leeks are very tender. If the cooking liquid is too thin, thicken it with a roux made with 1 tablespoon flour blended with 1 tablespoon softened butter. Add the lemon juice just before serving. Makes 4 servings.

LENTILS (*Lentilles*)

❧ LENTILS LORRAINE STYLE (*Lentilles à la Lorraine*)

The Lorraine district of France is known for hearty and delicious dishes. Lentils may be cooked in any way suitable for dried beans or peas.

1½ cups dried lentils
cold water
2 teaspoons salt
1 cup chopped onion
¼ pound salt pork, diced fine

3 tablespoons butter
1½ tablespoons flour
¼ teaspoon ground black pepper
chopped parsley

Wash the lentils and cover them with cold water. Cover and refrigerate overnight. Before cooking, drain the lentils and put them into a large kettle. Cover with cold water again and add the salt. Bring the water to boiling point, reduce heat, cover, and simmer about 2 hours or until lentils are tender, stirring several times. Drain well. Brown the onion and the salt pork in 1 tablespoon of the butter. Add the cooked lentils and 1 cup of their liquor. Soften the remaining 2 tablespoons butter and blend with the flour. Add to the lentils and cook 5 minutes. Add the pepper. Serve hot, sprinkled with chopped parsley. Makes 4 to 5 servings.

LETTUCE (*Laitue*)

⚜ BRAISED LETTUCE (*Laitues Braisées*)

4 heads Boston lettuce
1 teaspoon salt
boiling water
4 slices bacon or thinly sliced salt pork
2 tablespoons finely chopped white onion

2 tablespoons finely chopped carrot
⅛ teaspoon ground black pepper
⅔ cup beef stock or bouillon
chopped parsley
2 tablespoons butter, melted

Remove any damaged leaves from the lettuce, and wash it thoroughly, leaving the heads intact. Place in a large saucepan with 1 teaspoon salt and boiling water to cover. Cover and cook 2 to 3 minutes. Drain and press the heads lightly with a clean dry cloth to free them from water. Cut each head in half. Arrange the bacon or salt pork in the bottom of a buttered casserole. Sprinkle with the onion and carrot. Press the leaves of the lettuce heads close together and place them, flat side down, in the casserole over the vegetables. Cook a few minutes over low surface heat. Sprinkle with the black pepper. Add the bouillon. Cover the casserole with foil and bake 45 to 50 minutes. Transfer the lettuce to a warm serving dish and keep hot. Reduce the cooking liquid to one-half the original amount and pour it over the lettuce. Just before serving sprinkle with parsley and the melted butter. Serve promptly. Makes 4 servings.

MUSHROOMS (*Champignons*)

⚜ MUSHROOMS BORDEAUX STYLE (*Cèpes à la Bordelaise*)

Cèpes, commoner in France than in America, are an edible fungus. Mushrooms can be substituted in any recipe calling for cèpes.

1 pound fresh mushrooms or cèpes
3 tablespoons butter
salt and ground black pepper

1 tablespoon chopped shallots or chopped white onion
2 tablespoons hot olive oil or salad oil
chopped parsley

Wash the mushrooms. Break off the stems and set them aside. Slice the caps and sauté them in 1 tablespoon of the butter. Season with salt and black pepper to taste. Add the shallots or onion and sauté 1 to 2 minutes. Brown the remaining 2 tablespoons butter and pour it over the mushrooms. Keep warm. Chop the mushroom stems fine, and, in a separate skillet, sauté them in the hot oil until they are crisp. Season with salt and black pepper to taste and sprinkle over the sliced mushrooms. Garnish with chopped parsley. Makes 4 servings.

❦ Mushrooms Provençal Style (*Cèpes à la Provençale*)

Prepare Mushrooms Bordeaux Style, replacing the shallots or onion with 1 small clove garlic, chopped fine, and the butter with the same amount of oil. Makes 4 servings.

❦ CREAMED MUSHROOMS (*Champignons à la Crème*)

1¼ pounds mushrooms
3 tablespoons butter
1 tablespoon flour
1 cup hot light cream
¾ teaspoon salt
1/16 teaspoon ground white pepper
¼ teaspoon lemon juice
4 pieces hot toast
chopped parsley

Wash the mushrooms. Remove the stems and reserve them for other uses. Cut the large caps in halves or quarters; leave the small ones whole. Heat the butter in a 1½-quart saucepan, add the mushrooms, and sauté them 8 minutes or until they are golden. Add the flour and mix in well. Stir in the cream and cook over low heat 15 minutes. Add the salt, white pepper, and lemon juice. Place on hot toast and sprinkle with chopped parsley. Makes 4 servings.

❦ MUSHROOMS WITH HERBS
(*Chanterelles ou Girolles aux Fines Herbes*)

Chanterelles are yellow mushrooms popular in France; they are also known as *girolles*. Other mushrooms can be substituted in recipes.

1 pound mushrooms
3 tablespoons butter
½ teaspoon salt
1/16 teaspoon ground black pepper
dash nutmeg
2 tablespoons chopped chives or parsley

Wash the mushrooms and slice them, using both caps and stems. Melt 2 tablespoons of the butter in a saucepan, add the mushrooms, cover, and simmer 5 minutes. Add the remaining 1 tablespoon butter and the salt, black pepper, and nutmeg. Cover and cook 2 to 3 minutes longer. Add the chives or parsley. Serve hot. Makes 4 servings.

⚜ MUSHROOM RAGOUT (*Ragoût de Chanterelles*)

1 pound mushrooms	¼ teaspoon dried thyme leaves
5 tablespoons butter	¼ cup dry red wine
1 shallot, or white part of 1 green onion, chopped	½ cup bouillon or chicken broth
2 tablespoons flour	salt and black pepper to taste
	chopped parsley

Wash the mushrooms, leaving the stems attached. Cut the larger ones into halves or quarters; leave the small ones whole. Melt 2 tablespoons of butter in a saucepan, add the mushrooms and the shallot, and cook 10 minutes. Drain the mushrooms, saving the liquor. Melt the remaining 3 tablespoons butter in a saucepan, and blend in the flour and thyme. Stir and cook until the mixture foams. Add the wine, the bouillon or broth, and the liquor drained from the mushrooms. Stir and cook 3 to 4 minutes or until the sauce has thickened. Add the cooked mushrooms and salt and pepper to taste. Sprinkle with chopped parsley. Makes 4 servings.

⚜ MUSHROOMS SAUTÉED IN BUTTER
(*Chanterelles ou Girolles Sautées au Beurre*)

This is the most popular way of preparing mushrooms. Mushrooms are excellent with game or eggs.

1 pound mushrooms	salt and ground black pepper to taste
3 tablespoons butter	3 drops lemon juice

Wash the mushrooms and slice them, using caps and stems. Melt the butter in a saucepan, add the mushrooms, and cook briskly 3 minutes. Reduce the heat and cook until mushrooms are golden. Sprinkle with salt, black pepper, and lemon juice. Serve promptly. Makes 4 servings.

⚜ STEWED MUSHROOMS (*Cèpes Étuvés*)

1¼ pounds mushrooms	¼ teaspoon salt
2 tablespoons butter	¼ cup boiling water or chicken stock or veal stock
1 teaspoon lemon juice	

Try to get mushrooms of approximately uniform size. Wash the mushrooms. Remove the stems and reserve them for other uses. If the caps are large, cut them in half; if small, leave them whole. Place the caps in a saucepan with the remaining ingredients. Cover and cook 3 to 5 minutes. Makes 4 servings.

HEARTS OF PALM (*Coeurs de Palmier*)

Palm hearts are the tender terminal fronds or stems of certain palm trees. In the United States they are available fresh in localities in which they are grown, and in cans in fancy food stores elsewhere. In Europe they are sold only in cans. Hearts of palm may be prepared in any way suitable for asparagus.

❧ HOW TO COOK HEARTS OF PALM

To prepare fresh hearts of palm, peel the stalks and boil them until tender in boiling salted water (¼ teaspoon salt to 1 cup water). Drain and serve hot with Béchamel, Velouté, or Mornay Sauce or Brown Butter (see Index). Or serve cold with Vinaigrette Sauce (page 56).

   To prepare canned hearts of palm, drain a 1-pound 10-ounce can, and cut the hearts in 1-inch pieces. Sauté in 2 tablespoons butter over low heat, shaking the pan from time to time, and turning once, using 2 forks so as not to break or bruise the pieces. (Do not brown.) Transfer the hearts of palm to a warmed serving dish, and pour melted butter or Brown Butter over them. Canned hearts of palm may also be drained and served cold with Vinaigrette Sauce. Makes 6 servings.

❧ HEARTS OF PALM AU GRATIN
   (*Coeurs de Palmier au Gratin*)

1 can (1 pound 10 ounces) hearts of
   palm
1 cup Italian Sauce (page 46)
¼ cup grated Parmesan cheese
½ cup soft breadcrumbs

2 tablespoons butter

Drain the liquid from the hearts of palm into a saucepan and set aside. Split the stems and cut them into 3-inch lengths. Heat them in the liquid from the can. With a perforated spoon, carefully transfer the palm hearts to a baking dish. Cover with the Italian Sauce and sprinkle with the cheese and breadcrumbs. Dot with the butter. Bake in a preheated hot oven (400° F.) 10 to 15 minutes or until browned. Makes 6 servings.

PEAS (*Pois*)

⚜ GREEN PEAS ENGLISH STYLE (*Petits Pois à l'Anglaise*)

2 cups shelled fresh green peas (2
  pounds in shells)
¼ teaspoon sugar
½ teaspoon salt, or salt to taste

boiling water
2 tablespoons butter
⅛ teaspoon ground black pepper

Wash the peas and put them in a 1½-quart saucepan. Add the sugar and salt
and pour in boiling water to a depth of ½ inch. Cook, uncovered, 5 minutes.
Cover and cook over moderate heat only until peas are tender. Drain off any
excess water. Shake the pan over the heat to dry the peas. Add the butter
and black pepper, and additional salt if needed. Makes 4 to 5 servings.

⚜ GREEN PEAS FRENCH STYLE (*Petits Pois à la Française*)

2 cups shelled fresh green peas (2
  pounds in shells)
2 tablespoons butter
12 small white onions
1 stalk parsley
¼ teaspoon sugar
½ teaspoon salt

¼ teaspoon dried chervil, or 1 teaspoon chopped fresh chervil
¼ cup boiling water
3 to 4 lettuce leaves, shredded
1 teaspoon flour
⅛ teaspoon ground black pepper

Wash the peas and place them in a saucepan with 1 tablespoon of the butter
and the next 6 ingredients. Strew the shredded lettuce over the peas. Cover
and cook over moderate heat until only 2 to 3 tablespoons water remains in
the pan, about 25 minutes. Blend the flour with the remaining tablespoon
butter and add to the peas. Shake the pan over the heat in a circular motion
to blend the roux with the pan liquid. (If stirred, peas will break.) Remove
the peas from the heat when boiling point is reached. Remove and discard the
parsley stalk. Serve promptly. Makes 4 to 5 servings.

⚜ GREEN PEAS HOME STYLE
(*Petits Pois à la Bonne-Femme ou à la Ménagère*)

2 cups shelled fresh green peas (2
  pounds in shells)
4 slices (3 ounces) lean salt pork
1 tablespoon butter
1 small white onion, chopped

2 teaspoons flour
⅓ cup stock or water
¼ teaspoon salt
⅛ teaspoon ground black pepper

Wash the peas and set them aside to drain. Rinse the salt pork in hot water and cut it into dice. Place it in a 1½-quart saucepan with the butter and onion. Stir and cook until pork and onion are golden. Sprinkle with the flour and mix well. Stir and cook 1 minute. Add the stock or water and the salt and mix well. Add the peas. Cover and cook 10 to 15 minutes or until peas are tender. Season with the black pepper. Makes 4 to 5 servings.

⚜ GREEN PEAS WITH MINT (*Petits Pois à la Menthe*)

2 cups shelled fresh peas (2 pounds in shells)
1½ tablespoons chopped fresh mint leaves
½ teaspoon salt
boiling water
2 tablespoons butter

⅟₁₆ teaspoon ground black pepper
4 to 5 whole mint leaves

Wash the peas, drain, and place in a saucepan with the chopped mint leaves and the salt. Pour in boiling water to a depth of ½ inch. Bring to boiling point and cook, uncovered, 5 minutes. Cover and cook 5 minutes or until peas are almost done. Drain off the water, add the butter, cover, and simmer 3 to 4 minutes or until peas are tender. Add the black pepper, and toss very lightly to avoid breaking the peas. Turn into a warmed serving dish. Garnish with the fresh whole mint leaves. Makes 4 to 5 servings.

⚜ SPLIT-PEA PURÉE (*Purée de Pois Cassés*)

2 cups dried split peas
4 cups cold water
¼ pound lean salt pork, diced
½ cup diced onion
½ cup diced carrots
½ teaspoon salt, or salt to taste

⅛ teaspoon ground black pepper
2 tablespoons butter

Wash the split peas and place them in a saucepan with the cold water. Brown the diced salt pork in a skillet and add it to the peas along with the onion and carrots. Soak 1 hour. Do not drain. Cover, bring to boiling point, reduce heat, and simmer 1½ hours. Add the salt and cook 30 to 40 minutes or until peas are well done. Push the peas through a coarse sieve. Stir in the black pepper and butter. This purée should be very thick. Makes 6 servings.

PEPPERS (*Poivrons*)

⚜ PEPPERS STUFFED WITH SAUSAGE (*Poivrons Farcis au Gras*)

6 medium-sized green or red sweet
  peppers
boiling water
salt
½ cup chopped onion
1 small clove garlic, crushed
1¼ pounds lean pork sausage
2 cups cooked rice

3 tablespoons chopped parsley
⅛ teaspoon ground black pepper
¾ cup beef stock or veal stock
¾ cup soft breadcrumbs
3 tablespoons olive oil or salad oil
¾ cup hot water, stock, or tomato
  juice
1½ cups Tomato Sauce (page 50)

Wash the peppers, cut off the tops, and remove the seeds and pith. Parboil the peppers 3 minutes in boiling water to cover with ½ teaspoon salt. Remove them from the water and invert them on a tray to drain. Cook the onion, garlic, and sausage together until sausage browns. Add the next 4 ingredients and salt if needed. Mix lightly but well. Stuff the mixture into the well-drained peppers. Arrange the peppers in an oiled baking dish and pour the hot water, stock, or tomato juice around them. Mix the breadcrumbs with the oil and sprinkle over the tops of the peppers. Bake in a preheated moderate oven (350° F.) 40 to 50 minutes or until crumbs are brown. Transfer the peppers to a warmed serving dish. Add the Tomato Sauce to the pan liquid, heat, and pour around peppers. Makes 6 servings.

⚜ PEPPERS STUFFED WITH RICE (*Poivrons Farcis au Riz*)

6 medium-sized green or red sweet
  peppers
boiling water
salt
½ cup chopped onion
1 small clove garlic, crushed

1 tablespoon olive oil or salad oil
1 cup peeled, seeded, and diced
  tomatoes
6 tablespoons raw long-grain rice
1 cup bouillon
¼ teaspoon ground black pepper

Wash the peppers, cut off the tops, and remove the seeds and pith. Parboil the peppers with ½ teaspoon salt 3 minutes in boiling water to cover. Remove the peppers from the water and invert on a pan to drain. Cook the onion and garlic in the oil until onion is limp. Add the tomatoes. Soak the rice 5 minutes in boiling water to cover, drain, and add to the onion and tomato mixture. Stir in ½ cup of the bouillon and ½ teaspoon salt, spoon the mixture into the pepper shells, and place them in a baking dish. Pour the boiling water remaining in the pan around the peppers. Cover with foil and bake in a preheated moderate oven (350° F.) 50 to 60 minutes or until rice is tender, basting occasionally with the remaining bouillon. Serve hot. Makes 6 servings.

POTATOES (*Pommes de Terre*)

⚜ CHÂTEAU POTATOES (*Pommes de Terre Château*)

1½ pounds potatoes
salt
cold water

¼ cup (½ stick) butter
⅛ teaspoon ground black pepper
chopped parsley

Peel the potatoes and cut them in pieces the size and shape of large olives. Place them in a saucepan with ¾ teaspoon salt and cold water to cover. Bring the water to boiling point and cook 1 to 2 minutes. Drain the potatoes and cool them in cold water. Drain and dry thoroughly. Melt the butter in a baking pan. Add the potatoes, and stir to coat them with butter. Sprinkle with black pepper and additional salt, if needed. Bake in a preheated moderate oven (375° F.) until potatoes are browned, 30 to 40 minutes. Sprinkle with chopped parsley. Makes 4 servings.

⚜ CREAMED POTATOES (*Pommes de Terre à la Crème*)

4 to 5 medium-sized potatoes
salt
boiling water
⅛ teaspoon ground white pepper

dash ground nutmeg (optional)
hot light cream
2 tablespoons butter

Boil the potatoes in their skins in salted boiling water to cover (1 teaspoon salt to 1 quart water) until they are done. Drain and cool. Remove the skins and slice the potatoes ¼ inch thick. Put the slices in a saucepan and sprinkle with ¼ teaspoon salt, the white pepper, and the nutmeg, if used. Add just enough hot light cream to cover the potatoes. Cook until the cream is reduced to about half the original amount. Add the butter and swirl the pan as the butter melts to blend it with the cream and thicken it slightly. Do not stir. Serve promptly. Makes 4 to 6 servings.

⚜ DAUPHINE POTATOES (*Pommes de Terre Dauphine*)

½ cup butter
1 cup water
2 teaspoons salt
1 cup sifted all-purpose flour
4 large eggs

7 to 8 medium-sized potatoes (2½ pounds)
½ to 1 teaspoon ground nutmeg
⅛ teaspoon ground black pepper

Place the butter, water, and salt in a 1-quart saucepan, bring to boiling point, and add all the flour at one time. Stir and cook over low heat 1 to 2 minutes, or until the mixture leaves the sides of the pan and forms a ball. Cool slightly. Beat in the eggs one at a time. (This is Chou Paste.) Peel the potatoes, boil them, and mash them until fluffy. Add the nutmeg and black pepper. (Do not add any milk or butter.) Add to the Chou Paste and mix well. Shape the mixture into 1-inch balls, or drop it from a tablespoon, or put it into a pastry bag and pipe it in 2-inch lengths. Fry in deep fat preheated to 375° F. 2 to 3 minutes or until browned. Drain on paper towels. Makes 6 to 8 servings.

⚜ POTATOES DAUPHINOIS (*Gratin Dauphinois*)

4 medium-sized potatoes
½ teaspoon salt
¹/₁₆ teaspoon ground black pepper
dash of ground nutmeg

1 cup grated Gruyère or Cheddar cheese
1 large egg, beaten
1 cup milk
2 tablespoons butter

Peel the potatoes, slice thin, and mix with the salt, black pepper, nutmeg, and ½ cup of the cheese. Turn into a buttered 10- by 6- by 2-inch baking dish. Combine the egg and milk, heat (do not boil), and pour over the potatoes. Sprinkle with the remaining ½ cup cheese. Dot with the butter. Cover and bake 15 minutes in a preheated moderate oven (350°F.). Remove cover and bake 25 minutes or until potatoes are soft and browned on top. Makes 4 servings.

⚜ DUCHESS POTATOES (*Pommes de Terre Duchesse*)

Duchess Potatoes are fluffy mashed potatoes into which beaten eggs have been incorporated. They may be served as a separate dish or the mixture put through a pastry bag while hot and formed either into cases for serving creamed dishes or into borders or rosettes for decorating a casserole or planked meat or fish. Duchess Potatoes are also used in making croquettes.

6 medium-sized potatoes (about 2 pounds)
boiling water
1 teaspoon salt

⅛ teaspoon ground black pepper
¼ teaspoon ground nutmeg
2 whole eggs
2 egg yolks

Peel the potatoes and cut them into quarters. Cook in a covered saucepan in 1 inch of boiling water with 1 teaspoon salt until soft but still firm. Drain well. Put the potatoes through a ricer or food mill. Beat until potatoes are smooth. Add the black pepper and nutmeg. Beat the whole eggs and the egg yolks together until they are light and foamy and add them to the potatoes. Whip until fluffy. Brush with beaten egg, milk, or melted butter. Bake in a preheated, very hot oven (450° F.) or under the broiler until browned lightly. Makes 6 servings as a separate dish.

For Duchess Potatoes used as a garnish, put the mixture through a pastry bag and shape as desired. Brush with 1 egg yolk beaten with 1 tablespoon milk or water and bake as directed in the recipe for the dish being garnished.

⚜ LYONNAISE POTATOES (*Pommes de Terre Sautée à la Lyonnaise*)

4 medium-sized potatoes
4 tablespoons butter
2 medium-sized onions

salt and ground black pepper
chopped parsley

Boil the potatoes in their skins until they are done. Cool until they can be handled. Peel, slice thin, and fry in hot butter until browned. Peel the onions, slice thin, and sauté in a separate skillet until brown. Add to the potatoes, sprinkle with salt and black pepper, and mix lightly. Turn into a serving dish. Sprinkle with chopped parsley. Makes 4 servings.

⚜ MAÎTRE D'HÔTEL POTATOES
(*Pommes de Terre à la Maître d'Hôtel*)

4 medium-sized potatoes
½ cup bouillon
2 tablespoons butter
¼ teaspoon salt
1/16 teaspoon ground black pepper

dash nutmeg
½ cup milk
2 teaspoons flour
chopped parsley

Boil the potatoes in their skins until they are done. Cool, peel, slice, and put into a skillet. Add the bouillon, 1 tablespoon of the butter, and the salt, pepper, and nutmeg. Bring to boiling point and cook, uncovered, 5 minutes. Add the milk and cook 2 to 3 minutes. Blend the flour with the remaining 1 tablespoon butter, add to the potatoes, and bring to boiling point. Turn into a warm serving dish. Sprinkle with chopped parsley. Makes 4 servings.

⚜ NEW POTATOES WITH BACON (*Pommes de Terre au Lard*)

2 small white onions, peeled
2 tablespoons butter, melted
2 slices lean bacon
1 tablespoon flour
¾ cup bouillon
2 tablespoons tomato purée

12 small new potatoes, washed and peeled or scraped
¼ teaspoon salt
⅛ teaspoon ground black pepper
chopped parsley

Cook the onions in the melted butter until they are lightly browned. Dice the bacon, add to the onions, and cook until it is brown. Sprinkle with the flour and cook until flour has browned. Stir in the bouillon and tomato purée and cook 4 minutes. Add the potatoes and the salt. Cover and cook 20 minutes or until potatoes are done. Season with the black pepper. Turn into a serving dish and sprinkle with chopped parsley. Makes 4 servings.

⚜ NOISETTE POTATOES

Peel potatoes and with a French melon-ball cutter scoop out balls about the size of hazelnuts. Fry in a heavy skillet in butter. Season with salt and ground black pepper to taste. Allow 6 balls per serving.

⚜ POTATOES NORMANDE (*Pommes de Terre à la Normande*)

2 slices salt pork, ¼ inch thick and
 4 inches long
1 medium-large onion
2 leeks, white part only
2 tablespoons butter

4 medium-sized potatoes
bouillon
¼ teaspoon salt
¹⁄₁₆ teaspoon ground black pepper
chopped parsley

Blanch the salt pork in hot water, drain, and cut into narrow strips. Slice the onion and leeks and fry them, without browning, with salt pork in 1 table-spoon of the butter. Peel the potatoes, slice thin, and add, along with enough bouillon barely to cover the potatoes. Add the salt and black pepper. Cover and cook until the potatoes are done, about 5 to 8 minutes. Add the remaining 1 tablespoon butter and swirl the pan as it melts to blend it with the sauce. Turn into a serving dish. Sprinkle with chopped parsley. Makes 4 servings.

⚜ POTATOES WITH ONIONS (*Pommes de Terre à la Boulangère*)

4 medium-large potatoes
4 medium-sized onions
¾ teaspoon salt

⅛ teaspoon ground black pepper
¾ cup bouillon, beef stock, or veal
 stock

Peel the potatoes and onions. Slice the potatoes ½ inch thick and the onions ¼ inch thick. Mix them together with the salt and black pepper and put them into a well-buttered shallow 1½-quart baking dish. Pour in the bouillon or stock. Cover and cook 15 minutes in a preheated hot oven (400° F.). Remove the cover and continue cooking until the liquid has evaporated and the vegetables begin to roast. Serve with lamb, beef, veal, or pork. Makes 4 servings.

⚜ PARSLEY POTATOES (*Pommes de Terre Persillées*)

12 potatoes, 1½ inches in diameter
¾ teaspoon salt
boiling water

3 tablespoons butter
¹⁄₁₆ teaspoon ground black pepper
chopped parsley

Peel the potatoes and put them in a saucepan with the salt and boiling water to cover. Boil, covered, 20 minutes or until potatoes are done. Drain well. Add the butter and black pepper and shake over low heat until butter is melted. Sprinkle with chopped parsley. Makes 4 servings.

⚜ POTATOES PONT-NEUF (*Pommes de Terre Frites, Dites Pont-Neuf*)

These are similar to the French-Fried Potatoes so popular with Americans.
Peel the potatoes and cut them into rectangular pieces the size of a man's little finger. Wash, drain, and dry them well. Fry a few at a time in deep fat preheated to 375° F. for 7 to 8 minutes until soft, but not browned. Remove from the fat and drain on paper towels. Increase the temperature of the fat to 390° F. and return the potatoes, a few at a time, to the hot fat. Cook 1 to 2 minutes or *only* until they are golden and crisp. Drain on paper towels. Sprinkle with salt and serve at once. Allow 1 medium-sized potato per serving. (*See illustration, page 370.*)

⚜ SAUTÉED POTATOES (*Pommes de Terre Sautées, ou Roesti*)

4 medium-sized potatoes	salt
3 to 4 tablespoons butter	ground black pepper

Boil the potatoes in their skins until they are done. Cool, peel, and slice them or cut them into fine strips. Melt 3 tablespoons of the butter in a 9- or 10-inch skillet, add the potatoes, and sprinkle them with salt and black pepper. Fry the potatoes until they are golden on both sides, adding the remaining 1 tablespoon butter if needed. Turn out onto a warmed platter. Makes 4 servings.

⚜ SAVOYARD POTATOES (*Pommes de Terre à la Savoyarde*)

2 medium-sized onions	1/16 teaspoon ground black pepper
3 tablespoons butter	1/4 pound Gruyère or Cheddar cheese,
4 medium-sized potatoes	sliced
1/4 teaspoon salt	1/2 cup bouillon or veal stock

Peel and slice the onions and brown them lightly in 1½ tablespoons of the butter. Peel the potatoes, slice thin, and put half in a buttered 8- by 8- by 2-inch baking pan. Cover with half the onions, sprinkle with half the salt and black pepper, and place half the cheese on top. Repeat, using the remaining potatoes, onions, salt, and black pepper. Dot with the remaining 1½ tablespoons butter. Pour in the bouillon or stock. Cover with the rest of the cheese. Cover and bake 20 minutes in a preheated moderate oven (350° F.). Remove cover and bake 20 minutes longer or until potatoes are done. Makes 4 servings.

⚜ SOUFFLÉ POTATOES (*Pommes de Terre Soufflées*)

Peel baking potatoes of uniform size and trim the surface so that they will be smooth and regular. Cut the potatoes into pointed ovals a scant ⅛ inch thick. For best results use a potato slicer. Wash the potatoes in cold water and dry them thoroughly. Fill a deep-fat frying kettle half full of cooking oil or salad oil, or rendered beef suet. Preheat to 275° F. Drop a few potato slices at a time into the hot fat. With a large perforated spoon raise the slices, one at a time, from the hot fat for a few seconds and return them to the kettle until they begin to puff, about 7 to 8 minutes. Using a sieve, remove the potatoes from the hot fat, drain them on paper towels, and cool them for at least 5 minutes. The second frying may follow immediately, or, if desired, the potatoes may be finished later in the day or even chilled and finished the next day. The potatoes will deflate but will puff again in the second frying.

For final frying, preheat fat to 400° F. Put a few slices at a time into a wire basket or medium-large sieve and lower it into the hot fat. Potatoes will puff into small oval-shaped balloons. Turn the puffs to brown them on all sides. Remove from the fat and drain on paper towels. Sprinkle with salt and serve immediately. Allow 2 pounds large potatoes for 6 servings. (*See illustration, page 370.*)

⚜ STRAW POTATOES (*Pommes de Terre Paille*)

Peel potatoes and cut them into fine julienne strips. Wash the strips and dry them thoroughly with a clean towel. Fry in deep fat preheated to 375° F. until crisp and golden brown. Drain on paper towels and sprinkle lightly with salt. Allow 1 medium-sized potato per serving. (*See illustration, page 370.*)

⚜ POTATO WAFERS (*Pommes de Terre Gaufrettes*)

Peel potatoes and cut them into thin slices with a special wafer cutter. Run cold water over the slices, drain, and dry thoroughly with a clean cloth. Fry, a few slices at a time, in deep fat preheated to 375° F., until slices are golden. Drain on paper towels. Sprinkle with salt. Allow 1 medium-sized potato per serving. (*See illustration, page 370.*)

⚜ Potato Chips

In the preceding recipe, slice the potatoes with a knife or potato slicer, instead of using the wafer cutter. Proceed as directed in the recipe. (*See illustration, page 370.*)

⚜ POTATO CAKES (*Pommes de Terre Galettes*)

2 cups mashed potatoes	1 large egg
1 tablespoon flour	1 tablespoon minced onion (optional)
½ teaspoon salt, or salt to taste	2 tablespoons milk or light cream
black pepper to taste	4 tablespoons shortening or salad oil

Combine the first 7 ingredients and shape into flat 3-inch cakes. Heat the shortening or oil, add the cakes, and brown them on both sides. Or, if desired, bake them on a buttered baking sheet in a preheated moderate oven (375° F.) 30 to 40 minutes or until browned. Makes 4 servings.

⚜ POTATO CROQUETTES (*Croquettes de Pommes de Terre*)

Prepare the mixture for Dauphine Potatoes (page 382). Add 2 tablespoons butter and 4 egg yolks. Mix well. Form the mixture into pear-shaped croquettes or into rolls or flat cakes. Beat 1 egg with 1 tablespoon milk or water. Roll the croquettes in breadcrumbs, dip into the beaten egg, and roll in crumbs again. Let the croquettes stand about 20 minutes to dry the crumbs. Fry until golden in deep fat preheated to 375° F. Drain on paper towels. Serve promptly. Makes 6 to 8 servings.

⚜ POTATO AND RAISIN CROQUETTES
(*Croquettes de Pommes de Terre aux Raisins*)

These croquettes may be served with game.

2 pounds (6 medium-sized) potatoes
boiling water
1 teaspoon salt
¼ teaspoon ground black pepper
3 whole eggs and 2 egg yolks

½ cup raisins or dried currants
flour
finely chopped almonds or fine dry
    breadcrumbs

Peel and quarter the potatoes. Cook until soft in a covered saucepan with 1 inch boiling water and the salt. Drain well and put through a potato ricer or food mill. Add the pepper. Beat 2 of the whole eggs and the egg yolks together until foamy and add to potatoes. Beat the mixture until fluffy. Stir in the raisins or currants. Sprinkle a pastry board lightly with flour and shape the mixture into pear-shaped croquettes or into balls, using 2 rounded tablespoons of the mixture for each croquette. Beat the remaining egg. Dip the croquettes into the beaten egg, then roll them in chopped almonds or breadcrumbs. Let them stand 20 minutes and then fry in deep fat preheated to 375° F. Drain on paper towels. Makes 6 servings. (*See illustration, page 370.*)

⚜ POTATO DUMPLINGS WITH CHEESE (*Knepfes au Fromage*)

3 medium-sized dry, mealy potatoes
3 large egg yolks
½ teaspoon salt
1 cup sifted all-purpose flour

½ cup (1 stick) butter, melted
1 cup grated Cheddar, Gruyère, or
    Parmesan cheese

Boil the potatoes in their skins until done. Peel them and mash until smooth. Beat in the egg yolks and salt. Continue beating until potatoes are fluffy. Stir in the flour, ¼ cup (½ stick) of the butter, and ½ cup of the cheese. Shape the mixture into 1½-inch balls on a lightly floured flat surface. Flatten the balls slightly with a fork. Poach them, about one-fourth at a time, for about 5 minutes in 2 quarts boiling salted water (1 teaspoon salt to each quart water). Drain well. Fry the balls in the remaining ¼ cup (½ stick) butter until golden. Sprinkle with the remaining ½ cup cheese and serve hot. Makes 6 servings.

❧ Potato Dumplings Polonaise (*Knepfes à la Polonaise*)

Prepare the mixture as in the preceding recipe, omitting the cheese. Shape it into balls, poach, and fry as directed. Sprinkle the dumplings with fine dry breadcrumbs fried in butter. Makes 6 servings.

❧ MOUSSELINE POTATO PURÉE
(*Purée de Pommes de Terre Mousseline*)

6 medium-sized dry, mealy potatoes
¼ cup (½ stick) butter
salt and ground black pepper to taste

dash ground nutmeg
about ½ cup milk or light cream

Peel the potatoes and cut them into halves or quarters. Cook them in boiling salted water to cover (1 teaspoon salt to 1 quart water) until they are soft but not mushy. Drain off the water and dry the potatoes over low heat. Put them through a potato ricer or food mill and return them to the pan. Mix with a wooden spoon until they are smooth. Add the butter, salt and pepper to taste, and the nutmeg and mix well. Heat the milk or cream and gradually beat in enough to obtain a fluffy consistency. Shake the pan over low heat for about 1 minute. Serve promptly. Makes 4 to 5 servings.

SALSIFY (*Salsifis*)

Salsify is also known as oyster plant, because the flavor resembles that of oysters. The roots are first boiled in Acidulated Water (page 162) or Court Bouillon (page 161) until tender and then prepared in various ways.

❧ HOW TO PREPARE AND COOK SALSIFY

The first step in preparing salsify is to choose smooth roots to avoid waste and work in scraping. Remove the stalks and save them for use in salads. Scrub the roots and scrape off all blemishes, using a small paring knife. As they are scraped, place the roots in cold Acidulated Water (2 tablespoons lemon juice or vinegar to 1 quart water) to prevent them from turning dark. Cut the large roots so that all pieces are 3 to 4 inches long or slice them about ⅛ inch thick. Blend 1 tablespoon flour with ¼ cup water until smooth and strain it into a saucepan. Add 1 quart water, 1 tablespoon vinegar, and ½ teaspoon salt. Bring the mixture to boiling point, add the salsify, and cook, uncovered, 50 to 60 minutes or until it is tender. Leave it in the cooking liquid until it is to be used, to prevent discoloration. Salsify can be served as a buttered vegetable, or prepared with a sauce, sautéed, or made into fritters. Allow 2 pounds for 6 servings.

⚜ SALSIFY FRITTERS (*Salsifis Frits*)

2 cups cooked salsify, sliced	¼ teaspoon salt
3 tablespoons chopped parsley	⅛ teaspoon ground black pepper
3 tablespoons lemon juice	Fritter Batter (page 24)
⅓ cup olive oil or salad oil	salt

Marinate the cooked salsify 30 minutes in the next five ingredients. Drain well. Dip each piece of salsify in Fritter Batter and fry in deep fat preheated to 375° F., until golden, about 4 minutes. Drain on paper towels. Sprinkle with salt. Serve hot. Makes 4 to 5 servings.

⚜ SAUTÉED SALSIFY (*Salsifis Sautés*)

Roll boiled salsify in flour seasoned with salt and black pepper (½ teaspoon salt and ¼ teaspoon ground black pepper to each ½ cup sifted flour). Sauté slowly in 2 to 3 tablespoons butter until browned, turning the pieces to brown both sides. Sprinkle with chopped parsley. Allow 2 cups cooked salsify for 4 servings.

⚜ SALSIFY WITH VELOUTÉ SAUCE (*Salsifis au Velouté*)

Make Velouté Sauce (page 40). Add 2 cups cooked salsify. Cover and simmer 10 minutes. Season to taste with salt, ground black pepper, and lemon juice. Serve sprinkled with chopped parsley. Allow 1½ cups cooked salsify for 4 servings.

SORREL (*Oseille*)

Sorrel is also called sour grass. The young leaves are used in salads. It is commonly used in France but not often in the United States.

⚜ SORREL PURÉE

Wash 3 pounds sorrel thoroughly. Cook it, using only the water that clings to the leaves, over moderately high heat for 10 to 15 minutes or until it is soft enough to push through a sieve. Drain well and press out as much water as possible. Rub through a sieve. Add 2 tablespoons butter, and salt and ground black pepper to taste. Makes 4 to 5 servings.

SPINACH (*Épinards*)

⚜ CREAMED SPINACH (*Épinards à la Crème*)

2 pounds fresh spinach, or 2 packages frozen spinach	¼ teaspoon sugar
2 tablespoons butter	salt and ground black pepper to taste
½ cup Béchamel Sauce (page 38)	2 tablespoons heavy cream
	croutons fried in butter

If frozen spinach is used, cook according to package directions. If fresh spinach is used, wash it thoroughly several times, drain, and place it in a saucepan. Cover and cook, without adding water, over moderately low heat *only* until spinach is wilted. Remove cover, press out water from spinach, and shake the pan over moderately low heat to evaporate the liquids. Chop the cooked spinach fine and heat with the butter 2 to 3 minutes. Add the Béchamel Sauce, sugar, and salt and black pepper to taste. Heat 1 to 2 minutes. Transfer to a serving dish and pour the heavy cream over it. Garnish with croutons fried in butter. Serve at once. Makes 4 to 5 servings.

⚜ SPINACH ENGLISH STYLE (*Épinards en Branches à l'Anglaise*)

2 pounds fresh spinach, or 2 packages frozen spinach, cooked	2 tablespoons butter
	salt and ground black pepper to taste

Drain the spinach and press out all the excess water, using the back of a large mixing spoon. Melt the butter in a saucepan, add the spinach, and sauté until it is hot. Season to taste with salt and black pepper. Serve hot. Makes 4 servings.

⚜ PURÉED SPINACH WITH EGGS (*Purée d'Épinards aux Oeufs*)

2 pounds fresh spinach, or 2 packages frozen spinach	½ teaspoon sugar
2 tablespoons butter	salt and ground black pepper to taste
⅔ cup Béchamel Sauce (page 38)	2 hard-cooked eggs
	pastry motifs (optional)

If frozen spinach is used, cook as directed on the package. If fresh spinach is used, cook 2 pounds as directed for Creamed Spinach. Rinse the spinach in cold water and press out the water using a large mixing spoon. Rub the spinach through a coarse sieve. Brown the butter and pour over the purée. Add the Béchamel Sauce, sugar, and salt and black pepper to taste. Heat 2 to 3 minutes, stirring frequently. Turn the spinach into a warmed serving dish. Put the yolks of the hard-cooked eggs through a sieve and put them in the center. Cut the whites in the shape of daisy petals and arrange them around the egg yolks to resemble a daisy. Surround the spinach with small pastry motifs (*fleurons*) if desired. Makes 4 servings.

SWISS CHARD (*Côtes de Bette*)

⚜ SWISS CHARD AU GRATIN (*Côtes de Bette au Gratin*)

2¼ pounds midribs of Swiss chard
boiling water
½ teaspoon salt

1 cup Béchamel Sauce (page 38)
¼ cup grated Parmesan cheese
2 tablespoons butter

Wash the Swiss chard and remove the green leafy part of the leaves, leaving only the midribs. (Save the leaves to use as a cooking green.) Scrape the midribs and cut them into 1-inch lengths. Place them in a saucepan with ½ inch boiling water and the salt. Cover and cook 10 to 15 minutes or until the midribs are tender. Drain well. Set aside. Butter a 10- by 6- by 2-inch baking dish and spread half the Béchamel Sauce over the bottom. Arrange the midribs over the sauce and cover them with the remainder of the sauce. Sprinkle with the Parmesan cheese and dot with the butter. Bake in a preheated hot oven (400° F.) 10 minutes or until the top has browned. Makes 6 servings.

TOMATOES (*Tomates*)

⚜ GRILLED OR SAUTÉED TOMATOES
(*Tomates Sautées ou Grillées*)

4 medum-sized firm tomatoes
salt and ground black pepper

8 teaspoons butter or olive oil or salad
oil
chopped parsley

Wash the tomatoes, cut them in half crosswise, and press them gently to remove the seeds. Sprinkle with salt and black pepper. Dot each half with 1 teaspoon butter or sprinkle generously with olive oil or salad oil. Place them in an oiled baking pan. Bake 15 to 20 minutes in a preheated hot oven (425° F.). If you prefer tomatoes sliced, cut them into slices ½ inch thick. Sprinkle with salt and black pepper and sauté in hot oil or butter in a skillet until cooked on both sides, about 10 minutes. Sprinkle tomato halves or slices with chopped parsley. Makes 4 servings.

⚜ TOMATOES AND POTATOES AU GRATIN
(*Tomates et Pommes de Terre au Gratin*)

4 medium-sized potatoes
salt and ground black pepper
4 medium-sized firm tomatoes

¼ cup bouillon
3 tablespoons grated Parmesan cheese
3 tablespoons butter

Boil the potatoes in their skins until they are done. Cool, remove the skins, and cut the potatoes into slices ⅛ inch thick. Place them in a buttered 10- by 6- by 2-inch baking dish. Sprinkle with salt and black pepper. Wash the tomatoes, cut them in slices ½ inch thick, and arrange the slices over the potatoes. Sprinkle with salt and black pepper. Pour in the bouillon. Sprinkle the top with the Parmesan cheese and dot with the butter. Bake in a preheated moderate oven (350° F.) 25 to 30 minutes or until browned. Makes 5 to 6 servings.

⚜ STUFFED TOMATOES (*Tomates Farcies*)

4 medium-sized firm ripe tomatoes
salt and ground black pepper
½ pound (1 cup) raw pork sausage
¾ cup finely chopped leftover roast
   beef, veal, or ham

¹⁄₁₆ teaspoon crushed garlic
2 tablespoons chopped parsley
¾ cup soft breadcrumbs
bouillon
2 tablespoons salad oil or olive oil

Wash the tomatoes, cut a slice from the stem end of each, and scoop out the centers, leaving the shells intact. Sprinkle the cavities with salt and black pepper and invert the tomatoes on a tray to drain. Cook the sausage and drain off and discard the fat. Mix the sausage with the meat, garlic, parsley and ¼ cup of the breadcrumbs. Moisten the mixture with a little bouillon if it seems too dry. Add salt and black pepper to taste. Stuff the mixture into the tomato shells. Place the tomatoes in an oiled baking dish. Blend the remaining ½ cup breadcrumbs with the oil and sprinkle over the tomatoes. Bake in a preheated moderate oven (350° F.) about 30 minutes. Makes 4 servings.

⚜ STUFFED TOMATOES PIEDMONT STYLE
(*Tomates Farcies à la Piémontaise*)

4 medium-sized firm tomatoes
salt and ground black pepper
⅓ cup raw rice
1½ tablespoons butter
⅔ cup hot water

½ cup grated Gruyère or Cheddar
   cheese
½ cup soft breadcrumbs
2 tablespoons olive oil or salad oil
parsley

393

Wash the tomatoes, cut a slice from the stem end of each, and scoop out centers. (Reserve the centers.) Sprinkle the cavities with salt and black pepper and invert the tomatoes on a tray to drain. Soak the rice 30 minutes in cold water to cover. Drain well. Melt the butter in a 1-quart saucepan, and add the rice. Stir and cook over moderate heat until rice is dry and begins to stick to the bottom of the pan. Add the hot water and ¼ teaspoon salt. Chop the tomato centers, push them through a coarse sieve, and add to the rice. Cover and cook 12 to 15 minutes or until the rice has absorbed all the liquid. Add the cheese and salt and black pepper to taste. Stuff into the cavities of the tomatoes. Place the tomatoes in an oiled baking dish. Combine the breadcrumbs with the oil and sprinkle over the tomatoes. Bake in a preheated moderate oven (350° F.) 30 minutes or until crumbs are brown. Serve with cooked rice tossed with melted butter and grated Parmesan cheese. Garnish with parsley. Makes 4 servings. (*See illustration, page 372.*)

⚜ STUFFED TOMATOES PROVENÇAL STYLE
(*Tomates Farcies à la Provençale*)

4 medium-sized firm tomatoes	1 tablespoon chopped parsley
salt and ground black pepper	1 small clove garlic, chopped fine
½ cup soft breadcrumbs	olive oil or salad oil

Wash the tomatoes, cut them in half, and scoop out part of the centers. Sprinkle the cavities with salt and black pepper. Combine the breadcrumbs, parsley, and garlic. Sprinkle generously over the tomatoes, filling the cavities and covering the tops completely. (Garlic is the predominating flavor in this dish.) Sprinkle the crumbs liberally with oil and place the tomatoes in an oiled baking dish. Bake in a preheated moderate oven (350° F.) 20 to 25 minutes or until crumbs have browned. Makes 4 servings.

TURNIPS (*Navets*)

⚜ CREAMED TURNIPS (*Navets à la Crème*)

2½ pounds turnips	¾ cup beef or veal stock
1 teaspoon salt	¼ cup light cream
boiling water	⅛ teaspoon ground black pepper
4 tablespoons butter	salt to taste
2 tablespoons flour	

Wash, peel, and slice the turnips. Place in a saucepan with the salt and boiling water to a depth of 1 inch. Bring to boiling point and cook, uncovered, 5 minutes. Cover and cook 15 to 20 minutes or until turnips are tender. Drain off water. Toss turnips lightly with 2 tablespoons of the butter. Melt the remaining 2 tablespoons butter in a 1-quart saucepan. Remove from heat, and blend in the flour. Stir and cook until the mixture foams. Add the stock and cream. Cook until the sauce is medium thick, stirring frequently. Add the black pepper and salt to taste. Pour the sauce over the turnips. Cook 1 to 2 minutes over low heat. Makes 6 servings.

⚜ GLAZED TURNIPS (*Navets Glacés*)

2½ pounds turnips, peeled and sliced
½ teaspoon salt
boiling water
1 cup boiling beef bouillon or stock

3 tablespoons butter
1 tablespoon sugar
⅛ teaspoon ground white pepper
chopped parsley

Place the turnips in a 1½-quart saucepan with the salt and enough boiling water to cover them. Bring to boiling point and boil, uncovered, 5 minutes. Drain off the water. Add the boiling bouillon or stock. Cover and cook 10 minutes. Remove cover and cook until all but 2 to 3 tablespoons of the liquid has evaporated. Add 2 tablespoons of the butter and the sugar. Shake the pan over medium-low heat until turnips are glazed. Add the remaining 1 tablespoon butter and the pepper. Toss lightly. Sprinkle with chopped parsley. Makes 6 servings.

⚜ STUFFED TURNIPS (*Navets Farcis*)

6 medium-sized purple-top white
  turnips
salt
boiling water

¾ pound pork sausage
1 teaspoon minced onion
2 tablespoons butter, melted
½ cup soft breadcrumbs

Trim off the top root from the turnips. Cut a slice from the top, leaving a border of purple around the top. Scoop out the centers, leaving a shell ¼ inch thick. Reserve the centers. Place the shells in a saucepan with ½ teaspoon salt and boiling water to cover. Bring water to boiling point, uncovered, and boil 5 minutes. Drain well and set aside in a baking dish. Place the turnip centers in a saucepan. Pour in ½ inch boiling water. Cover and cook until soft. Drain and mash. Crumble the sausage in a skillet, add the onion, brown lightly, and add to the turnip centers. Add salt to taste. Mix well. Stuff the mixture into the turnip shells. Combine the butter and breadcrumbs and sprinkle over the tops of the stuffed turnips. Bake in a preheated moderate oven (350° F.) 30 minutes or until tops are brown. Makes 6 servings.

ZUCCHINI (*Courgettes*)

Zucchini is an Italian type of squash with a thin dark-green skin and tender flesh. Though it falls into the summer squash category, it is actually available all year long. Zucchini may be prepared in many of the same ways as eggplant.

✤ STUFFED ZUCCHINI ORIENTAL STYLE
(*Courgettes Farcies à l'Orientale*)

3 zucchini, 6 inches long
1 cup cooked rice
1 cup finely chopped cooked beef,
    ham, pork, or veal
⅓ cup canned tomatoes or diced raw
    tomatoes

1 tablespoon finely chopped onion
salt and ground black pepper
1 cup soft breadcrumbs
4 tablespoons (½ stick) butter
tomato purée

Wash the zucchini, cut them in lengthwise halves, and scoop out the centers. Chop the centers very fine and mix with the next 4 ingredients and salt and black pepper to taste. Fill the zucchini with this mixture. Sprinkle with the soft breadcrumbs and dot with the butter. Bake in a preheated moderate oven (350° F.) 30 to 35 minutes or until crumbs are brown. Serve with tomato purée. Makes 6 servings. (*See illustration, page 371.*)

✤ RATATOUILLE NIÇOISE (*Ratatouille Niçoise*)

4 tablespoons olive oil or salad oil
1 small clove garlic, sliced thin
1 cup thinly sliced onion
3 green peppers, seeded and
    quartered

1 medium-sized eggplant, sliced ¼
    inch thick and peeled
3 small zucchini, sliced ¼ inch thick
4 medium-sized tomatoes, sliced thin
salt and ground black pepper

Heat 3 tablespoons of the oil in a flameproof baking dish. Add the garlic and cook 1 minute. Add the remaining vegetables in layers in the order listed, sprinkling each layer with salt and black pepper. Sprinkle the top layer (tomatoes) with the remaining 1 tablespoon oil. Cover and cook over low heat 35 to 40 minutes or until vegetables are tender. Remove cover, and cook 5 to 10 minutes longer to evaporate most of the pan liquid. Makes 6 servings.

Salads

In the French cuisine, there are two types of salads—simple salads and "composed" or combination salads. The simple ones are made of salad greens, such as lettuce, Belgian endive, chicory, Romaine, etc., dressed with oil and vinegar, and are served with roasts. Combination salads are made of various cooked vegetables, usually bound with mayonnaise. See also Salads in Chapter 4. (*See illustrations, pages 85, 86, 88, 369, and 372.*)

❧ GREEN SALAD WITH THICKENED VINAIGRETTE SAUCE
(*Salade à la Vinaigrette Liée*)

¼ teaspoon powdered mustard
½ teaspoon water
1 large raw egg yolk, or the yolk of
   1 hard-cooked egg
2 tablespoons salad oil or olive oil

2 teaspoons wine vinegar
1½ quarts bite-size pieces endive,
   chicory, or other salad greens
salt and ground black pepper to taste

Soak the mustard in the water 5 minutes to develop the flavor. Place it in the center of a salad bowl along with the egg yolk (if a hard-cooked egg yolk is used, mash it with a fork). Mix well. Gradually beat in the oil and vinegar. This dressing should be thin, not the consistency of mayonnaise. Pour over the salad greens and sprinkle with salt and black pepper to taste. Toss lightly but thoroughly. Makes 4 servings.

❧ WILTED GREENS WITH BACON (*Salade au Lard*)

4 slices bacon, or 4 thin slices salt
  pork, diced
4 tablespoons wine vinegar
ground black pepper to taste
¼ teaspoon sugar

3 cups bite-size pieces washed and
  dried chicory
3 cups bite-size pieces washed and
  dried dandelion greens
salt to taste (optional)

Cook the diced bacon or salt pork until brown and crisp. Add the vinegar, black pepper, and sugar. Heat and pour over the chicory and dandelion greens. Toss lightly but thoroughly. Add salt to taste if needed. Serve promptly. Makes 4 to 5 servings.

❧ ARTICHOKE SALAD À LA GRECQUE
(*Salade d'Artichauts à la Grecque*)

4 medium-sized artichokes
4 cups water
2 tablespoons lemon juice, or 3 tablespoons vinegar
⅔ cup olive oil
¾ teaspoon salt
1 rib celery, chopped fine

4 coriander seeds
½ teaspoon dried thyme
4 whole black peppercorns
4 small white onions
4 button mushrooms
1 carrot, peeled
black olives

Cut the artichokes into quarters, cut out the prickly choke, and trim off the pointed ends of the leaves until the leaves are about 1 inch long. Combine all the other ingredients except the mushrooms, carrot, and olives in a 2-quart saucepan. Bring the mixture to boiling point, add the artichokes, and cook, covered, 15 minutes. Add the mushrooms and cook 5 minutes or until the artichokes are tender. Cool the vegetables in the cooking liquid. Transfer the vegetables to a salad bowl. Cut the carrot into slices ⅛ inch thick and place them in the center. Arrange the olives around the carrot slices. Spoon some of the cooking liquid over the vegetables. Makes 4 servings.

❧ ITALIAN SALAD (*Salade Italienne*)

½ cup cold cooked sliced carrots
½ cup 1-inch pieces cold cooked green
  beans
½ cup cold diced cooked potatoes
¼ cup cold cooked green peas
1 teaspoon lemon juice
1 tablespoon olive oil or salad oil
¼ teaspoon salt or salt to taste

⅛ teaspoon ground black pepper
1 medium-sized tomato, diced
¼ cup mayonnaise
2 hard-cooked eggs
½ cup diced pickled tongue
4 rolled anchovy fillets
2 cold cooked beets, sliced

Combine the first 6 ingredients and sprinkle with the salt and black pepper. Mix lightly and marinate 3 to 4 hours in the refrigerator. Add the tomato and the mayonnaise, mix lightly, and mound the mixture into the center of a salad bowl. Chop the egg whites and yolks separately. Sprinkle the yolks on the center of the salad and surround them with the diced pickled tongue. Sprinkle the egg whites around the tongue. Garnish the edge of the salad with the anchovies and beets. Makes 4 servings.

❧ SALAD MARGUERITE (*Salade Marguerite*)

1½ cups cooked cauliflowerets
4 tablespoons Vinaigrette Sauce
  (page 56)
½ cup 1-inch pieces cooked green
  beans
½ cup cooked asparagus tips

1 cup sliced cooked potatoes
salt and ground black pepper to taste
4 tablespoons mayonnaise
1 hard-cooked egg
½ teaspoon softened butter

Select 6 of the largest cauliflowerets and set them aside to use as a garnish. Marinate the remaining cauliflowerets 1 hour in 2 tablespoons of the Vinaigrette Sauce. Combine the green beans, asparagus, potatoes, and the remaining 2 tablespoons Vinaigrette Sauce. Marinate 1 hour. Combine all the marinated vegetables, season to taste with salt and black pepper, and mound them in a salad bowl. Mask with the mayonnaise. Cut petals in the shape of daisy petals from the hard-cooked egg white and arrange them in daisy fashion on the center top of the salad. Mash the egg yolk with the butter and put it in the center of the daisy. Garnish the salad in an attractive manner with the cauliflowerets reserved for that purpose. Makes 4 servings. (*See illustration, page 86.*)

❧ MIXED VEGETABLE SALAD WITH EGGS
   (*Salade Panachée aux Oeufs*)

cooked cauliflowerets
lemon juice
Vinaigrette Sauce (page 56)
watercress

grated carrot
mayonnaise
hard-cooked eggs

For each salad serving, sprinkle 4 cold, cooked cauliflowerets with ½ teaspoon lemon juice and 1 tablespoon Vinaigrette Sauce and marinate 1 hour. Place the cauliflowerets in the center of a salad plate and make a bed of watercress around them. Mix ½ cup grated carrot with 1½ teaspoons mayonnaise and ¼ teaspoon lemon juice. Spoon the mixture around the cauliflower on the watercress. Garnish with a half of a hard-cooked egg, sprinkled with salt and black pepper.

❧ MOLDED VEGETABLE SALAD (*Salade Moulé*)

carrots, pared
turnips, pared
boiling water
salt
2 cups aspic
3 medium-sized cooked potatoes,
    sliced

1 cup 1-inch pieces cooked green
    beans
¼ cup cooked green peas
6 cooked cauliflowerets
⅓ cup mayonnaise
⅛ teaspoon ground black pepper

Cut the carrots and turnips into olive-shaped pieces with a vegetable cutter, using enough to make 1 cup of each. Put them in separate 1-quart saucepans. Put into each pan ½ inch boiling water and ¼ teaspoon salt. Cover and cook until crisp-tender, about 10 minutes. Drain and cool. Decorate a 1-quart mold according to the following directions, using aspic as required, the carrots, turnips, potato slices cut in circles, and pieces of green beans. Combine the peas, cauliflowerets, mayonnaise, black pepper, and the remaining aspic. Chill until the mixture begins to set. Turn into the decorated salad mold. Chill until the salad is firm and ready to be served. Makes 6 servings.

❧ How to Decorate a Mold for a Gelatin (Aspic) Salad

Before starting to decorate a salad mold, drain all foods well and chill them. Allow 1¼ cups salad ingredients to each cup gelatin (aspic). Make the aspic with reduced, clarified chicken or veal stock, or with commercial gelatin and clarified chicken or veal stock (see following recipe). Cool the aspic over cracked ice or in the refrigerator or put it in the freezer for a few minutes.

    Rinse a mold with sloping sides in cold water and chill it. When the aspic is about as thick as fresh egg whites, put a small amount in the mold. Tip and roll the mold to coat the inside surface with a thin layer of aspic. Refrigerate the mold until the aspic is set. Impale the pieces of food to be used as the decoration on toothpicks, one at a time, dip them into the aspic, and arrange them in any design desired on the firm layer of aspic. Chill to set the design. Then coat with another layer of aspic and chill until firm. Fill the mold with any aspic mixture desired. Chill until it is firm and the salad is ready to be served.

❧ Aspic (Quick Method)

Soak 1 envelope (1 tablespoon) gelatin 3 minutes in 1 cup cold water or stock. Add ¾ to 1 cup stock or other liquid, heated to *just* below boiling point. Stir until the gelatin is dissolved. Use the lesser amount of liquid if the food to be coated is juicy or watery. Chill until the aspic is about as thick as fresh egg whites.

400

Water, fruit juice, wine, or a liqueur may be used as part of the liquid in making aspic. Wine or a liqueur gives the aspic a rather special flavor; for each cup of stock, replace 2 tablespoons with 2 tablespoons wine or liqueur, added just as the gelatin begins to cool.

⚜ SALAD NIÇOISE (*Salade Niçoise*)

2 medium-sized cold cooked potatoes, diced
1 cup 1-inch pieces cold cooked green beans
3 tablespoons Vinaigrette Sauce (page 56)
salt and ground black pepper to taste

1 clove garlic, cut in half
2 medium-small tomatoes, quartered
pitted ripe olives
anchovy fillets
1½ teaspoons capers
chopped fresh chervil (if available)

Combine the first 3 ingredients. Add salt and black pepper to taste. Rub the inside of the salad bowl with the garlic. Turn the salad mixture into the bowl. Decorate the salad with the quartered tomatoes, olives, anchovies, and the capers. Sprinkle with chopped fresh chervil, if available. Makes 4 servings.

⚜ SALAD ORLOFF (*Salade Orloff*)

1 rib celery, cut into julienne pieces
2 cooked artichoke bottoms, cut into julienne pieces
4 raw mushroom caps, cut into julienne pieces
½ cup julienne pieces cold cooked ham
½ cup julienne pieces cold cooked chicken

½ cup cooked spaghetti, cooled to lukewarm
4 tablespoons mayonnaise
1 tablespoon tomato purée
salt and ground black pepper to taste
2 medium-small tomatoes, peeled, seeded, and sliced
4 cooked fluted mushrooms
½ truffle, or 4 black olives

Put the first 6 ingredients into a bowl. Combine the mayonnaise and tomato purée and toss with the salad mixture. Season to taste with salt and black pepper. Arrange the salad on a serving plate. Decorate with tomato slices, fluted mushrooms, and truffles or black olives. Makes 4 servings. (*See illustration, page 86.*)

⚜ SALAD RACHEL, SIMPLIFIED RECIPE
(*Salade Rachel, Recette Simplifiée*)

¼ pound raw mushrooms, sliced thin
½ pound cooked asparagus tips
4 artichoke bottoms, sliced thin
2 tablespoons wine vinegar
6 tablespoons oil

¼ teaspoon salt
¹⁄₁₆ teaspoon ground black pepper
2 tablespoons brandy
2 tablespoons port

Place the mushrooms, asparagus tips, and artichoke bottoms in separate small bowls. Combine the remaining ingredients, pour 3 tablespoons of the mixture into each bowl of vegetables, and marinate 30 minutes. Reserve 4 of the largest asparagus tips for garnish. Cut the remaining asparagus tips into ½-inch pieces and place a mound of them in each salad plate. Arrange the mushrooms and artichoke bottoms in mounds on the salad plates. Garnish each plate with a whole asparagus tip. Makes 4 servings.

⚜ RICE SALAD DERBY (*Salade de Riz Derby*)

1 cup cold cooked rice	3 tablespoons Vinaigrette Sauce
⅓ cup cold cooked green peas	(page 56)
⅓ cup julienne strips cooked	1 tablespoon mayonnaise
mushrooms	chopped walnuts
⅓ cup julienne strips cooked ham	

Put the first 4 ingredients in a mixing bowl. Combine the Vinaigrette Sauce and mayonnaise, add to the rice mixture, and toss lightly. Add more Vinaigrette Sauce and mayonnaise if desired. Serve in a mound on a salad plate and sprinkle with chopped walnuts. Makes 4 servings. (*See illustration, page 85.*)

⚜ RUSSIAN SALAD (*Salade Russe*)

½ cup cold diced cooked carrots	¼ cup mayonnaise
½ cup cold diced cooked turnips	salt and ground black pepper to taste
½ cup cold diced cooked potatoes	⅓ cup julienne strips cold cooked ham
½ cup 1-inch pieces cold cooked green	⅓ cup julienne strips pickled tongue
beans	2 hard-cooked eggs, sliced
⅓ cup cold cooked green peas	4 rolled anchovy fillets

Combine the first 6 ingredients and mix lightly. Season with salt and black pepper to taste. Serve in a mound on a salad plate. Garnish with the ham, pickled tongue, sliced hard-cooked eggs, and anchovies. Makes 4 servings.

⚜ SALADS WITH HARD-COOKED EGGS (*Salades aux Oeufs Durs*)

Hard-cooked eggs (diced, sliced, or quartered) may be added to most vegetable, fish, shellfish, meat, or poultry salads. If they are used, additional seasonings may be necessary.

For an attractive salad that is easy to assemble, arrange wedges of lettuce in a salad bowl, sprinkle them with shredded cheese, and garnish as desired with sliced hard-cooked eggs and sliced tomatoes. Serve with Vinaigrette Sauce (page 56). Allow 1 wedge of lettuce per serving. (*See illustration, page 372.*)

⚜ TOMATOES STUFFED WITH CELERY OR FENNEL
(*Tomates Farcies au Céleri ou au Fenouil*)

8 medium-sized tomatoes
salt and ground black pepper
1¼ cups diced celery or fennel

3 tablespoons olive oil or salad oil
1 tablespoon lemon juice

Skin the tomatoes, scoop out the centers, and sprinkle the cavities with salt and black pepper. Combine the celery or fennel with the oil and lemon juice. Season with salt and black pepper to taste. Marinate 1 hour. Spoon into the centers of the tomatoes, having some of the filling heaped over the top. Makes 8 servings. (*See illustration, page 369.*)

SALAD DRESSINGS

Vinaigrette Sauce (page 56) is the basic salad dressing of France. It consists of 3 parts olive oil and 1 part wine vinegar, salt and pepper, and sometimes herbs and mustard. To this base other ingredients such as capers, olives, gherkins, hard-cooked eggs, anchovies, etc., may be added to create a variety of interesting dressings. The use of garlic in French salad dressings is usually confined to southern France. See also Cold Sauces in Chapter 3.

SALAD DRESSINGS BASED ON VINAIGRETTE SAUCE

⚜ Anchovy Dressing

To ½ cup Vinaigrette Sauce made without salt, add 1 finely chopped anchovy fillet or 1 teaspoon anchovy paste, 1 tablespoon finely chopped parsley, and 1 teaspoon finely chopped shallot or small white onion. Makes a generous ½ cup.

⚜ Chiffonnade Dressing

To ½ cup Vinaigrette Sauce, add 1 tablespoon each finely chopped green pepper, green olives, and gherkin pickle, and 1 hard-cooked egg, chopped. Makes about ¾ cup.

❧ Roquefort Dressing

Blend ¼ cup crumbled Roquefort cheese with 2 tablespoons Vinaigrette Sauce, then mix with an additional ⅓ cup Vinaigrette Sauce. Makes ¾ cup.

❧ CREAM DRESSING (*Assaisonnement à la Crème*)

Blend 1 teaspoon wine vinegar or lemon juice with ¼ cup heavy cream. Add salt and ground white pepper to taste. Serve over cabbage or Romaine (*cos*) lettuce. Makes ¼ cup.

❧ Cream Mustard Dressing

Blend 1 teaspoon Dijon-type prepared mustard with the basic Cream Dressing. Serve on cold cooked meats or fish or use for mixing meat and fish salads. Makes ¼ cup.

❧ MAYONNAISE DRESSING (*Assaisonnement à la Mayonnaise*)

Use with salads of cooked vegetables. See Mayonnaise, page 53

❧ EGG DRESSING (*Assaisonnement à l'Oeuf*)

3 hard-cooked egg yolks
½ teaspoon salt
⅛ teaspoon ground black pepper
2 teaspoons Dijon-type prepared
　mustard

1 cup olive oil or salad oil
2 tablespoons wine vinegar
1 hard-cooked egg white, shredded

Put the egg yolks through a sieve. Blend with the salt, pepper, and mustard. Gradually beat in the oil, a few drops at a time, until the mixture begins to thicken. Then the oil may be added a little faster, increasing the amount as the mixture thickens. Add the vinegar and beat well. Fold in the shredded egg white. Makes about 2 cups.

Dessert Sauces, Fillings, and Frostings

For convenience, a number of dessert sauces, pastry creams, cake frostings, and other preparations used with various kinds of desserts are grouped in this chapter. Others will be found with specific recipes in Chapters 16 and 17.

DESSERT SAUCES

The role of a dessert sauce is to complement the dessert. Simple desserts are best when served with sauces that contrast sharply with the flavor of the basic dish. Certain rich desserts require light, delicate sauces, not too pronounced in flavor.

❧ APRICOT SAUCE I (*Sauce à l'Abricot I*)

½ pound dried apricots
water
½ cup sugar

¹⁄₁₆ teaspoon salt
apricot brandy, cognac, or Kirsch to
taste

Wash the apricots and cook in water as directed on the package. Put the cooked apricots through a food mill, or purée them, about ¾ cup at a time, in an electric blender. Add the sugar and salt. Cook, stirring, 4 to 5 minutes over moderate heat. Add the apricot brandy, cognac, or Kirsch to taste. Serve over puddings or plain cake. Makes approximately 1½ cups sauce.

To store, pour the sauce into a jar and cover with 1 to 2 tablespoons apricot brandy, cognac, or Kirsch. Cover tightly and store in the refrigerator.

⚜ APRICOT SAUCE II (*Sauce à l'Abricot II*)

This is especially good over hot desserts.

1½ cups apricot jam or marmalade
½ cup water
2 tablespoons sugar
¹⁄₁₆ teaspoon salt

1 tablespoon apricot brandy, Kirsch, cognac, Grand Marnier, Cointreau, or rum

Combine the first 4 ingredients in a 1-quart saucepan. Mix well. Cook, stirring, until the sauce reaches the boiling point, then cook over low heat 5 to 8 minutes, stirring constantly. Add the apricot brandy, Kirsch, cognac, Grand Marnier, Cointreau, or rum. Makes approximately 1¾ cups sauce.

To store, pour the sauce into a jar and pour 1 to 2 tablespoons of one of the liqueurs over the top. Cover the jar tightly and place in the refrigerator.

⚜ ORANGE SAUCE

½ cup sugar
1 tablespoon cornstarch
¹⁄₁₆ teaspoon salt
1 cup orange juice

1 tablespoon grated orange rind
½ teaspoon grated lemon rind
2 tablespoons (¼ stick) butter
¼ teaspoon vanilla extract

Combine the first 3 ingredients in a 1-quart saucepan. Add the orange juice. Stir and cook until the mixture has thickened and is clear. Remove from heat and stir in the remaining ingredients. Serve over plain cake, puddings, sweet waffles, etc. Makes 1¼ cups sauce.

⚜ RED-CURRANT SAUCE

2 cups red currants   1½ cups sugar

Combine the currants and sugar, mix well, and let stand about 1 hour or until the currants form juice. Cook over low heat 5 minutes. Increase the heat and boil about 15 minutes. Rub though a fine sieve. Makes about 2½ cups.

⚜ RED-CURRANT JELLY SAUCE

Put an 8-ounce glass of red-currant jelly into a small saucepan. With a fork, break up the jelly and mix with 1 tablespoon hot water and 2 tablespoons

Kirsch. Stir the mixture over low heat until the jelly has melted and blended with the water and Kirsch. Makes 1 generous cup.

❧ RASPBERRY SAUCE (*Sauce aux Framboises*)

2 cups fresh raspberries
2 to 3 tablespoons sugar

1 teaspoon lemon juice
¼ teaspoon vanilla extract

Crush the raspberries and put them through a sieve. Add the remaining ingredients and mix well. Serve over ice cream, plain cake, and puddings. Makes approximately 1 ½ cups.

❧ STRAWBERRY SAUCE (*Sauce aux Fraises*)

2 cups fresh strawberries
2 tablespoons sugar
¼ teaspoon vanilla extract

Kirsch or dry white wine to taste
   (optional)

Crush 1 cup strawberries and mix with the sugar and vanilla extract. Slice the remaining cup strawberries and fold in. Add Kirsch or dry white wine to taste, if desired. Makes 2 cups sauce.

❧ BRANDY SAUCE

1 large egg, separated
about ¾ cup sifted confectioners'
   sugar
dash of salt

½ cup heavy cream, whipped
3 tablespoons apricot brandy or peach
   brandy

Beat the egg white until it stands in soft stiff peaks. Gradually beat in the sugar. Add the salt to the egg yolk and beat until fluffy and lemon-colored. Fold in the beaten egg white, then the whipped cream and brandy. Chill. Serve over hot or cold puddings or plain cake. Makes approximately 1 ½ cups sauce.

❧ CHOCOLATE SAUCE (*Sauce au Chocolat Chaude*)

½ pound semisweet chocolate
⅓ cup hot water
1 teaspoon cornstarch

1 tablespoon butter
½ teaspoon vanilla extract

Break the chocolate into small pieces and put it in the top part of a small double boiler. Add the water. Place over hot water until the chocolate is melted, stirring occasionally, then stir and cook over low direct heat 1 to 2 minutes. Blend the cornstarch with the butter, add, and cook the sauce until it is smooth and slightly thickened. Remove from heat. Stir in the vanilla extract. Serve warm over Profiteroles (page 489), plain cake, or ice cream. Makes approximately ¾ cup.

⚜ CUSTARD SAUCE (*Crème à l'Anglaise*)

4 large egg yolks
½ cup sugar
¼ teaspoon cornstarch
1 cup hot milk
1 cup hot light cream

3-inch piece vanilla bean, or 1
   teaspoon vanilla extract
dash salt
cognac, Cointreau, Kirsch, rum, or
   sherry to taste (optional)

Beat the egg yolks lightly in the top of a 1-quart double boiler. Mix the sugar with the cornstarch and gradually add to the egg yolks, beating well after each addition. Stir a little of the hot milk into the egg yolks, then add the remaining hot milk and cream. Add the vanilla bean (if used) and the salt. Stir and cook over hot water (not boiling) until the custard coats a metal spoon. Let cool, stirring frequently. If vanilla bean was not used, add the vanilla extract. Strain through a fine sieve. Store in a tightly covered jar in the refrigerator. If desired flavor to taste with cognac, Cointreau, Kirsch, rum, or sherry. Makes approximately 1¾ cups.

⚜ HARD SAUCE

½ cup softened unsalted butter
1 to 1¼ cups sifted confectioners'
   sugar

1 tablespoon brandy, rum, or liqueur

Stir the butter until it is fluffy. Gradually beat in the sugar and brandy, rum, or liqueur. Serve over warm puddings. Makes about 1 cup sauce.

⚜ VANILLA SAUCE

½ cup sugar
4 teaspoons cornstarch
¼ teaspoon salt
1 cup water

2 tablespoons butter
2 tablespoons heavy cream
1 teaspoon vanilla extract

Combine the first 3 ingredients in a 1-quart saucepan. Mix well. Add the water. Stir and cook over low heat 5 minutes or until the sauce is clear and has thickened. Remove from heat and stir in the butter. Add the cream and vanilla extract. Serve over plain cake or puddings. Makes about 1 cup.

VARIATIONS

⚜ Lemon-Vanilla Sauce

Omit the cream in the recipe for Vanilla Sauce and add 1½ tablespoons lemon juice and 1 teaspoon grated lemon rind.

❧ **Vanilla-Rum Sauce**

Add 2 tablespoons rum to Vanilla Sauce.

PASTRY CREAMS

❧ **FRENCH PASTRY CREAM** (*Crème Pâtissière*)

½ cup sugar
4 teaspoons cornstarch
dash of salt
1 cup milk or light cream

3 large egg yolks, beaten lightly
1 teaspoon vanilla extract
⅓ cup heavy cream, whipped

Combine the sugar, cornstarch, and salt in a heavy saucepan. Gradually blend in the milk or light cream, mixing until smooth. Bring to a boil over medium heat, stirring frequently with a wire whisk or wooden spoon. Boil 1 minute, stirring to prevent scorching the cream. Remove from the heat. Stir a little of the hot mixture into the egg yolks, and then add them to the remaining hot mixture. Bring *just* to boiling point (do not boil), stirring constantly. Remove from heat and add the vanilla extract. Place a piece of waxed paper directly over the cream, cover, and refrigerate until the cream has cooled completely. Add the whipped cream, and beat with a rotary beater until the mixture is smooth. Makes about 1½ cups.

❧ **ALMOND PASTRY CREAM** (*Crème Pâtissière d'Amande*)

1 cup blanched almonds
½ cup sifted confectioners' sugar
3 tablespoons softened butter

2 large egg yolks
1 tablespoon Kirsch or rum

Put a few almonds at a time in the jar of an electric blender and blend until they are ground very fine, repeating until all are ground. Or put the almonds through a food chopper twice, using the fine blade. Put the almonds in a 1-quart mixing bowl. Add the sugar and mix well. Set aside. Stir the butter with a spoon until it is creamy. Beat 1 egg yolk at a time into the butter, and beat in the Kirsch or rum. Blend into the almond and sugar mixture. Makes approximately 1¼ cups.

❧ **CHANTILLY CREAM** (*Crème Chantilly*)

1 cup heavy cream
2 tablespoons sifted confectioners' sugar

½ teaspoon vanilla extract
brandy, rum, or liqueur to taste
(optional)

409

Combine the cream, sugar, and vanilla extract and beat until the mixture stands in soft peaks. Flavor to taste with brandy, Cointreau, Kirsch, rum, or other liqueur, if desired. Makes 2 cups.

⚜ CREAM BOURDALOUE (*Crème Bourdaloue*)

This is sometimes used to replace French Pastry Cream.

⅔ cup sugar
⅓ cup cornstarch
⅛ teaspoon salt
1 cup milk
1 large whole egg

1 large egg yolk
2 tablespoons dark rum or Kirsch
½ teaspoon vanilla extract
2 tablespoons butter

Combine the sugar, cornstarch, and salt in the top of a double boiler. Blend in ¼ cup of the milk. Heat the remaining milk and add to the mixture, stirring constantly. Cook over moderately low heat 5 minutes, being careful not to scorch the mixture. Remove the pan from the heat. Beat the whole egg and the egg yolk together only until they are blended. Then gradually beat in a little of the hot mixture, and stir into the remaining hot mixture. Cook over hot water (not boiling) 5 to 7 minutes or until the cream is very thick. Remove from heat. Add the rum or Kirsch, vanilla extract, and butter. Cool. Makes 1½ cups.

⚜ THICK CUSTARD FILLING

½ cup sugar
2 tablespoons cornstarch
1 tablespoon flour
dash of salt

3 large egg yolks
1 cup light cream
1 cup milk
1 teaspoon vanilla extract

Combine the first 4 ingredients in the top part of a double boiler or in a heavy saucepan. Beat in the egg yolks and ¼ cup of the cream. Heat the remaining cream with the milk over direct heat or in the top of a double boiler *only* until hot (do not boil). Add to the sugar and egg mixture. Cook, stirring constantly, over hot (not boiling) water or low heat until the custard is very thick. Cool before using, stirring frequently to prevent a skin from forming over the top. Use as a filling for cakes, pastries, Swiss Roll (page 473), etc. Makes 2 cups filling.

CAKE FROSTINGS AND FILLINGS

Frostings on cakes are sometimes more important than the cakes themselves. They give cakes eye appeal, help them to keep moist, and add richness and flavor.

⚜ HOW TO FROST CAKES

General Instructions, Layer and Loaf Cakes

Have both the frosting and the cake cold. Brush off all the loose crumbs with a pastry brush and trim off all the ragged edges with kitchen scissors. Select a flat plate 2 to 3 inches larger than the diameter of the cake. Cut 4 strips of waxed paper 10 by 3 inches, and place them, overlapping, around the edge of the cake plate.

For Layer Cake: Place a cake layer, inverted, in the center of the plate. (If all the layers are not the same thickness, place the thicker or thickest layer on the bottom.) Using a flexible plastic, rubber, or metal spatula, spread the top of the bottom layer smoothly with frosting almost to the outer edge. Place the next layer, right side up, on the frosted layer. If more than two layers are used, cover each with frosting and place the next on top, but do not frost the top of the cake until later. If the layers tend to slide before the frosting is set, anchor them with toothpicks. Spread the sides of the cake with a thin layer of apricot jam or frosting to hold the crumbs. Then spread the frosting from the top edges down the sides, covering each side completely. If the frosting is creamy or fluffy, swirl it as you spread. Spread the remaining frosting over the top of the cake to the edge, swirling it as you spread. If coconut, chopped nuts, or chocolate granules are used, sprinkle the top and sides of the cake before frosting is set.

For Loaf Cake: Place the cake in the center of the cake plate. (If the diameter of the top of the cake is larger than that of the bottom, invert the cake on the plate.) Spread a thin coating of apricot jam, almond paste, or frosting around the sides and over the top of the cake to set the crumbs. Then spread the frosting from the top edges down over the sides, covering them completely. If the frosting is creamy or fluffy, swirl it as you spread. Spread the remaining frosting over the top to the edges, covering it completely. Swirl the frosting as you spread. If coconut, chopped nuts, etc., are used, sprinkle them over the frosting before it is set.

⚜ FONDANT (*Fondant*)

2 cups sugar
⅛ teaspoon cream of tartar

1¼ cups water
1 teaspoon vanilla extract

Place all ingredients in a heavy-bottomed 1½-quart saucepan. Mix well. Cook over low heat, stirring constantly, until the sugar has dissolved. Remove the spoon when the mixture reaches the boiling point. Cover and cook 3 minutes. Steam condensing on the sides of the pan will wash down any sugar crystals that may have formed there. Place a candy thermometer in the syrup, being sure that the bulb does not touch the bottom or sides of the pan. Cook, uncovered, without stirring, until the thermometer registers 238° F., or until a soft ball forms when a little of the syrup is dropped into cold water. Wash away any sugar crystals from the sides of the pan with a swab or pastry brush dipped in cold water. Rinse a large platter in cold water, but do not dry it. Pour the fondant into the platter and place on a cooling rack to cool the fondant to 110° F., or until the platter can be held in the palm of the hand without discomfort. (Do not stir or agitate Fondant during the cooling period.) With a spatula or paddle, work the Fondant back and forth until it is white and creamy. Spoon it into a jar, cover tightly, and store in the refrigerator 24 hours or more to ripen. Fondant will keep several weeks if it is refrigerated. Use for stuffing dates and figs, for making mint patties, nut bars, chocolate-dipped bonbons, and for icing cakes. Makes 1¼ pounds.

⚜ Chocolate Fondant (*Fondant au Chocolat*)

To the recipe for Fondant, add 1½ squares (1½ ounces) unsweetened chocolate along with the sugar and water. Cook as directed. Sprinkle 1 teaspoon vanilla extract over the top of the Fondant before beating or working it. Makes 1¼ pounds.

⚜ Fondant Cake Icing

1 cup cooked Fondant
1 to 2 tablespoons liquid (water, simple syrup, maple syrup, strong coffee, lemon juice, orange juice, rum, brandy, Kirsch, or other liqueur)

flavoring to taste (vanilla extract, grated lemon rind or orange rind)
1 teaspoon egg white (optional)

Warm the Fondant in a very heavy-bottomed saucepan over very low heat, or in the top part of a double boiler over hot (not boiling) water, stirring constantly. (Be very careful not to overheat.) Add the liquid gradually, using only enough to thin the Fondant to pouring consistency while keeping it thick enough to mask the cake. Add the desired flavoring. To give the icing more sheen, add the unbeaten egg white just before putting the icing on the cake. Makes enough icing for the top and sides of an 8- or 9-inch cake. (For Fondant for Frosting Petits Fours, see page 480.)

⚜ LEMON BUTTER (*Beurre de Citron*)

This recipe is of English origin. Lemon Butter is used as a filling for tarts and cakes, or as a spread for toast or bread. It will keep several weeks in a tightly covered jar in the refrigerator.

5 large eggs
1½ cups sugar
1½ tablespoons grated lemon rind

dash salt
½ teaspoon vanilla extract

412

Place all the ingredients in the top part of a double boiler. Stir and cook over hot water (not boiling) 25 minutes or until the mixture has thickened. Makes 1¾ cups.

⚜ ROYAL ICING (*Glace Royale*)

This icing is used on cakes or Petits Fours made from Puff Pastry and on tarts with a top crust or lattice top.

1 large egg white

about ½ cup sifted confectioners' sugar

Put the egg white in a small mixing bowl and gradually beat in enough sugar to make the icing a runny mass that will be easy to brush on with a pastry brush. Makes approximately ½ cup.

⚜ ROYAL ICING FOR DECORATING (*Glace Royale pour Décors*)

Since this frosting is used for decorating purposes, it should be fluffy and stand in very stiff peaks. The more the frosting is beaten, the fluffier and lighter it becomes.

3 large egg whites
about 2 cups sifted confectioners' sugar

1 tablespoon lemon juice, or ½ teaspoon cream of tartar

Put the egg whites in a 2-quart, round-bottomed mixing bowl. Add ⅔ cup of the sugar and beat the mixture with a wooden spoon until it is creamy. Add the lemon juice or cream of tartar and beat well. Gradually beat in the remaining sugar, using an electric beater, if one is available. Continue beating until the icing stands in very stiff peaks when the beater is withdrawn. Cover the bowl of frosting with a damp cloth until you are ready to use it. Makes approximately 4 to 5 cups.

⚜ VANILLA BUTTER CREAM (*Crème au Beurre Vanillée*)

An excellent filling for cake and pastries.

½ cup sugar
1 tablespoon flour
2 tablespoons cornstarch
1/16 teaspoon salt

1 cup milk or light cream
2 large egg yolks
4 tablespoons (½ stick) butter
1 teaspoon vanilla extract

Measure out 1½ teaspoons of the sugar and reserve it for later use. Mix the remaining sugar with the flour, cornstarch, and salt in the top of a 1-quart double boiler. Gradually blend in ¾ cup of the milk. Cook over low direct heat, stirring constantly, 5 minutes or until the mixture is very thick, being

413

careful not to scorch the bottom of the mixture. Then cover and cook over boiling water 5 minutes. Mix the remaining ¼ cup milk with the egg yolks and stir into the hot mixture. Beat well with a wire whisk or a wooden spoon to prevent lumping. Cook over hot (not boiling) water 5 minutes, or until the cream is about as thick as mayonnaise, stirring and beating all the while to make a smooth mixture. Replace the hot water in the bottom part of the double boiler with ice cubes and cold water and cool the cream completely in the top of the double boiler. Blend the reserved 1½ teaspoons sugar with the butter and beat until the butter is very smooth and satiny. Add a teaspoon at a time to the cream and beat well after each addition. (This is important to prevent the cream from separating and curdling.) Beat in the vanilla extract. Makes approximately 1½ cups.

VARIATIONS

⚜ **Chocolate Butter Cream** (*Crème au Beurre au Chocolat*)

Add 1 square (1 ounce) unsweetened chocolate to Vanilla Butter Cream about 2 minutes before it has finished cooking. Stir until the chocolate is melted and thoroughly blended with the cream.

⚜ **Chocolate-Rum Butter Cream**
(*Crème au Beurre au Chocolat et au Rhum*)

Add 2 tablespoons dark rum to the Chocolate Butter Cream after the chocolate has melted.

⚜ **Coffee Butter Cream** (*Crème au Beurre au Café*)

In the recipe for Vanilla Butter Cream replace half the milk with double-strength coffee or mix 1 teaspoon instant coffee with the sugar.

⚜ **Kirsch Butter Cream** (*Crème au Beurre au Kirsch*)

Beat 1 to 2 tablespoons Kirsch into Vanilla Butter Cream along with the vanilla extract.

⚜ **Mint Butter Cream** (*Crème au Beurre à la Menthe*)

Beat 1 tablespoon crème de menthe into the Vanilla Butter Cream along with the vanilla extract.

⚜ **Mocha Butter Cream** (*Crème au Beurre au Moka*)

Add 1 square (1 ounce) unsweetened chocolate to Coffee Butter Cream while it is hot.

⚜ Rum or Brandy Butter Cream
(*Crème au Beurre au Rhum ou au Cognac*)

Beat 2 tablespoons dark rum, apricot brandy, or peach brandy into Vanilla Butter Cream along with the vanilla extract.

⚜ Praline Butter Cream (*Crème au Beurre Pralinée*)

Beat 4 tablespoons Praline Powder (page 418) into Vanilla Butter Cream along with the vanilla extract.

⚜ UNCOOKED BUTTER FROSTING

This can be substituted for Vanilla Butter Cream and may also be used to frost the outside of the cake.

¼ cup (½ stick) softened butter
about 2½ cups sifted confectioners' sugar

1 teaspoon vanilla extract
1 egg white

Stir the butter until it is creamy. Blend in 1 cup sifted confectioners' sugar and the vanilla extract. Beat the egg white until it stands in soft stiff peaks. Then, gradually beat in the remaining confectioners' sugar and fold the mixture into the butter and sugar mixture. Add additional confectioners' sugar if you wish a thicker frosting. Makes sufficient frosting for the filling, top, and sides of an 8-inch 2-layer cake or for the filling and top of a 9-inch 2-layer cake.

⚜ Uncooked Chocolate Butter Frosting

Use the recipe for Uncooked Butter Frosting, adding 1 square (1 ounce) melted unsweetened chocolate to the butter and sugar mixture. Proceed as directed in the recipe.

⚜ WATER ICING (*Glace à l'Eau*)

Mix 4 to 5 teaspoons water with 1 cup sifted confectioners' sugar. Warm the mixture slightly. Use to glaze certain types of cakes, pastries, and Petits Fours. Makes approximately ⅓ cup.

⚜ WHIPPED-CREAM TOPPING

¼ cup sifted confectioners' sugar, or
2 tablespoons granulated sugar

1 cup heavy cream
½ teaspoon vanilla extract

Place all the ingredients in a mixing bowl and beat the mixture until it stands in soft peaks. Makes approximately 2 cups.

VARIATIONS

⚜ Coffee Whipped Cream

Mix 1 teaspoon instant coffee with the sugar used in Whipped-Cream Topping.

⚜ Mocha Whipped Cream

Mix 1 teaspoon instant coffee and 1 tablespoon cocoa with the sugar in Whipped-Cream Topping.

⚜ Orange Whipped Cream

Fold 2 tablespoons grated orange rind and ½ teaspoon grated lemon rind into the mixture for Whipped-Cream Topping.

GLAZES AND OTHER DESSERT PREPARATIONS

⚜ CARAMEL GLAZE

Melt 1 cup sugar in a small saucepan over low heat. Add 1½ tablespoons butter and stir until the mixture is golden brown. Makes enough glaze for the top of a 9- or 10-inch cake.

⚜ CARAMEL SYRUP

1 cup sugar
½ cup hot water

½ teaspoon vanilla extract

Melt the sugar in a heavy skillet or saucepan over moderately low heat, stirring constantly. Remove from heat and add the hot water. At this point the sugar will form hard lumps. Stir and cook until all lumps have dissolved. Remove from heat and let cool. Stir in the vanilla extract. Serve over pancakes, or as a sauce for ice cream, puddings, or cold desserts. Makes approximately ¾ cup.

⚜ CHOCOLATE GLAZE

6 squares (6 ounces) unsweetened
  chocolate
¼ cup light corn syrup

3 tablespoons water
2½ tablespoons unsalted butter

Break the chocolate into small pieces and set it aside. Place the remaining ingredients in a small saucepan. Cook the mixture, stirring, over moderate heat
until it reaches the boiling point. Remove from heat and stir in chocolate.
Continue stirring the mixture until the chocolate has completely melted. Use
this glaze to frost-glaze cakes, cookies, and Petits Fours (page 479). Makes
approximately ¾ cup.

⚜ GLAZING SYRUP

2 cups sugar
⅔ cup water

⅛ teaspoon cream of tartar
dash of salt

Combine all ingredients in a heavy-bottomed 1½-quart saucepan. Mix well.
Stir and cook until the mixture reaches the boiling point. Continue cooking,
without stirring, to 290° or 300° F. on a candy thermometer or until a little
of the syrup dropped into cold water separates into brittle threads. Remove the
syrup from the heat and dip the saucepan into cold water to stop further
cooking. Place the pan over boiling water to prevent the syrup from harden-
ing. Makes approximately 1¼ cups.

⚜ SUGAR SYRUP WITH RUM, COGNAC, OR LIQUEUR

HEAVY
(makes approximately 3 cups)
1½ cups sugar
2 cups water
½ cup rum, cognac, Kirsch, Cointreau,
  or other liqueur

LIGHT
(makes approximately 3¼ cups)
1 cup sugar
2 cups water
½ cup rum, cognac, Kirsch, Cointreau,
  or other liqueur

Combine the sugar and water in a 1½-quart saucepan. Mix well and bring to
boiling point. Cool to lukewarm and add the rum, cognac, Kirsch, or other
liqueur. Use as directed in specific recipes in this book. This syrup may be
stored in a covered jar in the refrigerator to use as needed.

⚜ CHOCOLATE CURLS

Let a square of unsweetened chocolate stand at room temperature until
warmed. Using a vegetable parer or a sharp knife, shave thin curls from the
top of the square.

❧ Chocolate Cigarettes

Let a bar (¼ pound) unsweetened chocolate warm to room temperature and shave long curls (cigarettes) from the back of the bar.

❧ HOW TO MELT CHOCOLATE FOR DECORATING PURPOSES

Melt semisweet chocolate over warm water (not hot). Cool until the chocolate is stiff enough to be piped through a decorating tube. If the chocolate is too thin, a little sifted confectioners' sugar may be added.

❧ MACAROON CRUMBS

Heat macaroons in a preheated moderate oven (350° F.) for 10 minutes. Remove from the oven and cool. Place macaroons in a plastic bag or paper bag and roll them into crumbs. Of if an electric blender is available, break the macaroons, a few at a time, into the bowl and blend a few seconds until the macaroons are in fine or coarse crumbs as desired.

❧ PRALINE POWDER

1 cup sugar
1 cup blanched almonds

½ teaspoon vanilla extract

Put the sugar and almonds in a heavy skillet. Stir and cook over moderate heat until the sugar is well caramelized. Stir in the vanilla extract. Turn out onto a buttered platter. Let cool until the mixture hardens, then break it into pieces and put them in a plastic bag or paper bag. With a heavy rolling pin roll and pound the pieces to powder. Store the powder in a tightly covered container and use as needed. Makes approximately 1 cup.

❧ VANILLA SUGAR (*Sucre Vanillé*)

Bury a vanilla bean in 5 pounds of granulated sugar in a canister equipped with a tight-fitting lid. Store at least 1 week before using. Replenish the sugar as it is used. Vanilla sugar may be used in any recipe specifying sugar and vanilla extract or vanilla bean. Makes 5 pounds vanilla sugar.

Desserts

Desserts (*entremets*), hot or cold, balance a meal, both gastronomically and from the standpoint of good nutrition. The type of dessert served is usually determined by the rest of the menu. Substantial meals should end with light desserts, such as poached fruit, or fresh fruit and soft cheese. Light meals welcome richer desserts, such as pastries, cakes, or rich puddings. This chapter includes all kinds of desserts except cakes, pies, and pastries, which are in Chapter 17.

CREAMS AND CUSTARDS

⚜ BAVARIAN CREAM (*Bavarois*)

1 envelope unflavored gelatin
¼ cup cold water
2-inch piece vanilla bean, or 1 teaspoon vanilla extract
1 cup milk
3 large egg yolks

½ cup sugar
dash salt
1 cup heavy cream, whipped (if vanilla extract is used instead of vanilla bean, add it to the cream before whipping)

Soften the gelatin in the water and set aside. Add the vanilla bean (if used) to the milk and heat only until milk is hot, stirring occasionally to prevent a skin from forming over the surface. Beat the egg yolks lightly in the top part of a double boiler or in a 1-quart saucepan. Gradually beat in the sugar. Add the salt. Gradually add the hot milk, including the vanilla bean. Stir and cook the custard over hot water (not boiling) or over very low heat until the custard coats a metal spoon. Remove from heat. Remove the vanilla bean, rinse it, and save it for use in another dessert. Strain the custard into a bowl and stir in the gelatin. Place in a bowl of ice water to chill, or chill in the refrigerator, until the custard begins to thicken. Fold in the whipped cream. Turn into a 1-quart mold. Chill until firm. When ready to serve, unmold onto a serving plate and serve with one of the fruit sauces (see Index). Makes 6 to 8 servings.

⚜ BAVARIAN CREAM WITH STRAWBERRIES
(*Bavarois aux Fraises*)

5 cups strawberries	⅓ cup cold water
1 tablespoon lemon juice	dash salt
¾ cup sugar	½ teaspoon vanilla extract
2 envelopes unflavored gelatin	2 cups heavy cream, whipped

Wash the strawberries. Reserve 10 to 12 of the finest; remove caps from the remaining berries. Drain the capped berries well, mash, and put them through a sieve. Stir in the lemon juice and sugar. Soften the gelatin in the cold water, place over hot water, and stir until melted. Add to the strawberries along with the salt and vanilla extract. Chill the mixture in a bowl of ice water until it begins to thicken. Fold in the whipped cream. Rinse a 2-quart mold with cold water and fill it with the strawberry cream. Refrigerate until the cream is firm, 3 hours or overnight. To serve, unmold onto a large round plate and garnish with the whole uncapped strawberries. Makes 10 to 12 servings.

⚜ STRAWBERRIES MARGOT (*Fraises Margot*)

Bavarian Cream with Strawberries	2 tablespoons sugar
1½ cups firm, ripe strawberries	½ teaspoon vanilla extract
1 cup heavy cream, whipped	pistachio nuts

Mold the Bavarian Cream with Strawberries in a 2-quart charlotte mold or other 2-quart mold. Chill until firm. Meanwhile, wash the strawberries, and remove the caps. Unmold the Bavarian Cream onto a serving plate. Combine the whipped cream, sugar, and vanilla extract and beat until the cream stands in stiff peaks. Frost the top and sides of the molded Bavarian Cream with some of the whipped cream. Put the rest of the cream in a pastry bag and pipe rows of cream across the top of the Bavarian Cream, around the edge of the top, and around the base. Arrange the larger strawberries as desired over the top, and the smaller ones at intervals in the cream around the base of the mold. Decorate with pistachio nuts. Makes 10 to 12 servings.

❧ CARAMEL CREAM I (*Crème Renversée au Caramel I*)

Caramel (see following recipe)
1 cup milk
1 cup light cream
3-inch piece vanilla bean, or 1 teaspoon vanilla extract

3 large whole eggs
2 large egg yolks
½ cup sugar
1/16 teaspoon salt

Coat a 1-quart casserole with Caramel according to the directions in the following recipe. Put the milk, light cream, and vanilla bean (if used) in a saucepan and heat, stirring to prevent a skin from forming over the top. Beat the whole eggs and egg yolks together until foamy. Gradually add the sugar and salt. Stir in the milk, cream, and vanilla bean (if used) or, if vanilla bean is not used, add the vanilla extract. Pour the custard into the caramel-coated casserole. Place the casserole in a pan of hot water. Bake in a preheated slow oven (325° F.) 50 to 60 minutes or until a knife inserted in the center comes out clean. Cool and chill. Just before serving, turn the cream out onto a serving plate. Makes 4 servings.

❧ Caramel

Melt ½ cup sugar in a small heavy saucepan over moderately low heat until it forms a golden syrup, stirring constantly to prevent burning. Add 2 tablespoons hot water. The syrup will harden, but cook the mixture until it has melted. Pour immediately into a 1-quart casserole, turning and rolling the casserole from side to side to coat it with the caramel. Set aside until ready to use.

❧ CARAMEL CREAM II (*Crème Renversée au Caramel II*)

½ cup sugar
¼ cup hot water
2 cups milk
3-inch piece vanilla bean, or 1 teaspoon vanilla extract

1/16 teaspoon salt
1 teaspoon cornstarch
3 large eggs, beaten

Stir and cook the sugar in a small saucepan over moderately low heat until it has melted and forms a golden syrup. Add the hot water. The sugar syrup will lump, but continue cooking until the lumps have dissolved. Heat 1¾ cups of the milk with the vanilla bean (if used) in a 1-quart saucepan or in the top of a

1-quart double boiler. Add the caramelized sugar and the salt. Blend the corn-starch with the remaining ¼ cup cold milk, beat it into the eggs, and add to the hot milk. Stir and cook over very low heat or hot water (not boiling) until the custard coats a metal spoon. Remove from heat. Remove and discard vanilla bean (if used), or add the vanilla extract. Stir frequently while custard is cooking. Strain before serving. Makes 6 servings.

⚜ CHESTNUT MONT-BLANC (*Mont-Blanc aux Marrons et aux Fruits*)

1 pound raw chestnuts
cold water to cover
1 cup milk or milk to cover chestnuts
1-inch piece vanilla bean, or 1
    teaspoon vanilla extract

⅔ cup sugar
¼ cup water
1 tablespoon butter
Chantilly Cream, or any fruit compote
    desired (see Index)

With a sharp paring knife, cut a slit around each chestnut shell. Place the chestnuts in a saucepan with cold water to cover and bring to boiling point. Remove the pan from the heat, and, without draining, remove the chestnuts from the water one at a time and peel off the shell before it has time to cool. Meanwhile scald the milk with the vanilla bean. Add the peeled chestnuts to the hot milk, bring to boiling point, reduce heat, and simmer until chestnuts are soft. Strain, discard the milk (reserving the vanilla bean), and put the chestnuts through a sieve, or purée them, a few at a time, in an electric blender. Combine the sugar, the ¼ cup water, and the reserved vanilla bean or the vanilla extract, if vanilla bean was not used. Mix well. Stir and bring to boiling point, reduce heat, and cook, without stirring, until a soft ball forms when a little of the syrup is dropped in cold water. If vanilla bean was used, remove it from the syrup and discard it. Add the puréed chestnuts to the syrup and mix until a thick paste is formed. Let cool until lukewarm. Stir in the butter. Butter a 1-quart ring mold and sprinkle it with granulated sugar. Pipe the paste through a pastry bag, fitted with the smallest round nozzle, into the mold, letting the mixture fall at random and handling it lightly to form a nest. While the nest is still warm carefully unmold it onto a chilled platter. Fill the center with Chantilly Cream or with any fruit compote desired. Makes 6 servings.

⚜ FLOATING ISLAND (*Île Flottante*)

½ cup ground roasted blanched
    almonds
dash salt
3 large egg whites
½ cup sugar

⅛ teaspoon almond extract
3½ cups Soft Custard (see following
    recipe)
dried currants or chopped pistachio
    nuts (optional)

Grind the almonds in an electric blender, half of them at a time, or grind them in a food chopper, using the fine blade. Set aside. Add the salt to the egg whites and beat them until they stand in soft, stiff peaks. Gradually beat in the sugar, beating well after each addition. Fold in the almond extract and ground almonds. Butter a 3-cup (¾-quart) ring mold well and sprinkle it with granulated white sugar. Fill with the meringue. Place the mold in a pan of hot water and bake in a preheated very slow oven (275° F.) 50 minutes. Meanwhile make custard according to the directions in the following recipe. Remove the pan from the oven and leave the mold in the pan of water until the meringue has cooled. Pour the custard into a serving bowl, and turn out the meringue ring over the custard. If desired, sprinkle with dried currants or pistachio nuts. Makes 8 servings.

⚜ Soft Custard

1 whole egg
3 egg yolks
⅓ cup sugar
⅛ teaspoon salt

2 teaspoons cornstarch
3 cups milk
3-inch piece vanilla bean, or 1
    teaspoon vanilla extract

Beat the whole egg and egg yolks together. Combine the sugar, salt, and cornstarch and gradually beat the mixture into the eggs. Blend in ¼ cup of the milk. Meanwhile, heat the remaining 2 ¾ cups of the milk with the vanilla bean (if used) and beat into the egg mixture. Stir and cook the custard over hot water until it coats a metal spoon. Remove from heat and cool. Strain the custard. If the vanilla bean was not used, add the vanilla extract.

⚜ LEMON CREAM (*Pouding au Citron*)

4 large egg yolks
½ cup sugar
1/16 teaspoon salt
¼ cup lemon juice

½ teaspoon grated lemon rind
½ cup heavy cream, whipped
½ teaspoon vanilla extract
finely shredded lemon rind

Beat the egg yolks in the top of a double boiler. Gradually beat in the sugar and salt. Add the lemon juice and mix well. Stir and cook over hot water (not boiling) until the mixture is thick and smooth. Remove from the heat and place over ice water to cool, stirring frequently. Fold in the grated lemon rind, whipped cream, and vanilla extract. Pile the mixture in 6 sherbet glasses. Garnish with a little finely shredded lemon rind. Makes 6 servings.

⚜ ORANGE CREAM (*Crème à l'Orange*)

4 large egg yolks
2 teaspoons cornstarch
¾ cup sugar
½ cup water
½ cup orange juice
¼ cup lemon juice

dash salt
1½ teaspoons vanilla extract
½ teaspoon grated lemon rind
1 teaspoon grated orange rind
½ cup heavy cream, whipped
shredded orange rind

Put the egg yolks in the top of a 1½-quart double boiler and beat them lightly. Add the next 5 ingredients and mix well. Cook over hot water (not boiling) about 25 minutes or until the mixture is medium thick and frothy, beating frequently with a wire whip or rotary beater. Cool. Add the salt, vanilla extract, lemon rind, and orange rind. Fold in whipped cream. Serve in sherbet glasses. Garnish with a little shredded orange rind. Makes 6 servings.

⚜ RICE CONDÉ (Riz Condé)

¾ cup raw long-grain rice
hot water
½ teaspoon salt
3 cups milk
¾ cup sugar
2-inch piece vanilla bean, or 1
    teaspoon vanilla extract

4 large egg yolks
2 tablespoons butter
2 tablespoons heavy cream
poached or canned fruit, or Apricot
    Sauce II, Raspberry Sauce, or
    Strawberry Sauce (see Index)

Soak the rice 30 minutes in enough hot water to cover it. Drain well. Add the next 3 ingredients and the vanilla bean (if used). Cover and cook over moderate heat until the rice is tender but not mushy. Remove and discard the vanilla bean (or, if it was not used, add the vanilla extract now). Beat the egg yolks until they are light and foamy and add them to the rice. Add the butter and cream. Mix well with a fork, being careful not to crush the rice. Heat 1 to 2 minutes or only long enough to cook the egg yolks. Turn the mixture into a mold and let stand until the mixture takes the shape of the mold. Unmold onto a serving plate. Garnish with poached or canned fruit, such as apples, apricots, cherries, peaches or pears, or with Apricot Sauce II, Raspberry Sauce, or Strawberry Sauce (see Index). Makes 6 to 8 servings.

⚜ RICE À L'IMPERATRICE (Riz à l'Imperatrice)

½ cup finely chopped glacéed fruit
3 tablespoons Kirsch
½ cup long-grain rice
hot water
3 cups milk
¼ teaspoon salt
3-inch piece vanilla bean, or 1½
    teaspoons vanilla extract

1½ teaspoons unflavored gelatin
2 tablespoons water
¼ cup sugar
2 large egg yolks
½ cup heavy cream, whipped
½ cup red-currant jelly

Combine the glacéed fruit and 2 tablespoons of the Kirsch and let marinate while preparing the rest of the ingredients. Soak the rice in hot water to cover for 30 minutes. Drain well. Add 2 cups of the milk, the salt, and the vanilla bean (if used). Cover and cook 20 to 25 minutes, or until rice is tender but not mushy. If rice becomes too dry before it has finished cooking, add a little more hot milk. Soften the gelatin in the water. Put the sugar and egg yolks in a saucepan and mix well. Stir in the remaining 1 cup milk. Stir and cook over low heat or hot water (not boiling) until custard coats a metal spoon. Add the gelatin and stir until it has dissolved. Strain the custard into the rice. Mix well and chill until the mixture begins to set. Fold in the marinated fruit and whipped cream. If the vanilla bean was not used, add the vanilla extract. Turn the mixture into a lightly oiled 1-quart mold. Chill until the rice mixture is set. Unmold onto a serving plate. Whip the jelly with the remaining 1 tablespoon Kirsch and serve over the dessert. Makes 6 servings.

⚜ STRAWBERRY CREAM (*Crème Printemps*)

2 cups strawberries (wild or
   cultivated)
3 tablespoons sugar
2 tablespoons Kirsch, or Kirsch to
   taste

2½ tablespoons confectioners' sugar
½ teaspoon vanilla extract
1 cup heavy cream

Wash and cap the strawberries, reserving 8 uncapped berries for a garnish. Mash the remaining strawberries, add the sugar and Kirsch, and marinate 1 hour in the refrigerator. Add the confectioners' sugar and vanilla extract to the cream and beat the mixture until the cream stands in soft peaks. Put the strawberries through a sieve and fold the purée into the cream. Serve in sherbet glasses and top each with one of the reserved strawberries. Makes 8 servings.

⚜ STRAWBERRY MOUSSE (*Mousse aux Fraises*)

1 quart strawberries
12 tablespoons sugar
1/16 teaspoon salt

3 large egg whites
½ teaspoon vanilla extract
½ cup heavy cream

Wash and cap the strawberries. Save 6 uncapped strawberries for use as a garnish. Crush the remaining berries and mix with 5 tablespoons of the sugar. Set aside. Add the salt to the egg whites and beat until they stand in soft stiff peaks. Gradually beat in 6 tablespoons of the remaining sugar. Fold in the crushed strawberries and the vanilla extract. Turn into a glass bowl and chill. Just before serving, add the remaining 1 tablespoon sugar to the cream and whip until the cream stands in soft peaks. Pipe the cream through a pastry bag or spoon it, as desired, over the top of the Strawberry Mousse. Decorate with the reserved uncapped strawberries. Makes 6 servings.

⚜ VANILLA CREAM (*Creme à la Vanille*)

2 cups milk
2-inch piece vanilla bean
½ cup sugar

2 teaspoons cornstarch
1/16 teaspoon salt
4 egg yolks, or 2 large whole eggs

425

Heat 1¾ cups of the milk with the vanilla bean only until milk is hot (do not boil). Put the next 3 ingredients into a 1-quart saucepan or 1-quart top of a double boiler. Mix well. Beat in the egg yolks or whole eggs and the remaining ¼ cup cold milk. Gradually add the hot milk including the vanilla bean. Stir and cook over very low heat or hot water until the custard coats a metal spoon. Cool. Remove and discard the vanilla bean. (If vanilla bean is not available, add 1 teaspoon vanilla extract at this time.) Pour the cream into a chilled glass bowl. Makes 4 to 5 servings.

⚜ Chocolate Cream

In the recipe for Vanilla Cream, mix 3 tablespoons cocoa with the sugar and cornstarch or melt 1 square (1 ounce) unsweetened chocolate over hot water (not boiling) and add it to the hot milk. Continue as directed in the recipe. Makes 4 to 5 servings.

⚜ SMALL POTS OF VANILLA CREAM
(Petits Pots de Crème à la Vanille)

Petits Pots de Crème are rich custards baked in individual ceramic pots designed for the purpose.

2 cups light cream
3-inch piece vanilla bean, or 1½
   teaspoons vanilla extract
6 egg yolks

½ cup sugar
⅛ teaspoon salt
Chantilly Cream (optional; page 409)

Heat 1¾ cups of the cream with the vanilla bean (if used). Beat the egg yolks until light and lemon-colored. Gradually beat in the sugar, salt, the remaining ¼ cup unheated cream, and the vanilla extract (if vanilla bean was not used). Gradually beat in the hot cream. Strain the mixture into crème pots or custard cups. Place them in a baking pan. Pour hot water into the pan to a depth of 1 inch. Cover the pots with crème-pot covers or cover the custard cups with foil. Bake in a preheated slow oven (325° F.) 20 to 25 minutes or until a knife inserted in the center comes out clean. Cool and chill before serving. Garnish with Chantilly Cream, if desired. Makes 6 servings.

⚜ Small Pots of Caramel Cream *(Petits Pots de Crème au Caramel)*

Place ½ cup sugar in a small heavy saucepan. Stir and cook it over moderately low heat until the sugar melts and is straw-colored. Add 2 tablespoons water. The melted sugar will lump, but stir and cook it until it is smooth. Remove the pan from the heat and spoon 1 tablespoon of the syrup into each of 6 little crème pots or 6-ounce custard cups. Finish filling them with rich custard made by the recipe for Small Pots of Vanilla Cream. Bake and serve according to directions in the recipe. Makes 6 servings.

⚜ BREAD CUSTARD FRITTERS (*Beignets au Pain*)

Cut a loaf of unsliced bread into slices ¾ inch thick. Trim the crusts from the slices and dip the slices into rum-flavored Custard Sauce (page 408). Roll each in flour and dip them, one by one, into beaten whole egg. Fry about 3 minutes in deep fat preheated to 370° F. The outside will be crisp and the inside soft and sweet. Serve with rum-flavored or plain Custard Sauce. Allow 1 slice of bread per serving.

⚜ ZABAGLIONE (*Crème Sabayon*)

6 large egg yolks
6 tablespoons sugar

⅔ cup Marsala or sherry

Put the egg yolks in the top of a double boiler. With a rotary beater or an electric beater, beat the egg yolks, then gradually beat in the sugar, and continue beating until the mixture is thick and pale lemon color. Gradually beat in the wine. Place over hot water (not boiling), and continue beating until the mixture foams and begins to thicken, being careful not to overcook it. Strain into sherbet glasses and serve hot at once, otherwise the Zabaglione will fall flat. If desired line each glass with 3 ladyfingers or strips of sponge cake or pound cake. Zabaglione may also be served as a sauce. Makes 4 servings as a dessert or 6 servings as a sauce.

CHARLOTTES

⚜ APPLE CHARLOTTE (*Charlotte aux Pommes*)

firm-textured bread, sliced ¼ inch
  thick
1 cup (2 sticks) butter, melted
6 to 8 large cooking apples
¼ cup water
¼ cup (½ stick) butter
½ cup sugar

¼ teaspoon salt
1 tablespoon lemon juice
½ teaspoon vanilla extract
½ cup raspberry jam
¼ cup light rum
2 tablespoons sugar
1 glacéed red cherry

For best results, use bread 2 to 3 days old. Remove the crusts. Cut some of the slices into 12 wedges and dip them in the melted butter. Sauté in a skillet until golden brown on each side, adding a little more butter if needed. Fit the wedges into the bottom of a 6-cup charlotte mold or deep casserole. Cut

427

bread slices in strips 1¼ inches wide, enough to line the inside of the mold. Dip the strips in melted butter and fit them, overlapping, around the inside of the mold. Trim off all protruding ends. Peel, quarter, and core the apples and cut them into thin slices. Place them in a pan with the water and the ½ stick of butter. Cover and cook over very low heat until the apples are soft and all the water has evaporated. Add the ½ cup sugar, salt, lemon juice, and vanilla extract. Mix well. Heat again if apples seem watery; they should be thick enough to remain in a solid mass in a spoon. Turn the mixture into the prepared mold. Cut enough bread wedges to cover the top of the mold, dip them in melted butter, and place them on top of the apples. Place the mold on a baking sheet in order to catch any butter that drips over the sides and to prevent the bottom from browning too much. Bake in a preheated hot oven (400° F.) 40 minutes or until the top has browned. Remove the Charlotte from the oven and let it stand 20 minutes before removing it from the mold. Place the jam, rum, and the 2 tablespoons sugar in a small saucepan, bring to boiling point and boil 1 minute, stirring constantly. Strain and spoon over the warm Apple Charlotte. Garnish the center with a glacéed cherry. (*See illustration, page 439.*) Makes 6 servings.

⚜ APPLE MOUSSELINES (*Mousseline de Pommes en Coupes*)

1 envelope unflavored gelatin
1¼ cups milk
⅔ cup sugar
1 teaspoon cornstarch
¹⁄₁₆ teaspoon salt

3 large egg yolks, or 2 medium-sized
    whole eggs
1 cup unsweetened applesauce
½ cup heavy cream, whipped
2 tablespoons Kirsch or Kirsch to taste
6 glacéed cherries

Soak the gelatin in ¼ cup of the milk while making the custard. Place the sugar, cornstarch, and salt in the top of a 1-quart double boiler or in a 1-quart saucepan. Mix well and beat in the egg yolks or whole eggs. Gradually stir in the remaining 1 cup milk. Stir and cook over hot water or very low heat until the custard coats a metal spoon. Remove from heat and add the softened gelatin. Mix well. Place over ice water until the custard begins to set. Fold in the applesauce, whipped cream, and Kirsch to taste. Serve in sherbet glasses. Top each with a glacéed cherry. Makes 6 servings.

⚜ CHARLOTTE RUSSE (*Charlotte Russe*)

about 19 ladyfingers
Bavarian Cream (page 419)
⅓ cup heavy cream

2 teaspoons sugar
¼ teaspoon vanilla extract
glacéed cherries

Line a 1-quart charlotte mold or a straight-sided mold with waxed paper, having a circle on the bottom, cut to fit, and a strip around the sides, cut to fit. Split the ladyfingers. From one of the halves, cut a 1-inch circle and place it in the center of the bottom of the mold, rounded side down. Cover the rest of the bottom with ladyfingers that have been shaped to a point at one end. Place them close together around the circle with the pointed ends toward the center, so they radiate from it like the petals of a daisy. Stand the remaining ladyfingers, close together, all around the sides. (If they tend to fall out of place, butter the paper lining around the sides very lightly.) Fill the mold with Bavarian Cream. Chill at least 3 hours. When ready to serve, unmold the Charlotte on a round serving plate. Combine the cream, sugar, and vanilla extract, and beat until the cream stands in soft stiff peaks. Put into a pastry bag and pipe around the mold as desired. Decorate with glacéed cherries.

Charlotte Russe may also be molded in an 8- or 9-inch springform pan. Do not line the pan with paper or put ladyfingers on the bottom. When the Charlotte is almost set, cover the top with ladyfingers in the same way that they were arranged over the bottom of a charlotte mold, rounded sides up. Chill until firm. To serve, remove the sides of the springform pan and place the mold on a plate. Decorate as desired with whipped cream and glacéed cherries. Makes 6 to 8 servings.

❧ INDIVIDUAL CHARLOTTES (*Petites Charlottes*)

1½ cups sliced strawberries or
    raspberries
⅔ cup sugar
dash salt
1 tablespoon cornstarch
1 cup light cream or milk

3 egg yolks, lightly beaten
1 teaspoon vanilla extract
½ cup heavy cream, whipped
12 to 16 ladyfingers
Chantilly Cream (page 409)

Combine the strawberries or raspberries with 2½ tablespoons of the sugar and refrigerate until the Charlottes are ready to be served. Mix the remaining ½ cup sugar, the salt, and the cornstarch in the top of a 1-quart double boiler or in a 1-quart saucepan. Stir in ¾ cup of the light cream or milk. Cook over boiling water or low heat until the mixture has thickened. Combine the remaining ¼ cup light cream or milk with the lightly beaten egg yolks and blend with the sugar mixture. Stir and cook over hot water (not boiling) or very low heat until the mixture is thick. Cool. Add the vanilla extract to the heavy cream and beat until the cream stands in soft peaks. Fold into the mixture. Split the ladyfingers and stand 4 halves in each of 6 to 8 sherbet glasses. Spoon the cream into the glasses, filling them half full. Chill. Just before serving, finish filling the sherbet glasses with the sweetened sliced strawberries or raspberries. Put Chantilly Cream in a pastry bag and pipe a rosette on the top of each serving. Makes 6 to 8 servings.

MERINGUES

⚜ ITALIAN MERINGUE (*Pâte à Meringue Italienne*)

1 cup sugar
¼ teaspoon cream of tartar
½ cup water

⅟₁₆ teaspoon salt
3 large egg whites
½ teaspoon vanilla extract

Combine the first 3 ingredients in a 1-quart saucepan. Stir and cook slowly until the sugar has dissolved and the water begins to boil. Cover and boil 3 minutes, or until the steam has washed down any sugar crystals that may have formed on the sides of the pan. Remove cover and boil rapidly, without stirring, to 242° F. on the candy thermometer or until the syrup spins a thread 6 to 8 inches long. Add the salt to the egg whites and beat until they stand in stiff peaks, but stop before they are dry. Using a rotary or an electric beater, gradually beat in the hot syrup. Add the vanilla extract and continue beating until the meringue stands in very stiff peaks. Use as a pie or pudding topping, to frost cakes, and to make frozen parfaits and sherbets. Makes 2½ cups.

⚜ SWISS MERINGUE (*Pâte à Meringue Suisse*)

This meringue is hard after it is baked. It is used to make shells to be filled with Chantilly Cream, Fruit Cream, and other cream fillings.

¼ teaspoon salt
¼ teaspoon cream of tartar
4 large egg whites

1 cup fine granulated sugar
½ teaspoon vanilla extract

Place the first 3 ingredients in a mixing bowl. Using an electric beater, beat the mixture at high speed until the egg whites are stiff enough to hold their shape. At low speed, beat in the sugar, 2 tablespoons at a time. Beat the mixture until it is very stiff, shiny, and moist. This is very important for making successful meringues.

⚜ Individual Meringue Shells

Mark 12 circles 3 inches in diameter on a piece of brown paper. Butter the paper lightly and dust it with cornstarch. Using a pastry bag, spread each circle with a layer of Swiss Meringue ¼ inch thick. With more meringue, build a border to a height of 1½ inches, leaving the center unfilled. Place the paper on a cooky sheet. Bake in a preheated very slow oven (250° F.) 1¼ hours. Turn off heat and let the meringue shells cool in the oven ½ hour. Remove from the oven and continue cooling. When the meringue shells are cold, transfer them to a tin box and cover tightly. Use as needed for cream fillings, fruits, and ice cream. Makes twelve 3-inch shells.

⚜ Meringue Pie Shell

Make Swiss Meringue, using only 2 egg whites and half the quantities of the other ingredients. Using a round 9-inch cake pan as a guide, mark a 9-inch circle on brown paper. Butter the paper lightly and dust with a little cornstarch. Spread the circle with a layer of meringue ¼ inch thick. Build a border with the remaining meringue to a height of 1 ½ inches. Place the paper on a cooky sheet. Bake in a very slow oven (250° F.) 2 hours. Let cool in the oven ½ hour. Remove from the oven and finish cooling. Remove the shell from the paper. Fill with cream filling, fruit, or ice cream. Makes one 9-inch meringue shell.

⚜ ALMOND MERINGUES (*Meringues aux Amandes*)

1 recipe for Swiss Meringue (page 430)

⅓ cup finely ground blanched almonds
2 tablespoons cornstarch

Make the mixture for Swiss Meringue, but use only ¾ cup of the sugar in the mixture. Combine the ground almonds, cornstarch, and the remaining ¼ cup sugar. Fold into the Swiss Meringue mixture. Shape and bake the meringues according to the directions for baking Swiss Meringues. Makes 12 shells.

⚜ CHESTNUT MERINGUES (*Chamonix*)

sweet chestnut purée (available at specialty food stores)

8 baked round Individual Meringue Shells (page 430)
Chantilly Cream (page 409)

Pipe chestnut purée into the baked Individual Meringue Shells, using a pastry bag. Put 1 heaping teaspoon Chantilly Cream in the center of each. Serve as a dessert. Makes 8 servings.

⚜ MERINGUES GLACÉES

Sandwich Individual Meringue Shells together with a filling of vanilla ice cream. Serve with Strawberry Sauce, Chocolate Sauce, or other desired sauce (see Index). Allow 1 Meringue Glacée (2 shells) per serving.

⚜ SNOW EGGS (*Oeufs à la Neige*)

1/16 teaspoon salt
3 large eggs, separated
12 tablespoons sugar

1 ½ cups milk
1 ½-inch piece vanilla bean, or 1 teaspoon vanilla extract

431

Add the salt to the egg whites and beat until the whites are stiff. Gradually beat in 9 tablespoons of the sugar, beating well after each addition. (To test for stiffness, rest an egg on the meringue. If the egg does not sink, the egg whites have been beaten enough.) Heat the milk, the remaining 3 tablespoons sugar, and the vanilla bean (if used) in a shallow saucepan. Bring to boiling point and reduce heat to simmering. (If vanilla bean was not used, add the vanilla extract.) Using an English dessert spoon or oval-shaped soup spoon, shape the meringue into ovals the size and shape of an egg, and drop them into the simmering milk. After poaching 2 minutes, turn them carefully with a fork and poach 2 more minutes. (If they are cooked longer, they will collapse.) With a large perforated spoon remove the meringue eggs from the milk and drain them on a clean dry towel. Set aside. Strain and reserve the milk. Beat the egg yolks in the top of a 1-quart double boiler or in a 1-quart saucepan. Gradually beat in the reserved milk. Stir and cook over hot water or very low heat until the custard begins to thicken. Remove from heat, strain, and chill. To serve, pour the custard into a glass bowl, and float the meringue eggs over the top. Makes 4 to 5 servings.

DESSERT OMELETTES AND SOUFFLÉS

⚜ JAM OMELETTE (*Omelette à la Confiture*)

4 large eggs	apricot jam or marmalade
2 teaspoons sugar	confectioners' sugar
1½ tablespoons butter	¼ cup 100-proof rum (optional)

Place the eggs and sugar in a mixing bowl and beat lightly with a fork. Melt the butter in a heavy 8-inch skillet or omelette pan. Pour in the egg mixture. Cook over moderately low heat. As the omelette cooks, lift the edges and turn them toward the center so the uncooked mixture flows under the cooked portion. Cook only until the bottom is light brown and the top is set. Spread the top with apricot jam or marmalade. Fold half the omelette over the other half. Place on an oven-proof platter and sprinkle with confectioners' sugar. Put under broiler heat only long enough to caramelize the sugar, leaving the oven door ajar. If desired, heat the rum, ignite, and pour it, flaming, over the omelette. Serve promptly. Makes 3 servings.

⚜ SOUFFLÉ VANILLA OMELETTE (*Omelette Soufflé à la Vanille*)

2 large egg yolks	4 large egg whites
¼ cup confectioners' sugar	1 tablespoon granulated sugar
½ teaspoon vanilla extract	

Beat the egg yolks until light. Gradually beat in the confectioners' sugar and vanilla extract. Beat the egg whites until they stand in soft stiff peaks. Then beat in the granulated sugar. Fold the egg whites into the yolks. Heap the mixture onto a well-buttered heatproof platter and smooth the mixture with a spatula. Use the spatula to make a furrow about 2 inches deep down the lengthwise center of the omelette. Bake in a preheated slow oven (300° F.) 30 minutes or until the omelette is well puffed and browned. Sprinkle the top with confectioners' sugar just before omelette is done. Serve at once, for the omelette collapses more quickly than a soufflé. Makes 2 servings.

⚜ Soufflé Omelette with Lemon or Orange
(Omelette Soufflé au Citron ou à l'Orange)

In the recipe for Soufflé Vanilla Omelette, add the grated rind of either 1 lemon or 1 orange to the egg yolks along with the vanilla extract. Continue as directed in the recipe. Makes 2 servings.

⚜ VANILLA SOUFFLÉ *(Soufflé à la Vanille)*

3 tablespoons butter
4 tablespoons flour
1 cup hot milk
3 large eggs, separated
⅓ cup sugar

1½ teaspoons vanilla extract
¼ teaspoon almond extract
¼ teaspoon salt
Chantilly Cream (page 409)
⅓ cup toasted slivered almonds

Melt the butter in a 1-quart saucepan. Remove from heat and blend in the flour. Stir and cook ½ minute or until the mixture is bubbly. Remove from heat and beat in the milk, using a wire whisk. Stir and cook over moderate heat until thickened. Beat the egg yolks with half of the sugar and add to the cooked mixture. Add the vanilla and almond extracts. Let cool. Add the salt to the egg whites and beat them until they stand in soft stiff peaks, then beat in the remaining sugar. Carefully fold into the custard. Butter a 1½-quart soufflé dish, sprinkle it with sugar, and gently turn the mixture into it. Place the dish in a pan of hot water. Bake in a preheated slow oven (325° F.) 1 hour or until the center is firm when pressed with the index finger. Spread with Chantilly Cream, sprinkle with the slivered almonds, and serve promptly. Makes 6 servings.

⚜ Chocolate Soufflé *(Soufflé au Chocolat)*

Make the recipe for Vanilla Soufflé, adding 2 squares (2 ounces) unsweetened chocolate to the mixture just before adding the egg yolks. Stir until chocolate is melted.

⚜ **Coffee Soufflé** (*Soufflé au Café*)

Make the recipe for Vanilla Soufflé, replacing half of the milk with strong coffee.

PUDDINGS

⚜ **ENGLISH PLUM PUDDING, OR CHRISTMAS PUDDING**
(*Pouding de Noël*)

1½ cups seeded raisins
¾ cup dried currants
¾ cup finely chopped figs
⅓ cup chopped citron
⅓ cup chopped candied orange peel
⅓ cup chopped candied lemon peel
1 cup Madeira or sherry
½ cup fine dry breadcrumbs
½ cup brandy or rum
¾ cup sifted all-purpose flour
1½ teaspoons salt
½ teaspoon ground cinnamon
¼ teaspoon ground cloves
1 teaspoon ground nutmeg
1 teaspoon ground ginger
½ pound suet, ground
4 large eggs, separated
⅓ cup sugar

Hard Sauce (page 408) or Custard Sauce flavored with Kirsch or brandy (page 408)

Marinate all the fruit several hours or overnight in the Madeira or sherry. (The longer the fruit is soaked in the wine, the better the pudding.) Soak the breadcrumbs 10 minutes in the brandy or rum. Sift the flour, salt, and spices together into a large mixing bowl. Add the suet and mix well. Beat the egg yolks well, and gradually beat in the sugar. Add to the flour mixture. Add the marinated fruit and breadcrumbs and mix well. Beat the egg whites until they stand in soft stiff peaks and gently fold them into the mixture. Butter a 1½-quart mold generously, sprinkle it with sugar, and turn the pudding mixture into it. Cover the mold and place on a trivet in a deep kettle. Pour in hot water, having it come halfway up the sides of the mold. Cover the kettle and bring the water to boiling point. Continue cooking 3½ hours, adding additional water to the kettle as needed. Serve with Hard Sauce or Custard Sauce flavored to taste with brandy or Kirsch. Decorate with holly. (*See illustration, page 437.*) Makes 12 servings.

✣ HOT DIPLOMAT PUDDING (*Pouding Diplomate Chaud*)

2 tablespoons seedless raisins or
   currants
hot water
¼ cup mixed diced glacéed fruit
2 tablespoons Kirsch or rum
2 cups milk
2-inch piece vanilla bean, or 1
   teaspoon vanilla extract

3 whole eggs
2 egg yolks
½ cup sugar
⅟₁₆ teaspoon salt
6 macaroons or ladyfingers
Vanilla Sauce (page 408) or
   Zabaglione (page 427)

Soak the raisins or currants 5 minutes in hot water to cover them. Drain them well and mix with the glacéed fruit and the Kirsch or rum. Let the mixture stand until ready to use. Heat the milk with the vanilla bean (if used). Beat the whole eggs and egg yolks together lightly. Gradually add the sugar, mixing well. Add a little of the hot milk to the eggs, then add the salt and the remaining hot milk, including the vanilla bean (if used; if not, add the vanilla extract). Spread half the marinated fruit in the bottom of a buttered 1-quart casserole. Break 3 of the macaroons or ladyfingers into pieces and scatter the pieces over the fruit. Repeat, using the rest of the fruit and macaroons or ladyfingers. Pour the egg and milk mixture over all. Cover the casserole and place it in a pan of hot water. Bake in a preheated slow oven (325° F.) about 50 minutes, or until a knife inserted in the center comes out clean. Remove the pudding from the pan of hot water, and let stand 10 minutes. Unmold it on a serving dish. Serve warm with Vanilla Sauce or Zabaglione. Makes 6 servings.

✣ HAZELNUT PUDDING (*Pouding aux Noisettes*)

⅔ cup roasted shelled hazelnuts or
   filberts
½ cup sifted flour
½ cup (1 stick) butter, softened
2 cups hot milk
½ cup sugar

¼ teaspoon salt
4 large eggs, separated
1 teaspoon vanilla extract
light brown sugar
Vanilla Sauce (page 408), or whipped
   cream

Grind the hazelnuts or filberts medium fine. Set aside. Blend the flour with the softened butter and add to the hot milk. Add the sugar and salt. Cook, stirring, over moderate heat 5 minutes or until the mixture is smooth and thick. Cool slightly. Beat the egg yolks lightly. Add a little of the cooked mixture to them and then add to the remaining cooked mixture. Stir in the vanilla extract and ½ cup of the ground nuts. Beat the egg whites until they stand in soft stiff peaks and fold them into the batter. Butter a 1½-quart casserole generously, sprinkle with light brown sugar and the remaining nuts, and turn the batter into the casserole. Place the casserole in a pan of hot water and bake in a preheated moderate oven (350° F.) 1 hour or until the pudding is well puffed and firm in the center. Serve warm with Vanilla Sauce or whipped cream. Makes 6 servings.

⚜ LIMOUSIN CHERRY PUDDING (*Clafouti Limousin*)

CHERRY FILLING
4 cups (1½ pounds) pitted sweet
   black or red cherries
1 tablespoon lemon juice
¾ cup sugar
⅛ teaspoon salt
2 tablespoons flour
2 tablespoons butter

PUDDING BATTER
1¾ cups sifted all-purpose flour
2½ teaspoons double-acting baking
   powder
½ teaspoon salt
1½ teaspoons vanilla extract
½ cup butter, softened
¾ cup sugar
1 large egg
⅔ cup milk

Combine the cherries with the lemon juice and put them in an 8- by 8- by 2-inch baking dish. Mix the sugar, salt, and flour and sprinkle over the cherries. Dot with the butter. Set aside while making the Pudding Batter. Sift together the first 3 batter ingredients. Set aside. Mix the vanilla extract with the batter and gradually blend in the sugar. Beat in the egg. Add the flour mixture alternately with the milk. Beat the batter ½ minute, then spread it over the cherries. Bake in a preheated moderate oven (350° F.) 50 minutes or until a toothpick inserted in the center comes out clean. Cut into squares. Serve warm or cold. Makes 6 to 8 servings.

FRUIT DESSERTS

⚜ BAKED APPLES (*Pommes à la Bonne-Femme*)

4 large tart baking apples
4 teaspoons butter
sugar

4 tablespoons dry white wine
2 tablespoons apricot jam or
   marmalade

Wash and core the apples, being careful not to break through the blossom end. Starting at the stem end, pare the apples about ⅓ of the way down. Place them in a 10- by 6- by 2-inch baking pan, pared side up. Put a teaspoon of butter in the cavity of each apple and finish filling the cavity with sugar. Pour 1 tablespoon dry white wine over each apple. Pour hot water into the pan to a depth of ¼ inch. Cover the pan with foil and bake in a preheated hot oven (400° F.) 25 minutes. Remove the foil and baste with some of the liquid in the pan. Continue baking, uncovered, 15 to 20 minutes. (The baking time depends upon the type of apple used.) Transfer the apples to individual serving dishes. Blend the apricot jam or marmalade with the liquid left in the pan. Heat and cook about 1 minute. Spoon over apples. Makes 4 servings.

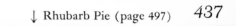

438　↑ Banana Fritters (page 448)　　　　　　　　　↓ Apricot Croûtes (page 447)

↑ Apple-Rice Meringues (page 446)

↓ Apple Charlotte (page 427)   439

↑ Pears with Chocolate Sauce (page 449)   ↓ Pineapple Ninon (page 450)

↑ Lattice-Top Apple Tart (page 493)

↓ Frosted Génoise (page 462) 441

442 ↑ Cream Puffs: with Chocolate Glaze, with Cream Saint-Honoré; Salambos; Chocolate and Coffee Eclairs (page 490)   ↓ Mocha Cake (page 468)

↑ Puff-Pastry Layer Cake (page 470)

↓ Swiss Roll (page 473) *443*

444 ↑ Small Babas au Rhum and Small Rum Savarins
(pages 474, 476)

↓ Plum Cake (page 469)

❧ APPLES ALICE (*Pommes Alice*)

3 large baking apples (Rome Beauty
  or Jonathan)
⅔ cup sugar
1⅓ cups water
2 teaspoons lemon juice
mixed glacéed fruit

about 1 cup French Pastry Cream
  (page 409)
milk
3 tablespoons ground blanched
  almonds (optional)

Peel the apples, remove the cores, and cut the apples into crosswise halves.
Combine the sugar, water, and lemon juice in a 1½-quart saucepan, mix well,
bring to boiling point, and simmer 5 minutes. Add half of the apples and simmer, uncovered, 15 to 20 minutes or until apples are tender. (The cooking
time depends upon the ripeness of the apples.) Transfer the apples to a baking
dish. Cook the rest of the apples in the same syrup. Fill the cavities with mixed
glacéed fruit. Thin French Pastry Cream with a little milk if it has thickened
on standing, then pour it over the apples. Sprinkle with the ground almonds
if available. Brown in a preheated hot oven (425° F.). If almonds are not
available, mix ¼ cup fine dry breadcrumbs with 1½ tablespoons sugar and
sprinkle over the apples. Brown in the hot oven as for almonds. Serve hot.
Makes 6 servings.

❧ APPLE DUMPLINGS NORMANDE (*Douillons à la Normande*)

4 medium-large cooking apples (Rome
  Beauty, Jonathan, Northern Spy,
  Winesap)
½ cup sugar
⅛ teaspoon salt
¾ teaspoon ground cinnamon

Plain Pastry Dough (page 24) using
  2 cups flour
4 teaspoons butter
2 teaspoons milk
sugar
Chantilly Cream (optional; page 409)

Wash the apples and peel and core them, being careful not to cut through the
blossom end. Mix the sugar, salt, and cinnamon and spoon 2 tablespoons of
the mixture into each of the apple cavities. Roll the pastry into a 15½-inch
square, ⅛ inch thick. With a fluted pastry cutter, cut the pastry into 4 squares
of equal size. Place an apple in the center of each and top with 1 teaspoon
butter. Bring the opposite corners of pastry together over the top, pressing
the sides together firmly. If any pastry is left, roll it thin, cut 4 1-inch circles,
and place one over the center top of each apple, pressing it down with the
index finger. Brush the surface of the dumplings with the milk and sprinkle
them lightly with sugar. Bake in a preheated hot oven (425° F.) 35 minutes or
until apples are tender and pastry is brown. Serve warm or cold, with Chantilly Cream if desired. Makes 4 servings.

❧ APPLE FRITTERS (*Beignets de Pommes*)

3 large firm eating apples
3 tablespoons sugar
1 tablespoon rum or Kirsch

½ teaspoon vanilla extract
Fritter Batter (page 24)

Peel and core the apples and cut them into crosswise slices about ¼ inch thick. Sprinkle the slices with 1 tablespoon of the sugar. Mix the rum or Kirsch with the vanilla extract and pour over the apples. Mix well, being careful not to break the slices. Let stand 1 hour. Drain any juice that may form in the bowl into the Fritter Batter. Dip a few apple slices at a time into the batter and fry in deep fat preheated to 375° F. until they are golden brown. Drain the fritters on paper towels and arrange them in a baking pan. Sprinkle with the remaining 2 tablespoons sugar and put into a preheated hot oven (450° F.) 5 minutes to glaze. Makes 6 to 8 servings.

❧ APPLE-RICE MERINGUE (*Pommes au Riz Meringuées*)

½ cup raw long-grain rice
water
2 tablespoons butter
1¼ cups hot milk
¼ teaspoon salt
3 tablespoons granulated sugar
2 large eggs, separated
3 large baking apples
½ cup granulated sugar

1 cup water
1 tablespoon lemon juice
2-inch piece vanilla bean, or ½
    teaspoon vanilla extract
½ cup plus 1 tablespoon sifted
    confectioners' sugar
red-currant jelly or apricot jam
    (optional)

Soak the rice 30 minutes in water to cover. Drain well. Melt the butter in a 1½-quart saucepan or in the top of a double boiler. Add the rice. Cook, stirring constantly, over moderately low heat 3 to 4 minutes or until the rice is dry and sticks to the pan. Add the milk, the salt, and the 3 tablespoons granulated sugar. Cover and cook over moderately low heat or boiling water until the rice is tender and has absorbed all the milk, about 15 minutes. Beat the egg yolks lightly, add a little of the hot rice to them, and then add the mixture to the rest of the hot rice. Toss the rice lightly with a fork to blend in the egg yolks and to separate the rice grains. Spread the rice on a heatproof serving dish. Set aside.

Peel the apples, remove the cores, and cut the apples in half crosswise. Combine the ½ cup granulated sugar, the 1 cup water, the lemon juice, and the vanilla bean or vanilla extract in a 9-inch skillet. Bring the mixture to boiling point. Add the apples. Simmer, uncovered, 15 to 20 minutes or until the apples are tender but still retain their shape, basting frequently. Arrange the apples over the rice. Beat the egg whites until they stand in soft stiff peaks.

Gradually beat in the ½ cup confectioners' sugar. Heap the meringue attractively over the rice and sprinkle it lightly with the additional confectioners' sugar. Bake in a preheated slow oven (325° F.) 12 to 15 minutes or until the meringue has browned lightly. If desired, top each serving with a little red-currant jelly or apricot jam.

To make this dish as illustrated on page 439, spoon rice on top of each poached apple half. Put the meringue in a pastry bag and pipe it over the rice, covering it completely. Brown as in the preceding directions. Makes 6 servings.

⚜ APRICOTS CROÛTES (*Croûtes aux Abricots*)

Cut stale Brioche or Savarin (see Index), or coffee cake into slices about ½ inch thick and brown the slices in butter. Top each slice with two canned or poached apricot halves, cavity side up. Place a glacéed cherry or a maraschino cherry in each half. Cover with hot Apricot Sauce II (page 406), flavored with Kirsch or rum. (*See illustration, page 438.*) Allow one slice Brioche, Savarin, or coffee cake and 2 apricot halves per serving.

⚜ BANANA BOATS (*Barquettes de Bananes*)

4 medium-sized firm ripe bananas, unpeeled
1 tablespoon sugar
2 to 3 tablespoons Maraschino

⅓ cup heavy cream, whipped with 2 teaspoons sugar
glacéed cherries

Wash and dry the bananas. Carefully cut them in half lengthwise and remove them from the peels, leaving the peels intact. Cut the bananas in ½-inch slices and add sugar and Maraschino to taste. Fill the peels with the whipped cream and top with alternate slices of bananas and slices of glacéed cherries. Arrange the Banana Boats on an oval-shaped dish. Makes 4 servings.

⚜ BANANAS WITH CHOCOLATE CREAM (*Bananes au Chocolat*)

Slice 2 large bananas or 3 medium-sized bananas and pour 3 tablespoons Grand Marnier over them. Sprinkle with 1 tablespoon sugar and chill 1 hour. Serve in compotes, topped with Chocolate Chantilly Cream (see following recipe), and decorated with glacéed cherries. Makes 4 servings.

⚜ Chocolate Chantilly Cream

Fold 1 tablespoon cooled Chocolate Sauce (page 407) into ½ cup Chantilly Cream (page 409).

⚜ BANANA FRITTERS (*Beignets de Bananes*)

4 bananas	Sweet Fritter Batter (page 24)
4 teaspoons sugar	Vanilla Sugar (page 418)
4 teaspoons lemon juice	Raspberry Sauce (page 407)
3 tablespoons brandy or rum	

Peel the bananas, cut in half crosswise, and split each half lengthwise. Sprinkle with the sugar, lemon juice, and brandy or rum. Marinate 1 hour, turning occasionally. Drain well and dip into the Sweet Fritter Batter. Drop them, 3 to 4 at a time, into deep fat preheated to 375° F. Fry until golden brown. Drain on paper towels. Sprinkle with Vanilla Sugar. Serve hot with Raspberry Sauce. Or, if desired, serve these fritters as an accompaniment to meats. (*See illustration, page 438.*) Makes 6 servings.

⚜ JELLIED MIXED FRUIT WITH LIQUEUR
(*Fruits Rafraîchis au Kirsch*)

1 envelope unflavored gelatin	2 apricots, peeled and quartered
¼ cup cold water	2 nectarines or peaches, peeled and
1 cup boiling water	quartered
½ cup sugar	1 cup strawberries, caps removed
2 tablespoons lemon juice	½ cup sweet red or black cherries
3 to 4 tablespoons Cointreau, Kirsch,	Chantilly Cream (page 409)
Curaçao, or other desired liqueur	

Combine the gelatin and cold water and let stand 5 minutes. Stir in the boiling water. Add the sugar and lemon juice, and stir until sugar has dissolved. Chill in a pan of ice water or refrigerate until the mixture is as thick as fresh egg whites. Meanwhile, pour the liqueur over the apricots and the nectarines or peaches and let marinate until the gelatin has thickened to the desired consistency. Then gently fold them into the gelatin, along with the strawberries and cherries. Refrigerate until ready to serve. Serve in sherbet glasses, decorated with a rosette of Chantilly Cream. Makes 6 servings.

⚜ CHILLED MELON BALLS WITH FRUIT AND WINE
(*Melon Rafraîchis en Macedoine*)

Wash a melon (small watermelon, cantaloupe, honeydew, or other type) and wipe dry. Cut it in half and remove the fibers and seeds. With a French melon-ball cutter, cut the flesh into balls. Scoop out any remaining flesh to use in fruit cups, etc., leaving the shell clean. Return the melon balls to the shell. Add fresh pineapple wedges, strawberries, and pitted sweet cherries.

Sprinkle with port wine to taste. Chill. Allow ½ cantaloupe or ¼ honeydew or ½ small round refrigerator watermelon per serving. One large watermelon will serve 12 to 15 persons.

⚜ ORANGES STELLA (*Oranges Stella*)

With a pointed sharp paring knife, cut notches around the middle of a large orange as if cutting pointed teeth in a jack-o'-lantern, sticking the knife to the center of the orange each time a notch is cut. Then pull the orange apart, leaving two halves with notched rinds. Remove the orange sections with a grapefruit knife or paring knife. Marinate the sections in Cointreau for 1 hour, using 1½ tablespoons for each orange. Refill the orange shells with the orange sections just before serving. Using a pastry bag fitted with a star tube (No. 16), pipe a rosette of Chantilly Cream (page 409) in the center of each. Decorate with a crystallized violet, glacéed cherry, or fresh raspberry. Allow one orange half per serving.

⚜ PEACH MELBA (*Pêches Melba*)

3 large firm, ripe peaches
1½ cups raspberries
2⅓ cups sugar
1/16 teaspoon salt
1 cup water

1-inch piece vanilla bean, or ½
    teaspoon vanilla extract
vanilla ice cream
1 teaspoon lemon juice

Blanch the peaches a few seconds in boiling water, then dip them, one by one, in cold water, and slip off the skins. Cut the peaches in half and remove the pits. Crush the raspberries with a fork, add ⅓ cup of the sugar, and chill 1 hour. Combine the remaining 2 cups sugar, the salt, water, and vanilla bean or vanilla extract in a saucepan, bring to boiling point, and boil 2 minutes. Add the peaches and cook, uncovered, 10 minutes, or until peaches are tender but retain their shape. Chill in the syrup. Put the ice cream into 6 individual serving dishes or into 1 large serving dish. Drain peach halves and arrange them over the ice cream. Put the berries through a sieve, add the lemon juice, and spoon over the peaches. Makes 6 servings.

⚜ PEARS WITH CHOCOLATE SAUCE (*Poires au Chocolat*)

Allow half of 1 medium-large pear per serving. Peel and core the pear halves and cook until tender in sugar syrup, using ½ cup sugar and 1½ teaspoons lemon juice to each cup water. Cool pears in the syrup. With a perforated spoon, transfer each pear half to an individual serving dish. Cover the pears with Chocolate Sauce (page 407). Place a scoop of ice cream on each dish. Decorate with Chocolate Curls (page 417) or Chocolate Cigarettes (page 418). Serve with assorted cookies. (*See illustration, page 440.*)

❧ PEARS MOORISH STYLE (*Poires à la Mauresque*)

Arrange a cold poached half banana between 2 cold poached ripe pear halves in each individual serving dish. Cover with Chocolate Sauce (page 407). Decorate with rosettes of Chantilly Cream (page 409) and with halved glacéed cherries.

❧ CHANTILLY PINEAPPLE WITH RED-CURRANT SAUCE (*Ananas et Groseilles Chantilly*)

8 slices fresh pineapple
sugar

Red-Currant Sauce (page 406)
whipped cream, sweetened to taste

Dip the pineapple slices in sugar and let them stand 15 minutes. Arrange them on a round dish and garnish the slices generously with Red-Currant Sauce. Chill. Top with whipped cream. Makes 4 servings.

❧ PINEAPPLE NINON (*Ananas Ninon*)

1 large pineapple
4½ tablespoons granulated sugar
5 tablespoons Kirsch
1 cup wild strawberries or cultivated
    strawberries
1 medium-sized banana, sliced
¾ cup heavy cream

1½ tablespoons sifted confectioners'
    sugar
¼ teaspoon vanilla extract
glacéed cherries and glacéed
    pineapple
6 baked tartlet shells made of Sweet
    Pie Pastry (page 25)
Raspberry Sauce (page 407)

Wash and dry the pineapple. Remove the top, cutting it 1 inch below the green leaves. Insert a knife in the meat of the pineapple ½ inch from the edge, and cut around it as cleanly as possible. With a melon-ball cutter or sharp-sided spoon, remove the meat from the pineapple, leaving a shell with sides ½ inch thick. Cut the scooped-out pineapple into bite-size pieces and chill one or more hours in a mixture of 2 tablespoons each granulated sugar and Kirsch. Wash and drain the strawberries and remove the caps. Leave wild strawberries whole; cut cultivated strawberries in half. Mix with the sliced bananas and 2 tablespoons each granulated sugar and Kirsch. Chill 1 hour or longer. Sprinkle the inside of the pineapple shell with ½ tablespoon granulated sugar and chill 1 hour or longer. When ready to serve, fill the shell with alternating layers of fruit, having pineapple as the bottom and top layer. Combine the cream, confectioners' sugar, and vanilla extract and beat until the cream stands in soft peaks. Fold in the remaining 1 tablespoon Kirsch. Spoon a generous amount over the filled pineapple. Garnish with glacéed cherries and glacéed pineapple. Put the filled pineapple on a chilled plate for serving.

Fill the baked tart shells with the Kirsch-flavored cream and garnish them with glacéed cherries and glacéed pineapple. Place the tarts on the plate around the filled pineapple. Serve with Raspberry Sauce. (*See illustration, page 440.*) Makes 6 servings.

Compotes

A compote consists of not too ripe fruit cooked in a fairly heavy syrup. It may be cooked with a stick of cinnamon or a piece of vanilla bean, or vanilla extract may be added after the fruit has finished cooking. Red or white wine is often used to replace all or part of the water. The fruit is served in some of the syrup. Transfer the fruit to a serving dish with a slotted spoon and cook the syrup until it is reduced to about one-fourth to one-half the original quantity, then pour it over the fruit. Or the syrup may be thickened with a little cornstarch blended with a little wine or water or by the addition of apricot jam or red-currant jelly. A liqueur, such as Cointreau, Crème de Menthe, Kirsch, or Triple Sec, may be added to the syrup, or brandy or rum may be added, if desired.

⚜ APPLE COMPOTE (*Compote de Pommes*)

Select a type of apple that holds its shape when cooked, such as Rome Beauty or Jonathan.

4 large cooking apples
1 tablespoon lemon juice
2⅓ cups cold water

¾ cup sugar
1-inch piece vanilla bean, or ½ teaspoon vanilla extract

Peel the apples, remove the cores, and cut the apples into quarters. Mix the lemon juice with ⅓ cup of the water, and dip the apples into the mixture to prevent discoloration. Combine the remaining 2 cups water and the sugar and vanilla bean (if used) in a 1½-quart saucepan and bring the mixture to boiling point. Reduce heat and boil gently 5 minutes. Add the apples, cover, and cook, without boiling, 10 to 15 minutes or until the apples are tender and still hold their shape, basting occasionally or turning carefully. (The cooking time depends upon the ripeness of the apples.) Remove the vanilla bean if used; if it was not used, add the vanilla extract. Cool the apples in the syrup. Serve as a meat accompaniment or as a dessert. Makes 4 to 5 servings.

⚜ APRICOT COMPOTE (*Compote d'Abricots*)

¾ cup sugar
2 cups water
1/16 teaspoon salt
1 tablespoon lemon juice

2-inch piece vanilla bean, or 1 teaspoon vanilla extract
12 fresh apricots

451

Combine the first 4 ingredients in a 1½-quart saucepan with the vanilla bean (if used). Bring to boiling point and simmer 5 minutes. Peel the apricots, remove the pits, and add the apricots to the syrup. Cover and cook gently 5 minutes or until apricots are tender. With a slotted spoon, remove the apricots to individual serving dishes. Reduce the syrup to one-half the original amount. Remove the vanilla bean if used; if it was not used, add the vanilla extract. Pour over the fruit. Makes 4 servings.

❧ BANANA COMPOTE (*Compote de Bananes*)

¾ cup sugar
2 cups water
1/16 teaspoon salt
1 tablespoon lemon juice

2-inch piece vanilla bean, or 1 teaspoon vanilla extract
3 bananas
2 tablespoons apricot jam
2 tablespoons dark rum or rum to taste

Combine the first 4 ingredients in a 1½-quart saucepan, along with the vanilla bean (if used). Bring the mixture to boiling point and simmer 5 minutes. Peel the bananas, cut them into lengthwise halves, and add half of them to the hot syrup. Cover and cook 1 to 2 minutes. Transfer the bananas to a serving dish. Poach the remaining bananas in the same syrup. Reduce the syrup to one-fourth the original amount. Remove the vanilla bean if used; if it was not used, add the vanilla extract. Add the apricot jam and rum. Pour the syrup over the bananas and let them cool in the syrup. Makes 6 servings.

❧ CHERRY COMPOTE (*Compote de Cerises*)

1 pound sweet cherries
½ cup sugar
½ cup water
½ cup dry red wine

1 teaspoon cornstarch
1 tablespoon cold water
2 tablespoons Kirsch, or Kirsch to taste

Wash and pit the cherries. Tie 12 of the pits in a cheesecloth bag. Combine the sugar, water, and wine in a 1½-quart saucepan. Add the bag of cherry pits, bring the mixture to boiling point, and cook 5 minutes. Add the cherries, cover, and simmer 10 minutes. Using a perforated or slotted spoon, remove the cherries to a serving dish. Remove and discard the bag of pits. Reduce the syrup to one-fourth the original amount. Blend the cornstarch with the 1 tablespoon water, add to the syrup, and cook 1 minute or until the syrup is clear and slightly thickened. Add the Kirsch. Pour the syrup over the cherries, and let them cool in the syrup. Makes 4 servings.

❧ CHILLED FRUIT WITH KIRSCH (*Fruits Rafraîchis au Kirsch*)

½ cup sugar
1 cup water
2 teaspoons lemon juice
dash salt
2 apricots, peeled and quartered
2 nectarines or peaches, peeled and
    quartered

½ cup fresh pineapple wedges
½ cup sweet red or black cherries,
    pitted
½ cup strawberries, caps removed
2 to 3 tablespoons Cointreau, Kirsch,
    or Curaçao

Combine the first 4 ingredients in a 1-quart saucepan. Bring to boiling point, reduce heat, and simmer 5 minutes. Let cool. Place the fruit in a pretty glass or china bowl and embed the bowl in cracked ice. Pour the sugar syrup over the fruit. Sprinkle Cointreau, Kirsch, or Curaçao over the fruit before serving. Makes 4 to 5 servings.

❧ PEACH COMPOTE (*Compote de Pêches*)

In the recipe for Apricot Compote (page 451) replace the apricots with peaches. Makes 4 servings.

❧ PEACHES CARDINAL (*Pêches à la Cardinal*)

6 medium-sized firm ripe peaches
½ cup sugar
1¾ cups water
dash salt

4 teaspoons lemon juice
1 cup ripe red raspberries
2 tablespoons sugar
chopped blanched almonds

Wash the peaches. Plunge them into boiling water and then into cold water. Using a sharp paring knife, remove the skins. Cut the peaches in half, remove the pits, and if desired cut the peach halves in half. Combine the ½ cup sugar, the water, salt, and 2 teaspoons of the lemon juice in a saucepan. Bring to the boiling point, reduce the heat, and simmer 5 minutes. Add the peaches, cover, and cook slowly 5 minutes, or until peaches are tender when pierced with a fork. Chill in the syrup. With a perforated or slotted spoon, transfer peaches to compote glasses. Meanwhile, wash the raspberries, drain well, mash, and put them through a sieve. Add the remaining 2 teaspoons of lemon juice and the 2 tablespoons sugar. Stir until sugar is dissolved. Chill. Just before serving, spoon this sauce over the peaches, coating them completely. Sprinkle with chopped almonds. Makes 4 to 5 servings.

✤ PEACHES IN RED WINE (*Pêches au Vin Rouge*)

Peel peaches, cut them in half, remove the stones, and put the peaches in a large serving bowl or in individual fruit dishes. Sprinkle with sugar and red wine, using 1 teaspoon sugar and 1 tablespoon wine for each serving. Marinate 1 hour. Allow 2 large peach halves or 3 medium-sized peach halves per serving.

✤ PEAR COMPOTE (*Compote de Poires*)

¾ cup sugar
1½ cups water or dry red wine
1/16 teaspoon salt
1 tablespoon lemon juice
1-inch piece vanilla bean, or 1
   teaspoon vanilla extract

4 medium-sized firm ripe pears
fresh mint sprigs
3 to 4 drops red food coloring
  (optional)

Combine the sugar, water or wine, salt, and lemon juice, and the vanilla bean (if used), in a saucepan. Bring the mixture to the boiling point and simmer 5 minutes. Wash, peel, and quarter the pears, remove the cores, and add the pears to the hot syrup. Cover and cook gently (do not boil) 20 to 25 minutes or until pears are tender when pierced with a fork. (The cooking time depends upon the ripeness of the pears.) Remove the vanilla bean if used; if it was not used add the vanilla extract. Cool the pears in the syrup and then chill. Serve in compotes garnished with fresh mint. If the red wine is not used, add 3 to 4 drops red food coloring to the syrup if desired, to give the pears a pink color. Makes 4 to 5 servings.

✤ PEARS CARDINAL (*Poires à la Cardinal*)

In the recipe for Peaches Cardinal (page 453) replace the peaches with 4 to 5 pears, peeled and quartered and cooked in the syrup 20 to 25 minutes or until tender. Continue as directed in the recipe. Makes 4 servings.

✤ PLUM COMPOTE (*Compote de Prunes*)

In the recipe for Apricot Compote (page 451) replace the apricots with 2 pounds of plums. Makes 6 servings.

✤ PRUNE COMPOTE (*Compote de Pruneaux*)

Cook dried prunes according to the directions on the package for stewed prunes or prune compote. Allow 5 to 6 prunes for each serving.

⚜ RHUBARB COMPOTE (*Compote de Rhubarbe*)

1½ pounds rhubarb
¼ cup water
dash salt

¾ cup sugar
1½-inch piece vanilla bean, or ¾ teaspoon vanilla extract

Cut off the leaves and coarse big ends of the rhubarb stalks. Wash and peel the older stalks, but do not peel the young tender ones, since the peel gives the cooked rhubarb a pink color. Cut the stalks into 1-inch pieces. Add the water, salt, sugar, and the vanilla bean (if used). Cover and cook over very low surface heat 25 to 30 minutes. If the vanilla bean was not used, add the vanilla extract. Or, if desired, mix the salt with the sugar and sprinkle over the rhubarb, add the vanilla bean and bake in a covered casserole in a preheated moderate oven (375° F.) 45 to 50 minutes, or until rhubarb is tender. Do not stir. Remove the vanilla bean, if used. Serve as an accompaniment to meat or as a dessert. Makes 4 to 5 servings.

⚜ STRAWBERRIES CARDINAL (*Fraises à la Cardinal*)

2 cups firm ripe strawberries
1 cup ripe red raspberries
4 to 5 tablespoons fine granulated sugar

1 to 2 teaspoons lemon juice
chopped blanched almonds

Wash the strawberries, remove caps, and refrigerate 3 to 4 hours. Wash the raspberries, drain well, mash, and put through a sieve. Add sugar and lemon juice to taste. Stir until sugar is dissolved. Chill. Shortly before serving, put the strawberries in tall compote glasses and coat them with the raspberry purée. Sprinkle with chopped almonds. Makes 4 to 5 servings.

FROZEN DESSERTS

⚜ VANILLA ICE CREAM I (*Glace à la Vanille I*)

This is a basic recipe for a smooth, rich French Vanilla Ice Cream made in a crank freezer.

3-inch piece vanilla bean, or 2 teaspoons vanilla extract
1 cup milk
1 cup sugar

5 large egg yolks, lightly beaten
⅛ teaspoon salt
3 cups light cream, chilled

Add the vanilla bean (if used) to the milk and heat until milk is hot. Beat the sugar into the egg yolks, and gradually beat in the hot milk, with the vanilla bean (if used). Stir and cook over hot water (not boiling) about 8 minutes or until the custard coats a metal spoon. Chill. Remove and discard the vanilla bean, or add the vanilla extract if vanilla bean was not used. Stir in the salt and light cream. Strain the mixture into a 2-quart freezer can. Insert the dasher, cover, and put the can in the freezer tub. Adjust the can and the crank so that the handle turns freely. Fill the tub with cracked ice and rock salt, using 8 parts ice to 1 part salt, being careful that the ice and salt do not come up to the bottom of the lid, to prevent salt water from seeping into the ice cream. Turn the handle slowly and steadily until resistance is felt, then turn the handle rapidly until the ice cream is as thick as cornmeal mush. Drain off the excess brine. Wipe off the lid and remove it. Take out the dasher and scrape the ice cream from the sides of the can and pack it down, using a rubber spatula. Replace the lid and cork the opening in it. Repack in ice and rock salt, 4 parts ice to 1 part rock salt, covering the container completely. Cover the freezer with several thicknesses of newspaper, canvas, or burlap. Let stand 3 to 4 hours to ripen. Makes approximately 1½ quarts.

VARIATIONS

⚜ Chestnut Ice Cream (*Glace aux Marrons*)

Fold ½ cup vanilla-flavored chestnut purée and ⅓ cup whipped cream into Vanilla Ice Cream I shortly before the ice cream is firm.

⚜ Chocolate Ice Cream (*Glace au Chocolat*)

Make Vanilla Ice Cream I, adding 2 squares (2 ounces) melted unsweetened chocolate to the hot milk. Mix well.

⚜ Coffee Ice Cream (*Glace au Café*)

Make Vanilla Ice Cream I, adding 1 tablespoon instant coffee to the hot milk.

⚜ VANILLA ICE CREAM II (*Glace à Vanille II*)

This is a basic recipe for an excellent smooth ice cream developed for automatic refrigerators or freezers.

1¼ cups sugar	2 cups milk
¼ teaspoon salt	2 cups heavy cream
3 teaspoons vanilla extract	

Combine the first 4 ingredients and stir until the sugar is dissolved. Add the cream and mix well. Pour the mixture into 2 freezer trays or into an 8- by

8- by 2-inch pan. Let freeze until the mixture is a firm mush. Turn into a large mixing bowl and beat with an electric beater until the mixture is fluffy, starting with the beater at low speed and increasing the speed to the highest as the mixture softens. (Do not beat so long that the mixture melts.) Return the mixture to the trays or pan and freeze until the ice cream is firm, stirring once before it is completely frozen. Makes 1½ quarts.

❧ RASPBERRY OR STRAWBERRY ICE CREAM
(*Glace aux Framboises ou aux Fraises*)

Add 2 tablespoons sugar to 1 cup raspberry or strawberry purée. Fold into the beaten Vanilla Ice Cream II mixture just before returning the mixture to the freezer trays or pan.

❧ ICE CREAM PLOMBIÈRES (*Glace Plombières*)

Fill a shallow mold with alternating layers of Vanilla Ice Cream (commercial or homemade), ladyfingers soaked in Kirsch, and diced candied fruit marinated in Kirsch, having ice cream as the bottom and top layers. Cover with foil and place in the freezer until firm. To unmold, run a spatula between the mold and the ice cream and quickly dip (flash dip) the mold in a pan containing enough boiling water to come within an inch from the top of the mold. Quickly turn the ice cream out onto a serving plate. Return the ice cream to the freezer for an hour or more. If desired, decorate the mold with Kirsch-flavored Chantilly Cream (page 409) and glacéed cherries. Allow 1 quart ice cream for 8 servings.

❧ ICED VANILLA MOUSSE (*Mousse Glacée à la Vanille*)

2 tablespoons sugar
½ teaspoon vanilla extract

1 cup heavy cream
2 cups cold Soft Custard (page 423)

Add the sugar and vanilla extract to the cream. Beat until the cream stands in soft peaks. Fold into the Soft Custard. Turn into a 1-quart mold. Cover with foil. Freeze several hours or until firm. Makes 6 to 8 servings.

❧ PEACH OR APRICOT MOUSSE
(*Mousse aux Pêches ou aux Abricots*)

1½ cups diced peaches or apricots
¾ cup sugar
1 teaspoon lemon juice

½ teaspoon vanilla extract
dash salt
1½ cups heavy cream, whipped

Crush the peaches or apricots, add the sugar, and let stand 1 hour. Put the fruit through a sieve. Add the lemon juice, vanilla extract, and salt and fold the mixture into the whipped cream. Turn the mixture into a freezer tray, cover with foil and freeze, without stirring, 4 hours or until the mousse is firm. Makes 6 servings.

⚜ RASPBERRY OR STRAWBERRY MOUSSE
(Mousse aux Framboises ou aux Fraises)

1 quart raspberries or strawberries	1/16 teaspoon salt
1 cup sugar	1 quart heavy cream, whipped
1 teaspoon lemon juice	12 whole raspberries or 12 uncapped
1½ teaspoons vanilla extract	strawberries

Wash the raspberries or wash and cap the strawberries. Crush the berries with a fork, add the sugar, and let stand 1 hour. Put the berries through a sieve. Add the lemon juice, vanilla extract, and salt. Mix well, and fold into the whipped cream. Turn the mixture into a 1½-quart mold. Cover and place in the freezer. Let freeze, without stirring, until the mousse is firm. Serve garnished with the whole raspberries or strawberries. Makes 12 servings.

⚜ COFFEE PARFAIT *(Parfait au Café)*

1 cup sugar	3 large egg whites
¾ cup double-strength coffee	1½ teaspoons vanilla extract
¼ teaspoon salt	2 cups heavy cream, whipped

Combine the sugar and coffee in a 3-cup saucepan. Bring to boiling point, stirring constantly. Boil rapidly, without stirring, about 5 minutes or until the syrup forms a soft ball when a little is dropped in cold water (234° F. on a candy thermometer). Remove the syrup from the heat and cool about 1 minute. Meanwhile, add the salt to the egg whites and beat until they stand in soft stiff peaks. Pour the hot syrup in a fine stream over the beaten egg whites, beating the mixture all the while. Add the vanilla extract and continue beating until the mixture is thick and cool. Fold in the whipped cream. Turn the mixture into 2 freezer trays, or into a 9- by 9- by 2-inch baking pan. Cover with foil. Freeze, without stirring, until the mixture is firm. Makes 12 servings.

⚜ SAUTERNE SHERBET *(Sorbet au Sauterne)*

A sherbet is a light ice, which in France is usually served between main courses of a formal meal. It refreshes the palate and prepares it for the roast or other main dish which follows.

Sherbet is made with light syrup, fruit, and liqueur or wine. In France, it is served with a special conical scoop, placed point upward, in sherbet glasses, and sprinkled with the wine or liqueur that was used in the mixture.

1½ cups sugar
1½ cups water
dash salt
1 cup sauterne

2 tablespoons strained lemon juice
⅛ teaspoon cream of tartar
2 large egg whites

Put ½ cup of the sugar, 1 cup water, and the salt into a small saucepan. Mix well, bring to boiling point, and cook 5 minutes. Remove from heat and add the sauterne and lemon juice. Cool. Turn into a freezing tray and freeze until the mixture is almost solid. Put the remaining 1 cup sugar, ½ cup water, and the cream of tartar into a small saucepan. Mix well. Bring the syrup to boiling point and cook, without stirring, until it spins a thread (240° F. on a candy thermometer). Meanwhile, beat the egg whites until they stand in soft stiff peaks. Gradually beat in the hot syrup. With a rotary beater or electric beater, continue beating until the meringue is cool. Fold it into the frozen mixture and turn it into a 9- by 9- by 2-inch baking pan. Freeze until firm, without stirring. Serve in chilled sherbet glasses with 1 tablespoon sauterne poured over each serving. Makes 8 servings.

❧ ICED GRAND MARNIER SOUFFLÉ
(*Soufflé Glacé au Grand-Marnier*)

2 envelopes unflavored gelatin
⅓ cup Grand Marnier
4 large whole eggs
3 large egg yolks
¾ cup sugar
dash salt

1½ cups heavy cream, whipped
1½ teaspoons vanilla extract
⅓ cup heavy cream, whipped with 1
    tablespoon confectioners' sugar
glacéed cherries

Combine the gelatin and Grand Marnier and let stand 5 minutes. Place over hot water (not boiling) to melt. Beat the whole eggs and egg yolks together with an electric beater 2 to 3 minutes. Then gradually beat in the sugar and salt. Beat 12 minutes or until the mixture is very thick and lemon-colored. Beat in the melted gelatin. Fold in the whipped cream and vanilla extract.

Tie a 6-inch band of foil around a 1-quart soufflé dish to form a standing collar. Fill the dish with the soufflé mixture and chill until it is set. With a pastry tube, pipe rosettes of whipped cream onto the top of the soufflé. Garnish the rosettes with bits of glacéed cherries. Makes 6 servings.

17

Cakes and Pastries

The interesting variety of French pastries is based on certain basic doughs which are used in a variety of ways. These doughs include Génoise and sponge-cake mixtures, and Baba dough (given in this chapter), and Puff Pastry, Brioche Dough, Chou Paste, Plain Pastry Dough, and Sweet Pie Pastry (see recipes in Chapter 2). When one knows how to make all these, the preparation of the pastries in this chapter will be greatly simplified.

BASIC BAKING RULES

The first steps to successful baking are to be well organized and to become acquainted with the basic principles and standards for the dish you are making. Here are a few rules to follow:

1. Use a good recipe and study it before you start to work.
2. Use only the best ingredients. Have them at room temperature unless otherwise specified.
3. Have all ingredients and utensils assembled before you start to work.

4. Use standard measuring cups and measuring spoons. Make all measurements level.

5. Follow directions carefully.

6. Use an electric beater, if available, for beating the eggs in French butter cakes (Génoise) and sponge cakes. The eggs will beat to a greater volume in much less time.

7. Cool melted butter before adding it to cake batter.

8. Use pans that are the exact size specified. Pans too large or too small will cause failures in baking.

9. Use pans that are bright and shiny, inside and out, for baking cakes and cookies. They may be made of aluminum or stainless steel. Dark, dull pans cause cakes and cookies to brown too fast and to rise unevenly. Oven-glass pans may be used for cakes, but the oven temperature should be reduced by 25° F., to prevent overbrowning.

10. Prepare cake pans before mixing the batter. (See following directions on How to Prepare Cake Pans.)

11. Have your ovens checked regularly, and bake all dishes at the specified temperature and for the specified time. Do not open the oven door to test for doneness until the minimum time has elapsed.

12. Cool all cakes and cookies before frosting them, unless otherwise specified.

⚜ HOW TO PREPARE CAKE PANS

If pans are to be lined with paper, place the pan on a piece of unglazed brown paper or waxed paper, and trace around the bottom with a pencil. Cut out the paper. Grease the cake pan. Place the paper in the bottom. Then grease the paper lightly.

If the pans are only to be greased and floured, grease the bottom and the sides of the pan and sprinkle lightly with flour. Shake the pan to coat it uniformly. Invert the pan over the sink and knock it lightly to remove the excess flour.

Do not grease pans for sponge cakes; just rinse the pan in cold water and drain it well.

CAKES

⚜ GÉNOISE MIXTURE (*Pâte à Génoise*)

French Génoise usually has as its only leavening agent the air that is beaten into the eggs, but the original French version of this recipe specifies the addition of a small amount of baking powder. This is a fine-textured French butter cake. It is light like a sponge cake but has a firmer and moister texture and cuts more easily. Since this cake requires a great deal of beating, it is advisable to beat the eggs with an electric beater.

4 large eggs
¾ cup sugar
1 teaspoon vanilla extract
½ teaspoon double-acting baking
   powder

¾ cup, plus 2 tablespoons, sifted
   all-purpose flour
5 tablespoons butter, melted and
   cooled to lukewarm

Grease cake pans of the desired size (see pan sizes below), line with waxed paper, lightly grease and flour the paper, and set aside until the batter is mixed. Let the eggs stand in a bowl of warm (not hot) water 7 to 8 minutes so they will beat to a greater volume. Rinse a small-bottomed 2½-quart mixing bowl with warm water (not hot), drain the bowl well, and place it over a bowl (about 3-quart capacity) of warm water, making sure that the bottom of the smaller bowl does not touch the water. Break the eggs into the warm bowl, and with an electric beater, at high speed, beat them until they are foamy, about ½ minute. Then beat in the sugar, 1 tablespoon at a time, and the vanilla extract. Continue beating, at high speed, 6 to 7 minutes, or until the mixture is thick and pale yellow, and has quadrupled in volume. (The mixture almost fills the bowl.) Sift the flour again with the baking powder, and sift one-fourth of this mixture at a time over the beaten egg and sugar mixture. Carefully fold it in, using a flexible rubber spatula or plastic spatula. When all the flour mixture has been added, gently fold in the cooled melted butter, about 1 tablespoon at a time. Bake the batter in the prepared cake pans. Types and sizes of pans with the baking temperatures and approximate baking time for each follow:

Pan type	Pan size (inches)	Number of pans	Oven temperatures	Approximate baking time (minutes)
Tube	9 × 4	1	300° F.	60 to 70
Loaf	9 × 5 × 3	1	325° F.	50 to 60
Round layer	8 × 1½	2	350° F.	25

The cake is done when it rebounds to the touch when pressed gently in the center. Remove the cake from the oven, turn it out on a wire rack, remove the paper, and cool. Frost as desired. Makes approximately 12 servings.

⚜ **Frosted Génoise** (*Génoise Glacée*)

Bake a Génoise in two 8-inch layer-cake pans. When the cakes are cold, spread apricot jam or Vanilla Butter Cream (page 413), flavored to taste with

Kirsch, Cointreau, or Curaçao, between the layers. Spread the top layer with Fondant (page 411). (If Vanilla Butter Cream is used, flavor the Fondant to taste with the same liqueur.) Decorate the top as desired with candied fruits, almonds, or Chantilly Cream (page 409). (*See illustration, page 441.*) Makes one 8-inch 2-layer cake.

Génoise may also be frosted with Chocolate Butter Cream (page 414) between the layers and on the top and sides.

⚜ SAVOY SPONGE MIXTURE (*Pâte à Biscuit de Savoie*)

The classic French Savoy Sponge Mixture does not contain butter, but butter was specified in the French version of this recipe. The cake is a little richer and tenderer than the true Savoy Sponge.

3 large eggs, separated
¾ cup sugar
1 teaspoon vanilla extract
⅛ teaspoon salt
½ cup sifted all-purpose flour
⅓ cup sifted cornstarch

¼ cup (½ stick) butter, melted and
    cooled to room temperature
confectioners' sugar (optional)
Vanilla Butter Cream (optional;
    page 413)
Water Icing (optional; page 415)

Lightly grease an 8- by 8- by 2-inch cake pan and line it with waxed paper. Put the egg yolks in a small-bottomed 2½-quart mixing bowl. Place the bowl over a bowl of warm water (not hot), being sure that the bottom does not touch the water. Beat the yolks ½ minute with an electric beater, at medium speed. Gradually beat in the sugar, beating well after each addition. Continue beating, at high speed, for 2 minutes or until the mixture is pale yellow (almost white). Beat in the vanilla extract. Add the salt to the egg whites and beat them until they stand in soft stiff peaks. Set aside. Sift the flour again with the cornstarch and then sift all of the mixture over the beaten egg yolks and sugar. (Do not mix.) Add the beaten egg whites. Gently fold in the flour and the egg whites at the same time. Add the cooled, melted butter and carefully fold it into the batter. Turn the batter into the prepared cake pan. Bake in a preheated slow oven (300° F.) 45 to 50 minutes. Turn the cake out onto a wire rack to cool. If desired, sift confectioners' sugar over the top. Or, if desired, split the cake and fill it, layer-cake fashion, with Vanilla Butter Cream, and glaze the top with Water Icing. Makes one 8- by 8- by 2-inch cake or 6 to 9 servings.

⚜ ALMOND PITHIVIERS CAKE (*Gâteau d'Amandes dit Pithiviers*)

Puff Pastry (page 25)
⅓ cup almond paste
⅔ cup French Pastry Cream (page
    409)

1 egg yolk
1 tablespoon water
confectioners' sugar

You will need two-thirds of the Puff Pastry recipe for making this cake. Freeze the remaining pastry and the pastry trimmings for future use. Combine the almond paste and French Pastry Cream and beat the mixture with a rotary beater or wire whisk until it is smooth. Set aside. Roll the pastry in two circles ⅛ inch thick on a lightly floured flat surface. Cut the pastry into 8-inch circles, using an 8-inch round cake pan as a guide. Place one of the circles on an ungreased cooky sheet, and spread it with all of the almond paste and Pastry Cream mixture. Cover with the second circle of Puff Pastry. Moisten the edge of the pastry and seal it by pressing firmly all around with the thumb. Then crimp the edge with the tines of a fork dipped in flour. Beat the egg yolk with the water and brush it over the top of the pastry. With a sharp pointed knife, make curving lines out from the center and cut a small hole in the center of the pastry. Chill 30 to 40 minutes. Bake in a preheated very hot oven (450° F.) 12 to 15 minutes or until the pastry has begun to brown. Place another cooky sheet underneath the one on which the cake is being baked. Reduce the oven heat to 350° F. (moderate) and bake 25 minutes. Sprinkle sifted confectioners' sugar over the cake. Reduce the oven heat to 300° F. (slow) and bake 10 minutes. Makes one 8-inch cake or 6 to 8 servings.

❧ BIRTHDAY CAKE (*Gâteau d'Anniversaire*)

	For two 8-inch layers	For three 8-inch layers
large eggs	4	6
sugar	⅔ cup	1 cup
vanilla extract	1 teaspoon	1½ teaspoons
sifted all-purpose flour	¾ cup	1 cup
butter, melted and cooled	¼ cup (½ stick)	6 tablespoons
Chocolate Butter Cream (page 414)	¾ cup	1½ cups
apricot jam	about ½ cup	about ¾ cup
chopped blanched almonds	about ¼ cup	about ⅓ cup
Fondant Cake Icing (page 412)	about ¾ cup	about ¾ cup

Grease the 8-inch round layer-cake pans, line with unglazed brown paper or waxed paper, grease the paper, and set the pans aside (see How to Prepare Cake Pans, page 461). The eggs will beat to a greater volume if they are warm (not hot). Let the eggs stand 7 to 8 minutes in a pan of warm (not hot) water. Rinse a small-bottomed 2½-quart or 3½-quart mixing bowl in warm water and drain it well. Place the bowl over a larger bowl of warm water (not hot), making sure the bottom of the smaller pan does not touch the water. Break the eggs into the bowl, and with an electric beater (if available), at high speed, beat them ½ minute or until they are foamy. Then beat in the sugar, 1 tablespoon at a time, and then the vanilla extract. Continue beating, at high speed, 6 to 8 minutes, or until the mixture is thick, pale yellow (almost white), and almost fills the bowl (quadrupled in volume). Sift ¼ cup of the flour at a time over the beaten egg mixture. Carefully fold it in, using a flexible rubber spatula or plastic spatula. When all the flour has been added, gently fold in the butter, about 1 tablespoon at a time. Bake the batter in the prepared pans in a preheated slow oven (325° F.) 30 minutes or until the cakes rebound to the touch when pressed gently in the center. Remove the cakes from the oven, turn them out onto wire racks, remove the paper from the bottoms, and cool.

Spread Chocolate Butter Cream between the cake layers. Coat the sides with apricot jam, and sprinkle them with chopped almonds. Spread the top with Fondant Icing flavored with Kirsch. Make an appropriate inscription on the top with Fondant Icing put through a pastry tube fitted with a fine, plain nozzle. Arrange the desired number of candles over the top. Makes 12 to 16 servings.

⚜ BRIOCHE CROWN (*Brioche Couronne*)

Roll Brioche Dough (page 20) into a ball on a lightly floured pastry board and make a hole through the center with the index finger. Put a pinch of flour in the hole and rotate the finger, enlarging the hole with each rotation, until it is large enough to insert the hand. Continue to enlarge it by turning the hand round and round until the dough is of uniform thickness and well shaped. Place the dough on a buttered baking sheet. Brush with melted butter, cover, and let the dough rise in a warm place until it has doubled in bulk. Beat an egg yolk with 1 tablespoon water and brush it over the dough. With kitchen scissors, make a series of triangular snips around the inside of the ring. Bake the Brioche in a preheated hot oven (425° F.) 35 minutes or until it has browned. Makes one ring.

⚜ BRIOCHE LOAF WITH A TOPKNOT (*Brioche à Tête*)

Make Brioche Dough (page 20). Cut off about ¼ of the dough for the top-knot. Shape the remaining dough into a large ball, and put it in a buttered, fluted Brioche mold or in another wide-topped mold with high sides. Shape the reserved dough to simulate a pear. With the index finger, punch a hole in the center of the large ball. Push the pointed end of the pear-shaped dough into the hole. Cover and let rise for 30 minutes or until doubled in size. Make 3 or 4 radial cuts around the base of the topknot with a knife or scissors. Brush with 1 egg yolk beaten with 1 tablespoon water. Bake in a preheated hot oven (425° F.) for 45 minutes or until the Brioche is browned and done. Makes one Brioche Loaf.

⚜ CHRISTMAS LOG (*Gâteau Bûche de Noël*)

5 large eggs
1 cup sugar
¼ teaspoon salt
1 teaspoon vanilla extract
1¼ cups sifted all-purpose flour

2 tablespoons butter, melted and cooled
sifted confectioners' sugar
Vanilla Butter Cream (page 413)
Uncooked Butter Frosting (optional; page 415)

Line a greased 15½- by 10½- by 1-inch jelly-roll pan with waxed paper. Grease the paper lightly and set the pan aside. Place the eggs in a bowl of warm (not hot) water, and let them stand for 5 minutes so they will beat to a large volume. Place a small-bottomed 2-quart mixing bowl over a smaller bowl of warm (not hot) water, making sure the bottom does not touch the water. Break the eggs into a saucer, one at a time, and slip them into the warm bowl. Using an electric beater at high speed, beat the eggs 1 minute, or until they are light and fluffy. Gradually beat in the sugar. Add the salt and vanilla extract. Continue beating until the mixture is lemon-colored, as thick as whipped cream, and has quadrupled in volume, about 8 minutes. Sift and gently fold in the flour ¼ cup at a time, using a flexible rubber or plastic spatula. Add the cooled melted butter, and fold it in gently. Turn the batter into the prepared jelly-roll pan. Bake in a preheated moderate oven (350° F.) 20 to 25 minutes, or until a toothpick inserted in the center comes out clean. Cool the cake in the pan for 3 minutes. Run a metal spatula between the cake and the sides of the pan to loosen it. Meanwhile, sift confectioners' sugar over a clean towel. Turn the cake out onto the towel. Quickly remove the paper from the bottom of the cake and trim the crust from the edge. Roll up the cake and the towel together, and let the cake stand until it is cold. Unroll the cake and spread it with Butter Cream (any flavor desired). Roll up in jelly-roll fashion. Sprinkle the roll with sifted confectioners' sugar or frost it with Uncooked Butter Frosting. Makes 1 roll, 8 to 10 servings.

❧ GENOA LOAF (*Pain de Gênes*)

⅔ cup (¼ pound) blanched almonds
1 cup sugar
½ cup (1 stick) butter, softened
¼ teaspoon almond extract
⅛ teaspoon salt
3 large eggs

3 tablespoons Kirsch
1 cup, plus 2 tablespoons, sifted all-purpose flour
1 teaspoon double-acting baking powder

Blanch the almonds and put ⅓ cup of them at a time in the jar of an electric blender. Add ¼ cup of the sugar and blend about 20 seconds. If all the almonds are not ground fine, stir them with a fork and turn on the blender for another 20 seconds. Empty the contents of the jar into a bowl. Repeat, using the remaining ⅓ cup almonds and another ¼ cup of the sugar. (If an electric blender is not available, grind the almonds and ½ cup of the sugar in a food chopper, using the fine blade.) Put the butter in a mixing bowl and beat with an electric beater, at low speed, ½ minute. Then, at medium speed, gradually beat in the remaining ½ cup of the sugar, the almond extract, and the salt. Gradually beat in the ground almond and sugar mixture. Beat in one egg at a time. Add the Kirsch and beat ½ minute. Sift the flour with the baking powder and add it all at one time. Carefully fold it into the batter until all ingredients are blended. Line the bottom of a lightly greased 9- by 5- by 3-inch loaf pan with waxed paper cut to fit the bottom of the pan. Grease the paper and the sides of the pan lightly. Turn the batter into the pan and place in a cold oven. Set the oven control to 300° F., and bake the cake 1 hour and 20 minutes. Cool the cake in the pan for 20 minutes. Turn the cake out onto a wire rack, remove the paper, and finish cooling. If desired, sift confectioners' sugar over the top of the cake. Store in a tightly closed cake box. Makes one 9- by 5- by 2½-inch cake.

⚜ KUGELHOPF (*Kugelhopf*)

1 envelope active dry yeast
¼ cup lukewarm water
½ cup sugar
1¼ cups milk, scalded
¾ cup (1½ sticks) butter
1 teaspoon salt
1½ teaspoons vanilla extract
2 teaspoons grated lemon rind

4 cups sifted all-purpose flour
2 large eggs
½ cup raisins
¼ cup chopped blanched almonds
  (optional)
about 3 dozen whole blanched
  almonds (optional)
confectioners' sugar

Soften the yeast in the lukewarm water with 1 teaspoon of the sugar. Combine the hot milk and the butter and cool to lukewarm. Add the remaining sugar, the softened yeast, and the salt, vanilla extract, and grated lemon rind. Stir in 2 cups of the flour and beat well. Beat in the eggs, one at a time. Continue beating 5 minutes. Stir in the raisins and the chopped almonds, if used. (If the raisins are too dry, steam them in a sieve over boiling water for a few minutes.) Gradually add the remaining flour. Mix well. Cover the bowl and let the dough rise in a warm place (80° to 85° F.) until it has doubled in size, about 1½ hours.

Butter two 7-inch crown (Kugelhopf) pans generously. If desired, place a circle of whole blanched almonds in the bottom of each. Put half the dough in each pan. Cover and let the dough rise in a warm place until it has doubled in bulk. (The dough should have risen enough to almost fill the pans.) Bake in a preheated moderate oven (350° F.) 40 to 45 minutes. Cool the cakes in the pans 5 minutes, then turn them out onto cooling racks, crown side up. Sprinkle generously with confectioners' sugar. Makes two 7-inch cakes.

⚜ MARBLE CAKE (*Gâteau Marbre*)

1 recipe for Birthday Cake batter
  (page 464)
1 ounce (1 square) chocolate, melted
about ½ cup Vanilla Butter Cream
  (page 413)

about ⅓ cup Chocolate Butter Cream
  (page 414)
about ⅔ cup each Vanilla Fondant
  and Chocolate Fondant (page 412)

Divide the Birthday Cake batter in two equal parts. Into 1 part, fold the melted chocolate, using only a few strokes of a rubber spatula. Grease two 8-inch round layer cake pans lightly, line the bottoms with waxed paper cut to fit, and grease the paper lightly. Spoon the batter, alternating the colors, into the pans. Bake in a preheated moderate oven (350° F.) 25 minutes or until the cake springs back when gently pressed in the center with the index finger. Remove the cakes from the oven, turn them out onto wire racks, remove paper, and cool. Combine the Vanilla Butter Cream and Chocolate Butter Cream, mixing *only* enough to give the cream a marbled effect, and spread it between the layers. Mix the Vanilla Fondant and Chocolate Fondant lightly so that the colors do not merge and spread over the top and sides of the cake. Makes one 8-inch 2-layer cake.

⚜ MASCOT CAKE (*Gâteau Mascotte*)

Bake a Génoise cake (page 461) in two 8-inch layer-cake pans. When the cakes are cold, spread Praline Butter Cream (page 415) between the layers and over the top and sides. Cover the top and sides with chopped blanched almonds. Sprinkle generously with confectioners' sugar. Makes one 8-inch 2-layer cake.

⚜ MOCHA CAKE (*Gâteau Moka*)

Bake a Génoise cake (page 461) in two 8-inch layer-cake pans. When the cakes are cold, spread Mocha Butter Cream (page 414) between the layers and over the top and sides of the cake. Sprinkle the sides with finely chopped toasted blanched almonds, or with crystallized sugar, if it is available. Put the remaining Mocha Butter Cream in a pastry bag or tube fitted with a star nozzle, and pipe rosettes over the top. (*See illustration, page 442.*) Makes one 8-inch 2-layer cake.

⚜ MODANE LOAF (*Pain de Modane*)

1 envelope active dry yeast	⅓ cup sugar
lukewarm water	5 tablespoons softened butter
2½ cups sifted all-purpose flour	¾ cup mixed candied fruit
2 large eggs	¾ cup seedless raisins
2 tablespoons cold water	2 teaspoons unbeaten egg white
1 teaspoon salt	2 tablespoons confectioners' sugar
1 tablespoon grated lemon rind	1 tablespoon finely ground almonds

Soften the yeast in ¼ cup of lukewarm water. Stir in ½ cup of the flour. Mix until a soft ball of dough is formed. With the kitchen scissors, cut a cross (+) in the top of the dough and leave it in the bowl. Pour into the bowl enough lukewarm water to cover the dough. Then place the bowl in a larger bowl of lukewarm water. Cover the dough and let it rise 30 minutes or until it floats to the surface of the water. (This is called ferment or sponge.) Meanwhile, beat the eggs with the 2 tablespoons cold water and the salt. Stir in the remaining flour, ½ cup at a time. Stir in the ferment, lemon rind, and sugar. Using a wooden spoon, stir the dough and knead it with the back of the spoon for 5 minutes or until the dough leaves the sides of the bowl and the spoon clean. Add the butter and work it in until it is blended with the dough. Cover the bowl and let it rise in a warm place (80 to 85° F.) until it has doubled in size, about 1½ hours. Then knead in the candied fruit and raisins. Cover the bowl and chill the dough 8 to 9 hours or overnight. Punch down the dough while it is still in the bowl, and knead it with a wooden mixing spoon about 1 minute. Turn the dough into a greased 9½- by 5- by 3-inch loaf pan and spread it to the corners and sides of the pan. With the kitchen scissors, cut a gash about ½ inch deep in the lengthwise center of the dough to simulate the crack in the top of a baked loaf of tea bread. Mix the egg white, confectioners' sugar, and almonds, and brush over the top of the dough. Cover the pan and put it in a larger pan filled with lukewarm water. Let the dough rise until it comes to within ½ inch of the top of the pan (about 1½ hours). Bake in a preheated slow oven (325° F.) 1 hour. Cool the loaf in the pan 5 minutes. Turn it out onto a wire rack to finish cooling. Makes one loaf, 9½ by 5 by 3 inches.

❧ PARIS RING (*Paris-Brest*)

Make the recipe for Chou Paste (page 22). Put the paste in a pastry bag fitted with a large plain nozzle and pipe it in a circle on an ungreased baking sheet. Beat 1 egg yolk with 1 tablespoon water and brush it over the top of the paste. Sprinkle with chopped blanched almonds, and then sprinkle lightly with sugar. Bake in a preheated hot oven (425° F.) 30 to 35 minutes or until golden brown. Do not underbake. Turn off the heat. Make 3 or 4 small slits in the sides of the ring to allow steam to escape, and leave it in the oven 25 minutes to allow the center to dry out. Cool. Split the ring into 2 layers and fill with Praline Butter Cream (page 415). Sift confectioners' sugar over the top and sides. Makes 6 servings.

❧ PLUM CAKE

1 cup seedless raisins
1 cup finely diced glacéed fruit
¼ cup dark rum
½ cup (1 stick) butter, softened
¾ cup sugar

3 large eggs
1¼ cups sifted all-purpose flour
¼ teaspoon salt
½ teaspoon double-acting baking powder
confectioners' sugar

Soak the raisins and glacéed fruit in the rum 3 to 4 hours or overnight. Put the butter in a mixing bowl and gradually beat in the sugar. Continue beating

½ minute with an electric beater or 1 minute by hand with a mixing spoon or wire whisk. Beat in 1 egg at a time, beating 1½ minutes with an electric beater or 3 minutes with a wire whisk. Sift the flour with the salt and the baking powder and add one-third of it at a time to the mixture. Stir in the rum-soaked fruit. Line the bottom of a lightly greased 9- by 5- by 3-inch pan with waxed paper cut to fit the bottom of the pan. Grease the paper and the sides of the pan. Turn the batter into the pan. Place the cake in a cold oven. Set the oven control to 300° F. (slow) and bake the cake 1 hour and 20 min-. utes, or until a cake tester or a toothpick inserted in the center comes out clean. Cool the cake in the pan for 20 minutes and then turn it out onto a wire cooling rack. Remove the paper and finish cooling. Sift confectioners' sugar over the top. Store in a tightly closed cake box. Makes one 9- by 5- by 2½-inch loaf cake. (*See illustration, page 444.*)

⚜ POUND CAKE (*Gâteau Quatre-Quatre*)

1 cup (2 sticks) softened butter	1⅔ cups sugar
2 teaspoons vanilla extract	5 large eggs
½ teaspoon salt	2 cups sifted all-purpose flour

Have all ingredients at room temperature. Put the first 3 ingredients in the bowl of an electric mixer. (This cake may be mixed by hand, but it will then be slightly smaller.) Add the sugar gradually, mixing well after each addition. Beat in 4 of the eggs, one at a time. With a wooden mixing spoon gradually stir in the flour. With the same spoon beat in the remaining 1 egg. Grease *only* the bottom of a round 9- by 3½-inch tube pan and flour it lightly. Spoon the batter into the pan. Place in a cold oven, set oven control to 300° F. (slow), and bake 1½ hours or until a cake tester inserted in the center comes out clean. Cool the cake in the pan for 20 minutes. Turn onto a wire rack to finish cooling. Store in a tightly closed cake box. Makes one 9-inch round tube cake.

⚜ PUFF-PASTRY LAYER CAKE (*Gâteau Feuilleté à la Confiture*)

Puff Pastry (page 25)	Kirsch
¾ cup French Pastry Cream (page 409)	about ½ cup thick apricot jam
	confectioners' sugar

Divide the Puff Pastry into three equal parts. Roll each in a circle ⅛ inch thick on an ungreased cooky sheet, having a damp towel underneath the sheets to prevent them from slipping. Using an 8-inch round cake pan as a guide, cut an 8-inch circle out of each circle of pastry. Remove the pastry trimmings and reserve them for other uses. (This method of rolling the pastry keeps the circles round.) Prick the pastry all over with the tines of a fork. Chill the pastry on the baking sheets at least 30 minutes. Bake in a preheated very hot oven (450° F.) for 6 minutes, or until the pastry has puffed and begun to brown. Reduce the heat to 350° F. (moderate), and bake 30 minutes or until the pastry has browned. Carefully transfer the pastry layers to cooling racks. When cold, spread one layer with French Pastry Cream, flavored to taste with Kirsch, and place it on a flat plate 2 to 3 inches larger than the diameter of the layer. Spread the second layer of pastry with the apricot jam and place it over the Pastry Cream. Sift confectioners' sugar generously over the remaining layer and place it over the apricot jam. If desired, make lines across the sugar in any desired pattern. (*See illustration, page 443.*) Makes one 3-layer 8-inch cake, or 8 servings.

⚜ QUICK CAKE (*Sans-Façon*)

This easily made sponge-type cake will keep for several days in a tightly closed cake box. All ingredients should be at room temperature.

1 cup sifted cake flour	¾ cup sugar
1 teaspoon double-acting baking powder	1 teaspoon vanilla extract
	½ teaspoon grated lemon rind
¼ teaspoon salt	1 tablespoon grated orange rind
3 large eggs	½ cup strained orange juice

Sift the flour with the baking powder and salt and set aside. With an electric beater, set at medium speed, or with a wire whisk, beat the eggs until they are foamy. Gradually beat in the sugar and continue beating until the mixture has doubled in volume, 3 to 4 minutes with an electric beater; 8 to 10 minutes with a wire whisk. Add the lemon rind, orange rind, and orange juice. Mix well. Sift the flour mixture, all at one time, over the egg mixture. With a spatula carefully fold it in until the ingredients are *just* blended. Pour the batter into an ungreased round 9-inch tube cake pan. Bake in a preheated slow oven (325° F.) 45 to 50 minutes or until a cake tester inserted in the center comes out clean. Cool the cake in the pan for 20 minutes. With a spatula carefully loosen the cake from the sides of the pan and invert the pan on a wire cooling rack. Remove the pan. Serve, either cold; plain; dusted with sifted confectioners' sugar; with berries or other fruits and whipped cream; with a dessert sauce; or frosted with any desired cake frosting. Makes one 9-inch round tube cake.

⚜ SAINT-HONORÉ CAKE (*Gâteau Saint-Honoré*)

Plain Pastry Dough, using 1 cup flour (page 24)	Cream Saint-Honoré (see following recipe)
½ recipe Chou Paste (page 22)	½ cup heavy cream, whipped
½ cup sugar	1 tablespoon sugar
6 tablespoons boiling water	

Roll out Plain Pastry Dough in a circle ⅛ inch thick. Using a round 9-inch cake pan as a guide, cut a 9-inch circle from the pastry and place it on a double thickness of unglazed brown paper. Place the paper on a cooky sheet. Prick the pastry all over with the tines of a fork so that the pastry will lie flat when it is baked. Chill 30 minutes in the refrigerator or 15 minutes in the freezer.

Fit a pastry bag with a plain ½-inch nozzle and fill the bag with Chou Paste. Pipe a continuous border of paste around the top of the pastry circle ½ inch in from the edge. Bake in a preheated very hot oven (475° F.) 5 minutes. Reduce heat to 375° F. (moderate) and bake 10 minutes. Then reduce the heat to 350° F. (moderate) and bake 15 to 20 minutes or until the Chou Paste border is well puffed and the whole pastry circle has browned lightly. Transfer the pastry to a wire rack to cool. Remove and discard the paper on which the pastry was baked.

Pipe 12 miniature puffs of Chou Paste, the size of walnuts, onto an ungreased cooky sheet. Bake in a preheated very hot oven (450° F.) 10 minutes. Reduce the heat to 350° F. (moderate) and bake 15 minutes longer or until the puffs are brown. Transfer the puffs to a wire rack and make a slit in the side of each to prevent the puffs from becoming soggy. Cool.

Put the ½ cup sugar in a 1½-cup saucepan. Stir and cook the sugar over medium-low heat until the sugar has melted and is golden. Remove the syrup from the heat and stir in the boiling water, 1 tablespoon at a time. At this point the syrup may harden which is as it should be. Return the syrup to the heat and stir and cook until the syrup is smooth, and bubbles, a little smaller than dimes, have formed over the surface. Cool.

Place the pastry circle on a 12-inch serving plate. Cut off the tops of the miniature cream puffs, impale the bottoms on a fork, dip the underside in the caramel syrup, and arrange them close together on the Chou Paste rim of the pastry circle. Put a heaping teaspoon of Cream Saint-Honoré on each puff and replace the tops. Drizzle the remaining caramel syrup over the tops. Fill the center of the pastry circle with Cream Saint-Honoré. Sweeten the whipped cream with the 1 tablespoon sugar and pipe it over the top and in between the puffs as desired. Any Chou Paste and Cream Saint-Honoré that may be left can be used to make cream puffs for another meal. If desired, replace the Cream Saint-Honoré with French Pastry Cream. Makes one 9-inch cake and 8 large cream puffs.

⚜ **Cream Saint-Honoré** (*Crème Saint-Honoré*)

1 envelope unflavored gelatin	2 cups milk
¼ cup cold water	4 large egg yolks, slightly beaten
¼ cup sifted all-purpose flour	1 teaspoon vanilla extract
⅔ cup sugar	6 large egg whites
¼ teaspoon salt	3 tablespoons sugar

Mix the gelatin with the water and let stand to soften. Mix the flour, the ⅔ cup sugar, and the salt in the top of a 1½-quart double boiler. Stir in ½ cup of the milk. Heat the remaining milk only until hot, and add it to the

472

sugar and flour mixture. Stir and cook over direct moderate heat 4 to 5 minutes or until the mixture is very thick. Place the boiler over hot water, cover, and cook, stirring occasionally, 7 to 8 minutes. Gradually add 2 to 3 tablespoons of the hot mixture to the beaten egg yolks, and then gradually stir them into the remaining hot mixture. Mix well. Cook over hot water (not boiling) 5 to 6 minutes, stirring slowly to cook the cream uniformly. Remove the boiler from the heat and blend in the vanilla extract and softened gelatin. Strain the cream through a sieve into a 3-quart bowl and place the bowl in a pan of ice water to cool completely. Beat the egg whites until they are frothy. Then gradually beat in the 3 tablespoons sugar. Continue beating until rounded peaks are formed. Fold the egg whites into the cooled cream. Makes about 5 cups.

❧ SWISS ROLL (*Biscuit Roulé*)

4 large eggs
⅔ cup sugar
¼ teaspoon salt
1 teaspoon vanilla extract
1 teaspoon grated lemon rind
¾ cup sifted all-purpose flour

confectioners' sugar
Cream Bourdaloue (page 410),
   Vanilla Butter Cream (page 413),
   or jam
apricot jam and granulated sugar
   (optional)

Line a greased 15½- by 10½- by 1-inch jelly-roll pan with waxed paper. Grease the paper lightly and set the pan aside. Place the eggs in a bowl of warm (not hot) water and let them stand for 5 minutes so they will beat to a large volume. Place a small-bottomed ½-quart mixing bowl over a bowl of warm (not hot) water, making sure the bottom of the smaller bowl does not touch the water. Break the eggs into a saucer, one at a time, and slip them into the warm bowl. Using an electric beater at high speed, beat the eggs 1 to 2 minutes or until they are light and fluffy. Gradually beat in the sugar. Add the salt, vanilla extract, and lemon rind. Continue beating the mixture until the eggs are lemon-colored and as thick as whipped cream and have quad-rupled in volume, 8 to 10 minutes. Sift and gently fold in the flour ¼ cup at a time, using a rubber or plastic spatula. Turn the batter into the prepared jelly-roll pan. Bake in a preheated moderate oven (350° F.) 20 to 25 minutes, or until a toothpick inserted in the center comes out clean. Cool the cake in the pan for 3 minutes. Run a spatula between the cake and the sides of the pan to loosen it. Sift confectioners' sugar over a clean towel. Turn the cake out onto the towel. Quickly remove the paper from the bottom of the cake and trim the crust from the edge. Roll the cake and the towel together, and let the cake stand until it is cold. Unroll the cake and spread it with Cream Bourdaloue, Butter Cream, or jam. Roll it up jelly-roll fashion. Sprinkle the roll with sifted confectioners' sugar, or brush with apricot jam and then sprinkle with granulated sugar. (*See illustration, page 443.*) Makes 1 roll, 8 to 10 servings.

❧ TWELFTH NIGHT CAKE I (*Gâteau des Rois de Bordeaux*)

Twelfth Night Cake is made with Brioche dough in southern France, with Puff Pastry in Paris (see following recipe). It is served at Twelfth Night parties with a bean, almond, or lucky charm inserted in the dough before baking as a symbol of the Christ Child. Whoever finds the token in his piece of cake becomes the king or queen of the evening and leads the games and festivities at the party.

Shape 1 pound Brioche Dough (page 20) into a ball. Dip the index finger in flour and make a hole in the center. Enlarge this hole until a ring is formed. Make a slit in the under side and insert a lucky bean, almond, or charm in it. Place the dough on a greased baking sheet. Brush the top with 1 egg yolk beaten with 1 tablespoon water. With the point of a paring knife, mark the top in lattice fashion. If desired, arrange very thin small slices of candied lemon peel or orange peel over the top. Sprinkle with colored, coarse granulated sugar. Cover the ring and let it rise in a warm place (80° to 85° F.) 45 minutes or until the dough has doubled in size. Bake in a preheated hot oven (400°F.) 30 minutes or until done. Makes one cake or approximately 8 servings.

❧ TWELFTH NIGHT CAKE II (*Galette des Rois*)

Make the recipe for Puff Pastry (page 25) and roll it in a circle ½ inch thick, being careful not to handle the dough too much. Make shallow incisions near the edge all around the dough. Insert a lucky bean or charm in the dough and place the dough upside down on a baking sheet sprinkled with cold water. With a pointed knife, mark a lattice pattern over the top. Beat 1 egg yolk with 1 tablespoon cold water and brush it over dough. Bake in a preheated hot oven (425° F.) 10 minutes. Reduce heat to moderate (350° F.) and bake until the pastry is golden brown. Makes 8 servings.

Babas and Savarins

❧ BABA AU RHUM (*Baba au Rhum*)

1 envelope active dry yeast	1 tablespoon currants
¼ cup lukewarm water	½ cup sugar
3 tablespoons sugar	¾ cup water, apricot juice, or
¼ cup lukewarm milk	pineapple juice
2 cups sifted all-purpose flour	1 teaspoon lemon juice
3 large eggs	¼ cup dark rum (plus 2 tablespoons,
½ teaspoon salt	if desired)
⅔ cup butter, melted	fruit, ice cream, or Chantilly Cream
2 tablespoons raisins	(page 409) (optional)

Soften the yeast in the lukewarm water with 1 teaspoon sugar in a large mixing bowl. Add 2⅔ tablespoons sugar and the milk. Stir in the flour. Beat in the eggs, one at a time. Cover the bowl and let the dough rise in a warm place (80 to 85° F), until it has doubled in size. Punch down the dough. Add the salt, butter, raisins, and currants and with a wooden spoon work these ingredients into the dough. Put the dough into a well-buttered 8½-inch ring mold, filling it two-thirds full, or put it into 8 individual buttered ring molds or baking cups, filling each two-thirds full. Cover and let the dough rise until it fills the mold or molds. Bake in a preheated hot oven (400° F.); the larger mold 25 to 30 minutes, the smaller molds or cups about 15 minutes, or until a toothpick inserted in the center comes out clean.

While the Baba is baking, mix the ½ cup sugar, ¾ cup water, apricot juice, or pineapple juice, and the lemon juice in a saucepan. Stir and cook until boiling point is reached. Continue cooking, without stirring, for 5 minutes. Remove from heat and add the ¼ cup dark rum. Invert the hot Baba on a serving plate and pour the rum syrup over it. If desired, just before serving, heat 2 tablespoons rum in a small saucepan, ignite, and pour over the Baba, and bring it to the table flaming. The center of the Baba may be filled with fruit—such as pitted black cherries, berries, sliced bananas, apricots, peaches, piled high—or filled with ice cream. The small Babas may be filled with fruit, ice cream, or Chantilly Cream and topped with red cherries or angelica. (*See illustration, page 444.*) Makes one 8½-inch Baba or 8 individual Babas.

⚜ SAVARIN RING (*Savarin au Rhum*)

Make the dough for Baba au Rhum (page 474), omitting the currants and raisins. Butter an 8½-inch ring mold and fill it half full. Let the dough rise in a warm place (80 to 85° F.) until it reaches the top of the mold. Bake in a preheated hot oven (400° F.) 25 to 30 minutes or until a toothpick inserted in the center comes out clean and the cake is golden brown.

While the Savarin is baking, mix 1 scant cup sugar with ¾ cup water in a saucepan. Stir until boiling point is reached, then cook, without stirring, 2 to 3 minutes. Remove from heat and stir in ⅓ cup rum or Kirsch. Turn the Savarin out onto a large plate, and spoon the syrup over it. Let stand until all the syrup has been absorbed. Just before serving sprinkle with 2 to 3 tablespoons undiluted rum. Makes one 8½-inch Savarin Ring.

VARIATIONS

⚜ Savarin Chantilly (*Savarin Chantilly*)

Fill the center of a Kirsch-flavored Savarin Ring with 2 cups Chantilly Cream (page 409) mixed with 1 cup sliced strawberries sweetened with 1 tablespoon sugar. Garnish with 6 whole uncapped strawberries.

❧ Savarin with Fruit (*Savarin aux Fruits*)

In the recipe for Savarin Chantilly, replace the strawberries with the same amount of mixed stewed fruit. Garnish with Chantilly Cream (page 409).

❧ Small Rum Savarins (*Petits Savarins au Rhum*)

Put Savarin dough in 8 individual ring molds, filling them one-third full. Let the dough rise in a warm place (80 to 85° F.) until the dough fills the molds. Bake in a preheated hot oven (400° F.) 15 to 20 minutes or until browned. Remove the Savarins from the molds and while they are still hot, pour 2 tablespoons rum syrup (see Savarin Ring) over each. Let them stand until they have soaked up all the syrup. Arrange them on a round serving plate and fill the centers with Chantilly Cream (page 409) or Cream Saint-Honoré (page 472). Top each with half a glacéed cherry. (*See illustration, page 444.*) Makes 8 servings.

❧ STRAWBERRY TURBAN (*Turban aux Fraises*)

dough for Baba au Rhum (page 474)	1½ pints (3 cups) strawberries
¾ cup (12 tablespoons) granulated sugar	¼ teaspoon vanilla extract
	½ cup heavy cream
¾ cup apricot juice or water	1 cup fresh raspberries
1 teaspoon lemon juice	3 tablespoons confectioners' sugar
¼ cup Kirsch or Kirsch to taste	

Make the dough for Baba au Rhum, omitting the raisins and currants. Place the dough in a greased 8-inch ring mold. Cover and let it rise in a warm place (80 to 85° F.) until the dough has doubled in size. Bake in a preheated hot oven (400° F.) 25 minutes, or until a toothpick inserted in the center comes out clean.

While the Baba is baking, combine ½ cup of the granulated sugar, the apricot juice or water, and the lemon juice in a small saucepan. Stir and cook until boiling point is reached. Continue cooking without stirring for 5 minutes. Remove from heat and stir in the Kirsch. Invert the hot Baba on a serving plate, prick it all over with a fork and pour the hot syrup over it. Let it stand to soak up all the syrup.

Wash and cap the strawberries. Cut the larger berries in half; leave the small ones whole. Sprinkle with 3 tablespoons of the granulated sugar and spoon them into the center of the ring. Add the remaining 1 tablespoon granulated sugar and the vanilla extract to the cream and beat until the cream stands in soft peaks. If desired, flavor the cream with Kirsch to taste. Mound the cream over the strawberries. Wash and mash the raspberries and put them through a sieve. Add the confectioners' sugar and chill. Pour the purée over the cream just before serving. Makes 10 to 12 servings.

PETITS FOURS

In France the name *petit four* is given to a wide variety of small cakes, cookies, pastries, and other confections such as stuffed or candied fruits and glazed nuts. Frosted Petits Fours are made of Génoise cut into small fancy shapes and then frosted and decorated. See also Cookies, Puff-Paste Pastries, Chou-Paste Pastries, in this chapter; and Chapter 18, Simple Confectionery.

⚜ ALMOND ROCKS (*Rochers aux Amandes*)

2 large egg whites
dash salt
1 cup sifted confectioners' sugar

¼ teaspoon almond extract
¼ teaspoon vanilla extract
½ cup sliced blanched almonds

Pour 3 cups hot water in a 3-quart heatproof mixing bowl, and place the bowl over very low heat. Put the egg whites and salt in a 2-quart mixing bowl and place it over the bowl of hot water. With a wire whisk or an electric beater beat the egg whites until they are foamy. Then beat in the confectioners' sugar, about 2 tablespoons at a time, beating well after each addition. Turn off the heat under the bowl. Add the almond and vanilla extracts. Continue beating until the mixture stands in peaks when the whisk or beater is raised, 12 to 15 minutes for whisk; 8 to 10 for electric beater. Fold in the almonds. Drop the mixture by heaping teaspoons at a time onto buttered and lightly floured cooky sheets. Bake in preheated very slow oven (250°F.) 15 minutes. The outside of the rocks should be crisp and the inside soft. Cool on wire racks. Makes 1½ dozen.

⚜ CATS' TONGUES (*Langues-de-Chat*)

This is a typical French cooky, crisp and golden brown around the edges, white in the center, and the shape of a cat's tongue.

½ cup (1 stick) butter, softened
⅛ teaspoon salt
1 teaspoon vanilla extract

½ cup sugar
2 large unbeaten egg whites
1 cup sifted all-purpose flour

Mix the butter with the salt and the vanilla extract. Gradually blend in the sugar. Add 1 egg white at a time, beating well after each addition. Stir in the flour. Fit a pastry bag or a pastry tube with a plain nozzle (number 3). Fill it two-thirds full with the cooky dough. Pipe 2-inch lengths of the dough, 1 inch apart, on buttered and lightly floured cooky sheets. Bake in a preheated hot oven (400° F.) 6 to 7 minutes or until the cookies are golden brown around the edges. Cool on wire cooling racks. Store in airtight containers. Makes approximately 4½ dozen.

❧ PALAIS DE DAME (*Palais de Dame*)

These are small, round, button-shaped cookies.

¾ cup dried currants
¼ cup dark rum
⅔ cup sugar
½ cup (1 stick) butter, softened

1 large egg
1 teaspoon vanilla etxract
1½ cups sifted all-purpose flour

Soak the currants in the rum at least 2 hours. Gradually blend the sugar with the butter. Beat in the egg and the vanilla extract. Stir in the soaked currants. Add the flour, a little at a time, mixing well after each addition. Drop the dough in rounded ½ teaspoons at a time onto lightly buttered cooky sheets. Spread the dough slightly, keeping the cookies small and round. Bake in a preheated moderate oven (375° F.) 5 to 6 minutes or until cookies have browned lightly around the edges. Cool on wire racks. Store in airtight containers. Makes 5 dozen.

❧ PETITS FOURS WITH DATES (*Petit Fours aux Dattes*)

These Petits Fours may be made with Sweet Pie Pastry or with Puff Pastry trimmings.

Roll Sweet Pie Pastry (page 25) or Puff Pastry trimmings (page 25) ⅛ inch thick. With a 2-inch round cooky cutter, cut out circles of dough and wrap each around a whole pitted, dried date, having both ends of the date visible. Place the Petits Fours on ungreased cooky sheets. Beat 1 egg yolk with 1 tablespoon milk or water and brush it over the pastry. Bake in a preheated slow oven (325° F.) 12 to 15 minutes. Allow 2 Petits Fours per person.

❧ SWEET PASTRY PETITS FOURS (*Petits Fours en Pâte Sucrée*)

Sweet Pie Pastry (page 25)
1 teaspoon grated lemon rind, or 2
    teaspoons grated orange rind
1 egg, beaten

1 tablespoon milk
blanched almonds, seeded raisins, and
    candied fruit

Make the Sweet Pie Pastry according to the directions, but flavor it with grated lemon or orange rind by adding the rind to the flour and sugar mixture along with the shortening. Roll the pastry to ⅛ inch thickness on a lightly floured surface. With assorted cooky cutters, cut the pastry into various shapes. Place them on an ungreased cooky sheet. Beat the egg with the milk and brush the mixture over the pastries. Decorate as desired with blanched almonds, seedless raisins, and candied fruit. Bake in a preheated hot oven (400° F.) 15 minutes or until the pastries have browned. Cool. Makes approximately 2 to 2½ dozen.

⚜ FROSTED PETITS FOURS (*Petits Fours en Génoise Glacée*)

Petits Fours that are to be frosted are usually made of Génoise cut into small fancy shapes with a sharp knife or with assorted small cooky cutters. The pieces are coated with Apricot Glaze and covered with Fondant Icing.

⚜ HOW TO FROST PETITS FOURS

With a sharp knife carefully trim all ragged edges from a Génoise layer (page 461). Using a knife or small cooky cutters, cut the cake into 1½-inch squares, small rectangles, triangles, diamonds, hearts, etc. Insert a fork into each piece and dip it into Apricot Glaze (see following recipe), covering the top and sides. Place the pieces, with the uncoated side down, 1 inch apart on wire racks placed on baking sheets. Let them stand about 1 hour for the glaze to set. Using a large metal kitchen spoon, pour warm Fondant Icing (page 412) over 1 piece at a time, letting the icing run over the top and sides, covering them smoothly. (The baking sheet underneath will catch the excess icing, which should be scraped up, returned to the top of the double boiler, and reheated just until thin enough to pour.) Let the Petits Fours dry on the rack 1 hour or longer. If any are not sufficiently covered, frost again and let them dry. Decorate the tops as desired with glacéed fruit or nuts or with Confectioners' Sugar Flower and Leaf Frosting (page 480) put through a cake decorator's tube.

⚜ Apricot Glaze

1 cup sugar	¾ cup apricot jam
1 cup boiling water	

Combine the sugar and water in a saucepan. Stir and cook, uncovered, over medium heat until sugar is dissolved. Bring the mixture to boiling point, and boil 10 minutes. Heat the apricot jam in a saucepan until it bubbles around the edge of the pan. Remove from heat and push the jam through a sieve into the syrup. Mix well. Keep warm over hot water until ready to use, or reheat just before using to make the glaze thin enough to pour. Makes enough glaze for 2½ dozen Petits Fours.

⚜ Fondant Icing for Petits Fours

2¾ cups granulated sugar
¼ teaspoon cream of tartar
dash of salt

1½ cups water
4 to 5 cups sifted confectioners' sugar
½ teaspoon almond extract

Combine the first 4 ingredients in the top of a double boiler. Mix well. Stir and cook over direct low heat until sugar is dissolved. Increase the heat to moderate and cook, without stirring, to 226° F. on a candy thermometer. Cool to 110° F., or until the bottom of the pan can rest comfortably in the palm of the hand. With a wooden spoon, beat in the confectioners' sugar, using only enough to make icing that is still thin enough to pour. Stir in the almond extract. Let the icing stand over hot water to keep it at pouring consistency until it is to be used. If it thickens, add a few drops of hot water; if it is too thin, add a little more confectioners' sugar. If colored frosting is desired, add a few drops of red, green, yellow, or blue food coloring. Makes enough icing for 2½ dozen Petits Fours.

⚜ Coffee Fondant Icing

In the recipe for Fondant Icing, replace the water with the same amount of strong coffee, and use 1 teaspoon vanilla extract instead of the almond extract.

⚜ Kirsch Fondant Icing

Add 1 tablespoon Kirsch, or Kirsch to taste, to Fondant Icing.

⚜ Confectioners' Sugar Flower and Leaf Frosting

1 large egg white
2 to 2½ cups sifted confectioners'
　sugar

food coloring

Place the egg white in the smaller bowl of an electric mixer. Gradually beat in 2 cups confectioners' sugar. If frosting is not stiff enough to stand in stiff peaks when the beater is slowly raised, beat in more confectioners' sugar, about 2 tablespoons at a time, until desired stiffness is reached. To color the frosting, place 2 tablespoons frosting in each of 4 custard cups and keep them covered with a damp cloth to prevent drying. Color one portion green by adding 5 to 6 drops green food coloring; one yellow with 10 drops yellow food coloring; one pink with 4 drops red food coloring; one lavender with 2 drops blue food coloring and 4 drops red food coloring. Put a little frosting on the four corners of a piece of waxed paper and place it, frosting side down, on a cooky sheet (this keeps the paper from slipping). Put green frosting in a cake decorator's tube fitted with the leaf nozzle (No. 65) and pipe leaves onto the paper. Make flowers in the same manner, using a flower nozzle (No. 15) with yellow, pink, or lavender frosting. Let the leaves and flowers dry on the waxed paper, then remove them and arrange them on Petits Fours. If desired, freeze the leaves and flowers on a tray, wrap the tray for the freezer, and store in freezer until needed. Makes 2½ dozen flowers and leaves.

COOKIES

⚜ ALMOND WAFERS (*Tuiles aux Amandes*)

2 large egg whites
½ cup sugar
½ teaspoon almond extract
½ cup sifted all-purpose flour

¼ cup (½ stick) butter, melted
scant ½ cup coarsely chopped
   blanched almonds
confectioners' sugar

Beat the egg whites *only* until they are foamy. Gradually beat in the sugar. Continue beating 3 minutes, using a wire whisk or a wire hand egg beater. Beat in the almond extract. Fold in the flour and then the butter and almonds. Mix well. Drop the batter a heaping ½ teaspoon at a time onto lightly buttered baking sheets. Sift confectioners' sugar lightly over the tops. Bake in a preheated hot oven (400° F.) 3 to 4 minutes or only until cookies have browned lightly around the edges. With a spatula remove the cookies from the baking sheets and fold each over the handle of a wooden mixing spoon, having the top side of the cooky to the outside. Cool on wire racks. Store in airtight containers. Makes 2½ dozen.

⚜ CONVERSATION TARTS (*Conversations*)

Plain Pastry Dough, using 2 cups flour
  (page 24)

1¼ cups cold French Pastry Cream
  (page 409)
Royal Icing (page 413)

Line 6 individual tart pans, 3 by ½ inches, with Plain Pastry rolled 1/16 inch thick. Put about 3 tablespoons French Pastry Cream in each, filling them *just* to the top. Moisten the edges of the pastry with a little water. Cover the tarts with pastry rolled 1/16 inch thick and ½ inch larger than the circumference of the tart pans. Trim the edges of the pastry and crimp them with the tines of a fork. Brush Royal Icing over the tops. Roll the pastry trimmings 1/16 inch thick, cut them into narrow strips, about ¼ inch wide, and arrange 2 of the strips in the shape of a cross (+) over each tart. Brush the strips lightly with Royal Icing. Bake in a preheated hot oven (425° F.) 25 minutes. Remove from oven and cool. Makes 6 servings.

⚜ LADIES' FINGERS (*Cuisses-Dame*)

1¼ teaspoons grated lemon rind
¼ teaspoon salt
¼ cup (½ stick) butter, softened
¾ cup sugar
1 tablespoon lemon juice
1 tablespoon Kirsch

2 large eggs
2⅓ cups sifted all-purpose flour
⅛ teaspoon soda
6 tablespoons sugar
½ teaspoon ground cinnamon

Put the lemon rind, salt, and butter in a mixing bowl and mix well. Blend in ½ cup of the sugar. Add the lemon juice, Kirsch, and the remaining ¼ cup sugar and mix well. Beat in the eggs, one at a time. Stir in the flour, ⅓ cup at a time. Add the soda last, and mix it in well. Chill the dough in the refrigerator 1 to 2 hours, or until it is stiff enough to roll. Take out one-fourth of the dough at a time, keeping the remainder refrigerated. Roll each part on a lightly floured flat surface into a 6½- by 4½- by ¼-inch rectangle. Trim the sides and ends of the rectangles to straighten the edges. (Save the trimmings to reroll and make into cookies.) Cut each rectangle of dough into cookies 2 by ¾ inches. Cut 4 notches ¼ inch deep on only one side of each cooky; when the cookies are fried, they suggest fingers of a hand. Transfer the un-baked cookies to a lightly floured board or baking sheet. Cover the cookies, and let them rest at least 30 minutes. Preheat 1½ pounds vegetable shortening or 3 cups cooking oil in a 2½-quart deep-fat frying kettle to 375° F. Drop 4 to 5 cookies at a time in the hot fat, fry them 1 to 1½ minutes or until they rise to the top of the hot fat, then turn the cookies with a kitchen fork, and cook them 1 minute longer or until they have browned. Remove the cookies from the hot fat and drain them on paper towels or brown paper. Combine the 6 tablespoons sugar with the cinnamon and roll the fried cookies in the mix-ture. Store the cookies in an airtight container. If you wish to serve these cookies warm, heat them 5 to 6 minutes in a preheated slow oven (325° F.) as one would heat doughnuts. Makes approximately 6 dozen cookies.

⚜ ALMOND MACAROONS (*Macarons aux Amandes*)

1 cup (½ pound) almond paste
1 cup granulated sugar

3 egg whites, unbeaten
sifted confectioners' sugar

Blend the almond paste with the sugar, working the mixture with the hands until well blended. Then work in the egg whites, one at a time, mixing *very* well after each addition. This mixture should be of a consistency that will go through a pastry tube yet hold its shape on the baking sheet. Pipe the mixture through a pastry bag or drop it from the tip of a teaspoon in small mounds on unglazed brown paper on a baking sheet. Sprinkle each mound with a little sifted confectioners' sugar. Bake in a preheated slow oven (275° F.) 30 min-utes. Remove from the oven, place the paper on a moist cloth, and remove the macaroons. Makes approximately 2 dozen.

❧ MACAROONS NANCY STYLE (*Macarons de Nancy*)

1¼ cups blanched almonds
1 cup sugar
2 large egg whites, unbeaten

½ teaspoon vanilla extract
¼ teaspoon almond extract

Put ¼ cup of the almonds and 3 tablespoons of the sugar in the jar of the electric blender. Blend ½ minute or until all the almonds have been ground very fine, almost to a powder. Then turn the ground almonds into a mixing bowl. Repeat this process until all the almonds have been ground and the rest of the sugar has been used. Stir in the egg whites, one at a time, and then the vanilla and almond extracts. Mix well to form a stiff paste. Cut 2 pieces of un-glazed brown paper to fit each of 3 cooky sheets. Wet the paper and place 2 thicknesses on each sheet. Drop the paste in ½ heaping teaspoons onto the wet paper, 1 inch apart to allow room for spreading. Or if desired, put the paste into a pastry bag and pipe it in 1-inch mounds onto the wet paper. Bake in a preheated slow oven (300° F.) 30 minutes. To remove the macaroons from the paper, invert the paper of cookies on another cooky sheet or large board. Cover the back of the paper with a wet towel. When the paper is wet, lift the paper from the macaroons. Cool the macaroons and store in airtight containers. Makes approximately 5 dozen.

❧ COMMERCY MADELEINES (*Madeleines de Commercy*)

These little cakes were named for the town of Commercy, France, where they were a specialty of the pastry-makers. They are baked in madeleine pans, which are like muffin pans except that the individual cups are shell-shaped and shallow rather than round and deep.

1¼ cups sifted cake flour
½ teaspoon double-acting baking
　powder
¼ teaspoon salt
3 large eggs
1 teaspoon vanilla extract

⅔ cup sugar
2 teaspoons grated lemon rind
¾ cup (1½ sticks) butter, melted and
　cooled
sifted confectioners' sugar

Sift the first 3 ingredients together and set them aside. Beat the eggs in a 2-quart mixing bowl until light and lemon-colored. Add the vanilla extract. Gradually beat in the sugar. Continue beating until the volume has increased to four times the original amount. Gradually fold in the flour mixture and the lemon rind. Stir in the melted butter. Brush madeleine pans with additional melted butter. Spoon 1 tablespoon of batter into each shell, filling them two-thirds full. Bake in a preheated moderate oven (350° F.) 12 minutes or until a toothpick inserted in the center comes out clean. Remove the cakes from the pans to cooling racks. Sift confectioners' sugar over the tops. Makes 3 dozen Madeleines.

✣ ROUEN MIRLITONS (*Mirlitons de Rouen*)

This small pastry is a specialty of Rouen.

½ recipe Puff Pastry (page 25), or
    1 recipe Plain Pastry Dough, using
    1 cup flour (page 24)
apricot jam
2 large eggs
6 tablespoons sugar

½ cup fine Almond Macaroon Crumbs
    (8 Almond Macaroons 1½ inches in
    diameter; see page 482)
¼ teaspoon vanilla extract
¼ teaspoon almond extract
9 blanched almonds
sifted confectioners' sugar

Line 6 tartlet pans, 3 by ½ inches each, with Puff Pastry or Plain Pastry, rolled ¹⁄₁₆ inch thick. Prick the pastry all over with the tines of a fork. Then spread thinly with apricot jam. Beat the eggs until the yolks and whites are blended, then beat in the sugar. Stir in the macaroon crumbs, vanilla extract, and almond extract. Spoon the mixture into the pastry-lined tart pans over the apricot jam, filling the pans to within ⅛ inch from the top. Split the blanched almonds and arrange 3 halves in a cloverleaf design on each tart. Sprinkle with sifted confectioners' sugar. Put the pans in a preheated hot oven (400° F.) with a piece of foil in the bottom of the oven to catch any of the filling that may boil over. Bake 25 to 30 minutes or until the bottoms of the tarts have browned. Cool and serve cold. Makes 6 tarts.

✣ SMALL NEAPOLITAN CAKES (*Petits Gâteaux Napolitains*)

Roll Sweet Pie Pastry (page 25) into a circle ⅛ inch thick. With a 3-inch cooky cutter, cut out circles. Cut a hole ½ inch in diameter in the center of half the circles. Place all the circles on ungreased cooky sheets. Prick well with the tines of a fork. Bake in a preheated moderate oven (350° F.) 15 to 20 minutes or until golden. Cool on a wire rack. Spread each solid circle with apricot jam. Cover with the circles having a hole in the center. Coat with apricot jam and roll in granulated sugar. Garnish the center with a bit of Cream Bourdaloue, Chantilly Cream, or French Pastry Cream (see Index). Allow 1 cake per serving.

✣ ALMOND SANDCAKES (*Sablés de Trouville*)

These are crisp fan-shaped cookies.

½ teaspoon grated lemon rind
½ teaspoon almond extract
½ teaspoon vanilla extract
½ cup (1 stick) softened butter

½ cup sugar
½ cup ground blanched almonds
2 large egg yolks
1½ cups sifted all-purpose flour

Combine the first 4 ingredients and mix them until fluffy. Gradually blend in the sugar and ground almonds (grind the almonds in an electric blender if one is available). Beat in the egg yolks. Stir in the flour, a little at a time. Cover the bowl and refrigerate the dough 2 hours or until it is stiff enough to roll. Divide the dough into 3 parts and roll 1 part at a time ¼ inch thick on a lightly floured board, keeping the remaining 2 parts refrigerated until you are ready to roll them. With a pastry cutter, and using a 5-inch bowl, saucer, or lid as a guide, cut the dough into 5-inch circles. Then cut each circle into quarters, using a pastry cutter. With a wide spatula or a short-handled pancake turner, transfer the cookies to an ungreased cooky sheet. Bake in a preheated hot oven (400° F.) 5 to 6 minutes or until the cookies have browned lightly around the edges. Cool the cookies on a wire rack. Store in airtight containers. Makes 2 dozen.

⚜ VENDÉE SANDCAKES (*Sablés Vendéens*)

½ teaspoon grated lemon rind	2 hard-cooked egg yolks, sieved
¾ teaspoon vanilla extract	⅓ cup sugar
¼ teaspoon almond extract	1¼ cups sifted all-purpose flour
⅓ cup (¾ stick) softened butter	

Combine the first 5 ingredients and mix them until fluffy. Gradually blend in the sugar. Stir in the flour, a little at a time. This dough is stiff, but *do not* add any kind of liquid. Cover the bowl and let the dough stand 2 hours at room temperature. Divide the dough into 3 parts and roll 1 part at a time ¼ inch thick on a lightly floured board, keeping the remaining parts refrigerated until ready to roll them. With a pastry cutter and using a 5-inch bowl, saucer, or lid as a guide, cut the dough into 5-inch circles. Then cut each circle into quarters, using the pastry cutter. With a wide spatula or short-handled pancake turner, transfer the cookies to an ungreased cooky sheet. Make a design in the center of each with the tines of a fork. Bake in a preheated hot oven (400° F.) 5 to 6 minutes or until the cookies have browned lightly around the edges. Cool the cookies on a wire rack. Store in airtight containers. Makes 2 dozen.

PUFF-PASTE PASTRIES

For all the recipes in this section, use the recipe for Puff Pastry on page 25. Follow all the directions in this recipe to the letter.

⚜ COUQUES (*Couques ou Langues de Boeuf*)

Roll Puff Pastry trimmings ⅛ inch thick on a lightly floured board. Using a scalloped-edge 1½-inch biscuit cutter, cut the pastry into circles. Sprinkle a board with granulated sugar and roll each biscuit into the shape of an oval. Bake on lightly buttered cooky sheets in a preheated moderate oven (375° F.) 15 minutes or until the pastry has puffed and browned. Allow 2 pastries per serving.

⚜ CREAM HORNS (*Cornets Feuilletés à la Crème*)

Make the recipe for Puff Pastry. Roll the chilled pastry on a very lightly floured surface in an 18- by 12-inch rectangle ⅛ inch thick. Straighten the edges of the dough with a pastry wheel, then cut pastry into lengthwise strips 1 inch wide. This length is for a cornet tube form 4½ inches long. Starting at the small end of the form, wrap the pastry strips around the form, letting each row overlap the one below by about ¼ to ½ inch. (Do not extend the pastry beyond the tube form. Do not stretch or pull the pastry.) Moisten the end of the strip with a little water and press it gently to seal it.

Line a baking sheet with a double thickness of brown paper and place the cornets 2 inches apart on it. Refrigerate 30 minutes. Bake in a preheated hot oven (400° F.) for 20 minutes. Beat 1 egg white with 2 tablespoons water until foamy and brush over the surface of the cornets. Sprinkle them lightly with granulated sugar. Return the cornets to the oven and bake 5 minutes longer or until golden and glazed. Carefully transfer the cornets to wire cooling racks and cool them slightly. Then remove the cornets from the tube forms and cool completely. Fill with Chantilly Cream (page 409) or French Pastry Cream (page 409). Makes 12 horns (cornets).

Note: If metal cornet tube forms are not available in your locality, you can make your own forms. Cut a double thickness of heavy duty foil into a 9-inch square, and fold it over to form a triangle. Roll the triangle into a horn or cone shape, 4½ inches long and 1½ inches wide at the top. Fold the pointed ends of the foil at the top over the outside of the cone to secure it.

⚜ SMALL MILLE-FEUILLES (*Petits Mille-Feuilles*)

Make the recipe for Puff Pastry. Roll half the chilled pastry on a lightly floured board ⅛ inch thick into a rectangle 15 by 3 inches. Trim the edges. Repeat with the remainder of the pastry. Prick pastry well with the tines of a fork. Refrigerate 30 minutes on a cooky sheet lined with a double thickness of heavy brown paper. Bake in a preheated very hot oven (450° F.) 15 minutes or until pastry is puffed. Reduce temperature to 350° F. (moderate). With a spatula turn the pastry over and bake 15 minutes or until golden. Cool on wire racks. When cold, sandwich the two rectangles together with a filling of Cream Bourdaloue (page 410) and sliced blanched almonds. With a saw-edged knife, carefully cut the pastry into crosswise strips 1½ inches wide. Sift confectioners' sugar over the tops. Makes 10 strips.

⚜ NAPOLEONS (*Napoléons*)

1 recipe Puff Pastry, chilled
French Pastry Cream (page 409)
1 cup sifted confectioners' sugar
about 1½ tablespoons hot water

¼ teaspoon vanilla extract
1 square (1 ounce) unsweetened
  chocolate
2 teaspoons butter

Divide the chilled pastry in half, and roll one portion at a time into a 15- by 3-inch rectangle ⅛ inch thick, keeping the other half in the refrigerator. Trim the edges to make them straight. Line a baking sheet with a double thickness of brown paper and place the dough on it. Refrigerate 30 minutes. Repeat with the remaining pastry.

While pastry is chilling, make French Pastry Cream. Prick the chilled pastry with a fork all over the top. Bake in a preheated very hot oven (450° F.) 15 minutes or until the pastry is well puffed. Reduce the temperature to 350° F. (moderate). Using a wide spatula or a short-handled pancake turner, turn the pastry over. Bake 15 minutes or until golden. With a sharp knife, split the pastry rectangles in half to make 4 thin layers. Place the pastry, cut side up, on a cooky sheet. Bake 5 minutes longer. Transfer to wire cooling racks and cool completely.

In a small bowl, combine the confectioners' sugar, water, and vanilla extract. Mix until smooth. If the mixture thickens on standing, thin it to pouring consistency with a few drops of hot water. This is the glaze. Place one pastry layer, cut side down, on a wire rack on a tray, and pour half of the glaze uniformly over the surface. Let it stand 20 minutes or until the glaze is set. (Scrape up the glaze that has dripped onto the tray and return it to the bowl.) Pour the remaining glaze over the first layer of glaze, thinning it with a little water if it is too thick. Let stand 1 hour. Melt the chocolate with the butter over hot water (not boiling), mixing well. Cool. Using a pastry tube equipped with a straight tube used for writing, pipe 5 lengthwise stripes on the glaze. Pull a toothpick crosswise through the stripes, at ½-inch intervals, alternating the direction each time. Set aside.

Now place one of the remaining pastry layers, cut side up, on a serving tray or platter and spread it with one-third of the French Pastry Cream. Top with another of the remaining pastry layers, cut side down, and spread this with one-third of the Pastry Cream. Add the third layer, cut side down, and spread it with the rest of the Pastry Cream. Then cover with the glazed layer. Refrigerate at least 30 minutes. Cut the layered pastry rectangle crosswise into 10 servings, using a knife with a serrated edge. Makes 10 Napoleons.

⚜ GLAZED PALM LEAVES (*Palmiers Glacés*)

Roll Puff Pastry into a rectangle ¼ inch thick on a lightly floured flat surface. Sprinkle with granulated sugar. Fold each end of the dough to the center of the rectangle. Sprinkle with granulated sugar. Fold each end of the folded dough to the center of the rectangle, making 4 layers of dough on each side of the center. Then fold the two sides of the dough together as in closing a book. Place the dough on a large piece of foil or waxed paper. Roll the rolling pin down the dough lightly once. Fold the foil or waxed paper over the dough wrapping it completely. Chill 2 hours. Then cut the dough into crosswise slices ½ inch thick. Dip each slice in granulated sugar and place them 1 inch apart on a baking sheet lined with a double thickness of brown paper. Bake in a preheated very hot oven (450° F.) for 10 minutes. Reduce the temperature to 350° F. (moderate) and bake another 10 minutes. Place the baking sheet on another baking sheet (have it cold), reduce heat to 300° F. (slow), and bake 10 more minutes or until the pastry is golden brown. Allow 2 Palm Leaves per serving.

⚜ SMALL PUFF-PASTRY COOKIES (*Petites Galettes Feuilletées*)

Roll Puff Pastry trimmings into 1-inch balls, place them on a board, and flatten them to ¼ inch thickness. Then roll them in granulated sugar. Place on lightly buttered baking sheets. Bake in a preheated moderate oven (375° F.) 15 to 20 minutes or until the cookies have puffed and browned. Allow 2 per person.

⚜ SACRISTANS (*Sacristains*)

On a board sprinkled with granulated sugar instead of flour, roll Puff Pastry in a rectangle ⅛ inch thick, 8 inches long, and 5 inches wide. Trim the edges of the rectangle to get them straight, using a ruler as a guide. Beat 1 egg yolk with 1 tablespoon milk and brush over the dough. Sprinkle generously with finely chopped blanched almonds and granulated sugar or sifted confectioners' sugar. Cut the pastry into crosswise strips ¾ inch wide. Shape them like corkscrews by taking one end of the strip in each hand and giving the strip 2 or 3 twists. Place the strips on a moistened cooky sheet 1 inch apart, pressing down the ends firmly so they will not unwind. Cover and chill 1 hour. Bake in a preheated moderate oven (350° F.) about 25 minutes or until twists are golden brown. Allow 1 twist per person.

⚜ FROSTED PUFF-PASTRY STRAWS (*Allumettes Glacées*)

Puff Pastry trimmings   **Royal Icing (page 413)**

Roll Puff Pastry trimmings ⅛ inch thick into strips 6 by 4 inches. Trim the edges to straighten them. Spread Royal Icing over the top of the pastry. With a sharp, pointed knife, dipped in hot water or in flour to prevent the pastry from sticking to the knife, cut the pastry into crosswise strips 1½ inches wide. Transfer the strips to a moistened cooky sheet. Bake in a preheated hot oven (400° F.) 10 to 12 minutes, or until the strips have puffed and browned, being careful not to caramelize the icing. Allow 2 straws per person.

⚜ Frosted Puff-Pastry Straws with Almonds (*Condés*)

Make Puff-Paste Straws according to the directions in the preceding recipe, but before cutting the pastry into crosswise strips, sprinkle finely chopped almonds over the icing. Then sift confectioners' sugar lightly over the almonds. Cut the pastry into strips, and bake them according to the directions in the recipe. Allow 2 straws per person.

⚜ SMALL TURNOVERS (*Petits Chaussons*)

Roll Puff Pastry trimmings ⅛ inch thick. With a scalloped 3-inch cooky cutter, cut the pastry into circles. Put a rounded ½ teaspoon of apricot jam, peach jam, or French Pastry Cream on one side of each pastry circle, and fold the other half of the circle over the filling. Crimp the edges together with a fork dipped in flour. Prick the top of each to allow for the escape of steam. Beat 1 egg yolk with 1 tablespoon milk or water and brush the top of each turnover. Place on an ungreased cooky sheet. Bake in a preheated hot oven (425° F.) for 5 minutes. Reduce heat to 350° F. (moderate) and bake 12 to 15 minutes. Allow 2 turnovers per person.

CHOU-PASTE PASTRIES

⚜ PROFITEROLES WITH CHOCOLATE SAUCE
(*Profiteroles au Chocolat*)

½ cup hot water
½ cup (1 stick) butter
⅛ teaspoon salt
1 cup sifted all-purpose flour

4 large eggs
Chantilly Cream (page 409) or
    French Pastry Cream (page 409)
Chocolate Sauce (page 407)

Mix the first 3 ingredients in a 1-quart saucepan. Bring to boiling point. Remove from heat and stir in the flour all at one time, using a wooden spoon. Beat vigorously. Return to the heat and cook until the mixture leaves the sides of the pan and forms a very stiff ball. Remove the pan from the heat and beat in the eggs, one at a time, beating until each egg is completely absorbed before adding another. Pipe the dough through a pastry bag onto ungreased baking sheets in small mounds, 2 inches apart. Bake in a preheated hot oven (425° F.)

25 to 30 minutes or until the puffs are golden brown. Do not underbake. Turn off the heat. Make a slit in the side of each puff with a pointed paring knife to allow steam to escape, and leave them in the oven 20 minutes to dry out the centers. Cool. Split and fill with Chantilly Cream or French Pastry Cream. Arrange the puffs in a pyramid on a round plate or tray. Pour hot Chocolate Sauce over the pyramid. The hot sauce will soak into the cream puffs. Or if desired, arrange three or four small cream puffs on an individual serving plate and cover them generously with hot Chocolate Sauce. Makes 6 to 8 servings.

⚜ SMALL COFFEE OR CHOCOLATE ECLAIRS
(*Éclairs au Café ou au Chocolat*)

Make the dough (Chou Paste) as in the preceding recipe. Put it into a pastry bag fitted with a plain nozzle and pipe 1½-inch lengths of dough onto ungreased baking sheets. Bake and cool as given in the preceding directions. Fill with Coffee or Chocolate French Pastry Cream (page 409). Frost with Chocolate Fondant (page 412) or Coffee Fondant Icing (page 480). Allow 1 to 2 per person. (*See illustration, page 442.*)

⚜ CREAM PUFFS (*Choux à la Crème*)

Make the dough (Chou Paste) as directed in the recipe for Profiteroles. With a pastry bag fitted with a plain nozzle, pipe small buns onto an ungreased baking sheet. Bake and cool as in directions for Profiteroles. Fill with Cream Saint-Honoré (page 472). Sprinkle with confectioners' sugar, or frost with Chocolate Glaze (page 417). Allow 1 per person. (*See illustration, page 442.*)

⚜ PRALINE CREAM PUFFS (*Choux Pralinés*)

Pipe small mounds of Chou Paste onto ungreased cooky sheets. Brush with 1 egg yolk beaten with 1 tablespoon water. Sprinkle with chopped almonds and granulated sugar. Bake and cool as in directions for Profiteroles (page 489). Fill with Praline Butter Cream (page 415) and sprinkle with confectioners' sugar. Allow 1 to 2 per person.

⚜ SALAMBOS

Make small cream puffs from Chou Paste and fill them with Kirsch-flavored French Pastry Cream (page 409). Brush the tops of the Salambos with thin Water Icing (page 415). (*See illustration, page 442.*) Allow 1 to 2 per person.

DESSERT CRÊPES

✤ DESSERT CRÊPES (*Crêpes Fines*)

1 cup sifted all-purpose flour
½ teaspoon salt
1 tablespoon sugar
3 large eggs, beaten

2 cups milk
1 tablespoon rum or cognac
2 tablespoons butter, melted

Sift together the first 3 ingredients into a mixing bowl. Combine the eggs, milk, and rum or cognac and add to the dry mixture. Add the melted butter and mix only until ingredients are blended. Do not beat. Let the batter stand 2 hours to improve flavor and texture. Heat a 6-inch skillet or a French crêpe pan and brush the bottom lightly with melted butter. For each crêpe pour in 2 tablespoons of the batter. Quickly rotate the pan to spread the batter uniformly over the bottom. Cook over direct moderate heat 1 to 2 minutes or until the underside is brown and bubbles have formed over the top. Turn and cook ½ to 1 minute or until the other side has browned. When each crêpe is cooked, sprinkle it with confectioners' sugar. Stack the crêpes in pancake fashion in a pan lined with a clean towel and when all the crêpes are stacked fold the ends of the towel over them. Just before serving, heat the crêpes, without unwrapping, in a preheated moderate oven (350° F.) only until they are hot (about 10 minutes). Serve sprinkled with confectioners' sugar, or with syrup or honey. Or spread them with jelly or marmalade and roll them up. Or serve as Crêpes Suzette. Makes 18 crêpes or 6 servings.

✤ CRÊPES SUZETTE, CLASSIC METHOD (*Crêpes Suzette*)

18 Dessert Crêpes
Classic Crêpes Suzette Sauce (see
    following recipe)

brandy or Grand Marnier

Heat the Crêpes Suzette Sauce and place the crêpes in it, spooning it over them until they are well covered. Fold the crêpes into quarters. Heat brandy or Grand Marnier in a small saucepan, ignite it, and quickly pour it over the crêpes. Bring the dish to the table flaming. Serve the crêpes with some of the sauce spooned over them. The crêpes may be made ahead of time, but the sauce should be made just before it is used.

✤ Classic Crêpes Suzette Sauce

1 medium-sized navel orange
4 large-sized lumps sugar
4 tablespoons (½ stick) unsalted
    butter

1 teaspoon lemon juice
¼ cup Cointreau or Curaçao
¼ cup Benedictine or Grand Marnier

Wash the orange and dry it thoroughly. Rub the lumps of sugar over the skin, then place them on a board and crush them. Transfer the crushed sugar to a heatproof dish or to the inner pan of a chafing dish. Squeeze out the juice from the orange and discard the rind. (The rind is not used because the sugar has absorbed enough flavor.) Add the butter, orange juice, and lemon juice to the sugar and mix well. Cook until the sugar and butter have melted, then add the liqueurs and heat to boiling point. Makes sauce for 6 servings.

⚜ CRÊPES SUZETTE, QUICK METHOD

18 Dessert Crêpes (page 491)   brandy
Quick Crêpes Suzette Sauce (see
   following recipe)

Make the Dessert Crêpes ahead of time. Immediately before serving, wrap the crêpes in a towel, place in a baking pan, and heat in a preheated moderate oven (350° F.) only until the crêpes are hot (about 10 minutes). Remove the crêpes from the oven and spread them with Quick Crêpes Suzette Sauce. Fold or roll them and flambé with the liqueur and brandy as directed in the sauce recipe.

⚜ Quick Crêpes Suzette Sauce

½ cup (1 stick) unsalted butter,
   softened
½ cup sugar
1 tablespoon grated orange rind
⅓ cup orange juice

1 teaspoon lemon juice
¼ cup Cointreau, Curaçao, or Grand
   Marnier
¼ cup apricot brandy or peach brandy

Stir and beat the butter until it is creamy. Gradually blend in the sugar and orange rind. Add the orange juice and lemon juice and mix well. Spread the mixture on the warmed crêpes, fold or roll them, and place them in a heatproof dish. Heat the liqueur and brandy in a small saucepan, ignite, and quickly pour over the crêpes. Bring them to the table flaming. Makes 6 servings.

PIES, TARTS, AND TARTLETS

A pastry crust with a filling is called a pie in America, a *tarte* in France, and a tart in England. The small individual pies called tarts in America are known as *tartelettes* in France. In this book, the term tart is most often used for the larger and tartlet for the smaller. Oval or boat-shaped tartlets are called barquettes.

⚜ ENGLISH APPLE TART (*Tarte aux Pommes à l'Anglaise*)

Plain Pastry Dough for a 9-inch pie
  crust (page 24)
9 medium-sized cooking apples
¾ cup sugar
½ cup water

2 tablespoons butter
⅛ teaspoon salt
¼ teaspoon vanilla extract
¼ cup apricot jam
1 tablespoon water

Line a 9-inch pie plate with the unbaked pastry and set aside. Peel and slice 6 of the apples and put them in a saucepan with ½ cup of the sugar, the water, butter, and salt. Cover and cook until apples are tender. Put the apple slices through a sieve or purée them, one-quarter at a time, in an electric blender. Add the vanilla extract. Cool. Spread the cooled apple purée over the unbaked pie crust. Peel the remaining 3 apples, slice thin, and arrange them over the apple purée in a spiral, starting at the center and working out, with the slices overlapping. Sprinkle the apples with the remaining ¼ cup sugar. Bake in a preheated hot oven (425° F.) 30 to 35 minutes or until the apples are tender and the crust has browned. Mix the apricot jam and the 1 tablespoon water in a small saucepan, heat, and spread over the hot pie. Serve cold. Makes one 9-inch tart.

⚜ LATTICE-TOP APPLE TART (*Tarte aux Pommes Grillagée*)

Plain Pastry Dough for a 2-crust
  9-inch pie (page 24)
6 medium-sized apples (Rome Beauty,
  Jonathan, Stayman, or Winesap)
1 cup sugar

¾ cup water
⅛ teaspoon salt
2 tablespoons butter
1 tablespoon milk

Roll half the pastry ⅛ inch thick and line a 9-inch pie plate. Set aside. Peel the apples and cut each into eight equal parts. Put ¾ cup of the sugar, the water, and the salt into a saucepan, bring to boiling point, and add one-third of the apples. Cook, uncovered, until apples are tender. Using a perforated spoon transfer the apples to a plate to cool. Repeat twice, until all apples are cooked. Arrange the apples on the unbaked pie crust. Dot with the butter and sprinkle with the remaining ¼ cup sugar. Roll the remaining half of the pastry ⅛ inch thick, cut it into strips ½ inch wide, and arrange the strips over the apples in lattice fashion. Anchor the strips to the edge of the crust by pressing the pastry lightly with the index finger. Turn under the pastry that is overhanging and flute the edge with the thumb and index finger or crimp it with a fork. Brush the edge of the crust and the lattice pastry strips with the milk. Bake in a preheated hot oven (425° F.) 30 to 35 minutes or until crust is golden brown. Serve cold. (*See illustration, page 441.*) Makes one 9-inch tart.

❧ CHERRY TART (*Tarte aux Cerises*)

9-inch Plain Pastry Dough pie shell,
  baked (page 24)
1 cup sugar
3 tablespoons cornstarch
⅛ teaspoon salt
1 cup crushed pitted fresh sweet
  cherries

¼ cup water
3 cups whole pitted fresh sweet
  cherries
¼ teaspoon almond extract
chopped blanched almonds
  (optional)
whipped cream sweetened to taste

Bake the pie shell and set it aside. Combine the next 5 ingredients in a saucepan and mix well. Stir and cook over moderate heat until the juice is clear and thick. Remove from the heat, cover, and let cool to lukewarm. Add the whole cherries and the almond extract. Mix well. Turn into the baked pie shell. If desired, sprinkle chopped almonds around the edge of the pie. Serve topped with whipped cream sweetened to taste. Makes one 9-inch pie.

❧ Cherry Tartlets (*Tartelettes aux Cerises*)

Bake 6 3-inch Plain Pastry tartlet shells. Prepare cherries as directed in the recipe for Cherry Tart and divide equally among the 8 tartlet shells. Proceed as directed in the recipe.

❧ CUSTARD PIE (*Flan au Lait*)

9-inch unbaked Plain Pastry Dough
  pie shell (page 24)
4 large whole eggs, or 8 large yolks
⅔ cup sugar

¼ teaspoon salt
2½ cups light cream or milk
1½ teaspoons vanilla extract
ground nutmeg (optional)

Line a 9-inch pie pan with the unbaked pie shell and set aside. Beat the eggs or egg yolks with a fork. Add the sugar and salt and mix well. Stir in the light cream or milk and vanilla extract. Pour the mixture into the prepared pie crust. Sprinkle the top with nutmeg if desired. Bake in a preheated hot oven (425° F.) 15 minutes. Reduce heat to 350° F. (moderate) and bake 30 to 35 minutes, or until a silver knife inserted into the side of the custard comes out clean. The center may appear a little soft but will set later; if baked too long the custard will be watery. Serve cold. Makes one 9-inch pie.

❧ FRUIT TART (*Tarte aux Fruits*)

Sweet Pie Pastry for a 9-inch pie shell
  (page 25)
apricots, nectarines, or peaches
¾ cup sugar
⅛ teaspoon salt

1 tablespoon butter
½ cup apricot or peach jam or
  preserves
1 tablespoon water

Line a 9-inch pie plate with unbaked Sweet Pie Pastry rolled ⅛ inch thick. Flute the edge and prick the crust with the tines of a fork. Chill 30 to 40 minutes. Bake in a preheated moderate oven (350° F.) 8 to 10 minutes or until about half done. Meanwhile peel the fruit, cut in half, remove the pits, and flatten each half slightly so they will overlap easily. Reserve 2 tablespoons sugar for future use. Sprinkle 5 tablespoons sugar over the bottom of the partly baked crust, and on it arrange the fruit, cut side down, in a spiral from the center, having the halves overlapping. Mix the remaining 5 tablespoons sugar with the salt and sprinkle over the fruit. Dot with the butter. Bake in a preheated moderate oven (350° F.) 30 to 40 minutes or until fruit has colored lightly and is of syrup consistency. Remove the pie from the oven. Put the jam or preserves through a sieve into a small saucepan. Add the reserved 2 tablespoons sugar and 1 tablespoon water. Mix well. Stir and cook 2 to 3 minutes, then spread over the pie. Cool. This pie should be eaten the day it is made. Makes one 9-inch pie.

⚜ GOOSEBERRY TART (*Tarte aux Groseilles*)

Plain Pastry Dough for a 9-inch pie shell (page 24)
1 quart gooseberries
1 cup sugar
1 large egg yolk, beaten
3 tablespoons heavy cream
dash salt
½ teaspoon vanilla extract

Line a 9-inch pie plate with the unbaked dough, rolled ⅛ inch thick. Set aside. Wash the gooseberries and remove the tails. Drain well and mix with the sugar. Turn into the prepared pie shell. Bake in a preheated moderate oven (350° F.) 20 minutes. Combine the remaining ingredients and beat a few seconds. Spoon over the gooseberries. Bake 15 to 20 minutes longer or until the crust is lightly browned and the gooseberries are tender. Makes one 9-inch pie.

⚜ LINZERTORTE

This delicious tart is of Viennese origin.

1½ cups unblanched almonds, ground fine
1 cup sifted all-purpose flour
⅛ teaspoon salt
⅛ teaspoon ground cloves
¼ teaspoon ground cinnamon
1 cup (2 sticks) butter
½ cup granulated sugar
2 large egg yolks, beaten
raspberry or currant jam
1 egg white, slightly beaten
confectioners' sugar (optional)
slivered blanched almonds (optional)

Grind the almonds in a food chopper, using the finest blade, or in an electric blender, a few at a time, and set them aside. Sift together the next 4 ingredients. Add the butter and cut it into the flour mixture with a pastry blender or 2 knives. Blend in the ground almonds. Mix the sugar with the egg yolks and stir into the flour mixture. Knead the dough until all the ingredients are well blended and the dough is smooth. Pat two-thirds of the dough over the bottom and up the sides of a 9-inch ungreased cake pan with a removable bottom, having the dough thicker over the bottom than around the sides, and having it come halfway up the sides of the pan. Spread with jam. Pinch off pieces of the remaining dough the size of golf balls and roll them between the palms of the hands into rolls ⅓ inch in diameter and about 8½ inches long. Place them on a baking sheet and chill until they are firm enough to handle. With a spatula lift the rolls of dough and arrange them criss-cross style over the jam. Press the dough to the rim of the pan. Brush with lightly beaten egg white. Place on the lower shelf of a preheated slow oven (325° F.) and bake 1¼ hours. Place the tart on a rack to cool partly before removing the rim of the pan. Sprinkle with confectioners' sugar and, if desired, slivered blanched almonds. Makes one 9-inch tart.

⚜ Linzer Tartlets

Line six 3-inch tartlet pans with pastry for Linzertorte and proceed as directed in the recipe. Bake in a preheated slow oven (325° F.) 40 minutes.

⚜ ORANGE AND BANANA TART (*Tarte aux Oranges et aux Bananes*)

9-inch Sweet Pie Pastry pie shell baked (page 25)	9 tablespoons sugar
2 medium-sized navel oranges	4 tablespoons cornstarch
2 tablespoons Kirsch	1/16 teaspoon salt
2 medium-sized bananas, sliced	2 cups milk
2 tablespoons rum	4 large egg yolks
	1½ teaspoons vanilla extract

Bake the pie shell and set it aside to cool. Grate the rind of 1 of the oranges and reserve 1 teaspoon for later use. Peel the oranges, being sure to remove all the white skin, slice them thin, and marinate them in Kirsch for 1 hour. Combine the bananas, rum, and 1 tablespoon of the sugar and marinate 1 hour.

Blend the remaining 8 tablespoons sugar, the cornstarch, and the salt in the top of a 1-quart double boiler. Add ¼ cup of the milk and mix well. Heat 1½ cups of the milk and gradually stir it into the mixture. Stir and cook over moderate heat until the mixture is very thick. Beat the egg yolks, blend with the remaining ¼ cup milk, and add to the cooked mixture. Cook over hot water (not boiling), stirring constantly, until the cream is the consistency of mayonnaise. Remove from heat. Add the vanilla extract and grated orange rind. Cool completely, stirring occasionally to prevent a crust from forming. Spread the cooked mixture over the baked pie crust. Drain the oranges and bananas in separate bowls and arrange them over the pie in any design desired. This can also be put into 6 baked 3-inch tartlet shells to make Orange and Banana Tartlets. Makes one 9-inch tart or six 3-inch tartlets.

✤ PINEAPPLE TART (*Tarte à l'Ananas*)

9-inch Plain Pastry Dough pie shell,
    baked (page 24)
¾ cup well-drained crushed pineapple
1 cup pineapple juice
½ cup sugar

⅛ teaspoon salt
3 large eggs, separated
½ teaspoon vanilla extract
1 tablespoon sugar
½ cup heavy cream whipped

Bake the pie shell and set aside to cool. Drain the pineapple well and set it aside. Combine the pineapple juice, the ½ cup sugar, and the salt and cook over moderate heat 10 minutes. Put the egg yolks in the top of a 1-quart double boiler and beat them about ½ minute. Gradually beat in the hot syrup. Stir and cook over hot water (not boiling) until the mixture has thickened. Let cool. Beat the egg whites until they stand in soft stiff peaks and fold them into the custard mixture along with the vanilla extract. Spread the drained pineapple over the baked pie crust, and pour the custard over it. Chill. Add the 1 tablespoon sugar to the cream and beat until the cream stands in soft stiff peaks. Spread over the pie. Makes one 9-inch pie.

✤ RHUBARB PIE

6 cups (1½ pounds) diced rhubarb
1¼ cups sugar
1 tablespoon cornstarch
2 tablespoons flour
dash salt

2 tablespoons butter
Puff Pastry (page 25)
Vanilla Sugar (page 418)
Soft Custard (page 423)

Combine the first 5 ingredients and turn the mixture into a 2-quart casserole. Break the butter in pieces and scatter the pieces over the rhubarb. Roll the Puff Pastry ⅛ inch thick in a circle 2 inches larger in diameter than the casserole. Cut a strip of pastry 1½ inches wide from the outside of the pastry circle. Wet the edge of the casserole and press the pastry strip to it all around, having it extend over the edge ½ inch. Cover the casserole with the remaining pastry circle. Press the edges of the pastry circle and the pastry strip together, turn them under, and crimp them with a fork dipped in flour. Bake in a preheated hot oven (400° F.) 55 minutes. Sprinkle the top with Vanilla Sugar. Serve Soft Custard separately. Makes 6 to 8 servings. (*See illustration, page 437.*)

⚜ STRAWBERRY TART (*Tarte aux Fraises*)

9-inch pie shell made of Sweet Pie
   Pastry (page 25) or Plain Pastry
   Dough (page 24)
3 pints fresh strawberries
1 cup sugar
water, if needed
1½ tablespoons cornstarch

⅛ teaspoon salt
confectioners' sugar, sifted
1 tablespoon granulated sugar
   (optional)
½ cup heavy cream (optional)
Kirsch to taste (optional)

Bake the pie shell and set it aside to cool. Wash, cap, and slice enough strawberries to make 2 cups. Combine with ⅔ cup of the sugar. Cut the remaining berries in half, combine with the remaining ⅓ cup sugar, and let stand 30 minutes for juice to form. Put the sliced strawberries in a strainer over a bowl for about 15 minutes to drain. Do the same with the halved strawberries in a separate strainer. Measure the juice and add water, if necessary, to make 1 cup liquid. Blend the juice with the cornstarch until the mixture is smooth. Stir and cook in a small saucepan 3 to 4 minutes, or until thickened. Cool. Place the sliced strawberries in the baked pie shell, and arrange the halved strawberries on top, red rounded side up. Spoon the thickened juice over the top. Chill 2 hours. Sprinkle the edge of the crust with sifted confectioners' sugar. If desired, add 1 tablespoon sugar to ½ cup heavy cream, beat until it stands in soft stiff peaks, flavor to taste with Kirsch, and serve over the tart. Makes one 9-inch tart.

⚜ Strawberry Tartlets (*Tartelettes aux Fraises*)

Bake six 3-inch Sweet Pastry or Plain Pastry tartlet shells. Set aside to cool. Prepare strawberries as directed in the recipe for Strawberry Tart and divide them equally among the 6 tartlet shells. Proceed as directed in the recipe. Garnish with Kirsch-flavored whipped cream if desired. Makes 6 tartlets.

Flans

A flan is an open tart filled with fruit, cream, or other filling. The shell may also be filled with a savory filling and served as a light main course or an hors d'oeuvre. The flans in this section are desserts. (In the United States a flan is known as a pie or a tart.)

⚜ FLAN PASTRY (*Pâte à Flan*)

A flan ring is a metal hoop, with no top or bottom, usually about 1 inch high. They are available in various sizes and shapes—rectangular or square as well as round.

1 cup sifted all-purpose flour	½ cup (1 stick) unsalted butter, softened
1 tablespoon sugar	
¼ teaspoon salt	1 teaspoon grated lemon rind
	cold water, if needed

Sift the first 3 ingredients together into a mixing bowl. Add the butter and lemon rind and mix until a smooth firm dough is formed. Add 1 to 2 teaspoons cold water if needed. Wrap the dough in foil and chill 1 hour. Roll the dough on a lightly floured board in a circle ⅛ inch thick. Place the dough in a buttered 8- or 9-inch cake pan with a removable bottom or place it over a buttered flan ring on a buttered cooky sheet. Press it firmly down into the flan ring or against the inside of the cake pan. Turn the dough under the top edge of the pan or ring and make a fluted border with the thumb and index finger. If the shell is to be baked before it is filled, prick the dough with the tines of a fork and chill it 30 minutes. Cover the shell with foil and put a bean bag on top to prevent the crust from puffing out of shape. Bake in a preheated hot oven (400° F.) for 10 minutes. Remove the bean bag and foil, reduce heat to 350° F. (moderate), and bake 15 minutes or until golden. If the shell is to be baked with a filling, follow directions in the various flan recipes. Makes one 8- or 9-inch flan shell.

⚜ FLAN BOURDALOUE (*Flan Bourdaloue*)

1 cup almonds	2 large egg yolks
1½ cups water	2 tablespoons butter
¾ cup sugar	1 tablespoon Kirsch
3 tablespoons rice flour or cornstarch	8-inch cold baked Flan Pastry shell
1 large whole egg	(see preceding recipe)

Blanch the almonds and dry them in a preheated slow oven (300° F.) for 30 minutes. Put them through a food chopper, using the fine blade, or grind them fine, ⅓ cup at a time, in an electric blender. Put the ground almonds in a mortar, add the water gradually, and pound and beat with a pestle until the liquid is milky and almond-flavored. Strain the almond milk through cheesecloth. Set aside. Combine the sugar with the rice flour or cornstarch. Add the whole egg and the egg yolks. Mix well. Stir in ¼ cup of the almond milk. Heat the remaining almond milk and gradually add it to the sugar and eggs. Stir and cook over low heat until the cream is thick and smooth. (Do not boil.) Remove from heat and stir in the butter and Kirsch. Chill. When the cream is cold, turn it into the cold baked flan shell. Makes one 8-inch flan.

✣ FRANGIPANE FLAN (*Flan à la Frangipane*)

½ cup sugar
4 tablespoons flour
¹⁄₁₆ teaspoon salt
2 large whole eggs
6 large whole egg yolks
1 cup hot milk
1 cup hot heavy cream
1½ teaspoons vanilla extract

3 tablespoons unsalted butter
2 tablespoons almond paste, or ¼
    teaspoon almond extract
2 tablespoons almond macaroon
    crumbs
9-inch baked Flan Pastry shell
    (page 499)
toasted slivered almonds.

Combine the sugar, flour, and salt in the top of a double boiler. Beat in the whole eggs and the egg yolks. Add a little of the hot milk gradually to the egg and sugar mixture and then gradually blend in the remaining hot milk and the hot cream. Stir and cook over hot water (not boiling) until thick and smooth. Remove from heat and stir in the vanilla extract, butter, almond paste or almond extract, and macaroon crumbs. Cool, stirring occasionally to prevent a skin from forming. Turn into a baked flan shell. Garnish with toasted slivered almonds. Serve cold. Makes one 9-inch flan.

Simple Confectionery

The recipes in this chapter can all be easily made in the home kitchen.

❧ BRAZILIANS (*Brésiliennes*)

1 cup blanched almonds
1¼ cups sifted confectioners' sugar
1 teaspoon instant coffee
2 tablespoons dark rum

2 tablespoons milk
3½ squares (3½ ounces) unsweetened
  chocolate, grated
chocolate granules

Put ¼ cup of the almonds and 2 to 3 tablespoons of the sugar in the jar of an electric blender. Cover the jar and turn on the blender. Blend until the almonds are very fine, about ½ minute. Then turn the mixture into a mixing bowl. Repeat until all the almonds are ground. Add the remaining sugar to the mixture. Stir in the coffee, rum, milk, and grated chocolate. Let the mixture stand 15 minutes. Shape into ¾-inch balls and roll them in the chocolate granules. Place the candies on waxed paper and let them stand until dry, 1 to 2 hours. Store in an airtight container in a cool place. Makes 2½ dozen.

⚜ DISGUISED CHERRIES (*Cerises Marquises ou Deguisées*)

Holding brandied cherries by the stems, dip them into melted Fondant (page 411) flavored to taste with Kirsch. Cool on a marble slab or waxed paper. If desired, the fondant may be colored by adding food coloring (red, green, or yellow) drop by drop until the desired shade is obtained.

⚜ CHOCOLATE ALMOND BALLS (*Marquisettes*)

1 cup blanched almonds	2 tablespoons butter
1 cup sifted confectioners' sugar	2 large egg yolks
2 squares (2 ounces) unsweetened chocolate	½ teaspoon vanilla extract
	chocolate granules

Put ¼ cup of the almonds in the jar of an electric blender. Turn on the switch and run the blender ½ minute or until the almonds are ground very fine. Turn the ground almonds into a 1½-quart mixing bowl. Repeat until all the remaining almonds have been ground. Add the sugar and mix well. Put the chocolate and butter in a custard cup and place it in a pan of hot water until chocolate and butter are melted. Add to the almond-sugar mixture and mix well. Stir in the egg yolks and vanilla extract. Shape the mixture into ¾-inch balls. Roll the balls in chocolate granules and let them stand on waxed paper 2 hours or until they are dry. Store in an airtight container. Makes ¾ pound.

⚜ CHOCOLATE TRUFFLES (*Truffles au Chocolat*)

⅔ cup blanched almonds	2 squares (2 ounces) unsweetened chocolate, melted
½ cup Fondant (page 411)	½ teaspoon vanilla extract
4 tablespoons softened butter	chocolate granules

Put half the almonds in the jar of an electric blender. Let the blender run ½ minute or until the almonds are ground very fine. Turn the ground almonds into a 1½-quart mixing bowl. Repeat for the remaining almonds. Add the Fondant, butter, melted chocolate, and vanilla extract. Mix well, using the fingers. Shape the mixture into ¾-inch balls. Roll each in chocolate granules and let them stand on waxed paper 2 to 3 hours or until they are dry. Store in an airtight container. Makes ¾ pound.

⚜ FONDANT ALMOND PASTE (*Pâte d'Amandes Fondante*)

1 cup whole blanched almonds	chocolate granules or colored granulated sugar
1 cup ripened Fondant (page 411)	
½ teaspoon vanilla extract	

Put ¼ cup of the almonds in the jar of an electric blender. Turn on the blender and blend ½ minute or until the almonds are ground very fine. Turn the ground almonds into a 1½-quart mixing bowl. Repeat until all the almonds have been ground fine. Add the Fondant and vanilla extract. Mix until the ingredients are thoroughly blended and the mixture is a stiff paste. Shape the paste as desired and roll the shapes in chocolate granules or colored granulated sugar. If desired, use this paste to stuff pitted dried dates or pitted dried prunes, or with walnut halves. Makes ¾ pound.

⚜ FONDANT MINT PATTIES

Melt 1 cup Fondant (page 411) slowly over hot water. Add red, green, or yellow food coloring as desired, and peppermint or wintergreen flavoring to taste. Drop the Fondant on waxed paper from the tip of a teaspoon in patties the size of quarters. As soon as the patties are firm, loosen them with a spatula, since they may break if allowed to stand too long. Makes approximately ½ pound.

⚜ SALTED ALMONDS (*Amandes Salées*)

2 cups whole almonds, blanched   salt
1 egg white, beaten slightly

Add the blanched almonds to the slightly beaten egg white and stir until the almonds are completely coated. Spread them on a large baking pan. Sprinkle with salt. Bake in a preheated moderate oven (375° F.) until almonds are heated through, keeping the oven door open while baking and stirring frequently to prevent the almonds from burning. Makes 2 cups.

⚜ Salted Pecans or Walnuts

Replace the almonds in the recipe for Salted Almonds with pecan halves or walnut halves.

⚜ STUFFED DATES AND PRUNES (*Dattes et Pruneaux Fourrés*)

Slit plump dried dates or dried prunes down one side and remove the stones. Stuff Fondant (page 411) or Fondant Almond Paste (page 502) into the cavities. Roll in granulated sugar or dip in Glazing Syrup (page 417).

⚜ STUFFED WALNUTS (*Noix Farcies*)

Boil sugar and water to the crack stage (290° to 300° F. on a candy thermometer). Sandwich two walnut halves together with a small ball of white or colored Fondant Almond Paste (page 502). Dip in the syrup. Place on cooling racks to cool. Allow 2 to 3 per person.

GLOSSARY OF CULINARY TERMS

à la in the style of.

apéritif short alcoholic drink taken before a meal; appetizer or hors d'oeuvre.

appareil French term for a mixture used in the making of a dish. Such mixtures are of various kinds.

apricot glaze reduced, strained apricot jam used to coat cakes, petits fours, pastries, etc. The French term *abricoter* means to apply such a glaze.

aspic clear, brilliant jelly made from stock and used for glazing or dressing cold dishes. In French usage *aspic* applies to cold dishes molded with jelly; the term for jelly is *gelée*.

assaionnement salad dressing.

au, aux with, or cooked with.

au jus served with the natural juices (meat).

bain-marie vessel containing warm or hot water into which another utensil containing food is set while food is cooking.

ballottine piece of meat, poultry, etc., boned, stuffed, and rolled up—usually served hot. See also *galantine*.

barquette small oval or boat-shaped pastry shell. Barquettes may be filled with various mixtures for hot or cold hors d'oeuvre or small entrées, or with fruit, custard, etc., for dessert.

baste (*arroser*) to moisten with pan drippings, fat, or liquid while cooking.

beard, debeard (*ébarber*) to remove the "beard" from oysters or mussels; to remove fins and small fin bones from fish.

beat (*fouetter*) to mix by long and vigorous stirring with a spoon, fork, whip, or electric beater or mixer.

beurre butter; see Butters and Butter Sauces, pages 56–60.

beurre manié butter thickened with flour, used for sauces.

505

beurre noir butter cooked to a very dark brown and mixed with chopped herbs and vinegar; served as a sauce.

bind (*lier*) thicken with flour, starch, eggs, cream, etc.; mix chopped meat, vegetables, etc., with a sauce.

biscuit American usage, a raised bread baked in small, round shapes; English usage, a cracker or a sweet wafer or cooky; French usage, sponge cake.

biscuit glacée ice cream shaped in molds.

blanch (*blanchir*) to scald or bleach by putting into boiling water.

blanquette white ragout or stew made with lamb, veal, or poultry.

blend (*mélanger*) to mix gently.

boil (*bouillir*) to cook in boiling water.

bombe (*bombe glacée*) combination of ice creams or ices, fruits, creams, etc., made in a mold.

bone (*deosser*) to remove the bones from meat, poultry, or fish.

bouchées small puff-pastry patty shells.

bouillon strong, clear stock or broth.

bouquet garni herbs—usually parsley, thyme, and bay leaf—tied in a bunch and used for flavoring stews and sauces; the bouquet is removed before the dish is served.

braise (*braiser*) to brown meat or poultry in a little fat, then add a little water or other liquid and finish cooking with low heat.

brochette small spit or skewer used for broiling cubes of meat, shellfish, or vegetables. Food so cooked may be called *brochettes* or *en brochette*.

canapé bread cut in fancy shapes, fried in butter or toasted and spread with a savory topping; served as an hors d'oeuvre.

caramel browned sugar.

cassolette individual heatproof dish; food cooked and served in such a dish.

chop coarsely (*concasser*) cut or break up a food into large pieces.

coat a spoon (*napper la cuillère*) method of determining the thickness of sauces, etc., by dipping a spoon into the liquid; the thickness can be judged by the amount that adheres to the spoon.

cocotte small individual heatproof dish in which food is cooked and served; food so presented is called *en cocotte*.

compote fresh or dried fruits cooked in syrup (see Index).

coquille scallop shell; by extension a dish so shaped, or food cooked or served in a natural scallop shell or a shell-shaped container.

cream (*crème*) butter cream or custard cream used for frosting and for filling cakes and pastries; custard cream sauce. The French term for the cream that rises from milk is *crème du lait*.

crêpe thin French pancake. Crêpes may be filled, rolled, and baked for an entrée; sweet crêpes are served as a dessert with confectioners' sugar or a sauce.

croissant crescent-shaped roll made of puff pastry or yeast pastry.

croustade small or large case made of rich pastry or puff pastry, or a hollowed-out toast case, used for serving various creamed mixtures.

croûte bread crust, pie crust, or crust formed on anything. Meat, *pâtés*, etc., baked in a crust are called *en croûte*.

crouton small cubes or other shapes of bread fried in butter or toasted and served in soups or as a garnish.

daube stew cooked in a hermetically sealed casserole to preserve the flavor.

degrease (*dégraisser*) to skim off excess fat from the surface of a liquid.

diable, à la   deviled; method of preparing food. Sauce Diable (see page 45).
dice (*couper en dés*)   to cut into small cubes.

émincé   dish made with thinly sliced leftover cooked meat.
émincer   to cut meat or vegetables into very fine slices (*not* to mince).

fillet (*filet*)   strip of meat or fish without bone.
fillet of beef   tenderloin.
fines herbes   finely chopped parsley and/or other herbs, used as a garnish.
flambéed (*flambé*)   served with brandy or a liqueur poured on and set alight.
fleurons   decorations made of puff pastry in fancy shapes, used as a garnish and
   to ornament *pâté en croûte* and dessert pastries.
Florentine   cooked or served with spinach.
foie gras   livers of duck or geese fattened in a special way.
fold (*incorporer*)   to blend a light mixture gently into a heavier mixture; most
   often used of beaten egg whites.
fondu   melted.
fondue   name given to various dishes in which the main ingredient is melted or
   (for vegetables) cooked to a pulp.
forcemeat (*farce*)   meat or fish chopped fine and seasoned, used as a stuffing or
   garnish or in the making of other dishes.
four   oven.
fruits de mer   seafood.

galantine   boned poultry or meat, stuffed, rolled, and cooked in a gelatinous stock
   (see Index).
garnish (*garniture*)   various items of food used to decorate and to enhance the
   flavor of a dish.
gelée   (adj.) frozen; (n.) jelly.
glacé   frozen; iced; glazed; candied.
glacéed (*glacé*)   glazed; candied.
gratin, au   sprinkled with breadcrumbs and melted butter and browned. Cheese
   may or may not be added.
grill (*griller*)   to broil.

hacher   to chop or mince.
herbs   aromatic plants used in cooking, salads, etc.

jelly (*gelée*)   aspic; preserve made of fruit juice and sugar.
julienne   (food) cut in fine, short strips.

lard (*larder*)   to thread strips of pork fat into large pieces of meat with a larding
   needle.
lardon   strip of pork or bacon used for larding.

macédoine   mixture of small or cut-up fruits or vegetables.
Madère, au   with Madeira wine.
maître d'hôtel butter or **sauce**   butter sauce with parsley and lemon juice.
marinade   a seasoned liquid, cooked or uncooked, in which food is steeped for
   varying lengths of time.
marinate (*mariner, macérer*)   to steep in a marinade.

marmite cooking pot of metal or earthenware, with a lid. This utensil has given its name to certain soups; see Grande Marmite, Petite Marmite.

mask (*masquer*) to cover or mask with a sauce.

medallion (*médaillon*) round slice.

meunière, à la way of preparing fish, in which the fish is rolled in flour, fried in butter, and garnished with lemon juice and chopped parsley.

mince (*hacher*) to cut into small pieces.

papillote paper frill put on bones of cutlets, *suprêmes* of chicken, or croquettes in cutlet form; *en papillote*, baked in oiled or buttered paper, or, in America, in foil; method used for small cuts of meat or for fish.

Parmentier name applied to dishes that include potatoes, after Antoine-Auguste Parmentier (1737–1817), who popularized potatoes in France.

pastry base (*abaisse*) sweet pastry rolled to any desired thickness and used as a base for a dessert preparation. The French term is also applied to a layer of sponge cake similarly used.

pâte pastry, dough.

pâté originally a meat or fish dish enclosed in pastry, served hot or cold; now extended to meat or fish mixtures baked in a mold or loaf pan (see *terrine*) lined with strips of bacon and served cold (see pages 117–127).

pâtisserie pastries; the art of the pastry cook; pastry shop.

paupiette slice of meat spread with a filling, rolled, and braised.

petits pots de crème rich custards baked in individual custard cups (see pages 426–427).

petits fours small cookies, iced cakes, pastries, glacéed fruits, etc. (see pages 477–480). The name is said to have originated from the fact that the small cakes were baked in an oven that had been allowed to cool after large cakes had been baked.

pilaf rice cooked in stock with various seasonings; also spelled pilaff, pilau.

poach (*pocher*) to cook in liquid that has barely been brought to a simmer.

poivre pepper; *au poivre*, cooked or heavily seasoned with pepper.

pot-au-feu classic French soup, made with meat, poultry, and vegetables. The broth is served separately from the meat and vegetables, making two dishes in one (see Index).

profiteroles small balls of chou paste, baked, and filled either with cheese, puréed meat, and other savory mixtures for hors d'oeuvres or garnish, or with creams or ice cream as a dessert. For dessert, *profiteroles* may be frosted or served with a caramel or chocolate sauce.

puff pastry, puff paste (*pâte feuillitée*) delicate, rich pastry made with flour, water, and butter, rolled, folded, and chilled several times (see pages 25–26).

purée (*réduire en purée*) to mash solid foods by putting through a sieve, pounding in a mortar, or putting through an electric blender. A purée of anything is food that has been so treated.

quenelles dumplings made with various kinds of forcemeat bound with a panada or with eggs, used as a garnish or in soups (see pages 31–32).

quiche savory custard tart, originating in Lorraine.

ragout stew.

reduce (*réduire*) boil down to a sauce or other liquid in order to increase flavor and thicken the consistency.

rissole   pastry filled with forcemeat and fried in deep fat.
roux   cooked mixture of butter and flour used for thickening sauces (see page 36).

sabayon   see *zabaglione*.
sauté (*sauter*)   to brown or cook in a small amount of very hot fat.
scallop (*escalope, scaloppine*)   thin slice of meat or fish cut slantwise; the method is most often used with veal.
scallop (*pétoncle*)   bivalve mussel with ribbed, rounded shell (see *coquille*).
simmer (*mijoter*)   to cook at a very slow boil.
spices   seeds or other parts of aromatic plants used to season food (see pages 15–20).
subrics   croquette-type mixtures that are not dipped in egg and breadcrumbs but fried in butter in a shallow frying pan; served as hors d'oeuvre or small entrées.

tart (*tarte*), **tartlet** (*tartelette*)   pastry crust with fruit, custard, or other filling. In American usage the large version is called a pie, the small individual version a tart, but in French and English usage the large size is a *tarte* (tart) and the small a *tartelette* (tartlet). The terms "tart" and "tartlet" are used in this book.
Tartare, à la   way of serving chopped raw beef, seasoned with salt and pepper and with a raw egg yolk on top.
Tartare Sauce   mayonnaise-type sauce made with oil, finely chopped hard-cooked eggs, and chopped chives.
tartine   slice of bread spread with butter, jam, or other spread.
terrine   earthenware dish or mold in which pâté mixtures are cooked; the food cooked in such a dish (see pages 125–127).
torte, tourte   tart, pie.
toss (*faire sauter*)   to flip food over by tossing the pan.
tournedos (s. and pl.)   small round steak cut from the tenderloin of beef.
truss (*brider*)   to tie up or skewer a fowl for cooking (see page 310).

vol-au-vent   elaborate large or small puff-pastry shell filled with various creamed mixtures (see Index).

zabaglione (Italian; French *sabayon*)   rich wine custard served hot in cups or as a sauce (see page 427).
zest (*zeste*)   peel of citrus fruit.

INDEX

[Page numbers in italic type indicate reference to illustration.]

A

B

C

D

E

F

G

H

I

J

K

L

M

N

O

P

Q

R

S

U

V

W

Y

Z